W9-AHG-596

The fourth edition of *Exceptional Children and Youth* introduces a new full-color presentation, improved and expanded pedagogy, and new topic coverage, while retaining its personalized tone of respect and empathy for students with disabilities.

NEW to the Fourth Edition

PORTFOLIO ACTIVITIES

1. Interview a school psychologist in a local school district or the consultant in the area of learning disabilities at your state department of education. Identify the state criteria for identifying students with learning disabilities. Compare and record the ways these criteria can be interpreted by school districts across your state.

   Standards This activity will help the student meet CEC Content Standard 2: Development and Characteristics of Learners.

2. Select a lesson from a textbook in your content area. Adapt the material along the lines suggested in the text. What specific changes did you make? Who is the intended audience for your revised version of the lesson? Can you envision making these types of modifications in your classroom?

   Standards This activity will help the student meet CEC Content Standard 3: Individual Learning Differences.

3. How do successful adults with learning disabilities cope with the demands of their jobs and lives? Interview an adult with a learning disability. Invite him or her to talk to your class about the strategies he or she has used to succeed in life. What types of strategies are described? How might they be used by your future students?

   Standards This activity will help the student meet CEC Content Standard 3: Individual Learning Differences.

   To access an electronic template for these activities, visit our website through http://www.education.college.hmco.com/students/.

▲ *New* **Portfolio Activities** appear at the end of each chapter and connect to CEC Content Standards. These portfolio development activities link out to the textbook website where students can find templates for completing them!

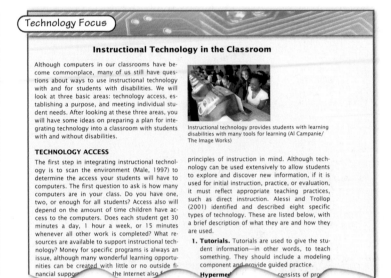

Technology Focus

Instructional Technology in the Classroom

Although computers in our classrooms have become commonplace, many of us still have questions about ways to use instructional technology with and for students with disabilities. We will look at three basic areas: technology access, establishing a purpose, and meeting individual student needs. After looking at these three areas, you will have some ideas on preparing a plan for integrating technology into a classroom with students with and without disabilities.

Instructional technology provides students with learning disabilities with many tools for learning (Al Campanie/The Image Works)

TECHNOLOGY ACCESS

The first step in integrating instructional technology is to scan the environment (Male, 1997) to determine the access your students will have to computers. The first question to ask is how many computers are in your class. Do you have one, two, or enough for all students? Access also will depend on the amount of time children have access to the computers. Does each student get 30 minutes a day, 1 hour a week, or 15 minutes whenever all other work is completed? What resources are available to support instructional technology? Money for specific programs is always an issue, although many wonderful learning opportunities can be created with little or no outside financial support

principles of instruction in mind. Although technology can be used extensively to allow students to explore and discover new information, if it is used for initial instruction, practice, or evaluation, it must reflect appropriate teaching practices, such as direct instruction. Alessi and Trollop (2001) identified and described eight specific types of technology. These are listed below, with a brief description of what they are and how they are used.

1. **Tutorials.** Tutorials are used to give the student information—in other words, to teach something. They should include a modeling component and provide guided practice.

▲ *New* **Technology Coverage** is integrated throughout the text with updates on special education technology issues, applications, and equipment. New "Technology Focus" boxes are featured in every chapter. In addition, marginal website icons are used to point readers to resources on the textbook website.

Case Study

An infant is born to a young couple—it is their second child. The little boy, named John, clearly has Down syndrome, but he also has very poor muscle tone and reflexes, difficulty swallowing and breathing, and a serious heart condition. The doctors are pessimistic—based on their preliminary evaluation, they believe that John will have serious or profound mental retardation and continuing medical and physical challenges—frequent surgeries are in his future. The young couple must make a decision to have lifesaving surgery performed on John to repair his heart. Heart-breaking and horrible questions are asked—Should John receive the surgery and live? Can we let our child die? If John lives with severe disabilities, how can our young family handle his needs—and our family's needs? What if the doctors are wrong in their assessment of John—does it, should it matter?

▲ *New* **Cases, Real-Life Stories, and Vignettes** are infused throughout the text to provide a better understanding of the lives and challenges of exceptional students, their families, and their teachers.

? Pause and Reflect

The right of students with disabilities to a free and appropriate public education is the result of years of advocacy and hard work on the part of parents, professionals, lawmakers, and people with disabilities themselves. Our current system is certainly not free of problems, but it is also important to recognize the accomplishments of the last thirty years. How do you think the current system of providing services could be improved, for the benefit of students, their families, and their teachers? •

▲ *New* **Pause and Reflect Boxes** after each major section create opportunities for students to reflect on, and respond to, the ideas in the chapter.

Tara Mould

Exceptional Children and Youth

An Introduction to Special Education

Fourth Edition

Nancy Hunt
California State University, Los Angeles

Kathleen Marshall
University of South Carolina

Houghton Mifflin Company
Boston   New York

To our students and their students

Publisher: Patricia A. Coryell
Senior Sponsoring Editor: Sue Pulvermacher-Alt
Senior Development Editor: Lisa Mafrici
Editorial Associate: Sara Hauschildt
Senior Project Editor: Margaret Park Bridges
Senior Manufacturing Coordinator: Marie Barnes
Executive Marketing Manager: Nicola Poser
Marketing Manager: Jane Potter

Cover Illustration © Ink Design

Copyright © 2005 by Houghton Mifflin Company. All rights reserved.

No part of this work may be reproduced or transmitted in any form or by any means, electronic or mechanical, including photocopying and recording, or by any information storage or retrieval system without the prior written permission of Houghton Mifflin Company unless such copying is expressly permitted by federal copyright law. Address inquiries to College Permissions, Houghton Mifflin Company, 222 Berkeley Street, Boston, MA 02116-3764.

Printed in the U.S.A.

Library of Congress Control Number: 2003110164

ISBN: 0-618-41592-0

123456789-DOW-08 07 06 05 04

Contents

Preface   *xiii*

PART **1**   **Building Blocks for Working with Exceptional Children and Youth**   **1**

1 An Introduction to Special Education   2

Terms and Definitions   3

Prevalence of Exceptional Children   6

Foundations of Special Education   6
  Early History: Great Teachers and Their Legacies   7
  Later History: Advocates for Social Change   7
  Legislation   12
  Litigation   18
  Disproportionate Representation of Minority Children   20

Individualized Education   24
  The Individualized Family Service Plan   24
  The Individualized Education Program   26
  The Individualized Transition Plan   30

The Pros and Cons of Labeling   30

Educational Setting   31
  The Framework of Support for Students with Disabilities   36

2 Risk Factors and Early Intervention   42

Terms and Definitions   43

Types of Risk   44
  Biological Risk   45
  Environmental Risk   55

Prevention   61
  Major Strategies for Prevention   61
  Early Intervention as Prevention   64

Early Intervention   64

Identification and Assessment of Infants at Risk   70
  Techniques for Identification and Assessment   71
  Can Disabilities Be Predicted from Risk Factors?   71
  The Resilient Child   73
  The Importance of Relationships   74

3 Families and Culture   78

Terms and Definitions   79
  The Macroculture and Microcultures   82
  Minority and Ethnic Groups   83
  Culture and Disability   83

Working with Culturally Diverse Families   84
  Knowing Yourself   84
  Developing Cultural Competence   84

v

Approaches to Studying Families 86
  The Family Systems Approach 86
  Ecocultural Theory 89

Family Reactions to Disability Across Cultures 89
  Factors Affecting Families' Reactions 93
  Impact of Exceptionality on Family Functions 97
  Exceptionality and Family Interactions 97
  Coping Strategies 100
  Sources of Support 101

The Role of the Family in Special Education Services 102
  The Parents' Rights 103
  Before Formal Schooling: The Early Years 105
  During the School Years 106
  Leaving School 109
  Transitions to Work and Higher Education 109
  Family Concerns for the Future 110
  Positive Aspects of Disabilities for Families 110

PART 2 **Learning About the Potential of Exceptional Children 115**

4 **Children with Learning Disabilities 116**

Terms and Definitions 117
  The Federal Definition 117
  Prevalence and Definition Issues 119

Causes of Learning Disabilities 120
  Internal Factors 121
  External Factors 123

Characteristics of Individuals with Learning Disabilities 123
  Learning Disabilities and Cognition: Approaches to Learning 124
  Learning Disabilities and Academic Performance 130
  Learning Disabilities and Social and Emotional Development 142

Teaching Strategies and Accommodations 144
  Assessment for Teaching 145
  Direct Instruction 148
  Strategy Instruction 150
  Special Skills Instruction 151
  Considerations for Culturally Diverse Learners 155
  Adapting Classroom Materials 156
  Curriculum 161

5 **Children with Mental Retardation 166**

Terms and Definitions 167
  Intelligence and General Cognitive Functioning 167
  Adaptive Behavior 168
  Manifestation During the Developmental Period 169
  Classification Issues 170
  Prevalence 172

Causes of Mental Retardation 173
  Biomedical Factors 174
  Social, Behavioral, and Educational Factors 175

Characteristics of Individuals with Mental Retardation   178
    Cognitive Development   178
    Language Development   180
    Physical Development   181
    Social and Emotional Development   182
    Effects on the Family   184

Teaching Strategies and Accommodations   186
    Early Intervention   186
    Curriculum   186
    Delivery of Instruction   192
    Materials   195
    Personal and Civil Rights   196

6   Children with Severe Disabilities   201

Terms and Definitions   202
    Severe Disabilities   202
    Severe and Profound Mental Retardation   203
    Prevalence   203

Causes of Severe Disabilities   204

Characteristics of Individuals with Severe Disabilities   206
    Cognitive Development   206
    Physical Development and Health   207
    Language Development and Communication   208
    Social Behaviors and Emotional Development   209

Effects on the Family   210
    Family Attitudes and Reactions   211
    Family Roles in Education   211

Teaching Strategies and Accommodations   214
    Normalization   216
    Inclusion   217
    Curriculum   220
    Transition Programming   223

Ethical Issues   233
    The Right to Life   234
    The Right to Education   236

7   Children with Behavior Disorders   240

Terms and Definitions   241
    The Federal Definition   241
    Measures of Behavior   242
    Classifying Behavior Disorders   243
    Prevalence   245

Causes of Behavior Disorders   246
    Environmental Factors   247
    Physiological Factors   248

Characteristics of Students with Behavior Disorders   249
    School Achievement   249
    Social Adjustment   251
    Language and Communication   252
    Severe Disorders   253
    Families   254

Attention Deficit/Hyperactivity Disorder   256
  Assessment and Diagnosis   256
  Characteristics of Students with ADHD   258
  Educational Programs for Students with ADHD   258

Teaching Strategies and Accommodations   259
  Identification and Assessment: The Classroom Teacher's Role   259
  Curriculum Focus   264
  Academic Programming   266
  Behavior-Change Interventions   268
  Discipline in the Schools   272

8   Children with Autism and Related Disorders   278

Terms and Definitions   279
  Defining Autism   279
  Autism Spectrum Disorders/Pervasive Developmental Disorders   280
  Dual Diagnosis   282
  Prevalence   284

Causes of Autism   284
  Historical Opinions About Causes   284
  Current Hypotheses About Causes   285

Characteristics of Individuals with Autism   287
  Cognitive Characteristics   287
  Physical Characteristics   290
  Social Interaction   290
  Language and Communication   291
  Behavior   293
  Family Interactions   295

Teaching Strategies and Accommodations   296
  The Importance of Early Intervention   297
  Applied Behavior Analysis   298
  Environmental Interventions   300
  Language-Based Interventions   302
  Biochemical Interventions   303
  Transition to Adulthood   305

9   Children with Communication Disorders   312

Terms and Definitions   313
  Communication   313
  Language   315
  Speech   316

Language Development   316
  Language Acquisition   317
  Speech Production   320

Types and Characteristics of Communication Disorders   320
  Language Disorders   320
  Speech Disorders   323
  Dialects and Language Differences   325
  Hearing Loss   326

Causes of Communication Disorders   326
  Prevalence   327
  Recognizing Risk for Language Disorders   328

Teaching Strategies and Accommodations 331
  Assessment 331
  Placement and Service Options 338
  Strategies for Working with Students with Communication
    Learning Needs 340
  Members of the Collaborative Team 341

10 Children Who Are Deaf and Hard of Hearing   351

Terms and Definitions 352

Causes of Hearing Loss 353
  Hearing and Hearing Loss 353
  Conductive Hearing Loss 354
  Sensorineural Hearing Loss 356
  Students with Hearing Loss and Additional Disabilities 356
  Prevalence 358
  Measurement of Hearing Loss 358

Characteristics of Students with Hearing Loss 359
  Language Development 359
  Cognitive and Intellectual Development 361
  School Achievement 362
  Social and Emotional Development 363
  Deafness and Culture 364

Teaching Strategies and Accommodations 368
  Early Identification and Intervention 368
  Developing Communication Skills 368
  Curriculum 378
  Assessment 380
  School Placement 380

Technological Advances 384
  Hearing Aids 384
  Cochlear Implants 386
  Assistive Listening Devices 386
  Telecommunication Devices 386
  Captioning 387

11 Children Who Are Blind or Have Low Vision   391

Terms and Definitions 392

Causes of Visual Impairment 394
  How We See 394
  Causes of Vision Loss 395
  Prevalence 395

Characteristics of Students Who Are Blind or Have Low Vision 396
  Language and Concept Development 397
  Motor Development 399
  Cognitive and Intellectual Development 399
  Social and Emotional Development 400
  School Achievement 401
  Effects on the Family 402

Teaching Strategies and Accommodations 405
  Early Intervention 405
  Identification and Assessment 406

Curriculum   408
School Settings for Students Who Are Blind or Have Low Vision   416
Education for Students with Additional Disabilities   418
Assistive Technology   418

12 Children with Physical Disabilities and Health Impairments   426

Terms and Definitions   427
Physical Disabilities   427
Health Impairment   428
Prevalence   428

Types of Physical Disabilities   428
Neurological Conditions   429
Musculoskeletal Conditions   435
Traumatic Injury   437

Types of Health Impairments   439
Asthma   439
Juvenile Diabetes   440
Cystic Fibrosis   441
Acquired Immune Deficiency Syndrome (AIDS)   442
Childhood Cancer   443
Attention Deficit/Hyperactivity Disorder (ADHD)   443
Multiple Disabilities   444

Characteristics of Individuals with Physical Disabilities and Health Impairments   444
Cognitive Development   445
Communication and Language Development   445
Social and Emotional Development   446
Effects on the Family   447

Teaching Strategies and Accommodations   449
Early Intervention   449
Educational Planning   450
Accessing Instruction   453
Integrating Technology   457

Adult Life   462

13 Children Who Are Gifted and Talented   468

Terms and Definitions   469
Early Scholars and Their Ideas on Giftedness   470
Current Definitions of Giftedness   471
Criteria for Identification   479

Factors Contributing to Giftedness   481
Hereditary and Biological Factors   481
Environmental Factors   481
Prevalence   482

Characteristics of Students Who Are Gifted and Talented   482
Cognitive Characteristics   483
Social and Emotional Characteristics   483

Physical Characteristics   483
Personal Characteristics   485
Special Populations of Gifted Students   485

Teaching Strategies and Accommodations   493
Early Intervention   493
Identification and Assessment: The Teacher's Role   494
Placement Alternatives   495
Program Models   502
Curriculum Modifications in the General Education Classroom   503
Is Special Education for Gifted Students Necessary?   509

PART **3   Current Issues in Special Education   517**

14 **The Special and General Education Relationship:
New Trends and Challenges   518**

Educational Reform: General Implications   519

Issues in Assessment   521
Purposes of Assessment   521
High-Stakes Testing   522
School Accountability: Perceptions of Disability   523

Access to the General Education Curriculum   524
Curriculum Standards   525
Universal Design for Learning   526

Providing Instruction   528
Teacher Preparation   529
Instructional Options   530

Glossary   G-0

References   R-1

Credits   C-0

Name Index   I-1

Subject Index   I-6

Preface

Our Focus

This fourth edition of *Exceptional Children and Youth* retains many of the qualities found in its previous editions but also moves forward to keep up with changes and new research in our dynamic field. Our values, as special educators and teacher educators, have not changed. In this book, we continue to focus on:

- *Respect* for our readers—future teachers and school professionals;
- *Respect* for our subjects—the exceptional students that they will teach;
- *Confidence* in the power of teachers to instruct and motivate;
- A belief in the *commonalities* between exceptional children and their typical peers;
- A *commitment to the unique learning characteristics* of many of the students we describe;
- The crucial role that *family involvement and support* plays in the development of exceptional children and youth.

You will see these important themes and philosophies interwoven throughout our narrative. In terms of writing style, we aim to present our content and transmit our values in a direct, clear, and friendly voice while also maintaining intellectual challenge and rigor.

Our Audience

We know that the readers of this book will be a diverse group—in profession, age, and experience. Most readers will be future teachers. In some states, these teacher candidates will be undergraduates. In others, our readers will be post-baccalaureate or graduate students. Some readers are currently teaching while changing or renewing their credential or license. Other professionals who work with and support exceptional students in schools will read this book as part of their professional preparation as well: for example, speech-language specialists, counselors, school nurses, and adaptive physical education specialists. Our readers mirror the schools where our children are taught, and our content must model the collaborative spirit that will serve those students most effectively. Our readers are also increasingly diverse in their own cultural and linguistic backgrounds, as are the children they are learning to teach. In addition, an increasing number of our readers will have disabilities themselves. Assisted by the laws and policies described in this book, they will have a unique affinity for their exceptional students. We welcome them all.

Our Approach

While the spirit and the values embodied in our book have not changed, the content must keep up with a field that reflects new science, social policy, and practice. Since the last edition of the text was published in 2002, the American education field has undergone important changes, such as the *No Child Left*

Behind legislation and discussion surrounding the reauthorization of the Individuals with Disabilities Education Act (IDEA), which is in process as we write. The fourth edition discusses these and other important developments that currently influence our field. In addition, each chapter of the text has been substantially updated.

Our Text Organization

Exceptional Children and Youth, Fourth Edition, is presented in three major parts:

- *Part One,* "Building Blocks for Working with Exceptional Children and Youth" introduces the major topics in special education. Chapters 1 through 3 address the history, development, and current status of special education, factors that put children at risk for a disability, early intervention, and the role of the child's family and culture in the educational process. These first three chapters are grouped together because these factors are critical elements for all areas of special education—and for all exceptional individuals.

- *Part Two,* "Learning About the Potential of Exceptional Children," discusses students with specific types of exceptionalities. We point out the similarities in learning characteristics among students with different categorical labels and the similarities in effective instructional procedures. In working with exceptional individuals, we encourage the reader to focus on the level of support a student needs to learn critical skills, to identify the most effective way to present those skills, and to recognize that categories and labels have limited value. Chapters 4 through 13 provide basic background on the definition and prevalence of the exceptionality. Most of each chapter is devoted to understanding the effects of the exceptionality on the student's learning and to educational issues such as placement, assessment, and appropriate teaching strategies.

- *Part Three,* "Current Issues in Special Education," contains Chapter 14, "The Special and General Education Relationship: New Trends and Challenges." Having assimilated the foundational knowledge in the field of special education, our readers will conclude their reading with a comprehensive look at the special education issues that are making the pages of today's newspapers.

Our Revisions to This Edition

This fourth edition represents our most thorough revision process yet—both in terms of content additions and pedagogical improvements. We are very excited about the following new additions and features:

- **New pedagogical structure:** The text has been revamped to include a systematic and helpful pedagogical structure in each chapter. As the reviewers of our text recommended, the book now includes *both student-oriented study tools* and *applied text features* such as teaching strategies, interesting excerpts from news media, and the real voices of many exceptional individuals. Please see the section below entitled "Special Learning Features" for a run-down of the specific features that you will find in each chapter.

- **More real-life stories, cases, and vignettes:** In order to truly understand the lives and challenges of exceptional children and youth, it is imperative to hear their real voices—and the voices of their families and teachers. During the revision process for this new edition, we spent much time collecting the most effective autobiographical pieces, stories, and cases to infuse throughout the text.

- **New full-color presentation:** A very exciting change in this edition is our move to full color (a change that has invigorated our approach as well as the attractiveness of the material to the reader). We believe this change will deepen the experience of the material for both the instructor and the student. You will note that new full-color figures, graphs, charts, and photos have been added to the text.

- **Detailed coverage of technology:** Throughout this new edition, you will see much attention paid to important technological resources that can aid exceptional students and those who support them. Each chapter contains several *marginal web icons* that direct readers to helpful web-based resources on exceptionality, and *Technology Focus* boxes that spotlight a specific assistive technology in each chapter. The text also includes screen shots of important websites and web resources on special education.

- **Emphasis on CEC standards and portfolio development:** As you can see on the text's inside covers, at the end of each chapter, and on the text website, the fourth edition is aligned with the Council for Exceptional Children's (CEC) Content Standards for Teacher Preparation Programs in Special Education. Each portfolio activity in the text fulfills one of the specific CEC content standards. These activities will allow students to understand, apply, and master the CEC Standards. In addition, an interactive electronic portfolio template is included on the fourth edition text website so that student can easily complete and submit these activities.

- **Enhanced coverage of multicultural and diversity issues:** Wherever relevant, we have included current research and information about multicultural and diversity issues related to special education, such as an analysis of the disproportionate numbers of minority children in special education programs, the role of cultural self-awareness in teaching students with diverse backgrounds, responses of different ethnic minority groups to parenting a child with a disability, and the underrepresentation of diverse students within gifted and talented programs.

- **Chapter-by-chapter updates:** Every chapter in the text has been thoroughly updated to reflect current research and scholarly thinking. In addition, each categorical chapter (Chapters 4–13) continues to have a clear emphasis on strategies for inclusive classrooms, and has been revised and updated to reflect changes in the field. The list below enumerates the specific changes that can be found in each chapter:

Chapter 1, "An Introduction to Special Education," introduces the "Framework of Support" for students with special needs and provides a template for "Unified Plans of Support." In addition, there is a reanalysis of disproportionality issues and a section defining assistive technology, which serves as the foundation for an expanded focus on technology throughout the book.

Chapter 2, "Risk Factors and Early Intervention" includes major revisions such as broadening our emphasis on prevention of disabilities through healthy pregnancy; new discussion of environmental toxins and on single parenting; emphasizing the delivery of early intervention in natural environments; and ending with a review of the importance of relationships.

Chapter 3, "Families and Culture," focuses on the reader's own experiences as a foundation for studying families. Expanded discussion of culture and cultural self-awareness leads the chapter. A family map has been included, and there is an expanded discussion of sources of support for families.

Chapter 4, "Children with Learning Disabilities," has been updated to reflect the new issues, positions, and research in the area of learning disabilities. We define and discuss the newly proposed definition of learning disabilities that focuses on response to intervention. We highlight the science of reading: specific updates address neurobiology and reading, phonemic awareness, and reading fluency. In addition, the new edition provides instructional guidelines and strategies in math and written language.

Chapter 5, "Children with Mental Retardation," has increased coverage of multicultural issues and concerns relative to the identification of children with mental retardation. We've also greatly expanded coverage of curriculum options for children and youth with cognitive disabilities. Academic content and transition programs are covered in greater detail. We also have increased coverage on self-management and include the ways these programs can be augmented by technology in community settings.

Chapter 6, "Children with Severe Disabilities," includes expanded coverage of environmental supports. We provide new coverage and examples of educational programs and technology, designed to promote the success of students with severe disabilities in the community and in secondary and post-secondary environments. We've also expanded coverage of families in this chapter.

Chapter 7, "Children with Behavior Disorders," has increased coverage of academic performance and academic strategies for students with behavior disorders. We include more personal perspectives of students in this chapter. We also address some of the ways technology can be used to assist students in managing their own behavior.

Chapter 8, "Children with Autism and Related Disorders," has expanded descriptive coverage of Autism Spectrum Disorders. We also provide more extensive information on several key classroom interventions for students with autism. This information includes recommended research-based guidelines and key components for effective teaching strategies.

Chapter 9, "Children with Communication Disorders," continues the work of making a complex topic accessible to the neophyte reader by assisting the reader in comprehending the importance of language across the special education eligibility categories. There is more explanation and more examples; broadened treatment of the link between language and behavior—or the lack of language with inappropriate behavior. There is also expanded presentation of the assessment of children from language minority backgrounds; more emphasis on strategies and classroom discourse; and expanded treatment of augmentative communication.

Chapter 10, "Children Who Are Deaf and Hard of Hearing," has been updated and streamlined; there is a focus on the successful DHH student; a moving story about a hard-of-hearing adult analyzing her educational experiences; and an important technology update.

Chapter 11, "Children Who Are Blind or Have Low Vision," now presents exemplary practices for early intervention with VI infants; broadened discussion of the expanded core curriculum and much expanded discussion and description of assistive technology for students who are visually impaired.

Chapter 12, "Children with Physical Disabilities and Health Impairments," now includes key updates in data and demographic information related to physical disabilities. We also include more strategies for including students with physical disabilities in instruction. These strategies include a focus on the use of technology to facilitate accessibility to the curriculum.

Chapter 13, "Children Who Are Gifted and Talented," has an expanded discussion of bias in test scores used for identification of gifted/talented students; disproportionate representation of traditional minority group students with teacher identification as a potential source of bias; new "A Closer Look" boxes on gifted and talented individuals, such as singer-songwriter Norah Jones and psychologist extraordinaire Robert Sternberg. The chapter ends with justification of special education for gifted learners.

Chapter 14, "The Special and General Education Relationship: New Trends and Challenges," is *new* to this edition. It is our look at the changing relationship between general education and special education. In this new chapter, we examine current issues, such as high-stakes assessment, curriculum standards, and teacher preparation. We discuss the effects these issues have on the education of all students. We also look at a range of instructional strategies designed to facilitate services in general education classrooms, such as co-teaching, peer-tutoring, and universal design.

Special Learning Features Within Our Text

 In the fourth edition, we continue to include specific *teaching strategies* that our readers can use in their work with individuals with disabilities. These strategies are based on both research and practice, and they are infused into the narrative of the textbook and also presented in the multiple *Teaching Strategies & Accommodations* boxes that you will see throughout the text. While an introductory course in special education is not generally considered a methods course, we want to lay the groundwork here for successful teaching strategies.

In addition, the fourth edition contains the following useful text features:

-  **New Technology Focus** boxes in each chapter spotlight the most current and important assistive technologies for each disability category. We have also tried to include visuals or photographs for many of these new technology tools.

- **New Portfolio Activities** at the end of the chapter, linked to Council for Exceptional Children Content Standards, provide ideas for learning more about a topic, volunteering with a group, or putting new learning into action through an activity.

- **The First Person boxes** in each chapter let the reader experience the topic of the chapter through the voice of someone who has "been there." Most of the First Person boxes have been updated and replaced for the fourth edition. We have worked hard to include the most insightful and engaging pieces available.

- 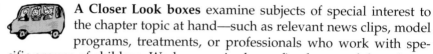 **A Closer Look boxes** examine subjects of special interest to the chapter topic at hand—such as relevant news clips, model programs, treatments, or professionals who work with specific groups of children. We have revised or refined most of these boxes for this new edition to make them as useful as possible.

Student Learning and Study Features

In addition to the features described above, *Exceptional Children and Youth* now contains an expanded set of student-oriented learning tools in each chapter, such as:

- **New chapter-opening outlines,** which provide an advance organizer for the reader.
- **New chapter-opening learning objectives,** listed at the front of each chapter.
- **New Pause & Reflect boxes,** interspersed throughout the chapters, usually at the end of each major chapter section. These breaks in the text allow the reader to pause and think about the information that has just been presented, usually in the context of a personal point of view.

- **New marginal web icons** point readers to relevant web-based resources that contain more detailed information on a variety of topics.
- **Chapter summaries** provide a detailed recap of each chapter's major points for review.
- **Marginal notes** pull out main ideas and definitions for easy reference.
- **Key terms** are included for review at the end of each chapter.
- **New Useful Resources** lists at the end of each chapter include descriptions of organizations, books, journal articles, and web sites related to each chapter topic that are relevant to the reader's personal interest and professional development.

Ancillaries That Accompany Our Text

Expanded Textbook Website **http://education.college.hmco.com**
Our newly revised textbook website has two primary functions: To provide a range of additional material for instructors to use in their teaching; and to provide opportunities for in-depth research and practice for students using the textbook.

For instructors, the following website resources are available:

- The Instructor's Resource Guide and Test Bank in an editable format (see the following discussion for a full description of the Instructor's Guide), PowerPoint Slides to help present key concepts and graphics to the class, which include text, art, and additional representations to support the text, additional information on CEC Standards, links to relevant websites that will extend knowledge of the course content, and case studies, including *The Story of Lucy and Nell* and other cases. A password to this website resource is available from your Houghton Mifflin publishing representative.

For students, the following website resources are available:

- Links to websites that will extend knowledge of the course content, case studies, ACE practice test items for each chapter, samples of documents referred to in the text, such as a sample Individualized Education Program (IEP), an interactive electronic portfolio template that will allow students to complete and submit chapter ending portfolio activities to the instructor, interactive glossary flashcards, and more.

Instructor's Resources Guide (available online or paper version available with adoption of the text)

Part 1 of the *Resources Guide* provides model syllabi for organizing course materials and activities for either a 10-week or a 15-week term. It is particularly useful for new instructors or those using this text for the first time. Part 2 includes chapter-by-chapter materials for the instructor and the student. For the instructor, complete coverage of the best available materials for teaching is provided— including learning objectives, chapter and lecture outlines, class activities, references, and resources that provide useful information (such as major publishers' names and addresses and the names and addresses of organizations that work with individuals who are exceptional). Part 3 is a complete set of assessment materials. The test bank contains multiple-choice and essay questions for each chapter.

Computerized Test Bank

Computerized versions of the printed *Test Bank* items are available upon adoption of the text on a hybrid CD ROM.

Special Education Resource Center

Find extensive professional resources in the "Special Education Resource Center" website (http://education.college.hmco.com). In addition to print and electronic resources, this site features assistive technology resources, links to professional organizations, school reform and standards content, current legislation, and teaching tools and supports.

Acknowledgments

We would like to acknowledge once more the contributions of the authors who contributed either complete or partial chapters in the first edition: Dr. Elaine Silliman and Janet Stack, University of South Florida, "Children with Communication Disorders"; Dr. Cay Holbrook and Dr. Mary Scott Healy, University of Arkansas, Little Rock, "Children Who Are Blind or Have Low Vision"; Dr. Emma Guilarte, University of South Carolina, "Children with Physical Disabilities and Health Impairments"; Dr. James Delisle, Kent State University, "Children Who Are Gifted and Talented"; and Dr. Philip Chinn, California State University, Los Angeles, "Exceptional Children from Diverse Cultural Backgrounds."

We continue to be blessed with a fantastic team at Houghton Mifflin, who provide us with ideas, structure, and support, and crack the whip at appropriate moments. Sue Pulvermacher-Alt, senior sponsoring editor in education, takes the lead; Lisa Mafrici, senior development editor, is our invaluable day-to-day correspondent and the "hub" of our team. Our development editor for this edition, Beth Kaufman, did so much to help us make this book more interesting and lively for the reader. She brought us the invaluable and sensitive eye of a parent of a child with special needs who is deeply interested in the material.

We would also like to thank our colleagues who reviewed various parts of the text and provided invaluable suggestions. They include: Shirley Cohen, Hunter College of CUNY; Carla S. Confer, University of Alabama; Karen S. Hurlbutt, University of North Dakota; Linda McCormick, University of Hawaii; Festus E. Obiakor, University of Wisconsin-Milwaukee; and Diana Rogers-Adkinson, University of Wisconsin-Whitewater.

Each of us has our own group of supporters at home whom we would like to acknowledge:

Nancy thanks her colleagues in the Division of Special Education at California State University, Los Angeles, for their hallway consultations and professional inspiration, particularly Brenda Naimy, Diane Fazzi, and Sharon Sacks, who were always generous with their expert knowledge of students with visual impairment; Vivian Correa of the University of Florida and Ellen Schneiderman of California State University, Northridge for their good ideas; Maria Gutierrez and Margie Moennich for their friendship and support, and Maggie, Lucy, Nell, and Dewey Gram for being a great family.

Kathleen thanks her colleagues at the University of South Carolina for their professional generosity, creative inspiration, and humor; her family, especially Richard, for boundless support and encouragement, and her graduate students, Rhett Siebert, Brandi Parenti, and Aaron Davis, for their many contributions to this text.

Thanks to our readers, too, for sharing our commitment to great outcomes for exceptional children and youth.

Nancy Hunt and Kathleen Marshall

PART 1

Building Blocks for Working with Exceptional Children and Youth

Part 1 introduces you to the major topics in the field of special education. You'll learn how special education has evolved during the past three decades and its implications for your future classroom. You'll learn about the factors that may affect individual students' educational experiences: their individual strengths, their families, their cultural backgrounds, and their exposure to risk. In your role as a teacher, you will need to take all of these factors into account. As you will see, the building blocks we discuss here are a vital foundation for your work with exceptional individuals.

Part Outline

Chapter 1
An Introduction to
Special Education

Chapter 2
Risk Factors and Early
Intervention

Chapter 3
Families and Culture

1

An Introduction to Special Education

Outline

Terms and Definitions
Prevalence of Exceptional
    Children
Foundations of Special
    Education
    Early History: Great Teachers
        and Their Legacies
    Later History: Advocates for
        Social Change
    Legislation
    Litigation
    Disproportionate
        Representation of
        Minority Children
Individualized Education
    The Individualized Family
        Service Plan
    The Individualized Education
        Program
    The Individualized Transition
        Plan
The Pros and Cons of Labeling
Educational Setting
    The Framework of Support
        for Students with
        Disabilities
SUMMARY
KEY TERMS
USEFUL RESOURCES
PORTFOLIO ACTIVITIES

Learning Objectives

After reading this chapter, the reader will:

- Define special education and use the terms of special education appropriately

- Describe how legislation and litigation have opened doors for exceptional individuals

- Describe the concept of individualized education, and the Individualized Education Program (IEP)

- Identify ways in which general and special educators work together to improve educational outcomes for *all* children

Most people come into teaching, or service to children in schools, with the hope that they can make things better for their students, and for their communities. Even the cynical among us enter our classrooms with a spark of hope that we can do good. But the realities of schools often make it hard to keep that spark alive. We must face working conditions that are often far from ideal; mountains of paperwork; demands from administrators and families; students who don't seem to want to learn; and tremendous pressure from school boards and state education agencies to improve student achievement and meet state standards in the subject areas.

What keeps us going? Our students, of course—the connections we make with them, and the successes, small and large, that come about as a result of our hard work (and theirs). But even the students in U.S. schools are becoming more complex. More and more, American schools are becoming places of great student diversity. The changes that result from this diversity are sometimes unsettling to us. Our students may not speak English in their homes, their traditions and values may be mysterious to us, and they may not learn the way we expect them to learn. Yet we are there to teach them *all*.

We are about to embark on the study of some of those children—those who present special challenges to their teachers by virtue of their disabilities and their special gifts and talents. With so much expected of teachers, so much responsibility resting on your shoulders, will you be able to teach and see progress in each of your students? In this book we hope to show you that the differences among children are simply variations on a theme of *commonalities*. You can reach and teach every one of them—and you will.

Terms and Definitions

Like other fields of study, special education has its own terminology. We use several terms to describe the group of students we work with. Among them is **exceptional**, used in the title of this book. We use this word to describe the range of students—those who are called blind, gifted, deaf—who receive special education services in the schools. It does not simply refer to students who are gifted, but to any student who may be an "exception" to the rule.

> Exceptional students are all those who receive special education services in the school.

Some of these students have a **disability** (students who are gifted do not usually fall into this category). A disability is a limitation, such as a difficulty in learning to read or an inability to hear, walk, or see. A **handicap** is not the same as a disability; a handicap results from the limitations imposed by the environment and by attitudes toward a person with disabilities. The American Psychological Association puts it this way:

> A disability is a limitation; a handicap results from the limitations imposed by the environment and by people's attitudes.

It is recommended that the word *disability* be used to refer to an attribute of a person, and *handicap* to the *source* of limitations. Sometimes a disability itself may handicap a person, as when a person with one arm is handicapped in playing the violin. However, when the limitation is environmental, as in the case of attitudinal, legal, and architectural barriers, the disability is *not* handicapping—the environmental factor is. This distinction is important because the environment is frequently overlooked as a major source of limitation, even when it is far more limiting than the disability. Thus, prejudice handicaps people by denying access to opportunities; inaccessible buildings surrounded by steps and curbs handicap people who require the use of a ramp. (Committee on Disability Issues in Psychology, 2003)

Some examples will help here. Some adults who are deaf, for example, admit that they are disabled—they hear very little. But they do not consider themselves handicapped. Their disability does not limit them in ways that they consider significant. They associate with a community of other deaf people with whom they can communicate freely; they do not often encounter people who manifest prejudice against them. Most are satisfied with their lives, their abilities and limitations. The deaf schoolchild, however, may be considered handicapped; she may not yet have learned how to communicate efficiently or to read English well, which considerably limits her ability to communicate with others and to achieve in school.

A young person who has experienced a spinal cord injury may emerge from the hospital unable to walk—a serious disability and perhaps a handicap. Through physical therapy and rehabilitation, however, that person can often learn strategies to cope with the handicap associated with the disability. Use of a wheelchair and adaptive devices in the car will enable him to become mobile again; modifications of workspace and the home may make those places accessible to him using a wheelchair. Nowadays, a physical limitation does not prevent a person from participating in sports, from wheelchair racing to mountain climbing.

Overcoming the attitudes of others toward a disability may be a more difficult fight. Will the behavior of friends and family change? Will job opportunities exist? Will new acquaintances think of him as a disabled person, or as a person who happens to have a disability?

People-first language focuses on the person, not the disability.

You will notice that we try to use **people-first language** in this book; first we describe the person and then the disability (see the Closer Look box entitled, "People-First Language"). For example, rather than say *an autistic child*, we suggest saying *a child with autism*. This is so that we can think about individuals who have disabilities, such as the young person just described, as *people* who happen to have a disability.

Naturally, within special education there is an emphasis on the prevention of disabilities and on starting to provide the help that children and families need as early as possible. **Early intervention** is the provision of services (instruction, therapies, and supports) to children from birth to age 3 and their families. Its goal is optimizing each child's learning potential and daily well-being and increasing that child's opportunities to function effectively in the community (Cook, Klein, & Tessier, 2004). We use the term *at risk* to describe those infants and young children who have a greater-than-average likelihood of developing a disability because of factors such as extreme prematurity, chronic poverty, or early medical problems. Some educators also use the term to describe older students who may be more likely to drop out of school; in this book, however, we use it to describe infants and young children only.

Early intervention helps reduce the impact of disabilities on young children.

What *is* special education, you may wonder, and what is so special about it? **Special education** is the educational program designed to meet the unique learning and developmental needs of a student who is exceptional. What is special about special education is the recognition of the unique nature of each individual and the accompanying design of an educational program specifically planned to meet that person's needs. Special education is not limited to a particular "special" place; most special educators believe that special education

Special education is the education program designed to meet the unique needs of exceptional children.

should take place in the most normal, natural environment possible. That may be in a baby's home, in a general education classroom, or in the Pizza Hut in the student's community; sometimes it may be in a hospital or a special school designed for a particular group of students, such as a school for students who are deaf. This book is designed to help you learn more about special education; we hope that it will help you find your own role in serving students who are exceptional.

❓ Pause and Reflect

In her book, *The Language Police* (2003), Diane Ravitch decries the use of people-first language because she thinks it is convoluted and indirect. What is your stand on this issue? Is this kind of language necessary? How might it be overdone? ●

A Closer Look   People-First Language

 In speaking or writing, remember that children and adults with disabilities are like everyone else—except that they happen to have a disability. Here are a few tips for improving your language related to disabilities and handicaps.

1. Speak of the person first, then the disability.
2. Emphasize abilities, not limitations.
3. Do not label people as part of a disability group.
4. Don't give excessive praise or attention to a person with a disability; don't patronize.
5. Choice and independence are important; let the person do or speak for himself or herself as much as possible
6. A disability is a functional limitation that interferes with a person's ability to walk, hear, talk, learn, etc.; use the word *handicap* to describe a situation or barrier imposed by society, the environment, or oneself.

Say	Instead of
child with a disability	disabled or handicapped child
person with cerebral palsy	palsied, CP, or spastic person
person who has	afflicted, suffers from, victim of
developmental delay	slow
emotional disorder, mental illness	crazy, insane
uses a wheelchair	confined to a wheelchair
student with Down syndrome	mongoloid
has a physical disability	crippled
condition	disease (unless it *is* a disease)
seizures	fits
paralyzed	invalid
chronic illness	sickly
has paraplegia, semiplegia, quadraplegia	paraplegic, semiplegic, quadraplegic

Source: It's the "person first"—then the disability, *Pacesetter* (September 1989), 13.

Prevalence of Exceptional Children

Prevalence figures reflect how many students need special services. These figures are used to allocate funds, to determine whether there are enough teachers, and for many other purposes. In the 2002–2003 school year there were 5,946,202 children from age 6 to 21 receiving special education services in U.S. schools (**http://www.ideadata.org/tables26th/ar_aa3.htm**). Figure 1.1 shows the breakdown of students by disability group. Notice that almost 52 percent of the total number of school-age students being served are classified as learning disabled, and about 90 percent of the total number fall into the four largest categories: learning disabilities, speech or language impairments, mental retardation, and emotional disturbance. Overall, about 9 percent of elementary and secondary students in the United States receive special education services (U.S. Department of Education, 2002).

Foundations of Special Education

Although there have always been exceptional children, documented attempts to teach them are relatively recent. As Hewett and Forness (1984) put it, "Throughout recorded history, perhaps the only categories that mattered were the *weak*, the *odd*, and the *poor*" (p. 3). Present-day concepts of disability are a reflection of the values and beliefs of contemporary culture, which emphasizes verbal and intellectual achievement, speed and mobility, and flawlessness in personal ap-

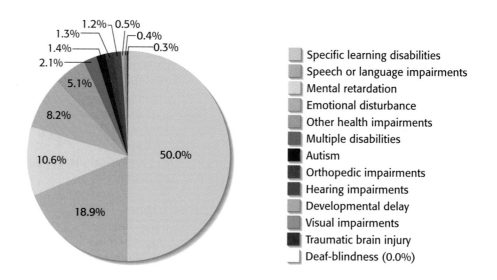

Figure 1.1

Percentage of Students Age 6–21 Served Under IDEA by Disability, 2001–2002 School Year

Source: U.S. Department of Education, Office of Special Education Programs, Data Analysis System (DANS). Available at http://www.ideadata.org.

Notes: Developmental delay is applicable only to children 3 to 9; data based on the December 1, 2001, count, updated as of August 30, 2002.

pearance. The first known attempts to teach children with disabilities came in the sixteenth and seventeenth centuries, when priests and other religious men and women taught small groups of deaf and blind children, usually the off-spring of the aristocracy (Moores, 2001).

Early History: Great Teachers and Their Legacies

A series of curious, innovative, and dedicated men and women in Europe and the United States pioneered the teaching techniques that are the foundation of special education. The work of **Jean-Marc-Gaspard Itard** in France was followed in Europe by that of **Edouard Seguin** and **Maria Montessori**; in the United States **Samuel Gridley Howe** and **Anne Sullivan Macy** were among the pioneers. Figure 1.2 provides more detail on these early teachers and some of their noteworthy students. Link to the Chapter One section in our textbook website at **education.college.hmco.com/student/** for more information and resources on great teachers of the past.

Later History: Advocates for Social Change

After an initial surge of interest within the United States in the education of children who were deaf, blind, or had mental retardation, school services for children with disabilities plateaued for many years. Families of children with disabilities either kept their children at home without going to school, or placed them in institutions. It was not until the 1960s that two events converged to reignite national interest in the needs of children with disabilities. The first of these was the election of John F. Kennedy as president in 1960. Kennedy had a sister, Rosemary, with mental retardation, and he was openly committed to improving the quality of life for people with mental retardation. He did two concrete things to accomplish this goal: He established the President's Commission on Mental Retardation, a group of expert researchers and practitioners who

The Kennedy family's commitment to improving services for people with disabilities helped lessen the stigma of mental retardation.

The Kennedy children in Hyannisport, Massachusetts around 1925. From left: Rosemary, John, Eunice, Joe Jr. and Kathleen. Rosemary was the inspiration for Eunice and John's commitment to people with mental retardation. (© CORBIS)

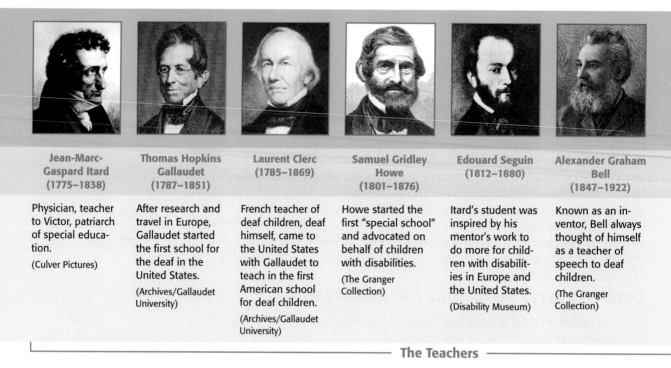

Jean-Marc-Gaspard Itard (1775–1838)	Thomas Hopkins Gallaudet (1787–1851)	Laurent Clerc (1785–1869)	Samuel Gridley Howe (1801–1876)	Edouard Seguin (1812–1880)	Alexander Graham Bell (1847–1922)
Physician, teacher to Victor, patriarch of special education. (Culver Pictures)	After research and travel in Europe, Gallaudet started the first school for the deaf in the United States. (Archives/Gallaudet University)	French teacher of deaf children, deaf himself, came to the United States with Gallaudet to teach in the first American school for deaf children. (Archives/Gallaudet University)	Howe started the first "special school" and advocated on behalf of children with disabilities. (The Granger Collection)	Itard's student was inspired by his mentor's work to do more for children with disabilities in Europe and the United States. (Disability Museum)	Known as an inventor, Bell always thought of himself as a teacher of speech to deaf children. (The Granger Collection)

— The Teachers —

Figure 1.2

Great Teachers and Their Students

identified the issues and priorities in the field, and he supported the use of federal funds to educate teachers of children with disabilities. Kennedy's greatest contribution was less concrete. His acknowledgment of mental retardation in his family and his dedication to improving services for people with disabilities played a large part in lessening the stigma of mental retardation and added prestige to the career of teaching children with disabilities.

The other event of the 1960s that influenced families and other advocates of children with disabilities was the civil rights movement, and the passage of the 1964 Civil Rights Act, which set the stage for advocacy for the civil rights of people with disabilities. The political and social demands of African Americans for equal rights and access to opportunities at all levels of society provided an example of what could be accomplished on behalf of disenfranchised groups to families and groups working with children with disabilities.

> With normalization, people with disabilities have the opportunity to lead typical lives.

In 1972, Wolf Wolfensberger articulated the principle of **normalization**—that people with disabilities should have the opportunity to lead a life as close to normal as possible. This philosophy implies that no matter how severe an individual's disability, he or she should have the opportunity to participate in all aspects of society. The normalization principle, which is "deeply embedded in services to individuals with disabilities" (Harry, Rueda, & Kalyanpur, 1999, p. 123), implied that special institutions for people with mental retardation, which tended to be segregated from the community, should be deemphasized.

> Deinstitutionalization has helped end the segregation of people with mental retardation from the community.

This movement, known as **deinstitutionalization**, has led to the establishment of many small group homes and other community-based residential facilities in towns and cities.

In schools, the application of the concept of normalization has led away from segregation—the education of exceptional children in special schools or

Anne Sullivan Macy (1866–1936)	Maria Montessori (1870–1952)	Victor, the "wild boy of Aveyron" (c. 1788–1828)	Laura Bridgeman (1829–1904)	Helen Keller (1880–1968)
Helen Keller's beloved "Teacher" who taught her to communicate. (AP Photo)	The first Italian woman M.D. Based her work with children with disabilities on that of Itard and Seguin. (© Hulton-Deutsch Collection/CORBIS)	Today he would be described as mentally retarded. (The Granger Collection)	Deaf and blind, Laura was taught to read and write by Samuel Gridley Howe. (The Granger Collection)	She became a widely admired writer, speaker, and public figure despite being deaf and blind. (Bettman/CORBIS)

Their Students

separate buildings—and toward the goal of education in the **least restrictive environment** (where the child with a disability has the most interaction with nondisabled children that is appropriate;—see the next section for more information on this). After the landmark special education legislation P.L. 94-142 (now known as the Individuals with Disabilities Education Act or IDEA) was passed in 1975, educators used the term *mainstreaming* to describe the participation of children with disabilities in the general education classroom. Today, the word **inclusion** is used. Inclusion refers to the placement of a child with disabilities in the general education classroom, with the supports that child needs also provided there. The 1997 amendments to IDEA placed renewed emphasis on educating students with disabilities in less restrictive environments. In particular, the law encourages opportunities for children with disabilities to participate in general education settings and in the general education curriculum. Inclusion of children with disabilities in such settings is important because *it raises expectations for student performance, provides opportunities for children with disabilities to learn alongside their nondisabled peers, improves coordination between regular and special educators, and increases school-level accountability for educational results* (National Center for Education Statistics, 1999).

> Inclusion refers to placement of a child with disabilities in the general education classroom, with the supports that child needs also provided in the classroom.

In practice, there appears to be a continuum of inclusion in today's schools, ranging from full-time, complete membership of the student with disabilities in the general education classroom to part-time participation for nonacademic subjects and activities. The practice of inclusion makes considerable demands on both the general educator and the special educator. The collaboration that must occur is often new to both, and it is a skill that requires time, patience, and willingness. Certainly, not everyone is in support of inclusion—in fact, the practice can be quite controversial. Many special educators strongly believe that inclu-

> The practice of inclusion requires collaboration between the general educator and the special educator, as well as time, patience, and willingness.

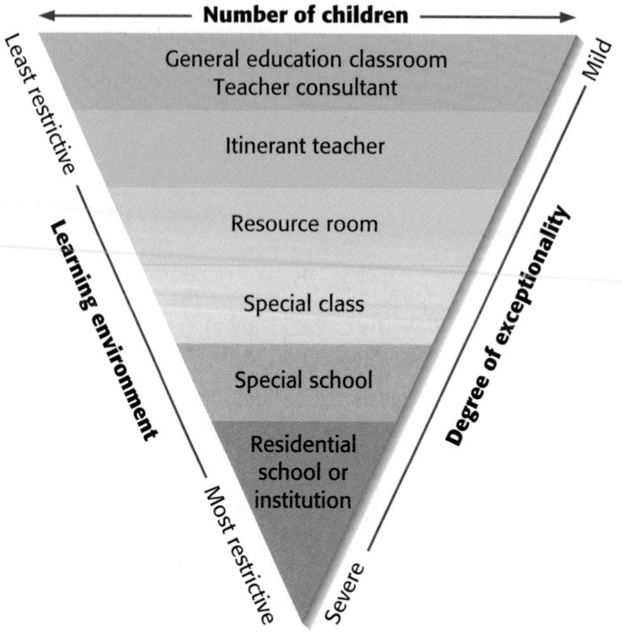

Figure 1.3

Learning Environments for
Exceptional Children: The
Continuum of Program
Options

Source: E. Deno, Special
education as developmental
capital, *Exceptional Children, 37*
(1970), 229–237.

sion should simply be one option in the continuum of program options and that
the individual needs of the child, rather than a "one-size-fits-all" philosophy,
should determine the child's placement (see Figure 1.3) Court decisions over the
past several years have affirmed the need for the continuum of program
options (U.S. courts affirm, 1996). In the ten years between the 1988–1989 and
1998–1999 school years, however, the number of students with disabilities
spending 80 percent or more of their time in the general education classroom increased from 31–48 percent. Along with that change has come a downward
trend in the percentage of students with disabilities educated in segregated settings (U.S. Department of Education, 2002).

General educators have sometimes objected to inclusive practices, maintaining that they are not prepared to meet the individual needs of children with disabilities, that the practice is too time-consuming, and that it takes time from
other children. But many special educators believe that placement in segregated
settings like a special school or even a special day class has interfered with the
social and academic growth of children with disabilities and has also limited the
opportunities of children who are not disabled to learn from those who are. Research suggests that the majority of general educators and administrators support the idea of inclusion, given the appropriate supports and collaborative
practices (Scruggs & Mastropieri, 1996; Villa, Thousand, Meyers, et al., 1996)
(see the Teaching Strategies box entitled, "Supports for General Education
Teachers"). Our hope is that this book, and the course it accompanies, will help
any member of the collaborative team—teacher, parent, psychologist, counselor,
therapist, nurse—have a clearer picture of students with disabilities and the
supports they need to succeed in the general education classroom.

Regardless of your personal experiences or beliefs about inclusion, it is important to understand what the "best practices" for including children with dis-

Teaching Strategies & Accommodations

Supports for General Education Teachers

A synthesis of research studies on inclusion has determined that the following supports are needed by general education teachers who are including students with disabilities in their classrooms:

- **Time.** Teachers report a need for one hour or more per day to plan for students with disabilities.

- **Training.** Teachers need systematic, intensive training—as part of their certification programs, as intensive and well-planned inservices, or as an ongoing process with consultants.

- **Personnel resources.** Teachers report a need for additional personnel assistance to carry out objectives. This could include a half-time aide and daily contact with special education teachers.

- **Materials resources.** Teachers need adequate curriculum materials and other classroom equipment appropriate to the needs of students with disabilities.

- **Class size.** Teachers agree that their class size should be reduced to fewer than twenty students if students with disabilities are included.

- **Consideration of severity of disability.** Teachers are more willing to include students with mild disabilities than students with more severe disabilities, apparently because of teachers' perceived ability to carry on their teaching mission for the entire classroom. By implication, the more severe the disabilities in the inclusive setting, the more the previously mentioned sources of support would be needed.

These needs may be greater for secondary teachers than for elementary teachers. Overall, it seems clear that many teachers have reservations or concerns about mainstreaming and inclusion and believe that substantial supports are necessary to enable these efforts to succeed. The ultimate success of mainstreaming or inclusion efforts, then, may well depend on the extent to which such supports are made available.

Source: T.E. Scruggs & M.A. Mastropieri, Teacher perceptions of mainstreaming/inclusion, 1958–1995, *Exceptional Children, 63*(1) (1996), 72.

abilities in general education classrooms are. They rest on three assumptions: *First,* that all teachers receive appropriate preparation and education about meeting the needs of children with disabilities; *second,* that children with disabilities are productive learners in the general education classroom; and *third,* that the appropriate supports are provided to both the student with disabilities and the teacher.

? Pause and Reflect

In thirty years, schooling options for families have changed from none—particularly for families of children with more severe disabilities—to a range of settings, including general education. Put yourself in the shoes of a parent of a child with a disability. What do you think you would want for your own child? ●

A good day at school means having fun with friends. (Elizabeth Crews/The Image Works)

Legislation

Federal law now mandates that children with disabilities be educated in the "least restrictive environment"—that setting which gives the child the greatest number of options for interactions with nondisabled peers and the same opportunities as those peers.

● *Public Law 94-142*   The law that has had the most profound impact on children with disabilities is Public Law (P.L.) 94-142, formerly known as the Education for All Handicapped Children Act (1975) and now known as the **Individuals with Disabilities Education Act (IDEA)**. It requires that every child between the ages of 3 and 21 with a disability be provided a free, appropriate public education in the least restrictive environment.

Before P.L. 94-142 was passed in 1975, only one-fifth of the children with disabilities in the United States were enrolled in school programs at all (U.S. Department of Education, 1995); the remainder were excluded from school, received inappropriate education, or were housed in institutions that did not provide educational programs. Now we are much closer to enrolling all children with disabilities in appropriate educational programs, although this is still an elusive goal. Congress has amended the law several times (see Table 1.1); as a result of the 1975 law and its amendments, children with disabilities and their families have well-defined rights. See the Closer Look box on page 13 for the principles that are the foundations of IDEA.

IDEA identifies specific categories that qualify a student for special education and related services. Under the law, the term "child with a disability" means a child:

- with mental retardation, hearing impairments (including deafness), speech or language impairments, visual impairments (including blindness), emotional disturbance, orthopedic impairments, autism, traumatic brain injury, other health impairments, or specific learning disabilities; and

P.L. 94-142, now known as IDEA, requires that children 3 to 21 with a disability be provided a free and appropriate public education in the least restrictive environment.

- who, by reason thereof, needs special education and related services (Knoblauch & Sorenson, 1998).

In addition to these categories, the 1997 amendments to IDEA allow states to classify children ages 3–9 as "developmentally delayed."

A child must meet two criteria to qualify for special education services under IDEA: He or she must have one of the disabilities listed above, and he or she must require special education and related services. The need for special education is determined through formal and informal assessment, which establishes whether the child's progress is behind that of typical children the same age. Not all children with disabilities do require services; many attend school

Table 1.1 Selected Foundations of Special Education Law		
1973	P.L. 93-112	Section 504 of the Rehabilitation Act
1975	P.L. 94-142	Education for All Handicapped Children Act (now known as IDEA)
1986	P.L. 99-457	IDEA amendments
1990	P.L. 101-336	Americans with Disabilities Act
1990	P.L. 101-476	IDEA amendments
1997	P.L. 105-17	IDEA amendments

A Closer Look   **Foundations of IDEA**

- **Zero reject.** No child, no matter how severely disabled, shall be refused an appropriate education by the schools.

- **Free appropriate public education.** Each student is entitled to special education and related services in public school at no cost. At the heart of this component of the law is the Individualized Education Plan (IEP). We describe the IEP further on pages 25–30 of this chapter and refer to its use in the classroom throughout this book.

- **Least restrictive environment.** Each child must be educated with nondisabled peers to the maximum extent appropriate. We discuss the differing perspectives on this concept later in the chapter (see page 9).

- **Nondiscriminatory evaluation.** Evaluation procedures must be conducted with fairness

in the child's native language, using multiple measures.

- **Due process and procedural safeguards.** Families and school districts can exercise their Fourteenth Amendment rights to due process under the law; that is, they may resort to mediation and appeal procedures when they do not agree with one another over issues such as the child's placement.

- **Technology-related assistance.** IEP teams must consider whether students with disabilities need assistive technology devices and services in order to benefit from special education and related services.

Source: Adapted from M. Yell, *The law and special education* (Columbus, OH: Merrill, 1998).

without any modifications to their program (Knoblauch & Sorenson, 1998). For example, some children with chronic health impairments do not require special services to keep up in school, despite frequent absences.

You can see that under federal law a great deal of emphasis is placed on what is called "categorical special education": providing services to children as if they fall into neat boxes, or categories. You may know from your own experience that this isn't the case in "real life"; children are much more complicated than that. You may find that, as you read through this book, the characteristics of a child you know are described in several different chapters. Keep in mind

FIRST PERSON

David

David learned to jump rope last week.

It may not seem like much of an accomplishment for a strapping fourth-grader. By the time kids reach the fourth grade, haven't they mastered rope jumping, and soccer, and dodge ball and capture the flag?

Not all of them.

Jumping rope can be a source of pride for an awkward boy who has spent most of his time on the sidelines, watching other children . . . and for my daughter and her friends, who taught him how to play.

I don't know much about David. Only the stories my daughter tells.

He sits near the teacher, in the front row, and struggles through even the most basic tasks. He giggles when nothing's funny, speaks out when he hasn't been called upon, mumbles to himself. He has a distracting habit of constantly wringing his hands. He spends part of each day away from class, with a special teacher.

"I think he's handicapped," my daughter says, not as judgment but as explanation. It takes me back to my days as a reporter and all the stories I wrote on "mainstreaming"—the practice of teaching disabled students alongside other children, instead of isolating them in classes labeled "special ed."

Over the years I'd duly noted the pros and cons: the advocates' claims that disabled kids benefit by making friends and learning social skills from other children, and the critics' concerns that handicapped kids might be shunned or belittled or take up too much of a teacher's time. What neither argument acknowledges is what I see: that the benefits of this social experiment flow not just one way, but back from the disabled child to mine.

Because, while David might be struggling to learn, he is teaching without effort—providing his classmates with new opportunities each day to learn and practice patience, tolerance, kindness, ingenuity.

I know it's not always easy, for him or for them. He is annoying at times, tagging along, interrupting conversations. I'm sure he tries the teacher's patience.

that the categories we use are for the convenience of lawmakers and educators; they are not iron-clad descriptors of the way children really learn and function. Harriet McBryde Johnson is a person who defies the application of categories. Let's allow her to speak for herself:

> It's not that I'm ugly. It's more that most people don't know how to look at me. The sight of me is routinely discombobulating. The power wheelchair is enough to inspire gawking, but that's the least of it. Much more impressive is the impact on my body of more than four decades of a muscle-

He fails, it seems, as often as he succeeds. That hurts, and he doesn't know how not to let it show. He cries sometimes. And on the playground, the older kids tease him.

But his classmates comfort him and rise to his defense. They encourage him when he's afraid to try something new. They teach him songs, tell him jokes . . . even if it means explaining the punch line over and over, until he understands it well enough to laugh.

And every day at recess, my daughter and her friends take out the long, red jump rope that David likes. They station him at one end, put the rope in his hand, take his arm and start it turning. Then as they jump, they swing their arms in big, wide circles, so David can keep pace by mimicking them.

Then it is his turn to stand alongside the rope and jump.

My daughter laughs with glee as she tells the story. I can imagine the grin on David's face, his fists clenched in determination, his pride as he launches himself airborne. And I can almost hear the shouts of his cheering section, yelling at him to lift his feet: *"Jump! . . . jump! . . . jump!"*

It has taken my daughter days longer than her classmates, but she finally has completed her computer lesson. Now everyone in class has finished and has received an award . . . everyone but David.

My daughter's sense of accomplishment is tinged by a tender sort of pity. "I wish everything wasn't so hard for David," she says, putting her award aside. "It's just not fair."

And I have to fight back tears . . . but not for David. You see, my daughter is no stranger to struggle. School has never come easy for her. She knows how it feels to be last, to be wrong . . . to miss the joke's punch line, to jump at the wrong time.

Fourth grade has been a good year for her. She has earned A's and B's, learned long division, won a solo in the school's musical, become a standout on her soccer team. But if you ask her now what she's proudest of, she's liable to tell you that it's teaching David that he can jump rope.

Because she has learned how one small achievement can lift you up, make you believe that big things are possible. And she wants David to learn that too.

Sandy Banks

Source: "Lessons from a Boy Named David" by Sandy Banks, *Los Angeles Times,* February 21, 1999.

Harriet McBryde Johnson is an attorney in Charleston, South Carolina, and a fearless advocate for people with disabilities. (Courtesy of Harriet McBryde Johnson)

wasting disease. At this stage of my life, I'm Karen Carpenter thin, flesh mostly vanished, a jumble of bones in a floppy bag of skin. When, in childhood, my muscles got too weak to hold up my spine, I tried a brace for a while, but fortunately a skittish anesthesiologist said no to fusion, plates and pins—all the apparatus that might have kept me straight. At 15, I threw away the back brace and let my spine reshape itself into a deep twisty S-curve. Now my right side is two deep canyons. To keep myself upright, I lean forward, rest my rib cage on my lap, plant my elbows beside my knees. Since my backbone found its own natural shape, I've been entirely comfortable in my skin.

I used to try to explain that in fact I enjoy my life, that it's a great sensual pleasure to zoom by power chair on these delicious muggy streets, that I have no more reason to kill myself than most people. But it gets tedious. God didn't put me on this street to provide disability awareness training to the likes of them. In fact, no god put anyone anywhere for any reason, if you want to know.

But they don't want to know. They think they know everything there is to know, just by looking at me. That's how stereotypes work. They don't know that they're confused, that they're really expressing the discombobulation that comes in my wake. (Johnson, 2003)

A disability rights attorney in South Carolina, Johnson recently debated Peter Singer, the Princeton philosopher who believes in "selected infanticide"— the killing of babies born with disabilities (Kuhse & Singer, 1985; Singer, 1996). Johnson's story would qualify for inclusion in at least two chapters of this book—she being both physically disabled—and gifted.

● *Major Amendments to IDEA*

Public Law 99-457   In 1986, Congress amended P.L. 94-142 with P.L. 99-457. This amendment extended the provisions of P.L. 94-142 to all children between the ages of 3 and 5 through the Preschool Grants Program. Now states receiving federal funds under these laws *must* provide a free and appropriate public education to preschoolers with disabilities as well. In addition, states are provided incentives to develop early intervention programs for infants with disabilities and those who are at risk for developing disabilities from birth through age 3. All states now provide early intervention for those infants. We will learn more about these provisions in Chapter 2.

> P.L. 99-457 extended the provisions of P.L. 94-142 to children between the ages of 3 and 5.

Public Law 101-476   These 1990 amendments used "people-first" language to rename the Education of the Handicapped Act the Individuals with Disabilities Education Act (IDEA). This law also recognized the importance of preparing students for life and work after school. It mandated the creation of an Individualized Transition Plan (ITP) that would prepare each adolescent student receiving special education services for life after school.

> IDEA now mandates an Individualized Transition Plan (ITP) for each student receiving special education from the age of 14.

Public Law 105-17   The 1997 amendments to IDEA provided the most significant revision of the law relating to the education of children with disabilities since P.L. 94-142 was passed in 1975. The law was amended to require that students with disabilities participate in state and district-wide assessment (testing) programs, with accommodations when necessary; that the Individualized Education Program (IEP) process place increased emphasis on the participation of students with disabilities in the general education curriculum; and that general education teachers be involved in developing, reviewing, and revising the IEP.

Latest Amendments to IDEA   IDEA is likely to be reauthorized by Congress in 2004. Several areas are being considered for changes. Congress will also determine what constitutes "full funding" for IDEA. States have never received the amount of money the federal government promised them to fund the law (Goldstein, 2003). For news of the IDEA reauthorization, go to **http://www .nichcy.org/reauth/index.html/**.

● *Section 504*   Are you taking this class in a building that has ramps leading up to it? Are there elevators as well as stairs and escalators? In the elevators are there Braille cells next to the numerals indicating each floor? Is there a wide stall, a low sink, and a low mirror in the restroom? Is one of the public telephones set low on the wall? Are there plenty of special parking places for people with disabilities outside?

Let us hope that all these adaptations make your school building accessible to students, faculty, and staff with disabilities. Most public facilities have not become accessible out of the goodness of anyone's heart. They are accessible because of Section 504 of the Rehabilitation Act of 1973, a civil rights law requiring that institutions not discriminate against people with disabilities in any way if they wish to receive federal funds.

Section 504 has had considerable impact on architecture and construction in the United States, since it requires changes in the design of buildings for public use for physical access. It has also been used to prohibit discrimination against a person simply because he or she is disabled. For example, if you had a newborn baby who needed corrective surgery to open a blocked trachea, would you hesitate to have the procedure performed? Well, that surgery cannot be denied to a baby with Down syndrome either, simply because she will have mental retardation. Section 504 prohibits discrimination on the basis of disability. To read more about disability rights laws, visit **http://www.usdoj.gov/crt/ada/cguide.htm**.

Students who may not qualify for services in the schools under the thirteen definitions in IDEA but still have a significant learning problem that affects their ability to perform in school may qualify for services under Section 504. Although there is no funding available under Section 504, it requires that the school create a special plan to accommodate the student's learning needs and create an accessible environment (Mastropieri & Scruggs, 2000). Figure 1.4 outlines the steps for consideration of IDEA and Section 504 eligibility.

● *The Americans with Disabilities Act*   On July 26, 1990, President George H. W. Bush signed into law P.L. 101-336, the **Americans with Disabilities Act (ADA)**, with these words: "Today, America welcomes into the mainstream of life all people with disabilities. Let the shameful wall of exclusion finally come tumbling down." The ADA is civil rights legislation for people with disabilities, and it is patterned on Section 504 of the Rehabilitation Act of 1973. The provisions of the ADA cover four major areas: *private-sector employment; public services,* including public facilities, buses, and trains; *public accommodations,* including restaurants, hotels, theaters, doctors' offices, retail stores, museums, libraries, parks, private schools, and day-care centers; and *telecommunications,* making telephone relay services available twenty-four hours a day to people with speech and hearing impairments. Table 1.1 (page 13) presented a summary of key legislation in special education. The homepage for the ADA is available at **http://www.ada.gov/**.

Litigation

Behind the laws pertaining to the education of exceptional children and youth is a series of court cases initiated by parent and advocacy groups to improve services for children. Two important state court cases preceded the passage of IDEA and addressed the need for schooling for children with disabilities, who at the time were not provided with any education at all. In *Pennsylvania Association for Retarded Citizens (PARC) v. Commonwealth of Pennsylvania* (1972), the parents of children with mental retardation sued to procure an education for their children. The courts decided in their favor and required Pennsylvania to provide a free, appropriate public education for students with mental retardation. In *Mills v. the Washington, D.C., Board of Education* (1972), a similar decision was reached in regard to all children with disabilities in the District of Columbia.

Section 504 of the Rehabilitation Act of 1973 requires that public facilities be accessible to people with disabilities.

The ADA protects the civil rights of people with disabilities in four major areas: private-sector employment, public services, public accommodations, and telecommunications.

PARC required Pennsylvania schools to provide a free and appropriate education to students with mental retardation.

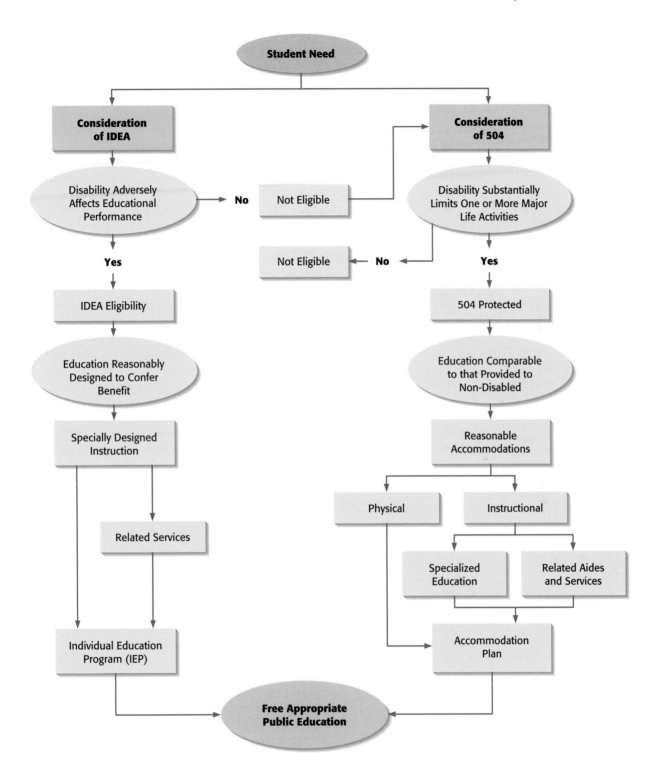

Figure 1.4

IDEA/504 Flowchart

Source: Council for Exceptional Children (1992). *Student access: A resource guide for educators.*

Since the passage of P.L. 94-142, there have been several cases in which the courts have interpreted various aspects of the law. The first case to reach the U.S. Supreme Court, *Board of Education of Hendrick Hudson School District v. Rowley* (1982), concerned the question of what constitutes an "appropriate" education. The parents of Amy Rowley, a deaf child, requested that she have a sign language interpreter so that she could benefit fully from her placement in a general education class. The court wrote that an "appropriate" education did not mean that the student must reach her maximum potential, but that she have a reasonable opportunity to learn. Since there was evidence presented that Amy Rowley could derive some benefit from general education class placement without a sign language interpreter, she was denied that additional service.

In *Irving Independent School District v. Tatro* (1984), the Supreme Court explored the school's responsibility to provide catheterization, a medical procedure, to a child with spina bifida who needed this service in order to remain in school. The Court decided that since this procedure could be performed by a school nurse and the child needed it to remain in school, it should be considered a related service rather than a medical service, and the schools must provide it.

In 1988, the Supreme Court, in *Honig v. Doe*, ruled that a student receiving special education services cannot be excluded indefinitely from school and from receiving the services specified in the IEP (see the next major section). In addition, the student cannot be expelled from school if the behavior in question is related to his or her disability.

The 1999 *Garret F.* ruling by the U.S. Supreme Court ensures that any and all services necessary for a student with complex health-care needs are covered by IDEA, as long as a physician does not provide the services (Maag & Katsiyannis, 2000). Table 1.2 summarizes these and other court cases that have significantly affected special education.

> The *Rowley* and *Tatro* cases concerned the schools' responsibilities to provide "related services."

> In *Honig v. Doe*, the Supreme Court ruled that a student receiving special education services cannot be expelled if the behavior in question is related to his or her disability.

Disproportionate Representation of Minority Children

The next three court cases we will discuss addressed the overrepresentation of children from minority backgrounds in special education classes. The issue of disproportionate representation of minority children has a long history and has not yet been resolved. Let's review the background on this issue.

What would you expect the racial breakdown of students receiving special education services to look like? In the United States, where 61 percent of the school-age population is white, 17 percent African American, 17 percent Latino, and 5 percent "other" (National Center for Education Statistics, 2003), shouldn't the representation in special education be approximately the same? In both the past and the present, this has not been the case, and the disparities between expectations and reality have presented a significant problem for our field.

In an often-cited article in *Exceptional Children,* Lloyd Dunn (1968) reported that a disproportionately high number of African American, American Indian, Mexican, and Puerto Rican children from low socioeconomic backgrounds were being placed in special education classes for students with mild mental retardation. Jane Mercer (1973) provided support for Dunn's findings when she reported that three times as many African American and four times as many Mexican American children were being placed in classes for students with mild mental retardation as compared to their numbers in the general school population. This situation is referred to as **overrepresentation**, or a representation

> Overrepresentation occurs when there are more students in a group than would be expected from the population.

Table 1.2 Important Litigation Involving Special Education

1954 *Brown v. Board of Education* In this case, the U.S. Supreme Court decided that the concept of "separate but equal" schools was unconstitutional and declared that all children must have equal opportunity for education.

1970 *Diana v. Board of Education* (California) This state case established that California schools could not place students in special education on the basis of culturally biased tests or tests given in the student's nonprimary language.

1972 *Pennsylvania Association for Retarded Citizens (PARC) v. Pennsylvania* This state case established the right of children with mental retardation to a public education in Pennsylvania.

1972 *Mills v. Washington, D.C. Board of Education* This state case established that all students with disabilities were entitled to a public education in the District of Columbia.

1979 *Larry P. v. Riles* (California) In this state case, it was decided that IQ tests could not be used to identify African American students with mental retardation.

1982 *Board of Education of the Hendrick Hudson Central School District v. Rowley* The U.S. Supreme Court, in its first decision interpreting P.L. 94-142, defined an "appropriate" education as one that provides a child with a reasonable opportunity to learn.

1984 *Irving Independent School District v. Tatro* The U.S. Supreme Court decided that procedures that could be performed by a nonphysician (such as catheterization) qualified as related services, not medical services, and must be provided by the school district, so that a child can attend school and benefit from special education.

1988 *Honig v. Doe* The U.S. Supreme Court ruled that a student receiving special education services cannot be excluded from school indefinitely (expelled), particularly if the behavior is related to the student's disability.

1999 *Cedar Rapids Community School District v. Garret F.* The U.S. Supreme Court ruled that services related to a student's complex health-care needs are covered under IDEA as long as a physician does not provide them.

greater than would be expected based on the actual number of students from that group in school.

Those findings are nearly thirty years old. But the overrepresentation and underrepresentation of individuals from certain ethnic cultures in categories of special education persist today (Donovan & Cross, 2002). Black students account for 14.8 percent of the school-aged population but 19.8 percent of the special education population in all disabilities. American Indian students remain overrepresented in special education services as well (U.S. Department of Education, 2002).

Underrepresentation occurs when fewer students receive services than would be expected based on their representation in the general school population. African American, Hispanic, and American Indian students, for example, are underrepresented in gifted and talented programs.

Underrepresentation occurs when there are fewer students in a group than would be expected from the population.

Factors Contributing to Over- and Underrepresentation   Why are some culturally diverse groups overrepresented in classes for children with disabilities and others not? Do the statistics accurately reflect the incidence of exceptionalities among culturally diverse students? In addressing these questions, we must consider the referral, assessment, and placement process. We must also concern ourselves with the access these children have to educational services, along with environmental and poverty factors.

One factor in overrepresentation may be how culturally diverse children are referred to special education. Teachers most commonly refer children for assessment, and referral is a subjective process, depending on local norms—that is, the child doing poorly stands out more in a class of children performing on grade level than within a class where all children are performing poorly (Donovan & Cross, 2002). The relatively high levels of referral for African American and Hispanic students initially led to the suspicion that bias caused teachers to refer students who were actually performing at an acceptable level. More recent work, however (MacMillan et al., 1996), has demonstrated that teachers refer children with significant behavior and academic problems—they do not appear to be referring students who are performing relatively well.

Fair assessment of children from diverse backgrounds is challenging and complex.

Another variable contributing to the overrepresentation of culturally diverse children in special education has been the use of assessment instruments that many believe are culturally biased, particularly the IQ test. There is a long history of debate about the appropriateness of IQ tests to determine eligibility for special education services, as you will see in the discussion of the *Larry P.* and *Diana* cases to follow, and there is little doubt that problems do occur: Misperceptions between the student and the evaluator, cross-cultural stereotyping, and item bias can lead to poor performance, particularly among students who have limited proficiency in English (U.S. Department of Education, 2001). The recent National Research Council report on minority students in special and gifted education programs concluded that approaches more closely tied to the design of interventions, such as performance-based assessments (based on how students are actually achieving in school) and curriculum-based measures (based on whether or not the student is mastering the curriculum, or standards), will be better tools to determine eligibility (Donovan & Cross, 2002). But the authors of that report acknowledge that a movement away from IQ, with its long history of use, will require major changes in training and procedures—and greater changes in beliefs and attitudes:

> Even more daunting is the change required in the thinking of professionals and the public about disabilities—a change from assumptions of fixed abilities and internal child traits to new assumptions about the malleability of skills and the powerful effects of instruction and positive environments. (p. 287)

Poverty is a third factor that affects representation rates in special education classes, and poverty occurs disproportionately in African American, Hispanic, and American Indian families. Poverty jeopardizes nutrition, quality of medical care, and living conditions. Poor women must often work even when a pregnancy is at risk. These factors can contribute to children being born premature or low birthweight. As you will learn in Chapter 2, children born at risk are more likely to develop learning problems and disabilities. In addition, poverty often contributes to stress and maternal depression, which affects the overall mental health of a family. Finally, studies have demonstrated that children from poor environments are more likely to be exposed to lead and other environmental toxins, are more likely to be exposed to alcohol and tobacco in utero, and have micronutrient deficiencies (Donovan & Cross, 2002). For more information on how poverty affects children, visit the Children's Defense Fund at **www.childrensdefense.org**.

Reasons for underrepresentation within special education classrooms are as varied as the reasons for overrepresentation and may differ according to the type of cultural diversity. The low national prevalence figures for Hispanics/ Latinos in classes for students with mental retardation and emotional disturbance, for example, may be related in part to the advent of bilingual education programs. These programs were only in their infancy at the time of the Dunn (1968) and Mercer (1973) studies, but sometimes provide an alternative to special education programs. Aware that the language of instruction in special education is primarily English, bilingual teachers may be reluctant to refer their students to special education, believing that their needs can better be met in a bilingual setting (Artiles, Harry, Reschly, & Chinn, 2002).

As with Latinos, there are several reasons why Asians may be underrepresented in classes for children with disabilities. First, due to norms and beliefs within their cultures, some Asian parents are reluctant to seek external assistance for a child with disabilities (Chan, 1986). Parents may be hesitant to grant permission to school personnel to test their child or to consider special education placement. A second variable is the fact that, as a group (with some exceptions), Asians in the United States enjoy a relatively high standard of living. With the exception of the second wave of Southeast Asian immigrants beginning in 1978, most of the Asian immigrants entering the country have middle- or upper-middle-class backgrounds with a relatively high educational level. The children from these families are at less risk of special education placement than many of the children from other culturally diverse groups, who come from backgrounds of poverty. In addition, educators may also have a tendency to stereotype Asian children as being very quiet. Thus, children who are seriously withdrawn may be passed off as having typical Asian behaviors and are not referred for possible special education placement.

The disproportionately low placement of American Indian, African American, and Latino children in classes for students labeled as gifted and talented is also an important issue. For a child to be placed in such a class, the child's potential must be recognized by someone, usually a teacher. He or she must then be referred, tested, and ultimately placed. A child will not be placed, however, if no one recognizes his or her abilities and makes a referral. We will discuss this issue at greater length in Chapter 13.

Litigation Relating to Over- and Underrepresentation   A number of critical court cases have addressed the issues of overrepresentation in special education and the appropriate assessment and placement of students from culturally diverse backgrounds. The landmark *Brown v. Board of Education of Topeka, Kansas* (1954) decision set the stage for several important court cases concerning children with disabilities. In the *Brown* decision, the U.S. Supreme Court ruled that separate schools for African American and white students cannot be considered equal and are therefore unconstitutional. This ruling provided the precedent for parents and advocates who maintained that children with disabilities were being unfairly denied equal educational opportunities.

Diana v. Board of Education (1970) was a state class-action suit that addressed the overrepresentation of children from non–English-speaking backgrounds in special classes in California. It was filed on behalf of nine Mexican American children who had been placed in classes for students with mental retardation based on the results of IQ tests given in English. Advocates for the children argued that their assessment had been unfair, since it was not conducted in Spanish, their native language. The case was settled with the agreement that children

In *Brown v. Board of Education*, the Supreme Court ruled that "separate but equal" schools were unconstitutional.

Diana v. Board of Education mandated that children be tested in their primary language for special education services.

must be tested in both their primary language and English when special education placement is being considered. When the children involved in the case were re-tested more appropriately, seven of the nine were no longer eligible for special education.

Larry P. v. Riles addressed the fairness of IQ testing for African American children.

In *Larry P. v. Riles* (1979), the issue was the disproportionate number of African American students in classes for students with educable mental retardation in California. The plaintiffs maintained that standardized IQ tests, which were used as the basis for placement of these students, were culturally biased against African American children. The *Larry P.* ruling eliminated the use of IQ tests to place African American students in classes for students with mental retardation in California. The overrepresentation of African American children in special education remains a cause of great concern, despite changes in assessment practices spurred by the *Larry P.* decision.

These cases are but a small sample of the numerous court decisions rendered on behalf of culturally and linguistically diverse students. They illustrate the inequities inherent in our educational system, many of which are so institutionalized that it often requires the threat of litigation to inspire changes.

IDEA reflects many of the decisions handed down by the courts through the years. The provisions in IDEA require testing in the native language by trained professionals, nondiscriminatory assessment, due process, least restrictive environment, appropriate education, individualization, and confidentiality. In addition, IDEA provides certain procedural safeguards for language minority students by requiring written or verbal communication be provided to parents or guardians in the language of the home. All meetings or hearings must have a qualified translator.

? *Pause and Reflect*

The right of students with disabilities to a free and appropriate public education is the result of years of advocacy and hard work on the part of parents, professionals, lawmakers, and people with disabilities themselves. Our current system is certainly not free of problems, but it is also important to recognize the accomplishments of the last thirty years. How do you think the current system of providing services could be improved, for the benefit of students, their families, and their teachers? ●

Individualized Education

With individualized education, each student has a program tailored to his or her unique needs.

At the core of the laws pertaining to the education of exceptional children is the concept of **individualized education**: Each student should have a program tailored to his or her unique needs. IDEA and its amendments have instituted a system of planning that can now extend from birth to the postschool years. Table 1.3 describes the components of individualized education. In the following sections we'll look at each of these individualized programs.

The Individualized Family Service Plan

The IFSP ensures that the youngest children and their families receive the services they need.

Exceptional children and their families can first receive individualized services through the **Individualized Family Service Plan (IFSP)**. Congress, recognizing

Table 1.3 Key Components of Individualized Education

Relevant Ages	Description
	The IFSP: The Individualized Family Service Plan must include the following components:
Children birth to age 3 and their families	▪ A statement of the infant's or toddler's present levels of development (physical, cognitive, speech/language, psychosocial, motor, and self-help) ▪ A statement of family's strengths, needs, resources, and priorities related to enhancing the child's development ▪ A statement of major outcomes expected to be achieved for the child and the family ▪ The criteria, procedures, and timelines for determining progress ▪ The specific early intervention services necessary to meet the unique needs of the child and family, including the frequency, intensity, and method of delivering services ▪ The projected dates for the initiation of services and expected duration of those services ▪ The name of the case manager (service coordinator) ▪ The procedures for transition from early intervention into the preschool program
	The IEP: The Individualized Education Program must include the following components:
Students ages 3 through 21	▪ A statement of the child's current educational performance levels ▪ Annual goals and benchmarks or short-term objectives ▪ A description of the special education and related services provided ▪ A statement describing the program modifications and supports the child needs to benefit from the general education curriculum ▪ A statement of the extent to which the child will be able to participate in general education programs ▪ The date on which services begin and their anticipated duration ▪ Appropriate objective evaluation criteria and evaluation procedures and schedules for determining, at least annually, whether the short-term objectives are being achieved ▪ A statement of transition services (ITP) needed by students who are 14 and over
	The ITP: Individualized Transition Plan might include the following components:
Students ages 14 through 21	▪ A statement of transition services needed (career planning, self-advocacy, social life, community participation, postsecondary education, leisure services, advocacy/legal services, daily living, physical care) ▪ Annual goals in each service area, accompanied by objectives designed to meet those goals ▪ Statements of educational and related services needed to enable the student to meet the goals and objectives ▪ Statement of interagency responsibilities and linkages, including the agency, purpose, contact persons, and the time by which the reponsibility or linkage must be established

Source: Adapted from Legal foundations: The Individuals with Disabilities Education Act (IDEA), *Teaching Exceptional Children* (Winter 1993), 85–87.

the importance of early intervention for young children within the context of the family, mandated that an IFSP be drawn up by an interdisciplinary team that includes family members. Table 1.3 lists the major components of the IFSP. It is meant to ensure that young children from birth to age 3 who are identified as having disabilities or developmental delay or who are at risk receive the services they need to develop skills and prevent additional disabilities. Chapter 2 will discuss the IFSP in greater detail. For more on the IFSP, IEP, and ITP, and sample documents, visit our website at **http://www.education.college.hmco .com/students/**.

The Individualized Education Program

The IEP outlines the educational plan for each student.

The **Individualized Education Program (IEP)** is the basis for special education programming in preschool, elementary, middle, and high school. IDEA calls for a team of people to draw up a written IEP at a meeting called for that purpose. The team is typically made up of the parent(s), the special education teacher, the general education teacher, the school principal, and any specialists who have evaluated the child or have been providing services to that child. When it is appropriate, the student is also present at the IEP meeting. Other school professionals become involved, too, when the student needs supportive services: The school nurse, speech-language specialist, adaptive physical education teacher, and other school professionals may participate in the IEP process. According to the law, the IEP must have the components listed in Table 1.3.

The Office of Special Education and Rehabilitation Services in the U.S. Department of Education has assembled a very specific, helpful guide to the IEP and the IEP process. What follows are excerpts from that guide.

Guide to the Individualized Education Program

Introduction

Each public school child who receives special education and related services must have an Individualized Education Program (IEP). Each IEP must be designed for one student and must be a truly *individualized* document. The IEP is the cornerstone of a quality education for each child with a disability.

To create an effective IEP, parents, teachers, other school staff—and often the student—must come together to look closely at the student's unique needs. These individuals pool knowledge, experience, and commitment to design an educational program that will help the student be involved in, and progress in, *the general curriculum.* The IEP guides the delivery of special education supports and services for the student with a disability. Without a doubt, writing—and implementing—an effective IEP requires teamwork.

The information below is based on what is required by our nation's special education law—the Individuals with Disabilities Education Act, or IDEA.

The Basic Special Education Process Under IDEA

The writing of each student's IEP takes place within the larger picture of the special education process under IDEA. Before taking a detailed look at the IEP, it may be helpful to look briefly at how a student is identified as having a disability and needing special education and related services and, thus, an IEP.

Step 1.   Child is identified [authors' note: by the family or the school] as possibly needing special education and related services. The state must identify, locate, and evaluate all children with disabilities in the state who need special education and related services. To do so, states conduct "Child Find" activities.

Step 2.   Child is evaluated. The evaluation must assess the child in all areas related to the child's suspected disability. The evaluation results will be used to decide the child's eligibility for special education and related services and to make decisions about an appropriate educational program for the child.

Step 3.   Eligibility is decided. A group of qualified professionals and the parents look at the child's evaluation results. Together, they decide if the child is a "child with a disability," as defined by IDEA.

Step 4.   Child is found eligible for services. If the child is found to be a "child with a disability," as defined by IDEA, he or she is eligible for special education and related services. Within 30 calendar days after a child is determined eligible, the IEP team must meet to write an IEP for the child.

Step 5.   IEP meeting is scheduled. The school system schedules and conducts the IEP meeting.

Step 6.   IEP meeting is held and the IEP is written. The IEP team gathers to talk about the child's needs and write the student's IEP. Parents and the student (when appropriate) are part of the team.

Step 7.   Services are provided. The school makes sure that the child's IEP is being carried out as it was written. Parents are given a copy of the IEP. Each of the child's teachers and service providers has access to the IEP and knows his or her specific responsibilities for carrying out the IEP. This includes the accommodations, modifications, and supports that must be provided to the child, in keeping with the IEP.

Step 8.   Progress is measured and reported to parents. The child's progress toward the annual goals is measured, as stated in the IEP. His or her parents are regularly informed of their child's progress and whether that progress is enough for the child to achieve the goals by the end of the year.

Step 9.   IEP is reviewed. The child's IEP is reviewed by the IEP team at least once a year, or more often if the parents or school ask for a review. [Authors' note: At that time the IEP is updated to reflect goals that have been met, and new goals are identified.]

Step 10. Child is re-evaluated. At least every three years the child must be re-evaluated. This evaluation is often called a "triennial." Its purpose is to find out if the child continues to be a "child with a disability," as defined by IDEA, and what the child's educational needs are.

A Closer Look at the IEP

Clearly, the IEP is a very important document for children with disabilities and for those who are involved in educating them. Done correctly, the IEP should improve teaching, learning, and results. Each child's IEP describes, among other things, the educational program that has been designed to meet that child's unique needs.

Contents of the IEP

By law, the IEP must include certain information about the child and the educational program designed to meet his or her unique needs. In a nut-shell, this information is:

- **Current performance.** The IEP must state how the child is currently doing in school (known as present levels of educational performance). This information usually comes from the evaluation results such as class-room tests and assignments, individual tests given to decide eligibility for services or during re-evaluation, and observations made by parents, teachers, related service providers, and other school staff. The statement about "current performance" includes how the child's disability affects his or her involvement and progress in the general curriculum.

- **Annual goals.** These are goals that the child can reasonably accomplish in a year. The goals are broken down into short-term objectives or bench-marks. Goals may be academic, address social or behavioral needs, relate to physical needs, or address other educational needs. The goals must be measurable—meaning that it must be possible to measure whether the student has achieved the goals.

- **Special education and related services.** The IEP must list the special edu-cation and related services to be provided to the child or on behalf of the child. This includes supplementary aids and services that the child needs. It also includes modifications (changes) to the program or supports for school personnel—such as training or professional development—that will be provided to assist the child.

- **Participation with nondisabled children.** The IEP must explain the ex-tent (if any) to which the child will not participate with nondisabled chil-dren in the regular class and other school activities.

- **Participation in state and district-wide tests.** Most states and districts give achievement tests to children in certain grades or age groups. The IEP must state what modifications in the administration of these tests the child will need. If a test is not appropriate for the child, the IEP must state why the test is not appropriate and how the child will be tested instead.

- **Dates and places.** The IEP must state when services will begin, how often they will be provided, where they will be provided, and how long they will last.

- **Transition service needs.** Beginning when the child is age 14 (or younger, if appropriate), the IEP must address (within the applicable parts of the IEP) the courses he or she needs to take to reach his or her post-school goals. A statement of transition services needs must also be included in each of the child's subsequent IEPs.

- **Needed transition services.** Beginning when the child is age 16 (or younger, if appropriate), the IEP must state what transition services are needed to help the child prepare for leaving school.

- **Age of majority.** Beginning at least one year before the child reaches the age of majority, the IEP must include a statement that the student has been told of any rights that will transfer to him or her at the age of majority. (This statement would be needed only in states that transfer rights at the age of majority.)

- **Measuring progress.** The IEP must state how the child's progress will be measured and how parents will be informed of that progress.

It is useful to understand that each child's IEP is different. The document is prepared for that child only. It describes the individualized education program designed to meet that child's needs.

Special Factors to Consider

Depending on the needs of the child, the IEP team needs to consider what the law calls special factors. These include:

- If the child's *behavior* interferes with his or her learning or the learning of others, the IEP team will consider strategies and supports to address the child's behavior. (See the "Closer Look" box entitled "Discipline Under the IDEA.")

A Closer Look   **Discipline Under the IDEA**

- Schools may suspend students with disabilities for up to ten school days, if such alternatives are used with students without disabilities, BUT. . .

- Schools must continue to provide educational services for students with disabilities whose suspension or expulsion constitutes a change of placement (usually more than ten days in a school year).

- Schools may remove students with disabilities to appropriate interim alternative educational settings (IAES) for behavior related to drugs, guns, and other dangerous weapons for up to forty-five days.

The law now requires the IEP team to conduct a "manifestation determination" once a disciplinary action for a student with a disability is contemplated. The IEP team must determine—within ten calendar days after the school decides to discipline a student—whether the student's behavior is related to the disability. If the behavior *is not* related to the disability, the student may be disciplined in the same way as a student without a disability, but the appropriate educational services must continue.

Source: B. Knoblauch & K. McLane, An overview of the Individuals with Disabilities Education Act Amendments of 1997 (P.L. 105-17), *ERIC Digest* (1999 update, E576, EDO-99-4).

- If the child has *limited proficiency in English,* the IEP team will consider the child's language needs as these needs relate to his or her IEP.
- If the child is *blind or visually impaired,* the IEP team must provide for instruction in Braille or the use of Braille, unless it determines after an appropriate evaluation that the child does not need this instruction.
- If the child has *communication needs,* the IEP team must consider those needs.
- If the child is *deaf or hard of hearing,* the IEP team will consider his or her language and communication needs. This includes the child's opportunities to communicate directly with classmates and school staff in his or her usual method of communication (for example, sign language).
- The IEP team must always consider the child's need for *assistive technology* devices or services.

The Individualized Transition Plan

As noted earlier, the IDEA mandated transition services for all students receiving special education services. Transition services are those that prepare the student for life after school, whether that be independent living, work, further education, or another option. Transition plans are now required from the age of 14. The **Individualized Transition Plan (ITP)** includes the components listed in Table 1.3.

The ITP helps prepare students for life and work after school.

? Pause and Reflect

The concept of *individualized education* may be the primary difference between special education services and general education. It would be a wonderful luxury if every child could have an IEP—a program of schooling designed to address and improve areas of weakness and strength. Do you think all children should have an IEP? What are the arguments for and against that idea? ●

The Pros and Cons of Labeling

We use terms that we call "labels" to describe groups of exceptional children. In this book, you will read about students with mental retardation, learning disabilities, physical and health impairments, speech and language impairments, and emotional disturbance, as well as students who are deaf and hard of hearing, visually handicapped, or gifted and talented.

Think of the labels that could be applied to you. Are you a Caucasian female? A Latino male? A Catholic, Protestant, Jew, Muslim? Would you want those labels to be the first piece of information other people learn about you? People with disabilities and their families and advocates have worked very hard to erase the "disability-first" perception of the disabled.

Why use labels at all? Many people feel that we should not. But labels do serve some useful purposes. First, they help us count individuals with exceptionalities. Just as the U.S. government wants to know your sex, race, and age in order to provide representation and services to your community, the federal government and the states count the number of students with disabilities in order to plan for and provide educational and supportive services.

Labels also help professionals differentiate methods of instruction and support services to different groups. Children who have visual disabilities learn to read with materials that are quite different from those used by children who have learning disabilities. Children who are deaf or hard of hearing need the support services of an audiologist and possibly a speech-language specialist. Gifted and talented students may learn more from a differentiated curriculum tailored to their learning strengths and needs (Clark, 2002). Many special educators would argue, however, that instructional methods do not vary significantly for students who are identified as having learning disabilities, mild mental retardation, or emotional disturbance, although the emphasis of instruction might vary from student to student, depending on individual student learning needs.

Labels enable professionals to communicate efficiently about children and their needs. But they are frequently misused and can carry an enormous stigma. Words like *hyperactive, autistic,* and *dyslexic* are often used freely to describe children who are having academic or behavioral difficulties in school. Using such terms may make a professional sound knowledgeable, but labels like these may alter the perceptions of others about the learning potential of such children. Moreover, labels often obscure individual differences among children (Hobbs, 1975); we assume that all children identified as "learning-disabled" are somehow the same. (Table 1.4 shows how labels have changed over time.)

Labels can lead to pre-judging and stereotyping.

Many professionals within special education see categorical labels as a necessary evil and would like to replace current labels with terminology that is directly related to instruction and that minimizes negative connotations (Adelman, 1996). For example, students with learning disabilities could be described as *students with intensive reading instruction needs*!

Many special education professionals would like to replace current labels with terminology directly related to instruction.

Pause and Reflect

List the labels that could be applied to you. Don't forget the labels that the media uses to describe groups, such as "soccer mom," "Gen X," "yuppie," and so on. Are there ways those labels can put you at an advantage? How might they work against you? •

Educational Setting

IDEA requires that each school district provide a range of program options for students with disabilities. As you saw in Figure 1.3, these programs range from what is considered the least restrictive to the most restrictive environment. Remember that the concept of "least restrictive environment" is based on the opportunities available for interaction between the student with a disability and nondisabled peers. In practical terms, this means that a family attending an IEP meeting must have the option of choosing from this range of programs in order to obtain the most appropriate education for the child. (See Figure 1.3 for examples of those settings.) The family and the school district must come to an agreement about the setting in which the child's educational needs can most appropriately be met.

The least restrictive environment, which may be different for each child, allows the most interaction with nondisabled peers.

Table 1.4 Terms Reflecting Social Changes

Areas of Disability	Past	Present
Mental retardation	Idiots, feebleminded, cretin, mentally deficient, educably retarded or trainably retarded, morons, high level or low level	Mild, moderate, severe retardation and intermittent, pervasive, extensive, and limited retardation
Learning disabilities	Dyslexia, minimal cerebral dysfunction, specific learning disabilities, learning disabilities	Learning disabilities
Emotional disturbance	Unsocialized, dementia, emotionally disturbed, acting out, withdrawn	Emotional/behavioral disorders (E/BD)
Attention deficit disorder (with or without hyperactivity)	Hyperactivity, specific learning disabilities	ADD (attention deficit disorder without hyperactivity) or ADHD (with hyperactivity) and combined
Head injuries	Strephosymbolia, brain-crippled children, brain-injured, closed head injury	Traumatic brain injury
Deafness	Deaf and dumb, deaf mute	Deaf or hard-of-hearing
Persons with orthopedic disabilities	Crippled children, physically handicapped	Physical disabilities
Learning disability in reading	Dyslexia, minimal cerebral dysfunction, specific learning disabilities	Dyslexia
Autism	Childhood schizophrenia, children with refrigerator parents, Kanner's syndrome, autoid	Autism; Autism Spectrum Disorders; Asperger's Syndrome
Placements for individuals with more severe disabilities	Asylums, institutions, residential schools, group homes	Community living, assistive living, and supportive employment
Placements for individuals with mild disabilities	Normalization, mainstreaming, regular education initiative, integration	Inclusion
Assessment	Testing, measurement	Assessment, norm-referenced or authentic/performance-based assessment
Preassessment	Diagnosis, child study teacher assistance teams	Prereferral teams, student support teams, student success teams

Source: G. Vergason and M. L. Anderegg (1996). Adapted from The ins and outs of special education terminology, *Teaching Exceptional Children, 29*(5) (May/June 1997), 36.

The concept of the least restrictive environment was originally envisioned as a relative one—that is, one that must be interpreted anew for each student on the basis of his or her unique learning characteristics. Some professionals today, however, interpret the least restrictive environment in a more general fashion and argue for the inclusion of students with disabilities in the general education classroom, along with curricular adaptations and the collaboration and teaming of professionals from special and general education. Others call for maintaining the continuum of educational services (Council for Exceptional Children, 1997; Leiberman, 1996) as represented in Figure 1.3. Let's consider an example.

Case Study

Ana is a student who has engaged in violent and self-destructive behavior. These behaviors have decreased in the special school for students labeled emotionally disturbed that she has been attending, but this is considered a relatively restrictive setting for Ana, since she has no opportunity there to interact with her typically developing peers. At her IEP meeting, her family and teachers decide that Ana's educational goals could best be reached in a less restrictive setting: a special class for students labeled emotionally disturbed on an elementary school campus. There she will have opportunities to participate in social and academic activities with her peers, with her special-class teacher planning and overseeing those experiences. With success she will have the opportunity for more and more interactions with others.

Advocates of inclusion might suggest that Ana be placed at her grade level in her neighborhood school, with a special education teacher or instructional aide available to monitor her behavior and make curricular adaptations as they are needed. They would argue that only with the models of appropriate behavior available in the general education class and the opportunities for meaningful social interaction provided there can Ana be motivated to change her behavior. This picture of inclusion can succeed only if professionals from special and general education team up to provide individualized educational services for Ana and each included student.

The majority of students identified as exceptional *are receiving their instruction primarily in the general education classroom* (see Figure 1.5). A number of different kinds of programs have been developed to ensure that these students and their teachers receive the support they need. Many involve **collaboration** between the special educator and the general educator—the foundation for successful inclusive practices. Marilyn Friend and Lynne Cook (2000) define collaboration as "a style for direct interaction between at least two coequal parties voluntarily engaged in shared decision making as they work toward a common goal" (p. 6). The "Closer Look" box entitled, "Defining Characteristics of Collaboration" describes the key characteristics of collaboration.

In inclusive settings, special and general educators also work together in team-teaching situations. **Team-teaching**, also called co-teaching, can involve shared instruction of a lesson, a subject area, or an entire instructional program. At the TRIPOD-Burbank program in southern California, for example, teachers of deaf students pair with elementary teachers in classrooms with three to six deaf students and twenty-two hearing peers. Both teachers sign and speak at all times, and many of the hearing students learn to understand and use sign language quite well. According to Vaughn, Schumm, and Arguelles (1997), co-teaching is "a bit like a marriage" (p. 5); it can be very rewarding once some of the common issues are worked out.

> Most exceptional students receive the majority of their instruction in the general education classroom.

> Team teaching can involve shared instruction of a lesson, a subject area, or an entire instructional program.

A Closer Look   Defining Characteristics of Collaboration

- Collaboration is *voluntary*. People cannot be forced to use a particular style in their interactions with others.

- Collaboration requires *parity* among participants. Each person's contribution is equally valued, and each person has equal power in decision-making.

- Collaboration is based on *mutual goals*. Professionals do not have to share all goals in order to collaborate, just one that is specific and important enough to maintain their shared attention.

- Collaboration depends on *shared responsibility* for participation and decision-making. Collaborators must assume the responsibility of actively engaging in the activity and in the decision-making it entails.

- Individuals who collaborate *share their resources*. Sharing resources of time, knowledge, and materials can enhance the sense of ownership among professionals.

- Individuals who collaborate *share responsibility for outcomes*. Whether the results of collaboration are positive or negative, all participating individuals are responsible for the outcomes.

Source: Adapted from M. Friend & L. Cook, *Interactions: Collaboration skills for school professionals* (White Plains, NY: Longman, 2000), pp. 6–11.

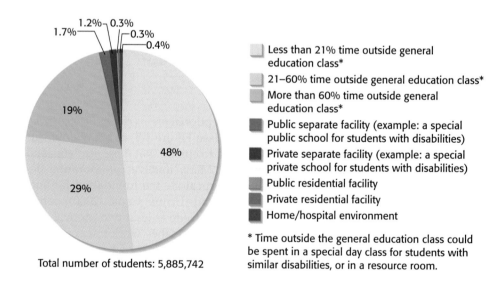

Total number of students: 5,885,742

1.2% 0.3%
1.7% 0.3%
0.4%
19%
48%
29%

Less than 21% time outside general education class*

21–60% time outside general education class*

More than 60% time outside general education class*

Public separate facility (example: a special public school for students with disabilities)

Private separate facility (example: a special private school for students with disabilities)

Public residential facility

Private residential facility

Home/hospital environment

* Time outside the general education class could be spent in a special day class for students with similar disabilities, or in a resource room.

Figure 1.5

Numbers of Children Age 6–21 Served in Different Educational Environments During the 2002–2003 School Year

Source: http://www.ideadata.org/tables26th/ar_abQ.htm.

Notes: Includes data from 50 states, the District of Columbia, and outlying areas.
Separate school includes both public and private separate school facilities. Residential includes both public and private residential facilities.

Co-teaching in an inclusion class can be an enjoyable learning experience for the special educator and the general educator. (Frank Siteman/PhotoEdit)

Another arrangement is the **teacher assistance team** (also known by many other names, such as the *student support team*) (Buck, Polloway, Smith-Thomas, et al., 2003). This is a group of teachers and other school professionals (such as school counselors) who work together to assist the general education teacher. Under some circumstances, a team concentrates on keeping children in the general education classroom instead of referring them to special education; a team like this is sometimes known as a **prereferral intervention team** (Safran & Safran, 1996). In other situations, team members provide consultation to teachers or direct services to students who are identified as having special needs but who are placed in the general education classroom.

These arrangements are designed to maintain the student's instruction within the regular classroom. Other kinds of services for students with special needs are called **pullout programs**, since they involve the student leaving the classroom to receive specialized instruction. The traditional organization of the resource room, for example, involves students leaving the general education classroom for specialized instruction in academic areas of need. In many parts of the country, however, this practice is changing, and the resource teacher is operating on the **consultation model**—meeting with teachers to plan instructional adaptations for students as well as providing direct instructional services within the general education classroom. Some other examples of traditional pullout programs are speech and language services, orientation and mobility for students

The prereferral intervention team works to keep students in the general education classroom.

Table 1.5 Settings for Delivery of Special Education

General education classroom	With supports as needed.
Resource room	A special education teacher provides instruction or support to identified students, either in the general education classroom or in a separate room.
Special classes in elementary or secondary schools	These classes group children by exceptionality—gifted, deaf, learning disabled—and a specialist teacher instructs them together. Individual students may leave the special class for part of the day to receive instruction in the general education classroom, but the majority of their time is usually spent in the special class.
Special schools	Designed exclusively for students with exceptionality. The related services that the students need are usually housed under the same roof. Special schools may be public or private.
Residential schools	Special schools where the students live during the school year. This is considered the most restrictive educational environment for exceptional students, since they have no opportunity to interact with their nondisabled peers.
Home- or hospital-based instruction	Provided by a special education teacher to students who, because of chronic illness or other needs, are taught at home or while they are hospitalized.

with visual impairments, and physical therapy for students with physical disabilities. Table 1.5 describes the settings in which special education is provided.

In today's schools, virtually all students with disabilities are receiving their education in a regular school building: The U.S. Department of Education (2001) put that number at more than 95.9 percent of students aged 6 to 21. At the classroom level, 48 percent spent less than 21 percent of their time outside the general education classroom (see Figure 1.5). The number of students receiving educational services in public and private separate school facilities, public and private residential facilities, and homebound or hospital settings decreases every year.

The Framework of Support for Students with Disabilities

Our definition of inclusion on page 9 speaks not just of *placement*, but also of *supports*. Placement in a general education setting by itself will not usually improve educational achievement for a child with an IEP. The general education teacher cannot provide individualized education to one or more students without the help of other professionals—usually specialists in the disability area, and others providing related services—the special education teacher, speech-language pathologist, adaptive physical education teacher, orientation and mobility specialist, school nurse, and so on. Some of the supports for the general education teacher are described in the previous box, "Support for General Education Teachers." But there is also a set of supports needed by the student with disabilities, which we describe in the **Framework of Support** (see Figure 1.6). The framework outlines the supports necessary to help a student meet the major goals of education: access to the core curriculum and standards designated by each state, and **social integration**—inclusion, acceptance, and the development of friendships. In Chapters 4 through 13 of our book, you will read about specific supports that may be appropriate for students with specific disabilities—but it is all based on the basic principle of special education: individualized

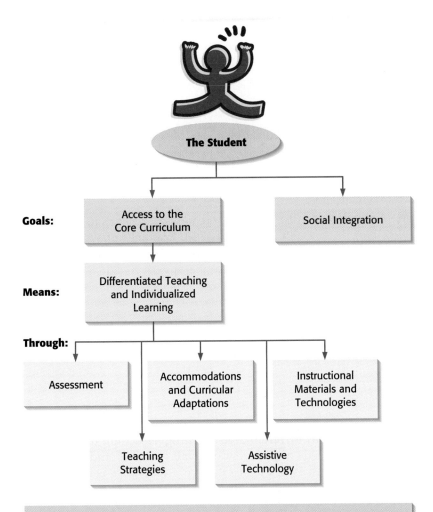

Figure 1.6

The Framework of Support

Source for definitions: Families and Advocates Partnership for Education (FAPE), *School accommodations and modifications,* http://www.fape.org.

Technology Focus

What Is Assistive Technology?

To ensure effective team decision-making, IEP team members must help family members understand that assistive technology includes both devices and services.

An *assistive technology device* is defined in the Individuals with Disabilities Education Act (IDEA) of 1997 as "any item, piece of equipment, or product system . . . that is used to increase, maintain, or improve the functional capabilities of children with disabilities" (U.S. Code, vol. 20, sec. 1401 [25]). Examples of frequently used devices in classroom settings include:

- Simple communication boards and wallets
- Sophisticated electronic communication devices
- Mobility aids, such as long canes and powered wheelchairs
- Expanded or adapted keyboards, touch windows, and speech recognition systems
- Magnification devices and computer screen reading adaptations

An *assistive technology service* is defined as "any service that directly assists an individual with a disability in the selection, acquisition, or use of

This young girl benefits from using a slantboard on her classroom desk—straightforward assistive technology. (Ellen Senis/The Image Works)

an assistive technology device" (U.S. Code, vol. 20, sec. 1401 [25]). Examples of assistive technology services provided in the public schools include physical therapy, occupational therapy, and speech therapy.

Source: Phil Parette and Gale A. McMahan (2002). Excerpt from What should we expect from assistive technology? Being sensitive to family goals, *Teaching Exceptional Children*, 35 (1) (2002), 56–61.

---

learning, which requires **differentiated teaching**—teaching that is designed to meet the individual needs of a student or small group of students. You can see that in order for the framework to be effective, *collaboration* between general educators, special educators, and families must occur.

The recent work of Pam Hunt and her colleagues indicates that the combination of collaborative teaming and Unified Plan of Support (see Figure 1.7), specifying academic adaptations and communication and social supports can increase academic skills, engagement in classroom activities, interactions with peers, and student-initiated interactions for both students with significant disabilities and students at risk for academic failure (Hunt, Soto, Maier, et al., 2003). It's hard work, but there are many satisfactions that can accompany being part of an effective team.

Sound challenging? Yes, it is challenging for all of us. But our commitment to normalization and inclusion for all students—especially, in our case, students with disabilities—requires that we give it our best effort. This book is about preparing you to make that effort, and helping you to recognize and ask for the supports that you and your students need.

Team Members Present:

Focus Student: _____   _____
School: _____   _____
Date: _____   _____

EDUCATIONAL AND SOCIAL SUPPORTS
For example: materials adaptations, curricular modifications, instructional modifications, peer supports, AAC systems, social facilitation, work and play partners.

SUPPORTS	Person(s) Responsible	Implementation Rating
		❑ fully ❑ moderately well ❑ somewhat ❑ not at all
		❑ fully ❑ moderately well ❑ somewhat ❑ not at all
		❑ fully ❑ moderately well ❑ somewhat ❑ not at all
		❑ fully ❑ moderately well ❑ somewhat ❑ not at all

Figure 1.7

Unified Plan of Support (UPS)

Source: From P. Hunt, G. Soto, J. Maier, & K. Doering (2003). Collaborative teaming to support students at risk and students with severe disabilities in general education classrooms, *Exceptional Children, 69*(3), 315–332.

SUMMARY

- Special education can be understood as providing an individualized educational program to meet a student's unique learning needs.

- When describing exceptional students, we distinguish between a disability (which refers to a student's condition) and a handicap (which refers to a limitation imposed by his or her environment). We also use people-first language, which decreases the negative impact of the labels that are commonly used to categorize exceptional children in school.

- Exceptional children make up about 12 percent of the school-age population, but advances in their education have been made only recently. Despite pioneering work by early advocates and educators, it was not until the civil rights movement of the 1960s that significant movement toward full acceptance and participation in society by people with disabilities began.

- In 1975 Congress passed a law that revolutionized education for students with disabilities: That law, the Individuals with Disabilities Education Act, is known as IDEA. IDEA and the Americans with Disabilities Act, passed in 1990, guarantee people with disabilities specific educational and civil rights. Among the most important are the individualized education program and the continuum of educational settings ranging from the least to the most restrictive environment.

- Progress has also been made through litigation. Cases such as *Diana v. Board of Education* and *Larry P. v. Riles* challenged the disproportionate representation of students from minority groups in special education.

- Special education professionals continue to be concerned about the disproportionate representation of students from culturally diverse backgrounds in special education services.

- The options for educational settings for students with disabilities include general education classrooms, resource rooms, special classes, special schools, residential schools, or other placements such as home or hospital.

- Both students and teachers need support from others—family and other school professionals—in order to make inclusion work.

- The Framework of Support provides a model for the kinds of supports that students may need.

KEY TERMS

exceptional

disability

handicap

people-first language

early intervention

special education

Jean-Marc-Gaspard Itard

Edouard Seguin

Maria Montessori

Samuel Gridley Howe

Anne Sullivan Macy

normalization

deinstitutionalization

least restrictive environment

inclusion

Individuals with Disabilities Education Act (IDEA)

Americans with Disabilities Act (ADA)

overrepresentation

underrepresentation

individualized education

Individualized Family Service Plan (IFSP)

Individualized Education Program (IEP)

Individualized Transition Plan (ITP)

collaboration

team teaching

teacher assistance team

prereferral intervention team

pullout programs

consultation model

Framework of Support

social integration

differentiated teaching

USEFUL RESOURCES

General Topics

- *Teaching Exceptional Children* is a journal of the Council for Exceptional Children, and it is filled with practical ideas for teachers. The May/June 1997 issue focuses on the history of special education in the United States.

- W. Anderson, S. Chitwood, and D. Hayden, *Negotiating the special education maze* (3rd ed.) (Bethesda, MD: Woodbine House, 1997) is a guide to helping parents and teachers understand the special education system.

- Julie B. Carballo, et al., *Survival guide for the first-year special education teacher,* revised (Reston, VA: Council for Exceptional Children, 1994). Developed by teachers who survived their first five years in the special education system, this guide offers tips on many aspects of teaching, from organizing your classroom to managing stress.

- Council for Exceptional Children (CEC) website available at **http://www.cec.org.** CEC is the major professional organization in special education, serving children with disabilities through their families, teachers, and other advocates.

- Veronica Getskow and Dee Konczal, *Kids with special needs: Information and activities to promote awareness and understanding* (Santa Barbara, CA: The Learning Works, 1996). This is a guide to promoting awareness and knowledge of childhood disability among children, teachers, and parents. It contains valuable suggestions for classroom activities aimed at nondisabled children.

● National Dissemination Center for Children with Disabilities website is available at **http://www.nichcy.org**. Here you will find a treasure trove of information, for teachers and families, about children with disabilities and their educational needs.

The Law and Its Implementation
● IDEA Practices is a website that provides information and support for implementing IDEA. Visit **http://www.ideapractices.org**.

● Wrightslaw is a website devoted to information about special education law and advocacy for children with disabilities. It's at **http://www.wrightslaw. com**.

The IEP
● *Guide to the IEP*. There is much more information available in the complete *Guide*. Copies are available online at **http://www.ed.gov/parents/ needs/speced/iepguide/index.html**.

● B. D. Bateman & M. A. *Better IEPs: How to develop legally correct and educationally useful programs* (3rd ed.) (Reston, VA: Council for Exceptional Children, 1998).

 PORTFOLIO ACTIVITIES

Standards All of the following activities will help the student meet CEC Content Standard 9: Professional and Ethical Practice.

1. Begin a portfolio journal in which you reflect on your own attitudes and feelings toward people with disabilities. Which of your feelings are based on experiences, and which on media reports or stereotypes? What do you hope to learn from this course that might change your attitudes?

2. Volunteer at a service agency that serves children with disabilities in the age range that interests you. Call your local United Way, March of Dimes, or children's hospital, and ask about volunteering opportunities. Include your responses to this experience in your portfolio journal.

3. How do people in your community refer to exceptional individuals? During the first few weeks of this semester, keep a file of newspaper clippings of articles that relate to exceptional individuals, special education, or related services. What types of issues are discussed? What types of language are used? What conclusions can you draw about the role of exceptional individuals in the community, their acceptance, and their visibility? Include these clippings in your portfolio.

4. Observe media coverage of people with disabilities or issues important to them. Do newspapers and television newscasts cover these topics in a fair and unbiased manner? Write a letter to the editor suggesting more coverage or more positive coverage, perhaps concerning access, bias, aging, employment, or medical advances. Include your letter in your portfolio.

 To access an electronic portfolio for these activities, visit our website through http://www.education.college.hmco.com/ students/.

2

Risk Factors and Early Intervention

Outline

Terms and Definitions
Types of Risk
    Biological Risk
    Environmental Risk
Prevention
    Major Strategies for
        Prevention
    Early Intervention as
        Prevention
Early Intervention
Identification and Assessment of
    Infants at Risk
    Techniques for Identification
        and Assessment
    Can Disabilities Be Predicted
        from Risk Factors?
    The Resilient Child
    The Importance of
        Relationships
SUMMARY
KEY TERMS
USEFUL RESOURCES
PORTFOLIO ACTIVITIES

Learning Objectives

After reading this chapter, the reader will:

- Understand the concept of *risk* as it applies to the development of young children

- List and explain the biological risk factors that can affect the development of young children

- List and explain the environmental risk factors that can affect the development of young children

- Describe how some disabilities might be prevented

- Define and describe *early intervention* for young children at risk, with developmental delays, and with disabilities

- Appreciate the importance of relationships in the healthy development of young children

Happily, the great majority of pregnancies result in healthy babies. Yet each woman, each couple conceiving a child, also takes a chance that the child will develop differently from "the norm" and as a result have special needs requiring extra help and support at home and at school.

Why do some pregnancies produce children with special needs? Why do some children who have difficult starts in life do just fine, whereas others who begin life under ideal circumstances develop problems? The answers are complicated—many times no medical or psychological expert can answer them for bewildered parents. But in this chapter we will describe some of the circumstances that place a child at risk for the development of a disability.

Many factors—known and unknown—can place a child at risk for the development of a disability.

The information in this chapter should have meaning for you as a teacher or other professional working with exceptional children. First, it should help you decide whether the cause of a student's disability has any bearing on the kind of instruction or support you will provide. Second, it should help you give more complete information to family members who come to you for advice and counsel. This information will be relevant to each of the specific disabilities discussed later in the book. We encourage you to review this chapter as you learn about children with specific disabilities.

We also expect that this information will have personal meaning for each reader. Some of you may be making decisions about whether or when to begin a family. Others may be watching your own children have children. We hope that the information presented here will help you to plan for a healthy family and to make intelligent, well-informed decisions that may enhance the possibilities for a healthy baby. Ultimately, the message of this chapter is that we can all have an impact on the prevention of disabilities in children. Each one of us has a responsibility to do whatever is within our power to *prevent* disabilities in the children of our country—and that is part of what this chapter is all about.

We must all help prevent disabilities in children.

Terms and Definitions

Imagine this scenario: You are a teacher in a high school for pregnant teenage girls. One of your students, Amanda, is 16 years old, has juvenile diabetes, and, at six months pregnant, is refusing to eat healthy foods. She has a history of difficulty keeping her blood sugar under control. Amanda is frequently lethargic, and, although academically capable, she is barely engaged with her classwork. At a meeting of school professionals to discuss her situation, the school nurse states emphatically to the group: "Look, this is a high-risk pregnancy—both Amanda and her baby are at risk. We have to do all we can to get this girl on track, for both of them!"

We hear the term *at risk* used frequently. People may be at risk for a heart attack, for failing a class, or for dropping out of school. In the story told above, Amanda's health appears to be at risk. Her baby, though, will be exposed to many risk factors, both biological (poor maternal health and nutrition) and environmental (young, single mother). These factors may affect her status at birth, and her performance in school when she is older. In this chapter, we will focus on risk to the fetus and the developing child. Let us define the term *risk* in this context. Psychologist and researcher Claire Kopp (1983) defined **risk factors** as "a wide range of *biological and environmental conditions* [emphasis added] that are associated with increased probability for cognitive, social, affective, and physical problems" (p. 1). Biological conditions generally arise from factors related to pregnancy or maternal and child health, such as low birthweight, exposure

Risk factors are biological or environmental conditions associated with cognitive, social, affective, and physical problems.

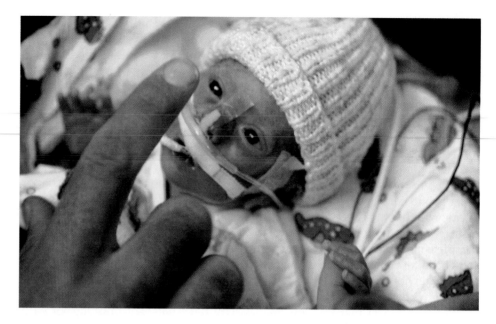

Premature infants like this little girl look so fragile that we are amazed that they survive. Most this size do, but they are at risk for chronic illness and disability. (AP Photos/World Wide Photos)

to drugs or toxic substances, or a chromosomal abnormality. Environmental conditions include negative influences in the child's physical or social surroundings *after* birth, such as extreme poverty, child abuse, or neglect.

The second part of Kopp's definition contains a crucial concept. These conditions are *associated with increased probability* for a variety of later problems. It is more likely that these problems will occur if there are risk factors present—but the presence of one or more risk factors *does not guarantee* poor development in children. The severity of the risk factor as well as the nature of the environment in which each child grows will determine whether developmental problems will occur.

Some children overcome both biological and environmental hurdles and, because of their own characteristics and the outside support that they receive, emerge as strong and productive adults. We refer to these children as especially *resilient.* You will see, however, that the existence of clusters or combinations of risk factors makes it more likely that developmental problems will occur and that *early intervention*—comprehensive, individualized services provided to children from birth to age 3 and their families—can have a significant positive impact on a child's development.

> **The presence of risk factors increases the probability of adverse outcomes but does not guarantee them.**

 **Pause and Reflect**

The material in this chapter should have applications to your own life, both personal and professional. Can you think of individuals you have known who might at one time have qualified as "at risk"? ●

Types of Risk

Since the concept of risk is wide-ranging, it is helpful to have a framework within which categories of vulnerable infants can be described. We will use the categories of **biological risk** and **environmental risk** to describe the potential impact of specific factors on young children (see Figure 2.1).

Environmental Risk
- Poverty
- Environmental toxins
- Child maltreatment
- Other

Combined Risk

Biological Risk
- Prenatal: from conception to birth
- Perinatal: 12th week of pregnancy–28th day of life
- Postnatal: after 28th day of life

Figure 2.1

Types of Risk

Biological Risk

Biological risk exists when events occur before, during, or after birth that may be associated with damage to the child's developing systems, increasing the likelihood that he or she will experience developmental problems. Biological risk factors can be divided into three categories that correspond with the earliest periods of development (Kopp, 1983): the **prenatal period**, from conception to birth; and the **perinatal period** (which overlaps the prenatal period somewhat), from the twelfth week of pregnancy through the twenty-eighth day of life (Gorski & VandenBerg, 1996). The **postnatal period**, for our purposes, will be defined as the twenty-eighth day of life through the first birthday. The accompanying Closer Look box provides the basic rules for a healthy pregnancy.

> Biological risk exists when prenatal, perinatal, or postnatal events increase the likelihood that the child will experience developmental problems.

A Closer Look   Basic Rules for a Healthy Pregnancy

- Plan for pregnancy by seeing a health-care provider before you conceive.
- Take a multivitamin containing 400 micrograms of folic acid daily before you become pregnant and through the first month of pregnancy to help prevent neural tube defects.
- Get early and regular prenatal care.
- Eat a variety of nutritious foods, including foods containing folic acid, such as orange juice, peanuts, beans, lentils, fortified breakfast cereals, and leafy green vegetables.
- Begin pregnancy at a healthy weight (not too heavy or too thin).

- Stop drinking alcohol before you try to conceive, and continue to avoid alcohol during pregnancy.
- Don't smoke during pregnancy and avoid secondhand smoke. It's best to quit before you become pregnant.
- Don't use any drug, even over-the-counter medications or herbal preparations, unless recommended by a health-care provider who knows you are pregnant.

Source: March of Dimes (November 2002). Fact sheet: Pregnancy after 35. www.modimes.org/professionals/681_1155.asp/. Retrieved 1/5/04.

● *Prenatal Factors*   Prenatal factors are those that affect embryologic and fetal development before birth. Adverse prenatal events often account for the most severe developmental outcomes among the infants who survive them. If they have their impact during the **first trimester** (first three months) of pregnancy, they may compromise the organs and body parts developing at that time; if they occur later in pregnancy, they may affect the growth and differentiation of those organs that are still developing, such as the brain and central nervous system. Prenatal factors include maternal illnesses and maternal use and abuse of substances, including drugs and alcohol. These factors—alcohol, drugs, illnesses, infections, and so on—are often called **teratogens**, substances that can cause birth defects. We will discuss some of the most common factors that research tells us can affect embryologic and fetal development during pregnancy (see Figure 2.2). The accompanying Closer Look box entitled, "Newborn Screening" discusses the benefits of routine screening of newborns for genetic diseases.

> Teratogens are substances that can cause birth defects.

Maternal Illness and Infection   Not every illness of the pregnant mother will affect her unborn child, but some illnesses and infections are known to have a devastating impact on embryologic and fetal development. As an example, let's look at **rubella** (sometimes called "German measles"), a highly contagious virus. Rubella is particularly damaging if contracted by a woman during the first sixteen weeks of pregnancy. It can result in blindness, deafness, heart malformation, and/or mental retardation in surviving infants, depending on the fetal organ developing at the time the rubella virus strikes. Moores (2001, p. 106) describes the impact of the virus:

> Illness of the mother during pregnancy can cause damage to the developing fetus.

> If a pregnant woman contracts rubella, particularly during the first trimester (three months) of pregnancy, the virus may cross the placental

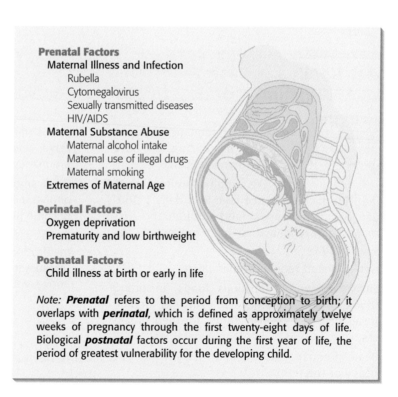

Prenatal Factors
  Maternal Illness and Infection
    Rubella
    Cytomegalovirus
    Sexually transmitted diseases
    HIV/AIDS
  Maternal Substance Abuse
    Maternal alcohol intake
    Maternal use of illegal drugs
    Maternal smoking
  Extremes of Maternal Age

Perinatal Factors
  Oxygen deprivation
  Prematurity and low birthweight

Postnatal Factors
  Child illness at birth or early in life

Note: **Prenatal** refers to the period from conception to birth; it overlaps with **perinatal**, which is defined as approximately twelve weeks of pregnancy through the first twenty-eight days of life. Biological **postnatal** factors occur during the first year of life, the period of greatest vulnerability for the developing child.

Figure 2.2

Examples of Biological Risk Factors

barrier and attack the developing cells and structures of the fetus, killing or crippling the unborn child. The virus can kill growing cells, and it attacks tissues of the eye, ear, and other organs.

Fortunately, immunization against rubella has virtually eliminated this disease as a cause of disability in the United States; it still constitutes a threat in parts of the world where immunization is not widely available.

Cytomegalovirus (CMV) remains the most common congenital infection in the United States (**congenital** refers to a condition the child is born with). Approximately 1–3 percent of all newborns are infected at birth because of trans-

A Closer Look   Newborn Screening

Hospitals across the United States take a blood sample from the heel of each newborn baby and test the blood for the presence of phenylketonuria (PKU), a metabolic disorder that, when left untreated, can cause mental retardation. More than forty states also screen for sickle cell disease, forty-eight screen for galactosemia, and over half the states require all newborns to be screened for hearing loss. Now there is the possibility of identifying an even wider range of potentially treatable diseases and genetic and metabolic disorders at birth—toxoplasmosis, maple syrup urine disease, propionic acidemia, cystic fibrosis, HIV, and many others—but hospitals and states are arguing over the necessity of such programs.

Why not just screen babies for all identifiable disorders at birth? Potvin (2000) lists the reasons:

- *Problems with the testing methodology.* Although there are still issues with screening methodologies, *tandem mass spectrometry* is an extremely sensitive new tool that can test for many disorders.

- *Difficulty providing necessary follow-up and counseling.* Once a disorder has been identified, families must be located for counseling and treatment.

- *No available treatment.* Not every disorder can be treated or cured.

- *Limited resources.* Testing is expensive, as are training and hiring new personnel.

- *Rarity of the diseases.* The incidence of these conditions is very low (for example, homocystinuria, a metabolic disorder, occurs about once in every 150,000 live births) and varies by race and ethnicity.

The inconsistency of screening procedures from state to state can cause problems for families. For example, Mubashir Younis was identified with propionic acidemia (PA) at birth in Massachusetts; he is now receiving treatment and is doing quite well. But Jordan Franks was born in Illinois, where PA is not screened for; he had a metabolic crisis at four days of age that might have been avoided had PA been identified at birth (Stagni, 2000).

The *Newborn Screening Task Force* report (2000) recommends that families be educated about newborn screening and involved in informed decision-making from the outset. Once a condition has been diagnosed, they should be made aware of the short- and long-term characteristics of the condition, treatment goals, and the health-care and social service resources that are available. Newborn screening can save lives and prevent illness and disability, but it comes with the responsibility of education and follow-up treatment.

Source: Newborn Screening Task Force (2000), Newborn screening: A blueprint for the future, *Exceptional Parent, 30*(10) 69–73; F. R. Potvin (2000), Newborn screening: Testing for disorders at birth, *Exceptional Parent, 30*(10) 90–93; and K. Stagni (2000), Newborn screening and parent support groups, *Exceptional Parent, 30*(10) 66–68.

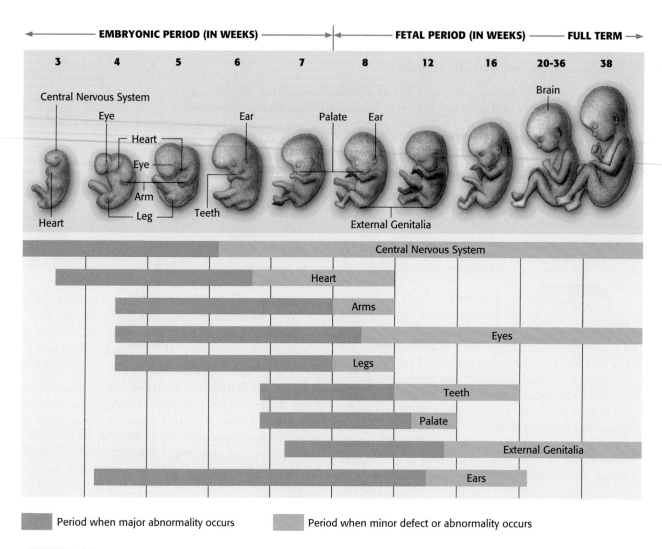

Figure 2.3

Sensitive Periods in Prenatal Development

Source: K. L. Moore (1998). Adapted from *Before we are born* (5th ed.), Elsevier.

mission of the virus from their mother during pregnancy. The virus can result in the infant's death or in aftereffects such as mental retardation, visual impairment, and hearing loss, which may not manifest themselves until later in the child's life (National Center for Infectious Diseases, 2002).

Sexually transmitted diseases (STDs) affect a mother and her partner and can have serious implications for the child. The term "STD" denotes the more than twenty-five infectious organisms that are transmitted through sexual activity. The most common STDs among pregnant women in the United States are bacterial vaginosis, herpes simplex, chlamydia, trichomoniasis, gonorrhea, hepatitis B, HIV, and syphilis (Centers for Disease Control, 2003). Active infection with STDs during pregnancy may result in a range of serious health problems among infected infants, including severe central nervous system damage, con-

> When STDs are identified and treated during the first trimester of pregnancy, harm to the fetus can be avoided.

A Closer Look   Facts About Pediatric HIV/AIDS

The global pandemic

- More than 2000 children worldwide are infected with HIV each day.

- In 2002, 5 million people were newly infected with HIV—800,000 of them were children.

- More than 42 million people are infected with HIV worldwide—3.2 million of them are children.

- In some parts of Africa, more than 60 percent of women aged 15–49 do not know that HIV can be transmitted from a mother to her child.

- Worldwide, approximately 28 million people have died of AIDS since the beginning of the epidemic—approximately 5.6 million of them were children.

- In 2002, 3.1 million people died of AIDS—610,000 (approximately 1600 per day) of them were children.

- In 2002, more than 720,000 babies were infected through mother-to-child transmission.

- In industrialized nations, the results of research and effective intervention have drastically reduced mother-to-child transmission of HIV to less than 2 percent. There are proven low-cost interventions that have the capacity to save thousands of children's lives in the developing world if we act now.

- More than 95 percent of people with HIV live in the developing world.

- Life expectancy at birth in southern Africa, which rose from 44 years in the early 1950s to 59 in the early 1990s, is expected to drop to just 45 between 2000 and 2010 because of AIDS.

- Worldwide, about 50 percent of all new HIV infections occur among young people 15–24 years old.

- More than 6000 young people worldwide aged 15–24 become infected with HIV every day—that is, about four every minute.

- Women now account for 50 percent of all the people living with HIV/AIDS worldwide.

- More than 13.1 million children have been orphaned by the AIDS epidemic since it began, and that number is expected to reach more than 25 million by 2010.

- It is estimated that an additional 45 million people will become infected by 2010 unless the world succeeds in mounting a drastically expanded global prevention effort.

The epidemic in the United States

- There are approximately 800,000 to 900,000 people currently living with HIV in the United States, and 200,000 of those people do not know that they are infected, putting them at the highest risk of spreading the infection.

- It is estimated that there are 40,000 new infections in the United States each year. At least half of these infections are among people under 25.

- In the United States, it is estimated that two adolescents are infected with HIV each hour.

- Mother-to-child transmission of HIV has accounted for 91 percent of all AIDS cases reported among U.S. children.

- Since the beginning of the epidemic, more than 450,000 people have died of AIDS in the United States.

- Since 1991, AIDS has been the leading cause of death among African Americans between the ages of 25 and 44.

- Approximately 75 percent of new HIV infections in the United States occur among blacks and Hispanics.

The material here was last updated in March 2003. For more information, call 888-499-HOPE (4673) or visit the Elizabeth Glazer Pediatric AIDS Foundation website at http://www.pedaids.org.

Source: Pediatric HIV/AIDS Fact Sheet, September 2003. Elizabeth Glazer Pediatric Aids Foundation www.pedaids.org. The estimates provided were compiled with data from the Centers for Disease Control and Prevention, Office of National AIDS Policy, UNAIDS, UNICEF, USAID, and the World Health Organization.

genital malformations, and death (Eng & Butler, 1997). For example, a mother with syphilis may have a child with congenital syphilis, which can result in death or severe mental retardation, deafness, and blindness. If the illness is identified during the first trimester of pregnancy, harm to the fetus can be avoided, but many infants with congenital syphilis are born to women who receive no prenatal care. Herpes, another STD, has symptoms such as cold sores and vaginal infections. Although the risk of transmitting herpes to an unborn child is relatively low, if transmission does occur during a vaginal delivery, it can have severe consequences for the infant, such as neurological, vision, and hearing impairment (Hutchinson & Sandall, 1995). Other STDs, including chlamydia, can also affect fetal development and the health of the newborn. STDs are a particular risk for adolescents and can be difficult to detect, since they are "silent—or present without symptoms—in women" (Centers for Disease Control, 1997, p. 1). Left untreated, STDs can cause infertility.

> AIDS and HIV can be transmitted during pregnancy, birth, and breastfeeding.

About 25 percent of U.S. women who have **acquired immune deficiency syndrome (AIDS)**, or those who test positive for the **human immunodeficiency virus (HIV)**, transmit HIV infection to their offspring during pregnancy, birth, or breastfeeding. Treatment with antiretroviral drug therapy during pregnancy can reduce the transmission rate to less than 2 percent (Lindegren, Steinberg, & Byers, 2000). Because early treatment is so important, most physicians are recommending testing for HIV early in pregnancy; that assumes, however, that the pregnant mother is receiving prenatal care. Learn more about AIDS in children in our Closer Look box, *Facts About Pediatric HIV/AIDS.*

AIDS weakens the immune system and ultimately results in death. Since HIV infection can cause central nervous system damage in children, HIV positive children may experience significant developmental delays. Improvements in treatments for infants and children with HIV appear to be lessening the severity of early symptoms (Abuzaitoun & Hanson, 2000), but children with HIV/AIDS in its more severe forms will qualify for special education services. Those services should focus on enhancing the quality of life for eligible children and their families (Boland, 2000).

The incidence of AIDS is rapidly increasing among women and children all over the world. In Sub-Saharan Africa, where antiretroviral drug treatment is not widely available, an estimated 28 million adults and children were living with HIV/AIDS at the end of 2001 (in comparison to 940,000 in North America) (information available at **http://www.unicef.org/aids**). In the United States, women infected with HIV are more likely to be young, poor, and urban (Lindegren, Steinberg, & Byers, 2000), so their children may be subject to multiple biological and environmental risk factors. Black and Hispanic women have particularly high rates of the disease. Lindegren and her colleagues warn that "despite encouraging evidence of increased survival because of effective therapies, transmission is ongoing, and young women are especially at risk" (p. 2). The accompanying Teaching Strategies box entitled, "Education of Children with HIV Infection" provides recommendations for those working with children with HIV/AIDS. You will read more about HIV/AIDS in Chapter 12.

Maternal Substance Abuse   Maternal drug use during pregnancy continues to generate great concern among professionals, politicians, and the general public. Doctors recommend that even the most common legal drugs, whether they are over-the-counter or prescription, should not be taken by pregnant women or be taken only with a doctor's recommendation. Many over-the-counter or prescription drugs have been associated with birth defects, particularly congenital mal-

Teaching Strategies & Accommodations

Education of Children with HIV Infection

As treatment for children with HIV improves, they are more likely to attend school and participate in school activities. The majority of children with HIV reaching school age will have normal cognitive function. The American Academy of Pediatrics makes the following recommendations for the education of children with HIV:

1. All children and youths with HIV infection should have the same right as those without infection to attend school and receive high-quality educational services.

2. Children and youths with HIV infection should have access to special education and other related services in accord with their needs as the disease progresses.

3. Mechanisms for administration of medications, including confidential methods for HIV infection, should be in place in all schools.

This includes appropriate facilitation of specific needs for fluids or bathroom privileges.

4. Continuity of education must be ensured for children and adolescents with HIV infection and encompasses the spectrum of traditional school, medical day treatment programs, and home schooling.

5. Confidentiality of HIV infection status should be respected and maintained, with disclosure given only with the consent of the parent(s) or legal guardian(s) and age-appropriate assent of the student.

6. The pediatrician/medical home providers should maintain appropriate communication with the school to facilitate the education of children in their care.

Source: For the complete policy statement, go to http://www.aap.org/policy/re9950.html.

---

formations such as heart defects, ear damage, and cleft lip and palate. The effects of others on the developing fetus have not been adequately investigated by researchers (American College of Obstetricians and Gynecologists, 2002).

Medical professionals' caution about over-the-counter and prescription drugs comes in part from the experience of many Europeans with **thalidomide** in the late 1950s. Thalidomide was prescribed to pregnant women for nausea; over time it was learned that taking the drug during the first trimester of pregnancy often caused shortened or missing arms and legs in the fetus (Graham & Morgan, 1997). The thalidomide experience taught medical researchers and practitioners that they must carefully monitor drugs ingested during patients' pregnancies.

But what effects do the illegal drugs used today have on infants? Babies of mothers who have used cocaine, heroin or methadone, marijuana, PCP, or amphetamines (substance-abusing mothers who use combinations of drugs as well as alcohol are referred to as **polysubstance abusers**) appear to be at significant risk, and may be particularly vulnerable to the effects of an unstable environment.

Cocaine and marijuana are currently the drugs most commonly used by women of childbearing age (Widerstrom & Nickel, 1997). Babies prenatally exposed to cocaine are more likely to be born early and to have a low birthweight and a smaller head circumference. Recently, Singer and her colleagues (2002) found that children prenatally exposed to cocaine had significant cognitive deficits and experienced a doubling of the rate of developmental delay during the first two years of life.

> The thalidomide tragedy of the 1950s demonstrated that great care must be taken with all drugs during pregnancy.

> Polysubstance abusers are those who use a combination of drugs as well as alcohol.

The long-term effects of prenatal drug exposure on the child are difficult to predict.

The long-term effects of exposure to illegal drugs on development are still being debated, but most researchers agree that preschool and school-aged children who were exposed to drugs *in utero* are at risk for developmental and language delay, and emotional, behavioral, and attentional difficulties (Jansson & Velez, 1999). In addition, substance abuse significantly affects the family environment; more than half the women who are dependent on cocaine, for example, will experience physical abuse, STDs, or separation from their children by imprisonment (Hans, 1999). Mothers who continue as substance abusers may neglect the most basic needs of their infants (Jansson & Velez, 1999). It appears that the substance-exposed children who are most likely to develop problems in life are those who also experience additional environmental risk factors, such as maternal stress, harsh discipline, family instability, and living in a single-parent family (Bennett, Bendersky, & Lewis, 2002).

Maternal alcohol intake during pregnancy can have grave effects on the developing fetus. For surviving children, it can result in **fetal alcohol syndrome (FAS)**. The child with FAS has altered facial features, such as a small head, widely spaced eyes, upturned nose, large ears, and a small chin; he or she will also have developmental delays in language and cognition, and may have behavioral problems such as oppositional and defiant behavior, poor judgment, and social withdrawal (Wunsch, Conlon, & Scheidt, 2002). Some children have the cognitive and behavioral characteristics associated with FAS but not the physical abnormalities; they are said to have **alcohol-related neurodevelopmental disorder (ARND)**. Alcohol-related birth defects (FAS and ARND) occur in nearly 1 in 100 births worldwide (Sampson, Streissguth et al., 1999), making them the leading cause of preventable mental retardation today (Wunsch, Conlon, & Scheidt, 2001). Although not all children of women who drink alcohol experience these significant aftereffects, researchers have not identified a "safe" level of alcohol intake during pregnancy. As a result, doctors now recommend that pregnant women—and those planning to conceive—drink no alcohol at all (National Institute on Alcohol Abuse and Alcoholism, 2003).

Maternal alcohol use during pregnancy can result in fetal alcohol syndrome or alcohol-related neurodevelopmental disorder.

Six-year-old Lance follows directions while being assessed in a Fetal Alcohol Syndrome Clinic. (AP Photos/World Wide Photos)

In the United States, about 23 percent of women smoke—many while they are pregnant (March of Dimes, 2000). Most of us realize that smoking damages the smoker's health, but prenatal exposure to tobacco also has a serious impact on the developing fetus. Maternal cigarette smoking during pregnancy is the single most important cause of low birthweight (Shiono & Behrman, 1995); pregnant women who smoke have a relatively high number of complications that can result in the death of the fetus, premature delivery, and physical abnormalities. Children of women who smoke during pregnancy are more likely to experience sudden infant death syndrome (SIDS) and have asthma; there is some evidence that they are also at higher risk for emotional and behavioral problems (American College of Obstetricians and Gynecologists, 1997).

> Smoking can result in pregnancy complications as well as low birthweight and physical abnormalities in the infant.

Extremes of Maternal Age   Mothers at the beginning and at the end of their reproductive span are at the greatest risk for potential pregnancy problems. Young mothers, particularly those in the earliest teenage years, are more likely to have pregnancy complications resulting in prematurity or low birthweight, as well as other medical complications that could endanger the life and health of their babies (Smith, 1994). Among the biological factors that place the infants of adolescent mothers at risk are poor maternal nutrition and low weight gain, a higher likelihood of sexually transmitted diseases, and, most important, limited access to prenatal care (March of Dimes, 2002). The children of very young mothers are also considered at risk because of the characteristics of their caregiving environment—their young mothers are less likely to finish school and have little work preparation; they may be less responsive to their baby's cues and are more likely to be accused of child abuse and neglect (Wakschlag & Hans, 2000).

> Young mothers and older mothers are at risk for different pregnancy complications.

Mothers over age 35 may present a different set of problems. They are more likely to have a child with **Down syndrome,** a condition caused by an extra twenty-first chromosome that results in mental retardation and physical anomalies in the child (see Table 2.1 and Chapter 5). Since the older a mother is, the more likely she is to have a baby with Down syndrome, the American Medical Association recommends that pregnant women aged 35 and older undergo amniocentesis or other prenatal testing. We will discuss prenatal testing procedures later in the chapter in the section on prevention of disabilities.

Women over 35 are also more likely to have health problems such as diabetes and high blood pressure, which can complicate a pregnancy. Older mothers, however, are also more likely to have access to early and consistent prenatal

Table 2.1 Maternal Age and the Risk of Having a Baby with Down Syndrome After a Previous Baby		
Age of Mother	**At Any Pregnancy**	**After Previous Child with Down Syndrome**
29 or below	1 in 1000	1 in 100
30–34	1 in 600	1 in 100
35–39	1 in 200	1 in 100
40–44	1 in 65	1 in 25
45–49	1 in 25	1 in 15

Source: S. M. Paeschel & A. Goldstein in *Handbook of Mental Retardation*, Second Edition, by Johnny L. Matson & James L. Mulick. Published by Allyn and Bacon, Boston, MA. Copyright © 1992 by Pearson Education. Reprinted by permission of the publisher.

medical care, and, given such care, many potential pregnancy complications can be managed, and a healthy baby is born. Early and ongoing prenatal care can minimize the effects of maternal age.

● *Perinatal Factors*   Perinatal factors are those that occur from the twelfth week of pregnancy to the twenty-eighth day of infant life. It is here that medical research and technology have had a profound impact on both the survival and the quality of life of small and sick babies. Nevertheless, perinatal stresses still increase the risk status and, at times, call for special treatment and follow-up.

Oxygen Deprivation   For a variety of reasons during pregnancy, labor, delivery, and newborn life, the infant can experience **hypoxia**, or a decreased availability of oxygen in the body tissues. Hypoxia can cause cells in the brain to die, resulting in brain damage and sometimes death. The long-term effects of oxygen deprivation can be severe or minimal, but among the disabling conditions associated with prolonged hypoxia are cerebral palsy, mental retardation, seizures, visual and auditory deficits, and behavioral problems. Most affected infants, however, experience mild episodes of hypoxia and therefore do not develop disabilities (Robertson & Finer, 1993).

Prematurity and Low Birthweight   Many of the prenatal risk factors discussed above increase the likelihood of **prematurity** and **low birthweight** (see Table 2.2). Most readers know those terms, but let's define them precisely. The average length of pregnancy, or gestation, is forty weeks. Babies born before thirty-seven weeks' gestation are called premature, or preterm. Although the timing of a birth is important, the baby's weight may be even more crucial. Babies born weighing less than about five and a half pounds (2500 grams) are said to be low birthweight. Those weighing three and a half pounds or less are considered **very low birthweight**. Babies born at twenty-five weeks gestation or less, usually weighing under one pound, are at the "threshold of viability"—their survival and their health are severely threatened (McDonald, 2002). Even full-term babies can be low birthweight; thus, prematurity and low birthweight may be independent of one another. Think of it this way: A premature baby, born at thirty-four weeks' gestation, might already weigh six pounds; a baby born on her "due date" might weigh only four pounds. Women who are poor and young are in particular danger of delivering prematurely; they are also more likely to receive little or no prenatal care and to be undernourished (Paneth, 1995; Scholl, Hediger, & Belsky, 1994). For an example of how premature birth affects children and families, visit our text website at **www.education.college.hmco.com/students/** and click onto "The Story of Lucy and Nell."

What are the dangers of premature birth? Premature babies are more likely to be low birthweight, and the lower the birthweight, the more likely a baby will have serious complications or die. In fact, low birthweight is a factor in 65 percent of infant deaths. Premature babies' systems are sometimes not ready to function independently; the babies need to gain weight but often have not developed the ability to coordinate sucking and swallowing, and their intestines are not yet ready to digest food normally, so feeding and weight gain are complicated; and their immature immune systems make them very vulnerable to infection. In addition, the lower the birthweight, the more likely it is that the baby will develop complications of prematurity, such as respiratory distress syndrome (extreme difficulty in breathing), brain hemorrhage (bleeding), and retinopathy of prematurity (an eye condition that can lead to blindness), all of which place their long-term development at risk.

> The perinatal period ranges from the twelfth week of pregnancy to the twenty-eighth day of life.

> Premature babies are born before thirty-seven weeks' gestation; low birthweight babies weigh less than five and a half pounds.

Table 2.2 Risk Factors for Prematurity	
Inadequate prenatal care	Multiple gestation births
Poor nutrition and weight gain	History of previous premature pregnancies
Maternal infections	Smoking
Adolescent mother	Substance abuse
Poverty	Congenital anomalies or injuries to the fetus
Acute and chronic maternal illness	Problems of the cervix and the placenta

Source: K. Rais-Bahrami, B. L. Short, & M. L. Batshaw, Premature and small-for-dates infants. In M. L. Batshaw (Ed.) *Children with disabilities*, Fifth Edition, 2001. Baltimore: Paul H. Brookes.

Advances in **neonatology**, the study of newborns, have dramatically changed the prognosis for even the tiniest surviving premature babies. The specialized care given to these fragile infants in the **neonatal intensive care unit**, the area of the hospital that provides care for sick and premature newborns, has ensured the survival of many babies who, even a few years ago, would have died. Until recently, babies weighing three and a half pounds and under (now called very low birthweight) routinely died; now most are routinely saved. The limits of survival have changed dramatically over the last few years; currently, the majority of infants born at twenty-four or more weeks' gestational age survive. Most of those babies weigh less than two pounds; the smallest survivors weigh around one pound. New drugs that successfully treat respiratory distress syndrome are helping to increase those numbers (Bradbury, 2002). However, premature babies are much more likely than full-term babies to have conditions such as cerebral palsy, mental retardation, seizures, and vision and hearing impairments.

> Advances in neonatology and high-risk infant care have ensured the survival of many low birthweight babies.

The number of premature survivors with disabling conditions increases as the birthweight drops. Current research suggests that from 10 to 30 percent of very low birthweight babies who survive are chronically ill or disabled. Their disabilities range from school learning problems, particularly those related to hyperactivity and attention, to severe disabilities (Hack & Fanaroff, 2000; Saigal, 2000).

● *Postnatal Factors*   Among the postnatal biological factors of the first year of life that place a child at risk for school learning problems are *chronic diseases and infections* and *severe nutritional deficiencies*. Among the diseases that can place a young child's learning at risk are asthma or chronic lung disease, meningitis (a life-threatening bacterial or viral infection), HIV, and ongoing ear infections (chronic otitis media). You will learn more about how chronic illness can affect learning in Chapter 10.

> Diseases like meningitis and conditions like chronic otitis media can result in disabilities that affect school performance.

Nutritional deprivation is usually associated with extreme poverty, and it is difficult to separate the effects of poor nutrition from the other deprivations of poverty (Sigman & Whaley, 1998). In many developing countries, however, there is dramatic evidence that malnutrition, and particularly iron deficiency, alter brain development in children (Donovan & Cross, 2002). In short, there is little doubt that chronic poor nutrition can affect brain development and thus cause learning problems in school.

Environmental Risk

The category of environmental risk includes risk factors related to the surroundings in which the child develops. Environmental factors can influence develop-

> Environmental risk includes all the risk factors related to the environment in which the child develops.

ment at any stage; our discussion will first refer to events that may affect the environment of the mother before her child's birth.

● *Environmental Factors That Influence Prenatal Development*
Studies from Hiroshima and Nagasaki, as well as ongoing observation of the after-effects of the fire at the nuclear reactor at Chernobyl, suggest a strong relationship between exposure to radiation in pregnant women and physical and psychological problems in their offspring (Kolominsky, Igumnov, & Drozdovich, 1999).

The effects of radiation depend on the distance from the source, the intensity of the source, and the time of the exposure during pregnancy (Graham & Morgan, 1997). Diagnostic X-rays that a pregnant woman might experience are rarely strong enough to harm the fetus.

Since many women today continue to work during pregnancy, they must consider the **occupational hazards** associated with some workplaces. Some occupations expose workers to low levels of radiation, and others expose them to low levels of lead and mercury. Exposure to these and other substances has been linked to reproductive loss and birth defects.

Traditionally, physicians and researchers have looked to mothers as the source of risk in their children, but some recent research has attempted to identify the role of the father in contributing to biological risk (American College of Medical Genetics, 1996). Older fathers account for a small percentage of all cases of Down syndrome (Skinner, 1990). Also, investigations of exposure to toxic substances in the environment have intensified because of the conviction of many veterans of the Vietnam War that their exposure to the defoliant Agent Orange increased the number of birth defects such as spina bifida and the incidence of childhood cancer in their offspring.

The mothers of these young children in Vietnam were exposed to Agent Orange, resulting in significant birth defects in their children. (Steve Raymer/CORBIS)

● *Postnatal Environmental Factors*   Once a child has been born, environmental factors continue to influence how he or she develops. The characteristics of the child's immediate caregiving environment are vital to optimal development. That environment must provide protection from exposure to dangerous toxins and disease as well as opportunities for learning and social growth and a stable home and family. We'll look at each of these areas.

Most researchers agree that the impact of biological risk events can be lessened or made worse by the characteristics of the environment. For example, although AIDS is classified as a biological risk factor and occurs in all sectors of our population, it is more likely to occur among those living in poverty. Children who are "at risk" develop as they do because of a complex interaction between their risk history and their caregiving environments.

Other agents within our environment can cause problems for children that may affect their school learning. Some of these, such as exposure to radiation, we are aware of, although hard data verifying the effects of these substances on the developing nervous system in children are difficult to come by.

Lead   One substance scientists are learning more about is lead. There are at least 2 million homes in the United States where lead-paint-covered surfaces are chalking and flaking, and almost every child in such a home has elevated levels of lead in the blood (Needleman, 1992). A recent study of Mexican women with high lead levels found that their children had relatively low levels of mental functioning at age 2 (Gomaa et al., 2002). Although poverty significantly increases the risk of lead exposure, excessively high levels of lead are found in children of all social classes and racial backgrounds.

> Early exposure to lead is associated with a greater likelihood of school problems.

Children with high lead levels have decreased IQ scores and poorer language and attention skills; their teachers find them more distractible and less well organized and persistent (Needleman et al., 1979). Long-term follow-up of these children indicates that early lead exposure is associated with a substantially elevated likelihood of having a reading disability, dropping out of school, delinquent behavior, and adult criminality (Needleman et al., 1991, 1996).

Other Environmental Toxins   Many of us are suspicious about the effect of environmental toxins on children, but research in this area is notoriously difficult to conduct. How does the researcher separate the effects of a toxic substance present in the environment—the air, water, soil, home, and community—from the effects of anything else? Some of the substances that have been studied are mercury, polychlorinated biphenyls (PCBs), and various pesticides. There is suspicion that these substances are **neurotoxins**—substances that adversely affect the structural or functional components of the nervous system (Center for Children's Health and the Environment, 2002). As such, they could have a relationship to the rising number of cases of attention deficit disorder, autism spectrum disorders, and other developmental disabilities, as well as asthma and cancer (Landrigan et al., 2002). The key word here is could—the research is not yet conclusive.

> Neurotoxins damage the developing central nervous system.

There are, no doubt, other substances within our environment that cause damage to the developing nervous system in children that have not yet been identified. Many of the causes of childhood learning problems, as we shall see in future chapters, are unknown.

Accidents   Accidents of all kinds are examples of environmental risks. Car accidents are the most common, but accidents may also happen on bikes, in swimming pools, and anywhere else that active, curious young children play and explore. Ac-

Accidents are the most common postnatal risk factor.

cidents that involve head trauma, oxygen deprivation, or spinal cord injury can cause severe physical disability as well as learning and behavior problems. Caregivers must be extremely watchful and observant of children's play areas.

The characteristics of the social environment are also crucial for optimal development: the nature of the medical technology available to support a sick newborn or child, the availability of public health services in the community, and the emphasis on educational achievement within the society as a whole. The next part of our discussion of environmental risk concentrates on the social aspects of poverty and family issues. You will see, however, that there is a great deal of overlap among these areas, and they are often interrelated.

Poverty—which can include both economic and social factors—is a major cause of environmental risk.

Poverty   Biologically normal infants who live in poverty may be at risk for problems of development because of characteristics of their caregiving environment. McLloyd (1998) identifies some of the risk factors associated with persistent poverty: higher rates of perinatal complications, reduced access to resources that might buffer the effects of those complications, increased exposure to lead, and less home-based cognitive stimulation. These inadequacies are more likely to exist in impoverished families—money *does* buy health care, food, and quality day care for working or absent parents—but they are by no means exclusive to poor families. The accompanying Closer Look box entitled, "Child Poverty in the United States" provides some basic information on the subject.

In the United States today one out of six children lives in poverty and three out of four poor children live in a working family. A baby is born into poverty every thirty-five seconds, and child poverty rates are two to nine times as high as those in other industrialized nations (Children's Defense Fund, 2002). The children of poverty are more likely to die in childhood, to be in special education programs, and to drop out of school; the girls are more likely to become pregnant during adolescence and the boys to engage in criminal behavior. Children who live below the poverty level are less likely to be in good health than those above the poverty line; they are also more likely to have limitations in their activity because of a chronic health condition (for example, asthma or diabetes) (Health Indicators, 2000). Problems with physical health can affect a child's cognitive status (McLloyd, 1998).

What is it about living in poverty that leads to poor outcomes for children? The obvious answer, lack of access to good medical care and nutrition, as well as to experiences and opportunities, is only partly right. Most of us can cite several examples of people who grew up in such circumstances who have reached significant levels of achievement in our society. Garbarino (1990) made the point that some families are economically impoverished but have a "socially rich family environment": family members, neighbors, and friends who provide support for both children and parents—the "informal helping relationships" that are the foundation of some communities. Other families are both economically and socially impoverished. According to Garbarino (1990, p. 90),

> these are the environments in which prenatal care is inadequate, intervals between births are often too short, beliefs about child care too often dysfunctional, access to and utilization of well-baby care inadequate, early intervention for child disabilities inadequate, and thus in which child mortality and morbidity are rampant.

These conditions are more likely to occur in our inner cities, where families must also live with the reality of frequent violence that respects no target—not even a small child. The stresses in such communities can become unbearable;

neighbors may be afraid and distrustful of one another, and little sense of community may exist.

Social impoverishment can occur at every economic level, but more affluent families can pay for supportive services when they are not available through friends and family. Many poor families, frequently headed by single mothers, are left with few resources to help with the considerable stresses of childrearing.

Families come in all shapes, sizes, and configurations. We can no longer assume that a child will grow up in a traditional nuclear family, nor do we insist that there is one "right" way to raise children. We do know, however, that certain characteristics of the caregiving environment appear to help children develop optimally. Emotional and physical safety, responsive and sensitive

A Closer Look — Child Poverty in the United States

Poverty matters.

Poor children are at least twice as likely as nonpoor children to suffer stunted growth or lead poisoning, or to be kept back in school. Poor children score significantly lower on reading, math, and vocabulary tests when compared with otherwise similar nonpoor children. More than half of poor Americans (55 percent) experience serious deprivations during the year (defined as lack of food, utility shutoffs, crowded or substandard housing, or lack of a stove or refrigerator). Poor households are more than fifteen times as likely to experience hunger.

How many U.S. children are poor?

11.7 million in the year 2001—or one in six (16.3 percent).

Are there poor children in working families?

Yes, three out of four poor children (74 percent) live with a family member who worked at least part of the year. One out of three poor children (34 percent) lives in a family where someone is employed full-time year round.

Are non-white children more likely to be poor?

Yes. Nearly one in three black children (30.2 percent) and more than one in four Hispanic children (28.0 percent) are poor in the United States compared to 9.5 percent of non-Hispanic white children and 11.5 percent of Asian and Pacific Islander children.

But . . . poor children defy the stereotypes.

There are more poor white non-Hispanic children (4.2 million) than poor black children (3.5 million) or poor Hispanic children (3.6 million), even though the proportion of black and Hispanic children who are poor is far higher. More poor children live in suburban and rural areas than in central cities. Poor families have only 2.2 children on average.

Are children in single-parent families more likely to be poor?

Yes. Two out of five children in families headed by single women (39.3 percent) were poor in 2001. Only 8.0 percent of children in married families were poor.

Ranked against other social problems, the hazards of poverty are high

A baby born to a poor mother is more likely to die before its first birthday than a baby born to an unwed mother, a high-school dropout, or a mother who smoked during pregnancy, according to the Centers for Disease Control. Poverty is a greater risk to children's overall health status than is living in a single-parent family, according to government researchers.

Source: Children's Defense Fund. http://www.childrensdefense.org/fs_cpfaq_facts.php.

caregivers, and stability of family members are all tied to the healthy development of children.

We will discuss issues related to families in the next chapter. But here it is important to describe two characteristics of families that place the child at risk: maltreatment and family instability.

Child Maltreatment   Child abuse and child neglect are grouped together under the term *maltreatment,* and reports of both are abundant in the United States today. Although hard economic times and high rates of unemployment no doubt increase the likelihood of child maltreatment (Garbarino, 1990), reports of the murder, abuse, and neglect of children are as old as recorded history and appear in all cultures.

Children with disabilities are overrepresented in samples of abused children, but it is difficult to determine how many children with disabilities are abused (Turnbull, Buchele-Ash, & Mitchell, 1994). Professionals suspect, however, that child abuse is responsible for a proportion of the cases of mental retardation, physical disability, and emotional disturbance in the United States today: One group estimates that over 18,000 children are seriously disabled every year as a result of abuse or neglect by parents or caregivers (U.S. Advisory Board on Child Abuse and Neglect, 1995).

In many states teachers are mandated to report suspected child abuse and neglect, so being informed about risk factors for child abuse and reporting requirements is crucial. (See also "Useful Resources" at the end of this chapter.)

Family Instability   Although we now know that the two-parent family is not a necessary condition for optimal child growth and development, it does seem clear that children need at least one stable caregiver throughout their childhood in order to develop well (Werner & Smith, 1982). That caregiver may not be a parent; often, a grandmother or other relative can provide the ongoing stability a child needs. As developmental psychologist Urie Bronfenbrenner reminds us in his often quoted statement, "The critical factor in a child's development is the active involvement of at least one adult who is simply crazy about the child" (1993, p. 47). Children who experience many changes in the adult makeup of the household appear to do less well in school (Hunt, 1982) and may be at greater risk for dropping out of school and engaging in criminal behavior.

It is important to emphasize that the existence of one risk factor alone does not ensure developmental problems. Rather, those problems occur because of multiple risk factors, most often a combination of biological and environmental events.

Research on risk factors has shown us that children with some of the previously described biological risks, such as prematurity, are more vulnerable to environmental stresses than other children are. It is the combination of biological and environmental risk factors that places that developing child in jeopardy for future school problems.

Family Structure   In a recent review of the data linking poverty and disability in children, Fujiura and Yamaki (2000) noted that the greatest concentration of poverty is found among single-parent households. Together, the environmental risk factors of single-parenthood and poverty, likely to be linked, become a significant predictor of childhood disability. Since both of these factors are more likely to occur in traditional minority groups, minority children are at disproportionate risk for disability, which may account for their disproportionate representation in special education (which we discussed in Chapter 1).

> Child abuse may be responsible for some cases of mental retardation, physical disability, and emotional disturbance in the United States today.

> Developmental problems most often stem from a combination of biological and environmental risk factors.

Single parenthood is a difficult topic. We all know many individuals who were raised by single parents and who have done very well in life. Some of our readers likely are single parents, struggling to become teachers or other professionals so that the lives of their children can be improved. Our intention is not to discourage their efforts—there are many exceptions to these findings.

But there are built-in challenges for the single parent. He or she can be many things, but two adults is not one of them. Children who grow up with two parents, or extended family members living in their homes, have the benefit of a relationship with more than one caring and caregiving adult. It means that there are two people to talk with, ask for help from, get angry at, and learn about adulthood from. Single parenthood decreases the amount of adult attention available to the child (Donovan & Cross, 2002), and ultimately increases the likelihood of poverty and disability. As we will see in Chapter 3, the presence of family often increases the social and emotional supports for both children and parents.

? Pause and Reflect

You have just read a long section with many examples of risk factors— but it is not a complete list, just the best-known examples. Can you think of other biological or environmental risk factors that affect child development? Is there research evidence supporting your examples? ●

Prevention

Fortunately, many steps can be taken to prevent or minimize the occurrence of risk factors and developmental problems in infants and children. Some of these steps can be taken for our children; some we can take ourselves; some are questions of public policy, and we can work within our political system to advocate for important changes (Simeonsson, 1994).

Major Strategies for Prevention

● *Inoculation*　Inoculation—vaccination against infectious diseases—starts in the first year of life and should continue through early childhood. Children are inoculated against diphtheria, tetanus, pertussis (whooping cough), measles, mumps, rubella, and polio, among other diseases. An effective, wide-reaching immunization program can virtually eliminate these diseases, many of which can also harm pregnant women. Many adults have not been immunized against rubella. Administration of a rubella titer test can determine whether you have had the disease, which can be easily confused with other common illnesses. If you have not had rubella, you will be doing a service to your community by becoming immunized against it, so you will not contribute to the spread of this destructive virus. It is not only women thinking of having children who should be immunized—men can spread this virus too!

Inoculation, or vaccination against infectious diseases, is a prevention strategy that should be available to every child.

● *Genetic Counseling*　Couples who have reason to be concerned they might have a child with a disabling condition will find that **genetic counseling** can provide them with helpful information. With information from a couple's family and personal health history, a genetic counselor can often discuss the likelihood that their child will inherit a genetic condition (see the accompanying Closer Look box entitled, "Genetic Counseling: 'The Science Is the Easy Part'").

Genetic counseling can also be a step in preventing disability.

What is genetic counseling? The mother of a 6-year-old with Down syndrome put it well when she said, "In two one-hour sessions, our counselor taught me everything I wished I had remembered from Biology 101, Psychology 101, and Philosophy 101." Genetic counseling draws on knowledge from these fields and others in an effort to provide the most accurate, up-to-date information on the causes and treatment of genetic disorders, the tests available for identifying them, a possible prognosis for a child with a genetic condition, and the prospects for future pregnancies.

A good genetic counselor should have first-rate knowledge of genetics. But he or she should also be able to communicate that knowledge in easy-to-understand language. And, according to Barbara Bowles Biesecker, genetic counselor and section head at the National Center for Human Genome Research, National Institutes of Health, genetic counselors must be able to listen as well as talk. "People are terrified when they get a diagnosis," she explains. "They often ask, 'Why did this happen?' They already know the scientific explanation; what they are really asking are the more soul-searching questions: How will I cope? Will I be able to love and accept this child?' Genetic counseling is much more complicated than explaining percentages. Actually, the science is the easy part."

Possibly the most important thing families can get from a genetic counselor is time—time to process a lot of information, time to grieve the considerable losses they may experience.

A genetic counselor can provide a tremendous amount of information about local and national resources. He or she may also be able to explain the practical implications of recent research results.

Genetic counselors are also familiar and comfortable with conditions other medical professionals rarely see. Whereas your pediatrician might see two children a year with your child's disability, a genetic counselor may see two a week. "One of the best things our counselor did was hook us up with other parents. Nobody can understand what we're going through except other CF parents," says the mother of a child with cystic fibrosis. Different families seek genetic counseling for different reasons. A couple with a newly diagnosed infant or young child, for example, will probably want a comprehensive expla-

nation of the child's condition and likely prognosis. They may also want to know the chances of this or another birth defect occurring in future pregnancies.

According to Phillip R. Reilly, clinical geneticist, lawyer, and president of the Shriver Center for Mental Retardation, the following people may benefit from consulting a genetic counselor:

- Families in which there is a known genetic disorder, such as cystic fibrosis, Huntington's disease, or hemophilia.

- Couples that come from the same ethnic group, when that group is known to have a high incidence of certain disorders. For example, Tay–Sachs disease is common among some ethnic groups, such as Ashkenazi Jews, and one in twelve African Americans carries the gene for sickle cell anemia.

- Families in which there have been multiple miscarriages, stillbirths, or a childhood death from unknown causes.

- Women older than 34 who are pregnant or planning a pregnancy.

- Relatives—especially siblings—of a child with a genetically transmitted disorder.

How do you find a genetic counselor? A pediatrician or the geneticist at your HMO or local hospital may be able to refer you to a qualified genetic counselor. Or contact one of the following organizations:

- National Society of Genetic Counselors
  233 Canterbury Drive
  Wallingford, PA 19086-6617
  http://www.nsgc.org

- Genetic Alliance
  4301 Connecticut Avenue, NW, #404
  Washington, DC 20008-2304
  (202) 966-5557 (phone), (202) 966-8553 (fax)
  (800) 336-GENE (helpline only)
  e-mail: info@geneticalliance.org
  http://www.geneticalliance.org

Source: From Genetic counseling—The science is the easy part by Naomi Angoff Chedd, *Exceptional Parent*, August 1995, pp. 26–27. Copyright © 1995. Reprinted with the expressed consent and approval of *Exceptional Parent*, a monthly magazine for parents and families of children with disabilities and special health care needs. Subscription cost is $39.95 per year for 12 issues; Call (877) 372-7368. Offices at 65 E. Rte. 4, River Edge, N.J. 07661.

The role of the genetic counselor is a neutral one; the counselor provides prospective parents with information and possible options, but the parents are then left to make their own decision about whether or not to have a child (Chedd, 1995). The prospective parents must often make difficult choices, since rarely can a genetic counselor guarantee what the outcome of a pregnancy will be.

● *Early Prenatal Care*   The easiest, most routine step a pregnant woman can take to reduce the risk for her baby may also be the most effective. Early **prenatal care**, the care an expectant mother receives from her physician during pregnancy, can provide a prospective mother with crucial but routine tests and observations that can drastically affect her baby's health. Blood tests that rule out the presence of sexually transmitted and other diseases, information about proper nutrition and activity level during pregnancy, and counseling and treatment based on the prospective mother's needs significantly lower the level of risk in each pregnancy.

> Early and consistent prenatal care is the most effective way to prevent many disabilities.

Despite the effectiveness of early prenatal care as a preventive measure, thousands of women give birth each year without ever seeing a doctor or visiting a clinic. Many of them are young, and most of them are poor. Babies born to women who do not receive prenatal medical care are more likely to be premature or sick at birth. There is also a higher likelihood of miscarriage, stillbirth, and early infant death in these pregnancies (Mechaty & Thompson, 1990).

The availability of free or low-cost prenatal care varies from state to state. Federal and state governments have, for the most part, failed to implement policy that would make these services available to all women, despite persuasive data that document the cost-effectiveness of such action. In countries where free prenatal care is routinely available, infant mortality and morbidity are considerably lower (Garbarino, 1990).

● *Prenatal Testing*   For those who have received genetic counseling or are concerned about the health of their growing fetus, two procedures can provide more information: **amniocentesis** and **chorionic villous sampling (CVS)**.

> Amniocentesis and chorionic villous sampling can provide information on the health of the fetus.

Amniocentesis was the first technique developed for prenatal diagnosis (Batshaw & Rose, 1997). It is performed between the fourteenth and eighteenth weeks of pregnancy by inserting a needle through the mother's abdomen into the amniotic sac and withdrawing less than one ounce of amniotic fluid. The amniotic fluid contains cells shed by the fetus, and these are cultured. A karyotype (a study of the number and description of the fetal chromosomes) is generally available in two weeks or less. Examination of the fetal chromosomes can lead to identification of chromosomal abnormalities such as Down syndrome. Evidence of neural tube defects like spina bifida can be seen in the analysis of the amniotic fluid cells. The risk to the fetus and the mother from amniocentesis is quite low.

In CVS, which is performed between the eighth and tenth weeks of pregnancy, a thin catheter is inserted through the vagina into the uterus and used to remove a small portion of the cells from the chorion, part of the developing placenta (Batshaw & Rose, 1997). Those cells, which contain genetic material from the fetus, are cultured. In two to three days a karyotype is obtained. Evidence of Down syndrome and other relatively common genetic abnormalities can then be determined. CVS is slightly less safe than amniocentesis; there is an approximately 1 percent greater risk of miscarriage following CVS than following amniocentesis (Burton, Schulz, & Burd, 1992), but with further research and refinement it may be used more frequently than amniocentesis.

One mother who had prenatal testing before the birth of her daughter, who has spina bifida, reminds us that prenatal testing is often helpful no matter what a couple's views are on the termination of pregnancy:

> I will always be grateful that when I finally gave birth to my daughter, it was in a setting where she could get the best of care from the moment of her first breath, and that my husband and I were fully prepared to welcome her into our lives with open arms. At the time of a prenatal diagnosis, it may be hard for families to see the value of the opportunity they have been given, but ultimately I believe families and their children benefit most by knowing about problems as early as possible. (Reichard, 1995, p. 131)

Early Intervention as Prevention

Early intervention is the set of services provided to children from birth to age 3 and their families that is designed for their unique characteristics and needs.

As we have emphasized, the presence of risk factors does not guarantee a developmental delay or disability. Early intervention plays an important role in preventing additional deficits in children who are at risk. The next pages will describe early intervention and the role it can play in the child's development.

 **Pause and Reflect**

Do you notice any attempts in your own community to prevent disabilities? What might they be? ●

Early Intervention

Early intervention may lessen the effects of risk factors on a child by enlisting the support of a team of professionals and family members in the child's care and development. What is early intervention? What are its goals? These are vital concerns for the parents or caregivers of a child with a disability or a child at risk for developing a disability. Hanson, Ellis, and Deppe (1989) define **early intervention** as "a comprehensive set of services that are provided to children from birth to age three and their families" (p. 211). Shonkoff and Meisels (2000) have a more detailed definition:

> Early childhood intervention consists of multidisciplinary services provided for children from birth . . . [to age 3] to promote child health and well-being, enhance emerging competencies, minimize developmental delays, remediate existing or emerging disabilities, prevent functional deterioration, and promote adaptive parenting and overall family functioning. These goals are accomplished by providing individualized developmental, educational, and therapeutic services for children in conjunction with mutually planned support for their families. (pp. XVII–XVIII)

The basic component of this intervention is a teacher (often called an early intervention specialist) who works collaboratively with professionals from a variety of disciplines, the family, and the child to provide information and support and model strategies designed to minimize the effects of the child's risk status or disability on his or her development.

Technology Focus

Assistive Technology for Infants and Toddlers

Research shows that assistive technology (AT) can help young children with disabilities learn valuable skills. For example, by using computers and special software, young children may improve in the following areas:

- social skills including sharing and taking turns
- communication skills
- attention span
- fine and gross motor skills
- self confidence and independence

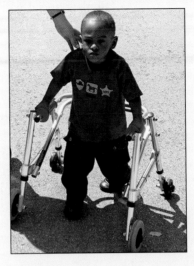

Using a support walker allows this boy to explore the playground. (Jeff Greenberg)

In addition, by using the right type of AT, some negative behaviors may decrease as a child's ability to communicate increases. Some common examples of AT include wheelchairs, computers and computer software, and communication devices.

Q: What types of AT devices can infants and toddlers use?

A: There are two types of AT devices most commonly used by infants and toddlers: switches and augmentative communication devices.

There are many types of switches that can be used in many different ways. Switches can be used with battery-operated toys to give infants opportunities to play with them. For example, a switch could be attached directly to a stuffed pig so that every time an infant touches the toy, it wiggles and snorts. Switches can also be used to turn many things off and on. Toddlers can learn to press a switch to turn on a computer or to use cause-and-effect (interactive) software.

Children who have severe disabilities can also use switches. For example, a switch could be placed next to an infant's head so that every time she moved her head to the left, a musical mobile hanging overhead would play.

Augmentative communication devices allow children who cannot speak or who cannot yet speak to communicate with the world around them. These devices can be as simple as pointing to a photo on a picture board or they can be more complicated—for instance, pressing message buttons on a device that activate prerecorded messages such as, "I'm hungry."

Q: Why is AT important?

A: Many of the skills learned in life begin in infancy. AT can help infants and toddlers with disabilities learn many of these crucial skills. In fact, with AT, they can usually learn the same things that nondisabled children learn at the same age, only in a different way. Communication skills at this age are especially important because most of what an infant or toddler learns is through interacting with other people, especially family members and other primary caregivers.

AT is also important because expectations for a child increase as those around them learn to say, "This is what the baby can do, with supports," instead of, "This is what the baby can't do." With AT, parents learn that the dreams they had for their child don't necessarily end when he or she is diagnosed with a disability. The dreams may have to be changed a little, but they can still come true.

Source: PACER Center, Inc. Families and Advocates Partnership for Education (FAPE) Project. http://www.pacer.org.

Readers are encouraged to copy and share this information, but please credit PACER Center.

Other key elements of early intervention are:

- It is *individualized*, or designed to meet the unique needs of each child and family.
- It is *interdisciplinary*, since children benefit from the expertise of a variety of specialists, including physical therapists, occupational therapists, nutritionists, social workers, physicians and nurses, speech therapists and audiologists, and others.
- But it is also cross-disciplinary and *collaborative*, since services should be coordinated with one another.
- It is primarily provided in *natural environments,* or those places that most closely resemble places that typical infants would be, such as the home.
- It is described in the *Individualized Family Service Plan* (IFSP).

● **Eligibility for Early Intervention**   As you learned in Chapter 1, early intervention services for infants and toddlers and their families are authorized by IDEA. The law identifies three groups of children aged birth to 3 who may be eligible for early intervention services. They are:

FIRST PERSON

Why Should Early Intervention Take Place in Natural Environments? A Parent's View

Our lives were like a pyramid before JP was born. We had a nice broad, solid foundation of family on which our lives were built. After JP was born, I felt like the pyramid flipped and we were trying to balance on the tip. We were almost instantly involved with cardiologists, geneticists, ear/nose/throat doctors, occupational therapists, speech therapists, physical therapists, and social workers. We were expected to become experts on Down syndrome, early intervention, insurance, Medicaid, and more.

As parents, we felt the urgency to do as much as possible, as quickly as possible. Time was our enemy. We wanted to do it all, hoping that something would "fix it quick." JP was just 6 weeks old when we first started receiving services in what was described as a traditional or medical model. Everything centered on this cute little fellow who did not even want to wake up to eat. Our son's life seemingly had become everyone's life. Our family lost its identity as a family, and his schedule dictated our schedules.

The therapists were very nice and highly recommended. Unfortunately, they worked with each other while I watched. The therapists did not often include me in the actual "hands-on"

- Children with developmental delay
- Children with an identified physical or mental condition that carries a high probability of developmental delay
- Children who are medically or environmentally *at risk* for developmental delay if early intervention is not provided

Early intervention includes efforts to improve the child's performance in all major functional areas—language, cognition, fine and gross motor skills, and social-emotional development. And because research shows that early intervention yields significant results (Guralnick, 1997), the availability and comprehensiveness of early intervention programs can have a great impact on the lives of children who are at risk and those with disabilities.

Research documents the effectiveness of early intervention services.

Our Technology Focus features assistive technology used with infants and young children, and the Teaching Strategies & Accommodations box focuses on early intervention strategies.

● *Models for Early Intervention Programs* Early intervention services are generally delivered through either a home-based program, in which the early intervention specialist provides services to the family in its own home,

therapy so I was not comfortable trying at home what they did in the therapy session. I did not know what to do, or when or how or why to do it. I was not an expert on child development, but I did know that a person who is developing slowly or has a disability needs lots of opportunities to practice. JP was not getting enough of those opportunities by going to the clinic just once or twice a week.

As parents, we wanted more, more, more for JP, but there was no way we could continue to add more appointments or specialists to our lives. We had four kids, I was working two part-time jobs, and my husband was trying to start his own business and go to school. "More" just would not have worked. We needed a different plan. We needed a plan that included JP as an active participant in our family—not the opposite. We wanted JP to enjoy playing with his brother and sisters and not have them resenting the extra time JP's therapy took away from family time. We wanted to count how many crackers JP could eat with his friends at church during snack, not the number of blocks JP placed in a bucket during three-minute intervals.

When services began to be provided in our natural environments, we got that new plan. Now, JP gets services at home with us and at his child care. It has been wonderful. This allows both our family and the child care providers to work (or should I say play) with him at home, church, grandma's, or anywhere else we may go during the day. We are able to take what we learn and use it anywhere. Supporting JP's learning in daily activities is now a *part* of our lives and *not* our lives.

Lorna Mullis

Source: Natural environments: A letter from a mother to friends, families, and professionals, copyright 2002 by Lorna Mullis, *Young Exceptional Children, 5* (3), 21–24. Reprinted by permission of the Division of the Council for Exceptional Children.

Teaching Strategies & Accommodations

Elements of Effective Early Intervention Programs

Cook, Tessier, and Klein (2000) identified eleven elements in the early intervention literature that are associated with effective early intervention programs. Among them are:

- A well-defined program model and philosophy with staff commitment to the approach being implemented

- A consistent system that promotes a high level of family involvement and support with an emphasis on caregiver–child interaction

- Extensive and cooperative team planning and program implementation

- Facilitation of functional skills to enable children to cope with environmental expectations as determined through individualized program and service planning

- Flexible adaptation of intervention techniques to determine those most effective in meeting child- and family-focused outcomes and objectives

- Strong emphasis on language and social skill development

- Incorporation of "best practices" as they are continually determined through practice and research in the field

- A well-designed system for staff and parent training and development

The best early intervention programs will reflect these elements. For the standards of practice advocated by the Division of Early Childhood of the Council for Exceptional Children, see S. Sandall, M. McLean, & B. J. Smith (Eds.) (2000). *DEC recommended practices in early intervention/early childhood special education.* Longmont, CO: Sopris West.

---

a center-based program, in which the family brings the child to an early intervention center, or another program for young children within their community. Often, services to infants and medically fragile toddlers are provided in the home; as children grow older and stronger, they are more likely to attend a program in the community.

The 1997 amendments to IDEA specified that whenever possible, services be provided to children in **natural environments**. In a Division of Early Childhood position statement (1998), a natural environment is "one in which the child would spend time if he or she did not have special needs" (p. 1). As a result of this mandate, services are likely to be provided in play groups, day care, Mommy and Me classes, libraries, parks, and other places in the community where young children and their caregivers can be found.

> Early intervention can be provided in the family home, at an early intervention center, or in the community.

The focus on natural environments flows from the principle of normalization we discussed in Chapter 1—in this case, young children in early intervention should be doing what their peers are doing, and they should be provided services in "normal" settings. But the concept is not without controversy (Bricker, 2001). In many states, the provision of services in natural environments has meant the end of center-based programs, where children with disabilities are in programs together, and their families have the opportunity to support one another.

> Family involvement and family support are the foundation of effective early intervention.

● *The Role of the Family in Early Intervention* With the growing appreciation of the importance of viewing the child within the context of the family, the focus of early intervention has shifted from the child to the entire family system. This broadened focus is reflected in the law, which mandates that each family receive an **Individualized Family Service Plan (IFSP)**, a written account of the personal and social services needed to promote and support each family member for the first three years of the child's life.

Each IFSP must include:

- A statement of the family's strengths, as well as needs, related to the child.
- A description of the major outcomes to be achieved by the child and the family.
- A description of the family's current resources, priorities, and concerns.
- A list of the specific services needed to meet the unique requirements of each child and family. These services may include family training, counseling, respite care, and home visits, as well as physical, occupational, and speech therapy, audiological services, and so on (Sandall, 1997a, 1997b).

> The IFSP is written not just for the child, but for the family.

Most families need information related to their child's condition, assistance in learning to identify their child's unique cues, guidance in handling the child in a more therapeutic and easy manner, and referrals for other services. The focus of early intervention is typically on facilitating and coordinating this range of activities so that the family may experience more satisfying and rewarding relationships with the child and the child may develop more fully (Chen, 1999).

Let's look at a hypothetical baby who would be eligible for early intervention services, Lea, who has Down syndrome. Down syndrome carries with it an extremely high probability of mental retardation, and often involves physical abnormalities (such as organ defects) as well.

Case Study

Lea is 8 months old and is recovering from heart surgery that successfully repaired a congenital heart defect. In the next year, Lea's physical health must be monitored closely to ensure her complete and successful recovery. Her family will need help facilitating Lea's speech and language development, which is usually delayed in children with mental retardation. Lea is not sitting or crawling, which suggests a delay in her motor development, and we know that her cognitive development is likely to be delayed. Because of Lea's varied needs, the design of her intervention program, or the outcomes on her IFSP, will benefit from the input of a team consisting of health-care professionals, a speech-language specialist, a physical therapist, and a teacher skilled in activities that will facilitate cognitive development. And we haven't even mentioned her parents' needs!

Lea will receive weekly home visits from an early intervention specialist and a speech-language pathologist, and her parents will take her to physical therapy twice weekly. Lea's parents will be given the name of their local Down syndrome parent group, and respite care will be provided so that they can attend the meetings. The team expects that Lea will be attending a center-based early intervention program by the time she is 18 months old, with one or both of her parents attending with her. (See Figure 2.4 for excerpts from Lea's IFSP.)

With the help of an **interdisciplinary team** of professionals, Lea's parents will make sure that she is off to a healthy start in life.

Pause and Reflect

In each state a different agency is responsible for services to children from birth to age 3. What is the agency in your state? How do parents find early intervention services in your state or country? ●

Family Strengths

Lucia and Omar Dean are totally committed to their first child, Lea. Mr. Dean has worked for United Parcel Service for five years. Mrs. Dean recently resigned from her job as a social worker to be a full-time mother. Their families are in a distant state, but the Deans are a part of a closely knit religious community, and have a great deal of support from friends.

Family Resources, Priorities, and Concerns

Mr. and Mrs. Dean have been focused on Lea's health after her heart surgery, and they are relieved that she is recovering well and beginning to move around more. They are unsure about what to expect from Lea, and frequently leave her alone in her crib to rest. Mrs. Dean has decided not to return to work so she can be with Lea, and she is very eager to get some ideas about how she can help her daughter. Mr. Dean is worried that his wife will be lonely at home, since their families live far away.

Outcomes

1. Lea's parents will learn more about Down syndrome and meet other parents of children with Down syndrome through participation in a parent-to-parent support group.
2. Lea's parents will feel confident in their ability to facilitate their daughter's healthy growth and development, particularly in the area of communication skills.
3. Lea will begin to use pointing and vocalizations to indicate her needs.
4. Lea's parents will learn more about the impact of her surgery and recovery on Lea's overall development, particularly her motor development.
5. Lea will sit and crawl independently.

Figure 2.4

Excerpts from an IFSP for Lea, an 8-month-old with Down syndrome

Note: On a complete IFSP, outcomes would be tied to strategies, criteria for measuring whether outcomes have been reached, service type and frequency, responsible agency, and so on. You can see a complete IFSP by visiting our website through http://www.education.college.hmco.com/students/.

Identification and Assessment of Infants at Risk

Three groups of infants and toddlers are eligible for early intervention services under the law.

Since most states have developed early intervention programs for infants and young children under IDEA, criteria must be designed to identify children who are eligible for these services. Remember that three groups of young children (from birth to age 3) are eligible for early intervention services:

- Those with an identified condition related to developmental disability, such as hearing or vision loss or Down syndrome
- Those who are experiencing developmental delay in motor, cognitive, communication, psychosocial, or self-help skills
- Those who are at risk for significant developmental delay because of biological and/or environmental events in their lives

Clearly, young children with identified disabilities are eligible. Also eligible are those children described as developmentally delayed. It is the group of children we discuss in this chapter, those who are categorized as biologically and environmentally "at risk," who have presented the most significant problems to the state teams working on eligibility criteria, and, based on our previous discussions in this chapter, we can begin to see why. We have developed a considerable list of biological and environmental risk factors, and there are many others we do not have the space to present. Deciding which risk factors or how many factors will qualify a child for services has presented a major challenge to the states. Many states require that multiple risk factors be used to qualify children for programs, since we know that as risk factors multiply, their combined effect is likely to be greater than that of any single factor.

Techniques for Identification and Assessment

We obtain information about a child's risk status from a number of sources: hospital and health records, family interviews, observation of the child, developmental and health screenings, and diagnostic assessment. **Screening** refers to quick and efficient procedures whereby large numbers of children can be evaluated to determine whether more in-depth assessment is required; screenings of young children's development, hearing, vision, and overall health can identify children with a high probability of delayed development. **Diagnostic assessment**, an in-depth look at the child's development, provides a more definitive picture of whether the child has special needs; in diagnostic assessment, formal assessment tools are used by a multidisciplinary team, with considerable input from the child's family (Meisels & Provence, 1989).

No one source of information should be used to make any decisions concerning a child's eligibility for services; "best practices" in assessment demand that multiple types of data from multiple sources be used for good decision-making. Foremost among these sources is the family. Meisels and Provence (1989) put it this way:

> One should not try to screen or assess young children without the active participation of those most expert about them—their parents. All parents know a great deal about their children, and the task of those conducting the screening and assessment is to enable parents to transmit that information productively. (p. 15)

"Best practices" in assessment demand that multiple types of data from multiple sources, especially the family, be used for good decision-making.

Can Disabilities Be Predicted from Risk Factors?

Despite the large number of studies that identify biologically at-risk infants and follow their development over time, researchers have found that their ability to predict which children will develop disabilities is relatively poor. Children with severe disabilities, often caused by massive central nervous system insult, are an exception to this rule, but they are the very small minority. Fortunately, many of the early complications of biological risk status are transient; that is, they disappear over time. Many infants can and do recover from the trauma of premature birth and early medical complications.

But, once again, the child's ability to recover from these early experiences appears to be mediated by the caregiving characteristics in his or her environment. Cohen and Parmalee (1983), for example, found that for most of their premature subjects, neonatal complications did not necessarily predict scores on the Stanford-Binet IQ test at age 5. But children whose developmental performance improved the most had caregiving that was more responsive and more reciprocal and that encouraged more autonomy than those children whose performance did not improve. We can begin to see why early intervention for infants at risk must focus on the infant within the context of the family.

> Children with responsive and consistent caregiving have the best chance of recovering from the effects of risk factors.

Arnold Sameroff has been studying the effect of environmental risk factors on children's development—particularly their mental health—throughout his influential career. Figure 2.5 shows his data, which indicates that the greater the number of risk factors (the specific factors are listed in the figure), the poorer the child's emotional health at age 4. In addition, each risk factor lowered the child's IQ by an average of four points (Sameroff, 1998). So it still appears to be true that the greater the number of risk factors, the poorer the outcomes for the child.

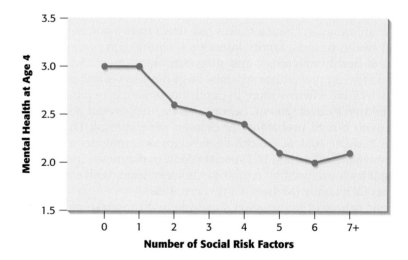

Number of Social Risk Factors

Types of Social Risk Factors:

1. History of maternal mental illness

2. High maternal anxiety

3. Parental perspectives that reflected rigidity in the attitudes, beliefs, and values that mothers had in regard to their child's development

4. Few positive maternal interactions with the child observed during infancy

5. Head of household in unskilled occupations

6. Minimal maternal education

7. Disadvantaged minority status

8. Single parenthood

9. Stressful life events

10. Large family size

Figure 2.5

Effect of Multiple Environmental Risk Factors on Mental Health at Age 4

Source: A. J. Sameroff (1998). Environmental risk factors in infancy. Reproduced with permission from *Pediatrics, 102*(5) (Supplement), 1287–1292. Copyright 1998.

Table 2.3 Characteristics of Resilient Children

Source	Characteristics
Individual	Good intellectual functioning
	Appealing, sociable, easygoing disposition
	Self-efficacy, self-confidence, good self-esteem
	Talents
Family	Faith
	Close relationship to caring parent figure
	Authoritative parenting: warmth, structure, high expectations
Extrafamilial context	Socioeconomic advantages
	Connections to extended supportive family networks
	Bonds to prosocial adults outside the family
	Connections to prosocial organizations
	Attending effective schools

Source: A. S. Masten & J. D. Coatsworth (1998). From The development of competence in favorable and unfavorable environments: Lessons from research on successful children. *American Psychologist, 53,* 212.

The Resilient Child

The impact of risk factors varies a great deal in different children, families, and environments. For example, there are many healthy young children doing well in school today who were born at very low weight; other low birthweight children are striving to overcome disabilities ranging from mild learning disabilities to severe mental retardation. Many children grow up in poverty and go on to lead productive adult lives; others develop school problems that lead to their dropping out of school or to special educational programming. On the other hand, few children born with serious chromosomal abnormalities grow up without developmental delays (although many of them can, as we shall see, become productive citizens).

So far in this chapter, we have identified a large number of biological and environmental risk factors that increase the likelihood of poor developmental outcomes in children. No single risk factor satisfactorily predicts or explains what will happen to a child, but the accuracy of our predictions increases with the number of risk factors that the child experiences, and the most vulnerable children of all are those who experience both biological and environmental risk factors. In fact, most children who experience a series of biological risk factors (with the exception of those that clearly damage the central nervous system) but grow up in a stable, supportive environment develop very well.

There are also the remarkable children who, despite a multitude of adverse biological and environmental events, overcome the odds and become healthy, productive adults (Masten & Coatsworth, 1998). (See Table 2.3.) Werner and Smith (1982) called them "vulnerable but invincible." What is it about these children that protects them from the school failure, emotional distress, early parenthood, and criminal behavior demonstrated by other children from similar backgrounds?

To find these protective factors, we look first within the child. Werner (1986, p. 16) defined the characteristics shared by the **resilient,** or "stress-resistant," children of several studies:

> (1) An active, evocative approach toward solving their developmental tasks, enabling them to negotiate successfully an abundance of emotionally hazardous experiences; (2) the ability, from infancy on, to gain other people's positive attention, and to recruit "surrogate parents" when necessary; (3) a tendency to perceive and interpret their experiences constructively, even if they caused pain and suffering; and (4) a strong "sense of coherence," a belief that their lives had meaning.

Werner described the most resilient subjects of her longitudinal study of the children of Kauai: One out of three grew up in chronic poverty, had experienced perinatal stresses or had congenital defects, was raised by a mother with little formal education, and lived in a family with serious instability, discord, or parental mental illness. But one out of four of these children "escaped the ill effects of such multiple risks and developed into stable, mature, and competent young adults who 'worked well, played well, loved well, and expected well'" (Werner, 1986, p. 13). There were ameliorative personal factors within these children and protective factors within their caregiving environments, among them a close bond with a primary caregiver and emotional support provided by other family members (such as siblings and grandparents) during early and middle childhood (Werner, 1999).

As Werner's research indicates, risk factors are not the only significant variables capable of influencing the course of children's development. Dunst (1993) suggests that it is not simply the absence of risk factors that helps us predict which children develop well; there are also "opportunity factors" that can occur within a family and community and that may enhance and strengthen a child's development. According to Dunst, research demonstrates that positive development outcomes are influenced by the power of factors such as high education level of parents, stimulating and warm caregiver–child interaction, and a supportive extended family. The influence of these opportunity factors increases when multiple factors are present.

You may know a person who could be considered resilient in your own life; in public life, figures like Oprah Winfrey or Maya Angelou, who have succeeded despite tumultuous childhoods, seem to qualify. Can you think of others?

The Importance of Relationships

A series of National Research Council reports has further emphasized the critical role played by the relationships that children experience as they grow. These researchers conclude that "the weight of successful development in the early years falls most heavily on the child's relationships with primary adult caregivers." And, despite their diversity, children require certain things from their relationships in order to flourish:

a. a reliable, supporting relationship that establishes a sense of security and safety,

b. an affectionate relationship that supports the development of self-esteem,

---

Resilient children can overcome the odds and become healthy, productive adults.

Personal factors and a close bond with a primary caregiver may help resilient children overcome early risk factors.

c. responsiveness of the adult to the child that strengthens the child's sense of self-efficacy, and

d. support for the growth of new capabilities that are within the child's reach, including reciprocal interactions that promote language development and the ability to resolve conflicts cooperatively and respectfully (Donovan & Cross, 2002, p. 121)

The fact that there are children who can experience many stressful biological and environmental events and emerge as healthy, competent adults—with the help of consistent relationships—provides us with hope and encouragement. Teachers, after all, have important relationships with children too. And teachers must take a hopeful stance in order to continue with their challenging work with children in high-risk situations. We must use the results of research to support other children and families so that they, too, can develop protective personal characteristics despite stressful caregiving environments.

SUMMARY

- Risk factors include a wide range of biological and environmental conditions associated with increased probability of developmental problems in young children.

- Risk factors can be categorized as biological risks and environmental risks. Biological risks are a threat to a child's developing systems and can include diseases, maternal substance abuse, and oxygen deprivation. Environmental risk stems from damaging physical and social surroundings of the child and his or her caretakers, such as exposure to lead, accidents, or limited access to health care.

- Some steps that help prevent risk status and disability include inoculation, genetic counseling, prenatal care, and prenatal testing. Early intervention is another means of preventing the negative impact of risk factors.

- Early intervention consists of a comprehensive set of services for infants and toddlers aged birth to 3 and their families that is designed for the unique needs and built on the unique strengths of each child and family. Early intervention has a strong family focus and can consist of services offered by a range of professionals across disciplines.

- Children at risk can pose a challenge for early intervention personnel because the range of possible risk factors is so great and because the presence of one or more risk factors does not guarantee a developmental delay. Techniques used to identify children for early intervention include screening and diagnostic assessment.

- It must be remembered that no absolute predictions can be made regarding children at risk. Some children are exceptionally resilient and succeed despite seemingly large odds. A strong bond with a caregiving adult and emotional support from other family members can help a child overcome biological and environmental stresses.

KEY TERMS

risk factors

biological risk

environmental risk

prenatal period

perinatal period

postnatal period

first trimester

teratogens

rubella

cytomegalovirus (CMV)

congenital

sexually transmitted diseases (STDs)

acquired immune deficiency syndrome (AIDS)

human immunodeficiency virus (HIV)

thalidomide

polysubstance abusers

fetal alcohol syndrome (FAS)

alcohol-related neurodevelopmental disorder (ARND)

Down syndrome

hypoxia

premature (preterm)

low birthweight

very low birthweight

neonatology

neonatal intensive care unit

occupational hazards

neurotoxins

inoculation

genetic counseling

prenatal care

amniocentesis

chorionic villous sampling (CVS)

early intervention

natural environments

Individualized Family Service Plan (IFSP)

interdisciplinary team

screening

diagnostic assessment

resilient

USEFUL RESOURCES

- The American Academy of Pediatrics has a website that provides information about childhood diseases and psychosocial risk factors in children. Visit **http://www.aap.org/family**.

- Some of the country's foremost researchers on the effects of environmental toxins on children have written a book for families: P. Landrigan, H. L. Needleman, & M. Landrigan (2002). *Raising healthy children in a toxic world: 101 Smart solutions for every family*. Emmaus, PA: Rodale Press.

- The Centers for Disease Control (CDC) has developed the CDC National Prevention Information Network (NPIN), devoted to disseminating information about the prevention of HIV/AIDS, sexually transmitted diseases, and tuberculosis. The web address is **http://www.cdcnpin.org**. The site has separate sections on children and youth; many resources are available in Spanish.

- Premature Baby–Premature Child is a website for families of children born premature. It's at **http://www.prematurity.org**.

- Two organizations committed to the development of high-quality professionals who will work with our youngest children are the Division of Early Childhood of the Council for Exceptional Children at **http://www.dec-sped.org** and the National Association for the Education of Young Children (NAEYC) at **http://www.naeyc.org**.

- The National Early Childhood Technical Assistance Center (NECTAC) is a consortium of six organizations providing assistance to early childhood specialists. Visit their website at **http://www.nectac.org**.

- Resources on child abuse and neglect can be found in Barbara Lowenthal's *Child abuse and neglect: An educator's guide* (2001), Paul H. Brookes Publisher, and at the National Clearinghouse on Child Abuse and Neglect Information at **http://www.calib.com/nccanch**.

● Zero to Three is an organization devoted to the healthy development of infants and toddlers. The website has good information for both parents and professionals. Visit **http://www.zerotothree.org** or write to the organization at 734 15th St. NW, Washington, DC 20005.

PORTFOLIO ACTIVITIES

Each of us has a personal and a social responsibility to help prevent disability in our communities. Here are some ways for you to help:

1. Participate in fundraising and awareness campaigns.

- Pledge or organize a team of volunteers for a fundraising event. Major fundraising organizations such as the March of Dimes, the United Way, UNICEF, the United Cerebral Palsy Association, or the Cystic Fibrosis Foundation would love your help.

- Working as a class, design posters illustrating risk factors and related prevention strategies for display in a community education program.

- Hold a "risk awareness" education day at your local high school or community center.

Write up the results of these activities and include pictures for your portfolio.

✓*Standards* This activity will help the student meet CEC Content Standard 3: Individual Learning Differences.

2. Promote early prenatal care and early recognition of risk and disability.

- Invite a genetic counselor from a local hospital to come and speak to your class or your parent group.

- Find out about the low-cost prenatal care services in your community and, in a small group, devise a plan to publicize them.

- Find out where you can refer parents who are concerned about their child's early development in your town or city. Make a list for your school and local pediatricians.

- Visit a neonatal intensive care unit. Write a narrative report of what you observed and present it to your classmates.

Write up the results of these activities and include pictures for your portfolio.

✓*Standards* This activity will help the student meet CEC Content Standard 1: Foundations.

3. Compile a resource guide for families of young children in your community. Include information about the risk factors described in this chapter and agencies in your area that might help families who experience such risk factors. Make your resource guide part of your portfolio.

✓*Standards* This activity will help the student meet CEC Content Standard 2: Development and Characteristics of Learners.

To access an electronic portfolio template for these activities, visit our website through http://www.education.college.hmco. com/students/.

3 Families and Culture

Outline

Terms and Definitions
    The Macroculture and Microcultures
    Minority and Ethnic Groups
    Culture and Disability
Working with Culturally Diverse Families
    Knowing Yourself
    Developing Cultural Competence
Approaches to Studying Families
    The Family Systems Approach
    Ecocultural Theory
Family Reactions to Disability Across
    Cultures
    Factors Affecting Families' Reactions
    Impact of Exceptionality on Family
        Functions
    Exceptionality and Family
        Interactions
    Coping Strategies
    Sources of Support
The Role of the Family in Special
    Education Services
    The Parents' Rights
    Before Formal Schooling: The
        Early Years
    During the School Years
    Leaving School
    Transitions to Work and Higher
        Education
    Family Concerns for the Future
Positive Aspects of Disabilities for
    Families
SUMMARY
KEY TERMS
USEFUL RESOURCES
PORTFOLIO ACTIVITIES

Learning Objectives

After reading this chapter, the reader will:

- Begin to appreciate how a family's cultural background colors their perception of "disability"

- Reflect on how the birth of an exceptional child affects the family

- Understand the legal basis for family involvement in special education

- Have ideas about how family members and professionals can learn to work together as partners

- Appreciate some ways in which an exceptional child contributes to the strength and richness of a family

Defining a family today can be more difficult than it used to be. Although for many of us the family unit still consists of two or more blood relatives residing together, there are plenty of exceptions: foster families (those created by the courts) and adoptive families are two that come to mind. For those of us living far away from relatives, close friends can create the kind of company and support that an extended family might.

Each family's cultural background—its combination of values, beliefs, history, traditions, and language—helps determine its response to the birth and raising of children, and to the birth and raising of a child with a disability. In the United States, a nation formed from the melding of thousands of groups from all over the world, the possibilities for variation in beliefs and traditions about child-rearing are nearly endless. And it is within this context that most of our readers will work, often with families whose values, beliefs, history, traditions, and language will be very different from their own. This chapter is designed to help you begin to learn about families of children with disabilities and to reflect on how their traditions and beliefs form their responses to their children and to you, the teacher. Without such reflection, there is no foundation for real partnership with families.

Terms and Definitions

How would *you* define family? How would *you* define culture? Your own experiences and your cultural *milieu* will color your ideas about both these terms. Families of exceptional children have their ideas about child-rearing, relations with the school, and disability colored by similar experiences. In this book, we broadly define **family** just as the U.S. Census Bureau (2002) does: A family is a group of two people or more related by birth, marriage, or adoption and residing together. Beyond this, you can expect to encounter many variations. A **household** is one or more people, including members of a family and others, who live under the same roof. An **extended family** consists of relatives across generations who may or may not live together. Many African American families report having "a wide network of kin and community" (O'Shea et al., 2001, p. 53) that provides them with support. So for many, the definition of family goes beyond biology.

> We define *family* as people living together who are related by birth, marriage, or adoption.

Clearly, it is not always the biological parent who raises the exceptional child. It may be one biological parent, a grandparent, a foster parent, another relative, or a family friend. Acknowledging these diverse possibilities, many professionals prefer to use the term **caregiver** to refer to the person who assumes that role. That term seems relatively impersonal to us, so in this chapter we use the word *parent* generically, to include all those caregivers who assume the responsibilities traditionally associated with being a parent.

This chapter is about the intersection between family and culture. And **culture** means different things to different people. Most anthropologists define culture broadly, as ways of perceiving, believing, evaluating, and behaving (Goodenough, 1987). Culture can be seen as a series of norms or tendencies that are shared, interpreted, and adapted by a group of people. The characteristics of a given culture may be described as specific behaviors or life patterns; however, every person is an individual, and groups of individuals within a culture represent a *range* of characteristics (Hanson, 1998). Culture, therefore, may guide the way you think, feel, behave, dress, and eat, but it does not ensure that every member of a culture will do things in the same way. The word culture can also

> *Culture* refers to the shared values, traditions, and beliefs of a group of people.

be used to describe many of the shared behaviors we experience in a number of different parts of our lives. For example, the shared language, dress, communication patterns, and food preferences of our ethnic background, as well as the behavioral, ethical, social, and dietary guidelines of our religion, reflect two aspects of culture. The cultural backgrounds of our own families and the families we work with will influence beliefs about child-rearing, education, and family life, as well as attitudes toward an exceptional family member. According to one useful definition, culture is a framework that guides life practices (Hanson, 1998). The term does not refer to a rigid or prescribed set of characteristics but "a set of tendencies or possibilities from which to choose" (Anderson & Fenichel, 1989, p. 8). The practices and traditions that arise from family culture may provide a source of pride and comfort to family members—and may sometimes be a source of misunderstanding or confusion for the professionals who work with them.

One component of culture that is very much related to school learning is the *language* of the family. Whether it be Spanish (the most common language spoken in American homes after English) (U.S. Census Bureau, 2002), American Sign Language, Cantonese, Swahili, Gujerati, or another language, the child's home language will affect both your ability to communicate with family members and the child's ability to profit from instruction in English. In 2002, the Los Angeles Unified School District's Home Language Survey identified eighty-six different home languages or dialects used by pupils in the district, which is the second largest in the United States (there are approximately 746,831 pupils in

FIRST PERSON

A Letter from a Parent of a Child with Disabilities

I believe that as professionals you can make a difference in our lives as parents of children with special needs.

You have the opportunity not to be intimidated when we blow off steam. You should not personalize these angry negative feelings. The great challenge for you is to give us the opportunity to fall apart once in a while.

You have the opportunity to decrease our profound sense of loneliness. . . . So often we want to talk about "it," but few people appear to want us to talk. You will often be the ONE person who will say: Tell me more. And then what happened? And how did that feel?

You have the opportunity to help us know our child. In the beginning, most of us know very little about their special needs. . . . You can model for us how to say the words, how to tell others. You can take us into our children's lives.

You have the opportunity to share books, pamphlets, and resources. Take the articles out of your file cabinets and off the shelves and spread them to the parents who have no idea where to find the stories and facts about our children.

You have the opportunity to help us recognize and celebrate our victories. They are often

kindergarten through twelfth grade there) (Office of Communications, 2003). Although your area may not be quite as diverse, you can be sure that it is becoming more so!

Felipe may have been born without limbs because of this mother's exposure to environmental toxins. Here he is surrounded by his loving family. (David H. Wells/CORBIS)

small for the "normal" population to appreciate. You know that awful-sounding "grunt" made by our child is truly a miracle. Often it is only you that knows that a new movement is significant and indicates a renewed sense of hope.

You have the opportunity to remind us how far we have come and how much we have accomplished. You, often more than our closest friends, know the details of our successes. Over and over, you can highlight those changes and celebrate the growth.

You have the opportunity to allow us those moments when our souls fall into deep despair. We will, at times, feel that we cannot and don't want to continue for another moment.

You can give us the space to be in that dark place. It is one of the greatest "interventions" you can give us.

If at times you can do some of these suggested activities, then you will have the opportunity to help us feel hope. We must feel hope if we are to get to our next appointment, or to face the next birthday party or to use the words *special needs*.

Partnership is a collaboration. Plopped right in the middle of that word you will find the word *labor*. Partnership is labor. It is hard work. You are the midwives helping us to give birth to a new relationship. Let us begin.

Janice Fialka

Janice Fialka is the mother of two children, Micah (who has developmental disabilities) and Emma. This excerpt is published in a collection of her writings entitled, *It matters: Lessons from my son*. To obtain a copy of this book or receive information about Fialka's speaking engagements, contact her at 10474 LaSalle Boulevard, Huntington Woods, ME 48070 or by e-mail at ruaw@aol.com.

Source: J. Fialka (1996). Excerpted and adapted from You can make a difference in our lives. *DEC Communicator, 23*(1), 8.

The Macroculture and Microcultures

The macroculture is the core culture of a country or area.

Have you noticed how your classmates, roommates, and friends from different ethnic groups seem to have quite a lot in common with you? If so, it is because you all belong to the **macroculture**, the core, or universal, culture of this country. Our macroculture evolved from Western European traditions. No longer limited to white Anglo-Saxon Protestants, the macroculture comprises many different ethnic groups, primarily middle class, that have a shared core of values and beliefs (see the accompanying Closer Look box entitled, "Shared Values of the American Macroculture"). Most educators, regardless of their ethnic background, belong to the middle class and subscribe to the values of the macroculture (Gollnick & Chinn, 2002).

Microcultures have their own norms while sharing core values with the macroculture.

The macroculture alone, however, does not define our pluralistic society. In your classroom you will find that all your students belong to subcultures, or **microcultures,** that have their own distinctive cultural patterns while at the same time sharing core values with the macroculture. There are many microcultures, and each of your students will belong to several. All your students and their families will belong to a microculture related to ethnicity. Some will be Chinese, Vietnamese, Cuban, or Haitian in national origin. All will also belong to a microculture related to socioeconomic status. Some may be middle class, others poor. All will belong to a language group. Probably all speak English to some extent. Some, however, may speak Spanish or Korean as their primary language. All will belong to a microculture related to gender. You will find that the boys are socialized to behave differently than the girls. All will belong to a microculture related to geographic region. If you live and teach in the Midwest, it is likely that your students are socialized differently than American children living in Hawaii. Consequently, the way an African American gifted female in your classroom thinks, feels, perceives, and behaves may be related to the fact that she is African American, or it may be directly related to her middle-class background, her close relationship to and beliefs in the Roman Catholic church, or the fact that she is a female.

A Closer Look   **Shared Values of the American Macroculture**

- Individualism and privacy
- Equality and equity
- Industriousness

- Freedom of choice
- Expert knowledge
- Social mobility
- Importance of education and learning

- Ambition
- Competition
- Self-reliance
- Independence
- Appreciation of "the good life"
- Perception that humans are separate and superior in nature
- Freedom of speech

Think about how these shared values affect our common perception of disability.

Sources: Klein & Chen (2001); Gollnick & Chinn (2002); Chan (1998); Zuniga (1998); Kalyanpur & Harry (1999); Harry, Kalyanpur, & Day (1999).

? Pause and Reflect

Evaluate these terms in your own life. How much do you identify with the larger American macroculture? And what microcultures do you belong to? ●

Minority and Ethnic Groups

Minority and *minority group* are terms often used in discussions about certain groups in this country. Although **minority** usually denotes a numerical minority, it may also suggest a subordinate power position in society (Gollnick & Chinn, 2002). **Minority groups** may be categorized according to ethnicity, gender, language, religion, disability, or socioeconomic status.

A *minority group* may be a numerical minority, or its members may hold a less powerful position in society.

Ethnicity refers to membership in a particular racial or national group. It denotes the common history, values, attitudes, and behaviors that bind such a group of people together (Yetman, 1985). Examples of ethnic groups in this country include Irish Americans, Native Americans, Chinese Americans, Latinos, and German Americans. Ethnic groups may be *ethnocentric:* They may view their own traits as natural, correct, and superior to those of other ethnic groups, whom they tend to view as odd, amusing, inferior, or immoral (Yetman, 1985). Used in a broader context, the term *ethnocentrism* describes the narrow perspective of individuals from various microcultures—or the macroculture. Harry (2002) writes that the more stigma there is attached to an ethnic group, "the more difficult it is for mainstream professionals to recognize cultural strengths that are different from their own" (p. 132). Although ethnicity is often the benchmark factor we think of when we use the term *culture,* culture and ethnicity are not the same, and many different microcultures interact with a person's ethnicity to form his or her cultural heritage (Keogh, Gallimore, & Weisner, 1997).

Ethnicity refers to membership in a racial or national group.

Culture and Disability

The recent work of Kalyanpur and Harry (1999) identifies some of the basic assumptions of the U.S. macroculture that influence our nation's response to disability, which is reflected in the special education system. The social construction of disability in the United States depends on a set of embedded beliefs. Among these beliefs is what is called the "reification" of disability—that is, we make disability into a *thing* that someone *has.* Disability is perceived as "a feature of the individual's constitution and exists as objective reality" (Kalyanpur & Harry, 1999, p. 10). Moreover, our perception of disability is rooted in our values. If reading and speaking well are highly valued, not being able to do those things becomes a mark of failure.

The perception of disability is rooted in the values of the culture.

Special education practices also have been influenced by the "medical model," which suggests that disability is physical, chronic, individually owned, and fixable. However, families from linguistically and culturally diverse backgrounds may have very different embedded values based on those of the microculture within which they were raised. They may see disability as having spiritual rather than physical causes; as a group phenomenon, shared by the family, rather than an individual one; and as temporary rather than fixed (Kalyanpur & Harry, 1999).

? Pause and Reflect

As you read the following sections, think about your own cultural identity. Reflect on your participation in the macroculture and micro-cultures. Why is this important to you as a prospective teacher? A thorough knowledge of who you are, how your beliefs and actions are influenced, and how you relate to students and family members who have different life experiences can lead not only to self-growth, but also to your ability to teach all children effectively. ●

Working with Culturally Diverse Families

Knowing Yourself

Self-examination is the first step to becoming culturally competent.

As the "Pause and Reflect" feature here suggests, one of the first steps to cultural awareness should be self-examination. Self-examination is not particularly difficult, but doing it honestly and objectively may be a little harder than you think. Begin by asking yourself who you are. Get a sheet of paper and provide information on your:

- ethnicity
- social class
- gender
- geographical background
- language background
- age
- religion
- teaching style

After you have completed the initial exercise, think about the importance you attach to each of these items. When you are a teacher, where do you think each of your students will fit in every one of these areas? How congruent will your values be with those of your students? Your values don't have to be congruent, but it is important to know who you are with respect to your students. Do you have biases and prejudices? Almost everyone does. You should be suspicious of the teacher who says, "I don't have a prejudiced bone in my body!" What is important is that we recognize these biases and not let them cause us to be unfair or insensitive to students, their parents, our colleagues, and others who are associated with the school.

Developing Cultural Competence

Cultural competence involves respect, willingness to learn, and appreciation of the many different ways of viewing the world.

To be able to work effectively with culturally diverse parents, it is important for teachers to be aware of their own attitudes toward people from diverse groups, and to be aware of the cultural assumptions on which beliefs are built. Because of their different backgrounds, parents will often look different, speak differently, and dress differently than you do. Professionals who work in schools must begin to develop **cultural competence**, "respect for difference, eagerness to learn, and a willingness to accept that there are many ways of viewing the world" (Hanson, 1998, p. 493).

Cultural competence is based on two key skills: awareness and communication. These skills become especially important when working with exceptional students and their families.

> Our cultural and ethnic identities help to shape our beliefs and practices, and who we are as individuals and family members. These identities are not the script for our behavior, but they do provide a texture and a richness—and they can bind us together in groups or separate us from one another. Knowledge and understanding of, sensitivity to, and respect for these cultural differences can significantly enhance the effectiveness of service providers in the helping professions. (Hanson, 1998, p. 21)

Regardless of their economic status, language skills, or educational level, parents are greatly concerned about the welfare of their children. They, better than anyone else, know the child's characteristics, strengths and weaknesses, and perceptions of the school. Cultivating a working relationship with culturally diverse parents requires respect for these understandings.

In special education, our work with families begins early, particularly if a disability is discovered when the child is quite young. As we discussed in Chapter 2, the development of the Individualized Family Service Plan (IFSP) involves planning not only for the child but also for the family. Therefore, our ability to communicate and relate to the family, to identify the information parents need, and to integrate our educational and social interventions with the participation preferences of the family are critical aspects of support for families (McWilliam & Scott, 2001; Sontag & Schacht, 1994). Our knowledge of how a family perceives not only a disability but also special services can affect the type of programming permitted and the extent to which services such as assistive technology are used (Hourcade, Parette, & Huer, 1997; Parette & McMahan, 2002). Linan-Thompson and Jean (1997) suggest that when communicating with linguistically diverse parents of students with disabilities, it is important to use the method of communication preferred by the parent, to have interpreters who are knowledgeable about special education as well as bilingual, and to provide information to the family in a variety of formats (such as videos, text, and so on).

Good communication with the family, despite cultural and language differences, is key to the child's learning.

Harry and colleagues (Harry, Kalyanpur, & Day, 1999; Kalyanpur & Harry, 1999) urge school professionals to build bridges between the values and experiences of families and those of the special education system by operating within a framework of **cultural reciprocity**—a two-way process of information sharing and understanding that can be truly reciprocal and that can lead to genuine mutual understanding and cooperation. See the accompanying Teaching Strategies box entitled, "Four Essential Steps for Developing a Posture of Cultural Reciprocity" to learn more about establishing such a framework for working with families.

Cultural reciprocity is built on mutual respect and information sharing.

A Cuban student in a Miami teacher preparation program was required to attend a social event with one of her students and his or her family in order to reflect on cultural reciprocity. She arranged to attend church with Jack, an African American boy, and his family.

> I was very nervous. I was on my way to a Baptist church in a predominantly black neighborhood. My stomach was in knots . . . I am of Catholic faith and was not sure what to expect. As I waited for the family, many people looked at me as if I were lost. I really did not fit in, I stood out like a sore thumb . . . I felt as if I were intruding. As people stared at me, I simply

Teaching Strategies & Accommodations

Four Essential Steps for Developing a Posture of Cultural Reciprocity

Step 1: Identify the cultural values that are embedded in your interpretation of a student's difficulties or in the recommendation for service.

Step 2: Find out whether the family being served recognizes and values these assumptions, and, if not, how their view differs from yours.

Step 3: Acknowledge and give explicit respect to any cultural differences identified, and fully explain the cultural basis of your assumptions.

Step 4: Through discussion and collaboration, set about determining the most effective way of adapting your professional interpretations or recommendations to the value system of this family.

_____

Source: B. Harry, M. Kalyanpur, & M. Day (1999). *Building cultural reciprocity with families: Case studies in special education* (pp. 7–11). Baltimore: Paul H. Brookes.

smiled and said "Hello." I just wanted to disappear. When I saw Jack's family, I felt more comfortable. They welcomed me very warmly and Jack shook my hand for the first time. It was then I felt I was in a very warm atmosphere. The church felt like one big family—very different from the church I regularly attend. At my church, when people walk in, they are very quiet and very careful not to make the slightest noise. At Jack's church, everyone was happy and no one whispered. This made me feel good. Jack's family interacted with everyone. I noticed that everyone greeted Jack—just like everyone else. No one treated him differently. Jack was accepted as he was. . . . What I saw was a close-knit community that was accepting of Jack's disability.

Many times we make assumptions about people based on race, religion, and other factors. . . . I thought people in the church would not be accepting of me because of my race and my religion—but I was wrong! (*Council for Exceptional Children*, 2001, p. 4).

Moving outside our own circles and experiences and into those of our students enriches our own lives and helps us understand cultural reciprocity (*Council for Exceptional Children*, 2001).

Approaches to Studying Families

The Family Systems Approach

The *family systems approach* assumes that what happens to one family member affects all family members.

Professionals writing about families with exceptional members have borrowed and expanded on a framework used by sociologists to understand family life; that framework is known as the **family systems approach**. Family systems theory is a framework for understanding the family as an interrelated social system

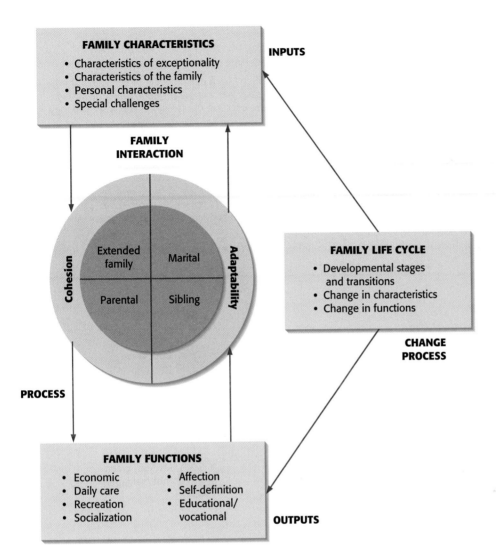

Figure 3.1

Family Systems Conceptual Framework

Source: A. P. Turnbull, J. A. Summers, & M. J. Brotherson (1984). *Working with families with disabled members: A family systems approach* (p. 60).

with unique characteristics and needs. It is based on the assumption that an experience affecting one family member will affect all family members (Turnbull & Turnbull, 2001).

The family systems approach, illustrated in Figure 3.1, suggests that each family has its own characteristics, interactions, functions, and life cycle, and the interaction within each family is unique. Family characteristics include the characteristics of the exceptional child, such as the nature, degree, and demands of the child's exceptionality, as well as the family itself—its size, socioeconomic status, ethnicity, religion, and so on. Family interactions are the relationships between and among family members; often, they are very much affected by a child's exceptionality. Family functions include all the tasks and responsibilities of family members. The family life cycle is the experiences of the family over time.

The family systems approach provides a helpful framework for viewing the child in the context of his or her family, in all its uniqueness and complexity, including the components related to traditions, values, and belief systems that we call culture. If you draw your own family map (see Figure 3.2), you will find that the components of family systems theory will come to life.

Directions for the Family Map

1. *Decide what family* you will picture (family of origin or procreation). If you have more than one family you may do both.

2. *Trace and cut out circles* on a plain piece of paper, making enough for yourself and each person or set of persons or things you want to include. *There are no restrictions on whom you include or how you symbolize them* (parents, siblings, neighbors, pets, your father's golf game—whoever or whatever has a significant effect on the family). If you wish, you may vary size, shape, or color of the units to express yourself more fully.

3. *Label each circle.* A single circle may have only one name or more than one if you see those people/things as a unit.

4. *Arrange the circles on the colored paper provided* so they express the relationships you observe in your family. When you feel comfortable with the total arrangement, firmly glue them in place.

5. Draw any *boundary or connecting lines* you feel complete the picture.

6. Attach a *page explaining what you have done.* Explain who the components are (age, sex, relationship to you, why included), why you arranged them as you did, the meaning of any connecting or boundary lines, and any special use of size, shape, or color.

7. Finally, *list any people you left out* that you might logically have included and *explain why* you left them out.

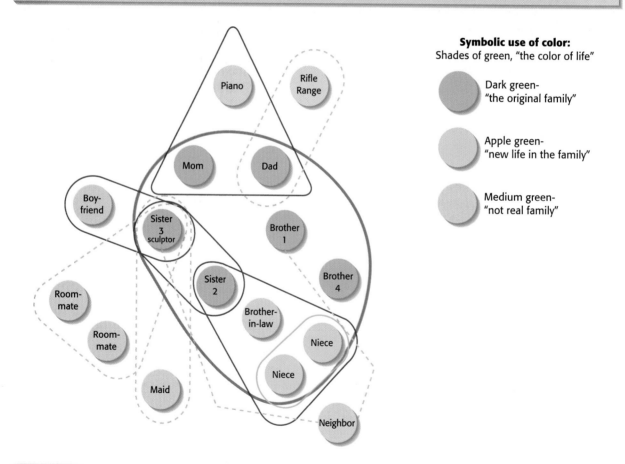

Figure 3.2

Complex Subsystems: Example of a Family Map

Source: Nancy V. Wedemeyer & Harold D. Grotevant (1982). Mapping the family system: A technique for teaching family systems theory concepts. *Family Relations,* Issue 8204, *31*:2, 185–193. (The authors would like to acknowledge Dr. Vivian Correa of the University of South Florida, who suggested the use of this article to teach family systems theory.)

Ecocultural Theory

Another framework through which the family and home can be studied is **eco-cultural theory**, which is based on two fundamental premises. First, families are in the process of adapting to the environment in which they live. This adaptation is based on the family's goals, dreams, and beliefs, as well as the physical, material, and sociocultural environment in which they live. The interaction of these two forces makes up the "ecocultural niche" of the family. The second premise is that to understand the influence of this ecocultural niche on the individuals within the family system, one must look at the family's daily routines and activities. Activities are defined and analyzed by the following five dimensions: the people present; the cultural goals, values, and beliefs of the participants; the motives, purposes, and intentions that guide the family's activities; the nature of the tasks involved; and the scripts, routines, and patterns of behavior used during the activities (Bernheimer, Gallimore, & Weisner, 1990; Dingle & Hunt, 2001). It is through these activity variables that early experiences are created and shaped (Reese, et al., 1995). Analysis of these family activities and routines can help us "weave interventions into the fabric of everyday life" (Bernheimer & Keogh, 1995). Ecocultural theory is the framework for "routines-based" early intervention practices (McWilliam & Scott, 2001).

> *Ecocultural theory requires that we recognize each family's daily routines and activities.*

> Theories of how families operate help us see the child and family in a wider view, in this case, part of a system or inter-related group, which usually maintains an orderly and functional daily routine that supports each family member's functioning.

? Pause and Reflect

It may be helpful to apply the family systems conceptual model (Figure 3.1) to your own family. Start with a family map (see Figure 3.2), which will help you reflect on your relationships with your relatives and close friends. Then think through the family systems model for your own family, remembering the basic idea: What happens to one member affects all members. Can you identify an event in one family member's life that had an impact on the rest of your family members? ●

Family Reactions to Disability Across Cultures

As you read this section, it will be important to keep in mind that disability is a **social construct** viewed very differently by families from diverse cultural backgrounds. (A social construct is the way in which an idea or concept is *constructed*—described and valued—within a culture.)

We all have fantasies about our unborn children—which the experience of having a real child soon erases. We may think of an adorable toddler holding our hand and walking contentedly by our side. We may look at other people's children behaving irritably or having a temper tantrum and think, "*My* child will never behave like that." We may picture our future offspring winning the science fair, writing the great American novel, or competing in the Olympics.

Most of the time, our children don't fit those fantasies. They may excel in ways that surprise us and show no interest in areas in which we imagined they would achieve. We seldom live up to our own dreams of being perfect parents, either. Our children love us anyway, and we usually come to accept each other, imperfect as we all are.

The discovery that a child is exceptional may come at birth or soon after, or it may come later in a child's life—perhaps, as with giftedness or learning dis-

Severe disabilities are likely to be identified earlier in the child's life.

abilities, at school age. Although parents may experience similar feelings at either point, the age of the child does appear to make a difference in the family's initial response. First we will discuss early diagnosis. Keep in mind that the more severe the disability, the earlier it is likely to be identified.

When a child with a disability is born into a family, the family's expectations are violated in at least two ways. First, the child may not look like or behave like the child they imagined. The doctor's predictions about the future may be dour and depressing or frightening in their vagueness. Grandparents and friends may not know how to react and may offer no congratulations, send no flowers, make no phone calls. Instead of imagining a bright future for the child, the parents imagine the worst—or don't know what to imagine. The family's cultural background may also influence how grandparents and extended family respond to the birth of a child with a disability. For some it may bring dishonor, with the sense that the parents have done something wrong for such a thing to happen; others accept disability as something that "just happens" (Klein & Chen, 2001).

Second, the parents' expectations for caring for the child may not correspond to reality. Nearly all families underestimate how much work is involved in having a new baby and how much of their own lives they are required to give up. Although all newborns are demanding, a baby with a disability may have special equipment, require special feeding techniques, be particularly irritable or fussy, and not respond predictably to being cared for. As a result, first-time parents may not be able to benefit from advice from friends and relatives, and experienced parents may not be able to rely on their experiences with their other children for some aspects of care-giving.

National and local organizations can provide both information and support to families.

When their children are identified with a disability, families who have access to other parents of children with a similar disability are fortunate: They can often provide both emotional support and specific ideas for easing the burdens of child care. Organizations founded by parents of children with a specific disability, such as the Association for Retarded Citizens-United States (ARC-US), the Cystic Fi-

Family reading creates an emotional bond and supports the development of literacy in children. This father and daughter, both legally blind, are reading a Braille book. (AP Wide World Photos)

brosis Foundation, or the Down Syndrome Congress, are often a great help to families with newly identified young children. (See our website at **http://www. education.college.hmco.com/students/** for a list of useful organizations.)

When parents of exceptional children look to the future, their dreams and expectations may also be violated. During childhood, the parents may be required to advocate for their child to ensure that he or she receives an appropriate educational program. As an adult, their child may still need their care. Parents must prepare for what will happen to that child—no matter what age—when they die.

This is not what we bargain for when we begin to dream about having a child. But it is not the catastrophe that it might seem to be at first glance, either. Many families become stronger and wiser for the experience of having an exceptional member. As usual, those virtues do not arrive without pain and struggle.

As an illustration, let us consider the story of a hypothetical family.

Tranh and Thu Le's baby is whisked away from them the minute she is born and soon surrounded by green-coated medical personnel who work over her quietly but urgently for many minutes. Returning from the huddle, their ashen-faced obstetrician tells them that their baby appears to have Down syndrome and is having difficulty breathing. The doctors suspect that she has a heart problem, and she is being taken to the neonatal intensive care unit, where she will undergo tests and be evaluated.

Before they can think about what questions to ask, Tranh and Thu Le are in the recovery room, looking at each other. Down syndrome? Doesn't that mean mental retardation? And a heart problem? Will she survive? Do we want her to survive? Will she need surgery? Why is this happening to us?

In describing the experience of learning that their child had a disability, many parents remember the initial feeling as one of *shock*. Parents sometimes describe themselves as standing over the situation, looking down on it and watching themselves. These feelings can be short-lived or persist for some time. Because of this, professionals are encouraged to repeat the information they have about the baby or child at another time, or in a different way, as often as possible over the first few days. It is crucial for professionals to be available to parents as they ask questions and as the import of the news slowly dawns on them.

As the shock diminishes, parents may begin to feel a deep *grief*. Their "dream child" is gone, and they don't know what they are left with. This is a feeling that many parents continue to experience for a long time, although it is not a constant feeling. For many, this grief is alleviated by the beginnings of an attachment to their child. Let's go back to our hypothetical situation.

Late that night, Tranh and Thu Le are able to visit their new daughter in the neonatal intensive care unit. The doctors have told them that their baby has a congenital heart defect that will require open-heart surgery. Although the baby is wearing a heart monitor and receiving some oxygen through a nasal tube, the nurse takes her out of her incubator and places her in Thu Le's arms. "She's adorable!" Tranh and Thu Le exclaim with surprise as they notice her fuzzy hair, her smooth skin, her tiny hands. Tranh notices that her nose is small and her eyes appear to have an upward slant. She opens those eyes, and suddenly the baby and her parents are looking at each other for the first time. Despite the sadness and anxiety in their hearts, Tranh and Thu Le fall in love with their new daughter. They decide to name her Angelica.

Another feeling that parents must often struggle with is *anger*. They look at friends and family members with normal, healthy babies and wonder why their baby couldn't have been that way. They look for someone to blame for their dilemma, and if they find no one, they may turn the anger inward and blame themselves, often without reason.

Despite the pain, most parents eventually reach a point at which they accept the fact that their child has a disability, a phase that Jan Blacher (1984a) describes as *adjustment and acceptance*: "a constructive adaptation to the child's handicap and realistic expectations of his or her progress" (p. 28). Although feelings of anger, guilt, and sadness do not disappear, the parents are able to recognize and rejoice in their child's progress and to act as advocates for their child.

Our story of Tranh and Thu Le is a hypothetical example of a family learning shortly after their child's birth that she has a disability. In some instances, early diagnoses like these do occur. Some disabilities are present at birth and are identified immediately or in the first few days of life. For many other families, however, the knowledge that their child has a disability comes much later. Learning disabilities, for example, typically do not appear until the child is in school and must begin to learn to read; children with autism may develop normally for the first months of life. Parents may suspect that something is wrong, but they sometimes have difficulty getting professionals to confirm their suspi-

> Feelings of shock, grief, and anger may recur throughout child-rearing, but most parents ultimately accept and adjust to their child's disability.

FIRST PERSON

The Joy He Brings

Five a.m. and our lives changed forever . . . for the better. He came into the world and demanded to be noticed—the beautiful face, the delicate features, and the diagnosis. How would we make it through the day?

Within a few short hours the medical staff, with heavy hearts, . . . pronounced him a healthy baby boy with Down syndrome. If they had only known the continuum of joy this child would bring to those whose lives he's happened by in the past ten years, they would have been in awe of the child before them.

Like a light that refuses to fade, Patrick burns his persona into those of us fortunate enough to take part in his life. From that first terrifying day of his birth, it has been he who has led the way in the transformation of how our family moves through life. There is a love of each other as individuals, celebrating in the idiosyncrasies in each of us that make our family like no other. There is humor as we move through our days, with happiness found in the most unlikely places. Patrick makes it so.

The uncertainty of how to parent a child with a diagnosis of Down syndrome was at first overwhelming, as the medical books and clinicians made their grave impressions. We quickly made our decision to parent *Patrick*, not the child with Down syndrome, and life stared anew. We partner with like-minded people in the process. Therapists, doctors, educators only get on our team if they're interested in Patrick as his wonderful self, not his perceived limitations. We all operate on the fly, with no experts and no paradigms—just learn as you go. The success has been dramatic.

The effects of life with Patrick have been profound. Our family of five has become a unit

cions. The worry that something is wrong with their child is very stressful for parents; they often veer back and forth between reassurance and deep anxiety.

Factors Affecting Families' Reactions

We know a great deal about families and how they work from our own experiences, and the components of the family systems approach provide us with a conceptual framework for discussion. Foremost among these is the first component, **family characteristics,** which includes the characteristics of the exceptional child as well as the family itself. Let us examine how knowledge of family characteristics has specific implications for families with a child with a disability.

● *Characteristics of the Child's Exceptionality*   Clearly, various abilities and disabilities will have differing effects on family life. For one thing, the *nature* of the exceptionality will determine the family reaction. The child who is deaf challenges the family to alter their communication system; will family members use sign language or speech for communication? If the choice is sign language, is each family member willing to take on the commitment of attending sign language classes? The child who is chronically ill places financial as well as emotional stress on the family; the child with a learning disability re-

The nature of the child's disability has an influence on family life.

---

of advocates, working to enhance the lives of individuals with special needs. Patrick's two sisters have empathy and respect, beyond their years, for these individuals. Along this journey, we have met wonderful friends with whom we might never have had the opportunity to connect had it not been for Patrick.

The effects of life with Patrick have also reached far into the community he calls home. His school had embraced his inclusion in every aspect of its culture. Teachers have been elevated in their profession by being forced to create new solutions to learning differences, and they have triumphed! Classmates, teammates, and fellow campers have been buoyed by his dogged determination and unwavering friendship.

As a future teacher, you set the culture of your classroom. Every child's experience will be a direct result of your embracing and owning him or her. If your focus is on the child, not the diagnosis, then you will know what each child needs . . . and every child has *special needs*. Things make sense when you look at a child as "How can I . . ." rather than "I can't because. . . ." Patrick's best teachers have been general education teachers who have said, "I can do this . . . let me try."

Remember the tremendous impact of your attitude. By valuing and embracing the differences in all children, you are teaching that inclusion is just the way we live. Your approach to teaching a special child has a far-reaching impact into the family unit, which is already anxious about the child's acceptance and ability to succeed. Every child can learn, and every child has the right to see success. Partner with parents and watch the results!

As for Patrick's future, we'll continue to rejoice in the many triumphs and agonize over the many difficulties, just as we will for our daughters. We'll work hard to ensure that a meaningful social and community life is surrounding him. The limits will only come from those who cannot see Patrick for being just wonderful Patrick. It is our job as parents to make sure they do not stand in his way.

Kate and Tom Myshrall
Worcester, MA

Source: Reprinted with permission of Kate and Tom Myshrall.

quires extra academic support and may cause a family to examine the emphasis they place on school achievement.

The *degree* of exceptionality may also have an impact on the family reaction. Children with more severe disabilities may look and behave quite differently than other children. Although on one hand these factors might stigmatize a family, on the other they clearly communicate that the child has a disability, relieving the family of the need to explain. Some disabilities, such as deafness and learning disabilities, are "invisible"; they are less likely to be apparent from looking at the child. Families of children with disabilities often describe the stress and frustration that accompany the constant explanations of their child's disability that are expected by family, friends, and strangers. Berry and Hardman (1998) provide a poignant example of family stress in their excerpt from Kathryn Morton's description of grocery shopping with her daughter Beckie: "I took her shopping with me only if I felt up to looking groomed, cheerful, competent, and in command of any situation. . . . To look tired and preoccupied with surviving . . . would have turned both of us into objects of pity" (Morton, 1985, p. 144).

> Parents are often required to explain their child's disability to others.

The *demands* of the exceptionality will also affect the family's ability to respond. Children who are medically fragile, needing special equipment such as ventilators, oxygen, or gastrointestinal tubes, present great caregiving demands on a family. Children in wheelchairs or those who use other equipment require special accommodations in their homes. Children with behavior and emotional disorders may be destructive of themselves, of others, or of objects within the home. Each exceptionality places its own unique constraints on family life (Hauser-Cram, et al., 2001). Even giftedness is no exception; the needs of the talented child for lessons, tutoring, or special attention may create difficulties for other children in the family.

> Disabilities place varying demands on family members.

● *Characteristics of the Family*   In addition to the nature and demands of the child's exceptionality, each family has qualities and characteristics that make it unique. Among these characteristics are **family configuration** and family size. Family configuration refers to the adults present in the family. These can include one or both parents, stepparents, or foster parents, and extended family members such as grandparents, aunts, uncles, cousins, or family friends. There may be one adult living with the child or many. For children of working parents, the caregiver during the parents' work hours may also be essential to the family configuration. Children who experience many changes in family configuration (such as several foster placements) appear to be particularly vulnerable to school problems later in life (Baker, Mednick, & Hunt, 1987; Werner & Smith, 1982). Related to family configuration is family size, which usually refers to the number of children in the family. Issues for only-child families may be quite different from those of larger families. Where brothers and sisters are involved, we must consider their needs in light of their exceptional sibling.

Another important family characteristic, one determined by income, education, and employment, is its **socioeconomic status (SES)**, which may affect the family's ability to participate in the child's educational program. Although most families have periods of financial strain, for some it is a more chronic problem than others. As this is being written, more than one in six of all urban children in the United States live in families whose income is below the poverty line (Children's Defense Fund, 2002). About 28 percent of children with disabilities live in poverty, as opposed to approximately 16 percent of nondisabled children (Fujiura & Yamaki, 2000). As we noted in Chapter 2, poverty can affect a child's

> Socioeconomic status is determined by family income, education, and employment.

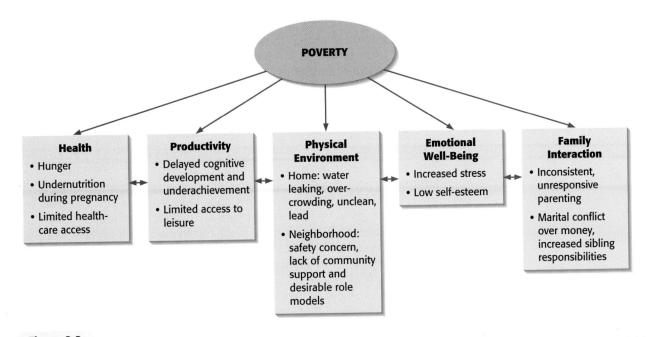

Figure 3.3

Impacts of Poverty on Five Family Life Domains

Source: J. Park, A. P. Turnbull, & H. R. Turnbull (2002). Impacts of poverty on family quality of life in families of children with disabilities. *Exceptional Children, 68*(2), 154.

health and nutrition as well as access to experiences. Park, Turnbull, and Turnbull (2002) describe the impact that poverty can have on **family quality of life**. These authors define family quality of life as family members having their needs met, enjoying their life together as a family, and having opportunities to pursue and achieve goals that are meaningful to them Figure 3.3 illustrates the impact of poverty on family well-being that Park, Turnbull, and Turnbull describe. As one mother explained it:

> If you have no money, it's very difficult to be—to do—to be together, to do fun things, to be at peace, to come home to a haven. . . . Because if you have no money, the bills not paid, you not gonna rest when you get home. You might have a good family, you know, a good husband, whatever. But, you don't have money, all that can go down the drain, so . . . money provides a way of release. You can go on a vacation, maybe, once a year, whereas if you don't have money, you won't be able to do that. You can—you can pay your bills. Whereas if you don't have money, you won't be able to do that. And when you can't do those things, you have this feeling of insecurity which floods over into other problems, emotionally. Anger, bitterness, and then it jumps off on the other family members and you got chaos. (Park, Turnbull, & Turnbull, 2002, p. 151)

As we have seen, a family's culture has a profound effect on its world view and on its attitudes toward an exceptional child. A child with a disability may be perceived quite differently from culture to culture. Many American Indian groups, for example, believe in accepting all events as they are; this value is based on the Indian belief that these events occur as part of the nature of life, and one must learn to live with the good and the bad in life (Coles, 1977; Joe & Malach, 1998). As the result of such values, attitudes toward children with disabilities are often open and accepting; difference and disability may be viewed as a natural part of life (Dorris, 1989). Other groups define a broad spectrum for "normal" behavior and therefore have difficulty with a school label such as "mental retardation" for their child (Harry, 1992a). In some Latino cultures, strong beliefs in the powers of good and evil, reinforced by religious beliefs, may lead a family to believe that the birth of a child with a disability has resulted from a curse put on the child or the effects of an evil spirit (Zuniga, 1998). Families with Anglo-European roots are more likely to resort to a traditional scientific explanation to understand the cause of a child's disability.

But each of us must take care not to make blanket assumptions about families' beliefs and practices based on their cultural background. According to Zuniga, "The central principle is to view each family as an individual unit to ascertain what meaning they ascribe to the illness or disability. Assumptions should not be made without first getting to know the family since so many variables contribute to views on causation and disability, particularly related to children" (p. 235).

A recent study by Cho, Singer, and Brenner (2000) described the responses of Korean and Korean American mothers to their child's disability:

> Without exception, all parents reported that the news that their children had disabilities precipitated an initial crisis. Several mothers described feelings of shame, self-blame, sorrow, denial, and anger. For example, a Korean American mother stated, "I was furious and ashamed to have an autistic child." A Korean mother reported, "I was hopeless and lost the meaning of my life when I learned that my daughter has autism." Many of the mothers described how they cried on and off during the first several months following the initial diagnosis. The duration of the initial crisis for parents could not be calculated because parents could not recall the precise time when the crisis was resolved . . . (p. 241).

These parents, like many others, reported that they resolved their initial negative feelings, and developed positive and loving views of their children. Those feelings returned, however, during times of stress, particularly when their child exhibited challenging behaviors. The authors point out that, for these parents, the process of resolving their feelings "was complex, including mixed positive and negative emotions during the same time period and return of earlier emotional and cognitive reactions" (Cho, Singer, & Brenner, 2000). We don't just feel one way, but often have several conflicting emotions, and they come and go and come again, precipitated by events in our lives.

Ecocultural theory would caution us not to focus solely on crisis in family life; most families continue with their established life routines and adapt and adjust to the demands of caring for their child (Gallimore, Bernheimer, & Weisner, 1999).

Religious background is another family characteristic that will affect the perception of disability. Churches, temples, and other religious communities often provide a significant source of support for families, and religious beliefs can shape a family's strategies for coping with a disability (Parakeshwar & Targament, 2001; Rogers-Dulan, 1998).

A family's religious beliefs can provide them with comfort and support.

Impact of Exceptionality on Family Functions

Think about the list you may currently have—either in your head or written down—of "things to do." Going to the bank, shopping for groceries, registering for a class, buying a book, calling a friend to arrange an outing, having your eyes examined—all these tasks are related to personal needs. If you are a parent, your own list is probably at the bottom of an infinite list of things to do for other family members.

Families with exceptional children are often responsible for complex **family functions**, which include all the tasks the family performs to meet its needs. Family finances can be strained by the need for ongoing professional evaluation and services. Taking care of the everyday needs of an exceptional child can be a full-time job in itself: Feeding, dressing, toileting, and transporting a child with a severe disability is labor-intensive. The socialization and self-definition needs of parents are often sacrificed to the needs of children, and families are expected to devote a great deal of time and energy to the educational and vocational needs of their exceptional child. When the needs of other family members are not met, stress may result.

When you work with the family of an exceptional child, you must take into account the needs of the entire family and the responsibilities for fulfilling other family functions that the parents must already shoulder. These responsibilities are challenging for any parent and sometimes feel overwhelming even in economically secure two-parent families; they are compounded in single-parent families and in those families where economic strains are real. Your expectations for families of children who are exceptional must be tempered by your appreciation of the responsibilities involved in meeting their overall needs. Your most useful suggestions to parents will help them incorporate effective strategies for facilitating their child's development into their daily routines; there will also be times when you can offer families additional supports to cope with the demands of their family life and the stress that results from unmet needs.

> Family functions include all the life tasks the family performs to meet its needs.

Exceptionality and Family Interactions

All the relationships within families can be touched by the presence of a child with exceptionality. Traditionally, conventional wisdom assumed that relationships would be affected negatively. More recently, researchers have begun to examine the possibility that the presence of such a child can affect **family interactions** in positive as well as negative ways, and we have consequently begun to alter many of our long-held assumptions and views.

> Family interaction addresses the relationships among family members.

● *Within the Family*   Research on the lifespan of a typical marriage suggests that most marital partners report a decrease in satisfaction with marriage in the years following the birth of children (Belsky, Lang, & Rovine, 1985). With the presence of any child adding to strain in a marriage, some researchers have assumed that the presence of a child with a disability in a family would lead to increased stress and family breakdown. A large-scale study completed in England by Pahl and Quine (1987) described a complex situation in which a number of specific factors led to unusually high levels of stress in parents of children with severe disabilities. Some factors were related to the child's disability, such as the child's behavior problems, and some to general family problems, such as parents' money worries. The highest levels of stress were reported by the families of children with the most severe disabilities. Breslau, Staruch, and

Sometimes children with HIV grow up in foster care. This foster mother and HIV-positive baby appear to be happily attached. (John Griffin/The Image Works)

Mortimer (1982) found that the best predictor of mothers' distress was the intensity of the child's daily needs—the amount of help, for example, that the child needed with eating, dressing, grooming, and so on. You can see that the weight of these factors within each family would vary depending on the nature of the child's disability and other family characteristics, and on the coping strategies and sources of support available to each family. While having a child with a disability can increase family stress, most families remain together despite those strains. In fact, some couples report that their marriage is strengthened by the presence of their child with a disability (Turnbull & Turnbull, 2001).

● *Between Parents and Children* Researchers have identified some differences in parent–child interaction when the child has a disability or is at risk for the development of a disability. (The interaction between mothers and their children is studied much more frequently than that of fathers and their children.) These differences vary according to the characteristics of each mother and each child and appear to change somewhat over time, particularly during the first year of life. In general, it appears that mothers of young children with disabilities dominate the communication interactions with their children more than mothers of children without disabilities, perhaps because it is more difficult to interpret infant cues and responses (Barnard & Kelly, 1990), or perhaps simply because their children talk less, since many children with disabilities have delayed language development. Kelly and Barnard (2000) believe that what is more important than the number of times the mother speaks to the child is whether the mother—or adult—and the child are responding to one another—with words or without—in contingent, sensitive, and empathic ways.

● *Among Siblings* What happens to the brothers and sisters of children with exceptionalities? Do they suffer from lack of parental attention? Are they given too much responsibility for caregiving? The impact of a sibling with a disability on brothers and sisters seems to depend on a number of factors, such as the attitudes and expectations of parents, family size, family resources, religion, the severity of the disability, and the pattern of interactions between siblings (Powell & Gallagher, 1993). It also seems to be more stressful for siblings when their parents are experiencing marital stress (Rivers & Stoneman, 2003), and when the sibling also has a behavior problem (Lardieri, Blacher, & Swanson, 2000). Traditionally, some studies have cited the negative aspects of the experience. Increased need for child care, for example, may make particular demands on older sisters (Stoneman et al., 1988). Brothers and sisters of children with disabilities may also react to related stress with changes in their behavior or feelings of loneliness, insecurity, or incompetence (Milstead, 1988).

Most professionals today believe that it is important to invite siblings to participate in decisions concerning their brother or sister with a disability, and sometimes to help with the exceptional child's educational programs. Of course, teaching is not appropriate for every sibling; some will enjoy the process and some will not. But many brothers and sisters are natural teachers of their exceptional siblings, and the family benefits from these positive interactions.

Brothers and sisters of children with disabilities can participate in their siblings' care and education.

● **The Extended Family**   Families with effective support systems seem to cope better with the stresses of daily life (Garbarino, 1990). For many, this group includes extended family members who provide help and support. The extended family includes grandparents, aunts, uncles, nieces, nephews, and other relatives. Extended family members may live with the parents and child or apart from them. They can be respite caregivers as well as sources of emotional (and sometimes economic) support to overstressed parents. Family support programs should consider the impact of a child with a disability on grandparents as well as on more immediate family members; many parents of children with disabilities worry about how their own parents will accept their grandchild (Seligman & Darling, 1997).

● **Families Under Stress**   Raising children today presents special challenges to families in environments that Garbarino (1997) calls "socially toxic"—usually violent urban areas. Garbarino believes that certain elements of these children's social world—violence, poverty, disruption of family relationships, substance abuse, the proliferation of guns, the threat of AIDS—have become poisonous to their development and undermine their sense of security. In addition, researchers tell us that adults are spending less time with children, and "the lack of adult supervision and time spent doing constructive, cooperative activities compounds the effects of other negative influences in the social environment for kids" (Garbarino, 1997, p. 14). The children who may be most vulnerable to the "social toxins" are those who already have the most developmental risk factors (see Chapter 2), especially those who live in poverty.

Families under stress may have less time in which to interact with their children.

Some families have difficulty withstanding these social stresses. Hanson and Carta (1996) call them **families with multiple risks** and suggest strategies for educators working with them (see the accompanying Teaching Strategies box entitled, "Principles of Support and Intervention for Children and Their Families").

Families with children with HIV infection, for example, must deal with many stressful issues (Lesar, Gerber, & Semmel, 1995). The negative social climate and stigma still associated with HIV and AIDS caused 70 percent of the families in the Lesar study not to disclose the cause of their child's illness to anyone outside their immediate families. The amount and nature of the social support they received were therefore diminished, leaving them isolated, and the intense caregiving demands of the child's illness isolated them further.

Teaching Strategies & Accommodations

Principles of Support and Intervention for Children and Their Families

1. **Providing opportunities for positive caregiving transactions.** Providing support at the earliest point for children and parents or caregivers in establishing positive and mutually satisfying relationships with one another holds promise for preventing or relieving sources of stress.

2. **Shifting focus from deficits to emphasis on individual and family strengths.** Services to children and families will be best served by identifying and supporting strengths, rather than by fault-finding and blaming.

3. **Recognizing and encouraging informal sources of support.** Friends, community members, teachers, and others may be natural supports for families.

4. **Becoming cross-culturally competent.** Professionals must be sensitive, respectful, and knowledgeable about the family's culture.

5. **Providing comprehensive, coordinated services.** Services to families must be community-based, appropriate, and valued by families; agencies must work together to provide coordinated services to families.

6. **Recognizing the need to offer families a broad spectrum of services.** Schools and other agencies must recognize that families with multiple challenges may require assistance in numerous areas before they can make use of other interventions that address specific child needs.

7. **Delivering flexible, usable services.** Service providers must individualize services based on family needs.

8. **Crossing professional boundaries and overcoming bureaucratic limitations.** Agencies and professionals must break through bureaucratic boundaries to work together on behalf of families.

Source: M. J. Hanson, & J. J. Carta (1996). Adapted from Addressing the challenges of families with multiple risks. *Exceptional Children, 62*(3), 201–212.

Coping Strategies

Despite the responsibilities and strains we have described, many families of children with disabilities survive and thrive:

Janice Fialka and John Cox from our First Person features are examples of such parents.

> These are the families who roll up their sleeves and get on with the task of finding the best available services for their child; who both accept the reality of the disability and are able to love the child for who he or she is; who manage to have successful marriages and emotionally well-adjusted children, both with and without disabilities. Many of them have enough energy left over from coping with the demands of their own lives to provide support to other families, and even to give encouragement now and again to weary educators and service providers. These families are said to have made a positive adaptation to their child with a disability. We meet these parents every day in the course of our educational or health practices. (Summers, Behr, & Turnbull, 1989, p. 27)

Recently, researchers have begun to study how people cope with stress and adversity. **Coping strategies** are the things people do to enhance a sense of well-being in their lives and to avoid being harmed by stressful demands (Turnbull et al., 1993).

Summers, Behr, and Turnbull (1989) note that a family's coping strategies have a great impact on how well they adapt to their child's disability. Families that cope successfully tend to use three key coping strategies:

- They attribute a cause to the event in order to establish a sense of personal control.
- They acquire mastery, or a feeling of control, in order to keep the adverse events from occurring again.
- They enhance self-esteem by finding the benefits or positive experiences that can result from adverse events (Taylor, 1983).

Turnbull and her colleagues (1993) describe these strategies as "cognitive coping"—"thinking about a particular situation in ways that enhance well-being" (p. 1). Thus, successful support of families incorporates strategies that increase not only the families' understanding of the causes of disability but also their sense of control over the events in their lives and their self-esteem related to the presence of their children with disabilities (Summers, Behr, & Turnbull, 1989).

> Coping strategies help people avoid the harmful effects of high levels of stress.

Sources of Support

Families find support during their toughest times from each other, extended family members, their communities, their churches, temples, and synagogues, and sometimes from counselors and therapists. When a family has a child with a disability, there are additional options that can help a family withstand stress and worry. The following are some examples.

● *Parent-to-Parent Support*   Parents often find their best support from other parents with children like theirs. One effective model for parent support is the **parent-to-parent model**, which links experienced parents of young children with disabilities to parents who are new to the programs and processes. Through phone conversations and group meetings, experienced parents listen, comfort, and share their experiences with others just beginning to learn about their children. Parents who have had similar experiences are often the most empathic and knowledgeable source of support for new parents.

At times, organizations, school programs, or agencies offer support groups for parents of children with similar disabilities or ages. These groups may have a specific goal, such as teaching advocacy skills, or they may be formed to provide parents with an opportunity to get to know other parents who have similar concerns. Parents often feel most comfortable among a group of peers and can discuss their very private fears and worries about their children with other parents who may have shared their experiences and feelings. Participation in support groups appears to help many parents feel less isolated; often parents report that until they participated in a group they felt they were the only people in the world with their problems. Participation in groups can also help parents form a network of new and understanding friends, and this helps families fulfill the often neglected socialization function that we previously mentioned.

> Support groups can provide comfort and information for parents.

Turnbull and Turnbull (1997) point out that support groups are common in early intervention programs, somewhat less so in school-age programs, and almost nonexistent for parents of older children and adults. Parents of older children and adults with disabilities often need information, communication, and sharing as well, and programs designed to meet their needs could fill a void that leaves many parents isolated. Technology has provided a boost to parent-to-parent support through the thousands of parent sites on the Internet.

The list of family resources at the textbook website will help you connect the families of exceptional children with other families and sources of support. Go to **http://www.education.college.hmco.com/students/**.

● *Respite Care*   For many families, the constant vigilance and caregiving required by a son or daughter with a disability can become overwhelming. A young child with intensive medical requirements, for example, may need to have equipment cleaned, adjusted, and monitored throughout the day; parents may even sleep lightly, perhaps with an intercom to the child's room next to them, in order to hear any "beeps" from equipment, indicating that the child (or the equipment) is having a problem. The child may be on several different medications or require special treatments that must be administered day and night. The child's care can be so complex that parents cannot simply leave the child with a babysitter. Children with unusual or demanding behavioral characteristics, such as those typical of some children with autism, for example, can also be particularly difficult to care for.

Most parents benefit from spending some time without their children in order to build up their spirits for the relentless requirements of being a parent. This is the case for parents of *all* children. For some families of children with very intensive caregiving needs, this time is much more difficult to obtain, and single-parent families are especially hard-hit. It is for families like this that the concept of **respite care** was developed. In respite care, trained substitute caregivers take over the care of the family member with a disability for a period of time that can range from an hour to a weekend. Respite care is usually provided in the family home, but it can also occur in the caregiver's home or in another facility such as a day-care center or group home. Families from culturally diverse backgrounds may not be comfortable with the notion of respite care or may prefer to have extended family members provide it. In those cases, the wishes of the family should be respected; some states allow family members to be paid for providing respite care.

Respite care is not yet widely available all over the country for families of children with disabilities; when it is provided, however, families report that it positively benefits their families and helps reduce stress levels (Abelson, 1999).

Pause and Reflect

Family members respond to the presence of disability in a child in many ways, depending on family characteristics such as cultural values and beliefs, and the characteristics of the child's disability. Sources of support for families can consist of their religion, other family members, and other parents. What about you? What are your sources of support during difficult times? ●

The Role of the Family in Special Education Services

As we saw in Chapter 1, the laws pertaining to the education of children with disabilities (IDEA and its amendments) call for parent partnership during every stage of the educational process. Parents choose to collaborate with professionals to varying degrees—some participate a great deal, some not at all.

The concerns of families with exceptional children change as their children grow and develop, moving from infancy through the school years. Sometimes, their children receive special education services from the first year of life through age 21. Let us take a look at the programs available for children with disabilities throughout the school years, and the provisions and expectations for parent involvement within those programs.

The Parents' Rights

Built into IDEA (see Chapter 1) is an acknowledgment of the parents' *right to be informed and to consent*. Before a child can be evaluated to determine whether he or she is eligible for special education services at all, parents must receive a written assessment plan that thoroughly describes, in clear, everyday language, what kind of evaluation will be conducted and for what purpose. They must sign and return the assessment plan before an evaluation can take place. In fact, parents' right to an informed consent must be considered at every educational decision point for their child. Ask yourself these questions when considering how this operates in the school in which you teach, or will teach:

> Parents have the right to be informed, to consent, and to participate in placement and program decisions.

- Are the written materials that explain procedures and alternatives available in the parents' native language? Verbally translating or paraphrasing this information may not constitute informed consent.

- Are the explanations on those written documents suitably simple and straightforward enough for a layperson to comprehend? Educators, like many other professionals, are notorious for their use of jargon; sometimes, we are so immersed in it that we assume that everyone else understands it, too.

- Do parents understand that they have the option *not* to consent? Sometimes, professionals who talk with parents do not emphasize this information, or it is "buried" in consent forms.

Parents also have *the right to participate in placement and program decisions* through the Individualized Education Program (IEP) process. Parents are equal members of the IEP team, as discussed in Chapter 1. They can express preferences for where their child will attend school and what the primary goals and objectives of their child's educational program will be. If parents do not agree with the IEP team's recommendations, no change in placement or program can be made until the disagreement has been settled.

When parents and school personnel disagree about a child's evaluation, placement, or program, parents must be informed of their **right to due process**. Either the parents or the school may call for a hearing (usually called a **due process hearing**) in order to resolve the conflict. Under the 1997 amendments to IDEA, **mediation** must be available to families and the school district before they go to a due process hearing, although participation in mediation in order to resolve disputes is voluntary. At the due process hearing, both parties may be represented by lawyers and have the opportunity to call witnesses who will testify for their point of view. The decision is made by an impartial hearing officer. Usually, both parties accept the decision of the hearing officer, but if either side still strongly disagrees, the decision can be appealed to the state educational agency and to state and federal courts.

> Due process procedures help parents and schools resolve disagreements about the child's schooling.

Because of the many opportunities for parent participation that IDEA provides, some professionals come to believe that parents are under an obligation to play a role in this process. This assumption is not correct. Parents also have the *right not to participate* in this educational decision-making. Some parents are not comfortable in such a situation; others are not able to take part, and so they waive their rights. Cultural considerations come into play here, too. Parents from some cultural groups may prefer to leave educational decision-making to the schools. When parents choose not to become involved in the IEP process, you must be sure that they understand all their options. Perhaps transportation is difficult for them, and telephone participation would be easier. Has it been made clear to them that an interpreter will be available? And is the interpreter competent and experienced? Korean American mothers from the Cho, Singer, and Brenner (2000) study reported great dissatisfaction with formal interpreters; they said that the interpreters were often not familiar with the terminology of special education, including the disability itself.

Teachers sometimes equate parents' noninvolvement in schooling with non-involvement with the child who has a disability (Prater, 2002). This is usually an inaccurate perception. Parents of children with disabilities, especially those with more severe conditions, have strenuous demands on their time and energy; they may see the time the child is in school as their only respite. In addition, family factors such as lack of child care, lack of a support system, or an inflexible work schedule may make participation in the child's educational programming nearly impossible for some families (Bauer & Shea, 2002). The cultural disconnect between the family and the school may also contribute to the family's lack of participation in school activities.

> Parents who are not involved in their child's education may be up against barriers to participation that school professionals do not understand.

As part of a study of Latino families of Puerto Rican and Mexican descent, Bailey and his colleagues (1999) asked parents whether they were aware of the range of services available to their young children with disabilities. Although the great majority of families were aware of services, they reported only a moderate level of satisfaction with them. The parents who were most dissatisfied had several reasons, among them feelings that they had been discriminated against, and the lack of spoken or written communication in Spanish. Those families who were most satisfied reported that there was one key professional who helped them navigate the system, as well as professionals who took time with them and were able to fully explain their child's condition and treatment options.

Kalyanpur, Harry, and Skrtic (2000) examined the cultural underpinnings of the legal mandate for parent participation in special education law, and noted that it is based on three core values of American culture: equity, individual rights, and freedom of choice. But not all parents grew up with those ideals, and some may not subscribe to them. In addition, they may not have the "cultural capital" required to navigate the educational system: language fluency, access to networks of support and information, access to school authorities, and so on. Again, as professionals, we must analyze the values and beliefs—often taken for granted—that underlie our expectations for children and families.

The earlier work of Harry and her colleagues (1992b, 1995) identified some of the factors that may contribute to the relatively low level of participation in special education procedures on the part of African American families. Harry's longitudinal study identified several factors that discouraged the parents' participation and advocacy for their children:

- *Late notices and inflexible scheduling of conferences.* Despite mandated timelines, parents did not always receive notice of meetings in a timely manner.

- *Limited time for conferences.* Meetings averaged only twenty to thirty minutes in length unless parents expressed many concerns.
- *Emphasis on documents rather than participation.* According to Harry and her colleagues:

  > When parents were asked how they perceived their role in the conferences, the majority consistently replied that their main role was to receive information about their child's progress and to sign the documents. . . . Observations revealed that parents' participation in conferences usually consisted of listening, perhaps asking a question (usually regarding logistical issues such as transportation), and signing papers. A typical view, expressed by one mother, was: "They lay it out [the IEP]. If you have questions, you can ask them. Then you sign it." (p. 371)

- *The use of jargon.* The use of unexplained technical terms by professionals can have a silencing effect on parents and may cloud their understanding of information and decision-making.
- *The structure of power.* When conferences are structured so that professionals report and parents listen, there is an implication that power lies in the hands of the professionals. Practices such as these violate the spirit of the law when they diminish parents' incentive to participate as partners in assessment, planning, and placement issues regarding their children.

Before Formal Schooling: The Early Years

In Chapter 2 we described the **early intervention** services that can be provided when a child under the age of 3 is identified with a specific disability or developmental delay, or is considered at risk for the development of a disability. Parents of young children in early intervention services are typically concerned with meeting the day-to-day needs of their child and learning more about the implications of their child's developmental status or disability. As we discussed in Chapter 1, the strengths and needs of the family are identified in the **Individualized Family Service Plan (IFSP)**, which is developed cooperatively by the family and the family service team (Sandall, 1997a, 1997b).

IDEA allows parents to stay actively involved in the education of their children with disabilities through participation on the IFSP team.

The teacher is reviewing IEP goals with this boy and his father. Working as a team will increase the likelihood of success. (Michael Newman/PhotoEdit)

During the School Years

Starting school is an important event in every child's life, and it means adjustments for every family. For parents of typically developing children, school entry usually means that they will play less of a role in their child's education. Although they will help with homework, confer with teachers, and possibly attend school meetings, the decisions about what their child will learn, how he or she will learn it, and where learning will take place are all made by the school. This process is quite different for parents of a child with a disability. Under the provisions of IDEA, educational decisions, including those relative to program planning and placement, are made by a team that includes one or both parents. This process may begin as early as age 3, when a child who has been in an early intervention program or who has been recently identified with a disability tran-

Teaching Strategies & Accommodations

Ideas for Involving Families at School

Many families, particularly those from culturally and linguistically diverse backgrounds, are hesitant to become involved in school activities. Here are some steps school professionals can take to meet the needs of families of children receiving special education services, and further the likelihood that families will participate at school.

- *Establish an advisory committee* composed of parents and professionals to outline and monitor the "family-professional" goals of the school.

- *Gather extensive information on the families' concerns, priorities, strengths, and needs.* Use a variety of informal and formal assessment instruments to gather information, emphasizing family interviews.

- *Identify family needs and preferences for school involvement.* The Family Information Preference Inventory (Turnbull & Turnbull, 1997) can be adapted to provide school professionals with information on the needs of families in the areas of teaching the child at home, advocacy, working with professionals on planning for the future, coping with family stress, and using resources.

- *Develop school manuals on policies and procedures, curriculum, and transition planning.* "User-friendly" materials that describe school practices, available in the parents' home language, can be a starting point for understanding and involvement.

- *Provide parents with videotapes, films, and slide presentations that focus on instruction and support.* See the list at the end of this chapter for resources.

- *Establish a materials lending library for parents and a toy lending library for their children.*

- *Invite parents to help with classroom projects.* Publish family recipe books or calendars in which every family contributes a recipe; write a class newsletter with and for families; begin home-school diaries; ask parents for help when the class is doing a special project.

- *Develop a system for providing regular feedback on the child's progress in school.* Notes are the standard, but think about phone calls, email, a classroom webpage, or videotapes.

- *Develop survival vocabulary lists in the native languages of your classroom families.* Include greetings, special education terms, body parts, action words, calendar words, and so on.

- *Provide parents with a current list of respite providers and babysitters who are experienced with children with disabilities.*

- *Post a bulletin board specifically for families, with photographs and announcements that might interest them.*

sitions into a preschool program. The transitions from home to preschool, and from preschool to kindergarten, require coordinated planning by the IEP team.

● *The Parent-Teacher Relationship*   The laws mandating educational programs for exceptional children require that parents and professionals work together, or collaborate, to meet the best interests of the child. Although most teachers see the importance of this collaboration, some may not have the skills or the persistence needed to help parents become involved. The "Closer Look" box in this chapter provides teachers with ideas for involving families at school, which may be helpful in this regard.

Harry (1992b) suggests that new roles for parents need to be developed to restructure parent-teacher communication:

> New roles for parents can increase the possibility of true partnership.

- *Include parents in transition planning*, discussing the expectations of the next environment (whether it be kindergarten or the workplace), issues of inclusion, or whatever the parents seem to need. Have parents visit potential receiving classrooms. Provide team meetings including family members and school professionals from the old and new environments.

- *Make extra efforts to include hard-to-reach families.* Provide single parents, fathers, and parents who live a long way from the school or do not have transportation an opportunity to share in their child's learning by organizing activities that do not require them to come to the school building.

- *Organize a telephone tree for the families in your classroom.* Use the telephone tree to remind parents of upcoming events including classroom learning units, field trips, celebrations, and open-house meetings.

- *Communicate personally with the family as frequently as possible.*

- *When you do communicate with the family, be a good listener.* Don't monopolize the conversation with school news—provide parents with a chance to share home news, too.

- *Consider making a home visit for families who cannot come to school.* If your school administrator and the family are comfortable with home visiting, it can be an invaluable link between home and school.

- *Provide a competent interpreter for conversations with families who do not speak English.* Don't use the child or someone you have pulled in from the hallway to interpret, except in an emergency. Having trained interpreters available lets parents know that the school is committed to successful communication with them.

- *Provide child care for important school meetings.* Some parents, particularly single ones, may not have a place to leave their children when they come to school.

All these ideas assume that resources AND a considerable amount of energy are available to improve home–school relationships. But research tells us that children whose parents are involved in school perform at a higher level (Carter, 2002)—so your efforts are very much worthwhile!

Source: C. C. Thomas, V. I. Correa, and C. V. Morsink (2001). Adapted from *Interactive teaming: Enhancing programs for children with special needs* (3rd ed., pp. 295–296).

- *Parents as assessors.* Parents' participation in the assessment processes that occur before the IEP meeting legitimizes their roles as providers of meaningful information about their children.
- *Parents as presenters of reports.* A parent report could be a formal part of the process, signaling to parents that their input is valued and necessary.
- *Parents as policymakers.* Harry recommends school-based, advisory parent bodies for special education programs, as well as active recruitment of parents as teacher's aides.
- *Parents as advocates and peer supports.* Parents serving in policymaking and support roles within schools may be more inclined to share their learning with other parents.

Technology Focus

Family Goals Determine Ultimate Success of Assistive Technology

Generally thought to be helpful to any student whose needs seem to require them, assistive devices or services are useful only if the student's family wants them. A recent study at Southeast Missouri State University (Parette & McMahan, 2002) focused on the need for IEP teams to be sensitive to family concerns, goals, and expectations for their child with disabilities. This is particularly important in the case of culturally and linguistically diverse families.

In establishing assistive technology (AT) goals, IEP teams need to consider certain factors relating to the family's perception of their child's disability and also their ability to understand and implement the devices. Some families, for instance, prefer that their children remain dependent on family and community resources rather than have them gain independence by means of the AT device or service. Some families may want their children to be included with their peers, but others may be afraid that the device will mark their child as out of the ordinary, and still others may feel doubly stigmatized by the AT, already having to cope with the stigma of their minority status.

The key to successful implementation of AT in the IEP is to consider the appropriateness of the device or service for a particular child, within the context of the family. The researchers formulated a detailed list of family goals and expectations re-

Adapted equipment makes all kinds of childhood experiences accessible (Jose Carillo/PhotoEdit)

garding AT, potential positive and negative outcomes, and possible IEP responses in light of those outcomes. They also provide a helpful set of questions team members can pose to families regarding acceptance of the device within the family and community, expectations of results to be gained from its use, and the resources available within the family concerning its implementation.

For more information, see P. Parette, and G. A. McMahan (2002). What should we expect of assistive technology: Being sensitive to family goals. *Teaching Exceptional Children, 23*(1), 56–61. This article contains the list of recommendations for dealing with family goals and expectations when considering applying an AT.

Source: Adapted from the ERIC/OSEP Special Project (2003). *IDEAs that work: News brief.* http://www.ericec.org.

Schools traditionally have difficulty engaging parents in meaningful participation (beyond Back-to-School night, the school picnic, or fundraising), then complain about lack of parental involvement. This is particularly true as children move into middle and secondary school. Perhaps Harry's suggestions for meaningful parental involvement would increase participation for all parents. Despite gains, most schools and school districts have a great deal of readjustment to do before parents feel like true partners in their children's education.

Leaving School

When the young person with a disability has completed school or reached age 22 (IDEA allows for schooling through age 21), the family must face a new bureaucracy and new issues. How will the child, now a young adult, spend his time? Is she prepared for employment? Can he find a job? How will she spend leisure time? What kinds of friendships and relationships will he have? Will there be a place for her in the community? Where will he live? Most of these issues confront any young adult seeking to separate from the family and achieve a sense of personal identity and independence, but they often assume a special degree of intensity and poignancy when faced by young adults with disabilities. Whitney-Thomas and Hanley-Maxwell (1996) found that parents of students with disabilities have less optimistic visions about their son or daughter's future than do parents of students without disabilities. They suggest that parents' feelings may realistically reflect the more narrow range of choices in adult life for students with disabilities.

Remember that the values and beliefs of the family will also affect their expectations for their adult child. Working in a culturally reciprocal manner with families is important at every stage of your student's life.

Transitions to Work and Higher Education

Although many in special education equate **transition** with employment opportunities, Halvorsen and coworkers (1989) broadened the concept to include the needs of the whole person across all life areas. Transition planning helps parents understand how their exceptional child will live as an adult.

Transition planning helps parents plan for their exceptional child as an adult.

In the past, many families had to make the difficult decisions about the needs of their young adult child with little help. To compound the problem, few alternatives were available for quality residential and employment opportunities for young adults with disabilities. Over the past fifteen years, however, the federal government has turned its attention to postschool choices for individuals with disabilities (Will, 1984), and since 1990, special education professionals have been required to focus on providing transition services to families at times of change. Preparation for the transition from school to work must begin long before school ends. In fact, many experienced parents and professionals believe that for some students, particularly those with severe disabilities, preparation should begin very early in the child's schooling (Falvey, 1995).

The services for students with disabilities provided since the passage of IDEA in 1975 have led to an increased number of those students attending higher education programs (U.S. Office of Special Education: available at **http://www.ed.gov/offices/OSERS/IDEA/overview.html**). Section 504 of the Rehabilitation Act of 1973 and the Americans with Disabilities Act (1990) require that higher education opportunities be extended to all qualified individuals with disabilities. You will read more about transition planning in the chapters to follow.

Family Concerns for the Future

The future of their children with disabilities is often a source of great concern for parents. Many parents, recognizing that they are not immortal, worry about what will happen to their child when they are no longer able to take responsibility for his or her care. Participation in the process of transition planning can allay some of the natural anxiety about future options (Clark & Patton, 1997). Along the way, the parents become aware of the resources available to help plan for the long-term future of their son or daughter. Families need information and support to confront the intricacies of financial planning and government benefits, guardianship, making a will, and finding and evaluating residential options for their son or daughter. Decisions relating to these crucial areas should be made, whenever possible, with the input of the son or daughter with a disability and should be based on his or her personal preferences. Even individuals with the most severe disabilities have ways of communicating personal preferences, and family members are most likely to be able to interpret their signals.

Pause and Reflect

The "shoes test" (Turnbull & Turnbull, 2001) is helpful in determining how you interact with parents. Put yourself in their shoes. How would you like to be treated? ●

Positive Aspects of Disabilities for Families

The ties that bind family members usually persist throughout a lifetime. When a son or daughter has a disability, those ties may involve more responsibility for decision-making and caregiving than a family anticipates. But despite these responsibilities, and despite the stresses and strains that can accompany them, many family members describe the benefits gained by living with a son or daughter or brother or sister with a disability. According to Ann and Rud Turnbull (1990, p. 115) and their colleagues, families have identified six of the ways in which young people with disabilities make positive contributions to their families:

An exceptional child can affect family relationships in positive ways, too.

- Being a source of joy
- Providing a means of learning life's lessons
- Giving and receiving love
- Supplying a sense of blessing or fulfillment
- Contributing a sense of pride
- Strengthening the family

Although it is important to stress that the journey isn't easy and families must be supported through their very real times of crisis, professionals in special education are finding that, given support, information, and strategies from professionals and other parents, most families can come to recognize and experience the positive contributions made by their family member with a disability. Our role is to support and inform families in that process.

SUMMARY

- Professionals in schools are increasingly called on to work with families and students from a variety of cultures. It is crucial that we begin to examine our own cultural experiences and attitudes so that we can respectfully engage family members with diverse backgrounds and experiences in a framework of cultural reciprocity.

- Theories of family life like the family systems approach and ecocultural theory shape our understanding of families and the demands of family life.

- The family systems approach uses the characteristics, interaction, functions, and life cycle of each family to describe its unique dynamics, including the initial reaction to the child who is exceptional, the child's impact on the family, and the family's ability to cope and find support.

- The initial reaction to a child with a disability may be influenced by the nature and degree of the disability, family size and socioeconomic status, and cultural and religious background.

- Some of the most important sources of support for parents are parent-to-parent support groups, respite care, and early intervention and special education services.

- IDEA provides a series of rights and opportunities so that parents can participate in decisions related to their child's schooling.

- Parents continue to play a key role through the school years. They have the right to be informed and to consent to the evaluation of their child, and to participate in placement and program decisions through the IEP process. Families are the focus of transition services for planning for their child's future needs.

- Each school professional must develop self-knowledge as the cornerstone of cultural competence, which will enhance our ability to work effectively with families from culturally and linguistically diverse backgrounds.

KEY TERMS

family
household
extended family
caregiver
culture
macroculture
microculture
minority
minority groups
ethnicity
cultural competence
cultural reciprocity

family systems
   approach
ecocultural theory
social construct
family characteristics
family configuration
socioeconomic status
family quality of life
family functions
family interactions
families with multiple
   risks

coping strategies
parent-to-parent model
respite care
right to due process
due process hearing
mediation
early intervention
Individualized Family
   Service Plan (IFSP)
transition

USEFUL RESOURCES

- The Pacer Center provides support for families to participate in all phases of their child's education. Many of their publications are available in Spanish and Hmong, as well as English. Visit them at **http://www.pacer.org**.

- Winifred Anderson, Stephen Chitwood, and Deirdre Hayden (1997). *Negotiating the special education maze: A guide for parents and teachers.* (3rd ed.). Rockville, MD: Woodbine House. This book is a step-by-step guide for parents of exceptional children as well as teachers and other professionals. Its emphasis on the collaborative relationships among special education providers is highlighted by many practical checklists, examples, and guidelines.

- The Children's Defense Fund–Parent Resource Network (PRN) provides access to a variety of national websites offering parents information on caring for their own children and on becoming involved in group efforts to help children in their own communities or states. Go to **http://www. childrensdefense.org/parentresnet.php**.

- *Conversations for three: Communicating through interpreters* is a video and booklet published by Paul H. Brookes that is an invaluable tool for training interpreters (who translate or interpret one language into another in a signed or spoken form) and those who work with them.

- *Exceptional Parent* magazine publishes articles especially for families of children with disabilities and provides a forum for the exchange of information by families with children with rare or unusual conditions. Write them at 65 E. Rte. 4, River Edge, N.J. 07661 or go to **http://www.eparent. com**.

- Family Village is a Web-based organization that integrates information, resources, and communication opportunities on the Internet for persons with cognitive and other disabilities. Visit them at **http://www.familyvillage. wisc.edu**.

- Family Voices is an organization composed of families and others interested in children with special health-care needs. Go to **http://www. familyvoices.org**.

- Federal Interagency Coordinating Council (FICC) available at **http:// www.fed-icc.org**. This new website for parents and families of children with disabilities identifies people throughout government who can help answer parents' questions about children and disability issues. See especially the "Family Stories" page.

- The Family Center on Technology and Disability offers a range of information about assistive technology used with children. Visit them at **http://www.fctd.info**.

- The work of Beth Harry and her colleagues has provided a voice for families who traditionally have not been heard in the special education system. See Beth Harry, Maya Kalyanpur, and Monimalika Day (1999), *Building cultural reciprocity with families: Case studies in special education* and Maya Kalyanpur and Beth Harry (1999), *Culture in special education: Building reciprocal family-professional relationships*. Both books are published by Paul H. Brookes, Baltimore.

- A good book for teachers is Martin Seligman (2000). *Conducting effective conferences with parents of children with disabilities*. New York: Guilford Press.

Books by parents of children with disabilities:

- Michael Berube (1996). *Life as we know it.* New York: Pantheon Books.
- Helen Featherstone (1980). *A difference in the family: Life with a disabled child.* New York: Basic Books. The author, a parent and educator, discusses openly and honestly how it feels to raise a child with a disability. This remains one of the most powerful books on the topic.
- Sandra Z. Kaufman (1999). *Retarded isn't stupid, mom!* Baltimore: Paul H. Brookes. This well-regarded book about the author's own experiences with her daughter Nicole has been updated to include descriptions of Nicole's experiences as an adult.
- Beth Kephart (1998). *A slant of sun.* New York: W.W. Norton.
- Mitchell Zuckoff (2002). *Choosing Naia.* Boston: Beacon Press.

 PORTFOLIO ACTIVITIES

1. Interview the parent or parents of a child or young person with a disability. How much of the caregiving role does the parent currently undertake? Have the demands of caregiving increased or decreased during the past ten years? Have the parents sought support services, or do they rely on informal support from other family members, volunteers, and so forth? After completing the interview, record and summarize your results and present them to your classmates. Brainstorm some possible resources for the family. Write an IFSP for the family for your portfolio—no matter what their child's age!

✔*Standards* This activity will help the student meet CEC Content Standard 1: Foundations and Standard 10: Collaboration.

2. What are the cultural groups (other than your own) represented in the area in which you live? Draw up a list of things you could do, based on what you have read in this chapter, to become more familiar with the values, traditions, and beliefs of those cultures. Present your list to your classmates, and include it in your portfolio.

✔*Standards* This activity will help the student meet CEC Content Standard 3: Individual Learning Differences.

3. Are you acquainted with the family of an exceptional child? If so, how do the components of the family systems approach apply to this family? Are they useful in identifying areas where services might be provided? Do they help you recognize the family's specific strengths and needs? Use the family systems framework to write a brief description of this family. If you're not familiar with a family yourself, read a book written by the parent of an exceptional child and apply these questions to that family. Some good choices might be found in the list we supply above. Include your work in your portfolio.

✔*Standards* This activity will help the student meet CEC Content Standard 1: Foundations and Standard 2: Development and Characteristics of Learners.

 To access an electronic portfolio template for these activities, visit our website through http://www.education.college.hmco. com/students/.

PART 2

Learning About the Potential of Exceptional Children

The chapters in Part 2 emphasize learning about the characteristics of individuals with specific abilities and disabilities. In addition to information on each category of exceptionality, Chapters 4 through 13 focus on helping you to understand the educational programs for each group of students. These chapters address several aspects of educational programs, including placement, assessment, and the selection and use of appropriate teaching strategies.

Part Outline

Chapter 4
Children with Learning Disabilities

Chapter 5
Children with Mental Retardation

Chapter 6
Children with Severe Disabilities

Chapter 7
Children with Behavior Disorders

Chapter 8
Children with Autism and Related Disorders

Chapter 9
Children with Communication Disorders

Chapter 10
Children Who Are Deaf and Hard of Hearing

Chapter 11
Children Who Are Blind or Have Low Vision

Chapter 12
Children with Physical Disabilities and Health Impairments

Chapter 13
Children Who Are Gifted and Talented

4 Children with Learning Disabilities

Outline

Terms and Definitions
  The Federal Definition
  Prevalence and Definition
    Issues
Causes of Learning Disabilities
  Internal Factors
  External Factors
Characteristics of Individuals
    with Learning Disabilities
  Learning Disabilities and
    Cognition: Approaches
    to Learning
  Learning Disabilities and
    Academic Performance
  Learning Disabilitiies and
    Social and Emotional
    Development
Teaching Strategies and
    Accommodations
  Assessment for Teaching
  Direct Instruction
  Strategy Instruction
  Special Skills Instruction
  Considerations for Culturally
    Diverse Learners
  Adapting Classroom
    Materials
  Curriculum
SUMMARY
KEY TERMS
USEFUL RESOURCES
PORTFOLIO ACTIVITIES

Learning Objectives

After reading this chapter about students with learning disabilities, the reader will:

- Describe the definition of a learning disability and discuss possible reasons for proposed changes in the definition

- Describe how the learning characteristics of individuals with disabilities affect academic performance in the areas of reading, language arts, and mathematics.

- Understand and explain the most effective approaches for presenting information to students with learning disabilities

- Identify ways to modify materials to facilitate accessibility for students with learning disabilities

- Reflect on the need for instruction and curriculum to address the specific learning characteristics of an individual child, including the relationship among instruction, assessment, and student performance

In this chapter we discuss students with learning disabilities, the largest group of children served in special education and the group most likely to be included in general education classes. Although these students require special education services, their learning needs are often balanced by excellence in other areas of life, and their ability to reach their potential can be dramatically enhanced by appropriate teaching and learning strategies.

Do you remember having to read aloud in school as a kid? Or sitting in a difficult math class, afraid of being called on to work out a problem at the board? Many of us remember vividly the feelings of panic, fear, and anxiety that those situations evoked, particularly if we were not good readers or if we were not confident in our understanding of geometry. Even now we can remember what it is like to feel inadequate in school.

Some students feel this way in school every day. The most ordinary classroom tasks may be problematic for them. These students feel, as you would, frustrated and confused about their inability to understand and perform in the classroom. Although they have average intelligence, they do not do well in school. Many students with learning disabilities read very poorly, and reading competently is the keystone of success in school. You know some of these students; let's find out more about them.

Terms and Definitions

Children with learning disabilities have probably always existed, but for many years educators failed to recognize their unique problems and characteristics. In 1963, a group of parents met in Chicago and invited the noted special educator Dr. Samuel Kirk to address them. When Kirk described the "specific learning disabilities" that their children shared, the parents seized on that term to describe and unite their children (Lerner, 1993). Although the term learning disabilities has been used for over forty years, the definition of learning disabilities continues to evolve.

The Federal Definition

A number of definitions of learning disabilities have been put forth over the years; most of them are quite general in order to accommodate the wide range of beliefs related to the origins of learning disabilities. The most widely used definition of **learning disabilities** was originally written in 1968 by the National Advisory Committee on Handicapped Children. It was slightly adapted for inclusion in Public Law 94-142 (1975), now Public Law 101-476, the Individuals with Disabilities Education Act (1990). It reads:

> "Specific learning disabilities" means a disorder in one or more of the basic psychological processes involved in understanding or using language spoken or written, which may manifest itself in an imperfect ability to listen, think, read, write, spell, or to do mathematical calculations. The term includes such conditions as perceptual handicaps, brain injury, minimal brain dysfunction, and developmental aphasia. The term does not include learning problems which are primarily the result of visual, hearing, or motor handicaps, of mental retardation, of emotional disturbance, or of environmental, cultural, or economic disadvantage. (USOE, 1977, p. 65083)

The current federal definition of learning disabilities refers to a disorder in one or more of the basic psychological processes of understanding and using language.

exclusionary definition

The federal law goes on to state that a student has a learning disability if he or she

1. Does not achieve at the proper age and ability levels in one or more of several specific areas when provided with appropriate learning experiences, and

2. Has a severe discrepancy between achievement and intellectual ability in one or more of the following areas: (a) oral expression, (b) listening comprehension, (c) written expression, (d) basic reading skill, (e) reading comprehension, (f) mathematics calculation, and (g) mathematics reasoning.

● *Key Elements in the Federal Definition*   The federal definition emphasizes that the performance of students with learning disabilities is often tied to their ability to receive or express information. Reading, writing, listening, and speaking are some of the ways we take in information or communicate what we know. The academic areas listed in the definition illustrate how this disability can be manifested. It is important to note that a child may have a learning disability in all of the skill areas mentioned or just in one area. For example, a student may find it difficult to learn to read and spell, yet do quite well in math. Some individuals can speak and write in an organized and effective manner, yet become quite confused when dealing with number concepts and algorithms. Knowing that a child has a learning disability tells you only that the child is experiencing some difficulty processing information. You must learn much more about the child before you can tell how much difficulty he or she is experiencing or what impact the disability has on specific academic subjects or tasks.

> Students with learning disabilities do not achieve at their age and ability levels in one or more specific areas.

Another key element of the federal definition is that the students demonstrate a severe **discrepancy** between achievement, or their performance in school, and their intellectual ability or potential. For example, a 9-year-old child with an average IQ who reads on the first-grade level would be exhibiting a discrepancy between what we expect (reading on the third-grade level) and the way he or she performs (reading on the first-grade level). A discrepancy is determined by examining the differences between scores on intelligence and achievement tests.

> A diagnosis of learning disabilities calls for a discrepancy between achievement and ability.

All that really is needed in most states to obtain a diagnosis of learning disabilities is a discrepancy between achievement and ability. The extent of the discrepancy necessary for identification varies from state to state because the size of the discrepancy is not spelled out in the federal definition. A significant discrepancy is usually equal to one or two years below expected performance level or two standard deviations below average performance. Although most states identify this discrepancy by comparing scores on standardized achievement tests with scores on intelligence tests, some states use a formula that takes into account factors such as IQ, achievement level, and age, whereas others use simple differences in grade-level performance. It is important to remember that this discrepancy has only to occur in *one* of the areas listed in the definition for identification to be made.

The definition also outlines what learning disabilities are *not*, in an element of the definition that has come to be known as the **exclusion clause**: "The term does not include learning problems which are primarily the result of visual, hearing, or motor handicaps, of mental retardation, of emotional disturbance, or of environmental, cultural, or economic disadvantage." Because a number of other disabilities or life situations may also cause problems in learning, some professionals feel that it is important to ensure that the difficulties a child is experiencing not be attributed to the fact that he or she comes from a deprived family or suffers from another disability. This clause can be used to help prevent the improper labeling of children from distinct cultures who have acquired learning styles, language, or behaviors that are not compatible with the academic requirements of schools in the dominant culture.

Because many children achieve below grade level, and it is often difficult to determine *why* a child is underachieving, the criteria for learning disabilities allow large numbers of children to be classified. This results in great diversity among the children identified as having a learning disability.

> The criteria for learning disabilities allow large numbers of children to be classified.

Prevalence and a New Definition

Learning disabilities was first included in public law as a disability area in 1975. Since that time the number of students identified as having a learning disability has grown by over 250 percent, from approximately 800,000 students to about 2,877,000 students (U.S. Department of Education, 1991; 2003). Because of concern about the increase in the number of children identified with learning disabilities, a new model of learning disabilities has surfaced (Gresham, 2001). This model removes the discrepancy clause from the definition entirely and focuses on a student's inability to achieve when provided with appropriate and research-based interventions (Fuchs, Fuchs, & Speece, 2002). For example, a student who is experiencing academic difficulty must receive interventions determined by the education profession to be effective treatments. The student must continue to have trouble learning the skills or content, after receiving instruction, in order to be evaluated for having a learning disability. As you can imagine, a lot of emphasis in this model is on the quality of instruction that goes on in the general education classroom.

A new definition based on the "responsiveness to intervention" model is now before Congress. In the proposed definition, the discrepancy component is removed. A school district may use a student's ability to respond to scientific, research-based treatments—such as intensive, individualized attempts to teach the foundations of reading—as the criterion for determining if he or she has a learning disability. The school is not required to evaluate whether or not a child has a discrepancy between ability and achievement. As it stands in the proposed definition, each state will determine the policies and the procedures it will use.

To find out about the status of the proposed definition of learning disabilities and the implications for both referral and assessment of students with learning disabilities, contact our website at **http://www.education.college.hmco.com/students/**.

The subjectivity and changeability of the definition of learning disabilities, as well as the definitions of other disabilities, remind us that the term "disability" is relative, and the definition of the term learning disability may change with increasing social and academic demands on our children.

? Pause and Reflect

Why do you think the number of children identified as having learning disabilities has increased so much in the past few decades? In your opinion, will a definition based on responsiveness to intervention affect the number of students identified each year? ●

FIRST PERSON

Advice About Being an LD Student

For any student with a learning disability, school often provides overwhelming challenges, which must be faced. Although as a student with a learning disability, I myself have experienced a great deal of pain and frustration, there are several survival techniques that help me cope. To be a student with a learning disability is to be a member of a minority, and as such, each of us should share our experiences so that others may develop strategies to help them through their struggles.

I believe one key idea is to find one's own definition of the dual identity within oneself as a learner and as a student. The learner is the one who makes an effort to be curious, involved, and motivated. Not all knowledge is taught in school. It is the student identity that gets labeled as disabled. The "learning disability" should not be allowed to overwhelm one's desire to attain knowledge. The learner in you must prevent it.

Another piece of advice besides developing a personal definition is developing one's self-esteem, to learn to have no fear of oneself. I felt like there was something wrong with me before I found out I had a disability; when I finally was diagnosed, it took me years to believe that I was not stupid or limited. However, I now understand that "to be categorized is, simply, to be enslaved," as Gore Vidal expressed. The label of *learning disability* should not be allowed to determine one's

Causes of Learning Disabilities

In most cases, the cause of a child's learning disability cannot be determined.

By virtue of the definition, a learning disability is not diagnosed until a student has experienced an academic problem in school. Typically, a learning disability is identified in the early elementary years, when a discrepancy between expected and actual academic performance can be established. In a great majority of cases, the cause of an individual's learning disability is unknown. This is true despite a vast amount of research investigating the possible causes of these disabilities. Many educators and researchers caution us about placing too much emphasis on finding the cause or causes of learning disabilities (Hallahan, Kauffman, & Lloyd, 1999). Knowing the cause of the disability does not necessarily tell us how to teach a student; in fact, some people believe that it may hinder the teaching process, particularly in the case of vague and poorly defined terms such as brain damage. The speculation and research about the causes of learning disabilities can be grouped into two categories: internal factors, such as organic, biological, or genetic factors, and external factors, sometimes referred to as environmental factors. Keep in mind, however, that when we are talking about possible causes of learning disabilities, we are referring mainly to hypotheses rather than facts.

identity, character, or self-image, nor one's potential.

Support from friends who can be trusted is crucial. It is destructive to believe that if you have a learning disability and your friends do not, you are too different from them to talk about your problems. Getting help or asking for support in the areas that present hurdles is essential. What is equally important is choosing carefully which voices or people have influence over you, your goals, your self-esteem, and your successes. Well-meaning or good-intentioned professionals or teachers can be just as hurtful to you as those who speak with prejudice and ignorance about learning disabilities. It is not a kindness to limit opportunities in education when a student experiences difficulty. A student with a learning disability can have just as much desire for success as a student without a disability.

But most of all, a student with a learning disability should always ask questions—of herself, teachers, evaluators, and tutors. The reason is that only when there is knowledge about your disability can there be the opportunity for self-advocacy. Being able to speak for yourself is crucial for getting the accommodations needed for your education and for full inclusion in the class by the teacher. The children's storybook character Winnie the Pooh said appropriately that "rivers know this. There is no hurry. We shall get there someday." The fact is that every student can learn in school, even with a learning disability; we all will get there someday.

Caitlin Norah Callahan

Source: Caitlin Norah Callahan, Advice about being an LD student. LD OnLine is a service of the Learning Disabilities Project at WETA, Washington, DC, in association with the Coordinated Campaign for Learning Disabilities. School partners include the Lab School of Washington and Arlington (VA) Public Schools. 1997 WETA.

Internal Factors

● **Brain Damage/Neurological Differences**   Since the brain is the center of learning, many professionals have assumed that students with serious learning problems have some type of brain damage. Although this explanation makes sense intuitively, there has been very little clear biological evidence. If brain damage exists, it has been too negligible to be identified through available technology, such as an electroencephalograph (EEG), a test used to measure brain activity. Today, however, there is renewed interest in neurological evaluations and brain research in the area of learning disabilities. One reason for this interest is advanced technology, which has allowed us to gain more detailed information. For example, some findings suggest that there are differences in the structure, symmetry, or activity levels of at least one hemisphere of the brain for individuals with and without learning disabilities. Bigler (1992) used a procedure called magnetic resonance imaging (MRI) to obtain a picture (similar to an x-ray) of the brains of individuals who had severe reading disabilities and also of some people who did not have learning disabilities. He found that some of the individuals with learning disabilities had structural irregularities in the left hemisphere of their brains. This structural difference was not present in all the individuals with disabilities, so Bigler could not draw any definitive conclusions.

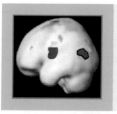
Brain function in children with no reading disability

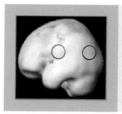
Brain function in children with developmental dyslexia

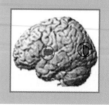
Children with dyslexia show increased brain function after training

Illustration of changes in brain images of individuals with dyslexia, following intensive instruction. (http://new-service.stanford.edu/news/2003/february26/dyslexia-226.html; copyright © 2003 by the National Academy of Sciences)

Current research in this area focuses on the different ways individuals with learning disabilities, particularly reading disabilities, process information while reading. We now can see the differences in brain activity between poor and fluent readers while they are reading text (Shaywitz & Shaywitz, 2001). It is the potential ability of instruction to address brain activity—to train skills mirrored by changes in neurological pathways—that is currently exciting researchers and other special education professionals. Some researchers (Temple et al., 2003) found that providing structured instruction, particularly in the areas of phonemic awareness (e.g., rhyming), can change the way the brains of children with reading disabilities process information. The preceding photos show a series of brain images that illustrate changes in a brain after intensive instruction in pre-reading skills.

● *Other Physiological Factors*   Medical researchers have suggested that other physiological factors have a role in causing learning disabilities. Many possible causes have been proposed over the years, including malnutrition and biochemical imbalances such as allergies or the inability of the blood to synthesize a normal supply of vitamins (Cott, 1972; Feingold, 1975). None of these theories, however, stood up to scientific experimentation (Arnold, Christopher, & Huestis, 1978; Kavale & Forness, 1983).

When we look back on the birth histories of students with learning disabilities, we do see that many of them experienced more **perinatal stress** than other babies. That is, during the perinatal period (from labor and delivery through the age of twenty-eight days) there were more traumatic events in their lives, such as difficult or prolonged labor and delivery, hypoxia during the birth process, low birthweight, or illness. Many babies with those same problems, however, do not have learning difficulties later in life, so perinatal stresses cannot be the sole cause of learning disabilities.

Several researchers have postulated that learning disabilities are inherited. As a teacher, you will often hear the parent of a child with learning disabilities say, "I had that same problem when I was in school—we just didn't have a name for it then." Although you may discover a lot of anecdotal evidence for inheritance, the empirical evidence is in dispute. The strongest evidence of a genetic basis for learning disabilities comes from studies of identical twins reared apart, which showed that both twins were likely to have a learning disability if one twin had a learning disability (De Fries, Gillis, & Wadsworth, 1993), and studies of the rate of disability occurrence within families (Lewis, 1992). Much more conclusive research needs to be done, however, before a link between heredity and learning disabilities can be established.

> No link between heredity and learning disabilities has yet been proved.

External Factors

If we look at learning disabilities as differences in **learning style**, or the way a student approaches learning, we may see the interaction between the student and the environment as a cause of learning disabilities. Some people believe that children identified as having a learning disability are really those children whose learning style is not compatible with the learning requirements of most school settings. In other words, rather than experiencing a deficit or disability, the students simply don't fit the mold. If teaching procedures and task requirements were different, the students wouldn't have a disability at all. Students with learning disabilities do often demonstrate a disorganized approach to learning; however, this may be a characteristic of the disability rather than a cause. Today, some educators believe that other external factors, such as inappropriate instruction, materials, and curricula, contribute to learning disabilities (Wallace & McLoughlin, 1988). This theory is attractive to many people because many students with learning disabilities *can* learn when they receive direct, systematic instruction. As we mentioned earlier, concerns related to appropriate instruction currently are receiving a lot of attention. Although skills that are missing or weak can be taught, a learning disability remains a lifelong problem.

> The learning styles of children with learning disabilities may be incompatible with school requirements.

Perhaps someday we will learn that some children, because of internal factors, are more vulnerable to external events and as a result develop what we now call learning disabilities. But since these learning disabilities range along a continuum from mild to severe and consist of many different types, it is probably foolhardy to search for *one* cause of a complicated group of learning problems (see the accompanying Closer Look box entitled, "Possible Causes of Learning Disabilities").

? Pause and Reflect

Often, children who have difficulty in school are relieved when they receive a diagnosis of learning disabilities. Before, they couldn't understand what the problem was—now, they have an explanation, even if they don't know the cause. Do you think knowing the cause of a learning disability is important to what we do in the classroom? Why or why not? ●

Characteristics of Individuals with Learning Disabilities

In this section, we will examine some of the ways learning disabilities can affect individuals. We will focus first on how people with learning disabilities receive,

A Closer Look — **Possible Causes of Learning Disabilities**

Internal factors

The following causes have been suggested, but little hard data are available:

- Brain damage
- Malnutrition and biochemical imbalances
- Perinatal stress
- Genetics

External factors

Many educators believe that external factors are major causes; others believe that they predispose children to learning disabilities. Major external factors include:

- Learning style
- Classroom factors (lack of motivation; inappropriate materials, methods, and curriculum)
- Environmental stressors (personal pain, family instability, poverty)

process, and produce information—in other words, how they learn. We will then look at the possible effects of learning disabilities on basic academic skills and on social behavior.

Learning Disabilities and Cognition: Approaches to Learning

Learning disabilities can affect cognitive processes—thinking skills used to process information.

As you remember, the federal definition of learning disabilities specifies that it is "a disorder in one or more of the basic psychological processes involved in understanding or using language." In this definition, *language* refers to the symbols of communication—spoken, written, or even behavioral. Although *psychological processes* is a vague term, think of it as referring to all the things we do when we take in information (listen, read, observe), try to learn information (classify, remember, evaluate, imitate), and produce information (speak, write, calculate, behave). These psychological processes are aspects of *cognition*, the wide range of thinking skills we use to process and learn information (Henley, Ramsey, & Algozzine, 1993).

In this section, we will look at five cognitive processes: perception, attention, memory, metacognition, and organization. These processes are vital to our ability to understand and use language. All students who have difficulty learning are probably experiencing a problem in one or more of them. Although everyone uses the same basic processes to learn information, we don't always use them the same way or with the same degree of efficiency.

● *Perception* Perception, as defined here, is the ability to organize and interpret the information we experience through our senses, such as visual or auditory abilities. Perception is important to learning because it provides us with our first sensory impressions about something we see or hear. When we hear a note or sound, we are able to identify and appreciate its uniqueness. When we see the letter *B*, we identify its structure (overall shape), orientation (direction of the letter), and component parts (one straight line and two curved lines). Later, if we observe the letter *D*, we are able to see that *D* has its own set of properties, and some are similar to those of *B* and some are different.

Teaching Strategies & Accommodations

Teaching Strategies for Students with Perceptual Difficulties

- If two pieces of information are perceptually confusing, do not present them together. For example, do not teach the spelling of *ie* words (*believe*) and *ei* words (*perceive*) on the same day.

- Highlight the important characteristics of new material. For example, underline or use bold letters to draw a student's attention to the same sound pattern presented in a group of reading or spelling words (m**ou**se, h**ou**se, r**ou**nd).

A student relies on his or her perceptual abilities to recognize, compare, and discriminate information. The ability to hold the image of a letter, word, or sound is necessary before information can be recognized, recalled, or applied. Let's look at an example of a young child who is just learning to read. If this child has difficulty discriminating sounds, she may confuse similar sounds, such as those made by the letters *m* and *n*. This confusion may make it difficult for the child to decode words by "sounding them out" and to make the connection between written letters and spoken sounds. In her mind, the relationship seems to change; sometimes she sees *m* and hears *mmm*; other times she sees *n* and hears *mmm*. This means she may begin guessing when asked to read a word such as *man*. (Is it *man, nam, nan,* or *mam*?) See the accompanying Teaching Strategies box entitled, "Teaching Strategies for Students with Perceptual Difficulties" for a few teaching strategies for children with perceptual difficulties.

Some children with learning disabilities reverse letters, words, or whole passages during reading or writing. Occasional letter or word reversal is typical of all young children. Children with learning disabilities, however, may continue to have difficulty with letter and word orientation and therefore continue to reverse letters and words throughout elementary school. Children who reverse words while reading typically reverse words that can be read in either direction (*saw* and *was*). You will seldom see a child try to read *firetruck* as *kcurterif*. The most common letter reversals are also those that are letters in either direction (*b* and *d*). If we think about how close these two letters are in the alphabet and recognize that often they are taught close together, we can understand why children often reverse them. The child hasn't had time to learn one completely before he is introduced to the other.

● *Attention*   The importance of attention to learning seems fairly obvious to most of us. It is the underlying factor in our ability to receive and process information. How can you take notes on a lecture if you can't tell what's important? How can you work a long division problem if you can't stay on task? **Attention** is a broad term that refers to the ability to focus on information. Many students with learning disabilities experience some level of attention difficulties. Students who experience severe attention difficulties may also be identified as having **attention deficit disorder (ADD)** or **attention deficit/hyperactivity disorder (ADHD)**. Attention deficit disorder will be discussed in more detail in

Attention deficits are frequently associated with individuals with learning disabilities.

Programs that incorporate peer tutoring allow each student to build on his or her academic and social strengths. (© Elizabeth Crews)

Chapter 7; this is a distinct disorder that can stand alone or coexist with many other categories of disability, including learning disabilities.

Attention deficits are one of the disorders teachers most frequently associate with individuals with learning disabilities. Many teachers describe their students with learning disabilities as "distractible" or "in his own world." These teachers are talking about kids who have trouble coming to attention and maintaining attention; something appears to be interfering with their ability to get on task and stay focused. Sometimes they are distracted by things in the classroom; other times they are subject to internal distractions, such as random thoughts or ideas.

Teachers are also perplexed or frustrated because a child seems to be paying attention but doesn't follow directions or can't summarize the main idea of a story. These problems may be a result of difficulties with **selective attention**, the ability to zero in on the most important part of a piece of information. For example, given the directions "Circle the correct answer," Keisha focuses on the fact that the word *circle* is underlined and proceeds to underline her answer. She attends to an inappropriate cue.

Again, once we understand the types of difficulties that can result from attention deficits, we can begin to restructure our teaching presentations to circumvent some of these problems or to teach some new attention skills. When children have difficulty attending to a task for a long period of time, we can address their work load. The accompanying Teaching Strategies box entitled, "Teaching Strategies for Students with Attention Difficulties" offers some suggestions for instruction.

● *Memory* If perception and attention are the skills that form a foundation for learning, then memory is the major vehicle for acquiring and recalling information. Think of all the memorizing that children must do during their years

Teaching Strategies & Accommodations

Teaching Strategies for Students with Attention Difficulties

Maintaining attention

- Break long tasks or assignments into smaller segments. Administer the smaller segments throughout the day, if a shorter assignment isn't acceptable.
- Present limited amounts of information on a page.
- Gradually increase the amount of time a student must attend to a task or lecture.

Selective attention

- Use prompts and cues to draw attention to important information. Types of cues include:
  1. Written cues, such as highlighting directions on tests or activity sheets
  2. Verbal cues, such as using signal words to let students know they are about to hear important information
  3. Instructional cues, such as having students paraphrase directions or other information to you
- Teach students a plan for identifying and highlighting important information themselves.

in school. **Memory** involves many different skills and processes. Some of these processes are used to organize information for learning; these are called **encoding processes**. When individuals encode information, they use visual, auditory, or verbal cues to arrange material; thus, encoding relies heavily on skills such as perception and selective attention. Students with learning disabilities who experience difficulty in perception and attention are also likely to have problems remembering correctly, because they may be encoding partial, incorrect, or unimportant information.

Students with learning disabilities may experience deficits in **working memory**—the ability to store new information and to retrieve previously processed information from long-term memory (Swanson, Cochran, & Ewers, 1990). Deficits in working memory translate into difficulties in the classroom. Students who don't use memory strategies try to learn information that is not broken down into manageable parts or that is unconnected to any previous knowledge. This makes it difficult for them to transfer the information into long-term memory and to retrieve it later on.

It is important to teach students memory strategies. Sometimes teachers try to associate materials with pictures, key words, or context clues to help students remember a number of facts or the relationships between them. Although many students with learning disabilities do not use tools for remembering, you can teach them some of these tools (see the accompanying Teaching Strategies box entitled, "Memory Strategies").

● *Metacognition*   **Metacognition**, the ability to monitor and evaluate performance, is another area in which students with learning disabilities often experience difficulty (Wong, 1991). Metacognition requires the ability to identify and select learning skills and techniques to facilitate the acquisition of informa-

> Encoding processes organize information so it can be learned.

> Students with learning disabilities often show deficits in working memory—the ability to store and retrieve information.

> Lack of metacognitive skills may hinder competent learning.

Teaching Strategies & Accommodations

Memory Strategies

Remember this number: 380741529

Look quickly at the number written above, then cover it completely with your finger. Wait one minute, and try to say the number out loud. Check your accuracy, but then ask yourself a more important question: What did I do to try to remember that long string of digits?

If that experiment didn't work, think of this situation. You are in a telephone booth, without a pencil and paper. You call directory assistance to get the number you need to call. How do you remember the number?

In either one of those situations, you probably used one of the following memory strategies:

- Chunking is the grouping of large strings of information into smaller, more manageable "chunks." Telephone numbers, for example, are "chunked" into small segments for easier recall; remembering 2125060595 is much harder than remembering (212) 506-0595.

- Rehearsal is the repetition, either oral or silent, of the information to be remembered.

- Elaboration is the weaving of the material to be remembered into a meaningful context. The numbers above, for example, could be related to birthdays, ages, or other telephone numbers.

- Another useful memory strategy is categorization, in which the information to be remembered is organized by the category to which it belongs. All the animals in a list, for example, could be grouped together for remembering.

tion; to choose or create the setting in which you are most likely to receive material accurately; to identify the most effective and efficient way to process and present information; and to evaluate and adapt your techniques for different materials and situations. Thus, metacognitive skills are critical to all aspects of learning. These skills supply many of the keys to learning from experience, generalizing information and strategies, and applying what you have learned.

Because most of these skills focus on planning, monitoring, and evaluation, students who do not have them may appear to plunge into tasks without thinking about them and never look back once they're done. Practicing a book report before delivering it to the class, making an outline of a paper before you begin writing, and jotting down the key points you want to make on an essay question before you begin writing all illustrate how metacognition can affect performance. As you probably know from personal experience, the students who practice, outline, and make notes are more likely to have coherent presentations or answers.

Fortunately, metacognitive skills can be taught. One technique that helps students plan, monitor, and evaluate—**self-monitoring**—is described in the accompanying Teaching Strategies box entitled, "Teaching Self-Monitoring." Self-monitoring teaches students to evaluate and record their own performance periodically. Written or auditory cues are provided for students, which prompt them to check their behavior.

● *Organization*   If we look at the many behaviors we consider to be characteristic of individuals with learning disabilities and examine the processes we have just discussed, we can see that the underlying thread is difficulty in **orga-**

Teaching Strategies & Accommodations

Teaching Self-Monitoring

The following procedure teaches self-monitoring of attention, defined as attention to task. The same technique can be used for a variety of skills.

- Teach students the difference between on-task and off-task behavior. Model the different behaviors and have students demonstrate them to you.

- Provide students with written or auditory cues (a timer, an audiotape with a tone or beep) that prompt them to check their behavior.

- Have students stop what they are doing when they hear the cue, ask themselves if they are paying attention, and record their response.

- Gradually fade the cues, then the recording sheets, as students learn to self-monitor independently.

nization. Because organization is a term we all use often, it is a useful and familiar framework to apply to learning disabilities.

Difficulties in organization can affect the most superficial tasks or the most complex cognitive activities. The simple acts required to come to class with a paper, pencil, and books; to get a homework assignment home and then back to school; and to copy math problems on a piece of notebook paper all rely on organizational skills. These may seem to be minor problems that can be easily addressed. Next to attention deficits, however, these simple problems of organization are mentioned most often by classroom teachers as sources of difficulty. It is important to recognize, however, that many students with learning disabilities cannot plan effectively. To some extent, metacognitive skills play a role in organization. Students must be able to understand the need to have a system of organization and develop a plan for carrying it out.

Another factor that may interact with metacognitive activity to produce organizational problems is **cognitive style**, the cognitive activity that takes place between the time a student recognizes the need to respond to something and the time she actually does respond. Students are often categorized along a continuum that ranges from impulsive to reflective. A child with an *impulsive* cognitive style responds rapidly, without considering alternatives, consequences, or accuracy. A *reflective* cognitive style describes a slower rate of response that includes an examination of the response and its alternatives or consequences. Many students with learning disabilities possess an impulsive cognitive style (Walker, 1985). This means that they are likely to respond without thinking. A student with an impulsive cognitive style may wave her hand vigorously to answer a question before you have even finished asking it. The tendency to jump the gun precludes the opportunity for engaging in organizational activity regardless of the type of task or its complexity.

Classroom interventions designed to improve organizational skills usually provide students with specific actions or guidelines for organized behavior. Examples include having a single notebook with designated places for homework, paper, and pencils; developing a list for students' lockers that identifies what is needed for each class; and preparing a standard end-of-the-day checklist for students to use in ensuring they have all required materials. Strategies like these

Homework Contract

Class: Ms. Washington Due Date: March 1, 2002

Assignment	Goal	Done?
Read pages 121-132 in reading book and answer questions 1-3 on page 132.	Read and answer all questions.	☐ Yes ☐ No Signature
Complete math problems 1-10 on page 176.	Complete problems 1-10.	☐ Yes ☐ No Signature
Write 3 sentences using Egyptian hieroglyphics.	Complete 3 sentences.	☐ Yes ☐ No Signature
Bonus I get five minutes of free time at the end of each period.	**Penalty** I have to sit out at recess to finish my work.	

(Student) (Teacher) (Witness)

Name: Date:

Figure 4.1

Organization Aid: KidTools Homework Contract

Source: G. Fitzgerald & L. Semrau (2000). Second Step KidTools [Computer Software]. Columbia, MO: University of Missouri-Columbia. Reprinted with permission.

have helped counteract the day-to-day organizational problems of many students with learning disabilities. Figure 4.1 is an example of a homework contract designed to address organizational skills and performance monitoring at the same time (KidTools, 2003). We will look more closely at complex organizational problems involving writing and thinking skills when we discuss academic interventions.

Learning Disabilities and Academic Performance

Before we look at the effects of learning disabilities on academic performance, let's review the key processes involved in cognition. Perception, attention, memory, metacognition, and organization are the five key processes. Together, they enable us to receive information correctly, arrange it for easier learning, identify similarities and differences with other knowledge we have, select a way to learn the information effectively, and evaluate the effectiveness of our learning process. If a student has problems doing any or all of these things, it is easy to see how all learning can be affected. We will look at three basic skill areas—reading, language arts, and math—and show how difficulties in these areas can affect other types of learning as well.

Reading is the most difficult skill area for most students with learning disabilities.

● ***Reading*** Reading is the most difficult skill area for the majority of students with learning disabilities. The term *dyslexia* is often associated with reading difficulties in students with learning disabilities. Although this term was initially used to refer to a specific and severe reading disability with clear neurological origins, the work often is used today, by some educators, to refer to more generalized reading disabilities (Shaywitz & Shaywitz, 2001). Because reading is necessary for almost all learning, the student with a reading disability often experiences difficulty in many other subjects as well. In addition, the emphasis on oral reading in the early school years may make the child with a reading disability reluctant to read, so he or she may progressively fall further behind in reading skills. Teachers are often faced with the challenge of not only trying to teach a child to read, but also motivating the child to *try* to read. A student with a severe reading disability may be reading on the first- or second-grade level, even though he or she may be 10, 11, or even 15 years old. As you can imagine, trying to inspire a teenager to "keep trying" in reading when he or she is so far behind can be a painful and difficult process.

If you think about everything you do when you read, you realize that it is a very complex process. To examine the potential effects of learning disabilities on reading, let's look at three of the major skills involved in the reading process: word analysis (identifying a word), reading fluency (rate and accuracy in reading), and comprehension (understanding what is read).

Word Analysis   In order to identify written words, we use a number of different skills. Some of the most important **word-analysis** skills include the ability to associate sounds with the various letters and letter combinations used to write them (phonic analysis), to immediately recognize and remember words (sight-word reading), and to use the surrounding text to help figure out a specific word (context clues). These skills rely heavily on perception, selective attention, memory, and metacognitive skills. Thus, word analysis is dependent almost entirely on the cognitive skills that are most problematic for individuals with learning disabilities.

If students do not have basic phonics skills, they cannot sound out words and will be very limited in the number of words they can read. This is particularly true given that many of these same skills are required in other word-analysis strategies, such as reading sight words. Recent research suggests the importance of assessing and teaching very young children skills in the areas of phonological and phonemic awareness (Foorman et al., 1998). There appears to be an important relationship between a young child's ability to hear and distinguish among sounds and his or her later ability to read. Researchers and teachers are investigating the most effective way to teach young children these important skills (Torgesen, 2000). A current hypothesis is that two major information-processing deficits are at the root of significant reading disabilities: difficulties in phonemic awareness and difficulties in rapid recall, or rapid naming of learning information (sounds, letters, words). This hypothesis is called the **double deficit hypothesis** and is the subject of much current research in the area of learning disabilities (Allor, 2002).

The most frequently recommended approaches to teaching reading to elementary students with learning disabilities include a structured presentation of phonics skills and rules (Carnine, Silbert & Kameenui, 1990). These approaches are called **code-emphasis approaches**. Because the students cannot identify sound/letter associations and patterns on their own, it is necessary to present these associations in a very clear way and provide students with lots of opportunities to practice and remember them.

> Teaching reading to students with learning disabilities involves a structured presentation of phonics skills and rules.

Many students with learning disabilities also run into obstacles when they try to use the sight-word approach to word analysis. Teachers often report spending an entire period working on a few sight words, only to find, the next day, that the child behaves as if he's never seen the words before. Learning most sight words, unless they are always in a specific context (such as the word *stop* on a stop sign), requires being able to identify and recall the aspects of the word that make it unique and to associate the correct sounds with the word. There are many specific strategies for teaching sight words (see the accompanying Teaching Strategies box entitled, "Teaching Word-Analysis Skills").

Teaching Strategies & Accommodations

Teaching Word-Analysis Skills

Phonics

Use structured phonics programs that:

- Teach most common sounds first
- Stress specific phonics rules and patterns
- Expose the beginning reader only to words that contain sounds he or she has already learned

Sight words

During instruction:

- Require the student to focus on all important aspects of the word (all letters, not just the first and last ones).
- Have the student discriminate between the new word and frequently confused words. For example, if you are introducing the word *what* as a sight word, make sure the child can read the word when it is presented with words such as *that*, *which*, and *wait*.
- Help the student devise strategies for remembering a particular word.

Context clues

- Control the reading level of materials used so that students are presented with few unfamiliar words.
- For beginning readers, present illustrations after the text selection has been read.
- Teach students to use context clues as a decoding strategy after they are adept at beginning phonics analysis.

Many students with learning disabilities depend heavily on context clues for guessing words.

Poor readers tend to use context clues as their major word-analysis strategy. Although context can be helpful when you come across one or two words that are difficult to decode, using context to figure out 50 or 60 percent of the words in a passage is ineffective. At the early elementary level, children may achieve some success with this method because of the many pictures in the story, and because they may hear the story read several times. Many students, therefore, develop patterns of guessing words. This is the most common reading pattern we see in all students with learning disabilities, and it is the most difficult to break. Some students try to guess their way through an entire story. Reading programs for students with learning disabilities often try to prevent or eliminate guessing by controlling the words students are expected to read so that only words the child knows how to decode are presented in stories; they also eliminate pictures and other cues from initial reading passages. Once the child gains confidence in her ability to use other word-attack skills and uses them effectively, then the use of context clues—which will become quite valuable when the student begins reading complex material—can be encouraged.

Fluency   Any child who has been asked to read aloud has faced the performance pressure to read in a smooth and accurate fashion in front of the rest of the class. **Reading fluency**, most frequently defined as the rate of accurate reading (correct words per minute), is more than a status symbol for children; it is an important indicator of reading ability. As you might expect, a child who has difficulty in word analysis will also have difficulty reading fluently. Obviously, the ability to recall information quickly, or rapid naming, is a fundamental component of reading fluency. Historically, interventions to improve reading fluency

Some children with reading disabilities benefit from individual and small-group instruction. (© James H. Pickerell/The Image Works)

have focused on having students practice reading a piece of text orally several times (called repeated readings). Sometimes the readings are first modeled by the teacher or a peer, and other times the student just practices improving his or her time and accuracy independently. Recent interventions focus not only on trying to improve the rate and accuracy of oral reading, but also on strengthening the ties between fluent reading and comprehension. Students are sometimes taught strategies that involve previewing text, summarizing paragraphs, reading with inflection, or monitoring errors to improve not only fluency but comprehension as well (Allinder et al., 2001; Vaughn et al., 2000).

Reading Comprehension   Students with learning disabilities may experience difficulties in **reading comprehension** because they lack the skills required for understanding text and have poor word-analysis skills. The child who has difficulty with reading fluency will have trouble understanding the gist of sentences and passages. It is important to adjust your expectations for comprehension if the child has difficulty in the actual reading of material. It is better to teach or assess reading comprehension skills on material the students can decode fluently or that is presented orally.

In addition to word-analysis skills, a number of other factors can affect a child's ability to comprehend text. Literal comprehension of material—the ability to identify specifically stated information—requires the ability to select important information from unimportant details, to organize or sequence this information, and to recall it. The ability to select and categorize information is also necessary for organizational comprehension, which includes identifying main ideas.

For more advanced comprehension activities, such as interpreting text, evaluating actions in a story, predicting consequences, and relating text to personal experience, students with learning disabilities can experience difficulty because of the role-taking skills required in some of these tasks and a reluctance to go beyond what is specifically stated in the text. For example, being able to put yourself in another's place (Why was hitting Joe a poor choice? What would you do if that happened to you?) requires seeing the similarities and differences between yourself and the character. Some students with learning disabilities cannot put themselves in another person's shoes and see things from another perspective.

Many difficulties in reading comprehension can also be traced to the lack of specific strategies used to help remember material or to self-check understanding (Malone & Mastropieri, 1992). If you are reading a book that is not particularly interesting, you may find after you've read a few pages that you haven't actually taken in anything you've read. If you are reading this book to prepare for a test, you may go back and reread the material, perhaps stopping every so often to paraphrase what you've read, rehearse the important points, or ask yourself questions to see if you really do understand it. All these learning strategies, which are essentially memory and metacognitive skills, help you to comprehend the text, and they become increasingly important as reading material becomes denser and more complex. Students with learning disabilities who do not use these active strategies are unlikely to have good comprehension.

Many teaching strategies that focus on reading comprehension emphasize the use of specific plans or behaviors to help students review material and check their comprehension periodically (Gajira & Salvia, 1992). Other techniques involve identifying and highlighting key information in the text, or recording the information using story maps (Gardill & Jitendra, 1999). Usually, the teacher will model these skills and then teach the student how to extract the key information necessary for good comprehension. Similar techniques are used to help students at the secondary level identify important information from textbooks, which are frequently several grade levels above their reading level. By using specific comprehension strategies and the conventions of the text (headings, vo-

> Students need to develop strategies that will help them remember material and self-check their understanding of it.

Teaching Strategies & Accommodations

Suggestions for Teaching Reading Comprehension

- **Predictions.** Predictions can be based on pictures, headings, subtitles, or graphs. They can be used to activate students' prior knowledge before reading, to increase attention to sequencing during reading, and can be evaluated after reading to help summarize content.

- **Questions.** Questions can be asked before reading to help students attend to important information, or students can be taught to transform subtitles or headings into questions to ask themselves as they read. Having students make up questions to ask each other after reading is a good alternative to the typical question-answer period and helps students develop study skills as well.

- **Advance organizers or outlines.** You can prepare an advance organizer on the text to help focus students' attention on key material in the text. Students can review the organizer before reading and take notes on it while reading. When it is completed, the students have a study sheet to review.

- **Self-monitoring or self-evaluation.** When students begin reading longer text selections, they can learn to stop periodically and paraphrase the text or check their understanding. This can be done by using an auditory self-monitoring tape or by randomly placing stickers or other markers throughout the text. When the student reaches the sticker, it is time to think about what he or she has just read.

cabulary words, questions in text), students can find and retrieve essential information (see the accompanying Teaching Strategies box entitled, "Suggestions for Teaching Reading Comprehension").

Reading continues to be the biggest obstacle faced by most students with learning disabilities. For this reason, the type of reading instruction used is critical. Snider (1997) found that students with learning disabilities who received thirty to forty-five minutes of instruction in the vocabulary-controlled, code-emphasis reading programs acquired necessary decoding skills and transferred those skills to the material they read in their classrooms. Because more and more students with learning disabilities are served in general education classrooms, teachers must investigate ways to provide reading skill instruction, particularly for young children, in a classroom setting.

● *Language Arts*   In this section, we will look at three general areas: spelling, spoken language, and written language. Because of the close ties of some of these skills to reading ability, they tend to be areas of great difficulty for many students with learning disabilities.

Spelling   Spelling requires all the essential skills used in the word-analysis strategies of phonics and sight-word reading. The student must either know specific sound and letter relationships or be able to memorize words. The difficulties students with learning disabilities have in learning and applying rules of phonics, visualizing the word correctly, and evaluating spellings result in frequent misspellings, even as they become more adept at reading. It is not uncommon to find the same word spelled five or six different ways on the same paper, regardless of whether the student is in the fifth grade or in college (for example, *ther, there, thare,* and *theyre* for *their*).

Many students with learning disabilities spell a word as if it were being approached for the first time, without reference to an image of the word held in memory. The majority of errors are phonetically acceptable, meaning that a reader can sound them out to read the word (Hom, O'Donnell, & Leicht, 1988). Other common errors include errors made in the middle of the word (vowel combinations are the most variable and confusing), scrambled words, and, in younger children, carryover from just-learned letter combinations. For example, a child may spell words such as *cake* and *late* correctly until she has a spelling lesson that contains the words *rain* and *pain.* The next time the child writes *cake,* she may spell it as *caik,* and *rain* may turn into *rane.* When a number of spelling patterns are presented to a child at one time, or if she doesn't have enough time to practice and recall individual patterns, the likelihood of confusion increases.

Many students with learning disabilities are asked to spell many words they cannot yet read. When this occurs, the students cannot be expected to succeed. If at all possible, it is best to combine spelling lessons with reading lessons. Use the sounds and words involved in reading as the sounds and words studied in spelling lessons. This will increase the probability that students will learn to spell with more confidence, and they will have many opportunities to practice sounds and words. For students of all ages, learning to evaluate spellings and developing a consistent mental representation of the word are critical skills. Recommended spelling strategies include teaching students to visualize the whole word while studying. Common spelling activities used by many classroom teachers, such as writing the words five times each, are useless if the student is copying the word one letter at a time. If students are encouraged to write the word, spell the word aloud, visualize the word, spell the word aloud with-

It is best to combine spelling lessons with reading lessons.

out looking at it, check the word's spelling, write the word without looking, and then compare their word to the original, the task will help develop needed memory and metacognitive skills.

Spoken Language Many students with learning disabilities experience difficulties in spoken or oral language, which can affect academic as well as social performance. These may include problems identifying and using appropriate speech sounds, using appropriate words and understanding word meanings, using and understanding various sentence structures, and using appropriate grammar and language conventions. Other problem areas include understanding underlying meanings, such as irony or figurative language, and adjusting language for different uses and purposes, called **pragmatic language skills** (Gibbs & Cooper, 1989; Henley, Ramsey, & Algozzine, 1993).

Although you may not think of oral language as an academic skill, the effects of language difficulties on academic as well as social performance can be significant. For example, a student who has difficulty identifying and discriminating speech sounds (such as the sounds of *t* and *d*) may have difficulty reading and spelling. Many other difficulties with oral language may translate into problems understanding not only spoken directions or lectures but also written language. A student who can only use or understand simple sentences (for example, "The dog licked the cat") will interpret the information incorrectly if given a more complex sentence ("The cat was licked by the dog"). Instead of realizing that these two sentences mean the same thing, the child may impose the simple subject-verb-object order on the second sentence and be convinced that the cat licked the dog.

Pragmatic language skills enable the child to use language effectively in different settings and for different purposes. This includes **functional flexibility**, or the ability to move easily from one form of language to another to accommodate various settings or audiences (Simon, 1991). Functional flexibility requires the individual to identify the type of language appropriate to the setting, to anticipate the needs of the audience, and then to adjust language structure, content, and vocabulary to meet these needs. It also requires an understanding that different types of language are used for different purposes. Individuals with learning disabilities may have difficulty with pragmatic language because they have difficulty attending to the cues (for example, other students' behavior) found in various settings. This can cause a problem if they don't pick up on when it is important to use respectful language, when it is OK to be relaxed and informal, or when it is appropriate to laugh or tell jokes. In addition, anticipating an audience's needs requires putting yourself in other people's positions and being aware of, for example, their prior knowledge about a subject or their desire for clarity or brevity when asking for directions or making a request. Students with learning disabilities may not monitor their effectiveness in communicating and therefore may not adjust their language to the setting.

It is important to provide students with many models of different language structures; however, it also is important to understand that using and interpreting oral language may require instruction. Interpreting oral language correctly involves reading nonverbal cues, such as raised eyebrows or posture, and understanding vocal cues, such as inflection and emphasis. The sentence "Just turn in your paper whenever you feel like it" can mean two entirely different things, depending on the emphasis and inflection used. Because the identification and use of these conventions require good perceptive and selective attention skills, many students with learning disabilities miss them.

Interpreting oral language correctly involves reading nonverbal cues, which can be difficult for students with learning disabilities.

Written Language   Students with learning disabilities often have great difficulty in written language or composition. Specific problems include inadequate
planning, structure, and organization; immature or limited sentence structure;

Students with learning
disabilities may have
difficulty planning,
organizing, and writing
their papers.

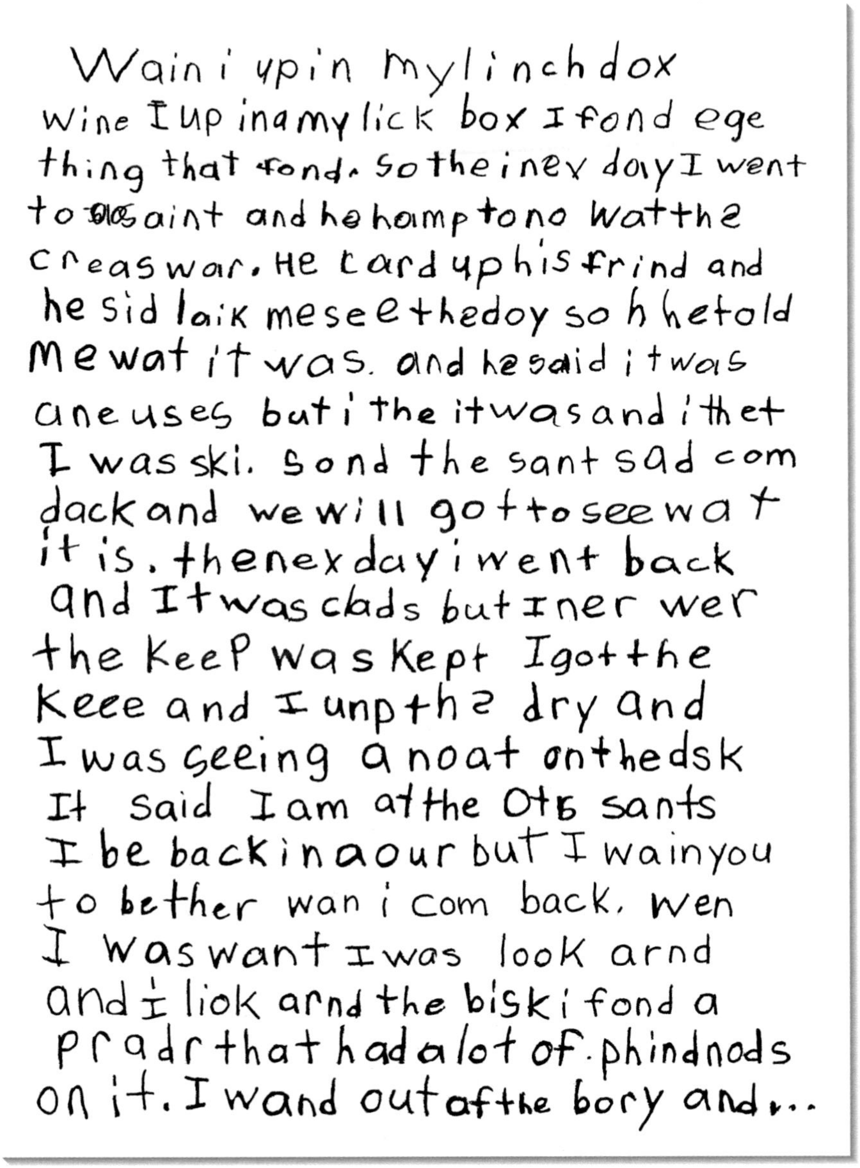

When I opened my lunch box

When I opened my lunch box I found an egg thing that flobbed. So the next day I went
to a scientist and he happened to know what the creature was. He called up his friend
and he said let me see the boy so he told me what it was and he said it was chicken
but I thought it was a snake. So the scientist said come back and we will go to see
what it is. The next day I went back and it was closed but I knew where the key was
kept. I got the key and I opened the door and I was seeing a note on the desk. It said I
am at the other scientist. I will be back in an hour but I want you to be there when I
come back. When I was waiting I was looking around and I looked around the desk I
found a paper that had a lot of phone numbers on it. I ran out the door and . . .

Figure 4.2

Phillip's Story

Source: Phillip DeKraft, copyright 2003.

limited and repetitive vocabulary; limited consideration of audience; unnecessary or unrelated information or details; and errors in spelling, punctuation, grammar, and handwriting (Carnine, 1991; Mercer & Mercer, 1993a; Newcomer & Barenbaum, 1991). Students with learning disabilities also lack the motivation and the monitoring and evaluation skills often considered necessary for good writing (Newcomer & Barenbaum, 1991). When we look at the skills necessary for good writing and consider the characteristics of students with learning disabilities, the types of difficulties we have identified are not surprising.

Some students who are adept in oral language may show restricted syntax and vocabulary in written language. If a student has difficulty reading and spelling and is fearful of making errors, these written language problems may reflect fear of failure rather than actual limitations in language ability. It is important to encourage these students to work on transferring oral to written language, to have plenty of opportunities to write without fear of failing, and to have access to word or vocabulary banks if necessary, in order to encourage and broaden written language skills. For some students, mechanical disabilities, though great, do not affect their productivity. "Phillip's Story" is the first installment of a story (and its translation) written by a boy who has a learning disability in written language and reading (see Figure 4.2 on preceding page). Phillip is entering the sixth grade next year; he is a bright kid who enjoys wrestling, playing the violin, and building things with his father and brother. As you can see, his spelling doesn't get in the way of his story-telling, yet it will pose quite a challenge for him in middle school.

For most students with learning disabilities, the educational emphasis for written language is on the development and use of organizational and metacognitive skills. From the first paragraph a child writes to a major paper written by a college student, the ability to organize and sequence thoughts, present a logical, cohesive text, and review and edit writing is critical. Word processors and spell-check programs are used often by students with learning disabilities to address mechanical and handwriting problems, but the words chosen and the structure of the writing still must come from the students themselves.

Because many students with learning disabilities approach writing tasks without a plan, instructional techniques often include providing students with a series of steps to follow as guidelines for writing. Some techniques may be quite specific; for example, students may be taught to develop a graphic representation of their thoughts and ideas to help them organize material before they begin writing. One example is an activity called webbing or creating a concept map. In this activity, students write their main topic in the middle of their paper—for example, cats. They then draw lines from the main topic that represent different subtopics (what cats look like, what they like to eat, and how they move). Under each subtopic, the student writes notes or words related directly to it (for example, soft, furry, long or short hair, different colors). Now the student can use this web to help write the paper: Each subtopic can represent a paragraph, and only related information will be included in the text (see Figure 4.3). Although the web example in the figure was generated by computer, Sturm and Rankin-Erikson (2002) found that hand-drawn concept maps, as well as those generated using Inspiration software, were effective in increasing the quality of writing of eighth-grade students. Other techniques may be more general so that they can be used in a variety of writing contexts, and they may include steps for planning, checking, and revising writing. Graham, Harris, and Larsen (2001) present a series of guiding principles for teachers to use when planning instruction in written language for classes that include students with learning disabilities. A summary of these principles may be found in the Teaching Strategies box entitled, "Six Principles for Writing Instruction" on page 140.

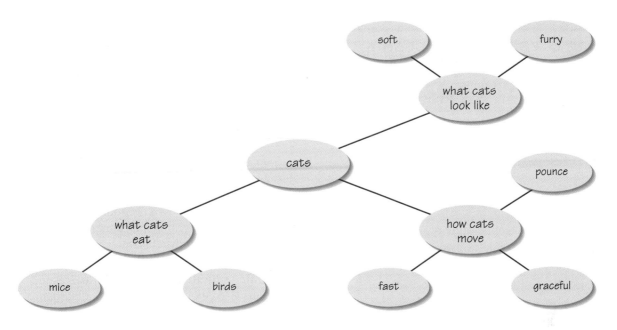

Figure 4.3

Webbing

● *Mathematics*   Although, in general, difficulties in math do not receive the same attention as problems in reading and language arts, students with learning disabilities often have a number of problems in this area. Specific problem areas include difficulty understanding size and spatial relationships and concepts related to direction, place value, decimals, fractions, and time and difficulty remembering math facts (Lerner, 1993). Remembering and correctly applying the steps to mathematical algorithms (for example, how to divide) and reading and solving word problems are significant problem areas (Cawley et al., 1996; Harris, Miller, & Mercer, 1995). Many students with disabilities use concrete and simple approaches to solving math problems (for example, counting) rather than more abstract, cognitive strategies (Jimenez Gonzalez & Garcia Espinel, 2002). Like all students, many students also make simple computational errors because of inattention to the operation sign, incorrect alignment of problems, omission of steps in the algorithm, or not checking or reviewing work.

Many students with learning disabilities approach math skills as a series of unrelated memory tasks (Engelmann, Carnine, & Steely, 1991). Because of the rapid presentation of skills in most math curricula and the early and extensive memory requirements, students who have difficulty conceptualizing the process or learning the facts just try to get through whatever skill is being worked on at the time. Let's look at an elementary classroom for a typical example of a problem that a student with learning disabilities might have in math. The teacher, Mr. Hernandez, has been teaching the students single-digit subtraction for two weeks. Jimmy, the little boy with a learning disability, understands the process of putting out markers for the big number and then taking away the same number of markers as the smaller number. Mr. Hernandez gives a test, and Jimmy completes only five of the twenty problems, but he gets them correct. Now Mr. Hernandez decides it's time for review, and he gives the students a worksheet with addition and subtraction facts on it. What do you think

Teaching Strategies & Accommodations

Six Principles for Writing Instruction

1. **Provide effective writing instruction.** Effective writing instruction consists of many components, including:

   a. a supportive and literate classroom environment

   b. daily practice on a range of writing tasks

   c. teacher modeling and direct instruction of writing skills

   d. teacher/student conferences

   e. cooperative learning opportunities for planning, drafting, and editing written products

   f. sharing written work with the class, careful assessment

   g. follow-up instruction and feedback

   h. integrating writing activities across the curriculum

2. **Tailor writing instruction to meet needs of individual children.** Adaptations may include student-specific topics for instruction, one-to-one supplemental instruction, and adapting task requirements (for example, length of writing assignment).

3. **Intervene early.** Recent research suggests that early intervention in handwriting and spelling skills can have positive effects on the quality and quantity of written compositions.

4. **Expect that each child will learn to write.** Research suggests that the teacher's expectations of a child's competency, coupled with supportive and positive classroom strategies, can facilitate the writing performance of students with learning disabilities.

5. **Identify and address academic and non-academic stumbling blocks.** Task-related behaviors (for example, attention, disorganization) as well as behavioral or emotional concerns may require intervention in order to promote positive and productive writing experiences.

6. **Take advantage of technological tools for writing.** Teachers can work with technology to both encourage and teach writing to students with learning disabilities. Simply using a word processor may help some children, whereas others may benefit from more sophisticated software used to teach planning, composition, or editing.

Source: Graham, S., Harris, K. R., & Larsen, L. (2001). Adapted from Prevention and intervention of writing difficulties for students with learning disabilities. *Learning Disabilities Research and Practice*, *16*, (44–48). Reprinted by permission of Lawrence Erlbaum Associates, Inc.

Jimmy does with all of his problems? He puts out markers for the big numbers and takes away the same number of markers as the smaller numbers. Perhaps Jimmy didn't attend to the signs. Mr. Hernandez points out to Jimmy that some of the signs are addition signs. Jimmy looks at him in confusion. Addition? What is that?

It is important to review and assess math concepts and strategies constantly so that students can build on previous skills.

Many students, like Jimmy, are just following the pattern of the week. It is important to constantly review and assess concepts and strategies for students with learning disabilities. It is likely that unless Mr. Hernandez reviews, has Jimmy practice, and encourages him to discriminate between operations, subtraction will become as vague a concept to Jimmy as addition is now. When teaching students with learning disabilities, teachers should always keep in mind the learning characteristics of their students and try to tailor instruction accordingly. Instruction in word problems, for example, should begin early with very simple problems; key words or information should be highlighted to

Facts	Pegword Associations	Visual Associations	Elaborations
$3 \times 3 = 9$	Tree and tree on a line		Remember the 2 trees sitting on a line.
$3 \times 4 = 12$	Tree with a door for an elf		Who would live in a tree with a door? An elf who bakes cookies, of course, as in the TV commercial.

Figure 4.4

Using Pegwords to Teach Multiplication Facts

Source: D. K. Wood & A. R. Frank (2000). Using memory-enhancing strategies to learn multiplication facts. *Teaching Exceptional Children 32* (5), 78–82.

help students identify what they need to solve the problem. Later, students can be taught to identify this information themselves. Consider also the importance of certain memory tasks. Students may be able to remember some math facts and may learn all of them if they are not forced into a timeframe—most students with learning disabilities aren't going to be able to learn the first three multiplication tables overnight.

One strategy, the use of **pegwords**, has become popular for teaching multiplication facts and has a body of supporting research (Greene, 1999; Mastropieri & Scruggs, 1991; Wood, Frank, & Wacker, 1998). A pegword is a word that rhymes with a number and is used in association with a picture to assist a student in remembering. For example, the number three has the pegword *tree,* which is presented with a picture of a tree. The multiplication fact "$3 \times 3 = 9$" is represented by the pegword phrase "Tree and tree on a line" and by a picture of two trees with a line underneath. Students must first learn the pegwords and visual symbols associated with each number. Then flashcards containing the math facts and pegword symbols are presented to the students (Wood & Frank, 2000). See Figure 4.4 for an example.

Current recommendations for instruction in mathematics include beginning your teaching, even of complex concepts, at the concrete level (materials that can be held and moved), then gradually moving to the semiconcrete level (pictures or graphics), and finally moving to the abstract level (numbers only) (Harris, Miller, & Mercer, 1995; Mercer & Mercer, 1993b). It is important for teachers to realize that advanced mathematical concepts, such as decimals, may take much more time to teach than they anticipate (Woodward, Baxter, & Robinson, 1999). For instruction in algorithms, word problems, and complex functions, the use of step-by-step written plans, or strategies for students to follow, helps them develop organization, memory, and evaluation skills. Instruction in mathathics can move from presenting simple algorithms for addition or subtraction to presenting more complex skills, such as solving algebraic equations (Maccini & Hughes, 2000; Mercer & Miller, 1992; Montague, Warger, & Morgan, 2000). Figure 4.5 presents one strategy for teaching mathematics.

Mathematics instruction for students with learning disabilities should move from concrete, to semiconcrete, to abstract levels.

STAR Strategy

1. **S**earch the word problem.
   a) Read the problem carefully.
   b) Ask yourself questions: "What facts do I know?" "What do I need to find?"
   c) Write down facts.

2. **T**ranslate the words into an equation in picture form.
   a) Choose a variable.
   b) Identify the operation(s).
   c) Represent the problem with the Algebra Lab Gear (CONCRETE APPLICATION).
      Draw a picture of the representation (SEMICONCRETE APPLICATION).
      Write an algebraic equation (ABSTRACT APPLICATION).

3. **A**nswer the problem.

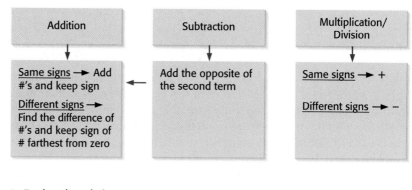

4. **R**eview the solution.
   a) Reread the problem.
   b) Ask question, "Does the answer make sense? Why?"
   c) Check answer.

Figure 4.5

Star Strategy

Source: P. Maccini & C. A. Hughes (2000). Effects of a problem-solving strategy on the introductory algebra performance of secondary students with learning disabilities. *Learning Disabilities and Practice, 15,* 10–21.

Learning Disabilities and Social and Emotional Development

Although you may typically think of students with learning disabilities as individuals who have difficulty in academic tasks, it is important to realize that most social behaviors also involve learning. The characteristics that interfere with a student's acquisition of reading or writing skills can also interfere with his or her ability to acquire or interpret social behaviors (Kavale & Forness, 1996). For example, individuals may have difficulties correctly interpreting or responding to social situations, reading social cues, acting impulsively without identifying the consequences of behavior or recognizing the feelings and concerns of others (Bryan, 1991; Carlson, 1987; Schumaker & Hazel, 1984). The individual who has difficulty identifying important information in academic work may also experience difficulty identifying important information in social situations. If a student has problems monitoring and evaluating his performance in spelling, he may also experience problems evaluating and adjusting his behavior on a date, in the classroom, or in the library.

Students with learning disabilities may have difficulty acquiring and interpreting social behaviors.

Normal variation makes it hard to tell which children will develop learning disabilities (Tom Pettyman/PhotoEdit)

Certainly, not *all* students with learning disabilities have problems with social behavior; however, many students with learning disabilities have problems relating to others and behaving acceptably at school. It is important to note that although some difficulties in social behavior may be related to learning characteristics, still others may be tied more directly to academic failure. The 16-year-old reading on the second-grade level may search for attention, acceptance, and control by engaging in inappropriate or even antisocial behavior. The search for a peer group, susceptibility to peer pressure, and problems anticipating consequences of actions may all contribute to the fact that adolescents with learning disabilities are often considered at risk for juvenile delinquency. Studies suggest that over half of the adolescents in the juvenile justice system have a disability—including learning disabilities (Bullis et al., 2002).

Having difficulty in academic work may also cause emotional distress. Of most concern is the self-esteem of students with learning disabilities. Research suggests that students with learning disabilities may not perceive themselves in a positive way—their self-esteem is lower than those of children without learning disabilities (Bryan, 1991; Vaughn, 1991). It has long been hypothesized that educational settings influence students' self-concept, and that pulling out children for specialized instruction would negatively affect children's perceptions of themselves. In a recent analysis of studies that compared students' self-concepts, Elbaum (2002) found that there were no predictable relationships between placement and self-concept in children with learning disabilities. Some children felt better when they received support services in the general education classroom, and some preferred going to a resource setting. Results such as these serve to emphasize, once again, the importance of looking at each individual child's needs when planning for instruction.

Although not all students with learning disabilities have low self-esteem, it certainly is understandable that an individual who must confront his or her disability on a daily basis would have difficulty feeling good about himself or herself, particularly in the area of personal competence.

Think for a moment about something you do not do well. Perhaps it is singing. If you really don't sing well, you may just avoid singing in public and it may present no real problem for you. What if, however, you had to sing every day, in front of all your friends? Not only do you have to sing in front of them, but you will receive a grade in singing. You've really tried, but you just can't carry a tune. Soon, all your friends are singing Mozart and you are still trying to get the scales right. Can you imagine how you would behave or feel in that situation? Perhaps you would begin to look for ways to avoid singing (lots of sore throats) or skip school altogether. You also might think of ways to avoid interacting with your friends, since you are so obviously different, and try to find other, nonsinging friends. Or, maybe, you would say you just didn't care—you never really wanted to sing anyway.

If we substitute reading or math for singing in the preceding story, you may understand how students with learning disabilities often feel. It may also help you as a teacher recognize the need to identify and develop your students' strengths as well as work on remediating their skill deficits. In addition, it may inspire you to think of ways to make school a positive experience for students, including ways to facilitate enjoyable and constructive interactions between the student or students with a learning disability and other students in the class. Seidel and Vaughn (1991) found that students with learning disabilities who dropped out of school reported strong feelings of social alienation and an absence of attachment to either teachers or classmates while they attended school. By demonstrating positive attitudes and encouraging positive interaction in the classroom, teachers may not only be helping students with learning disabilities feel better about themselves, they may be helping to keep them in school as well.

As you read through all the characteristics of individuals with learning disabilities, perhaps you thought, "Wow, I have difficulty with my organizational skills" or "My five-year-old reverses letters." It is very common to see your self, your parent, or your child in almost any description of individuals with learning disabilities—Why? Because we've looked at all the basic learning processes and academic skills—and, as we said earlier, all learning ability is on a continuum. Very few people are perfectly efficient learning machines, and not everyone relies on the same skills to learn information well.

❓ Pause and Reflect

What characteristics did you see that reflect your own learning characteristics or those of your students? Can you identify things you've done either as a student or a teacher to address those specific learning characteristics? ●

Teaching Strategies and Accommodations

How to assess and teach students with learning disabilities is a question that has been asked and debated for the past four decades. Many different philosophies can be found in the variety of educational programs for students with learning disabilities. In this section, we present assessment and teaching procedures that reflect what research has suggested to be best practice in the field. We will look at two major instructional approaches: direct instruction of specific skills and strategy instruction. Teaching models combining direct instruction and strategy instruction appear to be the most effective model for students with learning disabilities (Swanson, 1999). When integrated, these approaches reflect a similar philosophy about how students should be taught (direct instruction) and skills students should be taught (strategy instruction). We also will look at the instruction of support skills for students with learning disabilities, reflect on considerations for culturally diverse populations, and look at specific recommendations for adapting materials and presentations for students with learning disabilities.

Assessment for Teaching

There are two major purposes for assessment of students with learning disabilities. First, we assess in order to *identify* students who need special services and to determine the placement that best suits each child. Recall that we discussed this process in Chapter 1. Next we assess in order to *plan* the student's instructional program—to answer the question "What do I teach?" Assessment also allows us to evaluate the effectiveness of the program and the progress that the student is making; in fact, it can serve a variety of purposes.

● *Formal Assessment*   **Formal assessment** involves the use of standardized tests, the results of which can be used to compare the student's performance with that of his or her same-age peers. These tests assess the student's performance in math, reading, and several basic skill areas, and yield scores that reveal grade level and standing relative to other students. Achievement tests are used to document grade level of academic performance so that one can determine if a discrepancy exists between achievement and ability.

Although the information yielded by these tests may be useful in diagnostic contexts, it is not detailed or specific enough to provide a foundation for instructional planning. For that purpose, many teachers rely on informal measures.

● *Informal Assessment*   **Informal assessment** refers to direct measures of student performance and student progress in academic or behavioral tasks. There are many ways for a teacher to obtain information using informal assessment. Among them are *observations* of the student's work habits—for example, identifying the amount of time a child is able to pay attention to a task or activity. Observations can provide some information about why the child is unable to do well in certain tasks. For example, you might notice that a child works very rapidly on certain tasks and never reflects on or checks his or her work. You may notice that the child spends large amounts of time playing with the buttons on his or her shirt, or writing, erasing, and rewriting his or her words. This information may help you target specific areas for intervention.

Observations can also help prepare students to move into regular classroom settings. Because classroom teachers may have specific behavioral or learning requirements, the special education teacher or another professional can conduct an informal observation of the regular classroom into which the child will be placed. By noting specific requirements, such as length of seatwork time, types of tests, and behavior rules and requirements, the special education teacher can prepare the student for his move in a more effective manner. If Les is accustomed to sitting in his seat for a maximum of five minutes, and the classroom teacher usually has the students doing twenty minutes of seatwork at a time, it may be important to target longer in-seat behavior and increase sustained attention for instruction before Les makes the move. Figure 4.6 provides an example of an interview form used by a special education resource teacher to help her plan instruction for one of her students.

ASSESSMENT OF MAINSTREAMED ENVIRONMENT
TEACHER INTERVIEW

Teacher Sara Walker

Class Science 6th Grade

How much time are students required to listen to lecture or general instruction?
Generally the first 10-15 minutes of class is lecture or instruction.

How much in-class reading is required? What is the nature of the reading material?
A textbook is not used. In-class reading would consist of worksheets, dictionary, and encyclopedias (research materials). This is done daily for most of the class period—around 30 minutes.

What is the nature of classroom activities? (cooperative learning, independent work, discussion, pairs)
Mainly independent work and some discussion. Once a week there is a special speaker—students are required to take notes on speakers. Definitions or notes for science are often given during Lang. Arts period. Question: How much assistance do you give? Whatever is needed—I can meet with students at recess and before school.

How much homework is required and what is the nature of it?
At the beginning of the 4-week unit, a packet of assignments is given to students with a list of due dates. What is not completed in class should be completed for homework. Assignments are explained all on the first day of the 4 weeks. Assignments consist of wordfinds with unit vocab, research projects, essays or papers, labeling diagrams, answering questions. Students find answers from resources in room.

Do you assign projects or long-term assignments, and if so, how much structure or guidance is given?
(see above) In the beginning, teacher gives dates and explains expectations. Students are left on their own to complete them throughout the 4 weeks. (Some time is spent working in class.) On the day the assignment is done, students present them in class or teacher leads a discussion.

Do you give a final test at the end of the four-week unit?
No—grades are based on accuracy, punctuality, etc. of all assignments.

What are your behavior expectations?
That students are responsible and can work independently. Students should turn in assignments on time. Students work on tasks during class and participate in discussion. Students can move freely about the room without disrupting others.

Figure 4.6

Assessment of Mainstreamed Environment: Teacher Interview

Source: Kim Phillips (1993). Assessment of mainstreamed environment. Columbia, SC: Rosewood Elementary School, unpublished materials. Used by permission of the author.

Teachers can also use an observation form like this to target suggestions for the regular classroom teacher to use. Once differences between the classroom requirements and the abilities of the student have been identified, the special education teacher can suggest modifications to the classroom teacher to help the student gradually learn the behaviors necessary for successful classroom performance.

A teacher can also analyze a student's work for error patterns by using **informal inventories** of reading and mathematics skills and teacher-made tests based on the classroom curriculum (Lerner, 1993). Informal inventories consist of a series of sequential passages or excerpts, on different grade levels, that are usually taken from several curricula (Wallace, Larsen, & Elksnin, 1992). Research supports the importance of this type of assessment, also called **curriculum-based measurement (CBM)**, for student performance. Stecker and Fuchs (2000) found that when teachers used students' own curriculum-based measures to plan instruction, students performed significantly better than if more general informal measures were used. By using the informal curriculum-based assessment to assess a child's reading, writing, or math skills, the teacher can observe how the child approaches the task as well as the specific types of difficulties he or she is experiencing. For example, the teacher may note that a child misreads all words with a double vowel combination in the middle or never regroups when a zero is in a subtraction problem. Teachers should take frequent, if not daily, performance measures to evaluate how students are succeeding in the curriculum, and to know when to intensify or modify instruction.

> Using informal inventories, teachers observe how children approach classroom tasks.

Teaching Strategies & Accommodations

Designing Direct Instruction Programs in Reading

The following six steps may be used for designing direct instruction programs in reading:

1. Identify specific objectives based on importance of skills.

2. Whenever possible, develop strategies or plans for students to follow in accomplishing specific objectives (such as a strategy for decoding specific types of words).

3. Develop teaching formats and procedures before instruction begins; present only one concept at a time during each lesson.

4. Select examples for instruction; the role of examples is critical in direct instruction. If a concept is being taught, examples are used to teach students the critical attributes of the concept (for example, what makes a sentence

a sentence); if a skill or strategy is being taught, examples are used to teach when and how to use the skill and to provide practice and demonstration of skill application.

5. Sequence skills carefully before instruction; when presented with a new skill, students must know needed preskills. Other sequencing guidelines are based on the importance of the skill, the difficulty of the skill, and on reducing the potential for confusion between the new skill and other skills.

6. Provide sufficient opportunities for skill practice and continually review previous learning.

Source: D. Carnine, J. Silbert, & E. J. Kameenui, (1990). Adapted from *Direct instruction reading,* (3rd ed.). Copyright © 1990. Upper Saddle River, NJ.: Prentice-Hall, Inc.

Direct Instruction

In direct instruction, specific academic skills are taught using proven techniques.

The term *direct* is used in this text to refer to a philosophy and approach to teaching students with learning disabilities. **Direct instruction** commonly refers to (1) the identification and instruction of specific academic skills and (2) the use of teaching techniques that have been empirically demonstrated to be effective with students with learning difficulties. The identification and instruction of specific skills may seem to be a fairly obvious approach to teaching, but it represents a departure from many popular teaching approaches. The philosophy behind direct instruction is that any specific processing disabilities the child demonstrates can be managed through effective teaching procedures and that the most efficient use of instructional time is to focus on the academic skills in need of remediation (see the preceding Teaching Strategies box entitled, "Designing Direct Instruction Programs in Reading").

Direct instruction teaching methods address the organization and presentation of instruction. The approach is very teacher-directed and includes an initial presentation based on the teacher first *modeling* the skill or response, then providing guided practice (*leading*), and, finally, eliciting independent student responses (*testing*). Direct instruction provides students with positive examples of a response or strategy. Exposure to positive examples promotes the probability of correct responding and helps to eliminate confusion related to poor directions or student misinterpretation of the task. The modeling and leading steps are eliminated as instruction in a specific skill progresses (Engelmann & Hanner,

Teaching Strategies & Accommodations

Presentation Techniques for Direct Instruction

The direct instruction approach includes a number of presentation techniques designed to maximize student attention and involvement in learning (Lewis, 1993). Some of these presentation techniques include:

1. **Small-group instruction.** Recommendations include seating students in a small semicircle, facing the teacher.

2. **Using response signals.** The teacher chooses a signal that indicates it is time to respond (this could be a slight tap on the board or table or a snap of the fingers). The signal allows the teacher to delay the students' responses for a few seconds to encourage time to think about or reflect on the response. This delay or pause is called *wait time.*

3. **Choral or unison responding.** When using the model–lead–test format, the teacher can have the whole group answer together during guided practice and independent student response time. Individuals' responses would then follow unison responses. Unison responding helps to maintain students' attention, allows for more opportunities for practice, and provides numerous models of correct responding.

4. **Providing corrective feedback.** During instruction, errors are corrected immediately by modeling and then retesting responses; students also are praised when they make correct responses.

5. **Pacing.** Lessons are presented at a fairly rapid pace to maintain students' attention and interest in the lesson (Carnine, Silbert, & Kameenui, 1990; Engelmann & Carnine, 1982; Engelmann & Hanner, 1982).

LESSON 107

READING VOCABULARY
Do not touch small letters.
Get ready to read all the words on this page
without making a mistake.

TASK 1   Sound out first

a. Touch the ball for **best**. Sound it out.
Get ready. Quickly touch **b, e, s, t** as the
children say *beeessst*.

b. What word? (Signal.) *Best*. Yes, **best**.

c. Repeat task until firm.

best

ing

TASK 2   ing words

a. Point to **ing**. When these letters are
together, they usually say **ing**.

b. What do these letters usually say? (Signal.)
ing. Yes, **ing**. Repeat until firm.

c. Point to the words. These are words you
already know. See if you can read them
when they look this way.

d. Point to **ing** in **thing**. What do these letters
say? (Signal.) *ing*.

e. Touch the ball for **thing**. Read the fast way.
Get ready. (Signal.) *Thing*. Yes,
thing.

f. Repeat *d* and *e* for **looking, rēading**, and
something.

g. Repeat the series of words until firm.

thing

looking

rēading

something

Figure 4.7

Excerpt from Reading
Mastery II: Fast Cycle.

Source: Siegfried Engelmann
and Elaine C. Bruner (1995).
Reading Mastery II: Fast cycle,
Rainbow Edition, Presentation
Book C, p. 165. © 1995,
McGraw-Hill. Reprinted with
permission.

1982). See the Teaching Strategies box entitled, "Presentation Techniques for Direct Instruction."

Direct instruction appears to be the most effective means of teaching students with learning disabilities (Adams & Engelmann, 1996; Rosenshine & Stevens, 1986). Some of the commercial programs based on this approach include Corrective Reading—Revised (Engelmann et al., 1999) and Reading Mastery Plus (Engelmann et al., 2002). Figure 4.7 is an excerpt from Reading Mastery II, Fast Cycle, a direct instruction program (Engelmann & Bruner, 1995). All the commercial direct instruction programs contain specific scripted lessons for teachers and incorporate the teaching techniques just described. Other materials contain direct instruction techniques, including a variety of computer software and multimedia and videodisk programs. These programs use direct instruction to involve students in more active learning (Hayden, Gersten, & Carnine, 1992).

For more information on direct instruction programs and techniques, go to the National Institute for Direct Instruction's website at **http://www.nifdi.org**.

Strategy Instruction

A strategy can be defined as a set of responses that are organized to perform an activity or solve a problem (Swanson, 1993). In this section we will focus primarily on the strategy approaches used most often by teachers of students with learning disabilities. In addition to academic skills instruction, we will see that strategies are also used to teach specialized skills, adaptive skills, and life skills.

A **strategy instruction** approach to teaching students with learning disabilities involves first breaking down the skills involved in a task or problem—usually a procedure such as writing a paper—into a set of sequential steps. The steps are prepared so that the student may read or, later, memorize them in order to perform the skill correctly. Some strategies are developed so that the first letters of all the steps form an acronym to help students remember the purpose of the strategy and the steps involved (recall the STAR Strategy in Figure 4.6). Many strategies also include decision-making or evaluative components designed to help students use metacognitive skills (Deshler et al., 1983).

Strategy training involves more than just the presentation of steps, however. Careful assessment and direct instruction, including sufficient opportunities to practice the strategy, are considered essential in most strategy instruction. Students should first observe how to use the strategy, practice, and receive feedback before attempting to use it on their own. Strategies have been developed to address the needs of students with learning disabilities in a wide range of areas. Test-taking skills, study skills, reading comprehension, written composition, anger control, and math problem solving are all possible target areas for strategies. Some research suggests that the use of strategy instruction can be an important learning tool for students with learning disabilities. For example, elementary and secondary students with learning disabilities are found to write more reflective, complex, and well-written essays when using writing strategies (De La Paz & Graham, 1997; De La Paz et al., 2000). Students with disabilities who were taught to use strategies to complete math word problems improved their ability to complete the problem and arrive at the correct answer (Owen & Fuchs, 2002). Learning strategies have even been integrated successfully with some computer software to assist in the decision-making and problem-solving skills of older students with reading disabilities (Hollingsworth & Woodward, 1993).

The strategy instruction approach is intuitively appealing to educators. It teaches specific skills in a manner that controls for potential problems in a student's ability to identify important information or steps, organizes the steps for the student, provides a continual prompt for remembering, breaks the task into its component parts, and often focuses on metacognitive skills. In addition, we know that many students with learning disabilities do not use strategies or plans when approaching academic tasks. An important question, however, is whether or not students with disabilities can apply strategies they've learned in multiple settings. Although teachers often develop their own strategies, a number of commercially developed strategies and curricula based on strategies are available. One of the most well-known curricula designed for students with learning disabilities is the Learning Strategies Curriculum, which was developed at the University of Kansas Institute for Research in Learning Disabilities. This curriculum, which continues to expand, contains elaborate strategies and comprehensive procedures for teaching students ways to acquire information through skills such as paraphrasing, ways to store information through skills such as listening and notetaking, and ways to demonstrate knowledge through skills such as writing paragraphs and taking tests (Schumaker & Lyerla, 1991).

> Strategy instruction teaches specific skills by organizing steps, providing prompts, and focusing on metacognitive skills.

Each component of the Learning Strategies Curriculum contains a sequence of steps for learners to follow and practice so they can perform the tasks. Teachers are provided with a series of specific guidelines for teaching students how to perform these strategies. As we usually see with strategy instruction, students are taught not only specific behaviors but also how to evaluate and monitor their performance.

For examples and specific information on teaching the Learning Strategies Curriculum, visit the website at **http://www.ku_crl.org/iei/sim/lscurriculum.html**.

Special Skills Instruction

Many students with learning disabilities may receive instruction in specialized skills such as study skills or social skills. Instruction in these skills may be the only type of service required by some students with learning disabilities; for others it may be one component of a more comprehensive set of support services. Sometimes special skills instruction is incorporated into the regular classroom curriculum; other times, these skills are taught in special education settings—for example, in a resource class. This section gives an overview of instructional approaches to teaching study and social skills.

● *Study Skills*   As we have seen throughout this chapter, the difficulties experienced by many students with learning disabilities revolve around the ability to receive, process, and express information effectively. Study skills instruction addresses these areas as they relate directly to classroom activities. The purpose of teaching study skills is to give the student a set of tools for performing required classroom activities, not to teach the content of a specific course. Study skills instruction for students with learning disabilities might include teaching techniques for reading and remembering material in content-area texts, taking and reviewing notes, taking essay or multiple-choice tests, and preparing reports or projects. Students learn and practice these skills on materials from a variety of content areas. Study skills are frequently taught through the use of strategy training. The strategies are usually general enough so that they can be applied to many different types of tasks and content areas. For example, a strategy taught for taking an essay exam should work in any type of essay exam (English, history, science, or psychology). Other instructional techniques include teaching students to use graphic aids, such as charts, to apply time management and general organization aids to study behavior; to use structure or content outlines for taking notes; and to use alternative tools, such as tape recorders and computers (Smith, Finn, & Dowdy, 1993).

> Study skills instruction provides practice on different types of work so that students can use the skills in many classes.

As you learned in the previous section, curricula such as the Learning Strategies Curriculum include strategies for teaching study skills, and new strategies are continually being developed and evaluated. For example, Hughes et al. (2002) found that a new strategy for completing homework assignments (the PROJECT strategy) was very effective in giving adolescents a plan to use with weekly schedules and assignments across classes. Strategies such as these help to address the organizational challenges that are particularly problematic in middle and high school because of the number of courses, books, and assignments. Of course, a published curriculum is not necessary to teach study skills. If students are receiving a special course or series of classes in study skills, however, it is definitely helpful for the teacher to have an organized plan of instruction. Many teachers of students with learning disabilities develop original study skills curricula by drawing on existing programs and research and then adapt-

Technology Focus

Instructional Technology in the Classroom

Although computers in our classrooms have become commonplace, many of us still have questions about ways to use instructional technology with and for students with disabilities. We will look at three basic areas: technology access, establishing a purpose, and meeting individual student needs. After looking at these three areas, you will have some ideas on preparing a plan for integrating technology into a classroom with students with and without disabilities.

Instructional technology provides students with learning disabilities with many tools for learning (Al Campanie/ The Image Works)

TECHNOLOGY ACCESS

The first step in integrating instructional technology is to scan the environment (Male, 1997) to determine the access your students will have to computers. The first question to ask is how many computers are in your class. Do you have one, two, or enough for all students? Access also will depend on the amount of time children have access to the computers. Does each student get 30 minutes a day, 1 hour a week, or 15 minutes whenever all other work is completed? What resources are available to support instructional technology? Money for specific programs is always an issue, although many wonderful learning opportunities can be created with little or no outside financial support. Access to the Internet also falls in this category. Once you recognize how often your students have access to technology, you may determine if you can incorporate instructional technology into your classroom as a regular part of your curriculum for all students, as a special teaching or practice session for one or two children, or as a once-a-week extension of a cooperative learning activity.

ESTABLISH A PURPOSE AND INTEGRATE APPROPRIATE TECHNOLOGY

When you use technology for students with disabilities, it is important that you keep these basic

principles of instruction in mind. Although technology can be used extensively to allow students to explore and discover new information, if it is used for initial instruction, practice, or evaluation, it must reflect appropriate teaching practices, such as direct instruction. Alessi and Trollop (2001) identified and described eight specific types of technology. These are listed below, with a brief description of what they are and how they are used.

1. **Tutorials.** Tutorials are used to give the student information—in other words, to teach something. They should include a modeling component and provide guided practice.

2. **Hypermedia.** Hypermedia consists of providing access through a variety of navigational tools to a substantial database related to a specific topic. Hypermedia often is used to provide students with opportunities for topical discovery and the independent acquisition of information.

3. **Drills.** Drills are repeated opportunities for practice. Like the worksheets of old, drills on a computer can be a boring series of problems. Technology does, however, offer options for more interesting drill or practice activities, including those that provide corrective feedback to the student.

4. **Simulations.** Simulations are models of an activity or experience that allow students to learn through participation. Simulations can be used to establish a purpose for learning, to acquire a new skill, or to practice or apply a skill that has already been learned.

5. **Games.** Games in instructional technology have the same definition as games in a child's playroom. They are activities designed to be fun, to invoke a competitive spirit, and to establish a goal for the student to reach. Games can be used in all parts of the learning process, and are most often used to practice or apply skills or knowledge.

6. **Tools and open-ended learning environments.** A number of programs teach students to use technological tools for such things as graphing, organizing, and drawing. Students can use this technology to apply, illustrate, and practice skills, or to develop aids to new learning by developing outlines, etc.

7. **Tests.** The purpose of tests is to assess mastery. Tests given on the computer can be disguised in game formats or simulations, and may include learning tools such as providing corrective feedback. Many new programs can be very helpful to teachers by recording and graphing data on each student.

8. **Web-based learning.** Web-based learning includes everything from sending e-mail, to participating in discussion groups, to hypermedia. The purposes also vary widely, focusing more on group or individual exploration of topics than on direct instruction of new skills (Alessi & Trollop, 2001).

MEETING INDIVIDUAL STUDENT NEEDS

When technology is integrated in the curriculum, it is important to address the individual needs of students with disabilities. Gardner and Edyburn (2000) suggest that two of the important questions teachers should ask are:

1. What prerequisite skills and knowledge are required for my students to use the program?

2. Will special instructional strategies be required for my students to successfully use the program? (p. 207)

Special instructional strategies related to content may include teaching students specific steps to follow to evaluate their writing performance before presenting them with a program that prompts self-evaluation. Teachers must devote time to teaching students how to use a particular program. For students with disabilities, a series of commands, arrows, and several sets of directions can be overwhelming and confusing. Gardner and Edyburn (2000) suggest developing a strategy sheet or a written set of steps so that students have procedural prompts to guide them after instruction.

The following are websites with assistance, examples, and instructions for developing instructional technology:

TrackStar at http//hprtec.org/track

Web Toolboxes at http://www.ed.sc.edu/caw/toolbox.html

Federal search engine or guide to a range of educational resources (including some free materials) at http://www.thegateway.org

ing and applying those objectives and instructional techniques to the specific needs of their students. One of the most important goals of study skills instruction is to provide extensive practice on different types of work and to prompt the students to use the skills in other classes. Boyle and Weishaar (2001) found that high-school students learning a strategy for notetaking in content classes needed instruction and practice in using the strategy before applying it in their classes. These activities help to ensure that students will actually use the skills to do their coursework, which, of course, is the purpose of study skills instruction.

● *Social Skills*   As we've seen, some students with learning disabilities experience difficulties in emotional and social adjustment. Educators are concerned about the effects of these difficulties on the behavior and adjustment of young adults with learning disabilities.

Although differences in the social behavior and social skills of students with learning disabilities have been documented over the years, instruction or training in social skills is often neglected. It is hard enough to find time to provide academic instruction, and it may be difficult to justify teaching social skills in lieu of reading or biology. Another barrier to social skills instruction is the equivocal empirical support for its effectiveness. Reviews of social skills training programs suggest that few programs have resulted in any positive change in students' social performance or social acceptance (McIntosh, Vaughn, & Zaragoza, 1991). Because of the perceived need to teach social skills to students with learning disabilities, however, research continues in two major areas: what skills should be taught and how to teach the skills so students will be able to generalize them to real-life situations.

Many commercial curricula include or focus on social skills. It is important, however, for teachers to observe the student and his or her surroundings carefully before selecting skills for instruction. Skills necessary for success in a certain peer group or work setting may not be identified in a certain curriculum. For example, certain terms, forms of address, postures, and verbal skills will differ across regions, ages, and settings. If these particular skills are not identified and incorporated into the curriculum, the program may not be as successful as anticipated. It is helpful to conduct informal observations that allow a comparison to be made between the skills required in the target setting and the skills displayed by the students. The differences can then be identified and additional skills or adaptations integrated into the curriculum selected.

Social skills may be taught in a separate class, as you would teach history or math, or integrated into the regular curriculum as needed. For example, a teacher may notice that Antonio is always standing by the fence during recess and may decide that he might benefit from learning to play with other children. Another teacher might learn through experience that Sheila becomes very sullen and noncompliant whenever she receives any negative feedback or correction. The teacher may decide to teach Sheila some alternative ways to deal with criticism.

Generally, social skills programs involving multiple aspects of peer and adult interaction are taught in the classroom setting. However, social skills are difficult to transfer or generalize to other settings, and there is concern that the child who learns how to take turns and respond to questions in the classroom will not perform those behaviors in other classes or in the home and community. Nonetheless, Clement-Heist, Siegel, and Gaylord-Ross (1992) found that teaching job-related social skills in the classroom environment (for example, conversation skills, giving instructions) did result in a change of behavior in the actual work setting; even

Teachers must tailor the social skills curriculum to their students' particular environment.

more change was noted when students were given additional instruction on the work site. The results of this study support the importance of teaching in the actual setting, yet also provide evidence that change can be achieved even when community-based instruction is not possible. The social skills program, like many others, includes a "homework" component that encourages students to practice the skills in real situations or settings. Most homework activities involve a recording sheet for students to identify when and how they use the skill.

Effective social skills training programs have a number of components in common, including small-group or individual instruction, long-term training programs, and procedures that show students how to guide, monitor, or evaluate their own behavior (McIntosh, Vaughn, & Zaragoza, 1991). A number of social skills training programs are available commercially. One respected curriculum is the Walker Social Skills Curriculum: The ACCESS Program (Walker et al., 1988). The procedures used in this curriculum to teach social skills related to peers, adults, and self are based on principles of direct instruction and include training in a general learning strategy. This program, like many others, also includes extensive role-playing opportunities, feedback sessions, and self-evaluation or assessment activities. As you can see, social skills are taught essentially the same way as academic skills: Students are taught the skills directly; when appropriate, they learn a problem-solving or learning strategy; and numerous opportunities are provided for them to practice and evaluate their performance.

Considerations for Culturally Diverse Learners

It is difficult to have a learning disability; it is more difficult to have a learning disability and face cultural and/or linguistic differences in a classroom setting. As teachers, we must consider how cultural and linguistic differences affect the needs of individual students with learning disabilities. The characteristics may be the same, but additional challenges are faced by the students, and teaching strategies must be evaluated accordingly. For example, if students in your classroom are not native English speakers, they may speak and understand English at different levels of proficiency. Obviously, it is important for you to know each child's level of English proficiency in both receptive and expressive language. The way you present information to students can help to facilitate their understanding of both directions and content. Many of the teaching techniques we have just described, such as using clear, simple instructions, providing examples, and using response signals or cues, are quite helpful. Holding and pointing to the material you are presenting and modeling the way to answer questions provide context by giving the student cues about what is required (Fueyo, 1997). The students will be looking to you for prompts—the direct instruction format can provide needed modeling and guided practice. The specific difficulties encountered in reading and writing by students who are learning two languages may also require adjustments in how we teach these basic skills. In fact, many bilingual special educators advocate the use of the whole-language method of instruction, or direct instruction in a literature-based context, for students who are not native English speakers. These types of instruction allow students to use relevant books in their native language and help the teacher evaluate the student's performance in higher-level thinking, planning, and conversational skills (Lopez-Reyna, 1996).

Recent research suggests that the direct instruction approach to teaching phonological awareness and other reading skills may be quite important for bilingual children (McKinney et al., 2000). Gunn and coworkers (2000) found that a structured direct instruction reading program resulted in significant gains in skills such as word attack, vocabulary, and comprehension for young Hispanic children, even those who spoke little or no English, when compared to children who did not receive the intervention. The specific skill instruction characteristic of most special education programs appears to be quite important; however, any instructional method needs to be supported with motivating literature and with extensive opportunities to read, write, and discuss content in both native and new languages to facilitate development in both (Gersten & Woodward, 1994).

Many educators suggest supplementing direct instruction with motivating literature when teaching reading for bilingual students.

Adapting Classroom Materials

One of the best ways for teachers to address the needs of students with learning disabilities is to adapt instruction and materials. Although the way a textbook or worksheet looks may seem relatively inconsequential, students with learning disabilities face many unnecessary obstacles because of the way material is presented. Adaptation of materials may be as simple as redoing a skills sheet or as complex as restructuring a curriculum. An understanding of the basic approaches to learning by students with learning disabilities is necessary, as are time, motivation, and knowledge of course content. As we look at some basic guidelines, remember that you can make a number of different adaptations. If you keep in mind that students with learning disabilities often have difficulty perceiving, attending to, and organizing important information, you can go a long way in identifying what adaptations are needed. Couple this knowledge with the basic concepts of direct instruction discussed earlier, and you will be able to teach students with learning disabilities in a more effective manner. Our focus in this section is mainly on adapting written materials typically used in regular class instruction—materials that are not developed with students with learning disabilities in mind. We will look at organizing lessons from textbooks, preparing for lecture and reading activities in content areas, and general ideas for worksheet and test construction.

Lesson plans from a teacher's manual often have to be modified.

● *Modifications for Lesson Planning* Many textbooks include teachers' manuals to assist in the presentation of instruction. Too often, however, the lessons in the manuals are brief and potentially confusing because of the amount and structure of the content. You may need to modify these lessons before you present them to the class.

The accompanying Teaching Strategies box entitled, "Strategies for Lesson Planning" offers specific suggestions for modifying your lessons for students with learning disabilities. Keep them in mind as you review manuals before planning your lessons.

● *Modifications for Lectures and Reading Assignments* In many content courses, particularly at the middle- and high-school level, the teaching format may be limited to lecturing by the teacher and independent reading by the student. Even if projects or other activities are a regular part of the class, much of the material essential for tests and passing the course comes from the student's ability to identify and organize important information from what is presented orally or in the textbook. Adaptations, therefore, focus on clarifying important information and providing a clear organizational structure.

Teaching Strategies & Accommodations

Strategies for Lesson Planning

1. *Identify all the new skills being taught in the lesson.* More than one is too many. Sequence the skills according to the hierarchy of content and choose the first one in the sequence.

2. *Identify the preskills the student needs.* If the text does not provide a review of the preskills, prepare one.

3. *Review the introduction and actual teaching part of the lesson.* A surprising number of textbooks include very little instruction.

   - Is the skill or concept clearly identified and described at the beginning of the lesson?
   - Are there plenty of positive examples of the skill or concept being taught? Are there also negative or incorrect examples that require the student to discriminate and actually identify the fundamental parts of the skill?
   - Think of a rule or cue to help the student learn the skill more efficiently.

4. *Look at the opportunities for practice presented in the manual and student text.*

   - Is there a lot of guided practice and opportunity for response before the student has to work alone? Practice with the teacher gives the student a chance to learn the skill and allows the teacher to correct any errors right away. You may have to develop some practice examples.

5. *Examine application exercises or "written practice" activities.*

   - Do the independent activities reflect the skill that was taught?
   - Are the language and reading requirements appropriate for your student?
   - Is the right amount of independent work provided? Is there enough practice to show you that the student has mastered the skill, but not so much that the amount is overwhelming?

Lectures Adaptations for lectures involve helping students with learning disabilities identify important information and take notes in an organized way. Some ways to help students do this include:

- Providing students with an advanced organizer, such as an outline of the lecture, or with some questions to read before the lecture begins. The students can review the organizer and be better prepared to listen for key information.

- Preparing a simple outline that includes major topics but has room for the students to take notes under the different headings. This will help students organize and see the relationship between various pieces of information.

- Reviewing key vocabulary before the lecture begins or writing critical information on the board or on an overhead. Specifically tell students that information written on the board is important.

- Teaching students to recognize and identify the clues used most frequently to identify important information.

- Stopping every so often and asking students to paraphrase or talk about the topic.

Advance organizers or outlines can help students identify important information in lectures and take organized notes.

Reading Assignments   Adaptations for written texts include many of the same ideas just listed. Suggestions include:

- Providing advance organizers before reading, including both outlines and questions about the materials to help students read for important content. A number of content textbooks present questions or "what you will learn" guidelines at the beginning of chapters. If these exist in your text, remember to show students how to use them.
- Reviewing, highlighting, or boxing vocabulary or facts before reading.
- Cueing students to stop reading after every paragraph or every few paragraphs to review the material. The review could be written or oral paraphrasing or answering questions prepared for the different sections of the text.
- Teaching students to develop questions about the text themselves for use during or after reading.
- Having students answer questions reviewed at the beginning of the passage, having them paraphrase, and fill in outlines or other advance organizers after they finish reading the text.
- Using other activities, such as the webbing technique discussed in the section on written language, or developing pictures or other graphic representations of content.

For students who are able to understand grade-level content but who read at a far lower grade level, interaction with the regular classroom text may be quite difficult. For these students, adaptations of content area texts may include simplifying instructional content so that the reading requirements are reduced and only key information is presented. Classroom teachers or special education consultants or resource teachers may want to prepare annotated outlines that present only essential information. In some instances, this technique may be very difficult because of the density of the text (U.S. history or chemistry, for example). Alternatives include taping the lectures, persuading someone to record the text on tape, attempting to find a simpler version of the text (some programs have two levels of textbooks), or using a peer or adult tutor to read the text.

THE IMPORTANCE OF PLACE IN HISTORY

History contains four elements: place, time, people, and story. Place comes first. Place is the scene of the action, like the scenery for a play or a movie. But place is more than scenery. Place also shapes the story. Place changes over time, and it interacts with the people who create the story. The planet Earth is the major place of our history, though the Earth is affected by other parts of the solar system. The weather and the seasons affect all of history, and more recently, outer space and space travel are a part of the story.

Most of our attention will focus on the Western Hemisphere and on North America, in particular. The two areas we will study most thoroughly are the United States and the state of South Carolina.

Figure 4.8

Modifications of Material from an Elementary Textbook

Source: Archive Vernon Huff, Jr. (1991). The history of South Carolina. In *The building of the nation.* Greenville, SC: Furma.

Figures 4.8 through 4.10 show how one teacher adapted some material from an upper-elementary-level textbook. Figure 4.8 is an excerpt from the textbook, Figure 4.9 shows the material adapted as a review, and Figure 4.10 illustrates how the material has been adapted yet again for use as an advance organizer.

● *Modifications of Worksheets and Tests*   Much evaluation and practice in the classroom takes place through written performance. The content, structure, and appearance of worksheets and tests are important because they affect the ability of students with learning disabilities to perform as well as they can. The guidelines we provide in this section are simple ones designed to call the student's attention to relevant information and to remove confusing or distracting information. They may be used when creating your own material or when adapting existing material.

Directions on tests and worksheets should be simple and clear.

| **South Carolina History**
Chapter 1: The Land
Lesson 1A | Name: _____

Date: _____ |

1. The importance of place in history

   A. History contains four elements: _____ , time, _____ , and story.

Elements of History

	time		**story**

1. **Place.** Place tells where the action or event happened. Place is important because it can affect how the action or event occurs. Place is also important because it changes over time and it can affect the people who are a part of the event.

2. _____ tells when something happened.

3. **People.** The people are involved in the action or event.

4. _____ tells about the action or event and sometimes what caused it to occur.

WORLD BANK: Lesson 1A

continental drift   story   people   time   place

Figure 4.9

Textbook Excerpt Adapted as a Review

Source: Archive Vernon Huff, Jr. (1991). The history of South Carolina. In *The building of the nation.* Greenville, SC: Furma.

Directions should be simple and clear.

- Use bold print, capital letters, or other means of highlighting important words in the directions.
- If more than one type of direction is necessary for different sections on the worksheet or test, make certain the sections are clearly separated from each other. Each set of directions should be clearly identifiable and immediately precede the related section.

South Carolina History Chapter 1: The Land Lesson 1A	Name: _____ Date: _____

1. The importance of place in history

   A. History contains four elements. _____ , time, _____ , and story.

Elements of History

place	time	people	story

   1. **Place.** Place tells where the action or event happened. Place is important because it can affect how the action or event occurs. Place is also important because it changes over time and it can affect the people who are a part of the event.

   2. **Time.** Time tells when something happened.

   3. **People.** The people are involved in the action or event.

   4. **Story.** The story tells about the action or event and sometimes what caused it to occur.

Review what you have learned

1. What are the four elements that make up history? (1A)

   a. _____   b. _____

   c. _____   d. _____

2. Name one way that place is important when we learn about history. (A1)

   _____

Figure 4.10

Textbook Excerpt Adapted as an Advance Organizer

Source: Archive Vernon Huff, Jr. (1991) The history of South Carolina. In *The building of the nation.* Greenville, SC: Furma.

The *appearance* of the material should be organized and uncluttered.

- Avoid unnecessary pictures. If a picture or graphic is necessary to answer a question (for example, a map or a graph), make sure that the questions related to the graphic are on the same page and adjacent to the questions if possible.
- Make sure all writing is clear and legible and that adequate space is provided for responses.
- Break up long tests or exams into different sections to help students organize responses (and possibly to prevent them from skipping or omitting questions). If possible, allow room for answers directly under the questions. Try to minimize the amount of page flipping the students have to do. Students do need experience in standardized test formats (for minimum competency tests, basic skills tests, or SAT exams), so specific practice in these types of tests must be provided. Understand, however, that these formats are difficult for students with learning disabilities and may need to be introduced carefully.

Although types of questions or written activities will vary depending on grade level or subject area, the *format* of the presentation is always important.

- Avoid long columns of matching items—the ones that require drawing all those lines between the items on both sides of the paper. Either use another format or break the list into sections.
- Essay questions will create problems for many students with disabilities, and some guidelines may be necessary (outline, approximate number of sentences, strategy for answering essay questions).
- Some students with poor reading and writing skills may need to have the test read to them or have the whole test or worksheet on tape so that reading and writing are not necessary.

When preparing tests or other written assignments, it is important to remember that the goal of the assessment is to evaluate the students' knowledge of the subject matter. You don't want other skill difficulties to interfere with your understanding of what each student has actually learned.

Curriculum

It is beyond the scope of this chapter to discuss curriculum in any detail; however, many educators have suggested the need to restructure curricula to present content effectively to students with learning disabilities and to encourage the development of higher-order thinking skills (Carnine, 1991). Curriculum, whether you select or develop it, should reflect the components of effective instruction, as well as sequential presentation of content. References to important elements of curriculum, such as sequence, presenting one skill at a time, examples, and structure can be found in the guidelines for direct instruction, and in the academic characteristics sections presented earlier in the text. Researchers also found that organizing curriculum around the concept of "sameness" helps students learn more effectively (Engelmann, Carnine, & Steely, 1991). The underlying principle is using the same strategy or conceptual model for approaching all tasks in a skill or content area. For example, Kinder and Bursuck (1991) suggest that a model based on organizing knowledge into a "problem–solution–effect" structure should be applied to all social studies content. In this example, students organize their notes from text and lectures according to the problem–solution–effect rubric. By trying to organize content according to a basic structure or a few sets of structures, you can reduce the memory load of students and help them organize complex information.

A number of different teaching strategies and accommodations were presented in this section. It is important to consider two major points as you reflect on your own teaching ideas and plans for the classroom. First, consider that the interaction between students' abilities and teaching strategies is very important. If students have difficulty attending to information, then you must determine how to address that attention problem in your instruction and through your accommodations. If a child is not making progress in your reading program, you must figure out why and *adjust* the way you are teaching. Second, the teaching strategies presented here reflect current research and best practice—not just for students with learning disabilities, but for many children without learning disabilities as well. Not all children require or even benefit from such structured instruction, but many do—think about the ways these instructional strategies can be integrated into general education classrooms to support childen or to present complex content.

❓ Pause and Reflect

How can you adapt your teaching methods to address such issues as distractibility? Can you think of ways you could use direct instruction or strategy instruction to teach in a specific curriculum area? ●

A Closer Look   Growing Up with Learning Disabilities

Although a learning disability can be a significant challenge, it is not necessarily an obstacle to success and accomplishments in adult life.

- Many students with learning disabilities graduate from high school with a diploma and go on to postsecondary education. However, more students with learning disabilities drop out of high school and fewer attend community colleges or four-year colleges than students without disabilities (Murray et al., 2000; Scanlon & Mellard, 2002).

- The adaptive and social skills addressed throughout school are important for those students who plan to continue their education. Social and interpersonal skills training, career exploration, self-advocacy, and the use of accommodations such as taped lectures or untimed tests are examples of approaches that should be used before and after students begin postsecondary school (Gajar, 1992; Hitchings et al., 2001).

- Recent research suggests that students with learning disabilities who held two or more jobs in high school are almost twice as likely to be working or participating in postsecondary education after graduation as those who did not work (Berry, Lindstrom, & Vovanoff, 2000). Perhaps early work experience allows students to develop skills that help promote success later in life.

- Successful adults with learning disabilities take control of what is happening to them. Showing students how to use learning tools to create change and facilitate self-reliance may increase their probability for success (Gerber, Ginsberg, & Reiff, 1992).

- Personal attributes, including self-awareness, proactivity, and perseverance, are critical factors in achieving adult success. Students entering postsecondary placements need to be able to determine what services they need, (Mull, Sitlington, & Alper, 2001; Raskind et al., 1999).

Summary

- Students with learning disabilities demonstrate a discrepancy between potential and achievement that cannot be attributed to other disabilities or to environmental or cultural factors. Although there is no single known cause of learning disabilities, internal and external factors may be involved.

- Learning disabilities affect five major cognitive processes: perception, attention, memory, metacognition, and organization. Difficulties with each of these processes can lead to problems in academic areas such as reading, language arts, and mathematics.

- The social difficulties often caused by learning disabilities may stem from problems in learning appropriate behavior, or from repeated failures in school that lead to low self-esteem, helplessness, or acting out.

- Students with learning disabilities are assessed formally and informally to determine their academic skills.

- The most widely used instructional techniques for students with learning disabilities are direct instruction, strategy instruction, and special instruction in study and social skills.

- Many classroom materials and presentations can be modified for students with learning disabilities. When these students are included in regular classrooms, general and special educators must collaborate in making the necessary modifications and providing instruction.

Key Terms

learning disabilities
discrepancy
exclusion clause
perinatal stress
learning style
perception
attention
attention deficit disorder (ADD)
attention deficit/ hyperactivity disorder (ADHD)
selective attention

memory
encoding processes
working memory
metacognition
self-monitoring
organization
cognitive style
word analysis
double deficit hypothesis
code-emphasis approach
reading fluency

reading comprehension
pragmatic language skills
functional flexibility
pegwords
formal assessment
informal assessment
informal inventories
curriculum-based measurement (CBM)
direct instruction
strategy instruction

USEFUL RESOURCES

- Assis-TECH Inc. at **http://www.irsc.org/learn_db.htm**. This site is a source for the assistive technology devices for students with learning disabilities.
- Association for Direct Instruction at **http://www.adihome.org**. This organization provides information, assistance, and support to educators interested in using direct instruction and/or ordering related materials.
- National Center for Learning Disabilities (NCLD) at 381 Park Avenue South, New York, NY 10016, (212) 545-7510.
- Lawrence Clayton (1992). *Coping with a learning disability* (New York: Rosen Publishing Group). A book for families and teens that demonstrates being a teen with a learning disability can be a positive experience. It discusses family, personal, and peer emotional reactions and provides biographies of famous people with learning disabilities as positive role models.
- *The Gram.* Newsletter of the Learning Disabilities Association (formerly ACLD), 4156 Library Road, Pittsburgh, PA 15234, (412) 341-1515. This newsletter provides information about current legislation, educational programs, and research in the area of learning disabilities.
- LD OnLine at **http://www.LDOnLine.org**. This is a comprehensive website on learning disabilities, and the official website of the Coordinated Campaign for Learning Disabilities.
- Learning Disability Resources at **http://www.eoe.uga.edu/ldcenter/research/training.html**. This site has information and resources from the Research and Training Division of the Learning Disabilities Center at the University of Georgia.
- National Center to Improve the Tools of Educators (NCITE) at 805 Lincoln Street, Eugene, OR 97403-1211, (541) 346-1646, **http://www.uoregon.edu/~ncite**. This site offers numerous publications on academic skill instruction, a curriculum, and related research.
- National Institute of Child Health and Human Development (NICHD). Contact Dr. G. Reid Lyon, National Institutes of Health, 6100 Executive Boulevard, Room 4B05, Bethesda, MD 20892, (301) 496-6591. Publications related to understanding learning disabilities, reading and learning disabilities, and other areas of research are available at this location.
- *Reading and learning disabilities.* NICHCY briefing paper, National Information Center for Youth with Disabilities, 1995, (800) 695-0285. This paper includes a look at learning disabilities in children and youth, suggestions for parents on how to help their school-age children learn, and issues for adults with reading and learning problems.
- The Division for Learning Disabilities of the Council for Exceptional Children at **http://www.TeachingLD.org**. This website provides information on conferences, research updates, and organization publications. An interesting feature is interactive forums with experts in specific areas of learning disabilities.

PORTFOLIO ACTIVITIES

1. Interview a school psychologist in a local school district or the consultant in the area of learning disabilities at your state department of education. Identify the state criteria for identifying students with learning disabilities. Compare and record the ways these criteria can be interpreted by school districts across your state.

 ✓Standards This activity will help the student meet CEC Content Standard 2: Development and Characteristics of Learners.

2. Select a lesson from a textbook in your content area. Adapt the material along the lines suggested in the text. What specific changes did you make? Who is the intended audience for your revised version of the lesson? Can you envision making these types of modifications in your classroom?

 ✓Standards This activity will help the student meet CEC Content Standard 3: Individual Learning Differences.

3. How do successful adults with learning disabilities cope with the demands of their jobs and lives? Interview an adult with a learning disability. Invite him or her to talk to your class about the strategies he or she has used to succeed in life. What types of strategies are described? How might they be used by your future students?

 ✓Standards This activity will help the student meet CEC Content Standard 3: Individual Learning Differences.

4. Why are course content, teacher presentation, and the student's place in the classroom all vital to consider when planning a class that welcomes a student with learning disabilities? Based on what you've read in this chapter and your own experience, list classroom modifications in each of these areas that would be effective for all students. Be sure to consider social aspects of the class as well as academic ones, when listing your modifications

 ✓Standards This activity can help the student meet CEC Content Standard 5: Learning Environments and Social Interactions.

 To access an electronic template for these activities, visit our website through http://www.education.college.hmco.com/students/.

5

Children with Mental Retardation

Outline

Terms and Definitions
   Intelligence and General
      Cognitive Functioning
   Adaptive Behavior
   Manifestation During the
      Developmental Period
   Classification Issues
   Prevalence
Causes of Mental Retardation
   Biomedical Factors
   Social, Behavioral, and
      Educational Factors
Characteristics of Individuals
      with Mental Retardation
   Cognitive Development
   Language Development
   Physical Development
   Social and Emotional
      Development
   Effects on the Family
Teaching Strategies and
      Accommodations
   Early Intervention
   Curriculum
   Delivery of Instruction
   Materials
   Personal and Civil Rights
SUMMARY
KEY TERMS
USEFUL RESOURCES
PORTFOLIO ACTIVITIES

Learning Objectives

After reading this chapter about students with mental retardation, the reader will:

- Describe the role of adaptive behavior in the definition of mental retardation.

- Identify and discuss some of the learning characteristics of individuals with mental retardation.

- Identify and describe the range of educational goals that may be appropriate for individuals with mental retardation.

- Examine the importance of the community as an educational setting for individuals with mental retardation.

- Describe teaching methods and materials that can be used to help students with learning disabilities achieve their learning potential.

Students with mental retardation demonstrate a range of abilities and increasingly are included in the general education classroom. In this chapter we will look at how curriculum and teaching strategies are modified to help these students reach their potential in academic and life skills. We will also focus on the community as a source of instructional materials, employment, and independent living arrangements both during and after the school years.

Perhaps more than any other term used in the field of special education, the term *mental retardation* conjures up specific images of individuals or groups of individuals. We ask you to keep two basic concepts in mind as you begin this chapter. First, each individual with mental retardation is just that—an individual. You must let go of any negative preconceptions you may have related to how children with mental retardation look, how they act, or what they can achieve. Second, each and every child has promise; thus, you must identify the specific skills and interests that need to be encouraged and strengthened.

Terms and Definitions

The definition of **mental retardation** has been revised numerous times to reflect our evolving understanding. The federal definition, adopted in 1993, is as follows:

> Mental retardation refers to substantial limitations in present functioning. It is characterized by significantly subaverage intellectual functioning, existing concurrently with related limitations in two or more of the following applicable adaptive, or life-skill areas: communication, self-care, home living, social skills, community use, self-direction, health and safety, functional academics, leisure, and work. Mental retardation manifests before age 18.

The four following assumptions are essential to the application of the definition:

1. Valid assessment considers cultural and linguistic diversity as well as differences in communication and behavioral factors.
2. The identification of limitations in adaptive skills occurs within the context of community environments typical of the individual's age peers and is indexed to the person's individualized needs for supports.
3. Specific adaptive limitations often coexist with strengths in other adaptive skills or other personal capabilities.
4. With appropriate supports over a sustained period, the life functioning of the person with mental retardation will generally improve.

Intelligence and General Cognitive Functioning

The concept of intelligence is critical to the definition of mental retardation. Each reader of this book will have different ideas about what constitutes intelligence. Researchers, too, have difficulty agreeing on a definition of intelligence. It is what psychologists call a *construct,* defined by theorists and test makers and determined by their ideas, beliefs, and cultural values. Even though no universal agreement exists on what constitutes intelligence, a number of tests have been developed to measure it. The **Stanford-Binet Intelligence Scale** and the **Wechsler Intelligence Scale for Children, Third Edition (WISC-III)** are the

Mental retardation is characterized by subaverage intellectual functioning and deficits in adaptive behavior.

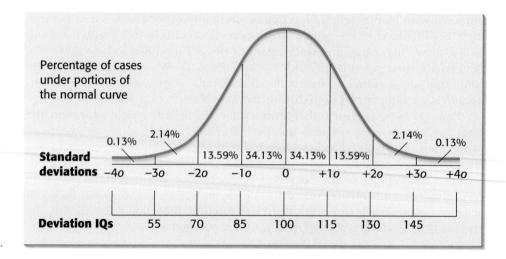

Figure 5.1

Theoretical Distribution of
IQ Scores

Source: S. A. Kirk & J. J.
Gallagher (1988). *Educating
exceptional children* (6th ed.,
p. 11). Boston: Houghton Mifflin.

two tests most widely used by American psychologists to assess intelligence. These tests include a number of subtests and yield a composite score, the score we typically refer to when we state a student's IQ. The WISC-III also yields two major subscores, one for verbal ability and one for performance ability. The intelligence test scores for the population at large can be represented in what is often described as a bell-shaped curve (see Figure 5.1). This distribution, also known as the normal curve, illustrates the range of scores that can be expected in any representative population. An average intelligence test score of 100 represents equivalence between mental age and chronological age.

The phrase *subaverage intellectual functioning* in the AAMR definition refers to performance on one or more intelligence tests resulting in an IQ score of about 70 or below. It is possible, however, for a student with an IQ score higher than 70 to qualify as having mental retardation if there are clear deficits in adaptive behavior. Conversely, it is possible for a student with an IQ score of 65 not to be identified as having mental retardation if he or she has good adaptive behavior. A critical point to remember is that the word *significantly,* which is used in the federal definition ("significantly subaverage intellectual functioning"), is subject to professional interpretation. It can also be decided that a child no longer has mental retardation if gains are made in adaptive behavior or in measured intelligence level. The term *mental retardation* can thus refer to a current state of functioning or performance rather than a permanent condition.

Adaptive Behavior

Adaptive behavior, the other key element of the AAMR definition, includes those social, maturational, self-help, and communicative acts that help each individual adapt to the demands of his or her surroundings (Beirne-Smith, Ittenbach, & Patton, 2002). They are *age-appropriate* and *situation-appropriate*; that is, they are different at each age and in each situation. Adaptive behaviors present a more comprehensive picture of a child's abilities than do IQ scores alone. Let us examine some examples of adaptive behaviors found in different developmental periods to see how they vary.

The most rapid and dramatic changes in adaptive behavior occur during the infancy and preschool period. The infant learns to reach, roll over, sit, stand, walk, and run; to finger-feed and then to use a spoon and drink from a cup; to draw others into close social relationships; and to communicate—first through vocalizing, and then, gradually, through understanding and repeating single words, two words together, short phrases, and finally sentences that increase in length and complexity. By preschool, many of these milestones have been mastered. The child becomes toilet-trained, and then many of the adaptive behaviors focus on social goals: learning to play and interact successfully with other children and with new adults, sharing, and making friends.

In the elementary school years the child must become socialized to the expectations of school and learn to adapt to those demands: to sit quietly until spoken to, to raise a hand to be recognized, and to follow the teacher's directions. Other adaptive behaviors are refinements of earlier milestones in motor, social, and language development; also included are academic skills that apply to everyday functioning in the environment, such as reading danger and warning signs. Adaptive behavior is not easy to measure. Expectations for age-appropriate and situation-appropriate behavior may differ from city to city, state to state, and culture to culture. Geography, local behavior norms, and cultural differences all interact to determine if a child's behavior is appropriate in a particular locale. These factors contribute to the variability of classification status from one school district to the next.

> Expectations for appropriate behavior may differ from place to place and culture to culture.

In order for a child to be classified as having mental retardation, he or she must demonstrate deficits in adaptive behavior that are comparable to the child's measured IQ. By incorporating the measure of adaptive behavior, the definition acknowledges that the child functions in various environments and potentially possesses many types of skills.

Adaptive behavior is usually measured through observation and interviews with the child's parents, guardians, or teachers. Two of the most widely used instruments are the **AAMR Adaptive Behavior Scale** (Nihira, Leland, & Lambert, 1993) and the **Vineland Adaptive Behavior Scales** (Sparrow, Balla, & Cicchetti, 1984). Adaptive behavior scales enable the teacher, parent, or observer to determine the child's competence in a wide range of functional behaviors. The AAMR Adaptive Behavior Scale measures two major areas—independent performance of daily living skills and inappropriate or maladaptive behaviors, such as self-abuse or destructive behavior. The Vineland Adaptive Behavior Scales, Interview Editions, measure the domains of communication, daily living skills, socialization, motor skills, and maladaptive behavior. Figure 5.2 shows a section from one of these scales.

Manifestation During the Developmental Period

Mental retardation must be present before the age of 18. This criterion is included in the AAMR definition to distinguish mental retardation from conditions in which adults suffer from impairment of brain functioning, such as from a head injury or stroke. The great majority of people with mental retardation—about 80 to 85 percent—are "invisible": They do not look "different." These individuals have mild mental retardation, and most of them are integrated naturally into the community. This fact adds to the difficulty of determining accurate prevalence rates and reveals one of the reasons why many children aren't identified until they reach school. Children with moderate mental retardation, however, are more likely to exhibit distinguishing physical or developmental characteristics and therefore are more likely to be identified at an early age or at

> Mental retardation must be identified before age 18, but a child can show gains in adaptive behavior or measured intelligence.

DOMAIN 1: Independent Functioning

A. Eating Subdomain

Item 1: Use of Table Utensils (circle highest level)

Uses table knife for cutting or spreading	6
Feeds self neatly with spoon and fork (or appropriate alternate utensils, e.g., chopsticks)	5
Feeds self, causing considerable spilling with spoon and fork (or appropriate alternate utensil, e.g., chopsticks)	4
Feeds self with spoon—neatly	3
Feeds self with spoon—considerable spilling	2
Feeds self with fingers	1
Does not feed self or must be fed	0

☐

Item 2: Eating in Public (circle highest level)

Orders complete meals in restaurants	3
Orders simple meals like hamburgers and hot dogs	2
Orders single items, e.g., soft drinks, ice cream, donuts, etc. at soda fountains or canteens	1
Does not order in public eating places	0

☐

Item 3: Drinking (circle highest level)

Drinks without spilling, holding glass in one hand	3
Drinks from a cup or glass unassisted—neatly	2
Drinks from a cup or glass unassisted—considerable spilling	1
Does not drink from a cup or glass unassisted	0

☐

Item 4: Table Manners (circle all answers)

If these items do not apply to the individual, e.g., because he or she is bedfast and/or has liquid food only, place a check in the blank and mark "Yes" for all statements.

	Yes	No
Throws food	0	1
Swallows food without chewing	0	1
Chews food with mouth open	0	1
Drops food on table or floor	0	1
Does not use napkin	0	1
Talks with mouth full	0	1
Takes food off others' plates	0	1
Eats too fast or too slow	0	1
Plays in food with fingers	0	1

☐

Subdomain total (add items 1–4)   ☐

Figure 5.2

AAMR Adaptive Behavior Scale

Source: K. Nihira, H. Leland, & N. Lambert (1993). *AAMR adaptive behavior scale: Residential and community* (2d ed.). Austin, TX: PRO-ED.

birth. Often the delay of certain developmental milestones, such as walking, the onset of speech, and the acquisition of self-help skills, alerts the parents and physician. Only about 7 to 10 percent of the people with mental retardation fall into this category.

Classification Issues

Scientists and educational professionals differentiate among individuals with varying degrees of mental retardation. As with most categories, or groups of exceptional individuals who share a common label, there is tremendous variety within the group of people identified as having mental retardation.

The American Association on Mental Retardation uses the terms *mild, moderate, severe,* and *profound* to denote degrees of mental retardation. People with mild mental retardation may require support services to enable them to graduate from high school, obtain appropriate job training, and get married and raise a family. Most individuals with mild mental retardation easily blend in to school and work environments. People with moderate mental retardation typically require support services and often supervision to enable them to live and work in independent or semi-independent community settings. People with moderate mental retardation have characteristics that are probably those you think of when you hear the phrase *mental retardation.*

Individuals identified as having severe or profound mental retardation require more extensive educational services. In this chapter, we will discuss the needs of students with mild and moderate levels of mental retardation. You will learn about individuals with severe and profound mental retardation in Chapter 6.

An ongoing classification issue in the area of mental retardation is the overrepresentation of students from minority populations among those classified as having mental retardation, particularly mild mental retardation. Children who are African American, and to a lesser extent, children with Native American heritage, are overrepresented in classes for children with mental retardation even when poverty is controlled—the trend exists even in wealth districts (Civil Rights Project, 2002). As you learned in Chapter 1, representatives from minority groups have objected to the use of IQ tests with children from both racial and language minority backgrounds (*Larry P. v. Riles, Diana v. State Board of Education*) because they believe that these children do not have equal access to the middle-class American cultural experiences that may be measured by norm-referenced IQ tests. Both the law and good practice dictate that no one test should ever be the sole grounds for diagnosis of a disability or for special class placement. Other factors, such as teacher and school authority bias, the influence or lack of influence of parents from minority backgrounds, the unequal distribution of school resources, and interpretations of actions related to testing policies, are all considered part of the complex overrepresentation issue (Civil Rights Project, 2002).

Some attempts to stem the overrepresentation of minority students in classes for children with mental retardation involve increasing the cultural awareness and cultural competence of all teachers before actual testing takes place. For example, Craig et al. (2000) suggest the use of teacher assistance teams. Such teams are trained to recognize cultural differences and evaluate instruction in an attempt to stem the rate of minority overrepresentation at the referral stage. Figure 5.3 lists guidelines for teacher assistance teams.

To learn more about the issue of overrepresentation of minority populations in special education, visit the website of the Civil Rights Project at Harvard University. Research reports, links to literature and resources, and conferences can be found at **http://www.civilrightsproject.harvard.edu**.

Although most states have used the same procedural guidelines to classify individuals with mental retardation for about twenty years (Denning, Chamberlain, & Polloway, 2000), increasingly stringent application of the adaptive behavior criterion has resulted in fewer children receiving the label of mild mental retardation. These children tend to have more comprehensive disabilities and are increasingly exposed to a curriculum that stresses preparation for life skills rather than the traditional remedial academic program. The expanded curriculum of life skills, vocational instruction, and basic academics now offered to many students with moderate mental retardation is often suitable to students in

> There are varying degrees of mental retardation.

> Increasing cultural awareness in teachers may help address overrepresentation of minority students in classes for students with mental retardation.

> With fewer children classified as having mild mental retardation, the mild and moderate categories are merging.

Questions About Cultural Context

1. What do we know about this student's linguistic, ethnic, and cultural background?
2. How would this child's family explain the student's behavior that is in question?
3. Do we notice the same or similar behaviors in other students with similar cultural backgrounds?
4. Is there any indication that the student's behavior has a cultural explanation?

Questions About Classroom Rules/Expectations

1. In what ways are students expected to respond to questions and directions?
2. In what ways are children expected to signal attention?
3. In what ways are students expected to behave toward authority?

Questions About Classroom Practices

1. In what ways is the teacher using flexible grouping?
2. In what ways is the teacher compacting curriculum?
3. In what ways is the teacher promoting interdependence?
4. In what ways is the teacher differentiating instruction?
5. In what ways is the teacher celebrating diversity?

Questions to Promote Culturally Competent Recommendations

1. Are there rules, expectations, and response behaviors that need to be explicitly taught to this student?
2. Are there classroom practices that need to be added, refined, or eliminated to more effectively support this student?
3. Do we need more information about this student's background and sociocultural context before we make recommendations for classroom adaptations?

Figure 5.3

Questions That Guide Culturally Competent Teacher Assistance Teams

Source: S. Craig, K. Hull, A. G. Haggart, & M. Perez-Selles, (2000). Promoting cultural competence through teacher assistance teams. *Teaching Exceptional Children, 32,* 6–12.

both groups and may make the distinction between moderate and mild mental retardation less important from an educational perspective.

Now that we've made these comments, we would like to caution you about making assumptions regarding the ability levels of students identified as having mild mental retardation. As a teacher, you will always need to make your own careful assessments about what and how to teach an individual child. In addition, keep in mind that the purpose behind labels and categorical grouping is to provide better educational services to children.

Prevalence

> Approximately 1 percent of school-age children have mental retardation; most are classified with mild mental retardation.

A strict interpretation of the normal curve (see Figure 5.1) would suggest a prevalence rate of about 3 percent for mental retardation; that is, 3 percent of the total population would be identified as having mental retardation. According to the *Twenty-fourth Annual Report to Congress on the Implementation of the Individuals with Disabilities Act* (2002), however, the U.S. Department of Education reported that 0.93 percent of the school-age population, or 10.6 percent of all students with disabilities, were identified as having mental retardation. Factors affecting the prevalence rate include the procedures and recommendations used in school re-ferral processes, changes in federal and state regulations over time, and the iden-tification and elimination of potential risk factors through early intervention.

? *Pause and Reflect*

In this section we discussed the importance of adaptive behavior to the definition of mental retardation. How do you think the ways we identify and measure adaptive behavior influence the composition of the population of children identified with mental retardation? How could adaptive behaviors differ among various communities or cul-tures around the country, and the world? ●

Causes of Mental Retardation

There are a number of possible causes of mental retardation, many of which can be linked to the risk factors described in Chapter 2. The American Association for Mental Retardation identifies four basic categories of risk factors: biomed-ical, social, behavioral, and educational (AAMR, 2002). Table 5.1 lists ten poten-tial causes that relate to the four areas of risk factors. The list includes causes for all levels of mental retardation. With the exception of category 9 (associated al-most exclusively with mild mental retardation), the conditions listed can result in any level of mental retardation.

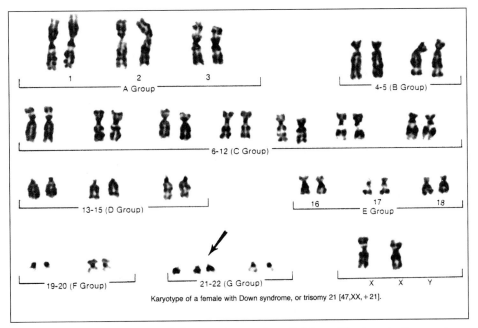

Karyotype of a female with Down syndrome, or trisomy 21 [47,XX, + 21].

An extra chromosome can result from an incomplete division of the twenty-three pairs of chromosomes during the formation of an egg cell. The extra chromosome at the 21st position results in trisomy 21—the most common form of Down syndrome. (From S. Pueschel [1983]. The child with Down syndrome. In Mel Levine, W. Carey, A. Crocker, & R. Gross (eds.), *Developmental behavior pediatrics*. Philadelphia: Saunders. Copyright 1983 by W.B. Saunders and Company. Reprinted by permission.)

Table 5.1 Causes of Mental Retardation

1. *Infections and intoxications.* Examples include rubella, syphilis, meningitis, and exposure to drugs, alcohol, or lead. The child may be exposed through the mother during pregnancy or may contract infections after birth. Unfortunately, fetal alcohol syndrome and drug addiction are major causes of mental retardation.

2. *Trauma or physical agents.* Injuries to the child that occur before, during, or after birth fall into this category. Hypoxia (deprivation of oxygen) and injuries received through child abuse are examples.

3. *Metabolic or nutritional disorders.* Examples of these disorders include phenylketonuria (PKU), Tay–Sachs disease, and galactosemia. In disorders of this type, the child's inability to metabolize or tolerate certain elements in food results in brain injury.

4. *Postnatal gross brain disease.* This refers to tumors that occur after birth.

5. *Prenatal diseases or conditions of unknown origin.* Examples of conditions found in this category include hydrocephalus and microcephaly. Hydrocephalus refers to the presence of cerebrospinal fluid in the skull, which increases the size of the skull while causing pressure on the brain; microcephaly describes a condition in which the skull is significantly smaller than normal.

6. *Chromosomal abnormality.* Chromosomal abnormalities refer to an unusual pattern of genetic material on one or more of the child's chromosomes. Two of the more well-known syndromes associated with chromosomal abnormalities are Down syndrome and fragile-X syndrome. Both of these syndromes usually result in distinct physical characteristics and mental retardation. Fragile-X syndrome is found mostly in males (because of the defective X chromosome). Females carry the chromosome and some may experience mild mental retardation. In some instances, these syndromes appear as recessive genetic traits; in others (such as the most frequently occurring type of Down syndrome), the abnormality is associated with other factors, such as the age of the mother.

7. *Other perinatal/gestational conditions.* Two prominent examples in this category are prematurity and low birthweight. Although many infants do not suffer negative effects from these conditions, both prematurity and low birthweight are risk factors for mental retardation. As you might expect, the more extreme these conditions are, the higher the level of risk.

8. *Presence of psychiatric disorders.* A few psychiatric disorders, such as depression, may be associated with mental retardation.

9. *Environmental influences.* This category includes causes that are described as cultural–familial. We will describe this category in greater detail later in this section.

10. *Other unknown causes.* Because it is difficult to identify the causes of mental retardation in many children, we suspect that there are causes that have yet to be discovered.

Source: H. J. Grossman (1983). *Classification in mental retardation.* Washington, DC: American Association on Mental Deficiency.

Biomedical Factors

Many causes of mental retardation appear to be related to biological factors, but cause is uncertain in over 50 percent of cases.

Table 5.1 shows that many causes of mental retardation appear to be tied to biomedical, or biological, factors, such as metabolic or nutritional disorders, postnatal brain disease, prenatal diseases, chromosomal abnormalities, perinatal/gestational conditions, and some psychiatric disorders. The more severe the level of mental retardation, the more likely it is that a cause can be pinpointed. For persons with moderate or severe mental retardation, biological causes can be pinpointed in 60 to 75 percent of the cases (Batshaw and Rose, 1997). Beirne-Smith, Ittenbach, and Patton (2002) point out that there is no certain cause in at least 50 percent of cases of mental retardation. This is particularly true for individuals with mild mental retardation.

As we mentioned in Chapter 2, prenatal care, genetic counseling, and appropriate immunizations can help prevent many disabilities, including mental

A Closer Look   Questions about Down Syndrome

1. **What is Down syndrome?** Although there are several types of Down syndrome, all types are a result of an extra copy or an extra part of the 21st chromosome in an individual's cells. This extra genetic material can result in mental retardation and distinctive physical features and characteristics. Down syndrome is associated with congenital heart defects, gastrointestinal difficulties, and a variety of physiological concerns.

2. **What causes Down syndrome?** Down syndrome is the most common genetic condition. Estimates of occurrence range from 1/660 to 1/1000 live births. Typically, we associate the occurrence of Down syndrome with increased maternal age. Although the incidence of Down syndrome is strongly correlated with the age of the mother, over 80 percent of children with Down syndrome are born to mothers younger than 35. Sometimes, Down syndrome is a chance occurrence.

3. **What are the educational opportunities for children with Down syndrome?** The possibilities for individuals with Down syndrome have increased greatly in the past few decades. Because of their distinctive physical characteristics, children with Down syndrome are identified at birth. Years ago, babies with Down syndrome were routinely placed in residential or institutional settings with little expectations for independent life in the community. Now, we know that most children with Down syndrome experience mild to moderate cognitive disabilities. All children, including those with Down syndrome, display a range of abilities. Some will do well academically, others will find community-based jobs or supported work, and others will become actors in television shows.

Sources: Medline Plus, 2003; National Down Syndrome Society, 2003.

retardation. The medical community continues to identify ways to prevent or ameliorate mental retardation through genetic research or very early (often prenatal) treatment. For example, the effects of hydrocephalus can be greatly minimized by surgery in which a shunt is implanted in the head of the infant prior to birth, allowing the fluid to drain away before brain damage occurs. Another example involves the identification of phenylketonuria (PKU), a metabolic disorder. All hospitals now require a test for PKU at birth. If the condition is present, the child is put on a specific diet and mental retardation can be avoided. One clearly identifiable cause of mental retardation is Down syndrome, an example of a chrommomsomal abnormality. Read the Closer Look box entitled, "Questions about Down Syndrome" to learn more about the effects of this condition on children and families.

For information, news, and research related to Down syndrome, go to the website of the National Down Syndrome Society at **http://www.ndss.org**.

Social, Behavioral, and Educational Factors

It often is difficult to pinpoint specific causal relationships between mental retardation and general environmental factors. The effects of social and educational factors such as social interaction, cultural differences, and socioeconomic conditions on cognitive abilities often appear to be correlational in nature. For example, although poverty alone does not imply poor nutrition, poor health care, or a poor social environment, many of these risk factors do tend to occur together.

You may have heard about the ongoing debate over the role of environment versus the role of heredity in determining intelligence. Do smart parents have smart children because the children inherit intellectual ability, or do their surroundings encourage the fullest possible development of their intelligence? Could students with mild mental retardation inherit low intellectual ability from their parents, or could a bright child be affected by adverse environmental conditions? The relative importance of heredity and the environment in intellectual development has been discussed, debated, and researched for many years.

The current thinking in this area represents a compromise. Each child probably comes into the world with a potential range of intellectual ability, and the environment in which the child is reared helps to determine the extent to which that ability is expressed (MacMillan, Semmel, & Gerber, 1994). In other words, it is likely that heredity and environment *interact* to result in the demonstrated in-

> The relative importance of heredity and the environment in intellectual development has been debated for years.

FIRST PERSON

John Kellerman's Story

Hello! My name is John Kellerman. I live in Tucson, Arizona, and work at Desert Survivors, a nursery that specializes in plants that are native to Arizona. I live with my mother, Teresa, my brother, Chris, and my dog, Winnie. I am 21 years old, and I have Fetal Alcohol Syndrome.

This means that my birth mother drank alcohol when she was pregnant with me, and the alcohol affected my development. It stunted my growth physically, but it also affected my mental and emotional development. I am not as smart and not as tall as other people my age. I like people, but I don't have many friends, because I don't know how to maintain a relationship. I like to be independent, but I have to be carefully watched by my mom, my brother, or my supervisor, because I cannot control my behavior all the time. Because of the alcohol damage to my brain (especially the frontal lobes), I don't have good control of my impulses and I have poor judgment when it comes to making

life decisions. Because of damage to the center of my brain (the corpus callosum), I have trouble organizing information and have trouble remembering things like rules and consequences. I also have trouble with concepts of money and time.

You see, all this makes life very difficult for me. I understand all about Fetal Alcohol Syndrome (FAS) and I understand why my birth mother drank. I understand why I have problems with memory, emotions, behavior, impulses, and learning from consequences. What I would like is for YOU to understand all this as well. My biggest problem is not my neurological dysfunction. It is being misunderstood by people who think my problems are due to lack of discipline or poor parenting. My mom really has tried to teach me proper social behaviors, but it just doesn't click all the time. I either can't remember the social rules (like don't stand too close, or ask first for a hug) or else I can't control the impulse to act.

tellectual ability of most children. Certainly, the environment (including teaching) can affect how any child's cognitive, behavioral, and physical skills develop throughout his or her lifetime.

When we look at the specific environmental and behavioral causes outlined by the AAMR (also presented in Table 5.1), however, we see specific maternal behavior related to the use of intoxicants that can have clearly documented effects on unborn children The link between these causes—maternal drinking, smoking, and drug use—can be easily and all too frequently linked to mental retardation in children. Alcohol consumption by a pregnant woman frequently results in fetal alcohol syndrome (FAS), a syndrome often accompanied by mental retardation, extensive behavior difficulties, and distinctive physical characteristics. FAS is now the leading cause of mental retardation in this country. In this chapter's First Person box, John Kellerman talks about FAS' impact on his life.

To learn more about FAS and to read many personal stories of lives touched by FAS, go to the website of the FAS Community Resource Center of Tucson, Arizona, at **http://www.come-over.to/FAS**.

Note: John was 21 years old when he drew this. He did not have long hair or a beard, but enjoyed imagining that he did. When asked about the missing arms and legs, he replied, "Oops, I forgot!"

John has a borderline IQ (68), with expressive language skills of a young adult, and the fine motor control of a young child. But he can play the drums rather well, and can give a speech on FAS with ease.

Self Portrait by John http://www.come-over.to/FAS/selfportrait.htm. Retrieved Jan. 5, 2004. Used with permission.

I get really frustrated with myself sometimes, and I feel bad when I make people uncomfortable or angry. I try hard and I want to please people, but my disability gets in the way of all that.

What makes my disability so hard to understand is that I have really good skills in certain areas, like verbal expression and vocabulary. I have learned how to "act" like an adult, but tests show that emotionally I am just a 6-year-old child inside. I have lots of knowledge, but I lack the common sense to use that knowledge wisely. I have the physical development of a man but the impulse control of a child. This makes the world a very dangerous place for me. I can easily be taken advantage of by others and can be led astray by just the promise of friendship or affection.

Do me a favor? Please ask every young woman you know to refrain from drinking alcohol during pregnancy. And please be forgiving if I am inappropriate. Remind me of what is right and wrong and I will try to remember. Show me healthy behavior and I will follow.

John Kellerman

Source: FAS Community Resource Center, Tuscon, AZ, www.fasstar.com.

? Pause and Reflect

In this section, we discussed the importance of the child's environment as a source of support for his or her inherited potential. Think of the ways you might enrich a young child's environment to support social, physical, and cognitive growth. ●

Characteristics of Individuals with Mental Retardation

Mental retardation is a developmental disability; that is, it affects a child's overall development in a relatively uniform manner. When we look at the effects of mental retardation on any individual, we must keep in mind not only the obvious things, such as severity and complicating factors, but also the child's own personality and determination. Characteristics are generalized descriptions of behavior. Any specific characteristic we present may or may not occur in a certain individual with mental retardation.

Cognitive Development

By definition, mental retardation can be interpreted to mean a low level of cognitive ability. Intelligence tests are used to provide an overall measure of cognitive ability, and persons with mental retardation are identified as having deficits in the ability to learn.

The ability to learn can be described in many ways. One aspect of learning is capacity—how much information can be processed at one time. Generally, children with mental retardation process smaller amounts of information than their typically developing classmates. Another aspect of learning is the ability to engage in problem solving. Individuals with mental retardation may rely on a limited set of problem-solving strategies, which can cause difficulty when new, different, or complex problems arise (Wehmeyer & Kelchner, 1994). Students with mental retardation may also have difficulty using cognitive skills such as metacognition, memory, and attention.

● *Metacognition and Memory*   Most students with learning problems, including mental retardation, have difficulty in the areas of metacognition and memory, particularly short-term memory. Metacognition refers to the ability to identify how one learns and to evaluate, monitor, and adapt the learning process. These difficulties in metacognition and memory, therefore, translate into problems in planning, evaluating, and organizing information.

Let's look at a student learning to use a calculator for multiplication. The student will say and practice the steps involved in pushing the calculator buttons several times (rehearsal, a memory strategy). He will determine if he needs more practice (performance evaluation, a metacognitive strategy). He will say the problem aloud as he enters it into his calculator (rehearsal, a memory strategy). He may then work the problem by hand to double-check his answer and his ability to use the calculator correctly (awareness of need to evaluate performance and method of evaluating performance, a metacognitive strategy). If he has done the procedure incorrectly, he might rehearse the skill some more or create some type of mnemonic device to help him remember the procedure (metacognitive awareness and memory strategy).

A student with mental retardation is more likely to have difficulty realizing the conditions or actions that will help her or him learn or retain the material (Merrill, 1990). Given the calculator activity, the student might not think to practice or rehearse the process first, not think to evaluate her or his performance or know how to do it, and not realize that more practice or a new memory approach might be helpful. Because of these cognitive effects, we must focus instruction on *how* to learn as well as on *what* to learn so that the student can achieve the greatest possible level of independence.

Memory and metacognitive skills are sometimes closely related. Before students can use strategies for aiding memory, they must be aware that such strategies are needed. Consequently, a very important way to improve the learning abilities of students with mental retardation is to teach a student when specific strategies for remembering should be used.

● *Attention* Mental retardation is often characterized by attentional deficits—the child has difficulty coming to attention, maintaining attention, and paying selective attention (Westling & Fox, 2000; Zeaman & House, 1963, 1979). In many instances, the problem is not that the child *won't* pay attention, but that he or she *can't* pay attention or doesn't know how to attend. It is possible, however, to minimize the effects of attentional deficits on learning.

A student with a deficit in coming to attention will experience difficulty focusing on the task at hand and, in the case of independent work, will have problems getting started. For some students this may be a result of having difficulty diverting their attention from distractions or previous activities. Other students may have difficulty recognizing the signs, directions, or task requirements for a new activity. It is often helpful for teachers to use clear and unambiguous signals that indicate the beginning or ending of activities and that specify task requirements. These signals may be phrases, such as "Eyes on me," or actions, such as clapping the hands.

Many students with mental retardation have a shorter attention span than other children their age. A child experiencing difficulty maintaining attention will do much better on long tasks (such as practicing problems in arithmetic) if the task is broken into shorter segments that can be done throughout the day rather than all at once. Sometimes, gradually increasing the amount of time a child is required to pay attention will help to lengthen a child's attention span. Children with mental retardation, like all children, will be able to attend longer to material that is interesting and attractive.

A student with problems maintaining attention may need frequent direction to reorient him or her back to the task at hand. One way teachers try to deal with this problem is to establish a signal that can be used instead of constant verbal direction. A clap, or a tap on the board or desk, can be used to remind the child to refocus. Teachers also try different types of written cues, including colored marks, underlining, arrows, and so on, to help children focus on starting points in written material.

In the area of selective attention—attending to the key issues—students with mental retardation often have difficulty identifying the critical aspects or content of information. A young child might not be able to identify the distinguishing characteristics or dimensions of a letter or word. An older student might miss the key words in the directions for a test.

> Teachers must focus instruction on how as well as what students learn.

Some ways you can accentuate important information for students include:

- Underlining key words, using color or exaggeration to help draw attention to the words
- Using key words to cue the student that what you are about to say is important
- Presenting less extraneous information during initial teaching
- Teaching the student to recognize and use the cues you have provided

● *Generalization*   Most students with mental retardation experience difficulty transferring skills from one context to another. In other words, once a student has learned a specific skill in the classroom using certain materials, he or she may have difficulty performing that skill another way, in another setting, or with other materials (Polloway & Patton, 1997). Sometimes, the problem of **skill transfer**, or **generalization**, can be relatively minor and easy to remedy. For example, some children simply become confused by a change in format or materials and just need to be told that they can use the same skill or strategy in the new situation. Another possibility is that the novel, or new, environments need to be adjusted in order to support the newly acquired skills. Children may be less likely to use a new skill (waiting and raising a hand to ask for a pencil), if it is not as efficient as an old one (getting out of a seat to take a pencil off the teacher's desk).

> Generalizing, or transferring skills from one setting to another, is often difficult for students with mental retardation.

Teachers also need to anticipate the possibility that students will need an explanation before performing a skill in a new setting or format. For example, a student who can work single-digit addition problems successfully but has only been presented with problems in a vertical format may not realize that the same process applies to problems in a horizontal format (2 + 3 = __). This child will need additional instruction, demonstration, and reinforcement.

You can maximize the potential for generalization by incorporating real-world materials into your instruction. For example, a student who has learned all the basic addition and subtraction skills may not realize that those same skills can be used to balance a checkbook, so you might have students practice using real checkbooks. Use real materials whenever they are readily available—it makes learning more meaningful for all students and helps to address the problem of poor skill transfer.

The child with moderate mental retardation may experience a great deal of difficulty understanding that the pencil-and-paper addition he or she does in the classroom is the same basic skill used in counting money or adding up points in a board game. For students with moderate mental retardation, the use of actual materials to teach needed or desired skills has even more importance. Teachers should never assume that a generalization of responses will occur without specific instruction. See the Teaching Strategies box entitled, "Strategies for Enhancing Cognitive Skills" for a summary of instructional strategies.

Language Development

> Children with mental retardation may experience a delay in language development.

One early sign of mild or moderate mental retardation is a delay in the acquisition of communication skills. Children with mental retardation acquire language at a slower rate than other children, usually have limited vocabularies, and tend to use a restricted number of sentence constructions. Speech problems are also found more frequently in children with mental retardation. A survey of

Teaching Strategies & Accommodations

Strategies for Enhancing Cognitive Skills—Metacognition and Memory

- Teach memory strategies, such as rehearsing and chunking information, if students are not using them.
- Teach students when to use memory strategies or provide cues for using them.

Attention

- Establish clear signals to orient students to the task or lesson.
- Break up long instructional segments or tasks into several short sessions.

- Gradually increase the amount of time you expect children to attend to a task.
- Accentuate key content and directions for the students through the use of response prompts or cues.

Generalization

- Teach students to use the skills they have learned in one class in other classes or settings.
- Use real-world materials to help students generalize basic skills to realistic situations.

---

services provided to elementary-age students with mild mental retardation found that 90 percent of the population surveyed had been identified as needing speech or language services, especially in the area of articulation (Epstein et al., 1989). Structural differences, such as tongue size or facial musculature, can affect the way some individuals pronounce certain sounds.

Individuals with mental retardation also may experience difficulty in nonverbal communication skills. Many children with mental retardation demonstrate appropriate nonverbal skills (proximity, gestures, eye contact), yet may display inappropriate skills or engage in appropriate skills at an unusual level (Bufkin & Altman, 1995). For example, a pat on the shoulder is appropriate during most interpersonal conversations. If someone were giving you a pat on the shoulder every few seconds, however, you would probably view the behavior as inappropriate. Nonverbal communication skills can be as important as verbal language in communication with peers and are an important focus of educational programs for many students with cognitive disabilities.

Physical Development

People with mild retardation may, as a group, be less physically fit than others—they may weigh somewhat less and be of smaller stature, have poorer motor skills, and have more health-related problems than their peers (Drew, Logan, & Hardman, 1992).

The physical health and motor skills of individuals with mental retardation are more likely to be impaired as the degree of mental retardation increases. Thus, people with moderate mental retardation are more likely to have noticeable physical differences than those with mild mental retardation. The same rule holds true when we consider the existence of additional disabling conditions, many of which, like cerebral palsy and epilepsy, involve physical ability and overall health. The greater the degree of mental retardation, the more likely it is that another disabling condition will accompany it.

People with mental retardation may have physical health problems.

Some of the specific syndromes that cause mental retardation result in accompanying physical impairments. The most common of these, Down syndrome, frequently results in structural heart defects, which in most cases can be corrected surgically. The incidence of hearing and visual impairments in children with Down syndrome is also considerably higher than in the general population. Although at one time these physical disabilities greatly shortened the prospective life span of people with Down syndrome, medical technology has enabled most individuals to live well into adulthood.

Many students with mild retardation require no extra programs or assistance to participate in sports or physical education activities. Other students, however, require more specialized physical activities, such as adaptive physical education, that include specific activities designed to improve strength and coordination. For many students, specific instruction in games or activities such as swimming or racquetball may be part of their educational program. Education geared not only to the activity itself, but also toward appropriate independent behavior in a gym or pool setting is important to helping students learn patterns of behavior that can be used both during the school years and into adulthood (Modell & Valdez, 2002). Many communities have organized activities designed specifically for persons with mental retardation or other disabilities, such as the Special Olympics. These programs provide additional opportunities for persons with mental and physical disabilities to compete in track and field events; however, integrated activities are always preferable to segregated ones.

Social and Emotional Development

Research has indicated some variability in the extent to which students with mild mental retardation are accepted and liked by their peers (Siperstein, Leffert, & Widaman, 1996). It is important to remember that every child or adolescent, with or without mental retardation, has personal and physical characteristics that can assist or detract from that individual's popularity and acceptance.

Students with mental retardation may have difficulty interpreting social cues.

Students with mental retardation may display delays in the development of communication, self-help, and problem-solving skills (Wehmeyer & Kelchner, 1994). As we suggested earlier, children with mental retardation also may have difficulty interpreting social cues, particularly if multiple cues are presented at once, or if incongruent cues and behaviors are present (Leffert, Siperstein, & Millikan, 2000). All these characteristics can contribute to ineffective interaction with others, but they can be addressed, in part, through specific training in communication and social skills. Some research suggests that the educational placement of students with mental retardation can affect their social acceptance by peers. For example, Buysse, Goldman, and Skinner (2002) found that young children with disabilities are more likely to have typically developing friends if they are in preschool settings that include large numbers of children without disabilities.

Most social behaviors are learned, just as other skills are learned. Sometimes, students with mild and moderate mental retardation display **immature behavior**, which generally reflect an inability to control emotions and delay gratification. Students with immature behaviors may have a low tolerance for frustration, cry easily, and do socially inappropriate things (Epstein et al., 1989). These behaviors may indicate a lack of appropriate social learning. A student with a problem in the area of selective attention, for example, may not have

Children learn social behavior from each other as they participate in everyday school and play activities. (Richard Hutchings/ PhotoEdit)

learned or may have difficulty identifying the relevant cues in a social situation, such as the nonverbal signals many of us use to judge how other people are reacting to us. When you enter a library, for example, you notice the low volume of speech and adjust your level of speech accordingly. If you don't, you probably notice the looks other people give you and then make the adjustment; if you do not, your behavior is interpreted as disruptive or inappropriate.

Studies have demonstrated that the behavior of students with mild and moderate mental retardation can be changed through behavior modification techniques and social skills instruction. With instruction, students can learn appropriate behaviors by modeling the behavior of peers in the classroom. This can pay off in improved social relations with others and an improved perception of self.

Many children with mental retardation may have the skills to perform appropriately, or according to the social norm in school or recreational settings, but they may display a lack of self-control or self-management of their performance. Self-control, self-awareness, and self-management of behavior are among the chief concerns of parents of children with cognitive disabilities (Kolb & Hanley-Maxwell, 2003). Many recent instructional programs demonstrate that students with mild and moderate mental retardation can learn self-management strategies to improve behaviors, ranging from recording and evaluating performance of academic tasks, to initiating appropriate social interaction, to improving on-task behaviors in the classroom (Firman, Beare, & Lloyd, 2002; Hughes et al., 2002; Mithaug, 2002). We discussed self-monitoring in Chapter 4, and the same types of procedures were not only found to be effective in teaching students to manage behavior, but also easy to implement in classrooms. Students used papers or notecards to check their performance and sometimes received external cues, such as a taped audio tone, to prompt self-evaluation.

Effects on the Family

The realization that a child has mental retardation may be either sudden or gradual, as you learned in Chapter 3. Sometimes, when a child is very ill at birth or when recognizable physical signs are present, the parents know about their child's disability before they leave the hospital. More often, however, the clues come slowly. The child may not sit, stand, and walk at the expected ages and may not understand language or use words at the expected times. But there are many differences in the way children develop, and parents often postpone acknowledging that their child is different from others.

It is in the school environment that most children with mild mental retardation are identified and the effects on the family are fully realized. Parents may confer with their child's teacher or receive a letter from the school administrator requesting permission to assess their child for possible provision of special education services. A discussion with the school psychologist after testing, or the IEP meeting, may be the first place that the parents hear the words *mental retardation* applied to their child.

For some parents, diagnosis, labeling, and the provision of special services will come as a relief; they usually are the ones who have suspected that their child has learning difficulties. Others will react negatively to the term mental retardation. These words evoke a special set of reactions from parents, perhaps because most people have little knowledge of mental retardation or of persons with mental retardation. Skinner et al. (1999) found that a majority of Latino mothers who wrote narratives about their relationship with their children with mental retardation reported that the children brought about positive change in their lives and were also viewed as a blessing from God. Although both cultural and religious background may influence a parent's reaction to a child with a disability, ultimately, each parent reacts in his or her own way.

Because the most identifiable causes of mental retardation increasingly are related to substance abuse by parents, parent reactions often now include responsibility and guilt. Some parents assume responsibility for their child's disability without cause; others clearly can link their behavior to their child's mental retardation. Often, mothers who abuse drugs or alcohol during pregnancy lose their children, at least temporarily, through the courts and foster care system. Read "My Thoughts on Being a Birth Mom to an Alcohol-affected Child" to hear one mother's perspective. Go to **http://members.aol.com/Alpha Mom33/birthmom.html**.

Another possible cause of negative reactions by parents is that their concept of mental retardation includes an inability to learn and limited potential for a fulfilling life. It can be particularly difficult for parents who have perceptions of this type to attach the label of mental retardation to their child—a child who seemed just like all the other children until he or she reached school. Accepting mental retardation, for many parents, involves a significant adjustment in their expectations and hopes for the child. Of course, these adjustments are often based on the parents' perceptions of mental retardation rather than their knowledge. Once parents acquire a more realistic concept of mental retardation, they are often able to raise their expectations and focus on the strengths and abilities of their child.

Greg and Tierny Fairchild have a young daughter, Naia, who has Down syndrome. The Fairchilds share their life—their decisions, struggles, and many joys—through words and pictures. The following excerpt from *Choosing Naia: A*

Most children with mild mental retardation are first diagnosed at school.

Family's Journey (Zuckoff, 2002) gives a glimpse of Greg's thoughts as he contemplates the future for his daughter:

> His basket filled with food and diapers, Greg ambled toward the Stop & Shop checkout line. It was morning, and the store wasn't crowded. He could have chosen any line, but he was drawn to one in particular. He placed his groceries on the moving belt and looked past the cashier to a smiling young woman at the far end of the counter. "Hello," Greg said. The young woman looked up from her work as a bagger. "Hi," she said sweetly. Greg wished he could tell her all the things in his heart. He wished he could ask a hundred questions about her life, her job, her family. How she got to work each day. Where she lived. What she did for fun. He wished he could ask about the friends he hoped she had. He wished he could tell her about his six-month-old daughter. He said none of those things. It would have seemed odd, intrusive. So he left it at hello. When her work was done and his groceries were neatly packed, Greg said, "Thanks." He gave her a warm smile. She smiled back. The bagger's name was Sarah, and she had Down syndrome. (p. 207)

To view a picture diary of the Fairchild family, go to **http://www.beacon. org/naia**.

Parents of children with mental retardation, like most parents of children with disabilities, often seek support from parent groups, gain knowledge from classes, books, and journals, and become aware of available services through contact with schools, associations, and service agencies (see the Helpful Resources section at the end of this chapter). In fact, parents of children with specific conditions, such as Down syndrome or Prader–Willi syndrome, often find that they must play the role of "expert" in presenting information specific to their children's syndrome to the educational community (Fidler, Hodapp, & Dykens, 2002). Balancing parenting roles and responsibilities and using resources effectively are important life-management strategies used by parents of children with disabilities (Scorgie, Wilgosh, & McDonald, 1999).

Many parents of children with mental retardation find that support groups help them manage stress and access resources.

The presence of a child with mental retardation can affect family interactions and relationships. A common concern of parents is that children with mental retardation will monopolize their attention and disrupt sibling relationships. Individuals with moderate mental retardation may demand more time of their parents than do other children. For example, it may take young children longer to acquire independence in skills such as eating and toileting, and parents may spend more time in schools with older children due to IEP development, curriculum planning, and behavior management issues. All families respond to these demands differently. Overall, the research in this area seems to suggest that siblings of children with mental retardation find ways to get the attention and social interaction they need (Stoneman et al., 1988). The interactions of siblings within families reflect the added child-care responsibilities of older siblings, and the sibling relationships are often characterized by a strong caregiving or dominant role on the part of the sibling without mental retardation. As individuals with mental retardation continue to receive educations that increasingly stress independent activities and functional skills, it will be interesting to see how sibling relationships change.

? *Pause and Reflect*

Teachers often assume that once a skill is learned, the child will be able to apply it in all situations. Yet, one of the characteristics of children with mental retardation is difficulty in generalizing or transferring new skills from one situation or task to another. Consider the many ways you can prompt students to apply skills in other settings. ●

Teaching Strategies and Accommodations

Teachers are expected to provide meaningful educational experiences—experiences that will help prepare students for life on their own—and to do it in the most inclusive setting possible. In many educational settings, the classroom teacher is responsible for the majority of service delivery to students with mental retardation. Interaction, communication, and professional cooperation between the special education teacher and classroom teacher are becoming the most important factors in the successful educational experience of students with mental retardation. Many current and upcoming educational issues, therefore, focus on the cooperative nature of educational programming and the development of challenging educational environments for full inclusion.

Early Intervention

Although diagnosis of severe mental retardation is typically made at birth or within the first year of life, children with moderate or mild mental retardation are more likely to be identified at a somewhat later age. The advent of Public Law (P.L.) 99-457, however, stresses early identification of children with disabilities and provision of appropriate services.

P.L. 99-457 (see Chapter 1) states that children identified as developmentally delayed, at risk, or having an identified disability between birth and the age of 3 are eligible to receive services. Most students in this age range receive services from the agency designated by the state to handle infant programs. Identified 3- and 4-year-olds are eligible for preschool programs through the local educational agency. As you might expect, one of the goals of early intervention is to reduce the effects of mental retardation on learning and basic skills acquisition. Early educational programming can provide students with a head start in basic skills and provide positive and successful learning experiences.

Curriculum

Educational programs for many students with mental retardation emphasize preparing students for life after school.

Curriculum options for students with mild and moderate mental retardation range from the basic learning skills (reading and math) and content-area skills (science and social studies) taught in the regular classroom, to functional life skills designed to help students learn the work, domestic, or leisure skills needed for independent living. Curriculum decisions should be based on the anticipated outcomes, or expected goals, of education for the individual student. The focus should be on the individual's abilities and preferences, and not on the particular level of mental retardation. For example, the anticipated outcome for a student who is capable of doing classwork in the regular class and has a high level of basic skills may be to graduate and possibly receive a high-school diploma. This student may be best served by taking basic academic courses in the regular curriculum, which might also include some vocational classes and training. The anticipated outcome for another student might be to live and work in a supervised community setting. This student would follow a full-time curriculum devoted to life skills, which might include training in social skills; interpersonal communication; domestic skills such as cooking, managing finances, and cleaning; using community transportation; and prevocational and vocational preparation, including on-the-job training.

> The focus of a student's instruction will often determine his or her educational setting.

It is important to keep in mind this wide range of potential outcomes and personal interests and abilities as we examine curriculum options for students with mild to moderate mental retardation. The three types of curriculum we will discuss are academic content, life skills, and transition programs. Although these are examined separately, you will see that many students could benefit from all three types of programs.

● *Academic Content*   Although you may not think of academics when you think of the term mental retardation, you may be surprised to know that many students with mild mental retardation participate in general education classes for all or part of the school day. In elementary school, students may attend basic content classes and receive extra support in reading or math through in-class instruction or through a resource program. Some students will benefit more than others from general instructional programs. In middle or secondary school, some students will continue in academic classes in pursuit of an academic diploma. Others will begin to take courses that are less academic and more vocational in nature, to best address their individualized educational goals.

Is a student with mental retardation expected to acquire the content delivered in the general education classroom? For example, is a student with mental retardation in a 10th grade biology class expected to do the same lab work, read the same text, and complete the same tests as the other students in the class? There is no single answer to that question—the response depends on the student and the course. In general, though, many students with mild mental retardation can participate at the elementary level, but more accommodations or adaptations of content may be necessary as students get older and the material becomes more abstract and difficult. Most of these accommodations should reflect an emphasis on the academic skills necessary for students to meet their life goals and independence. For example, science content could focus more on self health care and management, or plant care and gardening, especially if a related career is possible. This instruction may take place in the general education classroom, in a pull-out class that focuses on functional academics, or in the context of a specific vocational class—to continue our example, one that specifically teaches students to cultivate and harvest plants.

Functional academics are basic academic skills, such as reading, writing, and arithmetic, taught in the context of real-life or community activities. For example, reading skills might be presented within the context of reading menus, movie listings, clothing labels, signs, and directions; and arithmetic skills within the context of paying for food in restaurants or grocery stores, using a soft drink machine, planning a weekly budget, or balancing a checkbook. Functional academics taught in a separate class setting are more likely to be tied to specific tasks—for example, a class that focuses on cooking and the related reading, math, and health skills corresponding to planning, shopping for, and preparing meals. This type of curriculum should be integrated with using the target skills, for example, actually measuring ingredients for baking, so that the content is meaningful. At the elementary level, a functional curriculum would focus on content related to independent performance in home and community environments (preparing snacks, finding video games, keeping track of the baseball score, choosing a movie).

Older children with mild mental retardation, and many students with more moderate levels of mental retardation tend to have a curriculum plan that focuses more comprehensively on the skills necessary for everyday life. Although these students may experience a range of school experiences, most of their education may be guided by a life-skills curriculum.

● *Life-Skills Curriculum*   A **life-skills curriculum** is intended to provide the skills necessary to maximize a student's ability to live and work independently. Because students with moderate mental retardation may require support and have difficulty in transfer or skill generalization, they often can benefit from a comprehensive curriculum that includes self-care skills, community access skills, social interaction and communication skills, physical and motor development (including recreation and leisure skills), and specific job training (Beirne-Smith, Ittenbach, & Patton, 2002; Drew, Logan, & Hardman, 1992.)

Instruction in a life-skills curriculum encompasses the essential areas of everyday life. These areas are referred to as *domains*. Although you may see different terms used to describe these areas, they can be identified as domestic, recreation and leisure, vocational, and community living. The development of the curriculum involves:

- Looking at the specific skills that the student needs in these areas
- Identifying the specific skills in which the student needs instruction
- Providing that instruction within the context of the particular domain

In other words, the curriculum is generated by the student's environment rather than by a list of skills found in basal texts or regular curriculum guides. To identify the components of a curriculum, the teacher must assess the environment by observing and recording the exact skills needed in a specific home, recreation, or potential work setting. Once these skills are identified, the teacher will determine which ones the student already knows how to perform. Instruction will focus on those skills the students cannot yet perform independently. (See the accompanying, Teaching Strategies box entitled, "Environmental Assessment of Skills for Instruction" for an example of curriculum planning.)

Instruction involves presenting the skill in a naturally occurring context and integrating it with other skills found in that setting (Snell & Brown, 2000). All instruction is useful, meaningful, and motivating to the student; teaching is focused on usable skills that can be practiced often.

The community itself is playing an ever-increasing role in curriculum content for students with mental retardation. One goal of **community-based instruction** is placing students in job settings that are found in their local community. In addition, the community provides opportunities for the functional application of basic skills. For example, teachers can use menus, job applications, store names, movie theater marquees, bank books, bowling scorecards, and city maps (to name a few items) from the local community to assist in developing skills that can be used immediately and practiced repeatedly in the student's home environment. The regular classroom teacher should find that

A functional or life-skills curriculum provides the skills necessary for students to live and work independently.

The curriculum for students with moderate mental retardation emphasizes self-care skills, social interaction, recreation and leisure skills, and job training.

Community-based instruction allows students to receive instruction in meaningful and motivating settings.

Teaching Strategies & Accommodations

Environmental Assessment of Skills for Instruction

Student: Patricia Kelly, age 16
Environment: Home
Domains: Domestic/vocational

Rationale: Patricia is responsible for watching her two younger siblings (ages 8 and 10) every day from 3:30 to 5:30. Many of the skills required can also be used as a basis for employment in child-care fields. All the skills can be used to address future parenting needs.

Area 1: Recreation—Skills for Instruction

Suggest activities appropriate for indoor play.
Check toys and play materials to make sure they are safe and age-appropriate.
Check on children playing indoors every 15–20 minutes if they are not within sight.
Keep children in sight or hearing distance at all times when they are playing outside.
Recognize and prohibit rough or dangerous outside play.
Guide children in their selection of after-school snacks or prepare suitable snacks for them.
Play with children.

Area 2: Child Management—Skills for Instruction

Know household rules for indoor/outdoor play.
Remind children of rules when they return from school.
Enforce rules.
Know and use only management strategies suggested by parents.
Know and use a few plans or "tricks" for diverting children's attention.
Give accurate report of children's behavior to parents.

Area 3: Safety—Skills for Instruction

Identify and clear away unsafe debris, broken toys, etc., both inside and outside the house.
Check premises to ensure that potentially harmful materials are out of children's reach (matches, firearms, cleaning materials).
Be familiar with and experienced in administering emergency first aid procedures.
Know how to administer emergency procedures when a child is choking.
Distinguish between a mild incident and an emergency, and act according to plan.
Read labels to determine if a substance is poisonous.
Locate and use fire extinguisher and know fire evacuation plan.
Locate and call appropriate persons in case of concern or emergency (includes neighbor, parents, local emergency number).

using these resources facilitates learning and provides motivation for all the students in the class. A third role for the community is to serve as a source of activities. A series of local activities—using the post office, visiting the doctor and dentist, applying for a job, using the public recreation center, and eating at a favorite restaurant—could be the basic curriculum components for the school year, and all the academic, social, communication, and self-care skills needed for each activity could be taught as the class participated in that activity.

Because of the current emphasis on community-based instruction, many secondary students with moderate mental retardation are receiving instruction outside of the school setting for part of the school day. As we discussed earlier, community-based instruction can provide students with appropriate educational experiences and also maximize opportunities for social and physical integration.

During community-based instruction, a student learns work skills while he is on the job. (James Shaffer/ Digital)

● *Transition Programming*   Many people with mild mental retardation integrate themselves successfully into the life of their community with little or no outside assistance. They find jobs and do them well; they marry and begin their own families. Others, though, continue to need the help and support of social agencies. More and more, emphasis is being placed on the skills that young people need to make the transition from school to the working world. There is also a focus on the factors related to quality of life: social adjustment and integration into all aspects of the community. Research suggests the importance of community employment and living to the self-esteem of individuals with mental retardation (Griffin et al., 1996). The educational experiences that address the movement from school to work and from home or residential school to independent community living are referred to as **transitional programming**.

All secondary students with mental retardation now have a separate component of their IEP that identifies and describes the transition training they will receive. The transition plan, now mandated by IDEA, has resulted in the identification and promotion of effective transition practices (Hasazi, Furney, & DeStefano, 1999). Figure 5.4 provides an example of a transition plan. The importance of transition in the curriculum of students with mental retardation is likely to continue to increase as specific needs of adults with mild mental retardation are identified. Greater cooperation between the educational system, the business world, and adult social agencies will help to improve transition services.

Many professionals assert the importance of the student's voice in effective transition programming. **Self-determination**, which describes the active role the student takes, includes decision-making and self-advocacy, which may need to be taught to students with mental retardation. Many educators feel that a deep level of participation by the student is critical to a successful transition plan (Devlieger & Trach, 1999; Hasazi, Furney, & DeStefano, 1999). Spencer and Sands (1999) found that student, school, and family factors, including extent of inclusion, possession of job-related skills, ability to self-regulate, and family environment, were related to the level of student participation in transition plans.

Transitional programming addresses the experiences students need to move on to life after school.

Name DAVID RYAN		Date 7-1	
Transition Service Areas	**Person/Agency Responsible**	**Timeline**	**Comments**
A. Employment/ education goal: *Seek and secure a job*	*Transition coordinator, student*	*January of school year*	*Prepare career planning packet. Identify job sites.*
B. Home and family goal: *Prepare for marriage and family*	*Teacher*	*October of school year*	*Identify community resources.*
C. Leisure pursuits goal: *Attend special neighborhood events*	*Teacher, student*	*September of school year*	*Link interests with local options.*
D. Community involvement goal: *Know about wide range of services available in the community*	*Teacher*	*December of school year*	*Use community-based experiences.*
E. Emotional/physical health goal: *Seek personal counseling*	*Counselor, teacher*	*October of school year*	*Locate and contact community services.*
F. Personal responsibility and relationship goal: *Get along with others*	*Teacher, transition coordinator*	*January of school year*	*Identify interpersonal job skills required in warehouse setting.*

Figure 5.4

Individualized Transition Plan

Scenario: David is a 16-year-old male who is tired of school and wants to get a job. He is interested in finding a job working in a warehouse. His reading skills are adequate, and his math skills are weak. He also has some problems relating appropriately to peers. His probable subsequent environment: working in a nearby community, living at home, and having a car.

Source: M. E. Cronin & J. R. Patton (1993). *Life skills instruction for all students with special needs: A practical guide for integrating real life content into curriculum* (p. 57). Austin, TX: PRO-ED.

Transitional programming has become an integral part of the educational plans of most students with mental retardation. Recent research specific to the adjustment of students with mental retardation to the world of work suggests that more comprehensive and long-range transition support is necessary (Neubert, Tilson, & Ianacone, 1989). Steere and Cavaiuolo (2002) provide a specific example of an educational plan for independent employment and living (see Figure 5.5).

Delivery of Instruction

We see many commonalities in the instructional procedures used for students with mild and moderate mental retardation. A basic instructional technique focuses on the clear and straightforward presentation of tasks that have been carefully analyzed and sequenced. The process of breaking down a task or skill into its component parts is called **task analysis** (Alberto & Troutman, 2003). Teachers must be able to identify the skills required to complete a certain task (from preparing a sandwich to reading a newspaper article) and to develop an appropriate instructional sequence to teach them. The steps of a task analysis can be taught using a variety of techniques, ranging from physical guidance, to the use of verbal prompts, to observational learning. The level, or intensity, of instruction is directly related to the level of support required by the student. Researchers are constantly evaluating the most effective, most efficient, and least intrusive way to teach specific skills. For example, Biederman et al. (1998) found that children's simple observations of behavior were more effective than more intensive forms of instruction involving physical prompts when teaching children with mental retardation activities such as buttoning and putting puzzles together.

> Teaching students with mental retardation includes focusing on task analysis, a clear presentation of carefully sequenced tasks.

Prompts are clues or guides that maximize the probability that a student will answer correctly or attend to the appropriate material. Prompts are an important aspect of instruction in special education and are used extensively during initial instruction. If you underline the key word in a series of directions, you are prompting the student to attend to that key word. If you model the correct way to sound out a word, you are providing a prompt for the correct response. Prompts are then faded, or eliminated, over time. Prompts for teaching students with mental retardation may begin as physical prompts, such as a guiding hand. and then gradually move to verbal or visual prompts, such as a suggestion or picture. They may occur before or during skill performance; the timing of the prompt may have implications for skill acquisition and generalization. For example, Singleton et al. (1999) found that prompts occurring before skill performance resulted in quicker skill acquisition, and prompts occurring during skill performance facilitated maintenance and generalization.

> Prompting techniques are important strategies for teaching.

Many teachers focus on prompting students' awareness of their learning. Students with moderate mental retardation may need content-specific prompts, such as a series of pictures or photographs to remind them of what needs to be done. For example, a picture of a student raising his hand might prompt classroom behavior, or the words "wash, soap, dry" on the clothes' basket might prompt someone to follow the correct steps for doing the laundry. Browder and Minarovic (2000) found that nonreading students with moderate mental retardation were able to use sight word prompts and self-instruction to initiate work tasks in competitive employment settings. In another interesting study, Le Grice and Blampied (1994) taught students with moderate mental retardation to operate a video recorder and personal computer using color videotapes of a familiar staff member doing the steps of the skill. The videotape served as a sequenced

A.

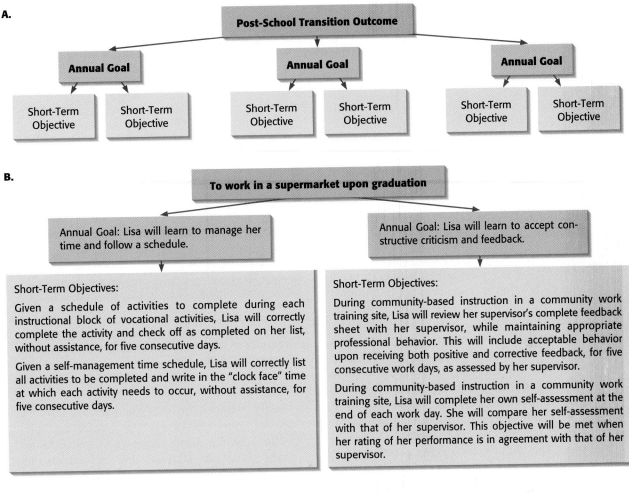

B.

C.

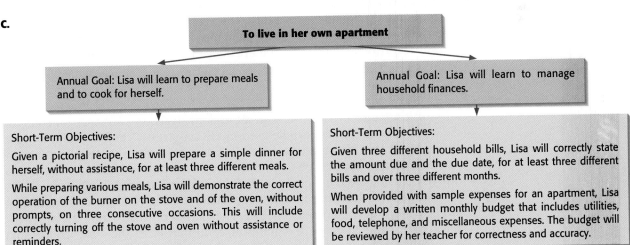

Figure 5.5

Educational Plans for Post-School Living: (A) Relationship of post-school outcomes to annual goals and short-term objectives; (B) Employment transition example; (C) Community-living transition example

Source: Steere and Cavaiuolo (2002). From Connecting outcomes, goals, and objecties in transition planning. *Teaching Exceptional Children, 34*(6) July/August 2002, pp. 56–57.

Technology Focus

Technology in Work Environments

A promising area of technology use for students with mental retardation is instruction in work and independent living skills. The two examples highlighted here involve using cues provided via technology to prompt and reinforce performance of new skills or behaviors in community settings. This technology helps to reduce the dependence of individuals with mental retardation on job support personnel during community-based instruction.

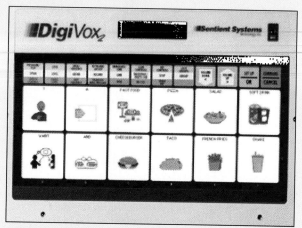

A Digivox, like this one, can be used to guide a student's performance of work-related skills by giving him picture and/or verbal prompts.

- Mechling and Gast (1997) used a Digivox, an augmentative communication device, to teach skills such as using a dishwasher to students with moderate mental retardation. The Digivox contains pictures or symbols that the student presses to release a corresponding digitized speech recording. A series of photographs of the student or teacher performing each step of the task was placed over the computer symbols, and the verbal directions for each step were recorded, enabling the students to use the Digivox to learn the series of tasks. The picture and synthesized speech cues helped to prompt the student's performance of each step of the vocational task.

- Davies, Stock, and Wehmeyer (2002) found that a multimedia palm-top computer program could also be used to provide pictoral and audio prompts for individuals during training in vocational tasks such as packaging software. The use of the Windows CE Visual Assistant Program allowed for individuals to receive both types of prompts for each step of the task analysis of two types of vocational skills. The researchers found that the use of the palm-top increased both independence and accuracy of skill performance.

series of prompts corresponding to the task analysis. We are only touching on the types of prompts that can be used in the classroom. The important thing to remember is that prompts can be easily integrated into regular classroom instruction. Recent applications of technology-based prompt systems used for vocational training are highlighted in the Technology Focus box here.

Cooperative learning is a strategy that provides children of various skill levels with a task to complete together. The teacher must structure the activity to allow each child to make a significant contribution to the task. Cooperative learning is a good strategy to keep in mind when teaching students with mental retardation in an integrated classroom (Sonnier-York & Stanford, 2002). Peer tutoring or peer support programs are related strategies for teaching students with mental retardation in general education settings. When teachers provide structured activities for peer tutoring groups, this increases the amount of time all students are academically engaged during a classroom period and can improve their academic performance (Copeland et al., 2002; Mortweet, 1999). Research

Teaching Strategies & Accommodations

Simple Strategies for Teaching Students with Mental Retardation

- Teach students in small groups (three or four students).
- Teach one concept or skill at a time.
- Teach steps or strategies for learning (a plan for remembering or sequencing information).
- Provide ample opportunity for practice (practice often, but don't overload).
- Use prompts to promote correct responding (examples, modeling, physical guidance).

emphasizes the importance of the special educator's presence in the general education classroom to support the general education teacher when students with moderate to severe mental retardation are served in inclusive settings (Snell & Janney, 2000). The special educator can work with the general education teacher to provide appropriate levels of attention, instruction, and behavior management to all the students in the classroom.

Students receiving instruction in a functional curriculum also have many learning experiences that require attention, remembering, and organizing. These activities can range from something as simple as learning a telephone number and address to remembering the steps involved in following a recipe, writing a check, or going shopping for groceries. Instruction also needs to be sequenced and structured carefully, with reliance on prompts to illustrate how to do the task as well as when to do it. Basic instructional guidelines are found in the Teaching Strategies box entitled, "Simple Strategies for Teaching Students with Mental Retardation."

It is important for all educational programs and other school activities to emphasize the importance of socialization and friendships between all students. Interaction with peers is a major focus of education—an important consideration for successful community integration in later years as well as during school. Students in self-contained programs may be mainstreamed into lunch or arts classes in order to provide at least minimal interactions with peers. Many educators, however, feel that more complete assimilation in regular classes is necessary. Sometimes, the need for special instruction and training must be weighed against the philosophy of integration and the need for social interaction as educators and parents try to decide on the most appropriate program for an individual child.

Materials

Because of the issue of skill transfer and generalization, the types of materials used in instruction can be very important, particularly when life skills or vocational skills are being taught. Both simulated materials and real-life materials have their uses. If you were teaching sight words found in the environment, an example of a simulated material would be the word *exit* printed in red capital letters on a rectangular card placed over the doorway of the classroom. An alternative would be to use the real thing and conduct your lesson using the actual exit sign over the door at the end of the hallway. Because not all teachers are able to take their students into the community for training on a daily basis, teachers and researchers have looked at ways to combine the use of simulated materials with real materials in natural environments. For example, Morse and Schuster (2000) found that a combination of community-based instruction and simulation training using a picture story board, a board on which representative pictures or cut-outs are used for illustration, resulted in successful instruction and maintenance of grocery-shopping skills. Branham et al. (1999) found that a videotape of individuals modeling certain skills, such as mailing a letter and cashing a check, was an even more effective addition to community-based instruction than classroom simulation. As our knowledge of the most effective ways to combine alternative instructional strategies with community-based instruction grows, we increase opportunities for teaching a wide range of important life skills.

Instruction using real materials can help students generalize skills.

The use of real materials in natural environments is, however, a critical component of effective instruction for many students with mental retardation. Real materials can motivate as well as facilitate generalization. As we've mentioned, using an actual checkbook folder and checks may be a good way to practice subtraction and addition skills that can easily be integrated into the regular curriculum. Many schools have had success at integrating the more functional objectives of a student's curriculum into their regular classroom curriculum.

Students who are in the regular classroom for the academic curriculum will probably use the same materials as everyone else. The resource or consulting teacher may work with the classroom teacher to develop strategies for helping the student interact with the text and other materials. Some materials are designed specifically for curriculum packages for students with learning difficulties. At the elementary level these materials are often found in programs for basic skills instruction (reading or math), such as the SRA Corrective Reading Series (a similar program is illustrated in Chapter 4). At the secondary level, these materials might include low-vocabulary, high-interest reading materials such as teen magazines or plays. The regular education teacher can ask the resource teacher or consultant about available materials or catalogs.

Personal and Civil Rights

The battle for personal and civil rights for people with mental retardation is not yet over.

The history of educating individuals with mental retardation includes acts and philosophies that ignore personal and civil rights. Today, many legal and ethical dilemmas remain unresolved. Many adults with mental retardation have to fight for access to fair housing, for the right to marry and have children, and for the opportunity to work in community settings.

It is difficult for most persons with mental retardation to wage an effective campaign for personal rights, since the mental competence of the individual is often determined to be unknown or insufficient and the parents or other legal surrogate must legally represent the individual. Often, the wishes of the parent and the individual may be different, resulting in decisions that are at odds with the individual's preferred outcomes. Another issue receiving a lot of attention today is the fact that the judicial system does not consider persons with mental retardation a protected class. This means that persons with mental retardation are eligible for, among other things, the death penalty. The apparent inequities in the legal system and the potential for abuse through representation suggest that advocacy is an important function for everyone interested in the fair treatment of *all* people.

A Closer Look — Employment Opportunities

People with mild mental retardation continue to face serious problems finding meaningful work. From the mid-1980s to the mid-1990s, hourly wages increased, as did the employment rate, but 65 percent of individuals with cognitive disabilities remained unemployed (Frank & Sitlington, 2000; Wehman, West, & Kregel, 1999). Employment options for persons with disabilities include (1) sheltered employment, (2) supported employment, and (3) independent competitive employment in community settings.

Sheltered employment

In sheltered employment, individuals with mental retardation are in segregated work settings, usually set up as assembly-line workshops, in which individuals work on assigned contracts. Typically, these contracts involve activities such as assembling items or putting packets together. The adults who work in sheltered workshops receive payment on a piecework basis; that is, they get paid for each task or product that is finished.

Supported employment

In supported work settings, people are placed in jobs that are either located in integrated settings or that facilitate social integration. The term *supported* refers to the training, supervision, and sometimes financial assistance that is provided to the individual and the employer in the work setting. There are a number of different models for supported employment, including the mobile work crew, the enclave, and supported jobs (Kiernan & Stark, 1986).

- The **mobile work crew** is a group of individuals with disabilities who learn a specific trade or set of skills that can be applied in the community, such as gardening and catering. The mobile work crew offers an avenue for supported employment in locations that have few businesses or work opportunities, such as in rural farming communities. A major disadvantage, however, is the fact that the crew continues to work as a segregated unit.

- An **enclave** is a small group of individuals with disabilities who are placed in a work setting, usually within a large business or corporation. They receive on-the-job training and support from job coaches, schools, or social service agencies and from within the corporation. Training may begin with an expected level of partial or limited skill performance; as individuals become more adept and receive more training, more work is required. The financial responsibility for paying individuals within an enclave will be gradually assumed by the employer.

- The **individual supported job model** involves one-to-one coaching and teaching of a single individual in a job setting. In an individual supported job model, a job coach, or employment specialist (Wehman & Targett, 2002) provides on-site training and ongoing problem solving. Typically, the level of support will diminish until only occasional visits are needed. Supported job models may lead to independent competitive employment as the need for support fades and the individual learns to perform effectively in the work setting.

Independent competitive employment

Most students with mild mental retardation, and many with moderate mental retardation, will find independent competitive employment. Agencies such as vocational rehabilitation may be tapped, but often individuals seek and get jobs independently. Many individuals with disabilities who find competitive employment independently work in low-paying jobs and are unsatisfied with their work (Edgar, 1988; Neel et al., 1988). These people may be more likely to quit their jobs or to continue to depend on their families for housing or support. Continued research on needed skills for adult employment, and the requirements for transition planning at the secondary school level will help to address these difficulties and result in more employment options and increased job satisfaction. Tools to identify and evaluate work performance, employee satisfaction, and needed support for both employers and employees are the focus of additional research designed to promote long-lasting and satisfying community employment for individuals with disabilities (Brady & Rosenberg, 2002).

A great place to learn more about the role you can play as an advocate for individuals with mental retardation is the website for the Association for Retarded Citizens (ARC) at **http://www.thearc.org**. It features an Action Alert and has a direct link to an Action Center for people interested in advocacy in action.

? Pause and Reflect

Most of us would agree that the basic goals of education are to prepare us for independent work, life in society, and personal satisfaction. These goals are no different for individuals with mental retardation. What are some things you could do and changes you could make in your home or in your place of work to support the individual independence of a person with cognitive disabilities? ●

SUMMARY

- The AAMR definition of mental retardation includes three criteria: subaverage intellectual functioning, impairments in adaptive behavior, and manifestation during the developmental period.

- Mental retardation is usually classified as mild, moderate, severe, or profound. Approximately 1 percent of school-age students are identified as having mental retardation. Of these, 80 to 85 percent have mild mental retardation. The causes of retardation include both biological and environmental factors.

- Students with mental retardation may have trouble learning how to learn (metacognition), remembering, coming to and maintaining attention, and generalizing. Language development may be delayed, although most differences are quantitative rather than qualitative. Students may be smaller and more prone to health problems, although physical differences generally are not visible. Students may also exhibit inappropriate social behavior.

- Parents and siblings adjust their familial roles to accommodate a child with mental retardation. Siblings often spend more time on child care, though not at the expense of peer relationships.

- A functional curriculum emphasizes independent functioning, incorporating academic skills such as reading in a real-life context. Teaching strategies that can be used by regular or special educators include task analysis, the use of prompts, cooperative learning, and the use of concrete materials. Computers provide drill and practice, word processing, tutorials, and other instructional assistance.

- Transition programs are designed to help students achieve as much independence as possible through employment, living arrangements, and social relationships.

KEY TERMS

mental retardation

Stanford-Binet Intelligence Scale

Wechsler Intelligence Scale for Children, Third Edition (WISC-III)

adaptive behavior

AAMR Adaptive Behavior Scale

Vineland Adaptive Behavior Scales

skill transfer (generalization)

immature behavior

functional academics

life-skills curriculum

community-based instruction

transitional programming

task analysis

prompts

self-determination

cooperative learning

sheltered employment

supported employment

mobile work crew

enclave

individual supported job model

USEFUL RESOURCES

- American Association on Mental Retardation (AAMR), 444 North Capitol Street, Washington, DC 20001-1512, (202) 387-1968, **http://www.aamr.org**. This website provides extensive information and resources about mental retardation, including research, books, policy, events, and a wide range of other services.

- ARC National Headquarters, 500 East Border, Suite 300, Arlington, TX 76010; (817) 261-6003. Information about programs and national policies affecting individuals with mental retardation and the ARC newsletter can be obtained from ARC headquarters.

- *The Capitol Connection Policy Newsletter*. Published by the Division on Career Development and Transition, the Council for Exceptional Children, 1920 Association Drive, Reston, VA 20191. This newsletter addresses interdisciplinary policy and practice in career preparation and transition to postsecondary education, employment, and responsible citizenship for special learners.

- Center for Applied Special Technology (CAST), 39 Cross Street, Peabody, MA 01960, **cast@cast.org**. This center provides information on assistive technology resourecs and educational applications.

- *Down Syndrome News*. Newsletter of the National Down Syndrome Congress; (800) 232-6372. This newsletter can serve as a source of information and support for professionals, parents, siblings, and individuals with Down syndrome.

- *Graduating Peter*. Gerardine Wurzburg, State of the Art, Inc., 2002. This excellent documentary, originally shown on HBO, chronicles the life of an adolescent with Down syndrome and the lives of his family as he attends inclusive programs in middle school and high school.

- *Sibling Information Network Newsletter*. A. J. Pappenikou Center on Special Education and Rehabilitation, University of Connecticut, 249 Glenbrook Road, Box U-64, Storrs, CT 06269.

PORTFOLIO ACTIVITIES

1. Visit your local high school and make an appointment with a job coach for individuals with mental retardation. Try to arrange an observation of a community-based job training session. Describe the observation and record the specific instructional strategies used by the job coach, the methods of job evaluation, and the social interaction between the trainee and his or her colleagues.

✓*Standards* This activity can help the student meet CEC Content Standard 7: Instructional Planning.

2. Send out a survey to local business people to find out their needs and attitudes regarding disabilities. Present data from the survey that address the following questions: Would they want to hire a person with a disability? What types of jobs would they suggest for individuals with mental retardation? What would the employers' expectations be? Support? Pay? Security?

✓*Standards* This activity can help the student meet CEC Content Standard 5: Learning Environments and Social Interactions.

3. Visit a group home and interview its residents and staff. Record or transcribe your interview. Find out what type of contact residents have with the community (for example, shopping in local stores, riding public transportation). Discuss their views on the value of community living.

✓*Standards* This activity can help the student meet CEC Content Standard 3: Individual Learning Differences.

4. Observe several secondary or elementary classrooms in a local school. Identify the teaching strategies and materials used in the classroom. What adaptations might the teacher have to make to accommodate and support a student with mild or moderate mental retardation? Talk with the teacher to see what types of instructional adjustments he or she may have made in the past. Create a notebook of suggested teaching strategies, materials, and adaptations for use in your classroom.

✓*Standards* This activity can help the student meet CEC Content Standard 4: Instructional Strategies.

To access an electronic portfolio template for these activities, visit our website through http://www.education. college.hmco.com/students/.

Children with Severe Disabilities

6

Learning Objectives

After reading this chapter, the reader will:

- Define normalization/social role valorization and describe how this philosophy influences the educational options available to students with severe disabilities.

- Describe the roles of both physical and social integration in the inclusion of individuals with severe disabilities into school and the community.

- Describe the ways a teacher can identify skills to be included in a student's life-skills curriculum.

- Identify ways an educational team can prepare a transition plan that will enable the student with severe disabilities to move to an integrated setting.

- Identify the community living options available to individuals with severe disabilities.

Outline

Terms and Definitions
    Severe Disabilities
    Severe and Profound Mental Retardation
    Prevalence
Causes of Severe Disabilities
Characteristics of Individuals with Severe Disabilities
    Cognitive Development
    Physical Development and Health
    Language Development and Communication
    Social Behaviors and Emotional Development
Effects on the Family
    Family Attitudes and Reactions
    Family Roles in Education
Teaching Strategies and Accommodations
    Normalization
    Inclusion
    Curriculum
    Transition Programming
Ethical Issues
    The Right to Life
    The Right to Education
SUMMARY
KEY TERMS
USEFUL RESOURCES
PORTFOLIO ACTIVITIES

Students with severe disabilities can benefit greatly from an educational program that prepares them for participation in the community. In this chapter, we introduce educational strategies designed to maximize these students' potential, and raise questions about the protection of their rights.

Although all children with disabilities experience significant challenges in their lives, children with severe disabilities face the greatest and most comprehensive challenges—typically both cognitive and physical. Today, the outlook and opportunities for individuals with severe and profound disabilities are now greater than you might think, certainly greater that many parents and professionals ever anticipated. Someone with severe mental retardation may be living in a home down the street from you, or may be the young man bagging groceries in your neighborhood grocery store. However, many of us are not afforded, nor do we seek, the opportunity to interact in a meaningful way with people who have severe disabilities. Although programs that prepare persons with severe disabilities to work, live, or interact with other members of the community are steadily increasing in both quantity and quality, there are still not enough of them. Often, schools provide our best models of integration; unfortunately, sometimes they demonstrate only segregation and a lack of tolerance. Schools can select programs, curricula, and activities that promote and develop knowledge, acceptance, and interaction among all individuals, including those who have severe disabilities.

Terms and Definitions

Individuals who are identified as having severe disabilities may display a variety of primary disabilities. In this section, we will look briefly at a general description of severe disabilities as well as the definitions of severe and profound mental retardation—terms included in the broader term of severe disabilities.

Severe Disabilities

Individuals with severe disabilities require extensive support in major life activities.

The Association for Persons with Severe Handicaps (TASH), a professional and family organization designed to provide advocacy and services for individuals with severe disabilities, describes people with severe disabilities in the following resolution statement:

> TASH addresses the interests of persons with disabilities who have traditionally been excluded from the mainstream of society. These persons include individuals with disabilities of all ages, races, creeds, national origins, genders, and sexual orientation who require ongoing support in one or more major life activity in order to participate in an integrated community and enjoy a quality of life similar to that available to all citizens. Support may be required for life activities such as mobility, communication, self-care, and learning as necessary for community living, employment, and self-sufficiency. (TASH, 2000)

To learn more about TASH and the organization's resolutions related to many facets of life for all individuals, including people with severe disabilities, visit its website at **http://www.tash.org**.

Although most disabilities can range in intensity from mild to severe (for example, learning disabilities, behavior disorders), the term **severe disabilities**

Communication, in all its forms, is the basis of all learning. (Ellen Senisi/The Image Works, Inc.)

is used in this chapter to refer primarily to individuals who have severe or profound mental retardation. The life supports and educational programs required by these individuals are typically more extensive than those required by individuals with other types of disabilities.

Severe and Profound Mental Retardation

The federal definition of **severe mental retardation** includes an IQ of less than 40 and the manifestation of deficits in adaptive behavior, with both areas of deficit originating during the developmental period—before the age of 18. **Profound mental retardation** varies only in the range of the IQ score, which is 20 and below. It is sometimes very difficult to determine the extent of mental retardation in an infant. This is particularly true when the child also has severe health or sensory impairments. Thus, the extent of mental retardation often cannot be determined until the child is much older. As you might expect, however, IQ scores, which are highly correlated with academic success, don't tell us much about individual children or adults when we are looking at scores of 30 or 18. IQ scores at this range do not yield information useful in providing educational support in everyday living skills. So, typical test information provides us with little usable data. Probably more than with any other group of students, it is important that we, as teachers, family, or friends, pay very close attention to what a student *can* do, and how he or she is trying to convey information. This information will guide us in planning instruction—not IQ scores. Individuals with severe disabilities are dependent on the people in their environment to provide opportunities for communication, growth, and a sense of belonging. Education will focus on what we need to do to support each individual's development.

Prevalence

The number of students served in the schools with severe disabilities could be recorded in several places, including the areas of mental retardation and physical disabilities. Typically, however, students with severe disabilities are identified through the category of multiple disabilities (NICHCY, 2002). During the 2000–2001 school year, 122,559 students with multiple disabilities received special education service (U.S. Department of Education, 2002).

❓ Pause and Reflect

If you look at the general definition of severe disabilities and the definitions of severe and profound mental retardation, you may notice a very basic difference. The TASH resolution focuses on the level of external support needed for individuals to participate in the community, and the federal definitions focus on individual performance or scores on assessment instruments. How do the different definitions cause you to look at the population of individuals with severe disabilities? Why do you think the TASH resolution intentionally focused on external rather than internal factors? ●

Causes of Severe Disabilities

There are numerous causes of severe and profound mental retardation, including genetic syndromes, physical trauma, and disease. Most of the causes of mental retardation presented in Chapter 5, such as fetal alcohol syndrome, may affect individuals differentially and can sometimes result in severe or profound levels of mental retardation. Some children with severe disabilities happen to be born with a cluster of disabilities, one of which is severe or profound mental retardation. The genetic syndromes we discussed in the last chapter, including Down syndrome, Klinefelter's syndrome, Turner's syndrome, fragile-X syndrome, and Tay–Sachs disease, result in a number of common physical, behavior, and intellectual characteristics and may cause severe mental retardation. The probability of having a child with some of these conditions can be determined through genetic counseling. Some, such as Down syndrome, can be detected through tests conducted during pregnancy, such as amniocentesis.

Other causes, such as physical trauma to the head caused by accidents or child abuse, can result in severe brain damage and mental retardation. Medical abnormalities, such as brain tumors, and diseases, such as meningitis, can also cause severe disabilities.

In most cases, the ways we teach students with severe disabilities will be the same regardless of the cause. As we mentioned, it is critical to attend to the particular skills and abilities of each child. However, there are times when knowing the cause of a disability can be important; for example, certain physical disabilities or health concerns are associated with specific syndromes, such as Down syndrome and cerebral palsy. As a teacher, you should become familiar with the characteristics of these conditions to avoid exposing your students to injury or health risks through some play or exercise activities. Sometimes, knowing the cause of severe disabilities can help teachers know what to expect and be better prepared for instruction (Hodapp & Fidler, 1999). For example, if we know that children with some syndromes are likely to show extreme self-abusive behavior, we will be better prepared both emotionally and instructionally to deal with these difficult circumstances.

Neither social and economic status, nor the general intellectual ability of the parents, seem to be related to the incidence of severe or profound mental retardation, which is estimated to be .7 percent, or 7 per 1000 births. Medical technology enables many individuals with severe disabilities to live much longer than in previous years; however, infants born with severe and profound mental retardation continue to be at high risk due to low birthweight and other complicating factors, such as respiratory complications, congenital heart defects, and accidental trauma (Hayes et al., 1997; Strauss et al., 1999).

? Pause and Reflect

Probably the most challenging prospect facing new parents is the possibility of having a child with severe disabilities. Mothers and fathers may rack their brains trying to identify causes; some may wonder why they did not seek genetic counseling. It is impossible to know or even anticipate how you would react if you had a child with a severe disability—it is possible, however, to reflect on the importance of family and community. What community resources and activities could be identified to support students and their parents currently meeting the challenge of living with severe disabilities? ●

FIRST PERSON

My Friend Carolyn

It is said that beauty is in the eye of the beholder. In Carolyn's eyes, everything is beautiful. She is always so happy that beauty seems to generate into the hearts of everyone around her.

Carolyn Dadd, 15, has moyamoya disease. She cannot walk, talk or feed herself, and she requires total care. She knows the people around her, though. I only wish more people could realize how capable she is.

I am 19 years old, and I have been Carolyn's sitter for the past seven years. I first met Carolyn when I was 12 and she was 9. I had never seen anyone quite like her. She was very small then, barely 60 pounds. Her smile was deep as if it sank back into her soul. When we met she raised her hand in a gentle motion to touch my face and laughed as if there was a joke beween us. Soon I found

myself laughing, too. That day started our friendship—one that I will cherish the rest of my life. It was obvious that Carolyn was different from anyone I had ever met, and that is exactly what I liked about her.

Jessica Morgan

Moyamoya disease is a progressive disease that affects the blood vessels in the brain. It is characterized by narrowing and/or closing of the carotid artery. This lack of blood may cause paralysis of the feet, legs, or upper extremities. Headaches, various vision problems, mental retardation, and psychiatric problems may also occur.

Source: "Good Things Come in Small Packages" by Jessica Morgan. From *Exceptional Parent,* July 2000. Reprinted with the expressed consent and approval of *Exceptional Parent,* a monthly magazine for parents and families of children with disabilities and special health care needs. Subscription cost is $39.95 per year for 12 issues; call (877) 372-7368. Offices at 65 E. Rte. 4, River Edge, N.J. 07661.

Characteristics of Individuals with Severe Disabilities

If you ask parents, siblings, and teachers of individuals with severe disabilities what the effects of those disabilities have been on the children themselves, you will get a wide range of answers. It is sometimes difficult to describe the effects of severe disabilities when you are personally involved. You keep thinking of the *person* with the disabilities—John is a hard-working student; Susan enjoys music; Mary is a little temperamental in the morning. Even when the disabilities are very challenging and sometimes overwhelming, you come to know and appreciate each individual.

Cognitive Development

The specific effects of mental retardation on cognitive development, which are discussed in detail in Chapter 5, include problems in such areas as selective attention, maintaining attention, short-term memory, metacognitive skills, and the maintenance, transfer, and generalization of skills. These problems may exist to an even greater degree in persons with severe and profound mental disabilities. Most people with severe or profound mental retardation experience disabilities across all cognitive skill areas.

The effects of severe disabilities on cognitive development are related partially to the learning experiences the person has throughout life, particularly in the early years. The frequent coexistence of physical or health impairments with severe cognitive disabilities often results in a reduction in the normal environmental interactions considered instrumental in the development of cognitive abilities. For example, an infant without severe disabilities, while lying in his crib, may accidentally hit the side of the crib with his hand and hear the noise it makes. After this happens a few times, the child will make the connection between his hand movement and the noise it makes against the crib. This is called an understanding of cause and effect. The realization that something you do can have predictable consequences is an important tool for learning to control and interact with the environment. Another example, recognized immediately by parents and infants, is the connection between crying and parental attention. The child may begin to hit his hand against the crib for the purpose of making the noise or cry in order to be held. He intentionally does something to get a specific result—attention from a parent. This purposeful behavior is referred to as a *means-end relationship*. The development of an understanding of cause and effect and of means-end relationships is critical for children to begin to explore their environments actively and with purpose; these skills are also considered important in language development (Iacono & Miller, 1989).

The child with severe or profound disabilities may experience difficulty learning these early skills in the typical way. A child with severe physical disabilities or with very delayed motor development may not be aware that it is her hand that is hitting the side of the crib—or she may not have sufficient motor control to direct it to happen again. A child with severe mental retardation may be unable to understand that her mother appears two or three minutes after she has started crying. As a result, the child may have difficulty making a connection between the things she does and the results of these actions or behaviors. The infant, therefore, may not acquire these important behaviors unas-

Understanding cause and effect and means-ends relationships is critical for most cognitive skills.

Grocery shopping is an important domestic life skill. Life skills are best learned in community settings. (Robin Sachs/PhotoEdit)

sisted and may not attempt to interact with the world around her. The child simply may not know that what she does makes any difference.

Many children with severe disabilities, however, do have the cognitive ability to learn communication, to indicate wants and needs, and to perform a series of steps necessary to perform domestic, community, or vocational skills. Students with severe mental retardation will have limited ability to perform academic-type tasks, so education does not focus on academic areas. Individuals with profound mental retardation may present educators or parents with great challenges in establishing specific communication skills, or teaching students to perform skills or tasks.

Physical Development and Health

Children with severe and profound mental retardation are usually much below average in physical size and may experience a wide range of physical and health-related difficulties (McDonnell, Hardman, & McDonnell, 2003). As we have mentioned, mental retardation to this degree of severity is typically accompanied by other disabilities.

Infants born with severe and profound mental retardation often experience significant delays in physical development. Because of this delay, the infant may have very limited physical movement at the beginning of life.

Sometimes, physical disabilities and health risks are associated with the specific syndrome or condition responsible for the mental retardation. Children with Down syndrome, for example, often require heart surgery at a very young age because of congenital heart defects, and they are at risk for respiratory problems. Children with severe mental retardation and cerebral palsy may have varying degrees of motor impairment; sometimes, the physical disabilities may affect mobility, speech, and regulated motor activity. A number of children will be prone to a seizure disorder such as epilepsy, although most types of seizures can be controlled or reduced by appropriate medication. Other syndromes or conditions may be degenerative in nature: The conditions will worsen over

Children with severe and profound mental retardation often experience health-related difficulties and severe delays in physical development.

time, and the child's health will become progressively worse, until death occurs. An example we have already mentioned is Tay–Sachs disease.

In some instances, the physical development of the child with severe or profound mental retardation is compromised as a side effect of extreme developmental delay. Intrusive procedures may be required on a regular basis to maintain comfort and sustain life. For example, a child who must be catheterized daily or fed through a stomach tube is exposed to more opportunities for infection and, therefore, illness.

A number of children with profound mental retardation may not be independently mobile and thus may not use their limbs with any regularity. This can result in atrophy of the muscles. Other individuals may have mobility, but also may require guidance and instruction to participate in physical activity of either a therapeutic or recreational nature. Therapeutic physical activity, including physical therapy, can increase strength and flexibility and prevent some health problems (Green & Reid, 1999). Physical activities not only have obvious health benefits, but also can serve an important recreational function and contribute to independent movement and psychological well-being (Modell & Cox, 1999).

Language Development and Communication

Severe and profound disabilities can have extensive effects on an individual's language development and communicative abilities. Some people with severe or profound retardation will have limited spontaneous oral language, others will have nonfunctional oral language, and some, no oral language at all. The presence or lack of spontaneous oral language does not, however, imply that no communication system can be taught. Research suggests that by far the most common form of expressive communication used by children with severe disabilities is direct behavior, such as dragging adults to the desired place or object, getting the desired object, or throwing away an undesired object (Harvey & Sall, 1999). Once again we see the strong and obvious relationship between behavior and communication. New communication skills, whether they are verbal or nonverbal, must be as efficient and as easy to use as the behaviors students are currently using. In other words, the communication must be **functional communication**—easy to use and easily understandable (Ostrosky, Drasgow, & Halle, 1999). The Teaching Strategies box entitled, "Guidelines for Developing Functional Communication Systems" presents a set of guidelines for developing functional communication skills for individuals with severe disabilities.

Nonverbal communication systems include sign language and language boards or communication boards. On communication boards, words or symbols that represent possible needs and requests are placed on a lap board, and the person communicates by indicating the appropriate word or picture. Many people with severe and profound mental retardation do find ways of communicating their wishes and controlling their environment by using nonverbal means.

Regardless of the method of communication selected, critical factors for effective communication include the preparation and interest of communication partners and an environment that supports individual interaction and communication (Butterfield & Arthur, 1995). Family interaction and support are critical, and the technical efficacy of a communication system must be weighed against the extent to which a family will encourage its use. In other words, the communication system must fit within the family dynamic and work for family members in order to be effective. Factors such as the weight and cumbersome nature of a communication board, the monotone sound and volume of a system using

> Many people with severe or profound disabilities can use a verbal or nonverbal communication system.

Teaching Strategies & Accommodations

Guidelines for Developing Functional Communication Systems

1. Take advantage of the existing communication skills of students with severe disabilities.

- Observe the communication strategies students already use to communicate. Ask yourself: What forms of communication does this student consistently and intentionally use to communicate? Observe these forms across settings, routines, and activities.

- Build on existing types of communicative behavior by teaching socially desirable and functionally equivalent forms of behavior that are more easily understood by others.

2. Select functional communication targets and identify powerful teaching opportunities.

- When selecting communication targets, ask yourself: Will learning this behavior help the student become more independent?

- Select potential teaching opportunities that will likely result in high levels of motivation by capitalizing on current student-initiated communicative occasions.

3. Facilitate the widespread use of the new forms of behavior.

- Identify the situations in which students currently use their existing communication forms (for example, generalized use of the existing form).

- Determine the consequences that might be supporting this generalization.

- Teach the new communication form in all situations where the student currently uses the existing form. Careful attention to, and reflection on, one's own behavior and prudent observation of student behavior are necessary.

4. Ensure maintenance of the new behavior.

- When replacing existing forms of communicative behavior, take care to ensure that the new form requires less physical effort and produces reinforcement more rapidly and more frequently than the old one.

Source: M. M. Ostrosky, E. Drasgow, & J. W. Halle (1999). How can I help you get what you want? *Teaching Exceptional Children, 31*(4), 58.

---

artificial language, and the simple visibility of assistive technology may interfere with a family's desired goals of social acceptance for their child and for themselves (Parette & McMahan, 2002).

Social Behaviors and Emotional Development

By definition, students with severe and profound mental retardation will have deficits in adaptive behavior. The extent to which appropriate adaptive behaviors, such as self-help skills and general social skills, are acquired will vary according to the severity of the disability, the type and breadth of educational programming, and the environment in which the person lives, works, or goes to school. For example, improvements in some areas of adaptive behavior have been found when persons with mental retardation live in group homes rather than institutional settings and work in competitive employment versus sheltered workshops (Inge et al., 1988; Sullivan, Vitello, & Foster, 1988).

Because the label severe disabilities can encompass a wide range of ability and performance levels, it is difficult to characterize "typical" social behavior. For a few persons, social development may be very limited, and target skills may include establishing eye contact or acknowledging someone's presence. Some individuals will have inappropriate behaviors, and interventions may then focus on reducing acting-out or tantrum-like behaviors (McDonnell, Hardman, & McDonnell, 2003). For others, social development goals may include appropriate social interaction in a community work setting. Often, a drawback to successful social interaction is the lack of a common communication system. Storey and Provost (1996) found that the use of communication books (essentially picture books) increased the amount of social interaction as well as interpersonal communication between individuals with severe disabilities and their nondisabled coworkers in a community work setting. The communication book provided a method everyone could use to "talk" to each other. Problems in communicative ability are also related to the presence of inappropriate or aberrant behavior (Sigafoos, 2000). Children with severe levels of aberrant behavior, such as self-injury, displayed fewer communication skills.

Although there is very little descriptive research available on the emotional development of persons with severe or profound mental disabilities, we know that all people experience an array of emotions. In some instances, we must learn to recognize the indicators of basic human emotions such as love, trust, fear, and happiness. For example, Yu and coworkers (2002) developed an observational recording system that allows observers to recognize distinct and reliable behavior indicators of happiness in individuals with severe and profound cognitive disabilities as they participate in work and recreational activities. The fact that researchers are devoting time to evaluating emotions such as happiness is an important sign the studies increasingly are focusing on improving the quality of life of individuals with severe disabilities. Some aspects of emotional development and expression are more easily observed. The management or appropriate demonstration of emotions such as anger or frustration is an important aspect of adaptive behavior. The development and nurturing of many emotions rest with the significant others in the person's life, including the family.

Pause and Reflect

As you think about the characteristics of individuals with severe disabilities, reflect on the important interaction between each person and his or her surroundings. Our expectations for individuals with severe disabilities—our ability to see children in schools and adults in community settings—is a result not only of philosophical changes, but also of our knowledge about the importance of appropriate environmental support. You are part of the environment—what is your role in supporting individuals with severe disabilities? ●

Effects on the Family

In this section, we will look at the joys and struggles of families of children with severe disabilities. We will also discuss the multiple roles that parents of children with severe disabilities must play.

Family Attitudes and Reactions

Many children with severe or profound mental retardation are diagnosed at birth, or shortly thereafter, and families must immediately confront the prospect of rearing a child with a severe disability (McDonnell, Hardman, & McDonnell, 2003). As you might expect, reactions to this diagnosis and the onslaught of ensuing emotions vary greatly. Parents have many questions about what the future holds for them and their other children: How can I care for this child? What will happen to her when I'm no longer around? How will my other children react to their brother? Some of these questions will be answered in time, some can be answered through education, and some can never be answered.

You may see many differences in the lives of families that include an individual with severe disabilities. It is interesting to note, however, that mothers of youngsters with severe disabilities, like all mothers, hope and expect that their children will be able to achieve independence (Lehmann & Baker, 1995). Although there are more services than ever before to assist families, many parents are concerned about the lack of community support and related services, such as respite care and speech therapy, that are available to them—services that are necessary for community inclusion and maximum independence for their child (Turnbull & Ruef, 1997). Parents of children with severe disabilities, especially those who have complex medical needs, are particularly vulnerable to stress. Factors such as availability of services, financial issues, care of other children in the family, and continuing medical care are weighed by parents as they try to make appropriate and life-altering decisions about caring for their child (Bruns, 2000).

Parents, of course, are not the only family members affected by the presence of a child with severe disabilities. Brothers and sisters will have their own reactions and ways of dealing with them. Reactions can range from resentment to extreme protectiveness; probably the whole spectrum of emotions will be experienced at some point during the sibling's lifetime. Although it is not unusual for siblings of children with mental retardation to experience high levels of stress, many children develop very close relationships with each other (Lindsey & Stewart, 1989).

Most children with severe or profound mental retardation are diagnosed at birth.

Family Roles in Education

The family of an individual with severe or profound disabilities can play an active role in educational programming from the very beginning. The passage of P.L. 99-457 in 1986 provided the legislative impetus needed for the establishment of federal programs for infants and young children with disabilities and their families (Campbell, Bellamy, & Bishop, 1988). The importance of early intervention and family responsiveness in the development of children with severe and profound mental retardation, as well as any type of disability, has been recognized for a long time. Parents who learn how to encourage language or communication, or who are trained to provide at-home occupational therapy, will feel more competent in dealing with their child, and will help that child to build an important and perhaps critical learning foundation. Educators must incorporate parents' goals and priorities, particularly in areas such as communication, curriculum content, and educational procedures (Stephenson & Dowrick, 2000). Dunst (2002, p. 140) identified the following four critical components of family-centered intervention models:

Early intervention programs provide crucial services for children with severe disabilities and their families.

1. Relational components
   a. Family friendliness/interpersonal skills
   b. Practitioner attitudes and behavior about family capabilities

FIRST PERSON

Keeping Sophia Healthy, Alive

If there is one clear thing about the quest to save 13-month-old Sophia Herzog Sachs' life, it is that it reaches out to us all. It includes Western pediatricians and Eastern herbalists. It includes neighbors as well as strangers. It includes prayer circles and those with just plain beliefs and wishes. The diagnosis is that this tiny charmer of a toddler with large brown eyes will die from Type A Niemann–Pick disease. And that is unacceptable to her parents, Karen Herzog, 42, and Richard Sachs, 49, who are Ashkenazi Jews—a population affected by the disease. In 20 years, Lucile Packard Children's Hospital at Stanford had not seen a single case. The nation's top center for what are called lysosomal storage diseases, the Mount Sinai School of Medicine, has seen only 40 cases in 20 years. None of the children lived. "It's awful," said Dr. Greg Enns, director of the Stanford genetics program and co-director of the University of California-San Francisco Lysosomal Disease Center, who spoke of telling the parents the shocking diagnosis. "As a pediatrician and as a parent, it is very difficult to see a family go through getting news like that." Not acceptable, the parents said again, and began their mission to seek life for their daughter. Niemann–Pick is an inherited metabolic disorder in which harmful quantities of a fatty substance accumulate in the spleen, liver, lungs, bone marrow and—in some patients, like Sophia—the brain. Referred to as a lysosomal storage disorder, it is named for

physicians Albert Niemann and Ludwick Pick, who in the 1920s identified two forms of the disease. Sophia's condition is so rare that only one in 30,000 Ashkenazi Jews have it, said Enns, who has treated other similar lysosomal disorders. In the close-knit south Palo Alto community of Greenmeadow, Penny and Richard Ellson rushed across the street to Herzog and Sachs when they learned about Sophia. Herzog mentioned an organic garden to ease Sophia's digestive problems. Ellson got on the phone, and on June 8 about a dozen people—neighbors and strangers—showed up in Herzog and Sachs' back yard, including master gardener Marcia Fein of the Foundation for a Global Community. Following Fein's organic design, they dug flower beds and planted neat rows of organic vegetables and herbs. It is called Sophia's Garden. "It has been very touching," Sachs said. But the garden is just a part of the action to help Sophia. "This is all a part of this larger picture to keep Sophia healthy and alive," said Sachs, president and creative director of Valley Design in Menlo Park. Sophia cannot crawl, but she babbles and has the look of a very curious little girl. "We feel her great energy and her wanting to be here," her mother says. In Sophia's room, where a long row of stuffed animals perch on top of a sofa, a tiny "altar" is filled with symbols of the diverse things that place the wind beneath people's wings. There are healing stones, a green Tibetan tara, tiny seeds from

Sophia: Surrounded by the people who love her and the toys she loves. (Courtesy of Sophia's Garden)

the Dalai Lama and a Buddha. On her crib are a Roman Catholic Mother Miraculous medal and an American Indian prayer wheel. The family has met with a rabbi, Chinese herbalists, shamans and a 94-year-old Chumash Indian healer. Last week, Sachs flew home from Paris, where he attended the third Scientific Lysosomal Storage Disorders Conference. He hopes Sophia can be included in a scientific trial. "We hit the ground rolling," Herzog said. "We have a window here to try to keep her well. They are gone by age 3." The plan to help Sophia is broad and "integrative," Herzog explained, pulling out a black and red chart that has "Sophia's care" written in a center circle. Inside about 30 surrounding connected circles are words such as: pediatric neurology, traditional Chinese medicine, homeopathy, Tibetan medicine, Feldenkrais, physical and occupational therapy, chiropractic, feng shui, ayurvedic, rabbi, Jewish Center, Western and Eastern herbs and so on. Enns, who had never seen a

Niemann–Pick Type A child until he met Sophia, said, "I applaud Sophia's family for being so persistent in their striving for the best care possible. They have her best interest in mind in trying to coordinate a complex team of physicians from all sides of the globe. I have a relatively open mind to other forms of therapy. Just because we don't understand how something works, doesn't mean that something can't work." But he also said he has "Western medicine-trained skepticism" and urges caution in ensuring that alternative treatments don't cause harm. Sophia's parents hope to establish a fund in her honor to encourage research and share information. Meanwhile, there is a daily whirlwind of e-mailing, organizing, documenting their own research and contacting research scientists from the home office that they call jokingly Sophia Central. It helps them not be simply terrified parents, they said, and most important, they think of Sophia not as dying, but healing.

Loretta Green

For additional information on Niemann–Pick disease, go to the following websites: the National Niemann–Pick Disease Foundation, Inc. at http://www.nnpdf.org; the National Tay–Sachs and Allied Diseases Association, Inc. at http://www. NTSAD.org; the Genetic Disease Foundation at http://www.geneticdiseasefoundation.org; the International Center for Types A & B Niemann–Pick Disease at Mount Sinai School of Medicine at http://www.mssm.edu/niemann-pick/ index.shtml.

Source: "PA Parents Try to Save Ill Daughter," by Loretta Green, *San Jose Mercury News,* July 1, 2002.

2. Participatory components
   a. Family choice and action
   b. Practitioner responsiveness and flexibility

Not everyone agrees with the present focus on the provision of early service in the home environment. Krauss (1990), for example, suggests that some families may resent the fact that the family must be evaluated before their child can receive services and may feel that their privacy is being threatened. Although you might think that most families would not feel this way, if you work with parents and families of infants or young children, it may be an important consideration to keep in mind.

One challenge faced by a number of families including children with severe disabilities is the realization that their child experiences a disability so unusual that there is little research, few educational resources, and no plan for parents to follow. When there is nothing for parents to do to support their child, they often experience frustration and despair, and search for interventions themselves. The First Person feature entitled "Keeping Sophia Healthy, Alive" describes the fight waged by one set of parents determined to pull together all possible resources and interventions, no matter how unusual, to save the life of their little girl, Sophia, who has Niemann–Pick disease, a metabolic disorder. To learn more about Sophia, her family, and their efforts to find treatments for Niemann–Pick disease, go to **http://www.sophiasgarden.org/**.

? Pause and Reflect

In this chapter on severe disabilities, we've chosen to include a separate section on families. Think about the challenges of everyday activities with a child who has severe disabilities—going to the grocery store, visiting friends, attending religious services. Also think of how difficult life can be when you have specific goals and dreams for your child and the older he gets, the greater the obstacles. What kind of support do you think is necessary for parents to maintain optimism and enthusiasm as they meet the challenges of parenting a child with severe disabilities? ●

Teaching Strategies and Accommodations

As we mentioned earlier, terms and criteria do little to suggest specific ways for educating persons with severe disabilities and do not address the educational or health-related issues of individual children. It is important to visit a student's classroom or to meet with him or her to learn who the child is and what his or her specific educational needs are.

When you meet a student or enter a class of individuals with severe disabilities, the first things that attract your attention are the differences. Puréed food, toilet training for people of all ages, unusual sounds, and strange equipment all stand out. When you meet a child, you may feel a sense of sadness because of her disabilities and what you may perceive as her limited possibilities for normal life experiences. All the implications of severe or profound mental retardation seem to be foremost in your mind as you get to know the child. Then something amazing happens as you spend time with her. In a very short time, what comes to mind are not the physical or cognitive limitations or the behavior characteristics. Instead, you think of the skills the child has learned to perform, the look in his or her eyes when excited, the way the child responds to your voice, and the wealth of skills the child will learn in the years to come. In short, you focus on *all* the characteristics of the individual rather than only the differences or disabilities.

The future of children with severe disabilities will depend in part on the vision and commitment of their families, their teachers, and their peers—of people like you. The extent to which children with severe and profound levels of mental retardation will become adults who are accepted, valued, and integrated into the mainstream of society is your responsibility as well as theirs.

The nature and content of educational programming for individuals with severe and profound levels of mental retardation have changed significantly in recent years. Most of the changes have come about because of new or different educational philosophies and greater expectations and goals for children, adolescents, and adults with severe disabilities.

McDonnell, Hardman, and McDonnell (2003) identify two categories of environmental support that we can use to facilitate the integration, independence, and success of individuals with severe disabilities. The first category is **formal supports**. Formal supports are the legal requirements, organizations, and agencies that offer people with disabilities and their families protection, resources, and assistance. Formal supports serve as a structure for financial and governmental incentives to individuals and communities. The second category is **natural supports**. Natural supports are the opportunities, activities, and responses offered by family, friends, and neighbors. As you read through this section, you will see that these parameters are useful ways of looking at interventions and programs for individuals with severe disabilities. Formal supports can provide important evidence of society's responsibilities and efforts to create quality life experiences for individuals with disabilities. The natural supports, however, touch each individual personally and serve as the foundation for necessary changes and modifications in formal support networks over time.

Strategies for teaching individuals with disabilities typically reflect a clear behavioral philosophy and focus on the analysis of behavior. Specific interventions include the task analysis and prompt systems introduced in Chapter 5. Another important paradigm shift in recent years is toward empowerment (Polloway et al., 1996). Person-centered planning, which allows individuals with severe disabilities to play an important role in decisions regarding their lives, is the underlying component of many educational programs (Reid, Everson, & Green, 1999). Because of the importance of decision-making in establishing personal input on life goals and activities, recent research is carefully examining ways to best tap into the preferences of individuals with severe disabilities. Discovering if Martin prefers bowling or watching videos, or if Anna likes orange juice or grape juice can be difficult if Martin and Anna simply take or do what is offered and don't have clear communication skills. Researchers are discovering systematic ways of presenting choices and creating response opportunities so that individual preference can be reliably and clearly demonstrated (Lim, Browder, & Bambara, 2001; Stafford et al., 2002). As we see in the Technology Focus box here, technology is contributing to the programmatic emphasis on eliciting choice.

Although there is some disagreement among professionals about the rate or extent of some of the changes we will be discussing, we now recognize the im-

New educational philosophies and higher expectations have changed educational programming for people with severe and profound mental retardation.

Technology Focus

Technology and Individuals with Severe Disabilities

Technological advances in the areas of communication and cognitive development have contributed significantly to the quality of life of individuals with severe and profound levels of mental retardation. Technology has opened many avenues of communication not previously available to people with severe physical as well as cognitive disabilities. A description of these advances in communication is provided in Chapter 12.

Technology also is playing an emerging role as a means of delivering and enhancing instruction for individuals with severe disabilities. Langone and Mechling (2000) used a computer-based program to teach students with severe disabilities to recognize photographic prompts for appropriate language use. In recent years, wearable computers have been developed. When attached to glasses or headphones, these may provide exciting options for community-based instruction and for performance feedback.

A new role of technology focuses on the ability of individuals with severe disabilities to participate in decision-making related to vocational opportunities. As we discussed in the text, the self-determination and identification of individual preferences are important components in educational programming. When personal preferences are tapped in areas such as food choice or in-school activities, tangible items can be used to elicit responses. Choices related to work-related tasks or environments are more difficult because the opportunities cannot be presented visually to the student. Enter the CD-ROM. Through video clips of different work environments, individuals with severe disabilities can view work settings and see the various tasks that might be involved at each site. Morgan, Gerity, and Ellerd (2000) and Ellerd, Morgan, and Salzberg (2002) found that using videos through CD-ROM technology allowed a student with severe disabilities to identify preferential work environments and to choose preferred tasks when presented with up to five job choices. The use of technology to extend sound instructional principles to new areas reflects one of its best and most promising applications.

---

portance and need for programs that emphasize normalization, social and physical inclusion, and life-skills curricula. Each of these areas will be discussed separately. As you will see, however, they are closely interrelated and together represent a continuing movement toward change for individuals with severe disabilities.

Normalization

One of the forces behind educational change for individuals with all levels of mental retardation is the movement toward normalization. The term **normalization**, or *social role valorization*, refers to an emphasis on conventional or normal behavior and attitudes in all aspects of education, socialization, and other life experiences (Wolfensberger, 1977, 1983). In other words, the focus of normalization is that all people should lead lives that are as normal as possible. For persons with mental retardation, this movement has great implications. Wolfensberger (1977) defined two dimensions of normalization: (1) direct contact or interaction with typically developing individuals and (2) the way an individual with disabilities is described to others.

The focus of normalization is that all people should lead lives that are as normal as possible.

The first dimension involves the way we treat people with mental retardation, and the things we decide to teach and encourage. It is important, for example, to consider a person's age and the usual criteria for normal behavior when we are interacting with someone or deciding what types of behaviors, skills, or recreational activities we will be teaching or doing. It may be easy and fast to feed a 10-year-old with severe disabilities, but it is not age-appropriate, and therefore, if it is at all possible, we should choose to implement a self-feeding program so that the child not only will become more independent but also will be expected to perform some of the skills of other children his or her age.

Sometimes, it may be beyond a person's physical or cognitive abilities to perform some self-care skills (eating, toileting, dressing) or other types of tasks with complete independence. In these instances, we encourage **partial participation**: we enable the student to perform the parts of the skill or task that are within his or her ability range (Snell, 1988).

The second dimension of normalization refers to the way we portray or present persons with mental retardation to others. This dimension includes the way we may refer to a student in our class, the words or phrases we include in writing about or describing persons with mental retardation, and the way we select clothing or hairstyles for our children or clients. The types of housing or educational environments in which we place persons with disabilities and the extent to which legislation protects and enforces basic human rights reflect our society's perceptions of individuals with disabilities. Persons with mental retardation should live in environments and structures that approximate normal living arrangements and that include a small group of friends, family, or caregivers (Taylor, Racino, & Walker, 1992).

In general, the move toward a normalized existence for individuals with severe and profound mental retardation depends on the increased willingness of the public to recognize and accept the humanity, value, and contributions of persons with mental retardation. Normalization has served as a foundation for many of the major social as well as educational changes that we have observed in the area of mental retardation over the past few decades. It is important for us, as educators, clinicians, and members of the community, to serve as advocates for normalized life opportunities for individuals with severe disabilities; it is also important for us to recognize the sometimes overwhelming challenges faced by families with members with severe disabilities. As Fern Kupfer, author of the article featured in the accompanying Closer Look box entitled, "Home Is Not for Everyone," discusses, every family is different and the same decision may not be the right one for everyone.

Inclusion

One term you will hear or see repeatedly in any educational program description or curriculum for students with severe mental retardation is *inclusion*, the incorporation of all individuals into the mainstream of society. There are several reasons why inclusion has become an important facet of instructional programming for individuals with mental retardation. First, it is proposed that individuals are more likely to develop functional patterns of behavior and higher levels of functioning if they have the opportunity to interact with people without disabilities. Second, it is considered to be every individual's right to access the opportunities and facilities that the community has to offer to the greatest extent possible. Third, an emphasis on inclusion will provide many individuals with

People with severe mental retardation may develop higher levels of functioning and independence when they interact with people without disabilities.

A Closer Look   Home Is Not for Everyone

Fifteen years ago I had a column in this space. Of course I was younger in the photograph (black-and-white, then) but serious looking and a little worn around the edges. The column I had written was titled "Institution Is Not a Dirty Word."

It was about my family's decision to place our child in a residential facility, an "institution" housing more than 50 severely mentally and physically handicapped children.

It was a decision that was not easily made. We loved Zachariah. But we couldn't continue to care for him at home. I had to explain to people that we did not "put him away," that we still saw him; that indeed, Zachariah was still our child.

I wrote the article—many articles and a book, in fact—to describe what it was like to have a child who never walked or talked, who would be in diapers all of his days, whose care precluded any semblance of normal family life for the rest of us.

I became a writer and a family advocate as a response to the anti-institutional bias in this country and the tendency to canonize the handicapped and the families—most significantly the mothers—who care for them at home. My point was this: there are good facilities for handicapped children in this country. There should be more.

Choosing to place your special-needs child in a group home, a residential facility or an "institution" does not mean that you are a bad mother.

Zachariah had Canavan's disease, which causes destruction of the myelin, the insulation around nerve cells. Although one doctor had written in the medical record when Zach was 3 years old, "I do not expect this little boy to live out the year," Zach survived until he was 16.

He was profoundly retarded, his days spent in wheelchairs and beds, with feeding tubes that made him gag, and eventually a body so cruelly curved by scoliosis that his back made the letter S. He also had huge blue eyes and a smile to beat the band. . . .

There was a time when I thought of Zachariah the first thing when I awoke in the morning and the last thing before I drifted off to sleep. I believed I would forever define myself as being his mother. But eventually I divorced, remarried, had a new job, stepchildren; my daughter when off to college, and I stopped speaking as a family advocate.

The phone call last week from a woman in Colorado made me sit down and write about this once again. She has a 3-year-old boy with a rare syndrome which includes autism. He has physical mobility but no language or cognition. "If he were in wheelchair," she said, "that actually would be easier." Her comment reminded me how mothers of handicapped children compare their children's disabilities.

She tells me how dysfunctional her family life is, how the special-education experts coming to her home are always devising new programs, how

the direct training and experiences they will need in order to achieve full or partial independence (Stainback, Stainback, & Ayres, 1996).

Inclusion also involves the acceptance of individuals with mental retardation by the community. Of course, acceptance and social interaction cannot be dictated, but they can be developed through encouragement, preparation, and opportunities. Obviously, it is easier to develop friendships and good working relationships with people who are living and working in the same environment as you are. It is also possible that early physical integration with typically developing peers will encourage the development of long-term friendships that will last through the school years. Interestingly, research suggests that students with severe disabilities who are included in general education classrooms are more likely to be accepted by nondisabled peers and less likely to be rejected by teachers than students with mild disabilities. Some research, however, suggests that these higher ratings of acceptance are related to nurturing attitudes of peers

little attention she is able to give to her new baby daughter.

Her son Andrew has severe eating problems which will soon necessitate tubal feedings. He wakes in the morning and spreads his feces along his bedroom wall. She would like to place her son in a facility, but social services offered only foster care, which would mean she would give up parental custody.

"I'm not an unfit mother," she protests. "If our family can't continue to care for Andrew, how can a foster family?"

Social services encourages her to keep Andrew at home. They talk about "least restrictive environment" and "inclusion." Most of the terms that deal with the severely impaired have been invented by special education professionals who have never lived with a child like Zachariah or Maria, or Andrew.

Years ago, we did put our retarded children "away"—we knew so little and were ashamed. Parents of Down syndrome infants were advised to put them in institutions and go on with their lives.

Then we learned the horror stories of institutional warehousing that resulted from this kind of ignorant social policy. But the progressive backlash that promotes the "home" as some kind of sacred shrine is also hurtful and wrong.

I said it 15 years ago, but it needs saying again: The view that "home" is the best place for every child has dangerous ramifications. Government funds are cut for human services under the guise of anti-institutionalization.

Well-meaning reformers who tell us how terrible the institutions are should be wary lest they become unwilling accomplices to politicians who only want to walk a tight fiscal line. It takes a lot of money to run residential facilities.

No politician is going to say he's against caring for the handicapped. But he can talk in sanctimonious terms about efforts to preserve the family unit, about families remaining independent and self-sufficient. Translated, this means, "You got your troubles, I got mine."

Each child is different. Each family is different. The hard truth is that the home is not the best place for every child. The harder truth is that even if it were, it might not be the best place for everyone else.

Fern Kupfer

Source: "Home Is Not for Everyone," by Fern Kupfer, *Newsweek*, December 8, 1997.

rather than true friendship behaviors and that although students with severe disabilities are less rejected, teachers are not confident that they can provide them with appropriate instruction (Cook, 2001; Cook & Semmel, 1999).

A key issue in inclusion is the extent to which people with severe mental retardation should be integrated into the school or community. Many professionals suggest that total inclusion should be the goal. An example of total inclusion in the public school setting would be the placement of students with severe disabilities in regular classes in order to promote socialization experiences. In many full inclusion programs, teachers attempt to adapt the general education content for the student with severe disabilities (Siegel-Causey et al., 1998). The Teaching Strategies box entitled, "Inclusion Curriculum Goals for a Student with Severe Disabilities" is an example of several eighth-grade science curriculum goals for a student with severe cognitive disabilities. Other professionals feel that inclusion to this extent may result in a reduced amount of needed edu-

Social interaction is an important part of school life. All students benefit from close personal friendships. (Cleo/PhotoEdit)

cational programming for students with severe disabilities, and that social integration can best be achieved in other settings. In addition, some parents are concerned about their child's safety and emotional well-being in integrated environments and prefer, at least initially, less risky program options.

The attitudes of the nondisabled persons in the community, school, or work setting are critical to successful inclusion. Various educational programs have been developed to give nondisabled persons some knowledge about individuals with disabilities, and many teachers do take the time to discuss individual differences and specific disabilities with their classes.

Curriculum

● **The Functional Curriculum**   Most of the curricula currently used in instructional programs for individuals with severe and profound disabilities stress instruction in life skills and are designed to maximize independent functioning. A curriculum that emphasizes preparation for life and that includes skills that will be used by the student in home, school, or work environments is called a **functional curriculum**. A functional curriculum includes instruction in all of the important areas, or domains, of adult life: domestic, community, recreation and leisure, and vocational. All types of instruction, including training in self-help skills and communication skills, mobility training, physical therapy, and occupational therapy, are integrated so that they complement one another and focus on functional activities rather than isolated practice tasks (Snell &

Inclusion Curriculum Goals for a Student with Severe Disabilities

Cory's Weather Station Activity

Curricular Goal: Increase understanding of weather instruments and meteorological concepts.

Assignments	Adaptations by Type and Description	Annual Goals	Monitoring	Outcomes
Check daily temperature readings, the type of cloud cover, precipitation, wind speed, humidity level, and barometric pressure.	*Teacher Support*—a behavior support plan used to increase participation was implemented by the teachers jointly. *Size*—reduced the number of steps required from 6 to 3 (check daily temperature reading, the type of cloud cover, precipitation).	Maintain socially acceptable behavior and read to get information.	Behavior rated on a monitoring card at the end of the class.	Participation increased to 100% and an unanticipated outcome that involved the improvement of his skills in dressing appropriately for the weather.
Record weather conditions on work sheets.	*Difficulty*—work sheets required approximated readings (e.g., estimate temperature to nearest 10-degree mark). *Input*—pictorial cues were provided on work sheets (e.g., picture of cloud conditions). *Output*—eliminated need to spell (e.g., color in thermometer to correct degree point).	Describe events and read to follow instructions.	Portfolio of work sheets and log of Cory's performance.	Increased ability to read and record thermometer numbers within 5 degrees and eliminated need for assistance to complete the work sheet.
Report readings to the class.	*Difficulty*—specific questions were asked that could be answered with short phrases. *Peer Supports*—modeling and input from peers were encouraged to promote greater participation.	Sustain communication and describe events.	Log of Cory's performance.	Increased answers from single words to short phrases, and increased use of adjectives, pronouns, and adverbs.
Record weather journal entries.	*Alternative Activity* (adapted content)— assigned to make a call to the national Weather Bureau to obtain their forecast and share this information verbally with the class.	Use telephone and describe events.	Log of Cory's performance and forecast report.	Became independent in dialing written phone numbers without assistance and improved speech.

Source: E. Siegel-Causey, C. McMorris, S. McGowen, & S. Sands-Buss (1998). In junior high you take earth science: Including a student with severe disabilities into an academic class. *Teaching Exceptional Children, 31* (1), 71.

Teaching Strategies & Accommodations

Examples of Functional Curriculum Domains

Domestic

Areas or subdomains: kitchen, bathroom, laundry room, bedroom

Community

Areas or subdomains: grocery store, bank, post office, restaurants, school

Recreation/Leisure

Areas or subdomains: park, YMCA, movie theater, bowling alley, fishing pond

Vocational

Areas or subdomains: specific job sites (hotel, restaurant, landscape)

Skill areas to be addressed across all domains: communication, transportation, social skills, attire, behavior expectations, word/sign/symbol recognition, area-specific skills (for example, using the stove, depositing money, bowling, greeting customers), decision-making skills

Drake, 1994). Each student must be taught the behaviors or tasks required in his or her home, work, or recreational setting (see the accompanying Teaching Strategies box entitled, "Examples of Functional Curriculum Domains").

Instruction in language is an important part of the functional curriculum for most persons with severe or profound mental retardation. This is especially true for individuals who will be going out to work or who are living in community settings. Caro and Snell (1989) have identified the following three major goals of programs designed to teach language or communication to persons with severe disabilities: (1) to increase the frequency of communicative behavior, (2) to expand the student's repertoire of communicative functions, and (3) to promote the spontaneous and generalized use of communication skills in everyday life. Instructional programs in language and communication must focus on functional communication, as we have already mentioned. Communication interventions should occur in natural environments, such as classrooms and playgrounds, and focus on purposeful communication, such as asking for a ball or a favorite snack.

The technique that is frequently used to identify skills for instruction is called an **environmental inventory**, or **environmental analysis** (Nietupski & Hamre-Nietupski, 1987). An environmental inventory involves a visit to the settings in which the student has to function. The environment might be a group home, the cafeteria in an elementary school, the local park, or the neighborhood bus station. A list is made of the specific skills needed by the average person to be successful in that environment. Then the skills of the individual student are compared to the needed skills, and specific behaviors or tasks are targeted for instruction. By using this procedure, the curriculum truly prepares the student to be successful in current or future life situations and channels valuable teaching time into meaningful instruction.

● *Community-Based Instruction*   One way that integration is incorporated into educational plans is through community-based instruction, which, as you learned in Chapter 5, involves actually conducting learning experiences in community settings. Students who are able to travel in the community will, for example, receive training on how to walk to their home or work site or how to

Integration is a natural outcome of community-based instruction.

take a bus. Instruction will take place on the very sidewalks or bus lines that the student will be using to travel. Community-based instruction provides students with direct training in skills they need to become integrated into society and also allows them to experience integration during the instructional process. The accompanying Teaching Strategies box entitled, "Scope and Sequence Chart for General Community Functioning" reflects the integration of community-based instruction in curriculum planning.

Transition Programming

As we've discussed throughout this text, *transition* refers to the process of preparing for and facilitating movement from one situation or place to another. In the area of severe and profound disabilities, the term usually refers to one of three types of movement: (1) movement from one level of school to another, (2) movement from a segregated school or home setting to an integrated or community-based school or residence, or (3) movement from school to a work setting, typically a work setting in the community. As we have seen, the educational and philosophical movements in the field today have been directed toward preparing individuals with severe disabilities for integration in local communities. The need for advance planning and continual instruction in the skills and behaviors needed to maximize the potential for successful experiences in future environments has resulted in the development of specific programs and extensive research focused on the transition process. The individualized transition plan prepares the child with disabilities for new environments. Consequently, transition programming permeates the educational programs of essentially all individuals with severe disabilities. Figure 6.1 illustrates the six areas of adult life that should be addressed by transition programs. How do we know if our programs have been successful

> The individualized transition plan prepares the child with disabilities for new environments.

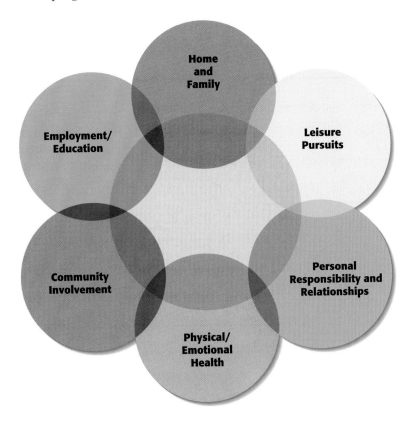

Figure 6.1

Domains of Adulthood

Source: M. E. Cronin & J. R. Patton (1993). *Life skills instruction for all students with special needs: A practical guide for integrating real life content into curriculum* (p. 13). Austin, TX: PRO-ED.

Teaching Strategies & Accommodations

Can Do: Scope and Sequence Chart for General Community Functioning

Goal areas	Kindergarten (age 5)	Elementary School	
		Primary grades (ages 6–8)	Intermediate grades (ages 9–11)
Travel	Walk or ride bus to and from school.	Walk or ride bus to and from school.	Walk, ride bus, or ride bike to and from school.
	Walk to and from school bus and to point in school (classroom, office).	Walk to and from school bus and to point in school (classroom, cafeteria, office, music room).	Walk to various destinations in school and in the community (neighborhood grocery store, mailbox).
	Cross street: stop at curb.	Cross street: familiar, low-traffic intersections.	Cross streets safely.
Community safety			Problem-solve if lost in new places.
			Use caution with strangers.
Grocery shopping			Buy two to three items at neighborhood store for self (snack) or classroom snack activity.
General shopping		Buy item at school store.	Buy item at school store.
Eating out	Carry milk/lunch money.	Carry milk/lunch money.	Carry milk/lunch money.
	Follow school cafeteria routine.	Follow school cafeteria routine.	Follow school cafeteria routine.
			Order and pay: familiar fast-food restaurants, snack stand.
			Buy snack/drinks from vending machine.
Using services	Mail letter at corner mailbox.	Mail letter at corner mailbox.	Mail letters.
		Use pay phone with help.	Use pay phone.

Source: A. Ford, R. Schnorr, L. Meyer, L. Davern, J. Black, and P. Dempsey (Eds.) (1989). *The Syracuse community-referenced curriculum guide for students with moderate and severe disabilities* (p. 78). Baltimore: Paul H. Brookes.

Middle school (ages 12–14)	High School (ages 15–18)	Transition (ages 19–21)
Walk, ride bus, or ride bike to and from school.	Walk, ride bus, or ride bike to and from school.	Walk, ride bus, or ride bike to and from home and community sites.
Walk to various destinations in school and in the community (store, restaurant, job site).	Walk to various destinations in school and in the community (store, restaurant, job site).	Walk to various destinations.
Cross streets safely.	Cross streets safely.	Cross streets safely.
Use public bus/subway for general transporation.	Use public bus/subway for general transportation.	Use public bus/subway for general transporation.
Problem-solve if lost in new places.	Problem-solve if lost in new places.	Problem-solve if lost in new places.
Use caution with strangers.	Use caution with strangers.	Use caution with stangers.
Buy items needed for specific planned menu.	Buy items needed for specific meal or special event.	Buy items needed for specific meal or special event.
Buy few items in store with limited money amount.	Shop for desired items in shopping center.	Shop for desired items in shopping center.
Purchase personal care items.	Purchase personal care items.	Purchase personal care items.
Budget/carry money for lunch/snacks.	Budget/carry money for lunch/snacks.	Budget/carry money for meals and snacks.
Eat in school cafeteria.	Eat in school/public cafeteria.	Eat in public cafeteria.
Order and eat in fast-food restaurants.	Order and eat in fast-food restaurants.	Order and eat in fast-food restaurants.
Buy snack/drinks from vending machine.	Buy snack/drinks from vending machines.	Buy snack/drinks from vending machines.
Use post office.	Use post office.	Use post office.
Use pay phone.	Use pay phone.	Use pay phone.
Ask for assistance in stores.	Ask for assistance in stores, information booths.	Ask for assistance appropriately in stores, information booths.

in these areas? How can we determine if someone is productive, happy, and healthy? A number of research investigations are conducted periodically to determine such factors as employment rates, graduation rates, and living arrangements of individuals with disabilities.

● *Transition Between Levels of School*   For the infant born with severe disabilities, transition programming in educational settings often begins immediately. As soon as the need for specialized services is recognized, interventions are put in place that are designed to prepare the child for success in future environments as well as the present one. Programs are available at day-care centers, through home-based instruction, and in preschools that are, in part, designed to help the infant or child move to an integrated setting or to prepare him or her for the next level of schooling.

The process of preparation for a new school situation will take place as long as the child is in the school system. If a child is already in an integrated setting, the change from elementary school to a middle school, or from junior high school to senior high school, will need to be addressed in the curriculum. All children must learn to cope with the new physical environment, the usually larger number of students, and the progressively greater freedoms that are present as they go from first through twelfth grade. The individual with severe mental retardation must be prepared to cope with these changes. For example, learning to use a locker may require a comprehensive instructional program (Felko et al., 1999). Although we don't typically think of students with severe disabilities in a college environment, some universities around the country participate in programs designed to integrate students with disabilities into the college setting (Grigal, Neubert, & Moon, 2002). The Teaching Strategies box entitled, "Danny's Schedule for Spring Semester at State University" provides a specific example of how university personnel can work together to create a viable post-secondary school environment for individuals with severe disabilities.

● *Transition from Segregated to Integrated Settings*   The education of students with severe or profound levels of disabilities has, on the whole, been segregated. The recent movement to end the practice of segregating students with severe disabilities is reflected in the transition plans of students of all ages. Many of these plans contain programming and educational goals intended to enable students to move to a partially or fully integrated school setting. In some instances, these goals may be to prepare students to move from a protective, residential school to a classroom in the local public school. For other students, the goals may be to move them from a separate lunch held in their classroom to a fully integrated lunch with all the other students in the school, or for them to join the regular classroom for certain nonacademic or even academic subjects.

Transition plans that include a focus on inclusion will probably contain many skills and experiences that address different aspects of communication, socialization, and independent movement. A student who has little or no experience interacting with nondisabled peers will not have the skills needed to benefit from new school situations. The transition plans may thus include trial experiences in the new school to help the student gradually become accustomed to the change.

As you might expect, the success of a student's transition into an integrated environment will depend not only on the appropriateness of the educational program the student receives before the move, but also on the support the student receives once he or she is in the school. Cooperative planning between the student's present and future teachers will help to facilitate a smooth transition.

Teaching Strategies & Accommodations

Danny's Schedule
for Spring Semester
at State University

Time	Monday	Tuesday	Wednesday	Thursday	Friday
7:00	Danny rides city bus to college campus				
8:00	Functional Academics with Special Education Teacher in classroom on college campus	Career Planning or Self-determination skills class with special educator	Free time—Danny gets to campus in time for Weight Training Class	Career Planning or Self-determination skills class with special educator	Functional Academics with Special Education Teacher in classroom on college campus
9:00		Ceramics Class in Art Building		Ceramics Class in Art Buildig	Independent Study and tutoring from Special Education Intern at Library
9:30	Weight Training Class at Fitness Center		Weight Training Class at Fitness Center		
10:00				Travel Training/ Community skills training with teaching assistant and two other students	
10:30		Travel Training/ Community skills training with teaching assistant and two other students			
11:00	Computer Tutorial with Special Education Intern (peer tutor)		Computer Tutorial with Special Education Intern (peer tutor)		Lunch with fraternity brothers
12:00	Lunch with other students and/or best buddy at student union food court	Lunch in community	Lunch with peer tutor at student union food court	Lunch in community	Review schedule for following week with special educator in classroom
1:00	Go to city bus stop on campus, go to job site	Travel Training and go to SPCA for volunteer work with teaching assistant and two other students	Go to city bus stop on campus, go to job site	Travel Training and go to SPCA for volunteer work with teaching assistant and two other students	Go to city bus stop on campus, go to job site
2:00	Works part-time at PetSmart		Works part-time at PetSmart		Works part-time at PetSmart
3:00		School bus picks Danny up on campus		School bus picks Danny up on campus	
4:00					
5:00	Parents pick Danny up from work		Parents pick Danny up from work		A friend picks Danny up from work

Source: M. Grigal, M. Neubert, & M. S. Moon (2002). Postsecondary options for students with significant disabilities, *Teaching Exceptional Children, 35*(2), 68–73.

Although many school personnel are becoming more receptive to the integration process (Stainback, Stainback, & Stainback, 1988), parents, special education teachers, and others involved in transition plans should always anticipate the possible resistance of other educators, or sometimes family members. Letting people know exactly what to expect and ways to deal with potential diffi-

Successful transition into an integrated environment depends on appropriate educational programs and support.

culties will alleviate anxiety. Often, visits to schools with existing integrated programs for students with severe and profound disabilities, or films of such schools, can help demonstrate effective programming.

Another factor critical to the successful movement of students with severe disabilities from segregated to integrated facilities is the role of parents. This

Teaching Strategies & Accommodations

Roles of Family Members in Transition: Strategies to Facilitate Culturally Appropriate Transition

Role: Family as . . .

Strategies for Service Providers for Issues Related to:

Guide

Continuity:

Child's home culture and practices are respected in new placement.

Family is involved in identifying and deciding how to manage conflicting practices and expectations.

Sources of potential discontinuity between home and the new program are identified; steps are taken to minimize them.

Information specialist

Communication:

Written material to families should be clear and concise.

Written and oral information should be free of jargon and technical language.

Written and oral information should be in the family's primary language.

Information exchange should match family preferences (e.g., face-to-face meetings, involvement of community leader, community elder, or extended family member).

Decision-maker

Collaboration:

Child and family preparation and training for transition should be culturally appropriate (e.g., small-group instruction, oral transmission of information, multigenerational involvement).

Families should be informed of their legal rights and responsibilities in a culturally sensitive manner.

Include opportunities for feedback from families throughout the transition process.

Ally

Family concerns:

Families are encouraged to share their concerns.

Family concerns are addressed in a culturally sensitive manner.

Families are consulted concerning culturally appropriate roles and level of involvement in transition; cultural brokers (e.g., a community leader) are involved as necessary.

Source: D. A. Bruns, & S. A. Fowler (1999). Culturally sensitive transition plans for young children and their families. *Teaching Exceptional Children, 31*(5), 26–30.

role may change over time. The accompanying Teaching Strategies box entitled, "Roles of Family Members in Transition: Strategies to Facilitate Culturally Appropriate Transition" outlines four roles of the family in the transition process. The strategies presented in the box can be used by service providers to ensure that parents are involved appropriately in all aspects of the transition process. Consideration of these roles and strategies also will help to facilitate a culturally sensitive transition program (Bruns & Fowler, 1999).

When it comes to decisions related to integrated placements, particularly if they involve changes in schools, parents may be concerned about the quality of programming in a new school or class situation and about the safety of their child, or they may be worried that their child will be rejected in the new situation. These feelings will be less pronounced if the parents have been planning for transitional placements during the course of the child's life. Parents may find support, encouragement, and strategies for helping to prepare themselves and their children through support groups composed of other parents of children with similar disabilities who have experienced the same concerns. Teachers and school administrators can help to get parents together if groups do not exist already in the community. Parents also might benefit from observing model programs that include integration and from communicating with personnel at the new school (Hanline & Halvorsen, 1989).

Support groups for parents can be located easily on the Internet. One comprehensive source of support group and information contacts is the Family Village website. Go to **http://www.familyvillage.wisc.edu** and click onto the Community Center to find support groups in your state and community.

Figure 6.2

Family Village Website

Source: http://www.family village.wisc.edu/index.htmlx.

Transition from segregated to integrated settings can involve residential as well as school settings. Until recently, the vast majority of individuals of all ages who experienced severe or profound levels of mental retardation lived in segregated residential facilities. Most of these were institutional or private settings such as nursing homes. During the past two decades, however, many of these individuals have moved to smaller and more integrated residences, such as group homes, or to live with their families. According to Taylor, Lakin, and Hill (1989), the number of children and youth in long-term residential facilities decreased from 91,000 to 48,450 in the years from 1977 to 1986. Similarly, according to the U.S. Department of Education's *Twenty-Fourth Annual Report to Congress on the Implementation of the Individuals with Disabilities Education Act* (2002), only 1.17 percent of students with disabilities ages 6 to 21 were served in residential or hospital environments during the 1999–2000 school year.

Transition to an integrated setting focuses on helping families keep and support their child in the home, and on enabling adults to live as independently as possible and to maximize interaction within the local community. Both the child who has been living at home and the child who has lived in a segregated facility must receive transition training for adult living. In many cases, it will be possible for individuals with severe mental retardation to live in group homes or apartments in a community setting. People living in independent or semi-independent housing must be prepared emotionally and technically. The skills involved in cooking, cleaning, dressing, recreational activities, and transportation must be taught and will usually require extensive planning and instruction. Preparation for these skills and in related ones must begin early, and then be extended to enable the individual to function in the specific home or apartment setting. See the accompanying Closer Look box entitled, "Living Settings for Individuals with Severe Disabilities" for a description of the range of living options for individuals with disabilities.

● *Transition from School to Work* Probably the most commonly perceived meaning of the term *transition* across the field of special education is the transition from school to work settings. Preparing students with severe disabilities to go into the work force, particularly the community work force, is a major educational goal.

Although it is suggested that transition programming from school to work begin at least five years before graduation from school, preparation is often a major component of the curriculum throughout the student's educational experience (Noonan & Kilgo, 1987; Wehman et al., 1987). The transition process will encompass not only skills directly related to a work situation but also the necessary skills involved in social interaction, self-help areas, and transportation.

An essential component of all school-to-work transition programs is community-based work experience. When possible, the student should try out several types of work experiences and play an important decision-making role in job selection (Brooke et al., 1995; Wehman et al., 1987). How receptive are business owners to training opportunities for students with severe disabilities? As you might expect, the receptivity will vary from person to person and from community to community. Aveno and Renzaglia (1988) approached sixty-one community businesses that could be potential job sites for persons with severe mental retardation (stores, restaurants, recreational facilities, etc.) and found that the business personnel had generally positive attitudes toward community

Joining the community work force is a major educational goal for many students with severe disabilities.

Individuals with disabilities often want to live in independent, community-based homes. For many people, these goals are realized through independent living arrangements. For others, the goals are adapted to include the most independent and normalized setting possible.

Institutions

Large, segregated residential buildings known as institutions were used for years to house thousands of individuals with mental retardation, mental illness, sensory impairments, or physical disabilities. After numerous allegations of neglect and abuse that often took place in institutions, a social and legal movement began in the 1960s and the 1970s to remove people from the institutional setting and relocate them in smaller, community-based settings. This movement, deinstitutionalization, led to the development of good community residential programs. However, the lack of existing support networks and adequate community-based housing also resulted in many displaced and homeless persons. Although institutions still exist, they are less frequently chosen as a residential placement of choice, and in some states are not considered at all.

Community-Based Residential Facilities

Some individuals who in the past lived in segregated settings have moved directly and successfully into the community. People with disabilities such as severe mental retardation may live in settings that range from nursing homes to community-based homes or facilities. Opportunities for community-based residences are continuing to increase for all individuals; however, the more complex an individual's health-care and personal maintenance needs are, the more likely it is that the person continues to live in one of the more segregated settings. Often, these settings are able to employ support personnel, such as nurses and therapists, and have available more elaborate medical equipment than a group home or apartment.

Intermediate-Care Facilities

An intermediate-care facility (ICF) is composed of a number of individuals with disabilities living together in a supervised setting. Some large ICFs do not provide for community integration, however, and may serve as permanent, segregated living settings for individuals with disabilities. These facilities may include cottage living or other congregated living options.

Small group homes house several adults with disabilities who live with a nondisabled person responsible for general supervision and coordination of activities. Such living situations require not only financial resources and trained personnel but also a receptive community. The resistance of some communities to the placement of group homes is one more obstacle to be overcome in the move toward normalized and independent living. The road to normalized socialization and integration within the community is an exciting option, but not an easy one.

A variety of living situations may also be found in apartment settings. For example, one or more individuals with disabilities may live independently in an apartment, with only periodic visits from a counselor or case manager. Another option may be a person with a disability living with a roommate without a disability. (The roommate may be a residential care provider—or just a friend.) Apartment living is one step closer to an independent, normal living arrangement for many young adults.

Living with Family

Another living option is the family home. Many individuals with disabilities continue to live in the family home during their adult years. Financial dependence, emotional dependence on the part of the family as well as the individual, and a lack of alternative living options may contribute to adults living in this setting.

integration of the students. Although the attitudes were generally supportive, Aveno and Renzaglia suggest that teachers recognize the need to develop strategies to help increase positive attitudes in the community. Recent research suggests similar findings. Hernandez (2000) also found that employers held generally favorable attitudes toward hiring individuals with cognitive disabilities, as long as appropriate supports were provided in the workplace. Teaching in community-based settings involves some of the same processes and people discussed in Chapter 5. For example, job coaches go with students to the work site to provide on-the-job instruction. Supported employment is a desired goal for many young adults with severe disabilities. Continued business and community support is needed, however, to provide adequate opportunities for supported employment to interested individuals (Brooke et al., 1995). In fact, research suggests that individuals with severe disabilities remain underrepresented in supported employment positions, compared to individuals with other, less severe, disabilities (Mank, Ciofi, & Yovanoff, 1998).

> Self-management procedures facilitate independent performance.

Teachers also should examine how to teach students to work independently in the employment setting. **Self-management procedures** have been taught to students with severe mental retardation to facilitate independent performance (Lagomarcino & Rusch, 1989). These procedures include self-monitoring or recording of completed tasks and giving praise or other reinforcement to yourself when a task or step of a task has been completed. The self-monitoring and prompt systems are the same as those we examined in the Technology Focus feature in Chapter 5. Whether high-tech or low-tech, a step-by-step prompting system is a useful instructional strategy. For example, a student might have a series of five photographs that are used as prompts for the five steps needed to complete a task, such as setting a table in a restaurant. A self-recording procedure might involve putting a check or another mark beside each picture as the task is completed. Students who can learn to monitor themselves accurately will require less direct supervision over time and therefore may be more likely candidates for permanent employment opportunities. Figure 6.3 illustrates a series of instructional prompts used to teach cooking skills to a class of middle-school students with severe disabilities.

Permanent employment in community settings is the ultimate goal of transition programming from school to work; it requires not only effective instructional techniques but also extensive coordination among the school, family, employers, and adult service agencies. Remember that the primary service providers for people with severe and profound mental retardation will change from the school to adult agencies once the students reach the age of 22. Work-related goals that are intended to extend into the student's adult life must include the cooperation and participation of case managers from the community service agencies.

In spite of the best efforts of families, advocates, and professionals, community-based employment options are not always available. The frequent alternative for individuals with severe disabilities in many communities continues to be sheltered workshop settings (as described in Chapter 5). In an attempt to foster integration and the social interaction of individuals with severe disabilities, a local artist in an Ohio community worked to transform an existing sheltered workshop to a collaborative art studio—individuals with and without disabilities collaborate on a range of artistic projects. Visit Passion Works Studio at **http://www.passionworks.org**. Access "A Passion for Art" to hear part of an audio documentary on Passion Works prepared by National Public Radio (NPR).

Pour milk into cup   Measure 1 cup   Pour milk in bowl

Pour milk for cup 2   Measure 1 cup   Pour milk in bowl

Figure 6.3

Picture Prompts: Making Pudding

Source: Reprinted with permission of Dr. Cheryl Wissick, University of South Carolina.

Pause and Reflect

In this section, we've examined some of the philosophical and practical components that contribute to effective educational programs for individuals with severe disabilities. As we've mentioned, the role of personal choice or preference—the voice of the individual—is finding increasing importance as educators and families work together to set goals, establish programs, and transition to other environments. Why do you think this emphasis on choice is so important? What does knowing individual preferences bring to our perceptions of individuals with disabilities—whether that choice seems as mundane as choosing between chocolate or vanilla ice cream or as relevant as choosing a restaurant or grocery store as a work environment? ●

Ethical Issues

The ethical issues that have arisen in the area of severe and profound disabilities revolve around the basic rights of all individuals: the right to life and the right to education. Professionals in the areas of medicine, education, and law have become involved with children with severe disabilities and their parents in attempts to resolve some of these issues and to find answers to some very disturbing questions. The fact that questions are raised at all relative to the human and constitutional rights of individuals with severe or profound levels of disabilities is difficult for many of us to understand. As we present these is-

Ethical issues in the area of severe disabilities include the right to life and the right to education.

sues, we will attempt to provide you with both sides of the controversies. It is inevitable, however, that our biases will be revealed through the discussion. We do not feel that it is appropriate for any professional in the field of special education to present noncommittal statements on issues that are so fundamental to the philosophy we espouse.

The Right to Life

Case Study
An infant is born to a young couple—it is their second child. The little boy, named John, clearly has Down syndrome, but he also has very poor muscle tone and reflexes, difficulty swallowing and breathing, and a serious heart condition. The doctors are pessimistic—based on their preliminary evaluation, they believe that John will have serious or profound mental retardation and continuing medical and physical challenges—frequent surgeries are in his future. The young couple must make a decision to have lifesaving surgery performed on John to repair his heart. Heart-breaking and horrible questions are asked—Should John receive the surgery and live? Can we let our child die? If John lives with severe disabilities, how can our young family handle his needs—and our family's needs? What if the doctors are wrong in their assessment of John—does it, should it matter?

Do all newborn infants have the right to live? Should lifesaving surgery be performed on infants who have an assortment of potentially painful and disabling physical and mental disabilities? Should heroic measures be taken to save the life of an infant with suspected severe mental retardation? Do parents, doctors, lawyers, or the government have the right or responsibility to make life-and-death decisions for these children?

These questions are at the heart of the ethical issue of the right to life of children born with severe mental retardation and physical disabilities. In essence, the questions are asked because judgments are being made at the time of a child's birth about the prospective quality of his or her life. **Quality of life** refers to the extent to which an individual can participate in, enjoy, and be aware of the experience of living. When a child with severe mental and/or physical disabilities is born, assumptions are also made about his or her prospective quality of life. Sometimes, these assumptions focus on whether or not the child's life is worth living, whether the mental or physical disabilities experienced by the child will enable him or her to have a meaningful life (Peushel, 1991). Often, these assumptions are accompanied by concern about the physical pain or discomfort the child is likely to experience, the prospect of a painful death later in life, or the likelihood of an existence characterized by endless surgical procedures and medical treatment. In other instances, the presence of moderate, severe, or profound levels of mental retardation may lead to negative assumptions about the child's quality of life. All these considerations come into play when medical decisions are being made about whether or not to treat children with severe disabilities when life-threatening conditions occur. In some cases,

> Quality of life refers to the extent to which an individual is aware of, participates in, and enjoys life.

the decision is made that, because of the prospect of poor quality of life, the infant should be allowed to die.

Although allowing any infant to die because of nontreatment is illegal (Orelove & Sobsey, 1987), such cases are rarely prosecuted, primarily because many individuals feel that these decisions can and should be made by the parents of the children and their physicians (Hentoff, 1985). When an investigation has occurred, it has usually resulted in extensive media coverage and publicity (Lyon, 1985), which has done little to encourage further prosecution. Certainly, any parent who chooses to withhold treatment, or in some instances nutrition, from a child is making an incredibly difficult decision. Nevertheless, the fact remains that if this type of decision were made for an infant without a disability, the persons responsible for allowing the infant to die would unquestionably be punished.

Orelove and Sobsey (1987) present five basic alternatives for the right-to-life issue: (1) to treat all nondying newborns, (2) to terminate the lives of selected infants who are not determined to be viable individuals, (3) to withhold treatment according to parental discretion, (4) to withhold treatment according to a quality-of-life determination, and (5) to withhold treatment judged not to be in the child's best interest. All these alternatives, with the exception of the first, involve subjective determinations that will result in the life or death of the child. Who, if anyone, has the right to determine if the child has the right to live? This, of course, is the root of the dilemma. Once this right has been placed in the hands of the parents or physicians, their personal criteria for the quality of life will serve as the basis for life-and-death decisions.

Most of the individuals who make decisions or provide guidance to parents about the potential quality of life for individuals with mental retardation, including parents, physicians, and lawyers, have had little, if any, experience living, working, or spending time with persons with any degree of mental retardation (Roberts, Stough, & Parrish, 2002; Smith, 1989). This lack of familiarity results not only in fear for the child's future, but often in misconceptions about the potential quality of life of individuals with varying levels of mental retardation.

Quality of life is defined many different ways when used to measure adult outcomes. Halpern (1993) suggests that the major criteria for quality of life are (1) physical and material well-being, (2) performance of adult roles, and (3) personal fulfillment. Objective, quantitative evaluations, such as specific job requirements, are important tools for identifying target instructional skills in the environment that may lead to successful performance. Qualitative or descriptive analyses of an individual's performance and personal fulfillment also are considered necessary for an accurate picture of that person's quality of life. Dennis and coworkers (1993) suggest that there is no single definition of quality of life. They, too, recommend that an individual's performance be evaluated within the context of his or her environment, using indices that reflect that person's culture, family or support system, and personal preferences. These indices may be different for each person, reflecting those facets of life that are important to the individual and his or her significant others. Storey (1997) asserts the need for broad, generally accepted operational definitions of quality of life, acknowledging that definitions might change according to the age and population. Because of advances in areas such as genetic and prenatal testing, the bioethical concerns related to the right to life for individuals with severe disabilities will only be magnified in the future, as will bioethical considerations for all of human life.

The Right to Education

We may take it for granted that all children and adolescents have the right to receive an education. Legally, this was not the case for individuals with severe and profound levels of mental retardation until 1975, when P.L. 94-142, the Education for All Handicapped Children Act (now known as IDEA), was passed. Even now, although the law states specifically that all children have the right to a free and appropriate education, controversy persists. The source of the controversy lies in the extent to which education is actually possible for some individuals with profound mental retardation. If, as some contend, there are children or adolescents who cannot benefit from educational programs, there remains the question of whether these individuals would qualify for school-based programs.

Some people feel that not all children will profit meaningfully from educational programming.

There are a few students whose disabilities are so extensive that they severely limit the amount of instruction to which they can respond. These students will receive educational programming that may be limited to sensory engagement and efforts to establish some type of communication skill or preskill, such as eye contact. Questions have been raised by some people about the need to continue educational programming for individuals with such profound levels of mental retardation. Their feeling is that it is misleading to describe every child as educable and that it must be recognized some students will not profit meaningfully from educational programming and should not be subjected to such programs. This point of view, when expressed by special educators, is supposedly applicable only to a very small number of children, and proponents stress that documented educational efforts must precede the label of ineducability.

Other professionals feel that no limits should be placed on instructional efforts and expectations.

Other special educators, however, feel that no child should be identified as unable to benefit from educational programming. There are a number of reasons for this point of view. Some express a fear that because such judgments are subjective and cannot be monitored across educational settings, a large number of students with profound levels of mental retardation will be labeled ineducable without receiving adequate or appropriate programming. Others have suggested that such determinations will undermine the progress made in the area of education for students with severe and profound levels of mental retardation by placing a limit on instructional efforts and expectations. Certainly, few individuals who taught several decades ago would have anticipated the amount of learning and skill now routinely acquired by individuals with all levels of mental retardation.

Perhaps the most important concern, however, involves the philosophy of education revealed when instructional effort is evaluated in terms of the amount or quality of student response. Ferguson (1987) proposes that education should be presented because of our commitment to individuals and should not be measured in terms of a cost-benefit standard. She suggests that it is our criteria for "meaningful" responses or functional skill acquisition that contribute to the constant delineation of a portion of the population as ineducable, or not capable of meaningful learning. In other words, she suggests that as long as we feel the need to justify education in terms of the types or amount of skills students are able to learn, we will always find a group of students who will be considered ineducable. According to Ferguson, the right to education does not have to be earned by the student; we should simply espouse the philosophy that we are committed to educating everyone.

? Pause and Reflect

Were you surprised, as you read this section, to discover the ethical issues related to the education and life of individuals with severe disabilities? As a fitting conclusion to this chapter, we ask you to think about your own parameters for quality of life and the relative or absolute value you place on life—difficult reflections for all of us. ●

SUMMARY

● Severe mental retardation is defined as an IQ score of 40 or below, and profound mental retardation as an IQ score of 20 or below accompanied by deficits in adaptive behavior. Severe and profound disabilities are caused by a variety of genetic and environmental factors and are usually identified at birth.

● The effects of a severe disability on the child include cognitive difficulty in making connections between the action and the environment, relatively small physical size and high risk of health problems, delays in or lack of oral communication, and limited social skills.

● Educational issues include normalization, integration, and an appropriate life-skills curriculum. Normalization involves age-appropriate treatment and providing environments and representations of individuals that are as close to normal as possible. Integration refers to both physical and social integration. The functional curriculum emphasizes preparation for life and instruction in integrated skills useful in school, work, or home.

● Transitional programming for children with severe and profound disabilities includes preparation for changes in schools, for movement from a segregated to an integrated setting, and for work after school.

● Basic rights, including the right to life and to education, have been questioned for people with severe disabilities. We have discussed both sides of the controversies.

KEY TERMS

severe disabilities

severe mental retardation

profound mental retardation

functional communication

formal supports

natural supports

normalization

partial participation

functional curriculum

environmental inventory (environmental analysis)

self-management procedures

quality of life

USEFUL RESOURCES

- The AbilityHub is a resource center for new programs and products in assistive technology. Their Assistive Technology Solutions are available at **http://www.abilityhub.com**. Go to the section on cognitive disabilities to access information on new products appropriate for individuals with mental retardation.

- PE Central–Adaptive Physical Education is available at **http://pecentral .org/adapted/adaptedmenu.htm**. This website is a resource page for articles or other printed information about adapting physical activities for individuals with disabilities.

- The Arc is an organization that provides information, resources, and training opportunities for individuals interested in learning more about individuals with cognitive disabilities. Go to its website at **http://www.thearc.org** for links to many helpful and informative sources related to the area of mental retardation.

- The Association for Persons with Severe Handicaps (TASH) is located at 26 West Susquehanna Avenue, Suite 210, Baltimore, MD 21204, (410) 828-8274. Visit their website at **http://www.tash.org**.

- Visit the Disability Rights Action Coalition for Housing (DRACH) website at **http://www.libertyresources.org/Advocacy/Housing/nac.htm**. to learn about the rights of individuals with disabilities regarding housing opportunities and related legislation.

- The following book can provide guidelines to teachers and other professionals interested in developing functional curricula: Paul Wehman and John Kregel (Eds.) (2004). *Functional curriculum for elementary, middle, and secondary age students with special needs* (2nd ed.). Austin, TX: Pro-Ed.

- This company provides information about educational and assistive robotic programs: Educational Electronic Robots, Elekit Company, 1160 Mahalo Place, Compton, CA 90220-5443, (310) 638-7970. Go to **http://www. owirobot. com/menu.html** to email them for further information.

 PORTFOLIO ACTIVITIES

1. Visit teachers or transition coordinators in several local schools who specialize in working with individuals with severe or profound mental retardation. Ask to observe the teacher working with students in community-based settings. Record your observations and compare the instructional strategies, types of tasks, and individual performance of the students in each setting.

   Standards This activity will help students meet CEC Content Standard 5: Learning Environments and Social Interactions.

2. Identify a task you do frequently as part of your daily or weekly routine, such as doing laundry or preparing a meal. Carefully observe and write down all the components of that task, including specific behaviors and

any decisions that must be made to complete the task. Prepare some ideas for how you could teach all these task components to an individual with severe disabilities.

✓ *Standards* This activity will help students meet CEC Content Standard 4: Instructional Strategies.

3. Locate several grocery stores or fast-food restaurants in your local community. Before visiting them, make a list of things you might need to know if you were teaching individuals with severe disabilities—for example, the location of specific food items, exits, and check-out lines in the grocery store; or methods of ordering, use of picture cues, and location of trays and condiments in the fast-food restaurants. Then visit each location. Create a chart or a graph of the similarities and differences at each location.

✓ *Standards* This activity will help students meet CEC Content Standard 3: Individual Learning Differences.

4. Compare and contrast functional or life-skills curricula for people with severe disabilities. Obtain the curricula from local public and/or residential schools. Identify the characteristics all the curricula have in common and any significant differences. Create a rubric for critiquing life-skills curricula.

✓ *Standards* This activity will help students meet CEC Content Standard 3: Individual Learning Differences.

 To access an electronic portfolio template for these activities visit our website through http://www.education.college.hmco.com/students/.

7
Children with Behavior Disorders

Outline

Terms and Definitions
    The Federal Definition
    Measures of Behavior
    Classifying Behavior Disorders
    Prevalence
Causes of Behavior Disorders
    Environmental Factors
    Physiological Factors
Characteristics of Students with
        Behavior Disorders
    School Achievement
    Social Adjustment
    Language and Communication
    Severe Disorders
    Families
Attention Deficit/Hyperactivity
        Disorder
    Assessment and Diagnosis
    Characteristics of Students
        with ADHD
    Educational Programs for Students
        with ADHD
Teaching Strategies and
        Accommodations
    Identification and Assessment:
        The Classroom Teacher's Role
    Curriculum Focus
    Academic Programming
    Behavior-Change Interventions
    Discipline in the Schools
SUMMARY
KEY TERMS
USEFUL RESOURCES
PORTFOLIO ACTIVITIES

Learning Objectives

After reading this chapter, the reader will:

- Describe how behavior disorders are defined and classified

- Identify techniques used to recognize and assess children with behavior disorders

- Explain how behavior-management strategies can be used to prevent or manage inappropriate behavior in children

- Identify strategies you can use to help students learn to manage their own behavior

In this chapter, you will learn how behavior disorders are identified and defined, the effects of these disorders on students and their families, and strategies that you can use to work with students who have them. We will also discuss some of the questions and problems surrounding the definition and identification of these disorders.

If you look at a crowd watching a baseball game or a soccer match, you will notice lots of people acting in a lot of different ways. Some people will stand up and yell, some may curse, one fan may be jumping up and down, and one fan may hide his eyes, because he just can't look. One person may be ignoring the game and reading the newspaper. Many will stand up during exciting parts of the game and sit down during the rest, so that others can see. Most people appreciate or at least tolerate these behaviors in their fellow fans. If, in a fit of excitement, one man throws a cup of ice in the air, well, that can happen sometimes. But, if someone runs down and jumps on the field—it is clear to everyone that a violation of appropriate behavior has occurred.

There are many differences in the ways people react to certain situations, act around other people, follow rules and regulations, and conform to society's expectations for behavior. As illustrated above, this is particularly true among adults, for we accept the fact that people choose their own lifestyles and behave in ways that are most comfortable to them. Typically, concern is voiced only when there appears to be a chance that someone will harm others or himself or herself, or does not appear able to cope with the daily activities of life.

Our outlook on conformity and acceptable patterns of behavior is different when we look at children, particularly children in school settings. The range of behaviors considered acceptable in school settings is limited so that children can benefit from educational programming. Our expectations of how children should feel and act are much more narrowly defined than are our expectations of acceptable adult behavior. Many children do, from time to time, behave in ways that appear to be out of bounds—beyond our typical standards of normal behavior. A child may get into a fight on the playground, or a teenager may come home from the shopping mall with purple hair and three eyebrow piercings. These children are not the focus of this chapter. As educators, we are concerned when inappropriate behavior persists, interferes with school performance, and appears harmful to the child or others.

Terms and Definitions

The children identified in this category of special education can be referred to in a number of ways. The terms used include *behavior disorders*, *severe emotional disturbance*, *emotional disturbance*, *emotionally handicapped*, and *behaviorally handicapped*. Professionals have many different opinions about which term is most appropriate; the term **behavior disorders** is used most frequently in the literature, but the term **emotional disturbance** is still used in the federal definition.

The Federal Definition

At the present time, the federal definition of emotional disturbance in IDEA includes two major criteria:

i. The term means a condition exhibiting one or more of the following characteristics over a long period of time and to a marked degree, which adversely affects educational performance.

a. An inability to learn which cannot be explained by intellectual, sensory, and health factors;

b. An inability to build or maintain satisfactory interpersonal relationships with peers and teachers;

c. Inappropriate types of behavior or feelings under normal circumstances;

d. A general pervasive mood of unhappiness or depression; or

e. A tendency to develop physical symptoms or fears associated with personal or school problems.

ii. The term includes children who are schizophrenic. The term does not include children who are socially maladjusted unless it is determined that they are emotionally disturbed. (US Department of Education, *Federal Register* 42 [163], August 23, 1977, p. 42,478).

> **Federal law cites five major criteria for determining whether a child has an emotional disturbance.**

This definition, like most definitions in special education, is the source of much debate and discussion. A great deal of the controversy revolves around the ambiguity of the terms used as diagnostic markers and concern that this ambiguity excludes children who require services. For example, phrases such as *inappropriate types of behavior* or *satisfactory interpersonal relationships* are difficult to translate into clear-cut measures of performance. It is not too difficult to imagine that different people would interpret these terms in different ways.

> **The ambiguities of the federal definition subject it to much controversy.**

It does seem likely that changes are imminent in the definition of emotional and behavior disorders, because the definition is less effective than it could be in providing guidelines for identification, assessment, and treatment.

Measures of Behavior

Behaviors can differ in frequency or rate, intensity, duration, and age appropriateness. Measures based on these factors are used to determine whether behavior is considered normal or abnormal. In other words, abnormal behavior can be normal behavior that is performed to such a degree that it becomes atypical.

● *Rate*   **Rate** refers to how often a behavior occurs in a given time period. Most children occasionally get out of their seats without asking permission, or get into fights. A child who gets into a fight every day, however, or who gets out of his seat every two minutes would be demonstrating an unusually high rate of these behaviors.

● *Intensity*   **Intensity** refers to the strength or magnitude of the behavior. For example, if a child hit his fist against the desk because he became frustrated, he might just hit it loud enough to make a noise, or he could hit it so hard he breaks either his hand or the desk. One instance would be considered a normal response; the other, more intense behavior would be considered problematic.

● *Duration*   The length of time a behavior lasts is referred to as its **duration**. Any child might have an occasional temper tantrum or cry if his or her feelings are hurt. But a tantrum or crying spell that goes on for an hour or two will be considered differently than a ten-minute outburst.

● *Age Appropriateness*   **Age-appropriate behavior** refers to the fact that some behaviors are considered quite normal in children of a certain age, but are considered problematic when they persist as the child ages or occur before they are expected. For example, clinging to a parent, throwing tantrums, or being afraid of monsters in the closet are behaviors we might expect from a 5- or 6-year-old, but not from a preteen.

Some children with emotional or behavior disorders exhibit *unusual* behaviors—behaviors we do not typically see at any level in other children. Children with unusual behaviors usually have a more severe level of behavior disorders. Examples of this type of behavior include unusual patterns of language, distinctive hand movements and walking patterns, and behaviors directed at harming oneself or others. We will look at these behaviors more closely when we discuss severe emotional or behavior disabilities later in the chapter.

An important point to keep in mind is that a single episode of what appears to be abnormal behavior does not mean that a child has a behavior disorder. Events within the child's life, as well as the changes and pressures of growing up, can result in an incidence of problem behavior, or perhaps even a few weeks in which the child seems to be exhibiting new and difficult behaviors. For example, we expect certain behaviors, such as talking back to parents and resisting being told what to do, to emerge during the beginning of adolescence. Although these behaviors may cause some difficulty in the family and at school, they reflect our expectations for teenagers. Educators are concerned about atypical behavior that exceeds expectations—that persists over several months and does not seem to have a readily identifiable cause (such as parents going through a divorce or a death in the family).

> A single episode of abnormal behavior does not mean that a child has a behavior disorder.

Classifying Behavior Disorders

Behaviors are usually classified into groups or categories. Sometimes, this is done for the purpose of diagnosis, sometimes for assessment, and other times for placement and educational interventions. For the most part, behaviors that seem related in some way are grouped together. Often, children exhibiting one type of behavior in a group or cluster will exhibit others found in that same cluster. Those children may be identified as having a specific type of syndrome or disorder. Other children display behaviors from a number of different groups. A number of classification systems are used with children having behavior or emotional disorders. In addition to the various behaviors described in this section, we have included a separate section on attention deficit/hyperactivity disorder (ADHD) later in this chapter. Although ADHD is not technically a behavior disorder, it has been considered a disorder of behavior because of its historical relationship with hyperactive behavior. ADHD is not a separate category of special education under IDEA; however, it is a common diagnosis for students in general education classrooms and warrants a clear and thorough discussion (see pp. 256–259).

● ***The DSM-IV-TR System***   One classification system is presented in *The Diagnostic and Statistical Manual of Mental Disorders of the American Psychiatric Association* (4th ed., 2000), known as **DSM-IV-TR**. This manual groups behaviors into diagnostic categories. In other words, the manual lists specific behaviors and other criteria that must be present before a disorder can be diagnosed. Because many behavior and psychiatric disorders are diagnosed on the basis of behavior alone, rather than by a specific test or medical diagnosis, these behavior descriptions can assist in the diagnosis of specific disabilities. Thus, a psychologist may collect observations and reports of a child's behavior in a number of settings over time and compare those behaviors to the categories in DSM-IV-TR to make a diagnosis.

> The DSM-IV-TR classifies behavior by diagnostic categories.

Social acceptance by class-mates is desired by every adolescent. The peer group can play an important role in identifying and support-ing appropriate behaviors. (Myrleen Ferguson Cate/PhotoEdit)

In some schools, the school or clinical psychologist makes the diagnosis of behavior disorders. In other schools, or in the case of a particular child, a psychiatrist or pediatrician may diagnose the disability. The professional status of the individual making a diagnosis is particularly important when severe problems are exhibited or when therapy or medication is part of the remediation process. For example, a physician will need to be involved for types of behavior disorders that may require drug therapy, such as depression or ADHD. An example of diagnostic criteria from DSM-IV is found in the section on ADHD in this chapter.

Visit the website of the American Psychiatric Association at **http://www. psych.org** to learn more about applying the information from the DSM series, to see the research agenda for DSM-V, and to learn more about current research in areas such as ADHD, depression, anxiety disorders, and autism.

● *Educational Classification Systems*   Other systems of classifying behavior are more informal and based on groupings of a more general nature. Rather than looking for specific disorders, we describe broad patterns of behavior or disorders, such as those described below. This type of classification system may be used for educational placement, service delivery, and program development. Although a classification system gives us an idea of the nature of a child's disability, it does not tell us the best treatment or educational procedures to use (Cullinan, 2000; Kauffman, 2001). As with all special education, appropriate interventions are selected based on the individual needs of each child.

Some of the systems currently used by schools and psychologists include scales based on the criteria found in the federal definition, such as the Scale for Assessing Emotional Disturbance (Epstein & Cullinan, 1998). Other scales and assessment instruments are based on systems developed and researched by professionals in the field.

For example, Quay and Peterson devised a classification system based on extensive observations of children and the patterns of behavior that surfaced. They used six types of behavior as the basis for their classification scheme: conduct disorder, socialized aggression, attention problems–immaturity, anxiety–withdrawal, psychotic behavior, and motor excess. The Revised Behavior

Problem Checklist (Quay & Peterson, 1983, 1996) reflects this classification system.

Achenbach and Edelbrock developed the Child Behavior Checklist (1979, 1991) that classifies behavior and then identifies these behavior clusters, as either externalizing or internalizing behaviors. **Externalizing behaviors**, also known as acting out or aggressive behaviors, encompass all those behaviors that are expressed overtly and that appear, in some way, to be directed toward others or the environment. These outwardly directed behaviors may represent impulsivity or a lack of self-control and can often be confrontational, aggressive, or disruptive. Children with externalizing behavior disorders typically stand out in a classroom because of the impact their behavior has on others. The child who throws tantrums or teases his or her neighbor will interfere with others' abilities to listen or participate in class; aggressive actions may result in more than one child on the floor or in tears.

Internalizing behaviors are self-directed behaviors, such as withdrawal, avoidance, or compulsiveness. A child with an internalizing behavior disorder may be sad or depressed, withdrawn or shy, or focused on disturbing fears or fantasies.

Because of the nature of internalizing behavior disorders, a child's problems may not be recognized immediately, if at all. This child, typically, will not be a disruptive influence in the class and will not exhibit behaviors that draw attention from peers or the teacher. The student's avoidance of social interaction and the presence of fears or interfering thoughts, however, can affect his or her ability to perform in school and to establish social relationships. Recently, in light of the publicity given to adolescent suicides, more attention has been directed to identifying children with this type of disorder. Again, it is important to examine the degree and appearance of the behavior, as well as the effects on the child when trying to identify internalizing behavior disorders. Many young children will exhibit excessively shy behavior when encountering new experiences or people (such as the first day of school). We might also expect a period of depressed or withdrawn behavior when a traumatic event such as death, divorce, or a move has occurred in a child's life.

In the rest of this chapter, we will be using the Achenbach and Edelbrock classification system of externalizing and internalizing behaviors to look at the effects of behavior or emotional disorders on children and their educational needs. This system is the least complicated, encompasses all behaviors, and focuses on the fundamental difference in children's behavior patterns.

From the teacher's perspective, the system helps to emphasize the relevance of *both* types of behavior. Unfortunately, the behaviors found in the internalizing dimension are not recognized as easily or determined to be problematic even though these behaviors can have a profound effect on a child. As you might expect, teachers are more motivated to identify problems that disrupt the classroom and cause daily conflict than to recognize a problem such as depressed or withdrawn behavior that affects only the child in question.

Prevalence

The prevalence rate of behavior disorders is estimated to be about 8.6 percent of the school-aged population with disabilities, although estimates have reached as high as 20 to 30 percent. In the United States and territories, 473,663 students, ages 6–21, were served for emotional disturbance during the 2000–2001 school year (U.S. Department of Education, 2002).

Some feel that many children with emotional or behavior disorders are not receiving needed attention.

Although these numbers may seem large, they actually represent a figure far lower than most estimates of the true number of students with behavior disorders. The vague criteria in the definition and the subjective nature of assessment often make a definitive diagnosis difficult; therefore, the percentage of students identified with emotional disturbance in one state could be very different from the percentage of children identified in another. There are probably many students with behavior disorders who are not receiving needed special education services.

? Pause and Reflect

Most children with behavior disorders are diagnosed based on the evaluations of teachers, parents, and school psychologists. When thinking about behavior disorders, it is helpful to understand your own ability to tolerate differences in behavior, as well as your perceptions of "too much" activity or "not enough" social interaction. What are your expectations of behavior for a child in your class? How flexible can you, or should you, be? •

Causes of Behavior Disorders

It is difficult to pinpoint the causes of most behavior and emotional disorders.

The causes of most behavior and emotional disorders are difficult to pinpoint. We often see children with very similar behavior patterns, yet very different learning and family histories. Sometimes, it is easy to pinpoint factors or situations that possibly contribute to behavior and emotional disorders; sometimes, there are no readily identifiable causal factors. Let's look at the following two examples of students with externalizing behavior disorders.

Case Studies

Sandy, age 10, was identified as behavior disordered at age 7. At that time, she began demonstrating a number of problematic behaviors: She used extremely violent and obscene language toward her teachers and classmates; threw loud and long temper tantrums; hit her teacher and threw things when she was denied a request; and said cruel things to the other children in the class. She was failing the second grade. About two years later, it was discovered that Sandy had been the victim of sexual abuse by her mother's boyfriend. Although the abusive situation had ended, Sandy's behavior persisted. The identification of the specific cause could not, by itself, heal Sandy's emotional distress or end the behaviors that she had acquired and practiced over time.

Bill, age 13, was identified as having emotional or behavior disorders for the past five years. He is very active, always out of his seat, and moving around. Although he can be compliant and cooperative, he flares up easily, becoming resistant and confrontational with teachers and principals. Bill constantly fights with other children. He seems to see every interaction as a challenge and responds with anger and aggression. He failed fourth grade and is barely passing his classes now. Most of the students in school dislike and avoid him. Bill lives with his mother and they apparently have a good relationship. Although Bill's behavior has improved some during the past few years, he is socially rejected and behind academically, and he still resorts to violent interactions when frustrated or when he feels challenged in any way.

Although Sandy's inappropriate behavior had a clear time of onset, Bill is an example of a child with a long history of problem behavior. He has trouble interacting with adults and peers, and is not doing well in school. Bill seems to see things somewhat differently than other children; he feels others are out to get him, he can't control his temper, and he always uses aggression to respond. Why does Bill act this way? Does he live in a violent home or neighborhood? Does he have problems dealing with reality? Or is he just a bad kid?

There are no simple answers to these questions for many students with behavior disorders. Sometimes, we (as teachers) can speculate or make assumptions about the role of parents, peers, or temperament, but often this is all we can do. It is very difficult to determine why one child has a behavior disorder and another child in the same situation does not.

In spite of numerous theories and hypotheses about the causes of behavior disorders, all we can do with certainty is identify factors that seem to coincide with the occurrence of behavior differences. These factors can be grouped into two major categories: environmental and physiological. Environmental factors focus on the child's interactions with people and things external to him or her; physiological factors focus on the inner biology or psychology of the child. The accompanying Closer Look box entitled, "Factors Associated with Behavior Disorders" summarizes these points.

Environmental Factors

Environmental factors that may contribute to behavior disorders include family factors, cultural factors, and school factors. Family factors often revolve around the level and consistency of discipline; the history of violence and arrests in the family; and the way parents and siblings deal with feelings and each other. Children who experience consistent behavior management practices, including positive as well as negative consequences for behavior, have a clearer idea of appropriate and inappropriate behavior. In other words, just as in the classroom, it is important for children at home to know the rules and be expected to follow them. Some other possible contributors to children's behavior can be the modeling of aggressive behavior by family members, neglect, or traumatic events such as death or divorce. Remember, however, that the way individual children respond to factors such as these can vary considerably. Also, it is important to note that many children with behavior disorders seem to have very supportive and loving family environments.

Cultural factors may include cultural norms for accepted levels of deviant behavior. Webb-Johnson (2003) suggests that one of the reasons African Ameri-

A Closer Look   Factors Associated with Behavior Disorders

Environmental Factors

- Family factors
- Cultural factors
- School factors

Physiological Factors

- Organic factors
- Genetic factors
- Specific syndromes with behavior correlates

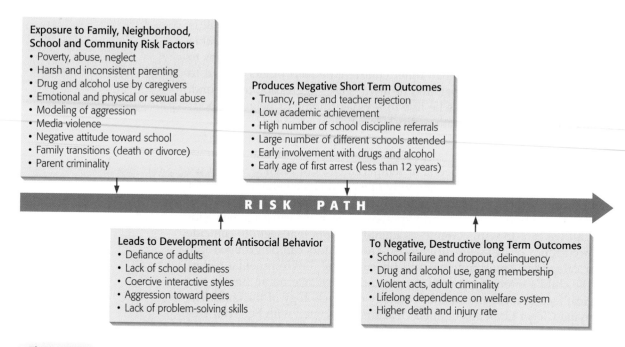

Figure 7.1

The Path to Negative Outcomes

Source: J. Sprague & H. Walker (2000). Early identification and intervention for youth with antisocial and violent behavior. *Exceptional Children, 66,* (3), 391.

can students are overrepresented in classes for students with behavior disorders is that many teachers misinterpret culturally acceptable behavior as inappropriate, leading to a cycle of attempted control by teachers and resistance by students. Some people suspect that other cultural factors influencing the occurrence of behavior disorders include the level of violence in the media. Figure 7.1 presents a diagram of the interaction between environmental risk factors and the development of inappropriate behaviors.

Physiological Factors

Physiological factors that may influence the development of behavior disorders include organic factors, such as dysfunctions of the central nervous system; genetic factors, such as a family history of schizophrenia; or specific syndromes, such as Tourette's syndrome, that are accompanied by unusual behavior patterns. A child's temperament has also been identified as a possible source of behavior differences. Again, with the exception of some syndromes with distinct behavior correlates, we must rely primarily on assumptions when dealing with physiological causes of behavior disorders.

It is interesting to note that a number of students receive drug treatment for behavior disorders. Although the cause of the behaviors may be unknown, certain drugs ameliorate symptoms for some people. Because drug treatments work on the symptoms rather than on the causes, drug therapy must be constant in order for the symptoms to stay suppressed. A prominent example is the use of drug therapy for attention deficit/hyperactivity disorder (ADHD). Although the

Drug therapy can be an important component of a treatment plan for some students with behavior disorders.

exact cause of this disorder is not known, certain drugs have been found to suppress its symptoms in some students. Young people with depression or who demonstrate psychotic behaviors may also receive medication. A medical model for treatment may be used with increasing frequency as we learn more about the role of physiological contributions to behavior disorders. Professionals stress, however, that effective programs include medication in conjunction with behavior and educational interventions (Forness, Sweeney, & Toy, 1996).

? Pause and Reflect

As you can see from our discussion of causes of behavior disorders, it often is difficult to pinpoint a clear cause of a child's inappropriate behavior. Even when we do find a traumatic event or sequence of events that precipitated behavior at one time, our interventions focus on the here and now. Factors in current environments must be addressed before behavior can be changed. Do you find it surprising that often there is no clear cause of a child's behavior disorder? ●

Characteristics of Students with Behavior Disorders

Behavior and emotional disorders, by definition, affect the way children interact with those around them as well as the performance abilities of the children themselves. In this section, we discuss some of the specific ways the child's life can be affected by behavior disorders.

School Achievement

Most children with emotional or behavior disorders are in the average range of intellectual functioning, yet do not do well in school. Their behavior in school interferes with learning and performing academic tasks. Although the extent to which behavior affects academic performance varies according to the individual child, poor schoolwork and underachievement in class are often cited as characteristics of children with behavior disorders. Researchers have found a relationship between more difficult academic task demand and the occurrence of antisocial behavior. In other words, the more difficult a task is, the more likely that the child will try to avoid working, or show frustration in inappropriate ways. Many children may whine or resist doing difficult math problems, for example, but few will throw their papers on the floor, break their pencils, or call the teacher names. (McEvoy & Welker, 2000). Low achievement in school also may be associated with poor work habits, lack of student participation, or poor attentional skills. Teachers can employ methods of instruction and classroom management that simultaneously support academic achievement and appropriate behavior. For example, allowing students to participate in choosing classroom tasks, providing plentiful opportunities for students to respond during class, and offering consistent praise for good performance can create increases in both accurate academic responses and appropriate classroom behavior (Jolivette et al., 2001; Sutherland, Wehby, & Yoder, 2002).

Most children with emotional or behavior disorders are in the normal range of intelligence but tend to do poorly in school.

FIRST PERSON

Jon: His Turn

Jon is a 13-year-old student with emotional/behavior disorders. Jon is in middle school; currently, he is in a self-contained class for students with behavior disorders. He was elated when he was asked to tell his story: Finally, we would listen.

I hope that this passage will help every E.D. teacher understand an emotional disability called "bipolar disorder" something that will haunt me for the rest of my life. I remember when I was first sent to an E.D. class it was September and I was going into fifth grade my first day was OK but as the days progressed things got much worse. I Started to get heavily depressed. Every day I went to school the biggest thought In my head was suicide but I could only keep it in my head for so long. It kept getting worse to the point that when I walk down the hall way to My classroom it was like walking into HELL! When I was in in kinder garden I got into trouble close to every day. My mother has told me about this many times. She used to say many of my family members used to say that something was Not quite right with me. The year I entered the Third grade was the year that Will live in infamy for me. It was the year that the monster inside me broke free. I still was not on any meds and when the littlest things happened such as getting Punished or having a lot of pressure put on me I would start crying then I Could not stop and I start thinking the words in my head what if what if what if. After that I look at things around me and somehow I don't remember where I am. Now I am on meds and doing better. I'm slowly but surely digging myself Out of my hole. There is a kid in my class that ticks me off but other then that School is going great. In this entry I would liked to thank my mom my dad And my psychiatrist Dr. Davis thanks to them I'm doing much better.

Source: This is a true story though the names and indentities have been changed to protect the privacy of the individuals depicted here. "Jon's story" is copied as originally written.

Research also suggests that students with behavior disorders perform approximately one standard deviation below the mean, or close to one year behind their expected achievement level. Glassberg, Hooper, and Mattison (1999) found that about 53 percent of a sample of students identified with behavior disorders also met the definition for learning disabilities at the time of testing. In addition, Anderson, Kutash, and Duchnowski (2001) found the academic prognosis for reading performance of children with behavior disorders was actually worse than the prognosis for children with learning disabilities. In spite of the fact that they actually received more special education services than the children with learning disabilities, children with behavior disorders made little progress in reading between kindergarten and the end of elementary school. There is no clear reason for this lack of progress; however, we can speculate that the amount of time teachers spend on managing behavior, and the resistance of students with behavior disorders to academic requirements may contribute to poor academic growth.

Some children experience difficulty adjusting to the behavior requirements of social situations, which leads to inappropriate or aggressive behavior. (Mary Kate Denny/PhotoEdit)

Social Adjustment

Children with emotional and behavior disorders by definition exhibit behaviors that affect their social and emotional development. Externalizing behaviors such as violence and aggression may be directed toward classmates, and many children with externalizing behavior disorders do not have the skills for reflecting on and restricting their behavior. As these children grow into adolescents, their lack of control can often lead to serious conflicts. The patterns of violent behaviors exhibited by students with behavior disorders change as students age. Violent behavior patterns may consist of bullying at the elementary level, fighting at the middle-school level, and using weapons or drugs at the high-school level (Furlong & Morrison, 2000).

Internalized behaviors such as withdrawal or depression may result in the children being teased or rejected by classmates, and may cause great difficulty when interacting with others. Research shows that children with behavior disorders are not accepted well by their regular classmates, even in adolescence—a time when some noncompliant behavior is the norm (Gresham & MacMillan, 1997).

Without education and intervention, the behaviors that characterize a behavior disorder will continue to affect the student after he or she leaves the school environment. What will happen when an aggressive child grows into an adult? Will he punch his coworkers or have a tantrum while driving or arguing with his girlfriend? If a student doesn't learn new ways to control and respond

Many adolescents with behavior disorders have been in trouble with the law.

to anger or frustration as he or she grows older, the probability of encounters with the law increases.

High-school classes for students with behavior disorders often include students who have been in trouble with the law. The number of teens with behavior disorders who have gone through the legal system at least once varies greatly from area to area; however, students with this diagnosis appear at higher risk for arrest both during and after the school years (Cullinan, 2002). Patterns of aggressive, rule-breaking, and risk-taking behavior are often found in students with behavior disorders, and these behaviors set the stage for illegal activities.

Research has investigated patterns of drug use and dropout rates of junior and senior high-school students with and without behavior disorders. Devlin and Elliott (1992) found that 51 percent of students with behavior disorders were in the high-drug-use category, 20 percent were in the medium-drug-use category, and 28 percent were in the low- or negligible-drug-use category. Compare these figures with those for students without behavior disorders: 14 percent in the high-use group, 10 percent in the medium-use group, and 74 percent in the low- or negligible-use group. Walker, Colvin, and Ramsey (1995) found that boys identified with antisocial behavior disorders experienced seven times as many arrests during their school years as boys identified as at risk for school failure. They also found the antisocial students were over five times as likely to drop out of school as the children at risk.

Language and Communication

As we look at the effects of emotional or behavior disorders on communication, we must remember that in many ways behavior *is* communication. Some behaviors are learned as a way of responding to situations or events, or as a way of getting a response; some are developed because an individual has no other effective means of expression; and some are developed to enable an individual to control a situation. When we talk about teaching students appropriate behavior, or reducing inappropriate behavior, we are also teaching students alternative ways of communicating information, feelings, or needs.

Inappropriate behavior does not imply that a student has poor language skills; in fact, some students with behavior disorders may be quite expressive and articulate. Other students with behavior disorders may have difficulty expressing themselves using verbal language, or they may experience mild forms of language difficulty and delay. Some students with behavior disorders are found to use fewer words per sentence, to have difficulty staying on a topic, and to have problems using language that is appropriate or meaningful in a given situation or conversation (Donahue, Cole, & Hartas, 1994). Students may also have difficulty organizing their thoughts to communicate effectively through oral or written language.

Language is crucial to academic performance, to interactions with peers and adults, and to the development of the sequential logical thought processes required in many self-management interventions, and it is an important component of any educational program. Communication, however, involves more than language. Name-calling, tantrums, and turning over desks, like all behaviors, are ways of communicating. Teachers should always keep in mind the potential communicative intent of the *behaviors* students are exhibiting and be ready to provide appropriate alternatives—new ways of expressing how they feel or what they want—so they can successfully overcome their existing, inappropriate, communication behaviors.

Severe Disorders

In the case studies presented earlier, we saw the great impact behavior disorders can have on a child's life. Yet the continuum of emotional or behavior disorders extends even further than what has been already described. Some individuals exhibit severe disorders of behavior—behaviors that require even more specialized attention and intervention, some of which are provided outside of the regular school setting. Others have unusual patterns of behavior, such as those found in autism (see Chapter 8), a psychiatric diagnosis such as childhood schizophrenia, or a combination of disabilities that also require specialized interventions and that can have profound effects on the individual's behavior in all areas of life.

Although children with very severe behavior disorders may either have externalizing or internalizing behavior disorders, they exhibit behaviors that are markedly severe and intended to harm others or themselves. Other children in this category may be so withdrawn as to resist any semblance of normal social interaction. Their functioning may be severely inhibited because of withdrawal, disoriented thoughts, or depression. In general, these children require extensive and intensive educational assistance. Some children with severe disabilities receive educational services in public school settings, whereas others still are served, at least for a time, in segregated or residential facilities.

> One child, John, who is barely 8 years old, lives in a residential facility for children with severe behavior disorders. He is exceptionally bright yet works at a primer level. By the age of 7, John had stabbed his mother twice with a knife, pushed his younger brother down the stairs and off a high chair, and tried to set fire to his room on three separate occasions. Although most of the time John seemed to be a friendly, outgoing child, his behaviors were determined to be so potentially harmful that he was placed in the residential setting.

Behavior patterns similar to John's are among the most difficult for professionals and parents to handle. The child seems to be normal or above average in so many respects, yet exhibits incredibly hurtful behavior without any warning or apparent reason. Treatment for John will need to be very complex, and most likely it is outside of the realm of school personnel. Teaching him to recognize and control his impulses will be a key focus.

Other students with severe behavior disorders may be the target of their own destructive behavior.

> Rhonda is 17 years old. Although she has always been moody and aggressive, she was identified as having behavior disorders only a few years ago. At that time, her behaviors became increasingly self-destructive and violent. She broke her hand by slamming it against her locker, gave herself cigarette burns on her arms, and, in the last year, made two suicide attempts. Although Rhonda was placed in a public school resource class initially, she was later placed in a residential setting for more intensive interventions and close supervision.

Such violent, self-destructive behavior is often interpreted as a plea for attention or a cry for help. Interventions for suicidal students include counseling, medication (when appropriate), helping them think more positively about themselves, teaching new and more positive ways to communicate anger, fear, or frustration, focusing on activities designed to demonstrate and accentuate their skills and abilities, and developing positive friendships.

The specific instructional strategies and therapies used for children with severe behavior disabilities will vary widely and must be tailored to the specific needs of the individual. In a number of instances, drug therapy will be a component of the treatment plan. In part, drug treatment is a response to recent discoveries that some disorders, such as certain types of schizophrenia or depression, appear to have a strong physiological component.

Cullinan (2002) suggests that the successful movement of children with severe emotional or behavior disorders from residential treatment facilities to their home and school environments must be accompanied by extensive liaison work between the facility and the home and receiving school. In order for these children to continue to improve and function independently, they must be able to cope with life in their everyday environments, not just in the residential facility. The more teachers understand about the environments into which children will be returning, the more they can prepare the students to handle those emotional and behavior requirements. We constantly hear media reports of increasing numbers of depressed teenagers and alarming rates of youth suicide. There are a number of websites you can visit to find out more about these issues. One website, that for the American Academy of Pediatrics, includes recent research data and suicide warning signs (**http://www.apa.org/**); another website, About Teen Depression, is targeted more toward parents. This website presents information on depression, alcohol, drugs, suicide, and treatment options (go to **http://www.about-teen-depression.com**).

Families

● *Relationships with Children with Behavior Disorders*   The effects on the family of a child with behavior disorders can be significant. Some parents struggle with the feeling that they are responsible for their child's behavior problem; many parents find dealing with the child's behavior to be emotionally and physically exhausting. Some parents, and siblings as well, feel they have to focus all their attention on a child with behavior disorders; others try to ignore the behaviors. Because a child's behavior is often taken to be a reflection of parenting skill, a child with behavior disorders may cause a parent to feel embarrassed and guilty. Parents may try to "make it up" to the child, or conversely become angry with him or her. Try to remember this the next time you stare angrily at a parent whose child is crying in the grocery store. Parents may be faced continually with fear of what their child will do next, or with feelings of helplessness.

A child with a behavior or emotional disorder may become a victim of abuse. Zirpoli (1986) found that children with behavior disorders are at increased risk for parental abuse. It is not clear whether abuse is more likely to cause behavior disorders or whether behavior disorders are more likely to cause abuse. Zirpoli, however, discusses the fact that the incidence of child abuse of children with all types of disabilities does not decrease after the age of 6, as it does with children without disabilities. One reason for this sad statistic may be that the presence of a lifelong disability is a continuing stressor on the family.

Because of specific stress factors and other individual needs of families, educational plans must take the family's needs into account. Some of the feelings of helplessness can be addressed when parents are given strategies to implement and carry over to the home, particularly in the area of dealing with crises—a need frequently expressed by parents of children with behavior disorders. For example, a family may be concerned about the tantrums their 10-year-old displays in public places when he is unable to get his way. Embarrassed by their child, the parents typically give in to him so that he will stop creating a public scene. The parents feel manipulated by their child and helpless. The teacher may come up with a set of techniques for the parents to try. These may include a checklist for the child to keep for himself while out in public. If all the appropriate behaviors are checked off, the child could be eligible for some privilege or allowed to choose where to eat lunch. Other strategies include helping the parents develop consistent and firm consequences to implement if a tantrum should occur and taking the child on a number of short trips to places that usually do not result in problems (for example, the post office as opposed to the toy store) so that lots of praise and encouragement can be given when no tantrums occur.

● *Parents and Schools*   The family of the child with emotional or behavior disorders plays a critical role in the development and implementation of effective educational programs. Strong parent-teacher relationships may be particularly important when the teacher and student are from different cultural backgrounds so that the parents believe the behavior goals are meaningful, and to ensure an absence of cultural bias in the goals the team selects (Cartledge, Kea, & Ida, 2000). If the parents do not buy into the child's behavior intervention plan, the child probably won't either. Many educators try to involve parents as much as possible when establishing consistent behavior-management strategies across home and school settings. Programs with a home-based component that include the delivery by parents of positive and negative consequences for behavior (privileges and restrictions) result in decreases in noncompliant and antisocial behaviors as well as in symptoms of depression in children (Eddy, Reid, & Fetrow, 2000; Rosen et al., 1990). Children are more likely to learn and apply new behaviors when they are receiving the same attention, consequences, and rules at home and at school.

One major factor in consistent behavior management is the degree of communication between the teacher and the parent. Parents of a child with behavior

> Teachers often involve parents in programs designed to teach behavior.

Children with behavior disorders may require certain levels of classroom structure to support appropriate school behavior. (Mary Kate Denny/PhotoEdit)

A key factor in consistent behavior management is communication between teacher and parent.

disorders should keep in close contact with their child's teachers so they can be aware of how he or she is progressing and how they can stress the same behavior patterns at home. Many teachers have devised daily or weekly checklists or behavior reports that are sent home to let parents know how the child behaved that day and what the parents can do to help reinforce good behavior. Parents may provide consequences for good school behavior, such as taking the child to a movie on Saturday afternoon after a week of good reports. This type of teacher-parent alliance may be particularly helpful with older children who value their weekend and afterschool time.

? Pause and Reflect

As we look at the characteristics of children and adolescents with behavior disorders, it is clear that there often is a strong interaction between behavior and academic performance. Perhaps you are surprised that so many children with behavior disorders also experience learning difficulties. How do you think inappropriate behavior could affect academic learning or difficulty in academics could affect behavior? ●

Attention Deficit/Hyperactivity Disorder

As mentioned earlier, **attention deficit/hyperactivity disorder (ADHD)** refers to a disorder that affects an individual's ability to attend to or focus on tasks and that may involve high levels of motoric activity. As you can see in the Closer Look box entitled, "Diagnostic Criteria for Attention Deficit/Hyperactivity Disorder" the symptoms of ADHD are grouped into two major categories: (1) inattention and (2) hyperactivity-impulsivity. The number of symptoms a child displays in each category will determine if the child has primarily an attention disorder (ADHD, predominantly inattention type), a hyperactivity disorder (ADHD, predominantly hyperactive-impulsive type), or a combination (ADHD, combined type) (DSM-IV-TR, 2000). You may hear the term *attention deficit disorder (ADD)* used by teachers or parents to refer to the inattention type of ADHD, or as a general description of attention problems.

Assessment and Diagnosis

Between 3 and 5 percent of children in the United States are identified as having ADHD (Barkely, 1998; Lerner, Lowenthal, & Lerner, 1995). The methods used to determine if a student has ADHD include interviews with the child, parents, and teachers, and behavior checklists. If you look at the DSM-IV diagnostic criteria in the accompanying Closer Look box, you will note that all children display some of these behaviors at one time or another. As with all behavior disorders, the clinicians look at the degree to which these behaviors are performed and how the behaviors affect academic and social performance before reaching a diagnosis. ADHD is diagnosed in individuals of all ages; however, the symptoms must have been present before 7 years of age (DSM-IV-TR, 2000). Research suggests that up to two-thirds of students with ADHD have an additional diagnosis—for example, learning disabilities or conduct-related behavior disorders (NIMH, 1999). Although assessment and diagnosis can be done by psychologists in the school setting, many children are referred to pediatricians for evaluation.

Some parents prefer a pediatrician's evaluation because the doctor can rule out other possible causes for the behavior, and because drug therapy is often used, which must be prescribed by a physician.

A Closer Look

Diagnostic Criteria for Attention Deficit/Hyperactivity Disorder

A. Either (1) or (2):

    1. six (or more) of the following symptoms of inattention have persisted for at least six months to a degree that is maladaptive and inconsistent with developmental level:

Inattention

    a. often fails to give close attention to details or makes careless mistakes in schoolwork, work, or other activities

    b. often has difficulty sustaining attention in tasks or play activities

    c. often does not seem to listen when spoken to directly

    d. often does not follow through on instructions and fails to finish schoolwork, chores, or duties in the workplace (not due to oppositional behavior or failure to understand instructions)

    e. often has difficulty organizing tasks and activities

    f. often avoids, dislikes, or is reluctant to engage in tasks that require sustained mental effort (such as schoolwork or homework)

    g. often loses things necessary for tasks or activities (e.g., toys, school assignments, pencils, books, or tools)

    h. is often easily distracted by extraneous stimuli

    i. is often forgetful in daily activities

    2. six (or more) of the following symptoms of hyperactivity-impulsivity have persisted for at least six months to a degree that is maladaptive and inconsistent with developmental level:

Hyperactivity

    a. often fidgets with hands or feet or squirms in seat

    b. often leaves seat in classroom or in other situations in which remaining seated is expected

    c. often runs about or climbs excessively in situations in which it is inappropriate (in adolescents or adults, may be limited to subjective feelings of restlessness)

    d. often has difficulty playing or engaging in leisure activities quietly

    e. is often "on the go" or often acts as if "driven by a motor"

    f. often talks excessively

Impulsivity

    g. often blurts out answers before questions have been completed

    h. often has difficulty awaiting turn

    1. often interrupts or intrudes on others (e.g., butts into conversations or games)

B. Some hyperactive-impulsive or inattentive symptoms that caused impairment were present before the age of 7.

C. Some impairment from the symptoms is present in two or more settings (e.g., at school [or work] and at home).

D. There must be clear evidence of clinically significant impairment in social, academic, or occupational functioning.

E. The symptoms do not occur exclusively during the course of a Pervasive Developmental Disorder, Schizophrenia, or other Psychotic Disorder and are not better accounted for by another mental disorder (e.g., Mood Disorder, Anxiety Disorder, Dissociative Disorder, or a Personality Disorder).

Source: American Psychiatric Association (2000). Diagnostic criteria for attention-deficit/hyperactivity disorder from *Diagnostic and statistical manual of mental disorders.* Fourth Edition, 1994.

Characteristics of Students with ADHD

The characteristics of children with ADHD will vary both across and within types of the disorder. When a child has inattention symptoms, his work may be messy, incomplete, and disorganized; directions may be forgotten or only partially followed; and he may be easily distracted and forgetful. The student with ADHD is likely to forget to bring pencils, paper, books, and lunch tickets to school—every day. Essentially, any activity that requires voluntary, sustained attention can be disrupted. For example, while you are giving directions for a test, the student may interrupt you to ask what is being served for lunch today. Long tasks or activities are particularly difficult, and the student may try to avoid them altogether. Your request for a student with ADHD to write a two-page essay in class could be met with (1) frequent trips to the bathroom or pencil sharpener; (2) a half-written sentence, with the student gazing out the window; (3) a "completed" essay consisting of three sentences and written in less than five minutes; or (4) the student attempting the task, crumpling up the paper, and sulking with his head on his desk. A student's attention deficits can eventually result in learning deficits, because of difficulty attending to material long enough to learn and practice it.

The behavior of students who experience impulsivity/hyperactivity symptoms reflects high and constant levels of activity. The characteristics of impulsive cognitive style that we discussed in Chapter 4 apply to students with ADHD. They may react quickly to situations, without considering the consequences, or they may shout out answers to questions without waiting for recognition or reflecting on their responses. The activity level demonstrated by many students with ADHD is much higher than that of other children, and it is constant. The child with hyperactivity symptoms is always moving—running, twitching, tapping, shifting, and jumping. Parents of young children with hyperactivity report that their children have trouble sleeping or eating (Fowler, 1995). The constant motion, combined with impulsivity, obviously is at odds with the behavioral requirements of school settings and often puts kids with ADHD at risk for accidents and social altercations.

Educational Programs for Students with ADHD

Although ADHD is not a category of special education identified in IDEA, many students with the disorder do receive special education or other educational support services. Students with ADHD who do not have another identified disability may receive services under the IDEA category "Other Health Impaired" or, more typically, under Section 504 of the Rehabilitation Act of 1973. It is likely, therefore, that if you have a student with ADHD in your classroom, he or she will have an IEP that identifies specific accommodations and educational needs. Educational strategies for students with ADHD focus on attention, organization, behavior management, and self-management. The specific interventions used for students with ADHD overlap considerably with the strategies we discuss in each of these areas in both Chapter 4 and this chapter. Students with ADHD need structure, consistency, and clear consequences for behavior; direct instruction procedures for social behavior and academic skills, strategy instruction, and self-monitoring instruction are examples of types of interventions that can be useful for children with ADHD. It is important for teachers and parents to remember that students with ADHD need to learn specific skills for organizing, attending, and self-management.

Drug therapy is frequently a part of educational programs for students with ADHD. It is successfully used in many, but not all, cases to allow students time to think, reflect, and learn. Approximately 70 to 80 percent of students with ADHD respond to medication (Barkley, 1998). However, drug therapy does not *teach* students necessary skills, although it may give the students the time needed to learn them. If you have a student in your class who is receiving drug therapy for ADHD, it is important for you to provide feedback to the parents and physician about the effects of the drug. Often, physicians must experiment with dosages before finding the correct one; your input will be important. The most common drugs used are psychostimulants, particularly Ritalin, Dexedrine, and Cylert (Barkley, 1998). Each child will react differently, and some side effects are indicated, so it is important to learn as much about each student's drug therapy regime as possible. New drugs, such as Concerta, allow for students to take one pill a day instead of taking a pill every few hours. Some children find this a positive alternative, since they don't have to take their pill during the school day. To learn more about ADHD, including research, resources, facts, and policy issues, visit the website of Children and Adults with Attention-Deficit/Hyperactivity Disorder (CHADD) at **http://www.chadd.org**.

❓ Pause and Reflect

It is important for you, as an educator or as a parent, to reflect on how each child interacts with his or her environment, and how you can adjust the environment to address the child's behavior patterns. With ADHD, sometimes medication, or drug therapy, can help the child better benefit from behavior and academic environmental supports—it may make the child more receptive to instruction. How can classrooms be adjusted so they are helpful to children with ADHD? ●

Teaching Strategies and Accommodations

Educational planning and programming for students with emotional or behavior disorders involve several interrelated issues: early intervention, assessment, placing children with behavior disorders within the school system, choosing a philosophical approach, designing curriculum and instructional strategies to enhance learning, and handling discipline in the school.

Identification and Assessment: The Classroom Teacher's Role

Identifying and assessing behavior disorders is not easy because of the ambiguity of the definition and the subjectivity involved in judging the appropriateness of behavior. For example, suppose I like my classroom busy and bustling, with chatter going on at all times, whereas you like your class perfectly still and quiet—no one moves without raising a hand. Further, suppose that little Bobby likes to roam around the class and talk. You and I will rate Bobby's behavior very differently. This point is important to keep in mind, because although there are many ways to assess behavior differences, including screening, rating scales, and psychological testing, the primary method of identifying students with emotional or behavior disorders is, increasingly, observations of the child's behavior.

Screening identifies children whose behavior interferes with academic achievement.

● *Screening*   There is so much variation in what behaviors and emotional reactions are considered developmentally appropriate among young children that it is difficult to identify emotional or behavior disorders in the early years. Many educators, however, believe that early intervention is critical, particularly for antisocial or noncompliant behaviors (Kamps & Tankersley, 1996). Although the average age of identifying children with behavior disorders in recent years is 6.5 years of age, the average age at which children begin receiving services is 8.5 years of age (US Department of Education, 2003).

Today, a major component of intervention is the prevention of behavior disorders, resulting in screening procedures being applied in preschool settings such as Head Start Programs (Feil et al., 2000). Young children with behaviors that greatly concern parents may be eligible for services under P.L. 99-457, as we discussed earlier, without being labeled behavior disordered.

- The purpose of screening is to identify children who exhibit behaviors that interfere with their classroom performance and academic achievement. Procedures designed to integrate screening and possible assessment for identification include the Standardized Screening for Behavior Disorders (SSBD), developed by Walker, Severson, and others (1988), and the Early Screening Project, an adaptation of the SSBD (Feil et al., 2000). These procedures involve what the authors call a multiple-gating procedure. That is, there are three stages, or gates, of the screening and assessment process. In the first stage of the SSBD, teachers rank all their students according to two types of behavior patterns: externalizing behaviors (such as stealing, throwing tantrums, damaging property, using obscene language, or physical aggression) or internalizing behaviors (such as shyness, sadness, thought disorders). This step requires teachers to look at all their students, therefore increasing the teachers' awareness of and attention to specific behavior difficulties that some children might be experiencing.

- In the second stage the three children who rank highest in the class on each of the two behavioral dimensions are assessed using comprehensive behavior-rating scales.

- If any of the children score beyond a certain point on the behavior-rating instruments, then the final stage, direct observation in various settings, occurs.

● *Assessment for Identification*   In addition to the IQ and achievement tests that are a part of all special education evaluations, a few specific types of instruments are employed if emotional or behavior disorders are suspected. After a child is referred, teachers, parents, and school psychologists observe him or her in school and home settings and complete **behavior-rating scales** designed to reflect patterns of behavior. Behavior-rating scales used frequently in the schools include the Conners' Behavior-Rating Scales and the Peterson–Quay Behavior-Rating Scales. An example of the Abbreviated Conners' Rating Scale for Teachers may be found in Figure 7.2.

Professionals urge that children be observed in a number of different settings, that ratings and observations be conducted by several different people,

Name of child _____ Grade _____

Sex of child _____ School _____

Age of child _____ Person filling out this scale _____

Please answer all questions. Beside each item below, indicate the degree of the problem by a check mark (√).	*Not at All Present*	*Just a Little Present*	*Pretty Much Present*	*Very Much Present*
1. Restless in the "squirming" sense				
2. Makes inappropriate noises when he or she shouldn't				
3. Demands must be met immediately				
4. Acts "smart" (impudent or sassy)				
5. Temper outbursts and unpredictable behavior				
6. Overly sensitive to criticism				
7. Distractibility or attention span a problem				
8. Disturbs other children				
9. Daydreams				
10. Pouts and sulks				
11. Mood changes quickly and drastically				
12. Quarrelsome				
13. Submissive attitude toward authority				
14. Restless, always up and on the go				
15. Excitable, impulsive				
16. Excessive demands for teacher's attention				
17. Appears to be unaccepted by group				
18. Appears to be easily led by other children				
19. Appears to lack leadership				
20. Fails to finish things he or she starts				
21. Childish and immature				
22. Denies mistakes or blames others				
23. Does not get along well with other children				
24. Uncooperative with classmates				
25. Easily frustrated in efforts				
26. Uncooperative with teacher				
27. Difficulty in learning				

Figure 7.2

Abbreviated Conners' Rating Scale for Teachers

Source: R. Sprague & E. Sleator (1973). Effects of psychopharmacologic agents on learning disorders, *Pediatric Clinics of North America, 20,* p. 726.

that observations be conducted over a period of time rather than during a single session, and that predisposing factors, including the influence of cultural differences and family expectations, be considered during assessment (Executive Committee of the Council for Children with Behavior Disorders, 1989). Although there are recommendations for administering behavior-rating scales, it is important to understand that there is no standard or uniform battery of tests, checklists, or procedures to follow for the identification of children or adolescents with behavior disorders. Each state education agency establishes its own guidelines and identifies the particular tests that can be used. Intelligence and achievement tests may be used to substantiate or rule out specific disability areas. Other assessment devices are largely subjective. All the information is examined to determine if the child has a behavior disorder. There is no specific test score, test average, or level of behavior agreed on by professionals as an appropriate criterion for identification.

Because classroom teachers play an important role in the identification of students with behavior or emotional disorders, it is important for them to understand the issues involved in defining and identifying children who fall into this category.

Teachers' personal biases can affect the referral and assessment process.

It is easy to see how the effects of personal bias and tolerance can influence behavior-rating scales. Each of the people involved in the rating process can have very different perceptions of what is normal or acceptable in terms of activity level or acting-out behavior; the raters may have different personal feelings toward the child, which could bias ratings; and the level of experience a rater has had with children can affect scoring—a parent with no other children might rate behavior differently than a parent with three or four other children.

Currently, researchers are studying the effects of gender and cultural bias on behavior ratings and student referrals (Reid et al., 2000). Cultural bias is of particular concern due to the growing overrepresentation of some populations, particularly African American students, in the number of students identified as having behavior disorders, as well as overrepresentation in the numbers of school suspensions and expulsions (Webb-Johnson, 2003). The Closer Look box entitled, "Cultural Diversity and Serious Emotional Disturbance (SED)" describes some of the factors to keep in mind when identifying and instructing children from culturally diverse backgrounds.

Visit the website of the Council for Children with Behavior Disorders at **http://www.ccbd.net** to view assessment and instructional practices for working with culturally and linguistically diverse children, youth, and their families.

● *Assessment for Instruction*   Although behavior checklists and screening procedures may help identify students with behavior disorders, they may not provide specific information about instructional objectives. Educators will conduct functional behavioral assessments to obtain information that can be translated into instructional goals when students with disabilities exhibit problem behaviors. The 1997 IDEA amendments require that a **functional behavioral assessment** (FBA) be administered to students with behavior problems in order to identify strategies that are positive and replacement behaviors that can serve the same function as the problem behaviors (IDEA Amendments, 1997). See the accompanying Teaching Strategies box entitled, "What Is a Functional Behavioral Assessment?" for more information about this type of assessment.

The information from the FBA will serve as the basis for a **behavior intervention plan** (BIP). The BIP should contain positive, behavior support strategies designed to teach and reinforce appropriate behavior (Kauffman, 2001). The BIP becomes a part of the student's IEP and reflects both behavior goals and interventions. Fundamental components of the Functional Behavioral Assessment, and ultimately the behavior intervention plan, include observations of what happens before, during, and after behavior. These components are refered to as the ABC's of behavior observation: A = antecedent (what happens before the behav-

---

A Closer Look | Cultural Diversity and Serious Emotional Disturbance (SED)

Misperceptions abound. Because many people lack understanding and cultural sensitivity toward cultures different from their own, teachers, administrators, ancillary personnel, and students may misinterpret culturally based behaviors and may view them as behavior disorders. What teachers consider "discipline problems" are determined by their own culture, personal values, attitudes, and teaching style. More often than not, disciplinary problems seem centered around interpersonal discourse. Tension and negative consequences seem to intensify among the various communication styles of diverse ethnic groups when teachers and their students do not share the same cultural backgrounds, ethnic identities, values, social protocols, and relational styles.

Cultural inversion and other behavior. Culturally different behaviors are not equivalent to social-skills deficits or behavior disorders. Standardized or European American-based social-skills assessments may not adequately reflect the social competence of culturally different students. The quick, high-intensity responses of African Americans, for example, may be seen as hostile, rude, or hyperactive. Acting-out, disruptive behaviors do not automatically signal conduct disorder and, in some cases, may be more a manifestation of "cultural inversion" where students are resisting the label of "acting white" by refusing to follow the established expectations of the classroom culture.

Cycles of misinterpretation and fear. Cultural misunderstandings can have negative effects for both students and teachers. Researchers noted the occurrence of vicious circles, explaining that when students find their playful acts are misinterpreted, they become angry and intensify the roughness of their activities; the result is greater fear on the part of whites. Students may feel empowered and rewarded by the effects of their actions on whites, particularly females. This false sense of power may lead them to escalate those behaviors, most likely at the expense of more productive behaviors that relate to school success.

Excessive compliance or cultural expectation? It also should be noted that exceptionally compliant behaviors are not necessarily indicative of the absence of some difficulty. For example, in one study Asian American students received positive teacher and peer ratings but also indicated they were least likely to question unfair rules or do anything if treated unfairly. This emphasis on conformity and "saving face" may cause teachers to make erroneous assumptions about the child's well-being and may lead to significant problems being overlooked.

Ecosystem importance. The tendency for some children to need more "wait time" or to be verbally unassertive (e.g., Native and Hispanic American) may be interpreted as unmotivated or resistant to instruction. Researchers assert the need for an "ecosystemic" assessment, which takes an ecological approach to consider all aspects of the child's environment.

The issue of culturally relevant assessment for SED is probably most relevant for African and Asian American students who are proportionately overrepresented and underrepresented in SED diagnoses, respectively. Researchers recommend that one use norms based on members of the cultural group of the student being assessed and that evaluation materials be reviewed by people who know the child well and can provide culturally based interpretations of the child's behavior. Other suggestions for linguistically diverse students are to assess students in both languages, attend to verbal and nonverbal communication, and to focus on ways to support the student rather than on simply documenting student deficits.

Source: G. Cartledge, C. D. Kea, & D. J. Ida (2000). Anticipating differences—celebrating strengths: Providing culturally competent services for students with serious emotional disturbance. *Teaching Exceptional Children, 32,* (2), 32.

Teaching Strategies & Accommodations

What Is a Functional Behavioral Assessment?

According to the IDEA Amendments of 1997, all students with behavior problems served under IDEA must receive a functional behavioral assessment (Yell & Shriner, 1997). Brady and Halle (1997) describe a functional behavioral assessment as a way to determine the uses or functions of behavior. They identify the following components of a functional behavioral assessment:

1. Interviews: The student, parents, teachers, and other caregivers should be interviewed about the occurrence of the behavior and the surrounding circumstances.

2. Direct observation: The student should be observed in the setting or settings in which the behavior occurs. Observations should include what happens before, during, and after the behavior occurrence.

3. Analog probes: The observer should manipulate specific variables, such as the setting or the number of opportunities for interaction (e.g., between the student and teacher) to get a better understanding of when and why the behavior occurs.

What Can We Learn from a Functional Behavioral Assessment?

1. When a behavior is most likely to occur: after lunch, during unstructured time, when the student is fatigued.

2. If something specific prompts the behavior: difficult seatwork, teacher correction, teasing.

3. What the student is trying to tell you: I want to be left alone, I want to get out of work, I am embarrassed, I love all this attention.

4. What usually happens after the behavior occurs: The student is ignored, put into time-out, or receives a lot of negative comments; the class laughs or works quietly; different consequences occur at different times of the day.

What Do We Do after a Functional Behavioral Assessment?

In the IEP meeting, the teachers, parents, student (if appropriate), and other relevant personnel develop an appropriate behavior-management plan based on the information from the functional behavioral assessment. Answers to the following questions will be used to develop the plan:

1. Can changes in the student's environment (seating, method of teacher questioning, shortening assignments) help to prevent the occurrence of behavior?

2. What new behaviors (requesting, self-removal from setting) can the student use to satisfy the same communicative intent of the problem behaviors?

3. How can we prompt use of the alternative behavior (signals, self-monitoring, modeling)?

4. What consequences shall we provide for (a) demonstration of new behavior and (b) demonstration of problem behavior?

5. How can we evaluate behavior change?

ior); B = the behavior itself; C = consequence (what happens after the behavior). If you work in a school setting, it is likely you will be asked to conduct these observations. Figure 7.3 is one school team's summary of the ABC's for one student.

Curriculum Focus

The curriculum for students with emotional and behavior disorders must address both behavioral and academic needs.

The curriculum for students with behavior and emotional disorders must address behavioral as well as academic needs. The teacher must include curriculum components that remediate behavior excesses or deficiencies as well as those that teach the regular school curriculum. To address both these major cur-

FBA - Sandra

Antecedents	Behaviors	Consequences
Math: Asked class to get ready for peer quizzing	Refuses to get with peer—says "I'm not doing this"	Goes to time-out
Geography: Class preparing to identify countries on class map— teacher asks her to study	Puts away map and refuses to study— say "buzz off" to teacher	Sent to office
Reading: Independent reading time	Reads more than any student in the class—very respectful	Teacher provides her with "A" grade and note to parents
Math: Class instruction, asked to state the next step in the problem	Told teacher to "drop dead"	Sent to office
Home Economics: Class working on their own recipes at their desks	Does research and studies—writes perfect recipes	No interaction— praised by teacher
Reading: Group reading of novel—take turns reading aloud	Refuses to follow along—closes book and sleeps	Teacher ignores so as not to disrupt group reading

Figure 7.3

ABC Chart for Functional Analysis

Source: T. M. Scott, C. J. Liaupsin, C. J. Nelson, & K. Jolivette (2003). Ensuring student success through team-based functional behavioral assessment. *Teaching Exceptional Children, 34*(5), 16–21.

riculum areas is quite a challenge for any teacher. Although the responsibilities of the classroom teacher and the special education teacher will vary depending on placement options and class size, the importance of collaboration in instruction and planning cannot be overemphasized.

Children with behavior disorders have the same placement options as other children with disabilities. These options range from the residential school to the regular classroom. Because of the nature of certain types of behavior disorders, such as aggressive and threatening behavior, some segregated service-delivery models have persisted in many school systems. These placement options are usually reserved as a last resort for students, usually adolescents, who are deemed unable to cope with the regular school environment.

The balance of instruction between academic skills, and interventions or programs designed to increase appropriate behavior is difficult to achieve. The extent of instruction in either area is generally dictated by the severity of the behavior disorder of the individual child. Most children with behavior disorders are now responsible for performing and succeeding in the general education curriculum. The ability of the special education teacher and classroom teacher to

Appropriate and engaging instruction is an important part of managing classroom behavior. (David Young Wolff/PhotoEdit)

work together is a critical factor in the successful adjustment of these students in general education classes. Specific social skills or behaviors, such as moving around the classroom, completing class assignments, or speaking appropriately to adults, need to be targeted for instruction, and all individuals involved in educational planning must agree on them.

Academic Programming

Although students with behavior disorders usually have many learning difficulties, only recently have research efforts been devoted to identifying the most effective academic interventions for these students (Vaughn et al., 2002). Most research in this area focuses on strategies for changing behavior, rather than strategies to improve academic performance (Gunter, Hummel, & Venn, 2000; Levy & Chard, 2001). Coleman and Vaughn (2000) found only eight publications in the past twenty-five years that addressed reading interventions for elementary students with emotional and behavior disorders. Those studies that do evaluate academic interventions specifically for children with behavior disorders focus primarily on basic instructional principles. For example, teaching students to read fluently at their grade level and providing ample repeated reading practice are recommended for improving both academic skills and behavior (Scott & Shearer-Lingo, 2002). In general, most teaching recommendations for students with behavior disorders are based on research done primarily with students with learning disabilities, some of whom also demonstrate behavior disorders. These instructional recommendations, therefore, mirror the interventions we discussed in Chapter 4. For example, teaching students to use learning strategies (Rogan, 2001) and utilizing mnemonic interventions such as mnemonic strategy instruction and memory aids such as keywords and pegwords (Scruggs & Mastropieri, 2001). In the area of reading comprehension, the use of story mapping instruction resulted in improved comprehension abilities for elementary-age students with behavior disorders (Babyak, Koorland, & Mathes, 2000).

Most of the instructional procedures recommended for students with behavior disorders include the direct instruction methods outlined in earlier chapters. Modeling/demonstration, leading or guided practice, and then providing independent practice or testing are the three teaching steps found in most effective instruction plans. Dawson, Venn, and Gunter (2000) compared teacher modeling of reading to computer modeling of reading using a voice synthesizer on the reading accuracy of students with behavior disorders. Although teacher modeling was more effective, the computer modeling also improved the students' reading rate and accuracy. This study reinforces the role of modeling in academic instruction for students with behavior disorders and identifies the computer as a viable option, particularly if a teacher does not use modeling in the classroom.

In the preceding paragraphs, we have looked at single components of instruction. Stein and Davis (2000) recommend the use of comprehensive direct instruction programs for students with behavior disorders—programs that include strategies for addressing both academic and social behavior. They base their recommendations on the philosophy of positive behavior support. **Positive behavior support** refers to an array of preventive and positive interventions designed to create and maintain a supportive and successful environment for individuals. Stein and Davis suggest that the specific, consistent, and structured interventions found in both the curriculum and methodology of direct instruction programs are crucial to providing effective instruction for students with behavior disorders. In Chapter 4, we provide an extensive description of direct instruction practices and corresponding programs. The accompanying Teaching Strategies box entitled, "Direct Instruction Checklist" provides a set of questions that teachers of students with behavior disorders can ask to evaluate their use of direct instruction.

> Direct instruction programs are recommended for students with emotional and behavior disorders.

Teaching Strategies & Accommodations

Direct Instruction Checklist

1. Am I using flexible instructional grouping as a technique to increase academic engaged time?

2. Am I maintaining high levels of engagement at high levels of student success?

3. Am I monitoring student performance frequently, providing immediate feedback to students and adjusting instruction according to student need?

4. Am I teaching all students to a high level of mastery?

5. Am I designing appropriate motivational strategies for my students?

Source: M. Stein and C. S. Davis (2000). Direct instruction as a positive behavioral support. *Beyond Behavior, 10,* 12.

Teaching Strategies & Accommodations

Students Talk to Teachers

Rich Curriculum

- Allow for more group activities and projects.
- Show enthusiasm when teaching.
- Allow for more discussion and expression of students in class.
- Relate the information to your students' lives (current and future).

Embracing Positive Behaviors

- Hold high expectations.
- Explain the "rules" clearly and provide consistent consequences regardless of labels or race.
- Encourage students to do their best regardless of their label or race.

Weaving Student-Centered Connections

- Understand issues students face today.
- Get to know students and their families.
- Get to know students in and out of school.
- Communicate with students at their level.
- Identify and connect students with services within and outside the school setting.

Source: L. Owens & L. A. Decker (2003). How to spell success for secondary students labeled EBD: How students define effective teachers. *Beyond Behavior, 12*(2), 21.

Clearly, educational professionals must recognize the importance of academic assessment and effective educational interventions for children with behavior disorders. Much research is needed in order to identify how to ensure that children with behavior disorders achieve academically. In the Teaching Strategies box entitled, "Students Talk to Teachers," high-school students with behavior disorders give their own recommendations for teaching. When discussing the recommendations, one student said:

> Teachers need to remember that we are still kids and they were kids once too. We were born in a more violent world—we listen to different music— we will learn more responsibility, but we are kids now. (Owens & Decker, 2003, p. 21)

Behavior-Change Interventions

Behavior goals for students with behavior and emotional disorders must be individualized to meet each student's needs; however, more general interventions designed to prevent behavior disorders may take place at the class or building level. These interventions can be described in terms of their intended effects. In the following sections, we examine three common curriculum goals and related teaching strategies: addressing inappropriate behaviors, developing appropriate cognitions, and teaching new behaviors.

● *Addressing Inappropriate Behavior* The current emphasis on prevention of behavior disorders, as well as the general societal concern about violence in schools, has led to new programs designed to reduce the probability of inappropriate behavior through the implementation of school-based programs. These programs include three levels of prevention identified by the United States Public Health Service and match each level with a specific type of behavior intervention. The three levels of prevention are primary, secondary, and tertiary. Primary prevention focuses on general, school-wide programs—often called universal interventions—that are designed to prevent problems among all children. Secondary prevention targets specialized group interventions for students who are at risk for more severe problems or who already exhibit mild behavior problems. Tertiary programs include specialized individual interventions designed for students who are at great risk for serious problems or who are already demonstrating serious behavior problems (Sprague & Walker, 2000). For each level, the complexity of the intervention is matched to the severity of the target behaviors. See Figure 7.4 for an illustration of the multilevel system of school discipline programs.

Early research suggests that the tri-level approach is an effective way to prevent or delay the onset of behavior problems for at-risk children. Universal interventions appear to reduce inappropriate and aggressive behaviors (Serna et al., 2000). Although the universal programs vary, most include both parent and school components. Most also include elements such as classroom management, peer tutoring, role playing, and problem-solving activities (Frey, Hirschstein, & Guzzo, 2000; Kamps et al., 2000). Secondary programs may include structured

> Many interventions are targeted at preventing the occurence of behavior disorders. Prevention includes primary, secondary, and tertiary levels.

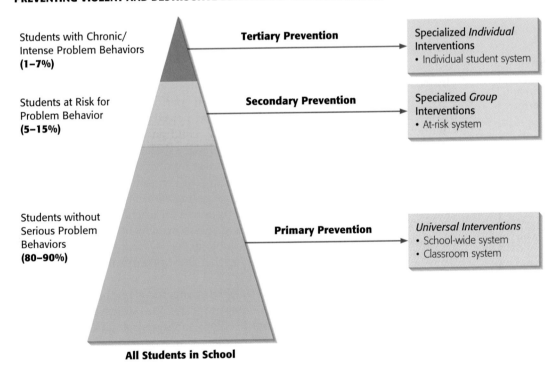

PREVENTING VIOLENT AND DESTRUCTIVE BEHAVIOR IN SCHOOLS: INTEGRATED SYSTEMS OF INTERVENTION

Students with Chronic/ Intense Problem Behaviors **(1–7%)**

Tertiary Prevention

Specialized *Individual* Interventions
• Individual student system

Students at Risk for Problem Behavior **(5–15%)**

Secondary Prevention

Specialized *Group* Interventions
• At-risk system

Students without Serious Problem Behaviors **(80–90%)**

Primary Prevention

Universal Interventions
• School-wide system
• Classroom system

All Students in School

Figure 7.4

Multilevel System of School-wide Discipline Strategies

Source: G. Sugai, J. R. Sprague, R. H. Horner, & H. M. Walker (2000). Preventing school violence: The use of office discipline referrals to assess and monitor school-wide discipline interventions. *Journal of Emotional and Behavior Disorders, 8,* 94–101.

group social skills and problem-solving activities, as well as group behavior management programs, such as the level system described in Figure 7.4. Tertiary programs likely will focus on the BIP that results from each student's functional behavioral assessment.

Figure 7.4, an integrated system of intervention, reflects the model of behavior change known as positive behavior interventions and supports (PBIS). PBIS focuses on developing coordinated, school-based change and incorporating consistent, positive interventions to create an environment that supports and recognizes appropriate behavior. Visit the Center on PBIS, created by George Sugai and Rob Horner, at **http://www.pbis.org** to learn more about the goals and procedures of this research-based model of behavior intervention.

● *Developing Appropriate Cognitions*   One of the recurring problems experienced by children with behavior disorders is difficulty interpreting events realistically and determining socially appropriate responses. For example, Hartman and Stage (2000) interviewed students with behavior disorders who were assigned to in-school suspension. The interviews revealed that the students had reacted negatively to their perception that teachers deliberately provoked them. Studies like this one suggest the importance of interventions with a positive and reinforcing focus. They also suggest that students need instruction in skills to help them identify and cope with both real and exaggerated concerns and thoughts. Regardless of the cause, children who have retreated from social activities and relationships usually receive instruction that will enable them to make slow and nonthreatening steps toward appropriate social behavior.

Because of the possible role of a child's thoughts in behavior disorders, it is difficult for the teacher, who cannot observe these thoughts, to manage the behavior without student participation. One way to address this problem is to provide **self-management instruction**.

> Instruction in self-management skills teaches students to attend to and record their own performance.

Instruction in self-management skills involves teaching children to pay attention to, monitor, and record their own performance (Levendoski & Cartledge, 2000). For example, children record on a piece of paper every time they talk without raising their hand. Alternatively, children can record a mark for every five minutes they exhibit appropriate behavior such as time-on-task or time without fighting. Self-management programs can involve the use of videotaping (Falk, Dunlap, & Kern, 1996) and role play to assist in self-evaluation. Students can observe and record behaviors and practice giving alternative responses.

Currently, technology offers numerous resources for teachers and other educational professionals to use when developing self-management programs for students with behavior disorders. See the Technology Focus feature for a summary of a great technological resource for parents, teachers, and other professionals.

● *Teaching New Behaviors*   Some programs focus on the instruction of new behaviors to take the place of the inappropriate ones. Interventions of this nature may involve teaching students problem-solving strategies to use when they begin to feel angry or upset. For example, a problem teachers often face is a child throwing a tantrum in the classroom when he becomes frustrated. Simply telling the child to stop, or even punishing the child, will not necessarily address the problem, because the child who habitually has tantrums does not know what else to do when he gets frustrated. Therefore, the teacher can give him a signal when he starts to become angry. When he sees the signal, the student has three choices: He can count to ten and take a deep breath to calm down, he can raise his hand and ask the teacher for help, or he can get up and

Technology Focus

Technology Application for Students with Behavior Disorders: Self-management Programs

Very little information is available in the literature on the effective use of technology for children with behavior disorders. Sources of information for teachers of students with behavior disorders are available on the Internet. One source of information is the Virtual Resource Center in Behavioral Disorders (VRCBD). The VRCBD is located on a website at the University of Missouri at Columbia (UMC) and is directed by Dr. Gail Fitzgerald and her colleagues (http://www.coe.missouri.edu/~vrcbd). This site includes information and a link for ordering CDs for the Teacher Problem Solving Skills series. In this series, teachers can find interactive training materials that use authentic videos of children and classrooms and case-based activities to teach and provide practice in understanding, assessing, and developing educational plans for children with emotional and behavioral disorders. Supplemental training materials, archives of national online conferences, and access to online discussion groups are provided on this website.

A second source of information at the University of Missouri-Columbia is the KidTools Support System (KTSS) directed by Dr. Gail Fitzgerald (UMC) and Dr. Kevin Koury of California University of Pennsylvania (http://KidTools.missouri.edu). KTSS programs are designed for children and youth with emotional, behavior, and learning disorders in the areas of self-management, organizational skills, and learning strategies. These

Staying Cool		Follow STAR?		
		Time	Yes	No
STOP	Hitting			
THINK	I can control myself. I wouldn't want anyone to hit me.			
ACT	Tell the person why I'm angry. Tell an adult if I have been hit.			
RESULTS	I will be cool. I will not be suspended. People will like me.			
Name: R. Schroeder			**Date:** 2/23/2004	

Figure 7.5 KidTools: Staying Cool

Source: G. Fitzgerald, & L. Semrau (2000). Second Step KidTools [Computer Software]. Columbia, MO: University of Missouri–Columbia. Reprinted with permission.

programs, KidTools and KidSkills, are multilevel and can be downloaded without charge from the website or ordered on CDs. The tools created by children are easily reproducible and can be personalized for individual students. Additional training materials for adults are available on the website, including information databases for all the tools and strategies. Figure 7.5 is an example made by one student using one of the planning tools in the KidTools series.

---

go sit in the reading corner for five minutes to relax. Now the child has options. Instead of throwing a book, he can choose an alternative behavior.

Viewing videotapes of appropriate behaviors, modeling by teachers and peers, and practicing appropriate responses are other activities that have been used effectively to teach new behaviors (Amish et al., 1988; Knapczyk, 1988). Recent research has examined the role of peers in helping students with behavior disorders to learn appropriate anger-management behavior. Presley and Hughes (2000) found that high-school students with behavior disorders demonstrated appropriate anger-management behaviors in role play after receiving a combination of individual instruction from peers, self-management instruction, and a traditional anger-control program.

Some behaviors (such as stealing and using obscenities) may seem more deliberate and manipulative and less a result of lack of control. Usually, behavior-management techniques that involve the application of specific consequences for appropriate and inappropriate behavior are used to address these types of behaviors. Although the predominant philosophy in behavior management is to focus on using positive interventions to teach new behaviors, punishing and exclusionary strategies (loss of recess time or time-out) are still used in many classrooms. All teachers must remember that negative approaches may produce negative reactions by students with behavior disorders; they should also realize that punishing a child does not tell him what he is supposed to do. Some research reveals that teachers tend to use these negative interventions most often with African American students (Ishii-Jordan, 2000; Townsend, 2000).

A major goal of programs for children with behavior or emotional disorders is to teach them a level of control that will enable them to perform appropriately in regular classes. One example of this type of program is the **level system**, which involves a stepwise progression through a predetermined set of behavior requirements, restrictions, and responsibilities. Through the demonstration of appropriate behavior over time, students can achieve higher levels of freedom and responsibility. Depending on the specific situation, the highest level reached could be eligibility for partial or full inclusion. This type of system has been shown to be effective even when the only consequence for appropriate behavior was increasing levels of independence and responsibility (Mastropieri, Jenne, & Scruggs, 1988). Some, however, have expressed concerns about the level system. For example, Scheuermann and Webber (1996) suggest that the least restrictive environment is an educational right, not something that can be earned only by students reaching a high level on the program. In addition, they report that a level system might emphasize a group, rather than an individualized curriculum, as mandated by law. Nevertheless, level systems are used frequently in self-contained classes for children with behavior disorders. See the accompanying Teaching Strategies box entitled, "Level System Evaluation Checklist" for an example of an evaluation checklist for level systems.

Regardless of your ultimate behavior goal for an individual student, several factors, such as consistency and clear consequences, are required for all behavior-management programs. It is also important for you, the parent, and the student to see the program as positive and practical. See the accompanying Teaching Strategies box (page 274) entitled, "Checklist for Positive Classroom Management" for a sample checklist. Although many behavior-management systems include tangible rewards for appropriate behavior, some students with behavior disorders have actually rated good grades as their most desired reward (Maratens, Muir, & Meller, 1988). This type of reward structure (independence, responsibility, grades) is likely to appeal more to regular classroom teachers than one dependent on tangible rewards (stickers, toys, food). Consequently, they may be more inclined to continue implementing the system in the regular classroom setting.

Discipline in the Schools

According to federal law, children cannot be punished for behavior that is a result of their disability.

Most schools have established programs for the purpose of disciplining children who exhibit inappropriate behavior. These programs may include suspension, in-school suspension, time-out, corporal punishment, and expulsion. Children with externalizing behavior disorders may seem to be prime candidates for experiencing some of these disciplinary actions, but federal law states that children

Level System Evaluation Checklist

Below is a level system evaluation checklist. The person who is most familiar with the level system being evaluated should complete the form.

Answer each of the following questions regarding your level system:

I. Access to least restrictive environment (LRE)

A. Are mainstreaming decisions made by each student's IEP committee, regardless of the student's status within the level system? YES NO If no, check below:

___ 1. Students are required to attain a predetermined level before they can attend a mainstream class.

___ 2. Mainstream classes are predetermined (e.g., P.E. for students on Level 2, P.E. and music for students on Level 3, etc.)

II. Placement in the level system

A. Are students initially placed in the level system at the level that is commensurate with their needs and strengths? YES NO

B. Is initial placement in the level system based on current, valid assessment? YES NO

III. Curriculum

A. Does each student have individual target behaviors designated in addition to those designated for the whole group? YES NO

B. Are group expectations considered by each student's IEP committee to determine if those expectations are appropriate for each individual student? YES NO

C. Are criteria for mastery of target behaviors determined individually? YES NO

D. Is the sequence of target behaviors developed individually for each student, based on that student's needs and areas of strength? YES NO

E. Are target behaviors differentiated as skill deficits or performance deficits? YES NO

F. Are reinforcers individualized? YES NO

G. Do you avoid using access to less restrictive environments/activities and nondisabled peers as reinforcers? YES NO

IV. Procedures

A. Are advancement criteria (criteria for movement from one level to the next) individualized for each student? YES NO

B. Are advancement criteria based on recent, relevant assessment data as well as expectations for age peers in general education environments? YES NO

C. Does each student's IEP committee determine whether advancement criteria are developmentally appropriate for a particular student? YES NO

D. Are behavior reductive strategies used separately from the level system (i.e., downward movement is not used as a consequence for inappropriate behavior or for failure to meet minimum criteria for a given level)? YES NO If no, check below:

___ 1. Downward movement is used as a consequence for inappropriate behavior.

___ 2. Downward movement is used as a consequence for failure to earn minimum points for a certain number of days.

V. Efficacy

A. Is each student's progress through the level system monitored? YES NO

B. Is there a problem-solving procedure if data indicate a lack of progress through the level system? YES NO

C. Do students consistently "graduate" from the level system? YES NO

D. Do behaviors that are addressed in the level system maintain over time and generalize across environments? YES NO

E. Do students who complete the level system maintain successfully in less restrictive environments? YES NO

F. Are self-management skills incorporated into the level system? YES NO

Source: B. Scheuermann, & J. Webber (1996). Level systems: Problems and solutions. *Beyond Behavior, 7*(2), 12–17.

Teaching Strategies & Accommodations

Checklist for Positive Classroom Management

1. The teacher interacts positively with the student.   YES   NO

2. The teacher communicates high expectations to the student.   YES   NO

3. Opportunities are provided for students to become acquainted.   YES   NO

4. Students are actively involved with peers through cooperative learning or peer tutoring.   YES   NO

5. Classroom procedures are taught to students, who demonstrate understanding of the procedures.   YES   NO

6. Students' instructional programs are appropriate to their needs, skill levels, and learning styles.   YES   NO

7. The subject matter is relevant to the students' lives and they understand the connection.   YES   NO

8. Students understand the teacher's instructional goals and why teaching strategies are being used to achieve these goals.   YES   NO

9. Students have been involved in some form of academic goal setting and recording.   YES   NO

10. The assessment system motivates the student to make a good effort.   YES   NO

11. Rules for managing student behavior are appropriate, succinct, stated positively, and applied to all.   YES   NO

12. Consequences for inappropriate behavior are clear to all students.   YES   NO

13. Consequences are educational, respectful, and implemented consistently.   YES   NO

14. Students demonstrate understanding of rules and consequences.   YES   NO

15. If a problem arises, the teacher meets privately with the student to discuss the problem and jointly develop a plan to help.   YES   NO

Source: Vern Jones (1990). Responding to student behavior problems. *Beyond Behavior*, 20. Council for Children with Behavior Disorders, Council for Exceptional Children.

---

cannot be punished for their disability. In other words, if a child's disability is considered to be related to his or her behavior, that child should not be punished for it. The IDEA amendments of 1997 present some guidelines for addressing the behavior problems of students with disabilities, including those with behavior disorders. One requirement in the 1997 amendments is that a school review, called a **manifestation determination**, must be conducted after a school behavior problem has occurred to determine if the student's behavior is related to the disability. If the ruling is that the behavior is not related to the disability, the student may be disciplined like any other child (IDEA Amendments, 1997; Yell & Shriner, 1997). In addition, children with behavior disorders must have a specific behavior-management plan, including disciplinary procedures in their individual educational programs. Any disciplinary actions, such as suspension, that change the student's placement are limited to ten days. Exceptions include the possession of firearms or drugs in school or at school functions, which allows administrators to place the child in a temporary alternative educational setting for up to forty-five days (IDEA Amendments, 1997; Yell & Shriner, 1997).

> Schools must develop guidelines that enable them to implement discipline without violating students' rights.

What effects do school-based programs have on behavior disorders? Few recent long-term outcome studies have been conducted on students with emotional and behavior disorders. Because many such students do not voluntarily continue to receive state or federal services after graduation, they are difficult to track after they exit school. Data from the National Longitudinal Transition Study suggest that in addition to personal and family variables, school variables, such as high functional competency in basic skills and a high-school diploma, were predictors of employment after high school (Rylance, 1998). Another area in which data exist is criminal activity. Research suggests that about half of all antisocial children become adjudicated as adolescents, and 50 to 75 percent of these adolescents go on to become adult criminals (Walker, Colvin, & Ramsey, 1995). This is dismal news, particularly when coupled with what we have already discussed about the high dropout rates of, and drug use by, adolescents with behavior disorders. With such concern about the prognosis for students with emotional and behavior disorders, it is easy to understand why there currently is such an emphasis on prevention.

？ Pause and Reflect

Probably the most challenging aspect of working with students with behavior disorders is thinking of how we can create positive, supportive interventions rather than negative, punitive interventions to address inappropriate behavior. Why does understanding the antecedents and consequences of behavior help us to figure out an effective, positive plan for behavior change? ●

SUMMARY

- Federal law lists five factors for identifying children who are emotionally disturbed: unexplained inability to learn, inability to relate satisfactorily to peers and teachers, inappropriate behavior under normal circumstances, pervasive unhappiness or depression, and a tendency to develop physical symptoms or fears associated with school or personal problems.

- Behavior can be evaluated in terms of rate, intensity, duration, and age appropriateness.

- It is difficult to determine the prevalence of behavior disorders because of differences in instruments used to measure behavior, in terminology and interpretation of definitions, and in the subjectivity of behavior-rating systems.

- The causes of behavior disorders are not known; however, certain environmental and physiological factors seem to relate to differences in behavior.

- The effects of behavior disorders on the child include underachievement in school, difficulties with social adjustment, and difficulties in self-expression or communication. Effects on the family include parental anger, stress, and guilt; helplessness; and an increased risk of child abuse.

- Assessment techniques include screening instruments, observation, and behavior-rating scales. States establish their own guidelines for selecting and administering tests, and professionals interpret the results based on the nature of the specific case and their own expertise. A teacher's conscious or unconscious bias can cause problems in assessment.

- Many educators recommend direct instruction programs and strategies for teaching students with emotional or behavior disorders.

- Regardless of a student's placement, regular and special education teachers should share the same expectations for appropriate behavior and use a consistent behavior-management system. The major strategies for working with students with behavior disorders involve developing appropriate cognitions, teaching new behavior, and eliminating inappropriate behavior.

KEY TERMS

emotional disturbance

behavior disorders

rate

intensity

duration

age-appropriate behavior

DSM-IV-TR

externalizing behavior

internalizing behavior

attention deficit/hyperactivity disorder (ADHD)

behavior-rating scales

functional behavior assessment

behavior intervention plan

positive behavior support

self-management instruction

level system

manifestation determination

USEFUL RESOURCES

- Russel A. Barkley (1992). *ADHD: What do we know?* and *ADHD: What can we do?* New York: Guilford Publications. Two comprehensive, informative, and practical videotapes on attention deficit/hyperactivity disorder; the tapes are appropriate for teachers and parents.

- Russel A. Barkley (1998). *Attention deficit hyperactivity disorders: A handbook for diagnosis and treatment.* New York, Guilford Press. A comprehensive discussion of ADHD from one of the leading authorities in the field.

- Mary Fowler (1995). *Maybe you know my kid.* New York: Carol Publishing Group. A parents' guide to identifying, understanding, and helping your child with attention deficit/hyperactivity disorder.

- Edward J. Kameenui and Craig B. Darch (1995). *Instructional classroom management: A proactive approach to classroom management.* White Plains, N.Y.: Longman. A text for classroom teachers about managing behavior within the context of instruction.

- Mitchell Yell (1998). *The law and special education.* Available at **http://www.ed.sc.edu/spedlaw/lawpage.htm**. This site provides access to the latest updates in special education legislation and case law.

- Resources in Emotional/Behavioral Disabilities appear at **http://www.gwu.edu/~ebdweb/index.html**. This is George Washington University's website for teachers and preservice teachers who relate experiences from a psychoeducational perspective.

- The Virtual Resource Center in Behavioral Disorders (VRCbd) provides professors, teachers, and parents with a wealth of training, assessment, and instructional materials for children with behavior disorders. Go to **http://www.tiger.coc.missouri.edu/urcbd**.

- Timothy E. Wilens (1999). *Straight talk about psychiatric medications for kids.* New York: Guilford Press. This book provides parents with specific information about childhood psychiatric disorders and the use of medications to treat them.

PORTFOLIO ACTIVITIES

1. Interview school psychologists from several local school districts. Discuss how the school district defines and identifies children with behavior disorders, and what tests and assessment instruments are used to identify students. Ask each psychologist about his or her perspective on the effectiveness of the assessment procedures.

✓ *Standards* This activity will help students meet CEC Content Standard 2: Development and Characteristics of Learners.

2. Ask school guidance counselors or conflict-management specialists for suggestions of strategies and programs that teach students self-control and problem solving. Ask them for some examples of curricula related to self-management, social skills training, and affective development. Critique several of the curricula and determine which you could integrate into a general education classroom.

✓ *Standards* This activity will help students meet CEC Content Standard 4: Instructional Strategies.

3. How do your expectations of classroom performance affect the ways you perceive students' behavior? Using a teacher's behavioral checklist, visit several classrooms at various grade levels. Observe and record the behavior of a few children in each class. Afterward, compare your observations and ratings with those of the classroom teachers. Are your perceptions and observations similar to those of the classroom teacher? Evaluate your own biases and their effects on your ratings. Make a list of behaviors that you think will be important in your own classroom.

✓ *Standards* This activity will help students meet CEC Content Standard 2: Development and Characteristics of Learners.

4. Interview a local pediatrician about the methods he or she uses to identify children with ADHD. Ask to see examples of behavior checklists and forms for classroom observations and parent interviews. Record the criteria the doctor uses. If possible, interview several pediatricians and compare their diagnostic methods.

✓ *Standards* This activity will help students meet CEC Content Standard 2: Development and Characteristics of Learners.

5. Observe a teacher conduct a functional behavior assessment for a student. Record the antecedents, behaviors, and consequences along with the teacher, and arrive at your own hypothesis about the function of the inappropriate behavior. Confer with the teacher and discuss his or her assessment. Identify suggestions for appropriate replacement behaviors.

✓ *Standards* This activity will help students meet CEC Content Standard 3: Individual Learning Differences.

 To access an electronic template for these activities, visit our website through http://www.education.college.hmco.com/students/.

8 Children with Autism and Related Disorders

Outline

Terms and Definitions
  Defining Autism
  Autism Spectrum Disorders/
    Pervasive Developmental
    Disorders
  Dual Diagnosis
  Prevalence
Causes of Autism
  Historical Opinions About
    Causes
  Current Hypotheses About
    Causes
Characteristics of Individuals
    with Autism
  Cognitive Characteristics
  Physical Characteristics
  Social Interaction
  Language and Communication
  Behavior
  Family Interactions
Teaching Strategies and
    Accommodations
  The Importance of Early
    Intervention
  Applied Behavior Analysis
  Environmental Interventions
  Language-Based Interventions
  Biochemical Interventions
  Transition to Adulthood
SUMMARY
KEY TERMS
USEFUL RESOURCES
PORTFOLIO ACTIVITIES

Learning Objectives

After reading this chapter, the reader will be able to:

- Describe communicative intent, and explain why this concept is important when working with children with autism

- Discuss how the goals of teaching students with autism compare to those of teaching other children

- Identify the types of collaboration necessary to provide effective early intervention programs for young children with autism

- Describe methods for determining the most effective interventions to use with individuals with autism and identify the most important characteristics of effective teaching strategies

Educational programs for children and adolescents with autism focus on instruction in functional communication, appropriate behavior, social interaction, and life skills. In this chapter, we discuss historical and current theories about autism and review effective interventions.

Arguably, no other area of special education has been the subject of as much speculation and controversy as autism. In most areas of disability, we can easily see that individuals perform somewhere on an ability continuum in physical, cognitive, sensory, or emotional skills. We can observe our own or others' performances and logically understand deficits or exceptional abilities. Autism, however, sometimes seems to defy logic. The characteristic behaviors of autism, coupled with the apparently uneven distribution and range of deficits and abilities displayed by individuals with autism, seem to undermine a clear and rational explanation. Consequently, autism has been attributed to many different causes, and a wide variety of sometimes bizarre treatments has been explored through the years by confused parents and professionals. Although science is leading us ever closer to a good understanding of autism, many questions remain. We do, however, know that individuals with autism, like individuals with other pervasive disabilities, are in a better position than ever before to assume fulfilling and productive lives.

Terms and Definitions

Defining Autism

Autism is a lifelong developmental disability that is best described as a collection of behavioral symptoms. Although autism has been recognized as a syndrome for many years, it was not identified as a separate category of special education until the IDEA reauthorization of 1990. The following is the federal definition of autism:

> Autism means a developmental disability significantly affecting verbal and nonverbal communication and social interaction, generally evident before age 3 that adversely affects a child's educational performance. Other characteristics often associated with autism are engagement in repetitive activities and stereotyped movements, resistance to environmental change or daily routines, and unusual responses to sensory experiences. The term does not apply if a child's educational performance is adversely affected primarily because the child has an emotional disturbance.
>
> A child who manifests the characteristics of "autism" after age 3 could be diagnosed as having "autism" if the criteria in the above paragraph are satisfied. (IDEA, Part B, p. 34.300-6A)

Autism was identified as a special education category in 1990.

The federal definition provides us with a general definition. The accompanying Closer Look box entitled, "Autism: A Parent's Perspective" presents one mother's description of autism. Her words give us insight into the meaning of terms such as repetitive activity and resistance to change.

As with all disability categories that rely on observational measures, the diagnosis of autism may be subjective. The *Diagnostic and Statistical Manual of Mental Disorders,* Fourth Edition (DSM-IV-TR), published by the American Psychiatric Association (2000), contains complex diagnostic criteria that parallel and

A Closer Look   Autism: A Parent's Perspective

Autism is when your two-year-old looks straight through you to the wall behind—through you, her father, her sister, her brother, or anybody else. You are a pane of glass. Or you are her own personal extension, your hand a tool she uses to get the cookie she will not reach for herself. Autism is when your eight-year-old fills a carton with three-quarter-inch squares of cut-up paper to sift between her fingers for twenty minutes, half an hour, longer, autism is when your eleven-year-old fills sheet after sheet with division, division by three, by seven, eleven, thirteen, seventeen, nineteen. . . . But that's enough, there are many books about autism now, anyone can read the symptoms. I need the image for what the symptoms can't convey: this child was *happy.* Is it not happiness to want nothing but what you have? Craving, the Buddha taught, was the source of all misery, detachment the road to the serene equilibrium of nirvana.

But nirvana at eighteen months? That's too soon.

Source: Claira Claiborne Park (1998). Excerpts from Exiting nirvana. *The American Scholar, 67*(2), 30.

attempt to quantify the behavioral characteristics present in the definition of autism. In addition, a simple five-step screening test called the Checklist for Autism in Toddlers (CHAT) is offered as a tool for pediatricians (Foote & Tesoriero, 2000). See the accompanying Closer Look box entitled, "Two Sets of Diagnostic Criteria." Because the tools various professionals use to diagnose autism can range from incredibly simple to quite complex, and because many professionals also have their own criteria for what autism "looks like," many parents have had a difficult time getting a diagnosis for their child (Maurice, 1993). These difficulties are diminishing, for the most part, as autism and related disorders receive more attention in the public, medical, and educational arenas.

Autism Spectrum Disorders/Pervasive Developmental Disorders

The difficulty of arriving at a clear diagnosis of autism is compounded by the fact that there are a number of disorders related to autism, referred to as **pervasive developmental disorders (PDD)** or **autism spectrum disorders**. The terms autism spectrum disorders and PDD refer to a collection of syndromes and conditions ranging from those in which only a few of the characteristics of autism are present or the characteristics are present in a very mild form, to autism itself. Over time, each of these syndromes is given specific names and the characteristics are more clearly delineated. The following disorders are considered to be part of autism spectrum disorders. You can see how the symptoms of the disorders overlap.

- **Autism.** Children exhibit severely disordered verbal and nonverbal language and unusual behavior patterns.
- **Asperger's syndrome.** Children experience nonverbal language problems, have a restricted range of interests, and have good verbal language.
- **PDD-NOS.** Children experience nonverbal language difficulties, but do not meet the criteria for other PDD disorders.

- **Rett's disorder.** A rare genetic neurodegenerative disorder that primarily affects girls, resulting in loss of social skills, language, and motor development, accompanied by distorted hand movements.
- **Childhood disintegrative disorder.** After a few years of normal development, children regress progressively in all areas, including language, social development, and motor development (DSM-IV-TR, Kutscher, 2003).

Physicians or other diagnosticians may want to delay the diagnosis of autism until these other, less severe associated disorders can be eliminated. Because autism is the only category among the pervasive developmental disorders specifically identified in IDEA, however, it is important for parents to get a confirmed diagnosis as soon as possible so that they can obtain appropriate services. Professionals are evaluating the effectiveness of diagnostic criteria and instruments for PDD to distinguish between autism and other pervasive developmental disorders and to determine the reliability of these instruments when used by different evaluators (Klin et al., 2000; Stella, Mundy, & Tuchman, 1999).

● *Asperger's Syndrome*   One of the most common autism spectrum disorders is **Asperger's syndrome**. Asperger's syndrome is increasingly being diagnosed and therefore there is a strong likelihood that you will have students with this syndrome in your classrooms. Approximately 26 to 36 out of 10,000 school-age children are diagnosed with Asperger's syndrome (Ehlers & Gillberg, 1993).

Individuals with Asperger's syndrome may have many of the social and behavioral characteristics of autism but, importantly, *without* any marked delays in language and cognitive development. They experience difficulties in social functioning and relationships, but not in intelligence or language skills. Learning disabilities, motor clumsiness, and hypersensitivity to sensory stimuli, such as loud sounds, are also common (Bock & Myles, 1999). The wide range of abilities can manifest in unique ways; a student may be as likely to become fixated on astronomy as on a piece of silverware. A child with Asperger's syndrome, therefore, is likely to be a student who does very well in some academic areas, yet not so well in others. He or she may work well alone and love to use the computer and the Internet, but resist working in cooperative learning groups or on group projects. Finally, this child may have few friends and may alienate adults and peers due to his lack of awareness of social requirements (Safran, 2002).

There is a debate among professionals questioning if Asperger's syndrome is really the same thing as autism in individuals with average to above average intelligence. The characteristics of individuals with Asperger's syndrome and with high-functioning autism (the term used to refer to people diagnosed with autism who do not have mental retardation) are very similar. Most researchers have found that IQ appears to account for almost all the performance differences (for example, levels of academic skills or language usage) among individuals in both of these categories (Freeman, Cronin, & Candela, 2002; Myer & Minshew, 2002). In other words, researchers suggest that children diagnosed with Asperger's syndrome are children with autism and high intelligence. So, the diagnostic dilemma continues. Be aware that children with a diagnosis of high-functioning autism or Asperger's syndrome will probably have the same characteristics. For children diagnosed with autism spectrum disorders, however, the diagnosis alone doesn't tell you much about the individual needs of the student; all children show extreme variability in their academic strengths

> Pervasive developmental disorders include autism and Asperger's syndrome.

A Closer Look   Two Sets of Diagnostic Criteria

**Diagnostic criteria for
299.00 Autistic Disorder**

**How Psychologists and Psychiatrists May
Define Autism**

A. A total of six (or more) items from (1), (2), and
(3), with at least two from (1), and one each
from (2) and (3):

1. qualitative impairment in social interaction, as
   manifested by at least two of the following:

   a. marked impairment in the use of multi-
      ple nonverbal behaviors such as eye-
      to-eye gaze, facial expression, body
      postures, and gestures to regulate social
      interaction

   b. failure to develop peer relationships ap-
      propriate to developmental level

   c. a lack of spontaneous seeking to share
      enjoyment, interests, or achievements
      with other people (e.g., by a lack of
      showing, bringing, or pointing out ob-
      jects of interest)

   d. lack of social or emotional reciprocity

2. qualitative impairments in communication as
   manifested by at least one of the following:

   a. delay in, or total lack of, the develop-
      ment of spoken language (not accom-
      panied by an attempt to compensate
      through alternative modes of communi-
      cation such as gesture or mime)

   b. in individuals with adequate speech,
      marked impairment in the ability to initi-
      ate or sustain a conversation with others

   c. stereotyped and repetitive use of lan-
      guage or idiosyncratic language

   d. lack of varied, spontaneous make-
      believe play or social imitative play ap-
      propriate to developmental level

3. restricted repetitive and stereotyped patterns of behavior, interests, and activities, as
   manifested by at least one of the following:

   a. encompassing preoccupation with one
      or more stereotyped and restricted pat-
      terns of interest that is abnormal either
      in intensity or focus

   b. apparently inflexible adherence to spe-
      cific, nonfunctional routines or rituals

and weaknesses (Griswold et al., 2002). Some of the educational approaches we
present later in the chapter are appropriate for children with Asperger's syndrome. Because these children may have highly developed language skills and
are often quite intelligent, interventions that focus on social skills development,
interpreting social cues, and working with others often are the interventions of
choice. A number of students with this syndrome are also treated with specific
medications prescribed to address behavioral characteristics such as hyperactivity, aggression, and compulsive or ritualistic behaviors.

Dual Diagnosis

Another difficulty in attempting to diagnose autism is the fact that it coexists
with a number of other conditions, such as **fragile-X syndrome**, an inherited
disorder caused by chromosomal abnormalities. Unlike autism, fragile-X syndrome is diagnosed through genetic testing. Affected children exhibit many of
the same behaviors as children with autism, such as communication delays,

c. stereotyped and repetitive motor mannerisms (e.g., hand or finger flapping or twisting, or complex whole-body movements)

d. persistent preoccupation with parts of objects

B. Delays or abnormal functioning in at least one of the following areas, with onset prior to age 3 years: (1) social interaction, (2) language as used in social communication, or (3) symbolic or imaginative play.

C. The disturbance is not better accounted for by Rett's Disorder or Childhood Disintegrative Disorder.

Source: American Psychiatric Association (2000). *Diagnostic and statistical manual of mental disorders* (4th ed. DSM-IV-TR) (pp. 70–71). Washington, DC.

How Pediatricians May Diagnose Autism

A child who fails to accomplish each of the following five measures almost certainly has classic autism.

Questions for parents

1. Does your child ever pretend, for example, to make a cup of tea using a toy cup and teapot, or pretend other things?

2. Does your child ever use his index finger to point, indicating interest in something?

Exercises for the child

3. Get the child's attention, then point across the room at an interesting object and say, "Oh, look! There's a [name of object]!" Watch the child's face. Does the child look to see what you are pointing at?

4. Get the child's attention, then give the child a miniature toy cup and teapot and say, "Can you make a cup of tea?" Does your child pretend to pour out tea, drink it, etc.?

5. Say, "Where's the light?" Does the child point with his index finger at the light?

Source: D. Foote and H. W. Tesoriero (2000). How doctors diagnose autism. *Newsweek*, July 31, p. 48.

---

stereotypic movements, perseveration, and hyperarousal. Children with autism, however, tend to display greater variability in their developmental profile and greater deficits in social and communication skills than children with fragile-X syndrome (Bailey et al., 2000). Nonetheless, there certainly is some overlap in diagnosis; 15 to 25 percent of children with fragile-X syndrome also meet the criteria for autism, and 4 percent of children with autism are diagnosed with fragile-X syndrome (Dykens & Volkmar, 1997).

The vast majority of individuals with autism (80 percent) also have mental retardation ranging from quite mild to profound (National Institute of Mental Health, 2003). Although the level of mental retardation certainly affects the ultimate ability levels of individuals with autism, as well as the specific educational goals and expectations, it typically does not affect the general educational approaches used in the classroom or other educational settings. Other common diagnoses that occur with individuals with autism and autism spectrum disorders are attention deficit/hyperactivity disorder in younger children and depression in adolescents and adults (Ghazuddin, 2002).

Prevalence

Estimates of the prevalence of autism fluctuate and often include the entire spectrum of autism disorders. In general, it is estimated that 1 in 500 births, or about 0.2 percent of children are diagnosed each year with autism or a related disorder (Rodier, 2000). During the 1999–2000 school year, 0.13 percent of all students ages 6 through 21, or 65,474 students, were served as students with autism (U.S. Department of Education, 2002). This number does not include the many young children with autism who may be served under preschool programs for children with developmental disabilities. The number of children identified as having autism has increased dramatically in recent years. Of course, the relatively recent identification of autism as a separate category in special education is partially responsible for this increase: As school districts became more practiced and prepared in classification procedures, more children were identified. For example, during the ten-year period following the special education categorization of autism, the number of children between the ages of 6 and 21 served with autism has grown from 5415 children during the 1991–1992 school year to the over 65,000 children served today. Some professionals, however, suggest that the rise in the number of children identified as having autism represents a true increase in numbers, and they speculate about possible environmental and medical causes.

Pause and Reflect

It may surprise you to know that twenty-five or so years ago, most people had not even heard about autism. Today, people with autism are featured in movies, television shows, and all other aspects of the media. Most people have heard the term and have an idea of what constitutes autism. What do you think is behind these changes in public awareness? Does awareness lead to other changes? ●

The National Center on Birth Defects and Developmental Disabilities has websites designed to answer children's questions about specific disabilities. These Kids Quest websites include one on autism spectrum disorder. Visit **http://www.cdc.gov/ncbddd/kids/kautismpage.htm** for a great resource for kids, including general information, reflective questions, Web links, and other websites about people with autism spectrum disorders.

Causes of Autism

Historical Opinions About Causes

Autism has been attributed to a wide range of possible causes.

The true causes of autism are unknown; however, research is bringing us ever closer to answering the questions about the reasons for the disorder and the unusual cognitive, behavioral, and communicative patterns that occur with it. Because of the unusual nature of the behaviors associated with autism, the disorder has been attributed to a wide range of possible causes.

Although theories about the causes of autism now rest firmly in the physiological realm—the neurological, genetic, and metabolic—this certainly was not always the case. Autism was first defined in the mid-1940s by Leo Kanner

(1943), who identified a cluster of behavioral characteristics that are essentially the same as those used today to diagnose children with autism. Kanner speculated about a range of possible causes, but it was Bettleheim (1967) who strongly felt that autism was a psychiatric response to an unsupportive and deprived environment. Naturally, the person responsible for the young child's environment was the mother, and it was she who was held responsible for the autistic state of her young child. How? It was assumed at the time that the child's withdrawal from social contact, abnormal focus on objects rather than people, and delayed language development reflected a lack of appropriate socialization and loving behaviors from the mother. In fact, the term *refrigerator mother* was used to describe the mothers of young children with autism—cold, unfeeling, icy. So, if you were a mother forty or fifty years ago and had a young child with autism, not only did you have the great challenge of trying to teach your toddler how to talk and play and smile, you also had to shoulder the burden of responsibility for *causing* these learning problems.

Fortunately, all we have learned about the nature of autism in the past decade or so has almost erased the stigma on parents, although, unfortunately, we still see some interventions based on the concept of parents as the cause of autism.

Current Hypotheses About Causes

Although there is still much speculation in the field, today our hypotheses about the causes of autism focus on physiological differences. The search for physiological causes for autism began in the 1960s (Rimland, 1964; Scott, Clark, & Brady, 2000) and has received increasing support in the past few decades. Most scientists agree that the collection of symptoms constituting autism, Asperger's syndrome, and pervasive developmental disorder arises from a set of inherited factors (Rodier, 2000). It also appears that most cases of autism begin very early in the embryonic development of the child. Children with autism

Today, hypotheses about the causes of autism focus on physiological factors.

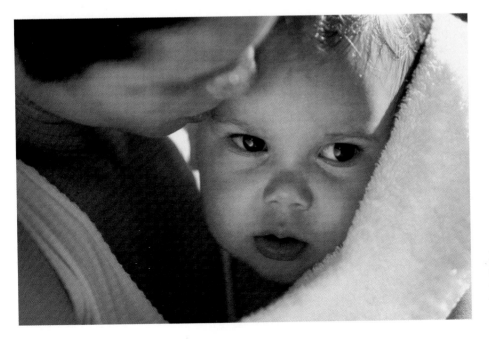

Parents may notice a lack of eye contact or social interaction in their young children with autism. (© Richard / CORBIS)

have specific differences in brain development, specifically in the brain stem (see Figure 8.1). Many also have specific genetic abnormalities. Although many genes appear to be associated with autism, no clear causal relationship between a specific genetic abnormality and the occurrence of autism has been established. Discovering the ultimate cause of autism will mean answering the following questions: What types of environmental or physiological insults trigger the brain differences? What factors influence the variety and intensity of characteristics related to autism? Is there a clear set of identifiable risk factors? The answers to these questions will depend on further knowledge about specific genetic and chromosomal factors, and they may lead to the discovery of the importance of environmental factors, such as drugs taken by the mother during pregnancy. Investigations designed to examine possible neurochemical factors common to children with autism have found only elevated levels of platelet serotonin, a neurotransporter, a finding that has led to highly speculative treatments and to attempts to determine the cause (Scott, Clark, & Brady, 2000).

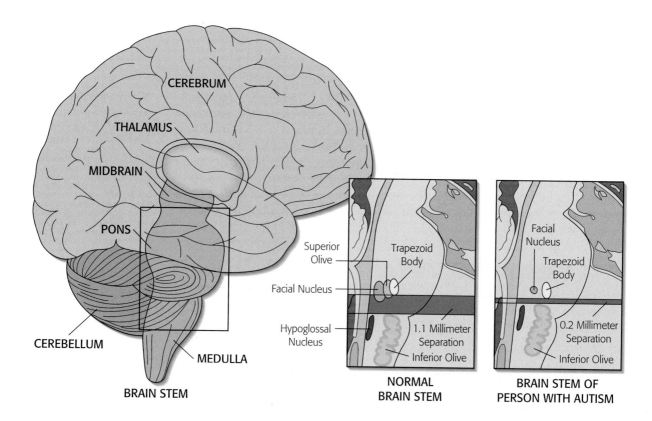

Figure 8.1

Autism's effects include changes to the brain stem, the region just above the spinal cord (*left*). The brain stem of a person with autism is shorter than a normal brain stem (*right*): The structures at the junction of the pons and the medulla (such as the facial nucleus and the trapezoid body) are closer to the structures of the lower medulla (the hypoglossal nucleus and the inferior olive). It is as though a band of tissue were missing. The brain stem of a person with autism also lacks the superior olive and has a smaller than normal facial nucleus. Such changes could occur only in early gestation.

Source: Patricia M. Rodier (2000). The early origins of autism. *Scientific American, 282*(2), 56–63.

Certainly, one of the puzzling factors about the onset of autism is that in close to 50 percent of children diagnosed, the defining characteristics don't appear until the child is a toddler, at which point some of the children begin to regress markedly in communication and social abilities (Davidovitch et al., 2000). Although this characteristic may be attributed to genes that are active only during specific times of a child's development, it has fostered increased, yet sometimes unsubstantiated, speculation about direct environmental influences, such as childhood inoculations or prenatal exposure to diseases such as rubella. No clear relationships between specific environmental factors and the onset of autism have been established.

? Pause and Reflect

The cause or causes of autism have eluded the professional community for many years, in part, because we were focused for too long on psychiatric rather than biological etiologies. You can see how the great increases in the number of children with autism would prompt additional research in this area. Why do you think that as we changed our perceptions of what causes autism, we also changed the nature of interventions we use with children and families? ●

Characteristics of Individuals with Autism

Individuals with autism often demonstrate unusual patterns of learning, speech, and behavior. There is great variability in the amount and intensity of symptoms among children who are identified as having autism. Children described as having autisticlike behaviors usually have only a few of these characteristics.

Cognitive Characteristics

Children with autism can be found at all levels of intellectual ability. As we stated earlier, about 80 percent of people diagnosed with autism are also diagnosed with mental retardation. Individuals with autism, even those without significant mental retardation, display unusual, uneven learning patterns, often consisting of relative strength in one or two areas of learning. Although a very small number of children with autism are truly gifted in one area, many do have learning strengths that are surprising in light of the child's overall level of functioning.

Most individuals with autism have mental retardation and display unusual learning patterns.

A child with autism may demonstrate ability in auditory memory, organization, or telling time and yet have extreme difficulty in other learning skills, such as reading or writing. For example, Michael, a young man with autism and moderate mental retardation, has a sight word vocabulary of only twenty-five words, yet can remember all the words to songs and commercials he heard over fifteen years ago. Although he cannot do even simple addition or subtraction when it is presented in number problem format, he can instantly add or subtract hours on his watch to accommodate changes due to Daylight Savings Time or Standard Time, before his watch is adjusted. He also can easily convert "military time" to standard time (for example, 1400

FIRST PERSON

Kevin Sribnick

When Kevin was an infant my parents thought he was deaf because he was so detached. One of my earliest memories was my father firing a cap pistol near Kevin to see if he would respond. He didn't. My parents took Kevin to doctor after doctor before he was diagnosed as autistic. I remember my mother saying she was happy to learn he wasn't deaf because there are so many wonderful sounds to hear. I suspect as Kevin got older and his inappropriate behaviors began to emerge, she had second thoughts about her preference. Kevin's early years were difficult for our entire family. He would only drink milk and would not eat until age 4. Finally my grandmother, who was visiting from New York, got him to eat solid food. As a young child, Kevin was quite destructive. I remember how distraught my mother was when Kevin used a lamp plug to scratch the sur-

face of two new coffee tables she had recently brought home. From then on she realized she would never be able to keep beautiful things in our home. Kevin would wander the house at night, frequently falling asleep wherever he happened to be when he finally closed his eyes. My brothers, sister, and I would take turns being responsible for finding him and bringing him to bed. Kevin would frequently have night terrors and the only way my parents could calm him was to take him for a drive, often at 2:00 a.m. in the morning. As is true for so many other children with autism, he could not tolerate change and would frequently have tantrums when something familiar was moved from its usual spot. By trial and error we would try to figure out what was missing and put it back into place. Because Kevin did not have any outward signs of a disability, strangers didn't understand

hours to 2:00 p.m.). These skills alone are not exceptional (most of us can convert time), but they are surprising when compared to other skills with which Michael has difficulty.

We have seen that many children with cognitive or learning disabilities have difficulty with memory tasks. Children with autism may have variable memory skills, but we do see some similarities with other children who have disabilities in some aspects of remembering. For example, individuals with autism, like children with learning disabilities and cognitive disabilities, do not appear to use active memory strategies such as organization and rehearsal of information (Renner, Klinger, & Klinger, 2000). Most typically developing kids have a good memory for things that happened to them. Children with autism, however, seem to recall events that happened to their peers better than they recall events that happened to themselves (Millward et al., 2000). This surprising learning characteristic seems incongruous with what we know about the social withdrawal of most children with autism. It is puzzling that children who don't seem to notice or may not interact with their classmates have such a good memory of what happens to the others around them.

his bizarre outbursts. We were very defensive and protected him from annoyed stares and unkind comments.

Despite all these problems, we loved Kevin very much. It became an early ritual that before any of us blew out our birthday candles, we would wish for Kevin to get better. As Kevin got older his behavior began to improve. He attended a school for children with mental and emotional disabilities and later worked in a sheltered workshop. Kevin learned to read simple phrases and add single digits. He became very close to me and would sit with me for much of the time while I studied for school. He also loved to swim. Being in the water always seemed to make him relaxed and happy.

Kevin lived at home until his mid-thirties. I would frequently keep him overnight on the weekends. We would make our supper together and listen to music. We both enjoy music from the late 1960s. I don't think the Moody Blues have a more devoted fan than Kevin. Five years ago, Kevin had a serious illness requiring hospitalization. I have never been so frightened in my entire life, and realized just how much Kevin means to me. Fortunately, he recovered completely.

Kevin is now 48 and for the last nine years has lived in an apartment with a caregiver and another man with autism. He continues to work and has become more self-sufficient. Kevin doesn't talk very much but does express all of his needs and preferences. He has become quite flexible when things are different from what he expects. Kevin and I always have lunch together on Sunday afternoons. Now that he lives independently, I have the opportunity to see how others view him. I recently read his quarterly service plan. As I read about Kevin's preferences and strengths, I realized that my little brother had become his own man. This year, my birthday wish will be for something else. Kevin is fine just the way he is.

Richard L. Sribnick, M.D.

Source: Personal account.

Children with autism also may be very rigid in their demands for environmental sameness and dependent on exact routines during the day (Koegel et al., 1995). For example, Mateo, a student who catches the school bus at 7:15 in the morning, will always leave the house at 7:10 a.m. and walk the exact same number of steps each time. If he leaves early, Mateo will walk very slowly so that he arrives and boards the bus at exactly 7:15. Some individuals will insist on sameness in their house or classroom, or in the sequence of events involved in going on a shopping trip or preparing lunch. Perry, a young man with autism living in a group home, became incensed one day and began raging at his housemates. The counselor living in the group home spent the afternoon searching for the problem. What was different? Had something been moved in Perry's room? Finally, Perry told the counselor that it had to do with toilet tissue. There had been a sale and the counselor bought two extra packages of toilet tissue. It was too much for Perry—too different from what the bathroom usually held. Not all individuals with autism will exhibit this characteristic, and some will require sameness in routine or order only certain things. As you might expect, this need for sameness may have significant implications when selecting instructional

> Children with autism are often very rigid in their demands for environmental sameness.

strategies and types of interventions. Once again, it is important to know and understand if and how this characteristic affects the child with autism in your classroom.

Physical Characteristics

Children with autism are usually described as average in appearance, if not as unusually attractive children. Most young children with autism look like any other typically developing young child. There do appear to be a few minor physical anomalies associated with autism, mostly related to the shape or placement of the ear (Rodier, 2000). These characteristics are truly minor, are not present in all children, and are difficult to observe unless one knows to look for them. There also appears to be an association between identified chromosomal abnormalities and minor physical anomalies. About 6.3 percent of children with autism have identified chromosomal abnormalities other than those associated with fragile-X syndrome. Children with these chromosomal abnormalities are more likely to have minor physical anomalies and to be cognitively delayed (Konstantareas & Homatidis, 1999).

Social Interaction

Many children with autism withdraw from social interaction or display significant deficits in social skills.

Individuals with autism typically demonstrate patterns of social behavior that reflect social withdrawal and avoidance of others. These patterns can include failure to make eye contact and to attend to others in the room, even if the other individuals are attempting to play with or talk to the child. The individual with autism simply may not react or may actively avoid other people's efforts at social interaction or communication. In fact, a characteristic description given by parents is that the child with autism appears to look through or past them (Maurice, 1993; Park, 1998). Historically, young children with autism were often misdiagnosed as being deaf, because their inattention was so marked that parents assumed they couldn't hear the noises around them, including their own names.

Many children with autism focus their attentions on objects instead of other people. They seem to disregard the desire for **joint attention**—the mutual sharing of experiences, activities, or even objects with friends, teachers, or parents (Scott, Clark, & Brady, 2000). As you can imagine, these characteristics can be particularly difficult for parents as they attempt to interact with and come to know their young child. Here is an example of one parent's observations:

> We start with an image—a tiny, golden child on hands and knees, circling round and round a spot on the floor in mysterious, self-absorbed delight. She does not look up, though she is smiling and laughing; she does not call our attention to the mysterious object of her pleasure. She does not see us at all. She and the spot are all there is, and though she is eighteen months old, an age for touching, tasting, pointing, pushing, exploring, she is doing none of these things. She does not walk, or crawl up stairs, or pull herself to her feet to reach for objects. She doesn't want any objects, instead she circles her spot. Or she sits, a long chain in her hand, snaking it up and down, up and down, watching it coil and uncoil for twenty minutes, half an hour, longer. . . . (Park, 1998, p. 30)

Not all individuals with autism are so completely withdrawn from social interaction with others, but most experience significant delays or deficits in social skills. A dual diagnosis of autism and mental retardation suggests high rates of poor adaptive behavior (Kraijer, 2000). Even those with less severe social deficits may have difficulty seeing things from the perspective of others and engaging appropriately in reciprocal social exchanges.

The importance of these characteristic social behavior patterns cannot be overestimated, because they affect virtually all areas of functioning—school, work, home, and play. For just about all individuals with autism and autism spectrum disorders, acquiring appropriate social skills and adaptive behavior comprises a substantial portion of educational programs at any age. As we will see, appropriate social interaction is closely intertwined with language, communication, and behavior.

Language and Communication

Difficulties and delays with language and communication are the hallmarks of children with autism. Some have delayed speech; it is not unusual for a child with autism to begin saying words at the age of six or seven. Sometimes, a toddler may begin talking at a normal developmental rate and then stop using previously acquired speech around age two (Davidovitch et al., 2000). Some children with autism may not acquire verbal language at all. A nonverbal child may use gestures, vocalizations, or facial expressions to communicate (Stephenson & Dowrick, 2000). Sign language or language boards are often used with nonverbal students to provide a means of communication.

If individuals with autism acquire oral speech, their speech patterns may take unusual forms. One common example is **echolalia**, the repetition of speech sounds. For example, if you asked a child, "What is your name?" the child would respond, "What is your name?" The child also may repeat certain words over and over—the jingle from a television advertisement or a sentence he or she has overheard. Although echolalic speech may seem to be nonfunctional—that is, not used for a specific purpose such as asking a question—it often does represent an attempt at direct communication. The student does not use typical forms of interpersonal communication, but the *intent* to communicate may be there. In fact, echolalic responses can indicate an attempt at the turn taking required in reciprocal speech (Scott, Clark, & Brady, 2000). In other words, the child may understand that a response is required but be unable to formulate an appropriate response, so he simply repeats what was just said. For example, in an attempt to manage his own disruptive behavior, Kyle will say over and over the words he's heard so often—Kyle, you've got to calm down. Although Kyle is repeating the words others have spoken, he uses them in a self-regulatory fashion—and calms himself down. Research continues to increase our knowledge base in this area, and interventions now include teaching students to adapt echolalic speech into useful, or functional, language.

Individuals with autism may present other types of language differences. Some may speak telegraphically, omitting articles, conjunctions, and tense markers ("Dan eat apple"). People with autism also may refer to themselves in the third person and avoid using pronouns altogether. As an example of both characteristics, Jim might say, "Jim watch TV" instead of "I want to watch TV." The speech of individuals with autism also is characterized by a flat or monotone quality.

> Differences in language and communication are the hallmarks of children with autism.

As you can probably see, many individuals with autism have a difficult time with reciprocal language—the use of language to give and receive information. **Reciprocal speech** combines the social or pragmatic aspects of communication, such as eye contact and turn taking, with the mechanical requirements of communication. It also involves skills in both **receptive language**, that is, understanding and interpreting information, and **expressive language**. Much research has been devoted to the observation and development of reciprocal speech in young children with autism (Savelle & Fox, 1988; Simpson & Souris, 1988). Some investigators have found that structured interventions that emphasize social interactive skills with peers or adults can increase both social and communication skills (Hwang & Hughes, 2000). It makes sense that teaching language in the context of social interaction will facilitate the acquisition and generalization of both types of behaviors. See Figure 8.2 for a sample protocol for language instruction in pronoun use.

We still have much to learn about the receptive communication skills of individuals with autism. As we mentioned earlier, individuals with autism often do not respond to language directed toward them. Sigafoos (2000) conducted research that reinforced our knowledge base on the relationship of poor communication skills to inappropriate behavior. Interestingly, he found stronger correlations between inappropriate behavior and receptive communication than between inappropriate behavior and expressive language. In other words, children with autism may be even more frustrated by their inability to understand information than their difficulty in expressing themselves. This implies that teachers need to assess the clarity and efficiency of their own communication strategies during instruction—you may increase appropriate behavior through good communication with your students with autism. See Table 8.1, "Considerations in Developing Communication Skills."

Table 8.1 Considerations for Developing Communication Skills in Children with Autism

- Make the communication an integral part of the child's life in and out of school.
- Communication, rather that rote responses, should be the goal.
- Emphasize spontaneous speech, whether pictorial, gestural, or verbal.
- Give the child many opportunities to communicate in all settings.
- Any socially acceptable attempt to communicate should be reinforced in all settings.
- Communication goals should be part of any plan to change maladaptive behavior.
- Initial communication goals should target obtaining items and activities that the student finds reinforcing.
- Communication goals should be developmentally and chronologically appropriate.
- Work together with all significant people in the student's environment to make the communication training as consistent as possible.

Source: From *Students with autism: Characteristics and instruction programming*, First Edition, by Jack Scott, Claudia Clark, and Michael Brady. © 2000. Reprinted with permission of Wadsworth, a division of Thomson Learning: www.thomsonrights.com. Fax 800 730-2215.

PROGRAM: Pronouns (I and You)

Program Procedure

1. *I*—Prompt the child to perform an action (e.g., physically guide the child to clap his or her hands) and say "What are you doing?" Prompt the child to say what he or she is doing with the correct pronoun (e.g., "I am clapping my hands"). Reinforce the response. Fade prompts over subsequent trials. Differentially reinforce responses demonstrated with the lowest level of prompting. Eventually, only reinforce correct, unprompted responses.

2. *You*—Sit across from the child. Establish attending and demonstrate an action (e.g., clap your hands). Say "What am I doing?" Prompt child to say what you are doing with the correct pronoun (e.g., "You are clapping your hands"). Reinforce the response. Fade prompts over subsequent trials. Differentially reinforce responses demonstrated with the lowest level of prompting. Eventually, only reinforce correct, unprompted responses.

3. *Randomize I and You*—Prompt the child to perform an action (e.g., give the child some juice to drink) and demonstrate an action (e.g., eat a cookie). Say either "What are you doing?" or "What am I doing?" Prompt the child to say what are you doing (e.g., "You are eating a cookie") or to say what he or she is doing (e.g., "I am drinking juice"). Fade prompts over subsequent trials. Differentially reinforce responses demonstrated with the lowest level of prompting. Eventually, only reinforce correct, unprompted responses.

Suggested Prerequisites:
>   Labels actions, possession, and pronouns (*my* and *your*).

Prompting Suggestions:
>   Model the correct response and use a time-delay procedure.

Question	Response	Date Introduced	Date Mastered
1. "What are you doing?" 2. "What am I doing?" 3. Either 1 or 2	1. Describes what he or she is doing with correct pronoun "I am…" 2. Describes what you are doing with correct pronoun "You are…" 3. Either 1 or 2		
1. I am			
2. You are			
3. Randomize I and You			
Helpful Hint: Be sure to ask your child to label pronouns in natural contexts.			

Figure 8.2

Pronouns: *I* and *You*

Source: B. A. Taylor, & K. A. McDonough (1996). From Selecting teaching programs (p. 133). In C. Maurice, G. Green, & S. C. Luce (Eds.). *Behavioral intervention for young children with autism: A manual for parents and professionals.* Austin, TX: Pro-Ed.

Behavior

Individuals with autism may display a unique range of characteristic, sometimes disturbing, behaviors. Some are typical of the types of behaviors you might see in any child, but they occur at greater rates and intensities and at unexpected times. Examples include throwing tantrums, crying, yelling or screaming, and hiding. You might expect a typical two-year-old to throw a tantrum if you take a toy away, or a five-year-old to start crying if he is reprimanded for leaving his toys out over night. You would not, however, expect a ten-year-old to throw a tantrum because a certain spoon is in the dishwasher, yet this is a behavior you might see from a child with autism.

One frequent cause of inappropriate behavior we've mentioned is the characteristic of rigidity, or need for structure, often present in children with autism. A common experience of parents of young children with autism is that the child will start crying or screaming because something is out of place. The parents and siblings then begin a long process of checking everything in the environment—every piece of furniture, book, lamp, rug—to identify and then fix the source of the child's dismay.

An unusual behavioral tendency demonstrated by some individuals with autism is the performance of repetitive patterns of behavior such as rocking, twirling objects, clapping hands, and flapping a hand in front of one's face. These repetitive, nonharmful behaviors are often referred to as **stereotypic behaviors**, or self-stimulating behaviors. Some people with autism display a number of stereotypic behaviors and perform them frequently, if not constantly. Others may engage in one or two behaviors, such as rocking during periods of inactivity.

Sometimes, the stereotypic nature of behavior is reflected in more disturbing actions. A few individuals with autism exhibit self-injurious or self-abusive behaviors, ranging from hand biting or head slapping to life-threatening behaviors such as head banging. The individuals seem oblivious to the pain and damage caused by these behaviors.

Why do individuals with autism display these behaviors, particularly harmful ones? Research suggests many possible reasons for self-injurious and other inappropriate behavior, including attempts at communication and efforts to manipulate the environment and avoid demanding or stressful situations (Chandler et al., 1999; Durand & Carr, 1985; Sigafoos, 2000). In other words, most of these behaviors have a definite use or function for the child with autism. Often, they represent the individual's best effort to tell you how he or she is feeling and to achieve some control over his or her environment.

> Individuals with autism often engage in repetitive behaviors referred to as stereotypic behaviors.

> Inappropriate behavior may reflect attempts by individuals with autism to communicate or to manipulate the environment.

Individuals with autism often engage in repetitive, stereotypic behavior, such as hand-flapping. (AP Photo/Ed Betz)

This knowledge of the relationship between behavior and communication is extremely important to those who make up the social support system of individuals with autism. Our first instinct as teachers is to try to eliminate inappropriate or harmful behavior. However, we must first assess the student's communicative intent and try to provide alternative behaviors or skills in language and communication when attempting to reduce inappropriate behaviors. Our job, therefore, is twofold: (1) determine the purpose or function of the behavior, and (2) identify and teach an appropriate, alternative behavior that will serve the same function. To accomplish these goals, we conduct functional behavioral assessments that include observations of the student performing the behavior in school or play settings (see Chapter 7). This procedure has been found to be effective in replacing inappropriate behavior with appropriate classroom behavior for students with autism (Chandler et al., 1999).

Family Interactions

Several times throughout this chapter, we refer to issues and challenges faced by families of individuals with autism. It is difficult to talk about autism without including parents in the discussion. Parents have been substantial contributors to the knowledge base in the field, both as ethnographers and as sources of objective evidence on the effectiveness of various interventions. Unfortunately, most parents are forced into the roles of treatment evaluator, teacher, and, in some cases, intervention designer. Because of the dearth of practical information about living with children with autism, difficulty getting an early diagnosis, inconsistency in treatment recommendations, and lack of early intervention programs, parents took the reins and brought the needs of children with autism into focus. This effort by parents is still under way, but now many parents and professionals are working together, and parent advocacy has resulted in a renewed demand for objective, empirical proof of an intervention's effectiveness as well as increased interventions for very young children.

> Parents are major contributors to the knowledge base in the field of autism.

Historically, the literature written by parents was filled with concerns about the difficulties they have experienced as they have tried to get an accurate diagnosis for their child (Maurice, 1993). We have already pointed to some of the specific reasons for diagnostic delays, a situation that is becoming less and less common, as early diagnosis and treatment are emphasized. It is important to recognize the importance of this issue, however, because parents may realize early on the level of effort they must put into getting appropriate services for their children. Even when a child receives an early diagnosis, the process is never an easy one. Parents report finding compassion and honesty to be important characteristics of the professionals who are in the role of delivering the diagnosis of autism (Nissenbaum, Tollefson, & Reese, 2002). The accompanying Closer Look box entitled, "Recommendations for Informing Families" provides simple guidelines for professionals based on the recommendations of parents of children with autism.

Once a diagnosis is obtained, parents are faced with a growing body of literature and testimonials about literally dozens of interventions, all of which should begin when the child is about two years old. So, sifting through the research and trying to find the intervention and desired service provider in the community as soon as possible become the next priorities. This process can be overwhelming to any parent (Morrice, 2002). Of course, families with limited resources or those living in rural areas may experience even more difficulty finding appropriate services. It is no wonder that parent support groups and

A Closer Look — Recommendations for Informing Families

Quick Reference of Recommendations for Practices When Informing Families Their Child Has Autism

1. Become knowledgeable about autism
2. Establish a family-friendly setting
3. Understand the family's needs
4. Use good communication skills
5. Provide a list of resources and interventions
6. Provide follow-up
7. Discuss prognosis
8. Provide hope
9. Recognize that it is not unusual for professionals to react to giving the diagnosis of autism

Source: M. S. Nissenbaum, N. Tollefson, & R. M. Reese (2002). The interpretative conference: Sharing a diagnosis of autism with families, *Focus on Autism and Other Developmental Disabilities, 17,* 30–43.

organizations such as the Autism Society provide valuable guidance and assistance as parents try to make their way through the intervention maze. Visit the website of the Autism Society of America at **http://www.autism-society.org** to learn more about advocacy, resources, research, and general information related to autism and autism spectrum disorders.

Once an intervention is chosen, the role of the parents and other family members will only increase. Almost all recommended interventions for young children with autism include intensive teaching, often within the child's home, and usually involving round-the-clock instruction, measuring, and evaluating by parents. So, by the time a child with autism is three or four, his or her family will have devoted at least two to three years of nonstop searching, investigating, and teaching. Because of the intimate role parents play in service delivery, great care is taken to understand and incorporate their needs and educational concerns in areas such as communication priorities (Stephenson & Dowrick, 2000).

? Pause and Reflect

The social and behavioral characteristics of children with autism, as well as their language skills, vary greatly from child to child, but always present challenges. How do you think you would react if a child with autism entered your family or your classroom? Where would you go for guidance and assistance? ●

Teaching Strategies and Accommodations

The majority of students with autism receive a functional, community-based curriculum.

The recommended focus of curriculum and instruction for individuals with autism overlaps with programs designed for students with severe disabilties. Individuals with autism and moderate to severe cognitive disabilities will require extensive behavior support and skills instruction, and will benefit from a functional, community-based curriculum that focuses on life skills. Other individuals with autism, those with mild cognitive disabilities or typical cognitive ability, may progress through a general education academic curriculum and receive less intensive behavioral, academic, and social support. In general, the areas of communication, socialization, and generalization of learning are particularly important in programs for individuals with autism.

Students with autism may receive special education services at all levels of the service delivery continuum, depending on each student's individual strengths and needs. Many young children receive services at home, and some attend a preschool program. As with all children with disabilities, decisions about educational settings for children with autism will be based on short-term and long-range educational goals for the child, and on his or her ability to perform in general education settings. You may find a child with autism and moderate mental retardation served in a self-contained class or in a high-school vocational training program. Or, you may find a child with autism receiving academic instruction in the general education class, with accommodations for language and in-class instruction in social skills. It is important to ensure that students with autism, regardless of the classroom setting, receive the level of instruction they require, particularly in the areas of social behavior and communication. These areas continue to be crucial throughout the transition plan of adolescents because they relate to job training and other preparations for life after school.

The Importance of Early Intervention

Although there is a great variety of available interventions for individuals with autism, the proponents of virtually all of them agree on one thing: the earlier the better. Arick and coworkers (2003) are conducting a long-term study of the effects of several early interventions on the social, behavioral, and language outcomes for young children with autism spectrum disorders. Preliminary results suggest a number of interventions may result in positive outcomes. Harris and Handleman (2000) found that all children who received intensive applied behavior analysis programs beginning before the age of four showed both clear gains in IQ and an increased probability of placement in general education classes. In terms of overall outcomes, children who received early intervention and who had higher IQs had the best prognosis.

Currently, there are general guidelines for early interventions designed for students with autism based on an analysis of early intervention research. The following recommendations for intervention were advanced by the National Research Council (2001):

1. Functional, spontaneous communication should be the primary focus of early education.
2. Social instruction should be delivered throughout the day in various settings, using specific activities and interventions planned to meet age-appropriate, individualized, social goals.
3. The teaching of play skills should focus on play with peers, and additional instruction in appropriate use of toys and other materials.
4. Instruction aimed at goals for cognitive development should also be carried out in the context in which the skills are expected to be used, with generalizaton and maintenance in natural contexts as important as the acquisition of new skills.

Children with autism should receive intensive intervention at an early age.

5. Intervention strategies that address problem behaviors should incorporate information about the contexts in which the behaviors occur; positive, proactive approaches; and the range of techniques that have empirical support.

6. Functional academic skills should be taught when appropriate to the skills and needs of a child. (NRC, p. 221)

These elements can serve as guidelines for both teachers and parents as they search for comprehensive preschool programs. Because of the requirements of PL 99-457, school districts must provide programs for individuals over age three identified with autism or other developmental disabilities, and many districts offer educational programs for children between the ages of birth and three (see Chapter 2). Increased awareness of autism and related disorders leads to parents receiving earlier diagnoses for their children and, therefore, demanding a greater number of comprehensive services. State educational agencies will be able to identify the range and type of services available in specific communities. Table 8.2 provides some guiding questions for parents to help match interventions to the specific needs of a child.

As children become school-aged, they will move from early intervention programs to school-based programs. Some of the specific programs or approaches described below are designed primarily for young children (e.g., the Lovaas method), while other approaches or interventions are appropriate for children of all ages (applied behavior analysis, social skills instruction). As we look at the sample of interventions presented below, you will notice some differences and some similarities. As was done with early intervention programs, research on interventions for school-aged children with autism was evaluated to determine the fundamental elements of successful programs for all students with autism. You can see that the following components mirror, in a general way, the factors of successful early intervention programs.

These six components (Iovannone et al., 2003, p. 153) are:

- Individual supports and services for students and families
- Systematic instruction
- Structured environments
- Specialized curriculum content
- A functional approach to problem behaviors, and
- Family involvement

Applied Behavior Analysis

Effective interventions for individuals with autism are based on applied behavior analysis.

The methods used most successfully for individuals with autism and other severe disabilities are based on the principles of applied behavior analysis (ABA) (Arick et al., 2003). As we discussed in Chapter 6, applied behavior analysis is not a specific intervention, but rather the application of scientific principles to the study of behavior. The application of ABA to intervention strategies focuses on clearly defining behavior within the context of the environment and then arranging the environment and providing consequences for increasing or decreasing specific behaviors. First you determine the role or function that the student's behavior plays in his or her environment, and then you identify alternative behaviors that can serve the same function. New behaviors are taught through

Table 8.2 Criteria for Selecting Early Intervention Programs: Questions for Parents

1. *Does your child have the necessary prerequisite skills for this program?*

   When you choose a teaching program, ask yourself what skills your child may need to perform the response. For example, you may want your child to request in sentences, but she may not be able to repeat words. Breaking a skill down into its component parts can help you identify what other skills you may need to teach first.

2. *Is this program developmentally age-appropriate for your child?*

   Programs should loosely reflect a sequence of development that would be expected of a typical child. When identifying a skill to teach, ask yourself if another child of similar age could perform the same skill.

3. *Will this skill help to reduce problem behaviors?*

   Choose teaching programs that are likely to have a positive impact on your child's behavior. For example, teaching communicative responses such as pointing and gesturing yes and no may reduce problem behaviors that serve a communicative function.

4. *Will this skill lead to the teaching of other skills?*

   When choosing skills to teach, identify those that are likely to build on one another. For example, teaching your child to imitate sequenced gross motor actions (e.g., imitating two actions in the correct order) will probably lead you to teach your child to follow two-step verbal instructions.

5. *Is this skill likely to generalize?*

   Choose programs and target responses that your child will have ample opportunity to practice beyond the teaching sessions. For example, you are more likely to ask your child to "Shut the door," or "Turn on the light," throughout the day, as opposed to "Stomp your feet." Responses that are associated with naturally occurring positive consequences are more likely to generalize.

6. *Will your child acquire this skill within a reasonable timeframe?*

   Priority should be given to teaching skills that your child is likely to acquire in a reasonable amount of time. For example, if your child does not speak, he will need to learn effective communicative responses. Your child can learn to point to desired items relatively quickly, in comparison to requesting in phrases. Skills that will be acquired in a reasonable timeframe will be reinforcing for you, your child, and your teaching staff.

7. *Is this an important skill for you and your family?*

   Choose skills that will have positive implications for your child's participation in family activities. Although matching colors is an important readiness skill, teaching your child to identify family members will have a greater impact on your child's participation in the family.

8. *Is this a skill that your child can use throughout the day?*

   Choose to teach skills that are functional for your child. For example, learning to follow simple instructions, using yes and no, pointing to desired items, and completing play activities are useful for your child and can be incorporated into his or her day.

Source: B. A. Taylor & K. A. McDonough (1996). Adapted from Selecting teaching programs (p. 64). In C. Maurice, G. Green, and S. C. Luce (Eds.), *Behavioral intervention for young children with autism: A manual for parents and professionals.* Austin, TX: Pro-Ed.

reinforcement-based opportunities for response. In other words, a specific skill, such as hand raising, could be taught to replace hand flapping, if teacher attention were the student's goal. The reason for the behavior is determined through a functional behavior analysis. The student would receive instruction in how and when to raise his hand. The teacher would carefully attend to the student whenever the appropriate behavior was performed—reinforcing the student's appropriate action. The occurrence of the original behavior (hand flapping) and the new, substitute behavior (hand raising) would be recorded and observed over time to determine if the reinforcement supplied by the teacher and others in the environment was resulting in increases in the desired, new behavior. Complex or multistep behaviors, such as some vocational tasks, may be taught in segments and then linked together. Other skills, such as getting dressed, are presented as a whole, with the student gradually increasing participation. Students with autism may require many instructional trials (discrete trials) and explicit training across environments. Visit our text website through **http://www. education.college.hmco.com/students/** to read more about applied behavior analysis in educational settings and to find more resources for further study.

● *The Lovaas Method*   The UCLA Young Autism Project, an intensive, three-year program for young children with autism, received much attention by parents and some professionals. This project uses interventions based on strategies developed by Ivar Lovaas over thirty years ago. The project developers present data that support significant change in children's cognition, language, and behavior (Smith & Lovaas, 1997). The project is based on the principles of applied behavior analysis; however, some professionals question the curriculum context (what skills are taught and where they are taught) and criticize the quality and validity of the program's experimental research (Gresham & MacMillan, 1997).

The Lovaas method, as this intervention is commonly called, requires intensive training of teachers or parents and begins when the child is two to three years of age. The trained interventionist provides intensive, discrete trial training with the child on a one-to-one basis in the child's home. A discrete trial is one episode in a set of repetitive instructional sessions, designed to teach a specific skill. Training is recommended for up to forty hours per week for a minimum of three years. Needless to say, this is an expensive and exhausting intervention approach, yet it is the treatment most commonly requested by parents of young children with autism. The existing empirical base of support has driven the widespread use of the program. In fact, the Lovaas program is one of the few specific educational approaches supported by the courts in litigation against school districts (Yell & Drasgow, 2000). Many school districts are attempting to create applied behavior analysis programs that provide substantial empirical support for learning, without requiring the expensive and limiting in-home training. The Teaching Strategies box entitled, "Recommendations for In-Home Behavioral Programs" provides guidelines for parents or teachers to use when selecting a behavioral program for very young children.

Environmental Interventions

● *Project TEACCH*   Other methods of teaching students with autism focus on arranging the environment to provide support and extensive opportunities for behavioral expression. The most prominent of these intervention approaches is Project TEACCH (the Treatment and Education of Autistic and

Related Communication Handicapped Children program) (Mesibov, 1994). The TEACCH program began as a statewide service delivery system in North Carolina over thirty years ago and it has spread across the United States and Europe. The intervention emphasizes encouraging and maintaining existing behaviors and structured teaching of developmentally appropriate new skills, often using one-on-one instruction, and focusing on the individual interests and needs of the student (Dawson & Osterling, 1997). Structured instruction takes place in context to support performance within designated environments. Structured instruction refers here to a carefully organized classroom or work environment, clear directions and predictable work patterns, and the use of physical, verbal, and picture prompts to promote correct responses. Supports are gradually withdrawn as students become more independent.

A fundamental component of the TEACCH program is the close working relationship between the professionals in the program and parents and families (Scott, Clark, & Brady, 2000). The program focuses on early intervention but continues throughout adulthood, providing safe and interactive learning environments for individuals with autism. Intervention research supports the effectiveness of TEACCH programs in producing satisfaction in increasing independence, and in reducing problem behaviors among the families and children and adults with autism (Mesibov, 1997; Persson, 2000), although some professionals question the research outcomes (Smith, 1996). To learn more about the TEACCH program, including recommended instructional strategies, visit this website: **http://www.teacch.com**.

● *Social Skills Interventions*   Although social skills training may be a component of many other types of instructional approaches, including applied behavior analysis and TEACCH, there is a current emphasis on training social skills as a distinct intervention. In addition, social skills interventions may comprise the major instructional emphasis for students with Asperger's syndrome or other autism spectrum disorders. Social skills may include initiating play activities, establishing eye contact, sharing toys, taking turns, and participating in cooperative recreational activities, such as games or reading stories. As noted in

Even in classroom or play settings, a child with autism may be oblivious to those around her. (Robin Sachs/PhotoEdit)

the recommendations of the National Research Panel, instruction in social skills and play skills should include peers. The emphasis of peer-focused social skills intervention involves creating an environment that simultaneously teaches and reinforces appropriate social behavior. Many of the social skills interventions for children with autism that include peers frequently incorporate peers in an instructional role. Usually the interventions include typically developing peers, but in some cases, peers with mild cognitive disabilities have participated in interventions. In the instructional role, peers receive training in modeling, prompting, and reinforcing the appropriate play behaviors and social interaction skills of children with autism (DiSalvo & Oswald, 2002: Kamps et al., 2002). Terpstra, Higgins, and Pierce (2002) also recommend providing specific scripts for peer trainers, as well as incorporating environmental support such as well-designed play spaces, following a regular schedule and routine, and determining play preferences and motivational activities to serve as a basis for play and other social activities.

Language-Based Interventions

A few popular instructional programs for individuals with autism are designed to prompt communication and link pictures or written language with verbal communication. These programs focus on incorporating the personal needs and circumstances of the individual child into the instructional program. The goal of these interventions may be simply to achieve more effective communication, to improve social interactions—including student-initiated interactions, or verbal guidance of appropriate alternative behaviors.

● *Picture Exchange Communication System*   The Picture Exchange Communication System (PECS) is a communication system based on teaching nonverbal children to use pictorial symbols to request information. Bondy and Frost (2001) formalized the PECS system and developed the training manual. The children gradually learn to combine the pictures to make picture sentences—eventually using language to accompany and, possibly, to replace the picture symbols. The PECS program uses a wide variety of pictures and an assortment of different picture boards on which to create phrases and sentences. Examples of PECS picture cards can be found in Figure 8.3. The picture boards are based on the concept of a traditional communication board; in this case, however, the emphasis is on student selection of the pictures and symbols used and the constant changing of these symbols to reflect immediate student needs. For students to use this technique, it must be an effective and efficient means of communication for the individual child; therefore, immediate responses by teachers, parents, and peers are necessary, particularly in the beginning of the program. The popularity of these picture collections with young children with autism resulted in a number of other picture groups designed to be used either for expressive language by children with autism or as a means of conferring messages to children. For example, the Picture Literacy Project at the University of Kansas (2003) developed a series of noun and action-word symbols that could be learned and used either for receptive or expressive communication. There are many other sources of pictures available to teachers and parents, most at little or no cost.

● *Social Stories*   Whereas the PECS system, and those like it, focus on symbols or pictures to foster language and social interaction, social stories are based primarily on verbal and written language. Gray (2003) created and de-

baseball

school bus

line up

jellybeans

pretzel

popcorn

Figure 8.3

Sample Picture Cards from the Picture Exchange Communication System (PECS).

Source: Picture Exchange Communication System (PECS), http://pyramidproducts.com. Retrieved November 2003.

fined social stories over a decade ago as a means of addressing the language and social needs of verbal children with autism spectrum disorders. In essence, a social story is a brief sequence of sentences designed to provide a self-instruction plan for the student. The social story uses four types of sentences, including descriptive sentences, perspective sentences, affirmative sentences, and directive sentences, to talk a child through specific situations, scenarios, or tasks. Each story is created by parents or teachers to reflect a specific challenge for the individual child. Sometimes, stories are designed to help a student engage in appropriate alternative behavior in problem situations; to prepare the child for a new experience, such as going to a new playground; or to help a child make decisions or remain calm. The complexity of the sentences, the length of the stories, and the vocabulary used will depend on the child. Winterman and Sapona (2002) found that the social story concept could be used by a nonverbal child with autism by utilizing picture communication symbols instead of sentences and creating picture stories.

Examples of social stories on a variety of topics are readily available to teachers and parents. Figure 8.4 provides an example of a social story on the topic of line leader. To read more about social stories and to see additional samples of social stories, visit the website of the Gray Center at **http://www.thegraycenter.org**.

Biochemical Interventions

Over the years, a number of interventions have focused on biochemistry, including diet-based interventions, vitamin-based therapies, and others. Most of these interventions lack supporting empirical data. The most recent of the proposed biochemical interventions involves the use of the gastrointestinal hormone secretin to reduce the symptoms of autism. In spite of personal testimony to the contrary, current research indicates that the administration of secretin produces no meaningful changes in the language or behavior of individuals with autism (Chez et al., 2000).

Pharmacological interventions are often a component of treatment protocols for individuals with autism.

Pharmacological interventions, on the other hand, are widely considered to be an important part of treatment protocols for many individuals with autism. Although not a primary educational intervention, drug treatment is often used to address some of the concomitant symptoms of autism, such as hyperactivity, depression, seizure disorders, agitation, aggression, and self-stimulatory behaviors (Heflin & Simpson, 1998).

Who Is Line Leader?

My name is Andrew. I am in the first grade. Sometimes, the children in my class form (one, two, three, etc.) lines.

The children in my class *stand* in a line when we are getting ready to go to another part of the school. Children do move a little when they stand in a line. Children may move to scratch, or fix their shirt, or their shoe. Sometimes, because they are standing close together, children may touch one another. Many times, it is an accident when children touch one another in line. They were not planning to touch another child.

The children in my class *walk* in a line to move safely in the halls. Walking in a line keeps children in order, too. If another group of students are walking in the hall going the opposite direction, the two groups can pass one another easily. That's why teachers have asked children to walk in lines for many, many years. It is a safe and organized way to move many children.

Usually, children stand and walk in lines for a short period of time. Once the children reach their destination, their teacher often doesn't need them to stay in the line anymore.

Sometimes, I may be the Line Leader. This means that the other children in my class will walk behind me.

Sometimes, I may be second, or third, or fourth, or another position.

Many children in my class like to be the Line Leader. My teacher knows who should be first in line. Teachers know about being fair, and try to make sure each child is Line Leader now and then.

It's important to follow directions about who is Line Leader. My turn to be Line Leader again gets closer every time the children in my class walk in a line!

Figure 8.4

Sample Social Story

Source: Carol Gray (2003). The Gray Center Website. Retrieved 7/14/03 from http://www.thegraycenter.org/sample_social_stories.htm.

Technology Focus

Vocal Output Communication Aids

There are many useful and important applications of technology for individuals with autism. Many of these applications focus on augmenting communication through electronic communication boards that include voice output. These devices are known as vocal output communication aids (VOCAs). The VOCA may look like a regular communication board, but pushing the picture or symbol will result in a digitized or synthesized speech reading of the symbol. Some VOCAs are more complex and may not provide vocal output until an appropriate two-word combination or sentence is created. These may include a combination of words and symbols or pictures. In addition to basic communication functions, some boards also contain educational programs that can be used for more traditional instruction. For example, a program can ask the student to find the picture or symbol of a particular word, match words, or find the word or sentence that describes a specific picture. Most VOCAs are portable, but typically too large for a child to carry around like a Palm Pilot. Most VOCAs can be placed on a desk or mounted on a wheelchair. It is important to note that most

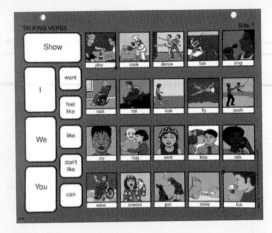

Figure 8.5 Voice Output Communication Aid (VOCA) Designed for Children with Autism

Source: Laureate Learning. Retrieved 7/11/03 from http://www.laureatelearning.com/images/tulg.gif.

VOCAs can be extremely expensive. Research has yet to evaluate if the use of VOCAs in any way supports language development or use in children with autism.

In addition to the interventions we have described above, many other treatments have been proposed. These treatments run the gamut from new, promising approaches, to historical, unsubstantiated interventions, and everything in between. Some of these interventions focus on the suspected psychopathology of autism, and address parental acceptance of children's behaviors and increasing the child's comfort as he or she attempts to communicate (Heflin & Simpson, 1998). Although these interventions may show up in any given community, many do not have empirical support. Some of the interventions appear to be logical and helpful; others may appear idiosyncratic and quite far-fetched. Yet because parents are often desperate for answers, they may be drawn to unproven and often expensive treatments. The support of good, empirical research is the criterion that must be used by parents and teachers to select an appropriate educational intervention for individuals with autism. See Table 8.3 for criteria to use when evaluating programmatic research.

Transition to Adulthood

Adults with autism have the same opportunities for independent performance at work and in residential settings as individuals with other disabilities. They may perform various types of work through competitive employment or sup-

> Adults with autism have the same range of opportunities for independence in work and residential settings as individuals with other disabilities.

ported work programs. Of course, the particular social and behavioral characteristics of autism may present great challenges in postschool environments, even for individuals without cognitive disabilities. Skills such as language use and appropriate social interaction may be targets for instruction throughout the lifetime of an individual. Instructional approaches such as applied behavior analy-

Table 8.3 Evaluating Evidence About Treatments for Autism

A great number of treatments for autism have surfaced over the years. Some professionals claim to have great success using these interventions to improve the performance of children, and some even suggest they can cure autism. All the claims can be quite confusing to parents and teachers trying to find the most effective educational programs. Part of making treatment decisions is determining the extent to which the evidence presented for treatment efficacy can be trusted. Green (1996) identifies the following factors to look for when evaluating evidence for various treatments.

Speculation vs. Demonstration

Is there actual proof that a treatment produces definite results (demonstration), or is there a recommendation based on someone's theory or hypothesis (speculation)?

Subjective Evidence vs. Objective Evidence

Is the evidence provided by individuals who are biased about the treatment results without controls for such bias (subjective)? Or, is the evidence presented in a quantitative form—the data are clearly defined and carefully observed and assessed via multiple measures by individuals without a stake in the treatment outcomes (objective)?

Indirect Measures vs. Direct Measures

Is the evidence provided in the form of an individual's perceptions, feelings, anecdotes, or impressions that behavior has changed (indirect), or has the behavior been directly observed, counted, or measured (direct)?

Noncomparative Information vs. Comparative Information

Does the evidence result from looking only at the performance of children receiving that intervention (noncomparative), or does it document improved performance when evaluated with students receiving other interventions or no intervention at all (comparative)?

Descriptive Research vs. Experimental Research

Is the information acquired through general descriptions or observations of performance (descriptive), or are observations arranged so that they can be conducted systematically and controlled (experimental)?

Statistical Significance vs. Clinical Significance

Do the results presented indicate only significance based on statistical analysis (statistical), or do they represent real educational importance (clinical significance)?

Source: G. Green (1996). Adapted from Evaluating claims about treatments for autism (pp. 15–28). In C. Maurice, G. Green, & S. C. Luce (Eds.), B*ehavioral intervention for young children with autism: A manual for parents and professionals.* Austin, TX: Pro-Ed.

A Closer Look — Comments on Job Preparation by a Young Woman with Autism

I like the idea of having job mentors. A mentor would be an individual already established in a career who could use his or her creative energy to guide and develop the creative talents of an autistic person and lead them to a satisfying job. One person *can* make a difference in how successful the person with autism will be. Another reason I like the idea of a mentor service is that high-functioning people prosper when there is that one special person who has the time to help out when problems arise or when something needs improving. Somehow that one person makes a difference.

Source: K. Hurlbutt, & L. Chalmers (2002). Adults with autism speak out: Perceptions of their life experiences. *Focus on Autism and Other Developmental Disabilities, 17*(2), 103–111.

sis and TEACCH are used through adulthood. Most adults with autism live with the family; others live semi-independently in group homes or apartments; and some adults live in more restrictive settings. Often, individuals with autism who live independently benefit from support services, even if it is only an occasional visit from a relative or care provider. In the First Person box here, a mother describes Jessy, her adult daughter with autism, and one of Jessy's many beautiful paintings is reproduced.

As we've said many times in this chapter, individuals with autism and autism spectrum disorders display a great range of abilities and learning and behavioral differences. Outcomes of educational programs for adolescents and adults will also vary greatly. Interviews with individuals who are clearly high-functioning adults with autism suggest that they have very strong opinions about what factors were important in facilitating their success, and that they would like to be considered experts and be asked to share their perceptions with the professional community (Hurlbutt & Chalmers, 2002). In the Closer Look box entitled, "Comments on Job Preparation" a young adult discusses the importance of a job mentor. Input from individuals with autism spectrum disorders, information from parents and teachers, and continued longitudinal research will help us navigate the many interventions and resources focused on the area of autism.

Pause and Reflect

In this section, we looked at many types of interventions—some very structured and intensive, others less so. If a student with autism were to be included in a general education program, which of these interventions do you think could be incorporated into the general education classroom? Do you think the age of the student would affect the type of intervention that could be more easily integrated with a teacher's typical teaching strategies? ●

FIRST PERSON

Jessy Park

RAGE FOR ORDER
The Paintings of Jessica Park

Paintings & Prints
Jessica Park
Exiting Nirvana
Calendar

Contact us at prints@jessicapark.com

Anecdotes must temper our yen for the miraculous, keep the account honest. Without them, Jessy's slow progress takes on too much of the aura of the success story everybody wants to hear. Suppose I say what is entirely true: that she has worked, rapidly and efficiently, for sixteen years in the Williams College mailroom; that she is hardly ever absent and never late; that she pays taxes; that she keeps her bank account accurately to the penny; that she has saved more money than any of her siblings; that increasingly she keeps house for her aging parents; that I haven't touched a vacuum cleaner in years; that she does the laundry, the ironing, some of the cooking, all of the baking; that she is a contributing member of her community and of her family. Who wouldn't hear, behind those words, others: miracle, recovery, cure? And I have as yet hardly mentioned the brilliant acrylics that seem to be, but are not, the crown of her achievements.

Indeed, they are remarkable. Black-and-white can convey the ordered exactitude of the outlines, the clarity and repetition of design elements, recalling the baby to whom shapes and colors were more significant than faces. There is no vagueness in her paintings, no dashing brush strokes, no atmospheric washes. It is hard-edge stuff, and always has been. Even in nursery school she never overlapped her colors, never scrubbed them together into lovely, messy mud. Her paintings then were as characteristic as these today, repetitive arrangements of shapes and patterns, always controlled, always in balance. What black-and-white can't convey is the incandescence of her colors, and even the finest reproduction could not convey their variety.

Jessy paints; paintings bring checks; the numbers in her bank account rise, as once the numbers rose (and occasionally fell) when she kept track of her behaviors on a golf counter. The checks are a significant motivator for her, as the growing recognition is for us, who must answer inquiries and learn to negotiate the world of galleries and shows social complexities forever beyond Jessy's ken. But for us, and for her, what's important about this demanding, absorbing activity, valued and rewarded by society, is not what it brings to her bank account or her reputation (a concept much harder to understand than stratification), but what it brings to her life. It interests people, predisposes them in her favor, encourages them to overlook behavior that needs overlooking. Autistic people need that. Yet its real meaning for her life is more ordinary: it gives her something to do.

Claira Claiborne Park

Source: Claira Claiborne Park (1998). Excerpts from Exiting nirvana. *The American Scholar, 67*(2), 37–39.

SUMMARY

- Autism is a lifelong developmental disability that is best described as a collection of behavioral symptoms. Symptoms include deficits in verbal and nonverbal communication, social withdrawal, repetitive and stereotypical behaviors, resistance to change, and unusual responses to sensory experiences.

- It is often difficult to diagnose autism because of the similarity between autism and other disorders, all referred to as pervasive developmental disorders. Asperger's syndrome is one of the many disorders related to autism.

- The cause of autism is not known; however, current research suggests that the cause or causes of autism are physiological factors. At one time, autism was thought to be an emotional or psychological disorder.

- Autism greatly affects the areas of communication, cognition, and social behaviors. Individuals with autism may display unusual speech patterns, such as echolalia, or may have no oral language. About 80 percent of people diagnosed with autism also have mental retardation. Most individuals with autism display stereotypic behaviors, such as rocking, twirling of objects, or hand clapping.

- Early intervention is a key factor for improving the prognosis of children with autism. Parents, therefore, play an important role in the education of their young children.

- The most effective interventions for individuals with autism are based on principles of applied behavior analysis; these programs involve the systematic instruction of discrete skills.

KEY TERMS

autism

pervasive developmental disorders

autism spectrum disorders

Asperger's syndrome

fragile-X syndrome

joint attention

echolalia

reciprocal speech

receptive language

expressive language

stereotypic behaviors

USEFUL RESOURCES

- Visit the Autism Society of America at **http://www.autism-society.org**. It is a national organization for parents, professionals, and individuals with autism. Branches exist in most states.

- Go to Families for the Early Treatment of Autism at **http://www.feat.org**. This website provides information to families and advocates about early intervention options.

- S. Harris and M. Weiss (1998). *Right from the start: Behavioral interventions for young children with autism: A guide for parents and professionals*. Bethesda, MD: Woodbine House. This text provides descriptions and guidelines for developing home-based programs for young children diagnosed with autism.

- C. Maurice (1993). *Let me hear your voice: A family's triumph over autism.* New York: Fawcett Columbine. This book tells one family's story about the emotional and physical struggle for appropriate interventions for two young children with autism.

- C. Maurice, G. Green, and S. C. Luce (Eds.) (1996). *Behavioral intervention for young children with autism: A manual for parents and professionals.* Austin, TX: Pro-Ed. This text is the standard in the field. It provides extensive and usable information about teaching programs and strategies for individuals with autism.

- Paul and Judy Karasik (2003). *The ride together: A brother and sister's memoir of autism in the family.* New York: Washington Square Press. In this interesting and touching book, two adult siblings of a man with autism recall the family experiences from early childhood to the present. An interesting aspect of this book is that both siblings do this, but in different ways. Judy writes the text, and Paul presents lengthy comic book-format presentations of their experiences with their brother.

- Dawn Prince-Hughes (Ed.) (2002). *Aquamarine Blue 5: Personal stories of college students with autism.* In this book, college students and university instructors with autism present essays about their academic life, academic abilities and disabilities, and social struggles and successes. Athens, OH: Swallow Press.

- Visit Rage for Order: The Paintings of Jessica Park at **http://www.jessicapark.com/index.html**. This website is dedicated to the life and work of Jessy Park—a young lady with autism who is an exceptional artist. On this website, you can view Jessy's artwork in full color, learn about upcoming art exhibits of her work, and preview the text of *Exiting Nirvana*, a book written by Jessy's mother, Claira Claiborne Park.

 PORTFOLIO ACTIVITIES

1. Interview several pediatricians about the process they use to diagnose a child with autism. Discuss and compare the specific criteria each uses and the medical and educational recommendations he or she gives to parents.

   ✓*Standards* This activity will help students meet CEC Content Standard 2: Development and Characteristics of Learners.

2. Attend a meeting of the Autism Society of America or an autism support group in your area. Talk with its members to identify the range and sources of services available in your area. Compile a list of these local activities, services, and contacts for parents of children with autism.

   ✓*Standards* This activity will help students meet CEC Content Standard 5: Learning Environments and Social Interactions.

3. Observe or participate in an applied behavior analysis or Lovaas training session for individuals who work with young children with autism. Describe how you think the training program does and does not address the specific characteristics of children with autism.

✓Standards This activity will help students meet CEC Content Standard 3: Individual Learning Differences.

4. Identify the services local school districts provide for preschool children with autism. Visit the classrooms or teaching sessions for each type of program and compare them. How do they differ? Summarize each program you observe and discuss which ones you would recommend to parents and why.

   ✓Standards This activity will help students meet CEC Content Standard 4: Instructional Strategies.

5. Visit a secondary school program that includes adolescents with autism. Map out the range of skills being instructed for each student with autism in the areas of communication, social skills, work skills, and academic skills.

   ✓Standards This activity will help students meet CEC Content Standard 5: Learning Environments and Social Interaction.

 To access an electronic portfolio template for these activities, visit our text website through http://www.education. college.hmco.com/students/.

Children with Communication Disorders

9

Outline

Terms and Definitions
  Communication
  Language
  Speech
Language Development
  Language Acquisition
  Speech Production
Types and Characteristics of
    Communication Disorders
  Language Disorders
  Speech Disorders
  Dialects and Language
    Differences
  Hearing Loss
Causes of Communication
    Disorders
  Prevalence
  Recognizing Risk for
    Language Disorders
Teaching Strategies and
    Accommodations
  Assessment
  Placement and Service
    Options
  Strategies for Working with
    Students with Communi-
    cation Learning Needs
  Members of the
    Collaborative Team
SUMMARY
KEY TERMS
USEFUL RESOURCES
PORTFOLIO ACTIVITIES

Learning Objectives

After reading this chapter, the reader will be able to:

- Understand and articulate the definitions of communication, language, and speech, and the relationships among those terms

- Define and describe the major categories of speech disorders in school-age children

- Define and describe language impairment in school-age children, and its relationship to school learning

- Describe an array of teaching strategies for children with communication disorders

- Appreciate the roles of members of the interdisciplinary team working with the student with communication disorders

Most of you reading this book are highly verbal individuals. You know how to change your communicative style to talk in different ways to different people in different situations. You know that talking to a toddler and talking to the school principal require distinct communicative styles. You can express a wide range of meanings, often in subtle ways, take your turn at speaking in all the many different situations you experience in a day, manage the flow and direction of conversations with both familiar and less familiar conversational partners, and fix breakdowns in understanding when they happen—for example, by asking for clarification. When it comes to reading and writing, you know how to read differently for different purposes—you can skim the newspaper versus reading a textbook—and you know what to do when you don't understand what you have read. You also know how to write for different purposes and audiences, how to adjust your style and form of writing for the occasion, and how to revise your meanings when you think they may not be clear to the reader. You are effective communicators. For you, communicating with others, either orally or through print, is relatively easy—at least in your native language.

Yet you have probably experienced difficulty in communication—the "fear and trembling" that can happen when a professor calls on you in class to answer a question, the frustration of having your speaking turn taken away when someone interrupts you, the inability to make sense of what you are reading, or the essay returned with a poor grade because the main ideas have not been communicated well.

Those who have experienced some disruption in the development and use of oral communication can experience similar difficulties every day, difficulties also reflected in their reading, writing, and spelling. Communication problems are common to many exceptional students studied in this book, such as those with mental retardation, learning disabilities, or behavioral and emotional disorders. For example, communication issues are at the core of autism, and students with a severe hearing loss or a physical disability may have difficulty acquiring effective oral communication skills.

The group of students emphasized in this chapter are different from other exceptional students. Most of them have normal sensory and motor functioning and normal intellectual potential. Their primary disability involves the communication process; however, their problems with communication are often subtle. In the following sections we'll examine the components of communication, language, and speech, and their development, and then look at how teachers work with students with communication disorders.

Terms and Definitions

Communication, language, and *speech* are related terms. Since they constitute the foundation for teaching and learning in school, we will examine their meaning more closely.

Communication

Communication is the exchange of ideas, information, thoughts, and feelings (McCormick, Loeb, & Schiefelbusch, 2003). It involves two or more people interactively sending and receiving messages. Communication has many purposes, and its power cannot be overestimated: "No matter how one may try, one cannot *not* communicate. Activity or inactivity, words or silence all have message value: they influence others and these others, in turn, cannot *not* respond to

We communicate— exchange ideas—through listening, speaking, reading, and writing.

Communication does not always involve speech. This nonverbal boy is learning to make a choice by pointing to a picture of his preference. Pictures are linked to the real objects to ensure that he understands the link. (© Bob Daemmrich Photo, Inc.)

these communications and are thus themselves communicating" (Watlawick, Beavin, & Jackson, 1967, p. 49).

We usually think of communication occurring through speaking, listening, reading, and writing. But it's important to think of communication as more than words. Don't people communicate with their clothing, their movement, and their facial expressions? Don't pets communicate to their owners when they are hungry or hurt? Even students with disabilities who lack the ability to speak express themselves in some way, as we will see in Chapter 12. Figure 9.1 displays some of the types of communication.

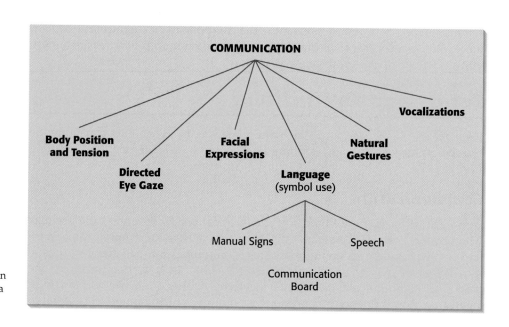

Figure 9.1

Types of Communication

Source: M. Diane Klein, Division of Special Education, California State University, Los Angeles.

Language

Language is the verbal system by which human beings communicate. As a system, it is bound by rules. Linda McCormick writes that "languages are abstract systems with rules governing the sequencing of their basic units (sounds, morphemes, words, sentences) and rules governing meaning and use" (2003a, p. 2). So different languages have different rules—of sequence, or order; of meaning; and of the ways language is used. For example, in Spanish adjectives usually come after nouns. For example, in English we say "I like hot food." In Spanish: "Me gusta comida caliente," which, translated word for word, is "I like food hot." If a student's first language is American Sign Language (ASL), he or she may omit articles (such as *a* and *the*), which are infrequently used in ASL, when using English. The rules of the first language of a student in your classroom will likely influence the way he or she she learns English.

So an important feature of language is that it is rule-governed. This means that patterns of regularity exist in the form or structure of language, or what is often called its *grammar*. For example, if you were asked to complete the following sentence: "Here is a bik; here are two _____," you would most likely respond *biks*, demonstrating your knowledge of language as ordered by rules (Berko, 1958). Linguists describe five interrelated components of language, each having a rule system: (1) **phonology**: phonological rules govern how we combine **phonemes**, the smallest units of sound that carry meaning, in permissible ways to form words; (2) **morphology**: morphological rules tell us how word meaning may be changed by adding or deleting **morphemes**—prefixes, suffixes, and other forms that specifically indicate tense and number, such as *-ed* to mark the past tense (miss*ed*) and *-s* to mark the plural form (dog*s*); (3) **syntax**: syntactic rules govern how words may be combined to form sentences; (4) **semantics**: semantic rules specify how language users create and understand the meaning of words and word combinations (McCormick, 2003a); and (5) **pragmatics**: pragmatic rules indicate how to use language appropriately within a social context in order to achieve some goal. Pragmatic goals might include finding information, fulfilling a need, or sharing a thought. All speakers of a language share the knowledge of how to use language in accord with the social rules of their speech community. Shared communication, called conversation or **discourse**, has specific rules for taking turns, responding appropriately, and managing topics. Figure 9.2 depicts the interrelationship of the primary components of language: They can be addressed separately but are interrelated.

We communicate verbally through language.

The form or structure of language is its grammar.

Rules of grammar have phonological, morphological, and syntactic components.

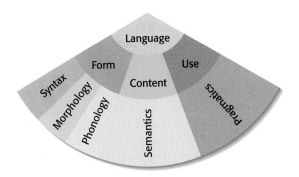

Figure 9.2

Components of Language

Source: From Robert E. Owens, Jr., *Language development: An introduction* Fifth Edition, © 2001. Published by Allyn and Bacon, Boston, MA. Copyright © 2001 by Pearson Education. Reprinted by permission of the publisher.

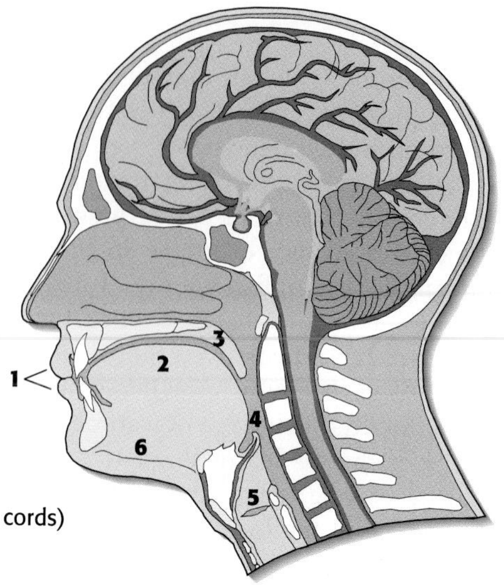

Figure 9.3

Structures of the
Speech Mechanism

1 Lips
2 Tongue
3 Soft palate (velum)
4 Pharynx
5 Larynx (contains vocal cords)
6 Jaw

Speech

Speech is the oral com-
ponent of the language
system.

Speech involves the physical action of orally producing words. It is a product of complex, well-coordinated muscular activity from respiration to phonation to articulation. Just to say "pop," for example, requires a hundred muscles coordinating their work at a speed of fifteen speech sounds per second (Haynes, Moran, & Pindzola, 1990). Figure 9.3 shows the structures of the speech mechanism, and begins to give us an idea of how complex speech is. Every language uses a set of sounds, or phonemes, from a larger set of all possible sounds. Languages do not all have the same number of phonemes. English uses approximately forty to forty-five phonemes. (For example, when you pronounce the letter "b," you use two phonemes: *b* and *ee*.)

Language Development

The next few pages cover very briefly what other books spend hundreds of pages explaining and discussing—the process of normal language development. Obviously, there is much more to learn about this subject than we can present here. If you have not learned this material through another course or your own reading, we have provided additional resources on normal language and speech development at the end of this chapter. The following brief overview provides the foundation for our understanding of communication disorders, which occur when language and speech do *not* develop as expected.

In about one thousand days, from birth to age 3, most children develop initial competence as oral communicators. How do children acquire communication skills so rapidly? What kinds of experiences must they have in order to learn to speak? How is their developing knowledge organized? How and why does this knowledge change during their school years? Theories of communication acquisition attempt to address these vital questions.

Language Acquisition

From the earliest times, humans have expressed curiosity about how language develops. According to Owens (2001),

> Psammetichus I, an Egyptian pharaoh of the seventh century B.C., supposedly conducted a child language study to determine the "natural" language of humans. Two children were raised with sheep and heard no human speech. Needless to say, they did not begin to speak Egyptian or anything else that approximated human language. (p. 31)

The oral communication process is complex, and there is no agreement on a single theory explaining how language develops. Most texts describe variations on four major theories of language development: These are summarized in Table 9.1. Contemporary strategies for teachers reflect a psycholinguistic or social interactional perspective, or a combination of both. Both perspectives stress the active, constructive nature of language learning and the interrelationships among biological, cognitive, social, and linguistic systems (Kamhi, 1992).

Psycholinguistic theories are primarily concerned with mental processes within the child—what goes on inside the child's head. Often, psycholinguists study the child alone. *Social interactional theories* (called *sociolinguistic* in Table 9.1) assume that mental processes originate as social processes and are progressively internalized by the child through interactions with a caregiver or teacher. This conceptual framework emphasizes the interpersonal context in which the

> Most major theories of language acquisition reflect a psycholinguistic and/or a social interaction perspective.

Table 9.1 Four Language Development Models

	Behavioral	**Psycholinguistic-Syntactic**	**Psycholinguistic-Semantic/Cognitive**	**Sociolinguistic**
Language form	Functional units (mands, tacts)	Syntactic units (nouns, verbs)	Semantic units (agents, objects)	Functional units: speech acts (requesting, commenting)
Method of acquisition	Selective reinforcement of correct form	Language-acquisition device (LAD) contains universal phrase structure rules used to decipher the transformational rules of grammar	Universal cognitive structures help child establish nonlinguistic relationships later expressed as semantic relations	Early communication established through which child expresses intentions preverbally; language develops to express early intentions
Environmental input	Reinforcement and extinction; parental modeling	Minimal	Cognitive relationships established through active involvement of child with environment	Communication interaction established first; parental modeling and feedback

Source: From Robert E. Owens, Jr., *Language development: An introduction,* Fifth Edition, © 2001. Published by Allyn and Bacon, Boston, MA. Copyright © 2001 by Pearson Education. Reprinted by permission of the publisher. (Chapter 2 of Owens's book provides a detailed description of each of these theories.)

child participates—how adults support the child as they collaborate to accomplish goals.

Although we do not know exactly how language is acquired, we do know when most children reach developmental milestones. There is variation in the age when individuals achieve these stages, but the process has a pattern and pace common among all languages and cultures. Table 9.2 summarizes five stages of language and communicative development from birth to age 12. For more information about language development, visit ASHA at **http://www. asha.org/speech/development/index.cfm**.

The age boundaries between phases, as well as the ages for the appearance of particular behaviors, represent data that have been compiled from many children and then averaged—so in working with individual children, teachers should use this information only as a general guideline. It's also important to be cautious when applying milestones to children from cultural minority groups, or children who are learning English as a second language, because they have not typically been included in research studies.

You can see from the information in Table 9.2 how swiftly development proceeds during the first three to five years of life. For example, by approximately 12 months, the infant has become a highly social individual and has begun the transition to conventional first words. At 24 months, the child has begun to use two-word sentences, and at 48 months she is using complex utterances. Such rapid learning is possible, in part, because of the typical child's communicative environment. If you are a parent or teacher of a young child, you know that there is almost nothing more interesting in this world than observing language develop! It is estimated that by age 4, in everyday interaction, the average child has been exposed to 20 to 40 million words and has spoken 10 to 20 million words (Chapman et al., 1992). By age 5, the basic system of oral communication has been acquired. This system continues to grow in more sophisticated ways during the school years because it is influenced by two new tools the child learns for thinking and communicating: reading and writing.

> We acquire the basic system of oral communication by age 5, and it forms the foundation for reading and writing.

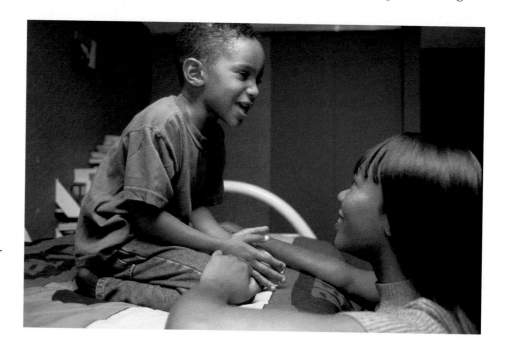

Children with language disorders may have no visible disability. Their challenges arise when they attempt to communicate. (© Richard Lord/The Image Works)

Table 9.2   Overview of Communicative Development: Birth to 12 Years

Age (Months)	Appearances
The examiner (1–6 months)	Responds to human voice; makes pleasure sounds (1 month)
	Produces strings of consonant-vowel or vowel-only syllables; vocally responds to speech of others (3 months)
	Smiles at person speaking to him/her (4 months)
	Responds to name; smiles and vocalizes to image in mirror (5 months)
	Prefers people games, e.g., peek-a-boo, I'm going to get you; explores face of person holding him/her (6 months)
The experimenter (7–12 months)	Recognizes some words; repeats emphasized syllables (8 months)
	"Performs" for family; imitates coughs, hisses, raspberries, etc. (9 months)
	Obeys some directives (10 months)
	Anticipates caregiver's goal and attempts to change it via persuasion/protest (11 months)
	Recognizes own name; engages in familiar routines having visual cues (e.g., bye-bye); uses one or more words (12 months)
The explorer (12–24 months)	Points to toys, persons, animals named; pushes toys; plays alone; begins some make-believe; has 4- to 6-word vocabulary (15 months)
	Begins to use 2-word utterances (combines); refers to self by name; has about 20-word vocabulary; pretends to feed doll, etc. (18 months)
	Enjoys rhyming games; tries to "tell" experiences; understands some personal pronouns; engages in parallel play (21 months)
	Has 200- to 300-word vocabulary; names most common everyday objects; uses some prepositions (*in, on*) and pronouns (*I, me*) but not always accurately; engages in object-specific pretend play and parallel play; can role-play in limited way; orders other around; communicates feelings, desires, interests (24 months)
The exhibitor (3–5 years)	Has 900- to 1000-word vocabulary; creates 3- to 4-word utterances; talks about the "here and now"; talks while playing and takes turns in play; "swears" (3 years)
	Has 1500- to 1600-word vocabulary; asks many questions; uses increasingly complex sentence constructions; still relies on word order for interpretation; plays cooperatively with others; role-plays; recounts stories about recent experiences (narrative recounts); has some difficulty answering *how* and *why* (4 years)
	Has vocabulary of 2100 to 2200 words; discusses feelings; understands *before* and *after* regardless of word order; play is purposeful and constructive; shows interest in group activities (5 years)
The expert (6–12 years)	Has expressive vocabulary of 2600 words while understands 20,000 to 24,000 word meanings; defines by function; has many well-formed, complex sentences; enjoys active games and is competitive; identifies with same sex peers in groups (6 years)
	Verbalizes ideas and problems readily; enjoys an audience; knows that others have different perspectives; has allegiance to group, but also needs adult support (8 years)
	Talks a lot; has good comprehension; discovers he or she may be the object of someone else's perspective; plans future actions; enjoys games, sports, hobbies (10 years)
	Understands about 50,000 word meanings; constructs adultlike definitions; engages in higher-order thinking and communicating (12 years)

Source: From Robert E. Owens, Jr., *Language development: An introduction,* Fifth Edition, © 2001. Published by Allyn and Bacon, Boston, MA. Copyright © 2001 by Pearson Education. Reprinted by permission of the publisher.

Speech Production

During the first 6 months of life, infants primarily produce vowel-like sounds with some glottal and back consonant-like sounds. At about 6 months of age their vocalizations begin to include more consonant-like sounds ("ba-ba-ba"). This stage is called *babbling*. These sounds tend to follow rather predictable patterns of development in all languages (Oller et al., 1976; Oller & Eilers, 1982). Social interactions with caregivers involving imitative vocal play and turn taking, along with developing cognitive capabilities such as increased memory span, play a role in the transition from babbling to speech, along with the increasing fine motor control necessary for phoneme differentiation.

? Pause and Reflect

We don't usually think about how we speak, and how we learn language, but it is the foundation of our work with so many school-aged children who have difficulties learning language—spoken or written. As the language needs of our students become more complex, teachers must know a great deal about how to develop vocabulary and concepts. How do you learn new vocabulary? How can you apply your own strategies to teaching your students? ●

Types and Characteristics of Communication Disorders

The IDEA definition of **communication disorder** is "a . . . disorder such as stuttering, impaired articulation, a language impairment, or a voice impairment that adversely affects a child's educational performance" (*Federal Register*, 1992). Disruptions to the communication process can affect language, speech, or hearing. Language disorders involve a delay in understanding others, participating in conversation, or using language appropriate to the listener or to the situation (ASHA, 1997). Speech disorders include phonological, fluency, and voice impairments. Figure 9.4 shows the relationship among communication disorders, language disorders, and speech disorders. Hearing loss, discussed in depth in the next chapter, also results in difficulties in acquiring and using language and speech.

Language Disorders

Although most children acquire language through natural interactions with the people around them, some do not. Those children experience either language delay (slower development) or language disorders (Fahey, 2000a). The American Speech-Language-Hearing Association (ASHA), the national professional organization for speech-language pathologists and audiologists, defines **language disorder** as

> A language disorder is the impaired comprehension or use of spoken or written language.

> the abnormal acquisition, comprehension, or expression of spoken or written language. The disorder may involve all, one, or some of the phonologic, morphologic, semantic, syntactic, or pragmatic components of the linguistic system. Individuals with language disorders frequently have trouble in sentence processing or in abstracting information meaningfully for storage and retrieval from long-term memory. (ASHA, 1980, pp. 317–318)

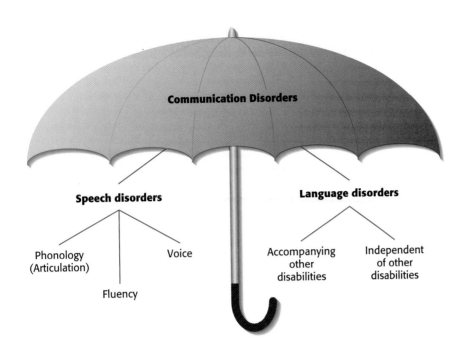

Communication Disorders

Speech disorders

Phonology
(Articulation)

Voice

Fluency

Language disorders

Accompanying
other
disabilities

Independent
of other
disabilities

Figure 9.4

Relationship of Communi-
cation, Language, and
Speech Disorders

Think about the five components of language described earlier—**phonology,
syntax, morphology, semantics,** and **pragmatics** (look at Figure 9.2 again). The
ASHA definition tells us that a language disorder can occur as a result of a problem with one or more of these components. Since they are interrelated, difficulties often occur in combination.

There has been considerable debate among professionals about how to classify children with language disorders (Kamhi, 1998). Should a child receive the
primary label of disability, such as learning disability, autism, or motor disabilities? Certainly, many children who qualify for special education services in those
specific disability areas have significant problems with language, spoken and
written. Or should professionals describe children by the specific area of language
that they have difficulty with—children with syntactical difficulties, for example?
These descriptions would cut across traditional disability areas, but many children do have problems with language that involve more than one specific area.

Polloway and Smith (2000) use a model that describes language disabilities by
degree of severity. Level I is severe language disabilities, and Level II, mild to
moderate language disabilities. Table 9.3 describes those categories in more detail.

For this discussion, we refer to children whose *primary* difficulty is in learning and using language. (The language problems of children with other disabilities will be described in the chapters that focus on specific disabilities.) These
children are sometimes referred to as those with **specific language impairment**
(McCormick, Loeb, & Schiefelbusch, 2003). Their problems with learning and
using language cannot be attributed to another disability—they have no other
apparent problems. Later in their school careers, however, students with specific language impairment are much more likely than children without language
impairments to have difficulties with reading and writing and, therefore, with
school achievement—so they may end up with the label of *learning disability*.
Table 9.4 describes some of the language problems associated with specific language impairment. Remember, in real life children do not appear in neat little

One way to classify
language disorders is by
level of severity.

Most students with a
specific language impedi-
ment do not have other
major disabilities.

Table 9.3 A General Model for Classification of Language Disabilities

Level I: Severe Language Disabilities
- A. Absence of language
- B. Nonspontaneous acquisition of language
- C. Severe language delay or distortion

Level II: Mild to Moderate Language Disabilities
- A. Oral language delay
- B. Oral language disorders
- C. Written language disorders
    1. Reading disabilities
    2. Graphic disabilities
    3. Expressive disabilities

Source: E. A. Polloway & Tom E. C. Smith (2000). *Language instruction for students with disabilities* (2nd ed.), p. 38. Denver: Love Publishing Company.

chapters as they do in this book. Their characteristics and needs are much more complex and challenging than the "categorical approach" we use here might suggest. Most current evidence supports the concept that students with language disorders follow the normal pattern of development, but more slowly and over a longer period of time (Bashir & Scavuzzo, 1992).

A language disorder involves difficulty *using* spoken language—that is, **expressive language**—and sometimes, *understanding* other people's spoken language—**receptive language**. If such problems persist (and longitudinal studies of preschool children with language delay have found that 28 to 75 percent of these children continue to have speech and language problems during the school-age years [Scarborough & Dobrich, 1990]), it is understandable that these students also have difficulty reading and writing. More than 50 percent of children with language disorders manifest significant problems with academic achievement over the course of their school careers (Nelson, 1998). This evidence suggests that, despite special education services, a substantial number of children will not catch up with their peers. In other words, a language disorder is usually an ongoing condition that persists into adulthood (Owens, Metz, & Haas, 2003).

● *The Link Between Language and Behavior* If you were in a foreign country in which you did not know the language, or the alphabet, but needed food or shelter, what might you do? Some of us would use gestures, or attempt to act out our needs—we would change our behavior in order to communicate, and our actions would communicate for us. This is exactly how researchers believe children without a communication system behave. If they cannot ask for what they need, or express their preferences, or initiate interaction with others, they act in such a way to communicate. They cannot use gestures or signs that represent their needs—after all, gestures and signs are linguistic symbols, too. So as the preschoolers sit down on the rug for "circle time," one boy pinches another on the leg (instead of saying, "Hi"). The little girl whose teacher is absent screams repeatedly (instead of saying, "Where's Mrs. Gonzalez?"). Sometimes, the function of the behavior is communication.

Table 9.4 Language Difficulties Associated with Specific Language Impairment	
Language Dimension	**Difficulties**
Phonology	Failure to capitalize on regularities across words
	Slow development of phonological processes
	Unusual errors across sound categories
Morphology/syntax	Co-occurrence of more mature and less mature forms
	Fewer lexical categories per sentence than peers
	More grammatical errors than peers
	Slow development of grammatical morphemes
	Many pronoun errors
Semantics	Delayed acquisition of first words
	Slower rate of vocabulary acquisition
	Less diverse repertoire of verb types
Pragmatics	Intent not signaled through linguistic means
	Difficulty gaining access into conversations
	Less effective at negotiating disputes
	Less use of the naming function
	Difficulty tailoring the message to the listener
	Difficulty repairing communication breakdowns

Source: From L. McCormick, D. F. Loeb & R. L. Schiefelbusch, (2003). *Supporting children with communication difficulties in inclusive settings: School-based language intervention.* Published by Allyn and Bacon, Boston, MA. Copyright © 1997 by Pearson Education. Reprinted by permission of the publisher.

We discussed the link between behavior and communication in Chapter 7, but it bears reiterating as we discuss students with language disorders. Communication is our way of controlling our environment. Without that means of control, students may behave inappropriately in an attempt to have an impact, and end up being considered "a behavior problem."

The link between communication and behavior has an important link with intervention. The field of **functional behavior analysis** has evolved as a means of designing interventions for students with communication and behavior problems based on that link. If a student behaves inappropriately, and we can determine the **communicative intent** of his or her behavior, perhaps we can substitute a more appropriate behavior—a picture card or another form of communication—for the undesirable one.

Speech Disorders

● *Phonological Disorders* Children with speech disorders may have difficulties performing the neuromuscular movements of speech as well as problems in the underlying conceptual knowledge of the sound system and the rules for its use. Speech problems can be described by their primary characteristics:

articulation, fluency, or voice (Fahey, 2000b). *Articulation* is the accurate and clear production of sounds within words. Educators would probably identify **phonological disorders** (formerly referred to as **articulation disorders**), which are problems in understanding and using the sound system, as the most common communication problem seen during the elementary years. Phonological difficulties are not unusual in children having difficulties in learning to read. They may interfere with the establishment of letter-sound relationships in reading and spelling (McCormick & Loeb, 2003). It is important to realize, though, that what appears to be a disorder may just be a normal difference in a child's rate of mastering certain phonological processes, particularly when the child is under 5 years old (Haynes et al., 1990).

Normally developing children simplify adult speech so that they may acquire it. For example, they often simplify the production of a multisyllabic word (such as *nana* for *banana*). Another common process is simplifying two consonants produced together (such as *pin* for *spin*). Other pronunciation errors include addition, omission, substitution, and distortion of phonemes. These processes are developmentally natural and are eventually discarded as the child becomes more skilled with the phonological system of the language.

Whether a child has a phonological disorder is determined by two factors: (1) whether the child is making phonological errors far longer than normal, and (2) whether the errors themselves are unusual; that is, they are not seen in normally developing children at any age. If a child's speech characteristics are embarrassing or lead to teasing from classmates, or if you are uncertain about whether a child has a phonological disorder, consulting with your school speech-language pathologist will help you come to a decision about whether to take action.

● *Fluency Disorders* **Fluency disorder** is a broad term that describes interruptions in the flow of speaking (ASHA, 1993a). The most familiar fluency disorder is **stuttering**. The primary symptoms of stuttering are excessive sound, syllable, and word repetitions, and sound prolongations and pauses. A child who stutters may also display a visible or audible struggle when talking.

In the past, it was believed that stuttering was a learned behavior: Children were conditioned to stutter because of stress in their environment. Today that explanation has been largely abandoned, for two reasons. First, there is substantial evidence of genetic transmission (Yairi, 1998). Second, in many children who stutter, their fluent productions of speech, as well as their disfluent productions, are characterized by brief but subtle malfunctioning of the laryngeal muscles (Conture, 1990). Some children go on to develop more severe forms of stuttering and clearly need treatment, whereas the stuttering of others—almost three-fourths of early stutterers (Lue, 2001)—does not progress in severity and resolves with or without treatment.

Because the onset of stuttering most typically occurs in the preschool to early elementary years, teachers need to know that referral to a speech-language pathologist is essential for appropriate diagnosis and the development of an intervention plan. Conture (1990) recommends that therapy begin immediately when (1) two or more sound prolongations are produced per every ten instances of stuttering; (2) eye gaze is averted more than 50 percent of the time when the child is in the speaker role; and (3) delayed phonological development is also present (see the accompanying Teaching Strategies box entitled, "Help for the Child Who Stutters"). Two organizations provide support and resources

The most common type of speech disorder is a phonological (articulation) disorder.

Fluency disorders are interruptions in the flow of speaking, such as stuttering.

Stuttering usually starts in the preschool or early elementary years.

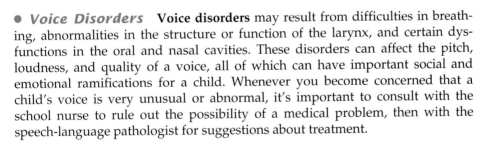

Teaching Strategies & Accommodations

Help for the Child Who Stutters

Teachers should:

- Refer the child suspected of stuttering to the speech-language pathologist
- Create relaxed communication environments for the child who stutters
- Reduce the pressure to communicate
- Slow down their rate of speech
- Discuss teasing with the child and the class
- Be willing to talk to the child, the speech-language specialist, and family members about stuttering

Teachers should *not:*

- Assume that a child's stuttering will go away
- Directly address the behaviors that the child uses to attempt to hide his or her stuttering

- Interrupt or finish the child's sentences
- Instruct the child to slow down, think before speaking, or just spit it out
- Assume a child is stuttering to gain attention
- React with alarm to speech blocks or repetitions
- Assume that a child who stutters has additional speech, language, or learning problems

Sources: D. F. Williams (1999). The child who stutters: Guidelines for the educator. *Young Exceptional Children, 2*(3), 9–14; and R. E. Cook, M. D. Klein, & A. Tessier (2000). *Adapting early childhood curricula for children in inclusive settings* (6th ed.). Englewood Cliffs, NJ: Merrill.

for people who stutter, their families, and teachers. They are the Stuttering Foundation of America at **www.stutteringhelp.org** and the National Stuttering Association at **www.nsastutter.org**.

● *Voice Disorders* **Voice disorders** may result from difficulties in breathing, abnormalities in the structure or function of the larynx, and certain dysfunctions in the oral and nasal cavities. These disorders can affect the pitch, loudness, and quality of a voice, all of which can have important social and emotional ramifications for a child. Whenever you become concerned that a child's voice is very unusual or abnormal, it's important to consult with the school nurse to rule out the possibility of a medical problem, then with the speech-language pathologist for suggestions about treatment.

> Voice disorders can affect the pitch, loudness, or quality of a voice.

Dialects and Language Differences

Not all speech differences are disorders. Other kinds of pronunciation differences may be dialect-related. A **dialect** is "a variation of a symbol system used by a group of individuals that reflects and is determined by shared regional, social, or cultural/ethnic factors. A regional, social, or cultural/ethnic variation of a symbol system should *not* be considered a disorder of speech or language" (ASHA, 1993a, p. 41). For example, one of the more common dialects in the United States is African American English (AAE). AAE includes not only the

> A dialect is a regional, social, or cultural variation of a symbol system; it is not a speech disorder.

spoken word, but also nonverbal factors such as body language, use of personal space, body movement, eye contact, narrative sequence, and modes of discourse (Terrell & Jackson, 2002). A dialect is *not* a communication disorder, but teachers need to be aware of how dialects are used in their students' communities to prevent misidentifying a language difference as a disorder. Teachers also need to be aware of dialects in order to recognize when a speech or language problem coexists with a dialect. Children's use of English will reflect the characteristics of their cultural and ethnic communities. Table 9.5 describes some of those differences in the use of English. We believe, along with many in the scholarly community (for example, Gee, 1990; Reid, 2000), that schools must build understanding in their students about the relationships between the home dialect and Standard American English in a respectful context. Ideally, our students will become fluent "code-switchers" who are able to move back and forth between the dialect of their native community and Standard American English.

Hearing Loss

The normal processing of spoken language is through hearing. Children with hearing loss frequently have significant communication problems; we will discuss hearing loss in greater detail in Chapter 10.

Pause and Reflect

As you might have discerned from your reading in this chapter up to this point, communication is a tremendously complex human process, and communication disorders are varied and multifaceted. This is also one of the most jargon-laden topics we cover in this book, and no doubt you are struggling to comprehend some of the terminology, if it is new to you. So let's make it more personal. Do you think you know someone with a communication disorder, or have you experienced one yourself? How do you think it feels to be unsure about such a basic human function as speech or language? ●

Causes of Communication Disorders

A number of communication disorders have known causes. In some cases, they are associated with genetic disorders such as congenital hearing impairment, fragile-X syndrome, or cleft palate and other structural malformations.

Communication disorders may have a genetic, physical, or environmental cause.

Other communication disorders appear to be caused by a range, and sometimes a mix, of biological and environmental factors (Downey et al., 2002). For example, maternal substance abuse affects fetal brain development and can result in delayed speech and language development. Head trauma and child abuse and neglect are also associated with communication disorders (Fahey, 2000a). Multiple factors may play a role in conditions such as autism, stuttering, and language disabilities, which "run in families, affect more boys than girls, and are found in identical twins" (ASHA, 1991, p. 21). However, specific genes for language or speech

In general, it is difficult to pinpoint the cause of a communication disorder.

have not been identified (Pembrey, 1992), and in many cases the causes of children's speech and language disorders are not clear or are unknown. That is the

Table 9.5 Contrasting Cultural Conventions in the Use of English

	Black English	Asian Speakers of English	Standard American English	Hispanic English
Morphological and Syntactical Components				
Plural *s* marker	Nonobligatory use of marker *s* with numerical quantifier. *I see two dog playing. I need ten dollar. Look at the dogs.*	Omission of plural marker *s* or overregulation. *I see two dog. I need ten dollar. I have two sheeps.*	Obligatory use of marker *s* with a few exceptions. *I see two dogs. I need ten dollars. I have two sheep.*	Nonobligatory use of marker *s*. *I see two dog playing. I have two sheep.*
Past tense	Nonobligatory use of *ed* marker. *Yesterday, I talk to her.*	Omission of *ed* marker or overregulation. *I talk to her yesterday. I sawed her yesterday.*	Obligatory use of *ed* marker. *I talked to her yesterday.*	Nonobligatory use of marker *ed*. *I talk to her yesterday.*
Pragmatic Components				
Rules of conversation	Interruption is tolerated. The most assertive person has the floor.	Children are expected to be passive; are discouraged from interrupting teachers; are considered impolite if they talk during dinner.	Appropriate to interrupt in certain circumstances. One person has the floor until point is made.	Official or business conversations may be preceded by lengthy introductions.
Eye contact	Indirect eye contact during listening. Direct eye contact during speaking denotes attentiveness and respect.	May not maintain eye contact with authority figure but may make eye contact with strangers. May avert direct eye contact and giggle to express embarrassment.	Indirect eye contact during speaking. Direct eye contact during listening denotes attentiveness and respect.	Avoidance of direct eye contact is sometimes a sign of respect and attentiveness. Maintaining eye contact may be considered a challenge to authority.

Source: V. Ratner & L. Harris (1994). *Understanding language disorders.* Eau Claire, WI: Thinking Publications.

case for the majority of children described in this chapter—particularly those with specific language impairment, or language difficulties not caused by any other disability or condition.

Prevalence

The federal government uses the label "speech or language impairments" to describe the students we are discussing in this chapter. The *Twenty-fourth Annual Re-*

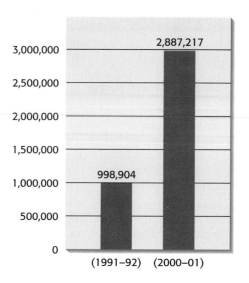

Figure 9.5

Growth in Number of Stu-
dents with Speech or Lan-
guage Impairments Served
Under IDEA, 1991–2001

Source: U S. Department of Education (2002). Twenty-fourth
Annual Report to Congress on
the Implementation of the Individuals with Disabilities Education Act. Washington, D.C.: U.S.
Department of Education.

port to Congress on the Implementation of the Individuals with Disabilities Education Act
(2002) reported that 1,093,808 children ages 6 through 21 were served by federally
funded programs in this category during the 2000–2001 school year, making this
the second-largest group of students served in special education programs. Only
the category of specific learning disabilities is larger. Figure 9.5 shows the growth
in the number of students served in this category over a nine-year period.

Recognizing Risk for Language Disorders

Teachers are often the first professionals to encounter children whose patterns
of language development place them at risk for subsequent academic and social
failure. Because you, as a future teacher, will have this unique "gatekeeping"
role, it is important to know what patterns may indicate risk at different points
in a child's school career. In the next sections, we discuss significant stages in
language development and identifiable risk indicators.

● *Preschool Years*   Under IDEA, many states now provide programs for
infants and toddlers who are at risk developmentally. If you are an early childhood education teacher, you will encounter very young children who appear to
have significant delays in the development of language and communication.
Some of these children may be late talkers (by definition, "late talker" refers to
delayed onset of speech). Late talkers usually improve in vocabulary between 2
and 3 and have normal language skills by age 5 or 6, but they may be more
likely to have reading and spelling weaknesses at ages 8 and 9 (Rescorla, 2002).
Others may have a **language delay**—delayed development in all areas of language. The child with language delay may have greater difficulties understanding what is being said, describing events, having conversations, and articulating
sounds, and may be less likely to use meaningful gestures for communicating
(ASHA, 2003; Owens, 2004). Discriminating between young children who are
late talkers and those with language delay—which may be categorized as specific language impairment as the child gets older—is a complex process, usually
requiring the expertise of a speech-language pathologist. Which category do
you think the following little girl would fall into?

Case Study
Darla is 2½, and she has not yet started to use any recognizable words. She is usually bright-eyed and cheerful, but lately she has begun to become frustrated easily and have frequent tantrums. Her parents are frustrated too, since Darla does not follow their simple requests and commands ("Come here," "Stand up," for example). Darla repeats sounds as she plays, and screams to get attention, but often her family cannot figure out what Darla wants. Her parents have come to their pediatrician for help.

It's true that there isn't enough information in this brief description for you to conclude much. But because Darla does not seem to understand what is said to her (in other words, she has poor receptive language), and is not pointing to what she wants (not using nonverbal forms of communication), it may be that she has a language delay. In any case, the safe path is for her pediatrician to refer Darla's parents for a speech and hearing evaluation.

As a teacher who may serve young children and their families, your understanding of risk for language delay becomes essential for effective early identification and intervention. Currently in the Los Angeles Unified School District, the second largest in the nation, language delay is the most common reason for referring children to early childhood special education services. At a national level, 55 percent of preschoolers receiving special education services are categorized with a speech or language impairment, making it the most prevalent disability category for children aged 3 through 5 (U.S. Department of Education, 2002). It is a serious problem, and early childhood teachers can play a key role in obtaining help for young children.

> Speech and language impairments are the most common reason for young children to be referred for special education services.

● *Kindergarten and the Early School Years* The profile of a language disorder changes over time. As children reach school age, patterns of difficulty can emerge that often involve learning to read and write. At this point, children with language disorders are often "relabeled" as learning disabled, or even as having emotional or behavioral disorders (Nelson, 1998). Again, teacher awareness of who may now be at risk is vital to assist children to remain in the general education setting whenever possible.

ASHA describes children with language disorders at school age as follows:

Children with communication disorders frequently perform at a poor or insufficient academic level, struggle with reading, have difficulty understanding and expressing language, misunderstand social cues, avoid attending school, show poor judgment, and have difficulty with tests.

Difficulty in learning to listen, speak, read, or write can result from problems in language development. Problems can occur in the production, comprehension, and awareness of language at the sound, syllable, word, sentence, and discourse levels. Individuals with reading and writing problems also may experience difficulties in using language strategically to communicate, think, and learn. ("Helping Children with Communication Disorders in the Schools: Speaking, Listening, Reading, & Writing" is available at **http://www.ASHA.org**.)

The issue of identification of language problems in kindergarten and the early school years is complicated when children enter school as English-language learners. It takes an experienced teacher with knowledge of the child's home language—often in consultation with a speech-language specialist—to determine whether the child's language problem exists in both the native language and in English. Only if the difficulty exists in both languages is there reason for concern.

● *Phonological Awareness as a Risk Indicator*   How does a teacher recognize risk for language and learning problems in these early school years? One important indicator is the child's ease in acquiring **phonological awareness**, or the ability to identify and manipulate phonemes, the sounds of language (Fitzsimmons, 1998). This ability is critical to emerging literacy.

Phonological awareness is the ability to recognize that words consist of sounds.

Phonological awareness is the child's explicit awareness that words consist of sounds, or phonemes (Snow, Burns, & Griffin, 1998). It is an aspect of **metalinguistic awareness**—the child's developing knowledge of his or her use of language, spoken and written. When we consciously analyze and compare the sound structure of words or the meaning of words and sentences in either oral or written language, we are using metalinguistic strategies for thinking critically about language. A strong connection exists between aspects of oral language development and the word-recognition skills necessary for learning to read (decode) and spell. In fact, in kindergarten, the best predictor of learning to read in first grade is a child's level of phonological awareness (Scarborough, 2001).

Metalinguistic awareness is the ability to think about language.

Children who are less sensitive to the sound structure of their language may also have a less-well-developed vocabulary, because words consist of collections of phonemes. During the early school years, despite experience with reading, these same children may encounter persistent problems in learning new vocabulary words. Most likely, they will also have serious difficulties with phonics approaches that require breaking words into their phonemic parts (for example, "What sound does *dish* begin with?" or "How many sounds does *fish* have?") and blending the parts into a whole. Difficulty with phonemic segmentation and blending will also affect the ability to engage in more advanced ma-

Teaching Strategies & Accommodations

Developing Phonological Awareness

● Beginning at the preschool level, teachers can integrate phonological awareness activities in meaningful ways by using children's literature that plays with the sounds in language, for example, through nursery rhymes and word games, and only then moving to judgments about sound similarities and differences (Catts, 1991b; Blachman, 1991a, 1991b; Griffith & Olson, 1992).

● A variety of writing experiences offers children rich opportunities to pay attention in a deliberate way to each letter in a word as they or the teacher actually write words (Treiman, 1993).

● All children need to show the developmental evidence that they can consistently engage in these earlier phonological awareness activities before explicit instruction in phoneme segmentation and blending is introduced.

● Finally, following mastery of segmentation and blending, children should be introduced to letter-sound correspondences.

nipulations of the phonological code, such as deleting, adding, or reversing phonemes, and in managing conventional spellings (Catts, 1991b; Ehri, 1989).

Research tells us that all students should have explicit instruction in phonological awareness to maximize success with word recognition in both reading and spelling (Snow, Burns, & Griffin, 1998). (For ideas, see the Teaching Strategies box entitled, "Developing Phonological Awareness.") Some forms of reading failure may be avoided if students are given explicit instruction in phonological awareness, and the instruction follows a developmental sequence.

> Reading fluency may be jeopardized by difficulties with phonological awareness.

❓ *Pause and Reflect*

The relationship between speaking, reading, writing, and listening is complex—most of us have strengths in one or another of those areas. Think about how life would be if one of those strengths was taken from you! What kind of accommodations would you need if you were not able to speak or communicate clearly? ●

Teaching Strategies and Accommodations

Assessment

Before teaching comes assessment—the process we use to determine who qualifies for services, and what will be taught.

● *Assessment for Identification of Communication Disorders*
Identification of students who are at educational risk for a speech or language disorder often begins with a concerned teacher or parent. Once the teacher has voiced that concern to the speech-language pathologist (SLP), he or she provides the teacher with prereferral criteria to guide their observation of the student in the general education classroom prior to the formal referral for a suspected language disorder. For an example of a prereferral form, see Figure 9.6.

In most educational settings, the speech-language pathologist has primary responsibility for the identification, assessment, and treatment of students with communication disorders. When classroom teachers and speech-language pathologists work collaboratively, they are more likely to serve the best interests of children with speech and language problems. (For more information about a career in speech-language pathology, see the Closer Look box entitled, "Collaboration: Who Is the Speech-Language Pathologist?".)

Speech-language pathologists do not engage in medical or psychological diagnoses. However, they do have the professional and ethical responsibility to (1) determine what may have caused the onset and development of the problem; (2) interpret whether other causal factors, such as the language demands of the classroom, may contribute to the maintenance of a speech or language problem; and (3) clarify the problem for a student and the family and counsel them appropriately (Luterman, 2001). Identifying causes may not be possible given the many factors that can influence the changing profile of a language disorder. Moreover, knowing that an initial cause, such as a birth injury or fetal alcohol syndrome, is related to the communication problem is not always useful for planning meaningful intervention for individual students—it doesn't affect the child's treatment.

> The speech-language pathologist identifies, assesses, and treats students with communication disorders.

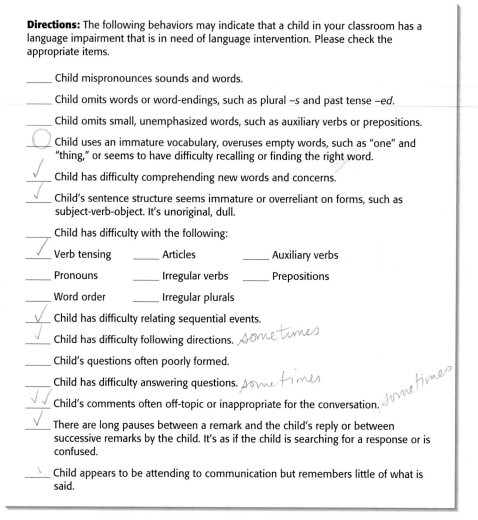

Figure 9.6

Prereferral Form: Identifying Children with Language Problems

Source: From Robert E. Owens, Jr. *Language disorders: A functional approach to assessment and intervention,* Third Edition, © 1999. Published by Allyn and Bacon, Boston, MA. Copyright © 1999 by Pearson Education. Reprinted by permission of the publisher

Assessment is an on-going, evolving process.

Regardless of the emphasis given to causal factors in assessment, there is common agreement that assessment is not a one-time snapshot of a student at a particular point in time. It is a portrait that continuously evolves because it incorporates diagnostic information with new information obtained from the ongoing monitoring of progress. Teachers, families, and speech-language pathologists should work together to paint that ongoing portrait.

Assessment of Students from Language Minority Backgrounds   The identification, assessment, and intervention for a language problem when a child comes from a non–English-speaking background is complicated—the example of Jesy in the Closer Look box entitled "Language Delay in Young Children" suggests just how complicated. As we described in Chapter 1, there is great concern among scholars and specialists that there is considerable misdiagnosis and overdiagnosis of such children (Artiles & Ortiz, 2002). In order to diminish the possibility of misidentification, a bilingual professional must conduct a careful assessment with children from language minority backgrounds in order to determine whether a language problem exists in the child's native language as well as in English. Only when the problem crosses both languages is it consid-

A Closer Look

Collaboration: Who Is the Speech-Language Pathologist?

Speech-language pathologists in the schools are members of the educational team. Their traditional role has been to be the "expert" specialist who serves students in special education with speech, language, or hearing problems. This service has typically been provided outside of the classroom in a pullout model of service delivery. Today, the speech-language pathologist's role is changing from one of outside expert to a truer educational partnership with both general and special education teachers. Because you are likely to work with these professionals, it's helpful to know about their background and training.

Speech-language pathologist is a professional title. Individuals holding this title must meet a number of academic and clinical requirements established by the American Speech-Language-Hearing Association (ASHA). This national organization is the professional, scientific, and credentialing body for more than 74,000 speech-language pathologists and audiologists. Approximately 45 percent of speech-language pathologists work in schools.

The professional credential is the Certificate of Clinical Competence (CCC). To be eligible for the CCC in either speech-language pathology (CCC-SLP) or audiology (CCC-A), individuals must have a master's or doctoral degree from an academic institution with an educational program accredited by ASHA.

In addition to these ASHA requirements for certification, forty-three states currently require licensing of speech-language pathologists and audiologists, similar to licensing for physicians and nurses. Licensure laws vary from state to state and are different from teacher certification. Many states have continuing education requirements as well to maintain the professional license.

The ASHA code of ethics states that only individuals who have the CCC, or are in the process of obtaining this certificate by working under an ASHA-certified supervisor, should practice speech-language pathology or audiology. However, to work in the public schools, a number of states require only a bachelor's degree in communication disorders, combined in some instances with teacher certification. Most states also require that, to continue working in the schools, a master's degree in communication disorders be obtained within a prescribed number of years. In all other settings, such as health-care facilities, the master's degree is the entry-level degree. Continuous efforts are being expended by ASHA and state professional organizations to have the master's degree also be the entry-level degree for school services.

Source: American Speech-Language-Hearing Association (1993). Implementation procedures for the standards for the certificates of clinical competence. *ASHA, 35*(3), 76–83.

---

ered a language delay or disorder; otherwise, the child may simply be a nonfluent user of English. Professionals must take great care not to identify such children with a disability label. There is considerable evidence that this occurs with some frequency (Ortiz & Yates, 2002).

Grace Zamora-Duran and Elba Reyes (1997) urge school professionals to look for "communicative competence" in their English-language learning students. Communicative competence includes the ability to comprehend language as well as to use it in a variety of contexts, including conversation with different speakers and formal and informal speaking. The checklist in Figure 9.7 will help you assess communication competence.

Research makes the strongest possible case that a teacher must have good working knowledge of the language and communication system and its many normal developmental and cultural variations in order to know who should be

A Closer Look   Language Delay in Young Children

Jesy Moreno started school last fall, a lucky recipient of one of the limited public preschool spots in Los Angeles. But one thing immediately set the small boy apart from most of his classmates: At age 4½, Jesy hardly spoke.

He could utter a few words—mostly names of family members—and he understood some of what was said to him. But carrying on a conversation was impossible, and he could not follow the simplest instructions.

There are thousands of youngsters like Jesy in Southern California—children who are not mentally retarded yet enter school lacking rudimentary communication skills in both their home language and English.

Expressed simply: The less children speak, the more limited their comprehension and vocabulary and the harder it is for them to learn to read and write, not to mention navigate the social complexities of school.

Even now, after a year of concentrated effort by his teachers, Jesy cannot count to 10 or name the colors in the classroom's crayon box. When another boy stole the wheels from a truck he had built, Jesy could not find the words to tell the teacher what had happened.

"Tell me, Jesy, what's wrong?" the teacher asked in Spanish, crouching to his level and over-enunciating her words, a practice everyone in the classroom follows with him.

"Ah, ah, *toda llanta,*" he answered haltingly. Um, um, all tire.

A classroom for children with language delays like Jesy's places new demands on a kindergarten teacher accustomed to teaching boisterous youngsters to raise their hands and wait their turn before speaking.

Slowly, the teacher begins coaxing words out of her students, using techniques ranging from songs to sign language. When she talks, she pronounces each word carefully, repeats frequently, then urges the students to answer questions with more than a nod. Every lesson has a hands-on component, every response is recognized.

"I reward every approximation of a word. I started the year with very concrete rewards—stickers on hands—and now I can use mostly verbal rewards," the teacher said.

After they make Lego models during a free play period one morning, the teacher draws them together on the floor and has each describe what they have made.

"What is this?" she prompts one boy. "*Que es esto?*"

"*Un ah-oh,*" he says, clutching an airplane-like structure.

"*Un aeroplano?*" Say "*aeroplano.*"

He tries.

"Good, good. *Muy bien!*"

Although nearly all the students are from Spanish-speaking families, they are taught mostly in English—with translation support from an aide—so they do not have the added burden of trying to learn two languages.

It is unclear whether children like Jesy can "catch up" to others their age through an intensive language-emphasis program. Most researchers agree that there are windows of language acquisition opportunity that, once missed, cannot be recreated.

Yet for Jesy's teachers, such deep concerns evaporated in one moment this spring: He stood at the phonics board in front of his preschool classmates and, with help from the teacher's aide, he slowly pieced together two sound cards—*ta* and *sa.* He stepped back for a moment, considered his creation, then said in a clear voice: "*ta sa . . . tasa*"—cup in Spanish. "Jesy!" the aide and his teacher shouted simultaneously.

Source: Adapted from Amy Pyle (1996). Teaching the silent student. *Los Angeles Times,* June 11, p. 1. Copyright © 1996, Los Angeles Times. Reprinted by permission.

✔	Grammatical	✔	Sociolinguistic	✔	Discourse	✔	Strategic
	Uses noun/verb agreement		Demonstrates various styles of social register in speech, for example, when interacting with peers or adults		Retells an event with attention to sequence		Joins groups and acts as if understands language and activities
	Uses pronouns correctly		Uses diminutives		Explains activity in present or near future		Demonstrates expressive ability
	Uses proper syntax		Uses terms of endearment		Shares experiences spontaneously		Counts on friends for help
	Uses verb tenses appropriately		Uses courtesy, etiquette terms, and titles of respect		Tells stories with personal emphases		Switches language to resolve ambiguities
	Uses dialectical variations		Uses appropriate variations in intonation		Switches language for elaboration		Observes and imitates language patterns
	Uses complex sentence structure				Switches language to clarify statements		Asks for information
					Switches language to experiment with new language		Reads to gain information
							Uses a dictionary
							Asks for repetition
							Takes risks and guesses at language meaning
							Attempts difficult words and constructions

Grammatical: Mastery of lexical items, rules of word and sentence formation, literal meaning, pronunciation, and spelling.
Sociolinguistic: Using language appropriately, in different social contexts, with emphasis on meanings and forms.
Discourse: Using language in an organized and effective manner.
Strategic: Using verbal and nonverbal strategies (such as paraphrasing, gesturing, or switching from Standard American English to a dialect) to enhance the effectiveness of communication and to compensate for breakdowns in communication.

Figure 9.7

Checklist for Skills Illustrating Communicative Competency

Source: G. Zamora-Duran and E. Reyes (1997). From Tests to talking in the classroom: Assessing communicative competence in *Reducing disproportionate representation of culturally diverse students in special and gifted education,* edited by A. J. Artiles and F. Zamora-Duran. Reston, VA: Council for Exceptional Children.

referred (Adger, Snow, & Christian, 2002). A delicate balance exists between failing to refer a child who needs assessment and referring a child who may be wrongly classified as disabled by the referral itself. Many researchers believe that this issue is at the heart of the disproportionate representation of students from non–English-speaking homes in special education services (Artiles & Ortiz, 2002).

● *Approaches to Assessment*　The specific approaches used in traditional language assessment may be determined by special education policies at state or local levels. However, speech-language pathologists generally use a combination of approaches, or tools, for information gathering, which can be classified as standardized (norm-referenced) or nonstandardized (descriptive) (ASHA, 2000). Some of these assessment tools are very useful for teachers as well. Typically, a speech-language pathologist uses some or all of the following assessment tools (ASHA, 2000):

- *Parent/staff/student interviews.* Parents, teachers, and the student can provide rich information on the student's functioning across a variety of settings. Parents can help particularly when the child is very young, or has severe disabilities; teachers can provide information on classroom functioning and peer interactions, and sometimes the student can describe specific problems that he or she faces.

- *Student history.* A review of records, interviews, and observation help professionals to understand background information so they can draw as complete a picture as possible of the student's current status and needs.

- *Checklists and developmental scales.* These tools can help the teacher or speech-language pathologist describe specific types of communication behavior.

- *Curriculum-based assessment.* The "use of curriculum contexts and content for measuring a student's language intervention needs and progress" (Nelson, 1998) can assist the teacher and speech-language pathologist in determining the student's classroom communication performance, particularly as it pertains to reading, writing, and speaking.

- *Dynamic assessment.* These procedures assess what the student is capable of doing with assistance. These approaches may help plan useful interventions (Bain & Olswang, 1995; Pena, Iglesias, & Lidz, 2001).

- *Portfolio assessment.* Defined as a collection of products, such as student work samples, language samples, dictations, writing samples, journal entries, and video/audio recordings, and transcriptions.

- *Observation/anecdotal records.* Observation and recording of communication behaviors by teacher, families, and the speech-language pathologist can be used to determine the *present level of educational performance* for the Individualized Education Program (IEP).

- *Standardized assessment information.* Standardized test results can be useful when a student's performance must be compared to that of his or her peers. ASHA says, "Although all areas of speech, language, and communication are interrelated, broad spectrum, norm-referenced tests may be used to measure such skills of language comprehension and production as syntax, semantics, morphology, phonology, pragmatics, discourse organization, and following directions" (ASHA, 2000, p. III-263).

Remember that standardized tests do not typically generate information that can be used to plan for the student in the classroom. Teachers and speech-language specialists must turn to other types of assessment to generate goals for teaching and learning. They have a professional obligation to be informed test consumers, though—that is, knowledgeable about the proven purposes and limitations of standardized tests.

● *Assessment for Teaching*   The kind of assessments that help teachers plan instruction are the *descriptive* assessments referred to in the paragraphs above—particularly curriculum-based assessment and portfolio assessment, which build on naturally occurring events in the classroom.

Another useful assessment, one based on careful observation, is a **language sample**. Language sampling can provide a picture of the student's current level of communication in the classroom (and in other environments, if samples are collected outside the classroom). During the course of a day, or several days, the teacher records 50–100 utterances of the target student. The utterances must be exactly what the student has said—it's easy to add the correct tense or make a singular a plural, since we tend to "hear" proper usage.

The language sample can provide the teacher with useful information. How long is the student's average utterance? Does the student respond to questions appropriately? What is the nature of the student's vocabulary? Teachers are often surprised by the results of an objective sample, since we usually understand so much more than what the student actually says.

An interesting way to use a language sample is to take two samples—one from a target child with communication problems, and one from a typical child of the same age who communicates effectively. A comparison of the two can help the teacher see where the target child needs to go. See Caroline Bowen's "Structural Analysis of a Language Sample" at **http://www.members.tripod .com/Caroline_Bowen/minisample.htm** for an excerpt from a language sample.

Ecological Assessment   Ecological assessment is based on the concept that the child's behavior (in this case, communication) is shaped by the environment in which he or she finds herself. An experience of mine from my classroom teaching years illustrates this point.

Case Study

In my kindergarten classroom I taught a beautiful little girl named Nancy Lopez. She was hard-of-hearing and came from a Spanish-speaking home. She was extremely sweet and compliant, and she seemed to understand much of what went on in the English-only classroom, but she was very silent. Perplexed, I called her parents in for a conference, and her father came in to speak to me. He brought Nancy's brother with him, and the two children went out to play while the adults talked.

While Mr. Lopez and I were talking, we heard the children playing through an open window. I soon noticed that there was a lot of talking—in Spanish—going on between the brother and sister, and much of it was coming from my sweet and shy little student. Nancy was speaking in long, animated paragraphs as she and her brother laughed and played.

I was mortified. Mr. Lopez must have thought (correctly) that I was incredibly naive. But the experience taught me an unforgettable series of lessons. Among them: it matters who the child is speaking to; it matters where the child is communicating, and, most importantly, the willingness and ability to speak English may be totally unrelated to the child's willingness and ability to speak her native language. Nancy was operating more like an English language learner than a hard-of-hearing child; we soon placed her in the general education kindergarten where she did very well. I provided support to her general education teacher as he needed it.

Table 9.6 Differences Between Ecological Assessment and Traditional Assessment

	Ecological Assessment	Traditional Assessment
Reference	Compares child's performance to the demands and expectations of activities and tasks in the child's environments	Compares child's test performance with that of a sample of similar children who were administered the same test items
Focus	Child's ability to meet setting and task expectations and participate in activities and routines in natural settings	Language forms and structures described in the normal development research as representative of children at the child's age or stage of development
Procedures	Observes the child's behavior in daily activities and interviews with persons who know the child well	Elicits the child's responses to a set of standardized tasks thought to represent major skills/abilities in the area
Assessment context	Natural settings: Assessment team includes parents and peers	Contrived settings: Independent assessments by discipline representatives
Best use of results	To generate individualized goals and objectives and plan special instruction	To determine child's status relative to same-age peers; for diagnosis and determination of eligibility for special education services

Source: From Linda McCormick, Diane F. Loeb, & Richard L. Schiefelbusch, *Supporting children with communication difficulties in inclusive settings: School-based language intervention,* © 2003. Published by Allyn and Bacon, Boston, MA. Copyright © 2003 by Pearson Education. Reprinted by permission of the publisher.

In an ecological assessment, Nancy would have been assessed in the classroom, on the playground, during one-to-one interaction, and, if possible, at home. The assessor would have to be bilingual to do a complete evaluation.

Table 9.6 describes the differences between standardized assessment and ecological assessment. If you're interested in learning more about ecological assessment, see the resources at the end of this chapter.

For the speech-language specialist, the assessment process functions to determine whether a speech or language disorder exists, and, if present, its severity and variability. Eligibility for special education and service options depends on how this evaluation question is answered and whether a diagnostic category, or label, can be assigned, such as speech impairment or language disorder. Although these categories may be global and imprecise, they allow us to understand the commonalities that make up a particular disability and to design assessment and intervention approaches for students who share common symptoms (Nelson, 1998).

> All students benefit when a teacher focuses on language development and expansion.

For the teacher, the assessment should provide a focus for instruction and language use during classroom activities and routines. The great majority of children—those with disability labels as well as the hard-to-find "average" child and those identified as gifted—will benefit from a teacher focus on language assessment and language development (Adger, Snow, & Christian, 2002).

Placement and Service Options

The placement and service options for students with communication disorders are similar to those already discussed in previous chapters, with one exception: an emphasis on the pullout mode of service delivery. Students with speech impairments or language disorders are often removed from the general or special education classroom for one-to-one or small-group treatment.

The thinking behind this service option for language intervention has had a practical basis. In a smaller group setting, the speech-language pathologist can control some of the many variables that affect a student's successful performance in the classroom. On another level, many children can be served, which gives the appearance of cost-effective services but in reality often results in caseloads exceeding 75 to 100 students per week.

The pullout model may not be "best practice" and has been criticized for several reasons (Kamhi, 1993; McCormick, 2003b). First, students' language learning may become increasingly isolated from the natural communication context of the classroom. Second, students tend to be stigmatized even further through their removal from the classroom and may suffer academically from missing important curricular content. Last, because speech-language pathologists were themselves isolated from the classroom and curriculum, teachers too often developed the unrealistic view that pulling students out was a way to "make them better and put them back" (Nelson, 1998). Also, when students leave the classroom, teachers lose the benefit of observing the speech-language pathologist at work, providing a model of language-building for interaction with students.

> The "pullout" model used with students with communication disorders is coming under increasing criticism.

In recent years, the trend has been toward integrated classroom-based services, in which language and communication instruction is provided within the context of daily activities *in the classroom*. When speech and language intervention is provided in the classroom, the general education or special education teacher can collaborate with the speech-language pathologist to provide the most effective intervention program for the child, in the natural setting in which the child will use the skills learned (see the accompanying Teaching Strategies box entitled, "Advantages of Integrated Classroom-Based Speech and Language Intervention").

Teaching Strategies & Accommodations

Advantages of Integrated Classroom-Based Speech and Language Intervention

- The student gains and maintains access to "regular" educational opportunities and learning outcomes.

- Opportunities for team collaboration are maximized, and fragmentation (gaps, overlaps, and/or contradictions) in services is avoided.

- The input and methods of all team members are synthesized as they address a shared vision for the student's participation in social, educational, and vocational settings.

- Skills taught through integrated intervention are likely to generalize because they were learned and practiced in the integrated, natural environments where they need to be used.

Source: From Linda McCormick, Diane F. Loeb, & Richard L. Schiefelbusch, *Supporting children with communication difficulties in inclusive settings: School-based language intervention,* © 2003. Published by Allyn and Bacon, Boston, MA. Copyright © 2003 by Pearson Education. Reprinted by permission of the publisher.

Although integrated, in-classroom intervention may be desirable, in many school districts across the country, students are still being "pulled out" of the classroom for speech and language services. There are many obstacles to changes in practice, and support for this change has come slowly. Professionals in speech-language pathology are currently working to revamp their roles in inclusive school settings, with many suggesting that they become part of an in-classroom intervention team with shared responsibility for student success (Ehren, 2000; Prelock, 2000). Barbara Ehren (2000) describes two major functions for the speech-language pathologist providing in-classroom services:

1. Work with the classroom teacher to make modifications in curriculum, instruction, and assessment so that students with speech and language difficulties can be successful in the general education classroom.

2. Engage the teacher as a partner in the process by enlisting his or her help in practicing new skills, setting new objectives, and assessing progress. (p. 225)

Teachers and speech-language pathologists must advocate for the practices they feel are most productive for their students and for themselves.

Strategies for Working with Students with Communication Learning Needs

Across the United States, but particularly in urban school districts, there is an increasingly large population of students who are English-language learners. Because of our changing population, every teacher should focus on English-language acquisition with his or her students. A focus on language potentially benefits *all* students, from the fifth-grader identified with a learning disability to the newly immigrated seventh-grader from Central America to the academically gifted child of any age. Integrating the teaching of both social and academic language—through listening, speaking, writing, and reading—into daily routines and curriculum may strengthen school learning for every child. Knowledge of language and language development strategies is crucial for all teachers in today's schools, so we can best develop our students' spoken and written language, and as the foundation for literacy instruction (Moats & Lyon, 1996).

● *Integrating Language and Literacy Learning* Focusing on language development in your classroom should lead to improvements in your students' literacy skills, since the two are so closely connected. Several principles of language and literacy learning guide the teacher's focus on classroom language learning:

1. All children naturally learn language through social interaction with adults and peers.

2. Children learn best when they are guided by a "big picture" or theme and when they understand the reasons for learning.

3. Real learning is functional; it is also "messy" because active choice and risk-taking are required.

4. Real learning is challenging and involves cooperating with others.

5. All children are capable of learning; the guiding premise is that the learner's ability to be successful is always the focus of assessment and instruction.

For students with language disorders, these principles mean that the goal for instruction remains one of *enabling communicative competence*. Guided by these principles, the focus of instruction is twofold: to support the student's abilities through the teaching of active "learning-how-to-learn" strategies and to help the student develop more effective communication.

Supporting Classroom Discourse The normal language routines of the classroom are referred to as **classroom discourse**. The most common pattern of classroom discourse is the pattern of *teacher initiation, student response,* and *teacher evaluation* (Falk-Ross, 2002). An example would be:

TEACHER: Who remembers where we left off yesterday?

JEFF: We had just finished the Bill of Rights.

TEACHER: Good Jeff, thank you.

Instructional discourse strategies are the ways in which teachers communicate to students expectations for learning, how they are to learn, how they know they are learning, and, most important, the meaning of learning. So when the teacher gives directions such as, "We are going to work on this list of vocabulary words because they could be on the test you are taking next week. Look up the meanings of the words in the dictionary; when you finish, write a sentence for each word and read your sentences to your partner," he is using a classroom discourse routine.

> Teachers use discourse strategies to communicate expectations for learning to students.

Another way of thinking about these discourse strategies is to consider them as a scaffold, or support for learning. **Scaffolding** refers to supporting a child so that she or he can understand or use language that is more complex than she or he could understand or use independently. Scaffolding occurs when a teacher (or another child, or a parent) breaks down directions step by step, asks questions about the elements of a story, elaborates on the themes or vocabulary of a story, asks "thought" questions, or restates or summarizes concepts or themes. As the child is able to use the language independently, scaffolding is gradually withdrawn. Russian psychologist Lev Vygotsky described the process of supporting a child to the next level of learning—his "zone of proximal development" (Vygotsky, 1978). The process of teaching and moving the child toward a higher level of knowledge and understanding is scaffolding. The supports provided by an adult or another child are gradually internalized and become part of the child's knowledge.

> Scaffolding is the guidance an adult or peer provides for students who cannot yet do a task alone.

Santamaria, Fletcher, and Bos (2002) described four scaffolding strategies that might be used for students with communication difficulties; they are presented in Table 9.7. Roland Tharp and his colleagues (2000) identified five guiding principles for effective teaching of students who are English-language learners that might also assist students with communication difficulties. They are described, along with scaffolding strategies, in Table 9.8.

Members of the Collaborative Team

A collaborative approach requires the willingness to cross disciplinary boundaries. Members of an educational team must be willing to maintain their existing roles, or expertise, and also to expand their roles, or even relinquish them, when appropriate, to meet students' needs. Classroom-based instruction and intervention mean that general and special education teachers and speech-language pathologists will work together in new ways to achieve the goals of an integrated curriculum. Typically, members of the team for a student with a communication disorder will be the classroom teacher, whether general or special education; the student's parents; an instructional assistant; and the speech-language specialist.

> New roles for the speech-language pathologist are emerging.

Despite the speech-language pathologist's intensive training and expertise, it is important that the classroom teacher not be intimidated by this able professional colleague. Typically, teachers are experts themselves in classroom learning, curriculum, and management—areas in which the speech-language pathologist has little training. Each collaborative partner has important contributions to make.

Table 9.7 Four Scaffolding Strategies for English Language Learners With Learning Disabilities

Scaffold Type	Description	Examples
Mediated activities	Support provided by teacher or more proficient peer, who intervenes and helps less proficient learner learn new information	Teacher-directed mini-lessons, buddy reading, cooperative learning groups
Tasks	Support embedded in the tasks, allowing students to focus on learning process and strategies, reducing information they must generate independently	Student-friendly instructions for task completion
Materials	Support provided through strategically designed prompts for learners	Story maps, paragraph frames, sentence starters
Comprehensible input	Language used in ways that make it understandable to the learner while developing second language proficiency	Information presented and available in student's first or second language to increase understanding

Table 9.8 Guiding Principles for Effective Pedagogy and Scaffolding Strategies

Guiding Principles	Scaffolding Strategies
Work collaboratively with students, create a community of learners	*Mediated:* buddy reading, cooperative learning groups, teachers and other adults facilitating center work
Develop language and literacy across the curriculum, use multiple techniques to promote second language acquisition	*Materials:* advanced organizers *Comprehensible input:* language that is understandable to students in their second language
Connect school to students' lives, incorporate cultural diversity into instruction	*Task:* information embedded in task that helps students perform task *Comprehensible input:* language that is understandable to students in their first or second language
Teach complex thinking, engage in cognitively challenging activities	*Mediated:* cognitively challenging teacher-directed mini-lessons
Teach through conversation, foster extended discourse	*Mediated:* teacher-directed mini-lessons, cooperative learning activities

Source for Tables 9.7 and 9.8: From Santamaria, L. J., Fletcher, T. V., and Bos, C. S. (2002). Effective pedagogy for English language learners in inclusive classrooms. In A. J. Artiles and A. A. Ortiz (Eds.), English language learners with special education needs (pp. 140–141). Washington, D.C. & McHenry, IL: Center for Applied Linguistics & Delta Systems Inc.

The happy connection between mother and child—or caregiver and child—is the foundation of communication development. (© DPA/The Image Works)

In fact, role expansion in a collaborative approach means that general education teachers, with the support of speech-language pathologists, can learn to incorporate communication goals and strategies for individual students into everyday classroom activities. Most important, effective role expansion depends on continuous planning and communication among all team members, as well as on changes in attitudes and expectations. Ehren (2000) makes specific suggestions for operationalizing shared responsibility in the classroom; see the accompanying Teaching Strategies box entitled, "Sharing Responsibility for Student Success."

> Teachers and speech-language pathologists can work together in collaborative teams.

Teaching Strategies & Accommodations

Sharing Responsibility for Student Success

1. Promote the writing of Individualized Education Program (IEP) goals that teachers and speech-language pathologists (SLPs) work collaboratively to achieve, as opposed to goals that are identified only with the teacher or the SLP.

2. SLPs should be prepared to make suggestions for modifications at IEP meetings. What can the teacher do to adjust assessment and instructional activities to accommodate a student's language disorder so that the student can benefit from classroom instruction?

3. SLPs should make specific suggestions to teachers on how to modify lessons, tests, and assigned work, and consider demonstrating appropriate modifications for the teacher.

4. Teachers and SLPs should agree on progress assessment procedures and work together to assess progress based on specific progress criteria.

5. Broadcast successes to other faculty members and administration. Brag about each other's hard work and mutual accomplishments.

Source: B. J. Ehren (2000). Maintaining a therapeutic focus and sharing responsibility for student success: Keys to in-classroom speech-language services. *Language, Speech, and Hearing Services in Schools, 31*(3), 225–226.

As schools shift toward more collaborative and integrated models of education, including inclusive models, we need to start with the basics: challenging our existing beliefs about how we work together, and what students are capable of when given appropriate support.

In working with students with communication disorders, as well as students with a range of other disabilities and all other students with language-learning needs, it might be helpful to consider three levels of language intervention strategies. Intervention becomes more focused and intensive at each level. Here are some examples that can be used by classroom teachers at each level.

Level One   Best practices for typical language learners; enrichment for students who are learning language successfully.

- Give your students plenty of opportunities to talk, and listen carefully to what they say. Students need to talk as much or more than teachers. You might consider tape recording one of your lessons, then listening for who is doing the talking. Teachers should allow a wide variety of students an opportunity to talk, and not monopolize all the talking themselves.

- Provide a "wait time" when a student is called on, and try not to interrupt. Students from some cultures unfold their narratives more slowly than others (Reid, 2000).

- Expand and extend your students' utterances. Respond to students' talk not with correction, but with an enriched, correct pattern (McCormick, 2003b). For example:

  STUDENT: This not lighting. Bulb broken.

  TEACHER: Your bulb isn't lighting up? Let's look at your circuit.

- Provide plenty of contextual supports for new language learning as well as new concepts: pictures, graphic organizers, films, hands-on experiences, and so on. Visual aids help all students, but are especially helpful for students who have difficulty with language.

- Have a place in your classroom where new vocabulary is recorded, and find opportunities to use new vocabulary in different contexts. Reward students for their use of new vocabulary as well.

- Through your dialogue with students, use *scaffolding* to move them to a higher level of speaking and understanding. Remember that scaffolding is "a process of enabling students to solve a problem, achieve a goal, or carry out a task that would be beyond their ability if they were not given help" (Reid, 2000, p. 28). Your goal is to improve students' levels of participation until they become independent.

Level Two   Procedures used with children who are not acquiring language at the same rate as their peers, or those who are learning English.

- Find the time for work on English-language development every day.

- Preteach critical vocabulary prior to student reading (Gersten & Baker, 2000).

- Provide the students frequent opportunities to use oral language in the classroom. Don't let the more fluent students monopolize the discussion. Oral language use should include both conversation and discussion of academic content.

Introduction to Augmentative and Alternative Communication

Personal achievement in life is a function of the ability to communicate.

Augmentative and alternative communication (AAC) refers to ways (other than speech) that are used to send a message from one person to another. We all use augmentative communication techniques, such as facial expressions, gestures, and writing, as part of our daily lives. In difficult listening situations (noisy rooms, for example), we tend to augment our words with even more gestures and exaggerated facial expressions.

People with severe speech or language problems must rely quite heavily on these standard techniques as well as on special augmentative techniques that have been specifically developed for them. Some of these techniques involve the use of specialized gestures, sign language, or Morse code. Other techniques use communication aids, such as charts, bracelets, and language boards. On aids such as these, objects may be represented by pictures, drawings, letters, words, sentences, special symbols, or any combination thereof.

Electronic devices are available that can speak in response to entries on a keyboard or other methods of input. Input can come from any number of different switches that are controlled with motions as simple as a push of a button, a puff of air, or the wrinkle of an eyebrow. The possibilities increase virtually every day! *Augmentative communication users don't stop using speech!* When speech is used with standard and special augmentative communication, not only does communication increase, but so do social interactions, school performance, feelings of self-worth, and job opportunities.

The goal of AAC is the most effective communication possible and, in turn, the greatest potential for personal achievement.

A WORD OF CAUTION

Selecting the communication methods that are best for an individual is not as simple as getting a prescription for eyeglasses. But, language is also complex, and we learn to use it every day. Indeed, developing the best communication system for a

This boy is using an augmentative communication device—a computerized picture keyboard. After he punches in his message, the computer will speak his words. (© Jeff Greenberg/PhotoEdit)

person with a severe speech and language problem requires evaluation by many specialists, all of whom may not have offices in the same building or even in the same city. Communication boards may need to be made. Vocabulary to meet the needs of a wide range of communication situations must be selected. Equipment may need to be ordered and paid for. Health plans or other third-party payors may need to be contacted.

And once all the parts of the communication plan are in place, the user must learn to operate each part of the system effectively and efficiently. Effective communication with its speech, standard augmentative, and special augmentative part is not learned out of a book. Professionals need to help the user and his or her communication partners learn a variety of skills and strategies, which might include the meaning of certain hand shapes and how to make them; starting and stopping a piece of electronic equipment at a desired word or picture; ways to get a person's attention; ways to help a communication partner understand a message; and increasing the rate of communication. *Communication planning is a life-long process.* And, problems will come up that threaten the plan. Without effort by the user, professional help, ongoing practice, and support from friends, family, and colleagues, the promises of augmentative communication may not be realized. And even with all the parts in place, chances are that problems will arise. Continue to find out what can be done to solve these problems.

Users of AAC will tell you the effort is worth it and that selection of their AAC system was the most important single event in their lives.

Source: American Speech-Language-Hearing Association. http://www.asha.org/public/speech/disorders/Augmentative+and+Alternative.htm.

FIRST PERSON

I Can Even Stutter Now!

Have you ever wondered what it would be like not to be able to communicate? It's very frustrating. It's very lonely. It hurts.

Think about it. You feel, you think, you know and understand the words, yet you cannot speak them. You hear everyone around you in an interesting conversation, but you cannot join in.

You cannot express any of the feelings or emotions that are just as deep inside of you as anyone else. You are furiously angry and you have to hold it in; or you are extremely happy and you can't show it. Your heart is so full of love you could just burst, but you can't share it.

I know what it is like because for years I could not communicate or express myself. I am a 19-year-old girl. I have cerebral palsy and cannot talk. I do not have coordination in my hands to write or use sign language. Even a typewriter was out of the question when I was younger.

I know what it is like to be fed potatoes all my life. After all, potatoes are a good basic food for everyday, easy to fix in many different ways. I hate potatoes! But then, who knew that but me?

I know what it is like to be dressed in reds and blues when my favorite colors are mint greens, lemon yellows, and pinks.

I mean really, can you imagine? Mama found me one night curled up in a ball in my bed crying, doubled over in pain. I couldn't explain to her where or how I hurt. So, after checking me over the best she could, she thought I had a bad stomachache due to constipation. Naturally, a quick cure for that was an enema. It didn't help my earache at all!

Finally, help came! I was introduced to Blissymbols.

My life changed! Blissymbols were originally developed for a universal language, but they have been a miracle for me and others like me. Blissymbols are a combination of the written word and a symbolized picture that anyone can learn and are displayed in a way that can be easily used. There was a tray strapped to my

- Focus on vocabulary building, but do not overwhelm students with new vocabulary—lists of seven or fewer words should be worked on over relatively long periods. Vocabulary should convey key concepts, be useful, relevant to the concepts being taught, and meaningful to the students (Gersten & Baker, 2000).
- Use more visuals as you teach. For students who are learning a new language, visuals such as semantic maps and story maps "help students visualize the abstractions of language" (Gersten & Baker, 2000, p. 463).
- Promote peer interactions, peer tutoring, and cooperative work groups. Students who are learning language, whether they are English-language learners or students with disabilities, will benefit from peer models, prompts, and supports.

wheelchair. It was covered with a sheet of paper divided into little blocks of words that I could use to form sentences. At last, I could communicate!

Naturally, one board could not hold all the words needed. I had to learn to make up my own, combining two or more words to mean another. As in "story sleep" for dream or "bad night horse" for nightmare.

My teachers started me on 10 words a day to see if I could learn them. I learned as fast as they could give me new words. I was ready to communicate! I could even stutter! That's what my uncle calls it when it takes three or four tries to point to one word. Once I mastered Blissymbols, I left the symbols behind and changed to words and sentences. Then I got my first computer. I programmed my Bliss board into it and much more. It also had a printer. Finally, I could write!

I didn't stop there. I went on to a more advanced system. I was doing the programming all by myself and even did some of the "funny" spelling.

The first thing I learned about computers was to think of them as a "hotel." My "hotel" had 99 floors or levels. Each floor had 128 rooms or spaces for programming. In each room, I could put one person, as in a letter or a number, or a whole family, as in a sentence; or I could just throw a wild party with several paragraphs. So you see my "hotel" had almost unlimited accommodations.

Did I stop there? Surprise, I got a new device. This one has the same basic features as my old one, but I can connect it to an Apple computer to either store the memory on a disk or just use the screen to make my paragraphs all in one, instead of having to say bits and pieces at a time. Everything in it is coded like my old device, but it is much easier to get the words or sentences out because everything is coded by pictures instead of numbers, and it is a lot easier to remember pictures. The new device makes it a lot easier for me to communicate with you or anyone else.

Communicating for me has opened a lot of doors. It even let me act in a play. I have been a guest speaker at a Kiwanis Club meeting. It has done a lot more, too. There's help out there, just don't give up.

Sara Brothers

Source: American Speech-Language-Hearing Association. http://www.asha.org/public/speech/disorders/I-Can-Even-Stutter-Now.htm. © 1997–2003.

- Teach communication skills to replace challenging behaviors (McCormick, 2003b). Remember that your student may not have the appropriate language to communicate his or her needs and feelings, and engage in challenging behavior as a result. Try to discern the communicative intent—what does the student want to say? Then teach the student more acceptable ways of communicating that intent.

Level Three   Interventions that are disability-specific:

- Incorporate sign language and fingerspelling for students with hearing loss. It often helps other students, too. If you're not an expert, buy a book and learn with your students. Teach *all* your students signs so they will use it with one another and develop new vocabulary.

- Build in concept development for students who are visually impaired. Concepts that sighted students learn through vision must be explicitly taught to students who are blind or have low vision.

- Through your school speech-language pathologist, investigate augmentative communication systems for students who cannot or do not speak. Students with physical disabilities can use picture boards and computer systems with adaptations (see Chapter 12). Students with autism might use systems like the Picture Exchange Communication System (PECS) described in Chapter 8.

- Students with developmental delay or mental retardation will benefit from exposure to short, direct sentences that contain functional vocabulary—words they need to function in everyday routines. Adding signs to those short sentences can be helpful, too—it makes the message more redundant.

Developing useful communication skills can be challenging, but it is not impossible—even for students with the most significant communication disorders. As an incentive, remember that the work you do to promote language growth and expansion will benefit *all* your students. As the teacher, you are crucial to what may be the most important goal for your students—learning to communicate effectively and therefore connect with others.

SUMMARY

- Communication is the exchange of ideas. Language is one type of symbolic communication; its code expresses ideas or content. Language is functional, or pragmatic. A community of language users agrees on the appropriate ways to behave as speakers and listeners.

- Speech is one component of the total language system. It involves the physical actions needed to produce meaningful spoken words.

- Language develops very rapidly and in generally the same sequence in all children, although the ages at which children reach particular developmental milestones can vary significantly. Several theories have been proposed to explain the acquisition of language and communication. It is likely that social interaction with others in the language community plays a vital role in speech and language development. By 5 years of age, the basic system of oral communication has been acquired.

- Language disorders involve difficulties in the comprehension and expression of the meaning and content of language. Speech disorders include phonological, fluency, and voice impairments. *Communication disorders* is a more general term used to include difficulties with speech and hearing, as well as language and speech disorders.

- Identification and assessment of students with communication disorders are typically the tasks of the speech-language pathologist.

- Placement options for students with communication disorders are increasingly focusing on inclusion in the integrated classroom. This has led to a shift in the philosophy, principles, and practices of educators. Instructional strategies focus on integrating language and literacy development and supporting the use of oral communication for a variety of functional purposes.

KEY TERMS

communication
language
phonology
phonemes
morphology
morphemes
syntax
semantics
pragmatics
discourse

speech
communication
   disorder
language disorder
specific language
   impairment
expressive language
receptive language
functional behavior
   analysis
communicative intent
phonological (articula-
   tion) disorders

fluency disorder
stuttering
voice disorder
dialect
language delay
phonological awareness
metalinguistic aware-
   ness
language sample
classroom discourse
instructional discourse
   strategies
scaffolding

USEFUL RESOURCES

- The website for the the American Speech-Language-Hearing Association (ASHA) at **http://www.asha.org** offers information and resources to professionals in the field and others interested in speech and language.

- Martha Scott Lue (2001). *A survey of communication disorders for the classroom teacher.* Boston: Allyn & Bacon. This book provides ideas and strategies for teachers of students with communication problems.

- Visit the website of the National Institute on Deafness and Other Communication Disorders at **http://www.nidcd.nih.gov**. This arm of the National Institutes of Health (NIH) supports research on communication disorders and serves as a resource in the field. The area entitled "Teachers and Kids" is particularly relevant for our readers.

- Two journals will be particularly interesting for those of you writing papers or working on projects in this area. They are *Language, Speech, and Hearing Services in the Schools*, published by ASHA, and the *Journal of Communicative Disorders*, published by the Division of Communication Disorders and Deafness of the Council for Exceptional Children.

- Visit the website of the Stuttering Foundation of America at **http://www.stuttersfa.org**. The Stuttering Foundation provides free online resources, services, and support to those who stutter and their families, as well as support for research into the causes of stuttering. They offer a very inexpensive video entitled *Stuttering: Straight Talk for Teachers.*

Resources on Normal Language Development

Earlier in the chapter we promised to provide you with further resources on normal language development. Here are two:

- Robert E. Owens (2001). *Language development*: *An introduction* (5th ed.). Boston: Allyn & Bacon.

- The American Speech-Language-Hearing Association (ASHA) website also covers this topic at **http://www.asha.org/public/speech/development** or **http://www.asha.org/public/speech/development/child_hear_talk.htm/**.

Resources on Ecological Assessment

- L. McCormick, D. F. Loeb, & R. L. Schiefelbusch (2003). *Supporting children with communication difficulties in inclusive settings: School-based language in-*

tervention (2nd ed.). Boston: Allyn & Bacon. Chapter 7, Ecological assessment and planning, provides an excellent overview of the topic; the ten-step planning process will be very useful for teachers.

● A. Losardo & A. Notari-Syverson (2001). *Alternative approaches to assessing young children.* Baltimore: Paul H. Brookes. This book describes a range of assessment procedures, including ecological assessment.

Resources on Augmentative Communication

● The website at **http://www.augcominc.com** is a compendium of resources and links.

● Linda Burkhart's "Simplified Technology" website has many useful resources and links for teachers and family members. Visit **http://www.lburkhart.com/links.htm**.

● *AAC: Augmentative and Alternative Communication* is a professional journal devoted to AAC issues.

 PORTFOLIO ACTIVITIES

1. Talk to a school speech-language pathologist and take notes on your discussion.

• Ask her to describe the students she sees: How many are there on her caseload? What speech and language needs do the students have?

• Ask her about her training: Does she have both a graduate and undergraduate degree in communication disorders? How many hours did she work with children before obtaining certification?

• Ask her about collaboration: Does she see children in their classrooms or in a pullout program? How does she find time to confer with their classroom teachers?

• Write a description for your portfolio of the role of the speech-language pathologist on the collaborative team.

✓ **Standards** This activity will help students meet CEC Content Standard 10: Collaboration.

2. Classrooms that include students with communication disorders should encourage multiple modes of communication. Students can express their ideas and feelings through painting, drawing, singing or the use of a musical instrument, creative writing, drama, e-mail—the possibilities are vast. Can you design a lesson or unit of lessons in which multiple modes of communication will be encouraged? At the preschool level? At the secondary level? You may include your lesson plan or unit plan in your portfolio.

✓ **Standards** This activity will help students meet CEC Content Standard 6: Language.

 To access an electronic portfolio template for these activities, visit our text website through http://www.education. college.hmco.com/students/.

Children Who Are Deaf and Hard of Hearing

10

Learning Objectives

After reading this chapter, the reader will:

- Understand how we hear and the major types of hearing loss

- Describe the relationship between hearing and language development

- Understand Deaf culture and the Deaf community, and the role they play in the education of children who are deaf

- Describe the communication options available for people who are deaf

- Identify the supports that a student with hearing loss needs in the general education classroom

Outline

Terms and Definitions
Causes of Hearing Loss
   Hearing and Hearing Loss
   Conductive Hearing Loss
   Sensorineural Hearing Loss
   Students with Hearing Loss and
     Additional Disabilities
   Prevalence
   Measurement of Hearing Loss
Characteristics of Students
    with Hearing Loss
   Language Development
   Cognitive and Intellectual
    Development
   School Achievement
   Social and Emotional Development
   Deafness and Culture
Teaching Strategies
    and Accommodations
   Early Identification and Intervention
   Developing Communication Skills
   Curriculum
   Assessment
   School Placement
Technological Advances
   Hearing Aids
   Cochlear Implants
   Assistive Listening Devices
   Telecommunication Devices
   Captioning
SUMMARY
KEY TERMS
USEFUL RESOURCES
PORTFOLIO ACTIVITIES

I often tell my students how I got into the field of special education. I was in college, an English major, and a boy I had a crush on worked part-time at St. Mary's School for the Deaf. I decided to try to get a job there, too, so I could "run into him" accidentally. Well, I did get the job, and I never once saw him at work in the two years that I worked in the school. But serendipity was at work—I found out what I wanted to do professionally for the rest of my life.

The little boys that I worked with were between 3 and 5 years old, and they lived at the school. (This was before the days of IDEA; parents who had no programs for their children in their communities were required to send their children to residential schools, often far from home.) Some spoke, some were silent, but they all used sign language as their preferred form of communication. The fascination I felt then with the possibility of teaching them more language has never left me. Do you remember the moment in the film *The Miracle Worker* when Annie Sullivan takes Helen Keller to the water pump, puts her hands under the water, and signs "water" into those hands? Helen's eyes light up. This is the moment she finally understands that water has a name, and that all things have a name. I wanted to see the eyes of those little boys light up as they learned to communicate.

Many of you share my interest in teaching language. It is at the heart of our instruction of English-language learners, of instruction for children with many of the disabilities we discuss in this book, and of foreign language instruction. In fact, teaching the complexity and richness of language is important for every learner. Sign language, used by many deaf students, is a source of great fascination as well. Join me now in learning about the students who taught me to be a teacher—those who are deaf and hard of hearing.

Nancy Hunt

Terms and Definitions

Deafness is a hearing loss that precludes the learning of language through hearing.

Hard of hearing describes a loss that is less severe than deafness.

Deafness is defined as a hearing loss "so severe that a child experiences difficulty in processing linguistic information through hearing, with or without amplification" (Northern & Downs, 2002, p. 341). People who are deaf usually rely primarily on their vision both for their understanding of the world and for communication. **Hard of hearing** is a term used to describe a hearing loss that, although serious, is less severe than deafness and usually permits the understanding of spoken language with the use of hearing aids. **Hearing impairment** is an umbrella term that refers to all degrees of hearing loss, from slight to profound. Since many individuals in the **Deaf community**—those adults bound together by their deafness, the use of American Sign Language (ASL), and their culture, values, and attitudes—dislike the term *impairment,* we will avoid it in this chapter and instead use the term **hearing loss** when referring to individuals who are deaf and hard of hearing. Table 10.1 defines some of the other terms that are important to this topic.

Please note that in keeping with today's conventions, throughout this chapter, the word *Deaf* is capitalized when it refers to Deafness as a cultural entity.

Table 10.1 Table of Terms

Residual hearing	The remaining hearing of a person with hearing loss that, with the help of a hearing aid, detects sounds within the environment and can be used to hear some sounds and learn speech
Congenital hearing loss	A loss that is present at birth
Acquired hearing loss	A loss that occurs after birth
Prelingual deafness	A hearing loss that occurs before the child develops spoken language
Postlingual deafness	A hearing loss that occurs after the child develops spoken language
Bilateral hearing loss	A hearing loss in both ears (although one ear may have more hearing than the other)
Unilateral hearing loss	Normal hearing in one ear and a hearing loss in the other

Causes of Hearing Loss

Hearing and Hearing Loss

The human auditory system, as shown in Figure 10.1, is complicated and extremely delicate. Sound energy creates vibration, and the vibration travels in sound waves through a passageway called the ear canal to the eardrum, or tympanic membrane, a thin layer of tissue between the outer and middle ear. The vibration of the eardrum sets off a chain of vibrations in the three small bones of the middle ear: the malleus, incus, and stapes. The sound is transmitted through the cochlea, a tiny, spiral-shaped structure in the inner ear. Finally, it reaches the brain via the auditory nerve, where it is interpreted as meaningful.

Because hearing depends on the transmission of sound waves across numerous tiny structures throughout the auditory mechanism, malfunctions or damage to any part of the system can result in temporary or permanent hearing loss.

Sound waves travel through the auditory canal to the eardrum, middle ear, cochlea, and (via the auditory nerve) to the brain.

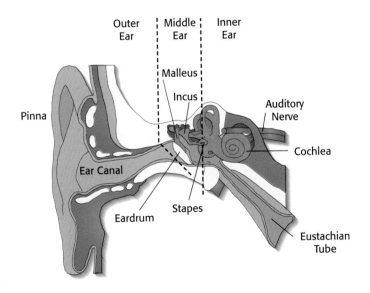

Figure 10.1

Structure of the Ear

Conductive hearing loss can be temporary, but recurrent conductive loss can affect language development.

Damage or obstruction in the external or middle ear that disrupts the efficient passage or conduction of sound through those chambers results in a **conductive hearing loss**. Most conductive losses can be successfully treated medically, but research has shown that recurrent conductive hearing losses in young children—even though temporary—can have serious long-term effects on their language development and school learning (Roberts, Wallace, & Henderson, 1997).

Sensorineural hearing loss is permanent and irreversible.

Damage to the cochlea or the auditory nerve in the inner ear is called a **sensorineural hearing loss**. A sensorineural loss is almost always permanent and irreversible (Northern & Downs, 2002). Most students with hearing loss in our schools have a sensorineural hearing loss, although some of them have a **mixed hearing loss**, with both conductive and sensorineural components. Table 10.2 is an overview of the two major kinds of hearing loss.

Hearing loss can range in severity from slight to profound. Children with losses described as mild and moderate are usually called hard of hearing; those with severe and profound losses are usually considered deaf. Even most deaf people, though, have some **residual hearing** (see Table 10.1) that can make a hearing aid helpful. See Table 10.3 for the effects of the varying degrees of hearing loss on children.

Knowledge of the cause of hearing loss in young children is important for several reasons. In the case of conductive losses, which are usually treatable, the cause dictates the treatment; in the case of sensorineural loss, which is permanent and often congenital, knowledge will help families gather information about the probability of hearing loss in any subsequent children and may help them master the feelings of stress related to their child's disability.

Conductive Hearing Loss

Otitis media—middle ear infection—is the most common cause of conductive hearing loss in children.

The most common cause of conductive hearing loss in children is middle ear infection, or **otitis media**. When, because of a cold or for some other reason, fluid gathers in the middle ear, it dampens or restricts the movement of the eardrum, and hearing loss may result. Middle ear infection, or simply the presence of fluid

Table 10.2 Characteristics of the Two Major Kinds of Hearing Loss

	Conductive Hearing Loss	Sensorineural Hearing Loss
Duration	Usually temporary	Permanent
Location of the problem	Occurs as a result of a problem in the outer or middle ear	Occurs as a result of a problem in the inner ear or the auditory nerve
Treatment	Treatable by a physician with medication and/or surgery	Not routinely treatable*
Impact on hearing	Tends to be a mild or moderate hearing loss	Tends to be a severe or profound hearing loss
Impact on learning	Depends on the length of the problem; can vary from no impact at all to significantly affecting language learning	Usually affects oral language development
Educational services provided	Special education services not routinely provided for this short-term hearing loss	Special education provided when the hearing loss affects the student's educational performance

*Sometimes treated by a cochlear implant (see p. 386).

in the middle ear, can cause mild to moderate hearing loss in children, and it should always be brought to the attention of the child's pediatrician. *Chronic* otitis media (ear infection that lasts for twelve weeks or longer, or returns repeatedly), with long-term effects on hearing, can also delay the normal development of language and speech in young children (Northern & Downs, 2002; Schoem, 1999). This language delay may, in turn, have subtle adverse effects over time on a child's achievement in school, long after the ear infection has disappeared.

Table 10.3 Degrees of Hearing Loss

Average Hearing Level	Description	Possible Condition	What Can Be Heard without Amplification	Handicapping Effects (If Not Treated in First Year of Life)	Probable Needs
0–15 dB*	Normal range		All speech sounds	None	None
15–25 dB	Slight hearing loss	Conductive hearing losses, some sensorineural hearing losses	Vowel sounds heard clearly; may miss unvoiced consonants sounds	Mild auditory dysfunction in language learning	Consideration of need for hearing aid; speech reading, auditory training, speech therapy, preferential seating
25–30 dB	Mild hearing loss	Conductive or sensorineural hearing loss	Only some speech sounds, the louder voiced sounds	Auditory learning dysfunction, mild language delay, mild speech problems	Hearing aid, speech reading, auditory training, speech therapy
30–50 dB	Moderate hearing loss	Conductive hearing loss from chronic middle ear disorders; sensorineural hearing losses	Almost no speech sounds at normal conversational level	Speech problems, language delay, learning difficulties	All of the above, plus consideration of other special education services
50–70 dB	Severe hearing loss	Sensorineural or mixed losses due to a combination of middle ear disease and sensorineural involvement	No speech sounds at normal conversational level	Severe speech problems, language delay, learning difficulties	All of the above; need for special education services
70+ dB	Profound hearing loss	Sensorineural or mixed losses due to a combination of middle ear disease and sensorineural involvement	No speech or other sounds	Severe speech problems, language delay, learning difficulties	All of the above; need for special education services

*dB stands for *decimals*, or units of loudness.

Source: Jerry L. Northern & Marion P. Downs (1991). Adapted from *Hearing in children*, 4th ed. Baltimore: Lippincott Williams & Wilkins.

Children should be treated by a physician when warning signs of middle ear infection appear, and especially when they persist over time. Some of those signs are fever, redness of the ear, rubbing of the ear, or, in a young infant, rubbing of the head against a mattress or blanket; reports of pain or itching; and, in extreme cases, dripping from the ear. Many middle ear infections can be effectively treated with antibiotics, and chronic cases are often treated with the insertion of small tubes into the ear, through which the liquid in the middle ear will drain out naturally (Northern & Downs, 2002; Schoem, 1999). Ear infections should always be treated promptly in babies and young children: Their long-term effects can be very serious. You, as a professional working with young children and families, can play an important role in the prevention of conductive hearing loss by encouraging prompt medical treatment when an ear infection is suspected.

Sensorineural Hearing Loss

Children with sensorineural hearing loss usually require special education services.

Conductive hearing loss can often be successfully treated in young children, and it is not usually the major cause of hearing loss that places school-age children in special education services. Children with sensorineural hearing loss, though, usually have a permanent condition that cannot be medically treated and that makes special education services necessary. Many cases are present at birth; there is hope that with universal newborn hearing screening children with congenital sensorineural hearing loss will be identified at birth or soon after, rather than as toddlers, when they are already behind typical children in language acquisition (Culpepper, 2003).

Parents often suspect that their child has a hearing loss at around 8 months old. It is still not uncommon, though, for pediatricians to tell parents "not to worry" (Prendergast, Lartz, & Fiedler, 2002); as a result, precious intervention time can be lost. While these figures are "slippery," the average age of confirmed diagnosis in one study was about 20 months (Kittrell & Arjmand, 1997); it is usually somewhat earlier for more severe losses, and later for mild ones.

Knowledge of the cause of a child's sensorineural hearing loss is often important for families. Parents may want to know if a child's hearing loss is hereditary. A genetic counselor can help a family know whether or not that determination can be made (Arnos, 1999). Also, many parents feel a strong desire to know the cause of their child's disability. In fact, Kathryn Meadow (1968) found that parents who knew the probable cause of their child's hearing loss were better able to cope with the complex feelings associated with the diagnosis. Summers, Behr, and Turnbull (1989) suggest that identifying the cause of disability may be a positive process of adaptation for families.

The major causes of sensorineural hearing loss in children change over time, depending on the occurrence of epidemics, the development of new drugs and medical treatments, and public health conditions. For example, most of the children who lost their hearing as a result of maternal exposure to rubella during the 1960s rubella epidemic have by now left special education services, and since the rubella vaccine was introduced in 1969, rubella has become a much less prominent cause of hearing loss. See the Closer Look box entitled, "Causes of Sensorineural Hearing Loss" for a list of the current most common causes of sensorineural hearing loss in children.

Students with Hearing Loss and Additional Disabilities

One out of four of children with hearing loss has additional disabilities.

Roughly one-fourth of the children who are deaf and hard of hearing and enrolled in special education programs have been identified with a disability in

A Closer Look   Causes of Sensorineural Hearing Loss

1. **Heredity.** In a great number of cases (probably about 60 percent) hearing loss is caused by heredity, or genetic factors (Moores, 2001).

2. **Meningitis.** Meningitis is a bacterial or viral infection that causes inflammation of the coverings of the brain and spinal cord. If the infection reaches the inner ear, it can destroy the delicate organs within, resulting in deafness. Meningitis is the major cause of *acquired* deafness in children. It may also be associated with other neurological disabilities.

3. **Prematurity.** Prematurity and the traumatic medical events frequently associated with premature birth and low birthweight are sometimes associated with hearing loss (see Chapter 2).

4. **Cytomegalovirus (CMV).** CMV (see Chapter 2) accounts for a small but increasing number of cases of childhood hearing loss (Schildroth, 1994). CMV is common; 44 to 100 percent of adult populations evaluated have been exposed to the virus (Strauss, 1999). When a pregnant woman contracts CMV, she can pass it to her fetus, which results in other disabilities as well as hearing loss.

5. **Other causes.** There are many other, less common causes of childhood hearing loss, including mother-child blood incompatibility, or RH incompatibility. This is decreasing as a cause of deafness because of rhogam treatments and improvements in blood transfusion techniques.

Although there are benefits to knowing the cause of sensorineural hearing loss, that information is frequently unavailable. In at least 30 percent of the reported cases of hearing loss, despite the best efforts of parents and counselors to determine the cause, it remains unknown (Moores, 2001).

---

addition to their hearing loss (Moores, 2001). Table 10.4 shows the numbers of children with hearing loss and additional disabilities. The most common are the cognitive-behavioral disabilities: mental retardation and specific learning disabilities. Part of the explanation for this relationship comes from the linkage between the cause of hearing loss and the additional disability. Moores (2001) reminds us:

> All of the major contemporary known causes of early childhood deafness may be related to other conditions to some extent. These include maternal rubella, prematurity, cytomegalovirus, mother-child blood incompatibility, and meningitis. Even in the case of inherited deafness, whether dominant, recessive, or sex-linked, the hearing loss may be only one manifestation of a syndrome that includes a wide range of conditions. (p. 118)

There may also be social or environmental causes for a condition in addition to hearing loss: An impoverished communication system, late entry to school, an inappropriate school program, and a lack of consistent behavioral limits, for example, could combine to allow the development of an additional disability.

Hearing loss is also frequently associated with other conditions that may be considered a student's primary disability, such as Down syndrome, cerebral palsy, and cleft palate (Chen, 1999). In addition, children who are both deaf and blind constitute a small but unique group of students who often have intensive

Table 10.4 Additional Disabilities of Deaf Children	
Specific Classifications*	**Percentage**
No disability in addition to deafness	60.1
Low vision	2.2
Legally blind	1.7
Learning disabled	10.7
Mentally retarded	9.8
Attention deficit disorder/hyperactivity	6.6
Emotional disorder	1.7
Cerebral palsy	3.4
Other conditions	12.1

*Percentages may total more than 100% because some students have more than one classification.

Source: Gallaudet Research Institute (2003). *Regional and national summary report of data from the 2001–2002 Annual Survey of Deaf and Hard of Hearing Children & Youth.* Washington, DC: GRI, Gallaudet University.

communication and mobility needs and are best served by a multidisciplinary group of professionals (Chen & Dote-Kwan, 1995). Family members can learn to interpret communication cues in infants with multiple disabilities that include both hearing and vision; these cues can serve as the foundation for a system of communication (Klein, Chen, & Haney, 2000).

Prevalence

In comparison to other groups of children served in special education programs, the number of children who are deaf and hard of hearing is small. Only 0.11 percent of the children served under IDEA in the 2000–2001 school year were labeled as hearing impaired (U.S. Department of Education, 2002). As many as 18.7 million Americans have some kind of hearing loss (Meadow-Orlans & Orlans, 1990), but the great majority of these are adult; one-third of adults over 70 has some degree of hearing loss (Desai et al., 2001).

A small percentage of all the children in special education programs are deaf or hard of hearing.

Measurement of Hearing Loss

If you work with students with hearing loss, you will most likely come into contact with a number of other professionals who interact with the child and family. As you review your students' records, you will see their reports.

The **otologist** is a physician whose specialization is diseases of the ear. He or she may participate in the diagnosis of hearing loss and treat the child later for related problems. The otologist is also the specialist many children see for chronic middle ear infections.

The **audiologist** has special training in testing and measuring hearing. Professionally trained audiologists have the skills and equipment needed to evaluate the hearing of any child at any age with a high degree of accuracy. Many audiologists also participate in the process of rehabilitation, or treatment of the effects of hearing loss, and prescribe and evaluate the effectiveness of hearing aids.

The audiologist is trained to test and measure hearing.

The traditional hearing test given by an audiologist is called a pure-tone test. You have probably had a test like this yourself, since hearing screenings are common in schools. In a pure-tone test the individual, wearing headphones, is exposed to a series of tones or beeps measured in decibels (units of loudness). The tones vary in loudness, or intensity, from soft to loud, and in pitch, or frequency, from low to high. The **audiogram** is the chart on which the audiologist records the individual's responses to the tones. People with normal hearing generally respond to very soft sounds, whether they are high or low in frequency (pitch). Figure 10.2 explains an audiogram. Note that each ear is tested separately. For more about audiograms, visit **http://www.audiology.org/consumer/guides/uya.php**.

There are a couple of simple principles that make interpreting an audiogram easier. First, the farther down on the audiogram the responses are recorded, the less residual hearing a person has, or the louder the tones have to be before the person responds to them. Second, the most crucial sounds for a person to hear are those that fall primarily between 500 and 3,000 Hertz, or cycles per second. Those are the "speech frequencies," the pitch range within which most speech sounds fall. Many professionals believe that children with hearing loss should hear speech sounds more than any other sounds. It is through amplification with hearing aids and the training of their residual hearing to respond to speech sounds that children can most efficiently learn to understand and express spoken language.

> The audiogram is the chart on which the audiologist records the individual's responses to sounds presented.

? Pause and Reflect

The preceding pages have provided you with some of the background information you will need to understand the implications of hearing loss in your students. Do you know an older person who might have a hearing loss? Would any of this background information help you to understand that person better? ●

Characteristics of Students with Hearing Loss

The impact of hearing loss on a person's ability to naturally acquire the spoken language of his or her community is often substantial. Those communication difficulties may then adversely influence school achievement, social and emotional development, and interaction with others.

Language Development

Hearing loss has its most pervasive effect on the development of spoken language. It does not appear to affect cognitive or intellectual development, but it can have a significant impact on school achievement.

If you were to become deaf right now, your primary disability would be your inability to hear. Your relations with your family and friends might be strained by your inability to understand everything they say through lip reading. You would be particularly uncomfortable at parties and restaurants, where the noisy background would make it difficult for you to use your residual hearing to follow the conversation. Television and movies would be harder to follow, and listening to

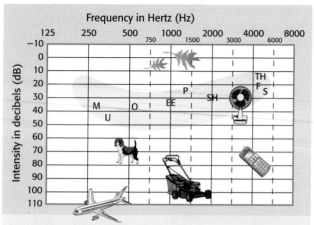

An audiogram is a picture of your hearing. The results of your hearing test are recorded on an audiogram. The audiogram above demonstrates different sounds and where they would be represented on an audiogram. The yellow, banana-shaped figure represents all the sounds that make up the human voice when speaking at normal conversational levels.

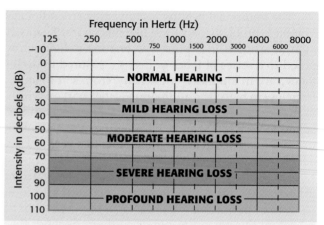

The softest sound you are able to hear at pitch is recorded on an audiogram. The softest sound that you are able to hear is called your threshold. Thresholds of 0–25 dB are considered normal (for adults). The audiogram above demonstrates the different degrees of hearing loss.

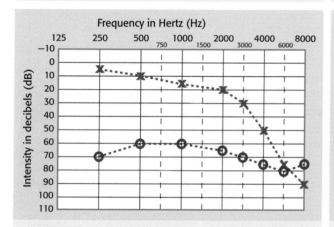

The audiogram above represents the hearing of an individual with normal hearing in low frequencies (pitch) sloping to a severe high frequency hearing loss in the left ear and a moderate to severe hearing loss in the right ear. The blue X's indicate the thresholds for the left ear and the red O's indicate the thresholds for the right ear.

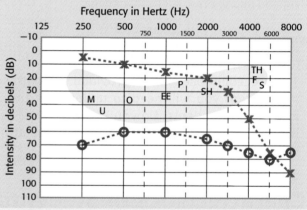

If we now superimpose the normal speech area on the audiogram, we can obtain some information regarding this individual's ability to hear speech. The listener is able to hear all the low and mid speech sounds, but is not able to hear the high pitch speech sounds (i.e., F, S, TH) in the left ear (blue X's). The listener is not able to hear any of the normal speech sounds in the right ear. This person would rely on the left ear for speech understanding and would probably experience difficulty hearing in noisy environments.

Figure 10.2

Understanding the Audiogram

Source: Allan S. Mehr (2003). Understanding your audiogram. In *Consumer Guides,* American Academy of Audiology, available at http://www.audiology.org/consumer/guides/uya.php.

music would bring you less pleasure. Well, you might say, that's what deafness is all about, isn't it? Well, yes—for those of us who have already acquired language. For the prelingually deaf child, deafness is much more than that.

Kathryn Meadow-Orlans (1980) said that for a child the primary disability of hearing loss is not the deprivation of sound, but the deprivation of *language*. Think about it. Young children with normal hearing learn how to talk by listening to the people around them use language meaningfully. They begin to understand and to say words. As they have more experiences listening and using language for different communicative purposes, and mature cognitively, their ability to communicate becomes much more sophisticated. But for the child who does not hear, or does not hear well, that listening experience does not occur, or occurs much less consistently. Unless sign language is used in the home, there are fewer occasions for practice in using language to communicate. Some children who are deaf, particularly those who have not been involved in early intervention programs, come to school at age 3 (and sometimes much later) without any speech or signing skills at all. So, although there are exceptions, many children who are deaf or hard of hearing start school with a language delay, and many of them never catch up to their hearing peers linguistically or academically while they are in school.

Carlos, for example, was a 15-year-old boy who was profoundly deaf. His family had recently moved from El Salvador to Los Angeles, and he had never been in school or had any communication development services. The language of his home was Spanish, but his family reported that he used no recognizable Spanish words. The language of the school was English (presented orally and accompanied by an English-order sign language system), but on entering school, Carlos used no recognizable English vocabulary, either signed or spoken. This boy was very bright and sociable; he had developed his own gesture language, and through this pantomime could communicate simple needs and actions. But catching up to the other students who were deaf in his class presented a formidable challenge to Carlos and his teachers.

The first language of children who are deaf and hard of hearing depends to some extent on the language they are exposed to in the home. The more residual hearing a child has, the more likely it is that the child will learn to speak the language of the home. Children who have little usable residual hearing, however, may develop a relatively unique "first language" based on what they are exposed to—spoken words and formal signs, for example—and what they invent themselves—gestures and "home signs" that may be understood only by the child and family members. On the other hand, deaf children of deaf parents who use American Sign Language may begin school with communication abilities that are developmentally appropriate for their age—and continue to excel throughout their school careers.

Many children with hearing loss begin learning *English* when they enter school. Research that has examined the acquisition of English literacy skills—speaking, reading, and writing—of children with hearing loss tells us that the English language of children who are deaf typically develops in the same order as that of hearing children, but at a considerably slower rate (Paul, 1998).

> Many children with hearing loss start school with a significant language delay.

> The more residual hearing children have, the more likely they will speak the language of their home.

> Many children with hearing loss do not learn English until they begin school.

Cognitive and Intellectual Development

The best information that we have today, based on the most recently conducted research, is that people who are deaf and hard of hearing as a group have normal cognitive and intellectual abilities (Paul & Jackson, 1993). However, that conclusion is a fairly recent one; for many years psychologists believed that

> Most people with hearing loss have normal cognitive and intellectual abilities.

the thinking and reasoning capacities of deaf people were "inferior" (Pintner & Patterson, 1917) or qualitatively different (Myklebust, 1964).

These earlier conclusions stemmed from the assessment process. People who are deaf or hard of hearing have, at times, been administered IQ tests that weigh verbal skills heavily; when they did not do well because of their limited understanding and use of English, they were judged to be cognitively below normal—sometimes even mentally retarded (Moores, 2001). Even when a relatively "fair" test is used, the person with hearing loss may not understand the test directions given by a psychologist who does not have the skills necessary for communicating with him or her. Like all assessment of students with disabilities, the assessment of students with hearing loss should take place in the language in which they are most expert, by a person who is also fluent in that language. Although psychologists and other test administrators have become more knowledgeable about testing people who are deaf and thus fewer abuses seem to occur today, great care should always be taken in interpreting test scores (Eccarius, 1997). As always, they are just one piece of the puzzle.

School Achievement

Despite normal abilities, most children with hearing loss do not achieve at grade level.

Despite the normal cognitive and intellectual abilities of most children with hearing loss, their average school achievement has been significantly below that of their hearing peers. Paul and Jackson (1993) report that "one of the most robust findings is that there is an inverse relationship between hearing impairment and achievement: the more severe the impairment, the lower the achievement" (p. 34). Donald Moores (2001) documents a slow but steady rise in achievement among the students whose schools participate in the Annual Survey of Children and Youth conducted by the Gallaudet Research Institute, but still, "achievement on the average seems to peak around the fourth-grade level in reading comprehension and the seventh-grade level in math computation" (p. 322).

Difficulties acquiring English often lead to poor reading skills for children who are deaf.

Why this discrepancy between ability and achievement? It hinges on the lack of mastery of the English language among students who are deaf. If a person can't comprehend and use the language fluently, then he or she can't read it, since even basal reading materials incorporate sophisticated grammatical structures (King & Quigley, 1985). Reading ability is crucial for success in nearly all academic areas.

Deaf students who are highly successful in school tend to have the following experiences:

- Heavy parental involvement
- Extensive family communication
- Early exposure to and intensive experiences with reading and writing
- An enjoyment of reading
- A relatively limited social life
- High parental and secondary school expectations
- Access to television viewing with captioning
- Positive self-image (Toscano, McGee, & Lepoutre, 2002)

Here's one student who speaks of the importance of ongoing and consistent communication:

. . . For 8 years my parents went to sign classes, and kept going, and going, and going. They needed to keep up with me, since it was my first language, and I progressed very quickly. . . . I have a brother, younger. But he can sign also. . . . My aunt knows some sign. Here and there some of my other relatives know some sign. Even though I am the only deaf person in the family, they all made the effort to include me. I know that doesn't happen everywhere, that you are included at the dinner table. They always made me part of the family conversation. Always. (Toscano, McGee, & Lepoutre, 2002, p. 13)

Social and Emotional Development

Traditionally, psychologists and other professionals concerned with the social and emotional development of individuals who are deaf have concentrated on the differences in this group from the "norms" set by hearing subjects. From this approach has arisen what Donald Moores (2001) calls a "deviance model," which implies that there is something deficient in the psychological makeup of people who are deaf. Many of these conclusions have arisen because of the psychological assessment of students with hearing loss by examiners who are not trained in using sign language and who administer tests that are not appropriate, thereby obtaining an inaccurate picture of the person's true capabilities.

> Inadequate psychological assessment labeled individuals with hearing loss as socially and emotionally deficient.

Moores (2001) describes a more accurate view of the social and emotional development of individuals with hearing loss. This perspective focuses on the development of a healthy, whole, well-integrated person rather than concentrating on what is different or deficient. It assumes that all humans have similar basic needs, which must be met satisfactorily for healthy personal development—among them, the need to communicate with others. For people who are deaf, this need for basic human communication is not always met. Think about this example: Parents of young children who are deaf often feel they do not have the command of communication necessary to explain complicated events, such as a relative's death, a separation, a forthcoming move, or marital problems, and so do not fully communicate the meaning of these experiences to their child. As a result, the child's world may change drastically from one day to the next with no explanation, leaving him or her anxious, frightened, resentful, or confused (Meadow-Orlans, 1980). The frustration that can arise from unsatisfactory communication can spill over into the child's behavior, relationships, and motivation.

> Frustration over inadequate communication may result in behavior or emotional problems for children who are deaf.

This is not to say that people who are deaf and hard of hearing, young and old, do not have problems like everyone else, only that those problems are not particular to hearing loss. Rather, they may arise from experiences within the family, school, and community where poor communication or no communication is the rule.

In summary, the primary effect of deafness on the developing child is to place the development of communication at risk. Because communication skills are so essential for school learning, when these skills are affected, school achievement is, too. But cognitive and social development need not be delayed in children with hearing loss when they are provided with a means and reason to communicate from an early age.

Pause and Reflect

It takes some thought and experience to fully appreciate the effect of deafness on language learning, and therefore on literacy development and school achievement. Can you think of any similar learning challenges from your own experience? ●

FIRST PERSON

Making the Grade: A Hard of Hearing Adult Looks Back on Her Education

I started my education in Illinois in a classroom for preschool children with hearing losses. This is where I learned to read as a 4-½ year old. Miss Bratlie went through the alphabet every day we met and next to each letter was a picture and a word beginning with that letter. I shall never forget the day that the "light bulb" came on. It was during the time that she was going over the alphabet. We had just done "Y" for yellow. Suddenly I understood that the word "yellow" was "yellow" and then I looked back at the word "orange" and figured out that the word was "orange." So I basically picked up reading by sight reading.

This wasn't because I had been hearing for 4-½ years. My mother discovered my hearing loss when I was 3-½ years old. She kept asking the doctors why I wasn't talking yet. They assured her I was fine and that in due time I would talk. One day I went out to play but she wanted me to wear a sweater. So she called me in her normal tone, but I didn't respond. So she called my name a little louder, and still I did not respond. So she kept calling my name louder until I responded. She said that when I turned around, I had the sweetest smile on my face and that was when she realized that I had not heard her until she had yelled.

I always did poorly on assessment tests. Usually it was because of my vocabulary—I didn't hear the bigger words used in everyday life. I think people tended to use a smaller vocabulary when talking to me. It was difficult for me to listen to table conversation at mealtimes (when I probably would have heard the bigger words) and eat at the same time so I tended to be in my own world a lot. My dear father has a voice in the range that is difficult for me to hear and I have to really concentrate to hear him. He often shared what was happening at work but I tended to tune him out. (I say all that because my brother and sister who have normal hearing scored at the top of their assessment tests as students. So I think they were enriched by family conversation.)

Deafness and Culture

Our discussions so far in this chapter have centered around definitions and descriptions that place deafness in the context of *disability*—and that tend to measure people who are deaf by the yardstick of people who are hearing. We speak of deafness as hearing *loss* or hearing *impairment*—yet, as one deaf professional put it: "How would women like to be referred to as male-impaired, or whites like to be called black-impaired? I'm not impaired; I'm deaf!" Many professionals in the field of deafness, particularly those who are deaf themselves,

The clinical perspective of deafness views it as a disability; many prefer that a cultural perspective be adopted.

Another reason for doing poorly on the assessment tests was that I was never taught how to pick out the main idea in a story or paragraph. When taking the test, I would read the selection then read the question and then reread the selection and try to figure out the answer to the question. Usually the question was related to the main idea, which I found to be difficult to answer. I think that current students are taught that the main idea is usually found in the first sentence.

The other major problem I had in classroom settings in high school was where the method of learning was through class discussions. I usually could not understand fellow students talking and thus didn't gain any information from the discussion. This again is an area where I wish I had a note taker available. I think students here have better advocates for them and probably would have help available. One other problem was that I had a few teachers who were tough for me to hear. I learned very little from their lectures. I have thought about what the solution would have been (of course, now they have FM systems available, which is fantastic) but I probably should have been more vocal about my classroom situation to my parents. I just chalked it up as something I had to cope with. I know that with my children that their usual response to my inquiry about what they learned that day is "NOTH-ING." Fortunately, their teachers often send home newsletters indicating what they are learning and I can quiz them on the subject matter and get a feel for their understanding and what they are learning or not learning.

It takes work by the student, teacher, and parents to help a student increase their vocabulary. I thought of 5 ways to help the student: (1) Hear it, if possible (I still mispronounce words because I don't hear them); (2) read it; (3) use it both in oral and written language; (4) learn Latin—helps to figure out new words and their meanings; and (5) write down synonyms even for words the student already knows. I have told my boys that most ideas or things have two words for them. For example, a ball can be called a sphere.

I hope that my perspective on education and the suggestions I have given can help parents understand the needs more clearly of students who are hard of hearing in the classroom. I know that our kids, with the right support, can "make the grade."

Debra Cappella

Source: www.handsandvoices.org.

have been urging teachers of deaf children to drop the clinical perspective, in which deafness is seen as a pathology, a deviance from the "normal" condition of hearing, a condition that must be "cured" or "fixed." These deaf professionals are exhorting the field to adopt the *cultural* perspective, which describes people who are deaf as members of a different culture—a culture with its own language, social institutions, class structure, history, attitudes, values, and literature—that must be studied, understood, and respected (Crittenden, 1993).

Adoption of a cultural perspective on deafness demands knowledge of **Deaf culture**, which Crittenden (1993) defines as "the view of life manifested by the mores, beliefs, artistic expression, understandings, and language particular to Deaf people" (p. 218). Deaf culture is the mainstay of the **Deaf community**, that group of people who share common goals deriving from Deaf cultural influences and work together toward achieving these goals. Crittenden (1993) describes the characteristics that members of the Deaf community share as follows:

> Deaf culture unites those in the Deaf community who share common goals.

- "Attitudinal deafness," the desire to associate with other deaf people with whom values and experiences are shared
- The use of American Sign Language (ASL), considered by members of the Deaf community to be their native language
- The similar life experiences of many people who are deaf in relation to family, schooling, and interaction with "the hearing world"
- The bond between deaf people, the friendships and relationships that grow out of those shared experiences

Members of the Deaf community may not be physically deaf (that is, they may be hearing people), but they must actively support the goals of the Deaf community and work together with people who are deaf to achieve them (Padden, 1980). Padden and Humphries's book *Deaf in America: Voices from a Culture* (1988) portrays members of the Deaf community. These authors, deaf themselves, write:

> In contrast to the long history of writings that treat [deaf people] as medical cases, or people with "disabilities," who "compensate" for their deafness by using sign language, we want to portray the lives they live, their art and performances, their everyday talk, their shared myths, and the lessons they teach one another. We have always felt that the attention given to the physi-

Understanding signing requires the development of concentrated visual attention (Terry Gilliam/AP Photo)

cal condition of not hearing has obscured far more interesting facets of Deaf people's lives. (p. 1)

Thomas Holcomb (1997) argues that it is important to offer deaf children opportunities to develop a Deaf identity from a young age, so that they see themselves as bicultural in a diverse world (see the accompanying Closer Look box entitled, "Deaf Culture and History"). David Stewart and Thomas Kluwin (2001, p. 119) describe how a teacher can integrate Deaf studies into the curriculum, and describe the basic premises of the study of deaf people:

- Deaf people are individuals first.
- The thoughts of a deaf person are shaped by a unique set of experiences that occur inside and outside of the classroom.
- A variety of information about deaf people is available from a variety of resources.
- There are diverse perspectives about deaf people that are related to their use of communication, interactions with deaf and hearing people, cultural affiliation with different ethnic groups, social patterns, use of technology, educational experiences, participation in the workforce, and more.
- Studying about deaf people is an opportunity for gaining knowledge about and appreciation for these perspectives.
- Deaf studies is a means for helping deaf students discover their own identity.

> Deaf studies can help deaf students discover their own identity.

A Closer Look   Deaf Culture and History

In March 1998 the Deaf community celebrated the tenth anniversary of the 1988 watershed political event at Gallaudet University, "Deaf President Now." Gallaudet students, faculty, and sympathetic deaf people from all over the country gathered to close down the university in protest because a hearing woman with little knowledge of deafness was named president. After a week of protests, the new president resigned and the university board of trustees named I. King Jordan, a man who became deaf early in life, president. In Jordan's first statement after he was named president, he stated, "We know that deaf people can do anything hearing people can do except hear" (Sacks, 1989). Many people who are deaf view that week at Gallaudet as a milestone in their history, and a powerful expression of the values of the Deaf community.

The Deaf President Now movement became a catalyst for a new study of the culture and history of deafness (Parasnis, 1996). If the values and culture of the Deaf community are to be integrated into the education of students who are deaf, then it is important to bring more teachers who are deaf into school programs. Deaf teachers can bring their own knowledge of Deaf culture and their own experiences to their students, as well as provide examples of successful adult life. In addition, many adults who are deaf are fluent ASL users but can also use manually coded English systems—they are bilingual.

Many professionals now believe that a knowledge and understanding of Deaf culture should be part of the school curriculum for students who are deaf, so that they are provided with opportunities to learn about other individuals with deafness and their achievements (Christensen, 1993; Schirmer, 1994).

Teaching Strategies and Accommodations

Students with hearing loss need the benefit of an interdisciplinary team of professionals who will cooperatively plan and implement their educational program, whether it is an Individualized Family Service Plan (IFSP) for the child from birth to age 3, an Individualized Education Program (IEP) for the school-aged child, or an Individualized Transition Plan (ITP) for the high-school student. First we will discuss the implementation of programming for the youngest children.

Early Identification and Intervention

Because hearing loss affects language development so directly, and the years from birth to age 3 are so critical for language, the early diagnosis of hearing loss is essential so that work with the family and language intervention with the child with hearing loss can begin.

The national trend to provide newborn hearing screenings may lower the age at which children with hearing loss are identified and begin intervention. There is hope that, ultimately, earlier intervention will improve the long-term outcomes for children who are deaf or hard of hearing (Joint Committee on Infant Hearing, 2000). Yoshinaga-Itano and coworkers (1998) compared the expressive and receptive language abilities of children identified before 6 months with those identified after 6 months; those identified earlier had significantly better language scores.

An early intervention program can serve many purposes for the family of a newly diagnosed child with hearing loss. Parents often need support from professionals in dealing with their reactions to the diagnosis of hearing loss; they also need information about the effects of hearing loss on language development. Families must make the important decision about how they will teach their child to communicate—will it be signs or speech? If signs are chosen, will it be American Sign Language (ASL) or manually coded English?

The early intervention professional will help the family continue to communicate naturally to the child about everyday experiences, sometimes with the addition of sign language. She will help the family and the child understand how hearing aids are used and what they can and cannot do. Children with hearing loss do not automatically know where a sound comes from the first time they hear it with their hearing aids; they must be taught the association, for example, between the noise they hear and the airplane flying overhead. The child, the family, and the teacher must collaborate to maximize every communication opportunity during the child's everyday routines and waking hours.

Developing Communication Skills

Most educators of children who are deaf or hard of hearing agree that early diagnosis, amplification, and intervention are of paramount importance for their students, but there is no such unanimity on the topic of how these children should be taught to communicate. Should speech alone be emphasized, or signs be added? How much emphasis should there be on the use of residual hearing? Which sign language system should be used? What should be the role of the na-

---

The early diagnosis of hearing loss is essential so that intervention can begin.

Newborn hearing screenings may eventually improve long-term outcomes for deaf children.

Table 10.5 Approaches to Communication Used with Students with Hearing Loss

Type	Name of Approach	Description
Oral English approaches	Auditory-oral	These programs teach children to make maximum use of their residual hearing through amplification (hearing aids or cochlear implants), to augment their residual hearing with speech (lip) reading, and to speak. This approach excludes the use of sign language.
	Auditory-verbal	The auditory/verbal approach is similar to the auditory/oral approach, except it does not encourage speech reading.
Simultaneous communication approaches	Manually Coded English (MCE)	Visual representations of English. MCE systems are typically used in educational settings with children rather than in social interactions among deaf adults.
	Signing Exact English (SEE II)	
	Signed English	
	Rochester method	Use of fingerspelling along with speech.
	Cued speech	A visual communication system combining eight handshapes (cues) that represent different sounds of speech. These cues are used simultaneously with speaking to aid in lip reading.
	Pidgin Signed English (PSE)	Use of ASL signs in English word order.
Dual-language approach	Bilingual (American Sign Language and English)	Supports development of ASL as a first language. ASL is a visual/gestural language with vocabulary, grammar, idioms, and syntax different from English that utilizes signs and facial/body grammar. English skills are developed as a second language through reading, writing, and spoken language specific to each child's potential and needs.
Total communication		A philosophy (rather than a specific method) that incorporates any of the above approaches based on what each child needs at any given time.

Sources: Laurent Clerc National Deaf Education Center, Communication choices with deaf and hard of hearing children. http://clerccenter.gallaudet.edu/supportservices/series/4010.html; Alexander Graham Bell Association for the Deaf and Hard of Hearing, So your child has a hearing loss: Next steps for parents. www.agbell.org/information/brochures_parent_so.cfm; Ellen Schneiderman, Ph.D., California State University, Northridge.

tive language of the student, be it Spanish, Russian, or ASL, in school learning? Before we attempt to grapple with these thorny issues, take a look at Table 10.5, which provides an overview of communication methods.

Most teachers of students who are deaf or hard of hearing have as their ultimate goal that their students become fluent, competent users of English. There is also increasing emphasis placed on the acquisition of fluency in ASL. Although the most intensive language teaching will take place in early intervention programs and in special schools and classes, the general education teacher who works with the deaf or hard-of-hearing student will also play a role in introducing and expanding English vocabulary, structures, and use. Because of this emphasis, teachers of students with hearing loss must focus on learning techniques related to language development, assessment, and teaching.

Traditionally, programs for students who are deaf and hard of hearing have differed in their approach to teaching communication skills. Some have emphasized the development of speech and auditory skills, while others have encour-

---

A Closer Look — Speech and Hearing Checklist

This checklist will help you to detect any hearing or speech problems in your child at a very young age. *Even if a hearing loss was not detected during your child's infant screening*, it is important to continually monitor speech and language development in order to identify a potential later loss as soon as possible.

Early detection is crucial because undetected hearing loss has a direct effect on the development of speech and language in young children. It is through the sense of hearing that infants begin to naturally learn their native language. If your child can't hear sounds or differences in sounds, then understanding words and speaking will be difficult. No child is too young to be tested or to be helped if a hearing loss is suspected. The earlier a child with hearing loss is identified, the less effect the loss will have on his/her speech development, social growth, learning ability, and classroom performance.

If your child fails to respond as the checklist for the appropriate age level suggests, have your child's hearing tested immediately. Don't delay! If your child does have a hearing loss, early detection means early solutions to hearing and speech problems through the help of medical intervention, education, and amplification. The earlier a hearing loss is identified, the less effect the loss will have on your child's future.

Average Speech and Hearing Behavior for Your Child's Age Level

Birth–3 Months

Startled by loud sounds
Soothed by caretakers' voices

3–6 Months

Reacts to the sound of your voice
Turns eyes and head in the direction of the source of sounds
Enjoys rattles and noisy toys

7–10 Months

Responds to his/her own name
Understands *mama, dada, no, bye bye*, and other common words
Turns head toward familiar sounds, even when he/she cannot see what is happening:

- Dog barking or paper rustling
- Familiar footsteps
- Telephone
- Person's voice

11–15 Months

Imitates and matches sounds with own speech production (though frequently unintelligible), especially in response to human voices or loud noises
Locates or points to familiar objects when asked
Understands words by making appropriate responses or behavior:

- "Where's the dog?"
- "Find the truck."

15–18 Months

Identifies things in response to questions, such as parts of the body
Uses a few single words; while not complete or perfectly pronounced, the words should be clearly meaningful
Follows simple spoken directions

aged the growth of signs along with those skills. Let us take a closer look at these philosophies, the oral approach and the manual approach.

● **The Oral Approach**   The **oral communication approach** is built on the belief that children who are deaf and hard of hearing can learn to talk and that speech should be their primary method of expression. Also, they should under-

> The oral approach is based on the belief that children with hearing loss can learn to speak.

2 Years

Understands yes/no questions

Uses everyday words heard at home or at day care/school

Enjoys being read to and shown pictures in books; points out pictures upon request

Interested in radio/television as shown by word or action

Puts words together to make simple sentences, although they are not complete or grammatically correct:

- "Juice all gone"
- "Go bye-bye car"

Follows simple commands without visual clues from the speaker:

- "Bring me that ball."
- "Get your book and give it to Daddy."

2½ Years

Says or sings short rhymes and songs; enjoys music

Vocabulary approximately 270 words

Investigates noises or tells others when interesting sounds are heard:

- Car door slamming
- Telephone ringing

3 Years

Understands and uses simple verbs, pronouns, and adjectives:

- Go, come, run, sing
- Me, you, him, her
- Big, green, sweet

Locates the source of a sound automatically

Often uses complete sentences

Vocabulary approximately 1000 words

4 Years

Gives connected account of some recent experiences

Can carry out a sequence of two simple directions:

- "Find your shoe and bring it here."
- "Get the ball and throw it to the dog."

5 Years

Speech should be intelligible, although some sounds may still be mispronounced—such as the /s/ sound, particularly in blends with other consonants (e.g., *street, sleep, ask*). Neighbors and people outside the family can understand most of what your child says and her grammatical patterns should match theirs most of the time.

Child carries on conversations, although vocabulary may be limited

Pronouns should be used correctly:

- *I* instead of *me*
- *He* instead of *him*

Don't Delay!

If your child does not exhibit the average behavior for his/her age, get professional advice from your doctor, your hospital, or a local speech and hearing clinic. No child is too young to be tested or to be helped if a hearing loss is suspected. Keep in mind that clapping hands or making loud noises behind a child's back are never accurate tests for hearing loss!

Source: Alexander Graham Bell Association for the Deaf and Hard of Hearing, "Speech and Hearing Checklist." www.agbell.org/information/brochures_checklist.cfm.

stand the speech of others through a combination of speech reading (lip reading) and residual hearing. The overall goal of oralism is that children with hearing loss learn intelligible speech and age-appropriate language (Connor, 1986). There are several different oral methods, but all high-quality oral programs share common goals:

- The earliest possible detection of hearing loss
- Amplification and intervention
- Intensive parent involvement in the child's education
- The use of residual hearing
- The exclusive use of speech, without sign language, for communication

Teaching speech takes considerable training and skill.

Teaching speech and auditory skills is theoretically part of the educational program for the majority of children with hearing loss. Teaching speech is one of the teacher's most complicated and challenging responsibilities, and doing it well takes considerable training and skill.

The teaching of listening skills, sometimes called **auditory training**, requires that the child be fitted with effective, appropriate hearing aids—preferably one in each ear. It begins with developing the child's awareness of all the sounds in the environment—doorbells ringing, dogs barking, people calling the child's name. The most important goal of training residual hearing, however, is to assist the child in understanding spoken language, and thereby support the development of oral language and speech (Flexer, 1994).

Auditory training itself does not enable the child to hear new sounds or words; it simply helps the child make sense of what is heard and use his or her residual hearing as well as possible. Attention to listening skills is important for the regular class teacher as well as the specialist, since there are safety issues involved for the student as well as language-learning issues. For example, attention to environmental sounds will help the student stay safe while riding a bike or crossing the street.

● **The Manual Approach**   The use of the **manual communication approach** by and with people who are deaf has a long history. According to Baker and Cokely (1980), "Wherever there were deaf people who needed to communi-

Adults are not the only teachers of sign. Here preschooler Lennette helps her classmate Noah. (Terry Gilliam/AP Photo)

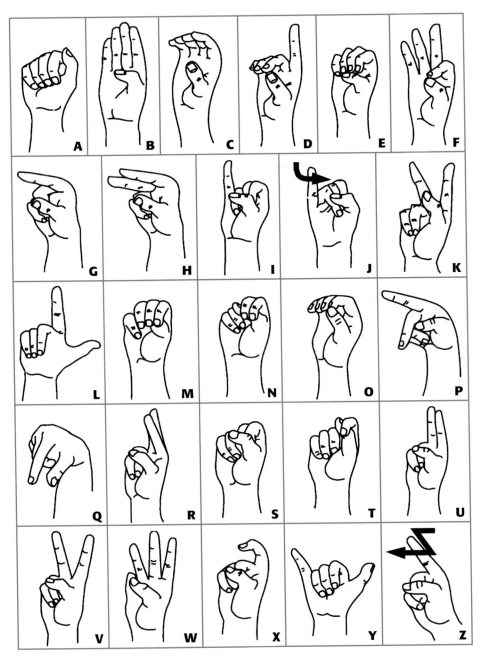

Figure 10.3

The Manual Alphabet

Source: T. Humphries, C. Padden, & T. J. O'Rourke (1980). *A basic course in American Sign Language.* Silver Spring, MD: T. J. Publishers. Reprinted by permission.

cate there have been signed languages that they and their ancestors have developed" (p. 48). The first to systematize a sign language for teaching purposes was the Abbé de l'Epée, a French monk who started the first school for deaf children in Paris in 1755 (Quigley & Paul, 1984).

Manual communication has two components: **fingerspelling**, in which words are spelled out letter by letter using a manual alphabet (see Figure 10.3), and **signs**, which are symbolic representations of words made with the hands. The Teaching Strategies box entitled, "Finger Spelling: Critical for Literacy Development" describes its importance.

The manual communication approach has two components—fingerspelling and signs.

Teaching Strategies & Accommodations

Fingerspelling: Critical for Literacy Development

Fingerspelling—representing the letters of the alphabet on the fingers—may be a critical bridge for deaf and hard-of-hearing children in learning English. Children should be exposed to fingerspelling on a regular basis. This exposure begins with the child's identification as deaf or hard of hearing. Infants and toddlers should be immersed in fingerspelling. They may not immediately understand the letters, but the exposure will prepare them for acquisition of reading and literacy.

Experts emphasize the importance of practice. It is important to make transitions between the letters of words as smoothly as possible. For example, do not fingerspell *CAT* as *C* pause *A* pause *T* pause. Instead, hold the wrist steady and practice until able to move easily between the letters *C-A-T*.

Two techniques—the sandwich technique and the chaining technique—are useful in reading to deaf children. In the sandwich technique, signs are "sandwiched" between fingerspellings. Individuals fingerspell the word or the phrase that appears in the book, then sign the word or phrase, then fingerspell it again (Blumenthal-Kelly, 1995; Humphries & MacDougall, 1997). In the chaining technique, the process is elongated. Individuals point to the word in the book, fingerspell it, sign it, then point to the printed word again.

Source: David R. Schleper (2000). Fingerspelling: Critical for literacy development, *Odyssey, 1*(3). Washington, DC: Laurent Clerc National Deaf Education Center, Gallaudet University. © by Laurent Clerc National Deaf Education Center. Reprinted with permission.

> American Sign Language uses the same vocabulary as English but has a different grammatical structure.

The sign language considered by many deaf adults to be their "native language" is **American Sign Language (ASL)**. ASL uses the same lexicon, or vocabulary, as English, but a different grammatical structure. Today, linguists consider ASL a legitimate language of its own, not simply a form of English (Stokoe, 1960). Because it does not correspond directly to English, and because there is no widely practiced method of writing in ASL, it has not traditionally been used as the primary language of instruction for children who are deaf. Instead, sign language systems that have been designed to represent English manually are generally used for educational purposes, since it is thought that their correspondence to reading and writing in English is closer. In these English-order systems, the intent is that every word and every inflection (for example, verb tense markers such as *-ed* and *-ing*) of English are signed.

● *Communication Controversies*   Since education of deaf children began in the sixteenth century, teachers have argued passionately about the best method of instruction. Advocates of the oral approach have maintained that teaching the child who is deaf to speak and to use residual hearing and speech reading to comprehend language provides the skills the individual needs to function both in the hearing world and in the community of deaf people. But teaching oral language and speech to a child who is profoundly deaf is an extremely difficult and laborious process.

The best results seem to occur when early diagnosis is combined with early amplification and early and consistent family involvement. Family involvement is the key. Typically, a preschool-aged child who is deaf speaks only a handful of words. Therefore, the family's commitment to teaching the child to talk is crucial in an oral program, and parents must be willing to experience the slow growth of communication skills in their child. For children who are hard of hearing, the growth of oral skills proceeds significantly faster; they frequently can learn oral language in the regular classroom, with support from a resource teacher or a speech-language specialist.

However, for many children who are deaf—those whose hearing loss is diagnosed after age 2, those with additional handicapping conditions, or those whose families are unable to supply them with the complete support that they need—the oral approach is frequently not satisfactory. During the 1960s and 1970s, dissatisfaction with the oral approach grew, and school programs using total communication proliferated. By 2002, about 53 percent of the students included in the Annual Survey of Deaf and Hard of Hearing Children and Youth attended schools in which some form of sign was used (Gallaudet Research Institute, 2003). Today, interest in oral methods is reviving with the advent of the cochlear implant, a treatment for profound deafness involving the surgical implantation of electrodes in the cochlea (see the Closer Look box entitled, "The Cochlear Implant Controversy") (Christiansen & Leigh, 2002).

Total communication was designed to use any and all methods of communicating with students who are deaf—speech, fingerspelling, English-order sign language, American Sign Language—depending on the learning needs of the student at the moment (Garretson, 1976). In practice, however, most professionals equate total communication with the simultaneous method—using speech and manually coded English together.

Today, the controversies in the field revolve not so much around whether speech or sign should be used but on which form of sign should be used in the classroom. Some professionals believe that advocates of the oral approach are operating under the clinical model of understanding deafness, where it is still seen as deviant; they believe that oralists want to turn children who are deaf into children who are hearing (Paul & Quigley, 1990). Proponents of viewing Deafness as a cultural difference rather than as a disability believe that American Sign Language should be the first language of all children who are deaf and that therefore it should be the first language taught in schools (Drasgow, 1998). These professionals, both deaf and hearing, use theories of first- and second-language acquisition of spoken language to support their argument that once fluency in the first language is acquired, second-language learning can and will follow (Drasgow, 1998). They propose teaching ASL first and then, when children have a solid ASL base, introducing English as a second language (Newell, 1991). Other professionals object to this model, suggesting that because there is no widely accepted written form of ASL, reading and writing skills in English will be introduced too late. Also, because ASL is used without speech, young children may not be given the opportunity to develop speech skills through listening and observation.

Only research, study, and the introduction of model programs will demonstrate whether teaching ASL as a first language in a bilingual program will ultimately succeed in improving the English literacy of children who are deaf, and in the process make them fluent ASL users who are comfortable in their own culture as well as in the "hearing world."

Recently, three researchers at the National Technical Institute for the Deaf, a college of the Rochester Institute of Technology, conducted a study of a group

Children taught with the oral method do best when early diagnosis is combined with early amplification and family involvement.

Many in the Deaf community believe that ASL should be the first language of all children who are deaf.

of deaf college students who were strong readers and writers (Toscano, McGee, & Lepoutre, 2002). The students used a variety of communication methods, including speech, sign language (ASL and manually coded English systems), cued speech, total communication, and fingerspelling; they had attended oral and sign language programs. These students described ongoing, committed involvement of parents in their schooling, particularly in the areas of reading and writing; their mothers were often the ones who taught them to read. Their families—not just their mothers, but fathers, siblings, and sometimes grandparents—went to great efforts to learn to communicate with them, and to ensure that the deaf children were included in all family conversations. The researchers concluded:

A Closer Look   The Cochlear Implant Controversy

A cochlear implant—"one of the twentieth century's most consequential developments in communication" (Niparko, 2000, p. 1)—is an electronic device designed to provide sound information for adults and children who have sensorineural hearing loss in both ears and obtain limited benefit from hearing aids. In the last thirty years, the technology has evolved from a device with a single electrode (or channel) to systems that transmit more sound information through multiple electrodes (or channels). The cochlear implant has been approved for use with children since 1990. A small but growing number of children with deafness are currently using cochlear implants; the annual survey done by the Gallaudet Research Institute reported that 7.4 percent of students in surveyed programs had cochlear implants, and over 90 percent of those implants were still in use (Gallaudet Research Institute, 2003). Because the implant is expensive and not routinely covered by medical insurance, some are concerned that it is only available to relatively affluent families.

Advocates such as Dr. Mary Jo Osberger, a researcher who has studied children with cochlear implants, assert that they can help children who do not benefit from hearing aids develop speech and language understanding and skills. She says that "no other sensory aid has had such a dramatic impact on improving the acquisition and use of spoken language by children with profound hearing impairments." Advocates argue that the earlier the children receive implants, the greater their chances of improvement.

Recent research suggests that the benefits of the cochlear implant vary greatly among individuals, but in general, children with cochlear implants surpass children who wear conventional hearing aids in speech perception, speech production, and speech intelligibility (Cheng & Niparko, 2000; Kirk, 2000). The best outcomes appear in children who receive their implants early in life, who undergo a period of intensive training after the implant, and who have had the implant for at least two years.

The Controversy

However, the implant has been called "cultural genocide" by many in the Deaf community who believe American Sign Language is the linguistic base for a separate culture. Their response is built on a legacy of failed attempts to teach deaf children oral communication—in their view, to be more like hearing children. In the view of Harlan Lane, a psychology professor at Northeastern University, "It's simply unethical to use force, surgery, or education to take children who would normally be members of a linguistic minority and try to make them into members of another linguistic group."

To many, the argument implies that deaf children belong to the Deaf community and not to their hearing parents, a view to which people like Donna Morere take exception. "There is a large segment within the community that identifies with Deaf culture and feels like hearing parents are not competent to make a decision like choosing a cochlear implant for their children," she says.

While communication may or may not have been easy, students were unanimous in their perception of positive support within the family unit. The development of strong reading and writing skills, therefore, cannot be said to be the result of the consistent use of a single communication method. (Toscano, McGee, & Lepoutre, 2002, p. 14)

No matter what the communication method, then, the ongoing involvement and support of families in communication and academic achievement appear to be what made the difference for these students: "the mode of communication is less important than the quality of communication" (Toscano, McGee, & Lepoutre, 2002, p.21).

Morere is in a unique position to see both sides of the debate. As a psychology professor at Gallaudet University—the only liberal arts college for the deaf in the United States—she has taught at the heart of the Deaf culture movement. Morere has normal hearing, but when her son Thomas was diagnosed as profoundly deaf, she was suddenly faced not with the abstract arguments of ethicists and anthropologists, but with the hard reality that her child could not hear. Initially, Morere says, she was persuaded by some of her colleagues at Gallaudet who cautioned her against opting for a cochlear implant. Her eventual decision to go ahead with the procedure is one she now says she wished she'd made earlier. "When I saw what the CI could do, I really regretted the little over a year that he didn't have it," she says. "I'm so relieved when Thomas can ride his bicycle in the street with other kids and instead of having to run after him and drag him off the street when a car comes, I can yell 'Car!' and he will ride his bike off the street," Morere says. "If that was all the cochlear implant accomplished, that would have satisfied me, but it's gone way beyond that."

The National Organization of the Deaf (NAD) is an education and advocacy group that has long worked on behalf of deaf individuals. In its recent position statement on cochlear implants, the NAD has provided a measured (but still passionate) view of the potential drawbacks and benefits of the implant. The paper's authors describe the importance of viewing people who are deaf according to a "wellness model," emphasizing the large number of deaf adults who live productive lives; they believe that "cochlear implants are not appropriate for all deaf and hard-of-hearing children and adults" (p. 2) and that they do not eliminate or "cure" deafness. The recommendations to parents are sound:

Despite the pathological view of deafness held by many within the medical profession, parents would benefit by seeking out opportunities to meet and get to know successful deaf and hard-of-hearing children and adults who are fluent in sign language and English, both with and without implants. The NAD encourages parents and deaf adults to research other options besides implantation. If implantation is the object of choice, parents should obtain all information about the surgical procedure, surgical risks, postsurgical auditory and speech training requirements, and potential benefits and limitations so as to make informed decisions. (pp. 3–4)

Local branches of the NAD would be a good place for families to start looking for such models.

Sources: Adapted from Mary Jo Osberger & Harlan Lane (1993). The debate: Cochlear implants in children. *Hearing Health*, 9(2), 19–22. The NAD Position Statement on Cochlear Implants is available at http://www.nad.org/infocenter/newsroom/positions/CochlearImplants.html.

Effective signed communication involves both the sign and facial expression, the punctuation of sign language. (© Ellen B. Senisi)

Curriculum

There is evidence that students with hearing loss do not learn the same subject matter as their hearing peers.

Students who are deaf or hard of hearing should learn the same subject matter in school as their hearing peers, but there is some evidence that they do not. Donald Moores (2001) believes that the emphasis on teaching communication skills in most programs for students who are deaf or hard of hearing has resulted in neglect of the traditional academic areas such as math, science, and social studies. Moores (2001) suggests that educators pay more attention to the teaching of traditional content areas in order to prevent their students with hearing loss from experiencing a major "knowledge gap." See the Teaching Strategies box entitled, "Themes in the Curriculum for Students Who Are Deaf."

Teaching Strategies & Accommodations

Themes in the Curriculum for Students Who Are Deaf

David Stewart and Thomas Kluwin (2001) believe that, because of lack of experiences and adequate opportunities for communication in their home environments, the curriculum for deaf students must reflect these themes:

- *Creating authentic experiences.* Teachers must engineer experiences for students that are directly tied to the teaching content.

- *Integrating vocabulary development.* Teachers must make words visible—write them, fingerspell them, provide pictures to illustrate them when possible—and teach them as part of broader concepts and in meaningful contexts.

- *Creating opportunities for self-expression.* Deaf students need opportunities to practice elaborate verbal skills, as well as opportunities for defining and refining ideas.

- *Providing deaf role models.* Deaf role models let deaf students know "this is what you need to do to succeed." Actress Marlee Matlin, former Miss America Heather Whitestone, percussionist Evelyn Glennie, and Gallaudet University President I. King Jordan are just a few who might be studied.

As we mentioned earlier in the chapter, in addition to the study of communication and the content areas, many professionals advocate for the study of Deaf culture in the school curriculum. There is hope that an understanding of the history and heritage of people who are deaf will help students "develop an appreciation for both their hearing and Deaf cultural and linguistic linkages with people throughout the world" (Luetke-Stahlman & Luckner, 1991, p. 347). See the Teaching Strategies box entitled, "Integrating Deaf Studies into the Curriculum" for additional information.

Today, the focus of the curriculum for most deaf students is in the area of literacy. The skills involved in learning to read and write and the application of those skills in life have not traditionally come easily to deaf students, and teachers and researchers are working to address the best ways for deaf students to acquire literacy skills (Luetke-Stahlman, 1999; Paul, 1998; Schirmer, 1994; Stewart & Kluwin, 2001). The Shared Reading Project has provided models of deaf adults reading books to deaf children that have demonstrated the importance of reading "aloud" (Schleper, 1997), and teachers of deaf children are taking the "best practices" for teaching reading from general education and applying them in their work with deaf children. For more information about the Shared Reading Project, please visit **http://clerccenter.gallaudet.edu/Literacy/srp/srp.html**.

> Teachers and researchers alike are focusing on improving the literacy of deaf children.

Teaching Strategies & Accommodations

Integrating Deaf Studies into the Curriculum

Grade Level	Content Area Topics	Deaf Culture Components
Kindergarten	Science/Social Studies: sound awareness and Deaf awareness	Basics for interacting with Deaf people
First grade	Social Studies: family life of the Deaf	Deafness and communication
Second grade	Social Studies: Deaf people in the community	Sensitivity activities, ASL as a language
Third grade	Sound, hearing measurement, and amplification	Deaf vs. hard of hearing, social interaction norms
Fourth grade	Reading: biography and history of Deaf people	Deaf history, Deaf identity, interview Deaf adult
Fifth grade	Health: hearing and deafness	Deaf community, organizations, and recreation
Sixth grade	Science: communication and assistive devices for the Deaf	Deafness and literature, Deaf values

Source: David A. Stewart & Thomas N. Kluwin, *Teaching deaf and hard of hearing students: Content, strategies, and curriculum,* © 2001 (p. 118). Published by Allyn and Bacon, Boston, MA. Copyright © 2001 by Pearson Education. Reprinted by permission of the publisher.

Stewart and Kluwin apply their "themes" (in the Teaching Strategies box on p. 379) to the teaching of literacy:

> The strategies that we described for teaching literacy are similar to those for teaching other subject matter to deaf students. Authentic activities must be incorporated into the learning experience, the students must be provided with opportunities to talk about what they are reading and writing, and modeling and guidance must be provided to help them overcome their lack of proficiency in the English language. (p. 109)

Assessment

Many tests are not reliable or valid for use with test takers who are deaf.

Undertaking an educational assessment with a student who is deaf or hard of hearing is a difficult endeavor, because the typical student's English-language competency is often significantly delayed for his or her age (Paul & Quigley, 1990). As a result, each test, with directions and questions written (or spoken) in English, becomes a test not of its content but of the student's mastery of English. When a student does not do well on a test, it is often because he or she does not understand the language of the directions or the test items. Rephrasing or paraphrasing the language makes the test standardization invalid, so the results cannot be used comparatively (Salvia & Ysseldyke, 2004). Although it is possible to work around these complicating factors, it takes skill and considerable experience in communication to obtain valid educational assessment results with students with hearing loss, particularly those who are deaf (Eccarius, 1997).

School Placement

Deaf and hard-of-hearing students can be found in every educational setting.

Students who are deaf and hard of hearing can be found in a wide variety of educational settings, from the general education classroom to the residential school. According to the Gallaudet Research Institute (2003), about 45 percent of the children with hearing loss were placed in the general education classroom, 32 percent were in separate classes on general education campuses, 14 percent in resource rooms, and 28 percent in special schools or residential schools (the numbers don't add up to 100 percent because some children were enrolled in more than one of these options). Let us discuss the most frequent placements. (See Figure 10.4 for a pictorial view.)

● **The General Education Classroom**   More and more deaf or hard-of-hearing students are included in the general education classroom—a 21 percent growth rate occurred between 1990–1991 and 1999–2000 (U.S. Department of Education, 2001). From that classroom base they may receive a variety of specialized services and supports. Their classroom amplification devices, whether they be personal hearing aids, cochlear implants, or classroom hearing aids connected to a teacher microphone, may be evaluated regularly by the school audiologist; they may receive direct services in speech, signs, or the development of auditory skills from the itinerant teacher with a specialization in hearing loss or from the speech-language therapist; perhaps they receive extra help with communication skills or academic subjects from the resource teacher, who is also a specialist in hearing loss. Students who participate in school programs with their hearing peers are likely to have more residual hearing than those who do not (Gallaudet Research Institute, 2002); they are also likely to have better communication skills.

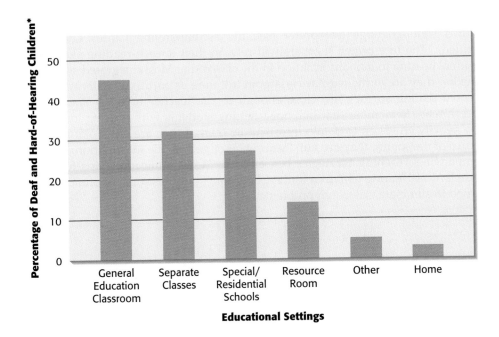

Figure 10.4

Educational Settings of Deaf and Hard-of-Hearing Children, 2001–2002
*Percentages may total more than 100% because of multiple responses.

Source: Gallaudet Research Institute (2003). *Regional and national summary report of data from the 2001–2002 Annual Survey of Deaf and Hard of Hearing Children & Youth.* Washington, DC: GRI, Gallaudet University.

A Closer Look)   **The Interpreter**

Interpreters provide an essential service to both students and teachers in classrooms. Oral interpreters silently repeat, with clear but unexaggerated lip movements, the message of another speaker. Sign language interpreters translate the spoken message into signs and fingerspelling.

Leah Ilan is an interpreter in Los Angeles who has a busy career as both an oral and sign language interpreter. Leah believes that the most important factors in the relationship between the classroom teacher and the interpreter are communication and trust, and that the better the interpreter knows the teacher, the better work she does. Leah finds oral interpreting somewhat more difficult than sign interpreting. She describes the job as "sounding out every single sound and making it visible—with the mouth, jaw, eyes, and facial expression. I use it all." Leah finds the need for concentration greater with oral interpreting, since the oral "consumer"—the person with hearing loss—relies on small parts of speech and word endings for comprehension. She hastens to add that sign interpreting is not easy; in fact, the preference now is that sign interpreters work in teams of two on long assignments. This allows sign interpreters periods of rest and avoids the appearance of hand and arm injuries such as carpal tunnel syndrome, which can limit or end their careers.

Some students with hearing loss will be integrated in the regular classroom with a sign language interpreter (see the accompanying Closer Look box entitled, "The Interpreter"); others will rely on their speech-reading skills and residual hearing to gain information in the classroom. Most integrated students, whether they are in the regular classroom full time or part time, will need preferential seating so they are close enough to the teacher or other speaker to speech read. Remember that in a noisy setting students with hearing loss must rely heavily on vision to obtain information; often if they are not looking at the source of the sound, they are not "hearing" it or getting the information. The accompanying Teaching Strategies box entitled, "Communication Tips for Deaf and Hard-of-Hearing Children in the Classroom" outlines some approaches designed to eliminate classroom problems.

Teaching Strategies & Accommodations

Communication Tips for Deaf and Hard-of-Hearing Children in the Classroom

Classrooms often move at a fast pace. Making sure that the deaf or hard-of-hearing child has access to everything that is going on will be of the utmost importance. Here are some considerations that may help facilitate communication in the classroom. Many of these strategies, which make the classroom a more visual environment, will be helpful for all children in the classroom.

For All Deaf or Hard-of-Hearing Students

- The student should have a clear view of the faces of the teacher and the other students.

- Do not seat the student facing bright lights or windows where a glare or strong backlighting will make it difficult to see the faces of others.

- Remember that the best place for a deaf or hard-of-hearing student may change with the teaching situation. Make sure the student feels free to move about the room for ease of communication.

For Students Depending on Spoken Language Communication

- When possible, seat the student close to the teacher's desk for the best listening and viewing advantage.

- Familiarize yourself with how to check a child's hearing aid.

- Do not exaggerate mouth movements or shout; this may cause distortion of the message through the hearing aid and greater difficulty for the student.

- If communication breakdowns occur, try repair strategies such as rephrasing the message, saying it at a slower pace, or writing the message when appropriate.

For Students Depending on Visual Communication

- Try to remove "visual noise" (visual interference) from communication situations (e.g., bottle on table, door open, paper in hand while signing, jewelry of signer, overhead projector in the way).

- When a sign language interpreter is being used in the classroom, make sure the interpreter has an opportunity to complete the message before moving on to the next point.

● *Special Classes*   A special class is composed of a group of students who are deaf and hard of hearing of similar age who are taught on an elementary, middle-school, or high-school campus by a specialist teacher of deaf and hard-of-hearing students. Many students with hearing loss attend special classes on public school campuses, because this placement provides a home base for integrating these students with their hearing peers.

Some students in the special class are integrated with their hearing peers for academic subjects, and others for subjects such as art, music, or physical education; still others may have contact with their hearing peers only at recess and lunch. The amount of time each student spends with hearing peers is specified on his or her Individualized Education Program (IEP). Although characteristics of the student are obviously of prime importance in the decision whether or not

Facilitating Classroom Discussions

- When possible, have students sit in a circle.
- Remind students to speak one at a time.
- Point to the student who will speak next. Wait for the deaf or hard-of-hearing student to locate the speaker.

Methods That Will Help Deaf or Hard-of-Hearing Students

- DO use as many visual aids as possible. Use written instructions and summaries, and write key words and concepts on the blackboard. Utilize captioned films when possible.
- DO use attention-getting techniques when they are needed: Touch the student lightly on the shoulder, wave your hands, or flash the lights in the classroom.
- DO set up a buddy system to help deaf or hard-of-hearing students with taking notes, clarifying assignments, etc.
- DO ask questions and spend individual time with deaf or hard-of-hearing students periodically to make sure they are following the instructions.

Don'ts to Keep in Mind

- DON'T change the topic of conversation quickly without letting the deaf or hard-of-hearing students know that the topic has changed.
- DON'T talk with your back to the class, your face obstructed by a book, or with a pencil in your mouth.
- DON'T call attention to misunderstandings or speech errors in front of the class. If this becomes a problem, discuss it with the child's family or other support personnel who may be working with the child.

Source: Material developed by Debra Nussbaum, audiologist, Kendall Demonstration Elementary School, Laurent Clerc National Deaf Education Center, Gallaudet University, Support Services Handout, Series Number 4009. © by Laurent Clerc National Deaf Education Center. Reprinted with permission.

to integrate, the availability of willing and competent general education teachers to work with the students with hearing loss is often what makes or breaks the opportunity for the student.

● *Residential Schools*   The deinstitutionalization movement (see Chapter 1) has had an important influence on the education of children who are deaf. Thirty years ago, most children with hearing loss attended large residential schools, either as day students or as residents. These schools hold a special place in the heart of the Deaf community. Many people who were deaf had left their homes to live at residential schools when they were very young; they learned to communicate there, made their lifelong friends there, met their spouses there, and settled in the surrounding area. They were anxious that their own deaf children attend these schools, too.

The nature of residential schools has changed dramatically since 1975, when IDEA mandated less segregated school settings.

The concept of the "least restrictive environment" in IDEA has mandated a less segregated school setting for most children who are deaf, and the nature of residential schools has changed dramatically since the law was signed by President Gerald Ford in 1975, much to the dismay of many members of the Deaf community. Student enrollment has declined notably (Moores, 2001). Some of the schools have closed; many of them have become centers for students who are deaf with multiple disabilities; most have become day schools.

Residential schools are often places where students can develop positive identities.

With a wider range of program options available in public schools, some professionals, often from outside the field of deafness, have seen very little justification for the removal of a child from his or her family in order to attend school. Nonetheless, many members of the Deaf community and professionals in the field of deafness continue to fight for the right to choose a residential school for a child who is deaf. The schools are sometimes seen as the birthplace of Deaf culture in this country, places where students who are deaf can develop their own positive identity rather than being forced to accept the values and norms of the hearing world.

❓ Pause and Reflect

There are so many specific instructional issues for students with hearing loss that it's a wonder so many of them are integrated into general education. After your reading, do you feel any better prepared to tackle the challenge of teaching a student who is deaf or hard of hearing? Why or why not? ●

Technological Advances

Hearing Aids

Hearing aids today are considerably more efficient than the hearing aids of old. They have been reduced in size, so they are more appealing cosmetically, and the majority of children are now fitted with behind-the-ear aids. More important, their capabilities have improved, and they can be designed to match each individual's hearing loss. Most children can benefit from wearing two hearing aids. New designs in hearing aids include those that have been miniaturized to the point that they fit completely in the ear. Although these tiny and lightweight in-the-ear hearing aids are just beginning to be recommended for young chil-

Modern hearing aids are much more efficient and compact than their predecessors.

Technology Focus

Technology Can Eliminate Communication Barriers

Many of the advances in services and opportunities for people who are deaf have occurred in the area of technology. Improved hearing aids, telecommunication devices and relay systems, and television captioning have made life more convenient and everyday experiences more accessible for many people with hearing loss.

For many years in telecommunications, the process of two people communicating over a distance was the same for everyone. You used a device called a telephone with a receiver for listening and a microphone for speaking. Your telephone was connected to a telephone line leading to a single telephone network, as was the telephone of the person you called. Communication took place exclusively by voice, without benefit of visual information, and was either inaccessible or "accessible with great difficulty" to individuals with hearing loss.

However, over the last five to ten years there has been a real paradigm shift in how people use telecommunications. Many of the new protocols, such as email, paging, and instant messaging, are mainstream and popular, and afford individuals with hearing loss the benefit of visual information either as a supplement to or replacement for voice communication.

Individuals with hearing loss now have a variety of ways to accomplish their home and business telecommuting needs:

- Auditory systems that enhance the traditional voice phone, known as *assistive telephone technology*
- Visual, text-based systems such as *two-way pagers* that permit users to both send and receive text messages. These small devices have thumb keyboards and vibrating alerts, and may also handle TTY, email, and fax among other functions.
- Auditory plus visual systems such as *Internet videoconferencing*
- *TTYs* and computers with TTY software
- *Email* and *instant messaging*
- The *Telecommunications Relay Service* (TRS), which provides a protocol for a hearing person with a voice telephone and a TTY user to communicate via a regular telephone line
- *Video relay service* that allows for sign language interpretation, rather than typing on a TTY, for relaying the speech of the hearing party

Source: Adapted from Linda Kozma-Spytek, Research Audiologist, *Accessing the world of telecommunications*, Technology Access Program, Gallaudet University. Available at http://tap.gallaudet.edu/AccessTelecomLKS/AcTel.htm.

dren or profoundly deaf users, they are prescribed more frequently for adolescents and adults, who often have great concerns about the visibility of their hearing aids.

In the last few years hearing aid technology has changed and improved dramatically (Sweetow & Luckett, 2001). Today's newest hearing aids are digitally programmable or fully digital—they can be programmed by computer and customized to match an individual's hearing loss and characteristics of the environment. The traditional analog hearing aid amplified all sounds to the same volume. That means that in the classroom, for example, the teacher's voice, children talking, and the sounds of the hallway outside would be heard at a similar volume. Digitally programmed hearing aids can improve the wearer's ability to hear in the presence of background noise, and can be set to work differently in different listening environments.

Digital hearing aids can be customized for each person's hearing loss.

In this inclusive classroom, the co-teachers are a general educator and a specialist in deafness. One tells the story aloud, and the other provides a word-for-word signed translation. (Will Hart/PhotoEdit)

Not all children need digital hearing aids, and they are considerably more expensive than analog aids. Families must discuss the pros and cons of this expense with their audiologist before committing to digital hearing aids (Sweetow & Luckett, 2001). It is likely that the appearance and the functioning of hearing aids will continue to improve through the refinement of digital-based technology.

Cochlear Implants

Researchers around the country have been surgically inserting **cochlear implants** in a relatively small number of profoundly deaf children with sensorineural hearing loss. Although the cochlear implant is not a cure for deafness, implants do appear to improve the perception of sound. The implants have become a source of controversy, however (see the Closer Look box on pages 376–377). For more information on how the cochlear implant works, please visit **http://www.pbs.org/wnet/soundandfury/cochlear/cochlear_flash.html**.

Assistive Listening Devices

Although a hearing aid makes all sounds in the environment louder, assistive listening devices increase the loudness of a desired sound—the teacher's voice, the actors on a stage, or the voice on the telephone. There are different types of assistive listening devices for different settings: Some are used with hearing aids, and some without. They can be used in classrooms, in theaters, at meetings—wherever they are needed. An audiologist can help a teacher or an individual determine which assistive listening device will be most helpful (American Speech-Language-Hearing Association, 1997).

Telecommunication Devices

Telecommunication devices for the deaf (TDDs) are telephones with small screens that display the message of the sender. The system works like this: One

While 6-year-old Erica gives her mother a kiss the transmitting coil of her cochlear implant is visible on her hair. The connection to the implant is on the interior side of the coil, and a speech processor is worn in a pocket on the body. For a fuller explanation of how the implant works, see http://www.pbs.org/wnet/soundandfury/cochlear/cochlear_flash.html. (J. D. Pooley/AP Photo)

person dials the number of a friend. The phone rings, and a light flashes in the home of the person receiving the call. When the receiver is picked up and placed in the cradle of the TDD, the two people can begin to type their communication into the TDD. The messages appear on paper, or, in the newest models, on a tiny screen on the TDD. Many agencies and businesses now routinely train their employees to use the TDD; they are used for business as well as social calls.

> Today most people with hearing loss can use TDDs.

Many people with hearing loss now prefer email and instant messaging—real-time conversation via the computer screen—to TDDs (Bowe, 2002). While many workplaces have a policy prohibiting instant messaging on the job, Bowe suggests that it is a *reasonable accommodation* under the Americans with Disabilities Act (see Chapter 1) to allow workers with hearing loss to use instant messaging to confer with coworkers and clients.

Captioning

Television captioning for viewers with hearing loss began as a system of open captioning in which captions that paralleled the verbal content of the television program appeared on the bottom of every viewer's screen. Today, though, a system called **closed captioning** exists. Viewers with hearing loss can buy a decoder that, when connected to their television set, allows them to receive broadcasts carrying a coded signal that the decoder makes visible (Withrow, 1976). Since July 1, 1993, all TV sets thirteen inches or larger that are sold or built in the United States have been caption-chip-equipped (Bowe, 1991), allowing viewers to select captioning of all available programs. Presently, captioned movies in the theater and captioned home DVDs are becoming more widely available (Wynant, 2003). As the population ages and hearing loss in the aging population becomes more common, there will likely be increased demand for these services. The National Center to Improve Practice in Special Education Through Technology, Media, and Materials is a good place to start looking for captioned materials (go to **http://www.2.edc.org/NCIP/library/v&c/toc.htm**). For open caption movie locations, visit **http://www.insightcinema.org**.

> Closed captioning allows viewers with hearing loss to receive captions that parallel the verbal content of many TV programs.

SUMMARY

- Deafness is hearing loss that prevents the learning of language through hearing. Conductive hearing loss results from damage to the outer or middle ear and can usually be corrected. Sensorineural loss involves damage to the cochlea or auditory nerve and as of now cannot be corrected.

- The most common causes of hearing loss are otitis media, inherited genetic factors, rubella, meningitis, and premature birth. Approximately 26 percent of children with hearing loss have additional disabilities.

- Hearing loss is measured by an audiologist using a series of tests, including pure-tone tests. The results of these tests are illustrated by an audiogram.

- Language is the most critical area affected by hearing loss, especially because hearing loss is usually not identified until after language normally appears.

- The cognitive abilities of students who are deaf and hard of hearing as a group are the same as those of hearing individuals. Despite this, students with hearing loss frequently underachieve in school because of the heavy emphasis on English-language skills.

- The Deaf community views deafness as a culture rather than a deficit and urges that understanding of Deaf culture be integrated into the curriculum for students.

- Manual communication includes fingerspelling and signs. American Sign Language (ASL) is considered a language of its own and does not correspond directly to English. Total communication uses oral, auditory, and manual modes of communication and advocates adopting whatever system seems most appropriate for a child at a given time.

- Many students with hearing loss attend general education classes and use amplification devices, special services provided by an audiologist or itinerant teacher, or an oral or sign language interpreter.

- Hearing aids and telecommunication devices have greatly improved in recent years, and technological advances continue to provide opportunities for people with hearing loss to communicate freely across long distances.

KEY TERMS

deafness

hard of hearing

hearing impairment

Deaf community

hearing loss

residual hearing

congenital hearing loss

acquired hearing loss

prelingual deafness

postlingual deafness

bilateral hearing loss

unilateral hearing loss

conductive hearing loss

sensorineural hearing loss

mixed hearing loss

otitis media

otologist

audiologist

audiogram

Deaf culture

Deaf community

oral communication approach

auditory training

manual communication approach

fingerspelling

signs

American Sign Language (ASL)

total communication

cochlear implants

telecommunication devices for the deaf (TDDs)

closed captioning

USEFUL RESOURCES

- The Center for Applied Special Technology (CAST) has developed *Bobby,* a system that can evaluate whether websites are accessible to users with hearing loss (and others with disabilities as well). Look for the Bobby icon (a picture of a British policeman, or Bobby, in his tall blue hat) to determine whether a website is accessible for students with disabilities, or *Bobby-approved* (visit **http:// www.cast.org/** and **http://bobby.watchfire. com/bobby/html/en/about.jsp**).

- Hands & Voices is a parent-driven, non-profit organization dedicated to providing unbiased support to families with children who are deaf or hard of hearing. They provide support activities and information concerning deaf and hard-of-hearing issues to parents and professionals. Access their website at **http://www.handsandvoices.org**.

- The Alexander Graham Bell Association for the Deaf (go to **http://www. agbell.org**) has published an excellent booklet for parents whose young child has been diagnosed with hearing loss. Called *So your child has a hearing loss: Next steps for parents,* it is available free of charge from Bell. It's an excellent introduction to hearing loss for teachers as well.

- Gallaudet University Press (at **http://gupress.gallaudet.edu**) publishes a range of books of interest to deaf and hearing readers; many are about sign language. For teachers, we recommend the book and video *Come sign with us* by Jan C. Hafer and Robert M. Wilson, which describes activities for teaching children sign language. For parents, there is *Literacy and your deaf child* by David A. Stewart and Bryan R. Clarke, *You and your deaf child,* by John W. Adams, and *The signing family: What every parent should know about sign communication* by David A. Stewart and Barbara Luetke-Stahlman. There is also an extensive collection of books for children that incorporate sign language.

- *Handspeak* is a sign language dictionary online that contains video illustrations of over 3000 signs (go to **http://www.handspeak.com**). Another excellent source for ASL vocabulary is the American Sign Language Browser at **http://www.commtechlab.msu.edu/sites/ aslweb/browser.htm**.

- The National Deaf Education Network and Clearinghouse (at **http:// clerccenter.gallaudet.edu/infotogo**) has a service called Info to Go that is an excellent source of additional information on deafness. Info to Go responds to a wide range of questions received from the general public, deaf and hard-of-hearing people, their families, and professionals who work with them. Phone: (202) 651-5051, TTY: (202) 651-5052, Fax: (202) 651-5054, email: Clearinghouse.Infotogo@gallaudet.edu.

- See Carol Padden and Tom Humphries (1988). *Deaf in America: Voices from a culture.* Cambridge, MA: Harvard University Press. This book, now a classic, focuses on the stories of people who are deaf and offers intriguing insights into those who share the culture of American Sign Language.

 PORTFOLIO ACTIVITIES

1. Explore Deaf culture and interact with deaf individuals:
   - Contact an adult service agency to find out how services are provided to deaf people.

- Volunteer to be a note-taker for a deaf student.
- Volunteer at a nursing home for elderly people who are deaf.

Write about your experiences in a journal that becomes part of your portfolio.

✓ **Standards** This activity will help the student meet CEC Content Standard 3: Individual Learning Differences.

2. How does your college or university provide support services to students with hearing loss? In particular, find out what types of career counseling are offered. How might these services be improved? With others in your class, create a list of career services that could be used by students who are deaf.

✓ **Standards** This activity will help the student meet CEC Content Standard 3: Individual Learning Differences and Standard 4: Instructional Strategies.

3. Devise a unit on deafness and Deaf culture to include in your curriculum. Its components might include the following:

- What is sound? How is it made?
- What are the parts of the ear? What causes deafness?
- How does a cochlear implant work?
- What are Deaf culture and the Deaf community?
- Invite a mime group, signing song group, or Deaf theater group to visit your classroom.
- Describe the types of manual languages and systems to transcribe them.
- What are the abilities, attitudes, and accomplishments of deaf artists?
- Who are some famous deaf people?
- Making communication work: What can deaf students tell their hearing friends so that they can improve their communication?
- Organize a Deaf Awareness Week at school.
- Explore jobs and higher education opportunities for deaf students.
- Offer sign classes by students with hearing loss for hearing students.
- Visit or host pen pal programs with students who are deaf in other programs, states, or countries.

Material adapted from Barbara Luetke-Stahlman and John Luckner (1991). *Effectively educating students with hearing impairments* (p. 352). New York: Longman. Copyright © 1991. Used by permission of the authors.

✓ **Standards** This activity will help the student meet CEC Content Standard 3: Individual Learning Differences and Standard 4: Instructional Strategies.

 To access an electronic portfolio template for these activities, visit our text website through http://www.education. college.hmco.com/students/.

Children Who Are Blind or Have Low Vision

11

Learning Objectives

After reading this chapter, the reader will:

- Understand and explain the legal and educational definitions of blindness and low vision

- Describe how we see, and the major causes of visual impairment in children

- Discuss how a visual impairment affects a child's learning and development

- Identify how education for students with visual impairments should be different from that of sighted students, and how it should be the same

- Describe some teaching strategies, accommodations, and assistive technology supports that can be used with students with visual impairments

Outline

Terms and Definitions
Causes of Visual Impairment
    How We See
    Causes of Vision Loss
    Prevalence
Characteristics of Students
    Who Are Blind or Have
    Low Vision
    Language and Concept
        Development
    Motor Development
    Cognitive and Intellectual
        Development
    Social and Emotional
        Development
    School Achievement
    Effects on the Family
Teaching Strategies and
    Accommodations
    Early Intervention
    Identification and
        Assessment
    Curriculum
    School Settings for Students
        Who Are Blind or Have
        Low Vision
    Education for Students with
        Additional Disabilities
    Assistive Technology
SUMMARY
KEY TERMS
USEFUL RESOURCES
PORTFOLIO ACTIVITIES

People who are sighted develop a concept of what it is like to be blind from maneuvering in the dark, or wearing a blindfold during childhood games. As a result of these experiences, most of us believe that we understand what it is like to be blind. We are probably wrong. In the first place, our experiences are based on the condition of total blindness. Contrary to popular stereotype, most people who are visually impaired respond to some visual stimuli, such as shadows, light and darkness, or moving objects. The majority of people with visual impairments can read print, either regular print or print that is magnified or enlarged; only 10 percent of students meeting the requirements of legal blindness use Braille as their primary learning medium (American Printing House for the Blind, 2002).

Second, some of our manufactured early experiences of "blindness" may have been negative or frightening because we lacked the skills that successful blind people have acquired. Most people rely on vision for protection and information. So, during the course of our childhood games we were usually tempted to peek or turn on the light for reassurance and confirmation. In contrast, people who are blind receive instruction in daily living skills and rely on their other senses to gain information about their world. Most people who are blind can move independently around their homes and travel in the community; they are productively employed and lead active lives. So our negative or fearful concepts of blindness probably do not reflect the real life of a person who is blind.

These common misconceptions about the ability of people who are visually impaired are important to remember when preparing to teach a child who is blind or visually impaired. We must look beyond our traditional view of blindness and our misconceptions to realize that, with specialized instruction, children with visual impairments are quite capable of succeeding in our classrooms.

Terms and Definitions

The term *visual impairment* covers all degrees of vision loss.

Like *hearing impairment*, we use **visual impairment** as an umbrella term that includes all levels of vision loss, from total blindness to uncorrectable visual limitations. The IDEA definition states that visual impairment, including blindness, is "an impairment in vision that, *even with correction*, adversely affects a child's educational performance. The term includes both partial sight (low vision) and blindness" (Knoblauch & Sorenson, 1998). It is helpful to think about the phrase *with correction* in this definition. Even with the best possible corrective lenses, these children have a vision problem that interferes with their learning at school. Many of us wear glasses or contact lenses that correct our vision. But we are not considered visually impaired, since our learning is not adversely affected.

Legal blindness refers to visual acuity of 20/200 or less in the better eye after correction, or a visual field of less than 20 degrees.

In schools we make a distinction between legal definitions and educational definitions. A person is considered **legally blind** when his or her **visual acuity**, or sharpness of vision, is 20/200 or worse in the better eye *with* correction, or when he or she has a visual field no greater than 20 degrees. (A person with 20/200 vision has to get as close as 20 feet to an object to see the same object that a person with typical vision can see from 200 feet.) If vision can be corrected through glasses or contact lenses to 20/200 or better, the person is not considered legally blind. The term *legal blindness* describes visual impairments that qualify a person for a variety of legal and social services. This definition is used to determine eligibility for governmental funding, tax deductions, rehabilitation, and other services. Although the legal definition is widely used, it is somewhat misleading, since many legally blind people have a good deal of useful vision. In fact, the majority of people who are legally blind read using large print!

Table 11.1 Educational Implications of Visual Impairments

Levels of Visual Impairment	Educational Implications
Total blindness	Students are totally blind or are able only to distinguish the presence or absence of light; they may learn best through tactile or auditory senses, although, if they do have some vision, they may use it effectively for orientation and mobility and other tasks.
Functional blindness	Students use their senses of touch and hearing as their primary means of learning, but may have some sight useful for orientation and mobility.
Low vision	Students are severely visually impaired but may be able to see objects at near distances, sometimes under modified conditions, or may have limited use of vision under average circumstances.
Blindness in one eye	Students with vision in only one eye may or may not be considered visually impaired, depending on the vision in the sighted eye; they may have difficulty with depth perception and may need special consideration in physical education or other classroom activities.

For educators, actual measurements of visual acuity are less important than a description of how the student functions in school. **Educational definitions** are generally based on the way a student uses his or her vision in an educational setting. For educational purposes, students who learn primarily through touch or listening are considered **functionally blind** and those who gain most of their information through their vision (and read large print) may be designated as having **low vision** (Hatlen, 2000a). Table 11.1 lists the levels of visual impairment and their educational implications. These definitions rely less on visual acuity measurements and more on **functional vision**—"what a person can do with his or her available vision" (Corn, DePriest, & Erin, 2000, p. 470). At times, students with exactly the same acuity will function very differently. In fact, professionals in the field of blindness and visual impairment often say that no two people see exactly alike (Augusto, 1996). Whereas one student might respond visually to educational tasks, the other might rely more on hearing or sense of touch, depending on his or her background, experience, type of visual impairment, and learning style. The real test of how well a student sees is how she accomplishes daily activities while using her sight as well as her other senses. Figure 11.1 presents the definitions pictorially, and Figure 11.2 illustrates the reading medium of students classified as legally blind.

Educational definitions of visual impairment are based on whether the student reads print or Braille.

Functional vision refers to how well a person uses his or her remaining vision.

? Pause and Reflect

You have read that use of the term *blind* does not necessarily mean that the person has *no* vision. How could you explain that idea to students in elementary school, so that they might have a more accurate picture of what their classmate with a visual impairment can see? ●

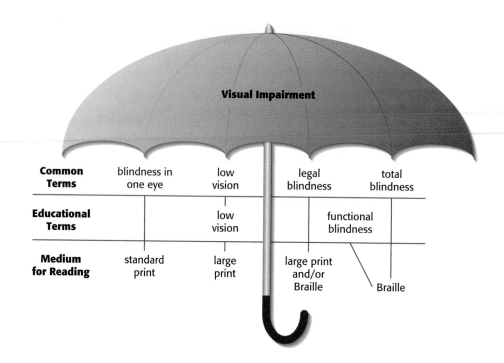

Figure 11.1

The Visual Impairment Umbrella

Causes of Visual Impairment

How We See

The eye is a small but extremely complex structure that contains an immense network of nerves, blood vessels, cells, and specialized tissues (Ward, 2000). For most people, this complicated structure works quite efficiently. Even if we need corrective lenses, most of us can see well. (Figure 11.3 shows the eye and its structures.) But impairments of vision can result from any interference with the passage of light as it travels from the outer surface of the eye, through the inner structures of the eye, and back through the visual pathways in the brain to the cortical brain centers.

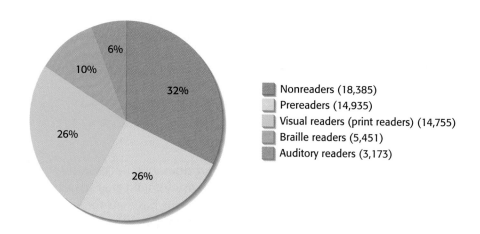

Figure 11.2

Reading Medium of Students Classified as Legally Blind

Source: American Printing House for the Blind (2002). *Distribution of federal quota.* Louisville, KY: American Printing House for the Blind.

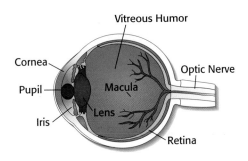

Figure 11.3

Structures of the Eye

When we look at an object, the light rays reflecting off it first pass through the outer membrane of the eye, the transparent, smooth **cornea**, through the **pupil** (the opening in the center of the eye), and through the **lens**, a transparent structure that lies between the iris and the tissue inside the eyeball, called the **vitreous humor**. The muscles in the **iris**, or colored part of the eye, expand or contract according to the amount of light available. The lens focuses the light rays so that they form clear images where they strike the **retina**, a layer of specialized cells at the back of the eye. The light rays activate the special cells on the retina; they then transmit signals of the images through the fibers of the **optic nerve**, which connects the eye to the brain, where they are interpreted. Damage to any of these structures, or a breakdown in the processing of visual information, can result in visual impairment. In the next section, we discuss some of the more common causes of visual impairment and their implications for learning.

> Light rays pass through the cornea, pupil, and lens and are then projected onto the retina, which sends signals of the image by the optic nerve to the brain.

Causes of Vision Loss

Most cases of visual impairment in school-age children are congenital in origin. Congenital conditions may be caused by heredity, maternal or fetal infection, or damage during fetal development or shortly after birth. Hereditary conditions that cause visual impairment include albinism, some forms of glaucoma, and retinitis pigmentosa. Other conditions, such as cataracts and underdevelopment or absence of parts of the eye structure, may be caused by damage during fetal development. It is important for classroom teachers to understand the eye conditions of their students, since the specific condition may affect what we expect for the child's visual functioning in the classroom. See the accompanying Closer Look box entitled, "Causes of Visual Impairment in Children" for additional details.

> Most visual impairments in children are congenital.

Prevalence

According to the *Twenty-fourth Annual Report to Congress* (U.S. Department of Education, 2002), students with visual impairments account for just 0.4 percent, or 25,927, of the total number of students aged 6–21 served under IDEA. As with many other disabilities, accurate counts are difficult because of differences in definition and classification (Huebner, 2000). However, even when the highest estimates are used, visual impairments are still among the low-incidence (or least frequently occurring) disabling conditions in children. Visual impairment is much more common among adults, especially those aged 65 and older.

A relatively large number of children who are visually impaired have additional disabilities as well—sometimes mental retardation, learning disabilities, physical and health impairments, and other disabilities accompany visual impairment. Although the exact number is hard to come by, it may be as high as 75 percent of children with visual impairments (Silberman, 2000).

> As many as 75 percent of students who are blind have additional disabilities as well.

A Closer Look — **Causes of Visual Impairment in Children**

- **Cortical visual impairment** results from damage to the brain rather than to the eye. If the occipital lobes in the brain are damaged, the brain cannot receive the images from the eye. Causes of cortical visual impairment include trauma and hydrocephaly. Children with this condition often have other disabilities as well (Ward, 2000).

- **Retinopathy of prematurity (ROP)** occurs most commonly in premature babies or even full-term babies suffering from respiratory distress syndrome (see Chapter 2) who require high levels of oxygen over an extended period of time for survival.

- In **optic nerve hypoplasia** and *optic nerve atrophy*, the optic nerve does not develop normally or degenerates, causing vision loss (Ward, 2000).

- **Albinism** is the congenital absence of pigmentation (including that of the eye), which can result in vision loss.

- **Glaucoma**, a leading cause of blindness across all age groups (Ward, 2000), occurs when fluid within the eye cannot drain properly, resulting in a gradual increase of pressure within the eye and damage to the optic nerve.

- A **cataract** is a clouding of the lens of the eye. Congenital cataracts occur in about 1 in 250 births (Ward, 2000). Children with cataracts will have difficulty seeing the board clearly and may need increased lighting or high-contrast educational materials.

- Diabetes can result in a condition known as **diabetic retinopathy**, another major cause of blindness in this country.

There are many other less frequently occurring causes of visual impairment on children and adults.

Pause and Reflect

There are many causes of visual impairments, and the cause effects what a person can see. Do you think you can change your own focus to what a student *can see*, rather than what she cannot? ●

Characteristics of Students Who Are Blind or Have Low Vision

> Negative attitudes and stereotypes can deprive the student with visual impairment of important experiences and opportunities.

Society's lack of knowledge or negative attitudes toward visual impairment may indirectly affect the child by depriving her of opportunities or experiences important for development. As you will read in the upcoming case study about Brenda, it is a fairly common belief that people who are blind cannot accomplish certain tasks. Unfortunately, this attitude may deprive them of the opportunity to compete with people who are sighted.

Even when differences are caused directly by the visual impairment, the degree to which the person's development is affected depends on the severity and cause of the visual impairment and on whether the child has additional disabili-

Case Study

Brenda is 9 years old and is in the fourth grade. She was born prematurely and is blind because of retinopathy of prematurity. Brenda has above-average intelligence and is on grade level in every academic subject. In some subjects, she requires more time than the rest of the class to complete daily assignments. During the first and second grades, Brenda's general education teachers decided that she should not be required to do all of the work that the rest of the class was required to. When the rest of the class was assigned twenty addition problems, Brenda was told to complete only ten. By the time Brenda was in the third grade, she would complain that the assignments she was given were too hard, or that she couldn't complete them because she was blind. Brenda's third-grade teacher, Ms. Garcia, was concerned and contacted a vision specialist teacher and Brenda's parents. They all agreed that this attitude could lead to a decline in Brenda's self-esteem and

confidence. At their meeting it was decided that Brenda would benefit from completing all class assignments.

Ms. Garcia re-examined the assignments she gave to her entire class realizing that if ten addition problems were enough for her to determine mastery for Brenda, they were enough for the other members of her class, as well. However, at this point in her education, it takes Brenda longer to complete the assignment than her classmates, regardless of the amount of material. Ms. Garcia, therefore, arranged her class schedule so that all students would have some time to complete assignments during school hours and could also take work home to complete.

It still takes Brenda more time to accomplish these assignments, but when she is finished she is confident that she can compete with the other students in her class. At the same time, she is learning strategies to help her complete her work more efficiently.

---

ties. Environmental factors, such as family background and the child's daily experience, are also significant. Kay Ferrell states that the factors which make a difference in how a child with visual impairments develops are *the opportunities to learn* and *the presence or absence of additional disabilities* (2000). As you read the following sections, think about the ways in which the areas of development are related to one another.

Language and Concept Development

Although communication through babbling and early sound production is generally the same for children who are blind and children who are sighted (Warren, 1984), developmental differences arise when children begin to associate meaning with words. In a classic study, Thomas Cutsforth (1932) researched the use of words and the understanding of their meaning by children who were totally blind from birth. He discovered that children who are blind often use words for which they could not have firsthand knowledge through other senses, such as when describing a blue sky. Cutsforth (1951) called this use of words without concrete knowledge of their meanings **verbalisms**.

Children who are blind may have other unusual language characteristics. For instance, they may ask frequent inappropriate or off-the-topic questions in order to maintain contact with partners or to respond to frightening or confusing situations (Fazzi & Klein, 2002). They may also engage in **echolalia**, the repetition of statements used by other people. Interventions should be responsive to the content of the child's utterance, but teachers should not reinforce language behaviors that would not be acceptable in a sighted child.

Children with visual impairments may be prone to verbalisms; they may use words without firsthand knowledge of their meanings.

Children with visual impairments should have direct experience with complex concepts.

Those of us who are sighted may take for granted the role that vision plays in learning and development, but Kay Ferrell (2000) reminds us that vision provides an incentive for communication and helps children develop concepts. Teachers and families of children with visual impairments *must make all the features of concepts explicit.* For example, an apple is not just red (or green or yellow); it is white on the inside, and the seeds are brown. Teachers working with children who are blind should be aware that even though a child may use verbal expressions that indicate an understanding of a concept, she may not really have the deeper understanding that comes with actual personal experience. If a child writes or reads a story about a big gray elephant but has had no firsthand experience with an elephant or the color gray, she is writing and/or reading

Teaching Strategies & Accommodations

Promoting Language Development

The following strategies will help professionals and family members support the development of verbal communication in young children who are visually impaired.

- *Make playful games out of vocal imitation and turn taking* (Lueck, Chen, & Kekelis, 1997). Repeating, rephrasing, and using pauses can encourage vocal turn taking and have positive effects on language development (Dote-Kwan, 1995).

- *Model appropriate ways to initiate and maintain social interactions.* Good social skills can be modeled and practiced during symbolic play routines (e.g., pretend kitchen and food preparation or talking on a play telephone).

- *Support the child's participation in a variety of everyday activities.* Hands-on experiences will support language development and provide topics of interest to talk about.

- *Provide extra information about things that are discussed.* Instead of merely labeling objects, events, and actions, describe the things that are of interest to the child. Also talk about and describe other's actions so that the child with a visual impairment does not become too self-involved in his or her own experiences or language use.

- *Avoid bombarding children with questions.* Since children with visual impairments often

rely on imitation to learn language strategies and may also have a tendency to become overreliant on questioning, modeling an overuse of questions could be counterproductive.

- *Express your own feelings verbally and help put the child's feelings into words.* Children with visual impairments cannot easily read frowns, smiles, and expressions of others. Other person's feelings need to be explained, and the child should be taught to express his or her feelings appropriately.

- *Try to expand on the child's existing language.* The child's attempt to communicate can be used as the basis for further communication. For instance, if a child says "ba-ba," the father can respond with "Yes, that is your bottle" and go on to describe it or its function.

- *Help children act out videos, stories, and songs to increase their understanding of embedded concepts* (Munoz, 1998). For example, preschool children commonly act out the events in the song "The Wheels on the Bus." Doing so helps children understand concepts such as windows going up and down.

Source: R. L. Pogrund & D. L. Fazzi (Eds.) (2002). *Early focus: Working with young children who are blind or visually impaired and their families* (2nd ed.). New York: AFB Press.

about something that she does not truly understand. The teacher may want to work more closely with the child on these concepts, providing rich and meaningful experiences (see the accompanying Teaching Strategies box entitled, "Promoting Language Development"). By the way, this may also be true of children who are sighted; teachers can never assume that children's use of concepts in verbal or written communications indicates a clear understanding of those concepts. The challenge to educators, therefore, is to provide *all* children with a wealth of opportunities that increase their experiences through all senses, thus increasing their understanding of the language they use.

Motor Development

From infancy, motor development is stimulated by vision. An infant who sees a brightly colored object or her mother's face reaches out for it and thus begins the development of gross motor skills. Children who are blind have difficulty in this area. Children who are sighted learn how to move by watching the movement of others and imitating it. Then, they practice variations of this movement and observe their own movement, which gives them the feedback they need to change and modify their movements. Children who are blind, however, cannot observe others and imitate their movements. They are slow to begin to move in response to the sounds around them (Orel-Bixler, 1999).

The acquisition of motor development skills may be delayed by lack of vision.

IDEA, as you have learned, provides that children with disabilities receive "related services" in order to fully benefit from schooling. Under this law, children who are blind may receive instruction in **orientation and mobility** (O&M), a set of skills involved in establishing one's location in the environment and moving safely through it (Anthony et al., 2002). When children who have visual impairments enter school, they should be able to move efficiently and safely through their environment with the support of the O&M specialist.

Cognitive and Intellectual Development

Blindness affects cognitive development in young children in much the same way as it affects motor development, by restricting the range and variety of their experiences, limiting their ability to move around, and diminishing their control of the environment and their relationship to it (Lowenfeld, 1981).

Blindness affects cognitive development by restricting the range and variety of a child's experiences.

With emerging research on newborns and infants, we are discovering more and more about the importance of vision in early learning. In early infancy the eyes are the child's primary avenue for exploring the world. The newborn uses vision to follow objects with her eyes, for example, and can stick out her tongue after watching someone else do it (Freidrich, 1983). The visual sense motivates the infant to interact with people and objects, guides that interaction, and verifies the success of the interaction. Vision thus stimulates motor activity and exploration, forming the basis for cognitive growth.

Some research has suggested that there are critical periods for certain kinds of learning (Bailey et al., 2001). If infants who are visually impaired miss out on those critical periods for reaching, crawling, or walking, for example, it may be difficult for them to "catch up" and develop at a normal rate later in life. School-age children may continue to experience difficulties in their developmental progress. Thus, early intervention for infants with visual impairments is designed to use the child's intact senses to provide the kind of experiences that will promote cognitive growth (Fazzi & Klein, 2002).

Social and Emotional Development

Most researchers agree that there is no unique psychology of blindness. The principles and issues related to the social and emotional development of people who are sighted are the same as those related to the social and emotional development of people who are blind (Tuttle & Tuttle, 2000). However, children who are blind do encounter unique difficulties in social situations. Primarily, the difficulties arise because of the way that the child is perceived by society and the way that the child perceives himself (Sacks, 1996).

For example, the child who completes class assignments develops a clear sense of accomplishment. Children who are visually impaired, however, are often allowed to turn in incomplete work or partial assignments, as in the case of Brenda. As a result, such children may believe that they are not "smart enough" to complete the same work that other children in the class do. The perception of other students in the class—and of the teacher—may also be that the child with a visual impairment cannot accomplish as much as the rest of the class.

> Children who are blind often encounter social difficulties because of how society perceives them and how they perceive themselves.

FIRST PERSON

Can Girls with Impaired Vision Be Mommies?

I was 26 the first time someone raised the question of whether I, who had been blind since age 5, could have and raise children. I had three advanced degrees and three years of teaching to my credit and had lived on my own (first single, then married) since age 21. Now, here I sat in the hospital with a pink-blanketed bundle in my arms, awestruck, wondering what I would do next.

I wanted some hands-on experience in diapering. I told a nurse who was going off duty, and when her replacement came in, the experience was brutal. She pushed my hands away gruffly and impatiently, saying she could do it better. I felt inadequate and embarrassed. This episode shook my confidence in my ability to cope with this incredible responsibility of being a mother.

Of course, within hours, I learned that the problem was the nurse's ignorance about blindness—not my ability to fasten a baby's diaper! I would also learn that the attitudes of others would continue to be the most significant problem unique to parents with impaired vision.

Sure, I had to make adaptations along the way—just as I had to make certain adaptations in riding a bike, climbing a tree, or going to college as a kid who couldn't see. I read books, I talked to other mothers. I invented solutions as I went along.

Organizing objects and clearly defining spaces were two keys in the first three years. Toys, books, food—everything that needed a Braille label got one. I pinned outfits together before laundering, so that my babies were color-coordinated, and I always put toys away in the same place. I carried my babies first in front carriers and later in backpacks, and when they became toddlers, I used child safety

Teenagers with visual impairments engage in fewer activities with peers and spend more time after school alone than their sighted peers do. Students with low vision in particular tend to involve themselves in more "passive" activities than their sighted or blind peers—and they sleep more (Wolffe & Sacks, 1997). The lack of independent mobility that sometimes accompanies visual impairment seems to have serious implications for friendships and social life in high school.

School Achievement

With appropriate assistance and placement, a student who is visually impaired and has no additional disabilities should be able to participate actively in all aspects of school and compete with sighted peers in academic areas. If a student with visual impairment is having trouble achieving academic goals, the teacher and the vision specialist should work together to determine if he is receiving proper instruction and has the needed adapted materials (Holbrook & Koenig,

harnesses to keep them close to me in public places.

My children have all been extremely verbal, as I've noticed many children of parents with impaired vision to be. They have also been early avid readers, probably a consequence of all my talking out of necessity and my obsession with being sure there were plenty of opportunities for learning.

It always amuses me that sighted people are so particularly focused on the fact that I cared for my children as babies. That was, without doubt, the easy part. A baby stays where you put her. Even when crawling or early walking, a baby is easy to keep within a defined area. It's when they become truly mobile—and later, truly individualized with their own opinions—that parenting, with or without sight, gets most challenging.

Sure, there have been some things we couldn't do. Someone else has to kick a soccer ball around with my eight-year-old, and someone else had to teach my older kids to drive. But no parent can do it all. On the other hand, I have taught other kids to bake cookies, write stories, sing songs.

Over the years I have known many other parents who are blind and seen many styles of parenting. Why should we expect anything less? Vision impairment is an equal opportunity disability and affects people of all temperaments and leadership capabilities.

What I know for sure is that when it comes to parenting, the same rules apply for people with impaired vision as for all others. Anyone who wants to have children should do so and will figure out the logistics as they go along. We have loved, laughed, and lived family life to the fullest in my household, and there is no person, no professional accomplishment, no privilege I could ever cherish more than my three children.

Deborah Kendrick

Source: Deborah Kendrick (1997). Can girls with impaired vision be mommies? *Envision*, 5–7.

2000). The sections later in this chapter on teaching strategies and technological aids will provide more information for this purpose.

Effects on the Family

The reaction of families to the fact that their infant or child is blind or has low vision depends on many factors. Most important, as we saw in Chapter 3, may be the degree of support available to the family through its informal network of relatives and friends and its formal network of agencies and professionals.

Several other characteristics of the family and the child may affect the parents' attitude toward their child's visual impairment (Ferrell, 1986):

1. *The severity of the handicap* may be an important issue, because many children with visual impairments also have additional disabilities. Parents of children whose visual impairment is severe or is complicated by other disabilities must respond to a variety of physical and developmental issues; in some cases they must also cope with anxiety about life-threatening medical procedures.

2. *The age of onset of the visual impairment.* The later the diagnosis of disability, the more difficult the news is for the parents; they have had more time for their hopes and expectations for their child to develop. On the other hand, the development of bonding, that crucial early parent–child tie that is so important to social and emotional development, may be affected when the infant is congenitally blind. Babies who have visual impairments are less likely to make eye contact with their mothers, which can reduce the amount of the "mutual gazing" that occurs between infants and mothers. In addition, these babies may smile less regularly and consistently at their parents. Smiling in infants is important to elicit social interactions with other people and serves as a means to include the infant in the social relationship (Warren, 1984).

3. *How the information or diagnosis concerning visual impairment was initially received.* Stotland (1984), the parent of a child who is blind, says, "Ask any five parents of visually impaired children how they first learned their child had vision problems and you will get five different horror stories. These stories will range from blatant misdiagnoses to inaccurate predictions of total blindness, to expressions of pity" (p. 69).

4. *Support from medical professionals and educators* is critical in the initial discovery of a child's visual impairment. Parents must feel comfortable asking questions and expressing concerns and emotions if they are to accept their child's visual impairment.

> Parents' attitudes toward their child's visual impairment are affected by its severity, age of onset, delivery of diagnosis, and medical and educational support.

A child with visual impairment creates a dynamic within the family that affects it in many ways long after the initial diagnosis. These effects might include changes in daily routines, social interactions, and parent involvement at school (J. B. Chase, as quoted in Wolffe, 2000). As we saw in Chapter 3, there are often high expectations on the part of school professionals for parental involvement with their child and with the school.

Families of children with visual impairments are often able to incorporate their child into the family routine, ensuring that the child feels she is a vital member of the family. In some cases, family members allow more time for the child to complete a particular task, such as clearing the dishes from the table. Family members can also use special adapted materials for more complicated tasks—for example, Braille labels on the washing machine and dryer. Participation in family routines helps children learn to complete tasks that they have started, to perform as independently as possible, to take responsibility for their actions, and to feel like a contributing family member.

Outside their daily routines, families often must deal with changes in their social relationships as an indirect result of their child's visual impairment. Parents, for example, may have difficulty coping with the attitudes and misconceptions of their friends. Deborah Barton (1984), the parent of a child who is blind, recalls, "When my child started walking and talking, my friends considered him a genius and thought of me as a saint. They misinterpreted what they saw, and I let them. They praised Jed for ordinary behavior ('he's walking,' 'he likes peanut butter,' 'he doesn't whine') and talked about me as if I was a cross between Madame Curie and the Flying Nun" (p. 67). Although at first this kind of acknowledgment might seem welcome, it is difficult for parents to endure misconceptions such as these over time because they indicate a lack of understanding of their child's needs and abilities.

Social interactions between the child who is visually impaired and children who are sighted may also require special attention and effort. Families of children with a visual impairment must be even more careful to provide social activities for that child outside of the family so that good social skills are established throughout the early years of a child's development. Unfortunately, some parents of sighted children may be reluctant to invite the child who is blind to participate in activities such as birthday parties or slumber parties because of their lack of understanding about blindness. Parents of children with visual impairments may need to initiate some of this social interaction and to educate the parents of their child's sighted peers. When inexperienced adults begin to learn about the abilities and needs of a child with visual impairment, they can model acceptance and understanding for their own children. See the Teaching Strategies box entitled, "Promoting Social Inclusion at Home and at School" for ideas that family members can use to promote social relationships.

School is another area in which family participation and adaptation are important. Parents or caregivers should participate in the IEP team, which gathers as

Parents may have difficulty dealing with the attitudes and misconceptions of others.

This boy uses the long cane to assist his mobility—but having a couple of friends around helps too. (© Peter Byron/PhotoEdit)

Teaching Strategies & Accommodations

Promoting Social Inclusion at Home and at School

- Encourage the child to explore the environment by providing many hands-on experiences. Take him or her on outings to various community sites (such as parks, playgrounds, and restaurants) and on shopping trips (to the grocery store, shopping mall, or video store), for example.

- Allow the child to be an active participant in each hands-on experience. For example, when grocery shopping, have the child choose a favorite snack or select a favorite fruit from the produce section.

- Provide opportunities for the child to participate in structured group activities that facilitate socialization, such as swimming lessons, gymnastics, story hour at the public library, and rhythm and music groups. Many of these activities can be done with a family member.

- Encourage the child to take risks and try new activities. Provide opportunities for the child to experience a variety of multisensory activities (such as tasting new foods and feeling a variety of textures; playing rough-and-tumble games; engaging in climbing activities; and playing in water, sand, and snow).

- Provide opportunities for the child to assume responsibility for classroom jobs or home chores on a consistent basis. Young children can be responsible for putting away their toys, putting their dirty clothes in a clothes hamper, helping to set the table for a family meal, clearing the table after eating a meal, or helping to take out the trash or recycle bins.

- Form partnerships with other parents and teachers and become involved in play groups and community groups (such as a church, Tiny Tots, dance classes, music lessons, ice skating, and skiing).

Source: S. Z. Sacks & S. K. Silberman (2000). Social skills. In A. J. Koenig & M. C. Holbrook (Eds.), *Foundations of education,* Vol. II, (2nd ed., pp. 633–634). New York: American Foundation for the Blind.

Family participation in the child's education, especially on the IEP team, is crucial.

much information as possible concerning the child's abilities and needs, including the degree to which the child uses remaining vision. The family plays a crucial role in providing the professionals with information on how the child uses his vision. Once decisions have been made regarding adaptive materials and curricular activities, parents become vital participants in their child's education. If, for example, a child is learning to travel independently with a cane, the parents can reinforce this skill by communicating closely with their child's teachers to monitor progress and to learn about the skill from them (Perla & O'Donnell, 2002). In doing so, they encourage independence for their child. If a child is learning Braille, parents can learn it too. Close communication between parents and teachers and direct involvement of parents in the education of the child are critical to educational success.

? Pause and Reflect

Though many adults with visual impairments become content and productive, there is no doubt that visual impairment significantly affects a child's development. How does what you have read so far fit in with your preconceptions of visual impairment, and how does it differ? ●

Teaching Strategies and Accommodations

Understanding the following issues will help teachers and parents provide an appropriate education for children with vision loss.

Early Intervention

Professionals have long recognized the need for intervention programs for infants and their parents as soon as a visual impairment is diagnosed. For babies with congenital blindness, this diagnosis comes at birth or soon after; for babies with lesser degrees of visual impairment, the diagnosis may occur later in infancy. Children with a moderate degree of impairment may receive a diagnosis only after they encounter difficulty in completing school tasks.

Kay Ferrell (1986) has described several reasons for early intervention with infants who are visually impaired. First, as discussed earlier, vision is an important component of early cognitive development, and there may be particular periods of early development when optimal learning occurs. Early intervention may also prevent the development of secondary disabilities. Failure to develop language, ear–hand coordination, or attachment to a significant adult may form the foundation for disabilities in addition to visual impairment that will emerge later in the child's life, such as cognitive delay or behavioral and emotional problems.

> Early intervention with infants with visual impairments may prevent the development of secondary handicaps.

Early intervention can take numerous forms. Teachers of young children with visual impairments will encourage parents to continue to talk to their baby, to "show" things to the baby by allowing her to touch and explore them, to teach the baby to listen for clues to what is happening around her, to play games that involve moving and identifying parts of the body, using the baby's hands to find her head, nose, ears, tummy, knees, and so on. Early intervention specialists can also help parents make the most of the learning opportunities that arise in the routines of daily life with their baby. This role is important, since parents sometimes alter their interactions with a child who is visually impaired. They may assume that a child who cannot see is less interested in his or her environment or does not need the stimulation of playing with household objects and toys or of playing baby games with parents.

Hatton, McWilliam, and Winton (2002) have described exemplary practices for early interventionists serving infants with visual impairments and their families:

- Establish reliable alliances (Turnbull & Turnbull, 2001) with families and other service providers based on family and child strengths, respect for diversity and culture, and collaboration.

- Collaborate with families and other professionals to complete the Individualized Family Services Plan (IFSP) process.

- Serve as an effective member of the early intervention team, help families and other team members understand medical information, and be familiar with service coordination responsibilities.

- Approach early intervention from a support, rather than provision of services, perspective.

- Make home visits that promote functional outcomes for both the child and family.

Infants with visual impairment and additional disabilities need intensive intervention.

Infants who are visually impaired and have additional disabilities, as well as especially intensive intervention needs, and their parents need a great deal of support (Chen, 1999). Reading the cues of a baby who is blind and may be deaf, mentally retarded, or physically disabled can be complex. How can a mother tell when the baby is pleased or sad? What are the baby's preferences? How do the family members and the baby build relationships? Effective intervention for these families requires an early intervention specialist who knows each disability area well and can build on the family strengths to foster communication and loving relationships (Klein, Chen, & Haney, 2000).

Identification and Assessment

Assessment of students who are visually impaired is difficult, mostly because of lack of standardized tests for this population.

Educational assessment for students who are visually impaired is especially difficult for three reasons: the lack of standardized assessment instruments, the need for adaptations of existing assessment instruments to meet the needs of students with visual impairments, and the need for a fair interpretation of test results. The lack of standardized assessment instruments is a direct result of the small number of students with visual impairments. It has been impossible to standardize tests on this population because of the great diversity of children with visual impairments caused by differences in age of onset and degree of visual impairment, and differences in educational experiences.

● *Identification in School*   Every state mandates vision screening in the schools to determine which students have visual problems that warrant further assessment. At least one in four school-age children have eye problems that need professional attention (Prevent Blindness America, 2003), and that number is considerably higher among children with other disabilities. (Part C of IDEA requires a vision and hearing screening for all children from birth to age 2 who are referred for the evaluation of a disability [34 CFR 303.322].) To learn more about the prevention of eye problems, visit **http://www.preventblindness.org/ children/ch_eye_problems.html**.

The Snellen Chart is the most common visual screening test.

The most common visual screening test is one you have probably taken yourself, although you may not know the name of it—the **Snellen Chart**. The person being examined is positioned twenty feet from the chart, on which eight rows of letters ranging from large to small are printed, and is asked to read the letters with each eye (while the other eye is covered). If that individual has difficulty reading any of the letters on the chart, the school nurse or other person conducting the screening usually makes a referral for a more comprehensive evaluation of vision.

The Snellen Chart is used to screen for distance vision problems only. If you suspect that one of your students has a near vision problem (which would affect reading) or another kind of vision problem, then urge your school nurse to conduct or recommend a more complete visual evaluation for that student. (See the accompanying Closer Look box entitled, "Detection of Vision Problems.")

There are a number of ways to screen for visual impairments in very young children or those who do not know the letter names. The most common are the Snellen E Chart and Apple/House/Umbrella Screening. There are also a variety of means for evaluating the vision of students with severe handicaps that the experienced examiner will be able to use (Harley & Lawrence, 1984). No student should be excluded from vision screening because he or she cannot provide traditional responses. Continuous observation of the student in the classroom and in other natural settings should accompany the screening, plus referral of identi-

A Closer Look | Detection of Vision Problems

Teachers are often the first to detect vision problems in their students. Symptoms of visual impairment may include:

- *Physical changes in or about the eyes and face.* Physical changes may include an eye that tends to wander or eyes that are bloodshot or show recurrent redness or watering. Children may complain that their eyes hurt or feel "dusty." Frequent rubbing of the eyes, facial distortions, frowning, and an abnormal amount of squinting or blinking may be other symptoms of trouble. Children may show a preference for using only one eye, or for viewing at a distance or at close range, or they may tilt their heads or bring objects unusually close to their eyes.

- *Changes in vision.* Children may complain that objects look blurry or that they are unable to see something at a distance. Note also an inability to use vision in different situations or with different illumination.

- *Changes in behavior.* Children may become irritable when doing desk work or have a short attention span when watching an activity that takes place across the room. They may report headache or nausea after close work, hold books close to the eyes, or lean down close to the book. If the teacher suspects a visual impairment, he or she should immediately notify the parents and refer the student to the school nurse or physician for evaluation.

Source: Adapted from I. Torres & A. L. Corn (1990). *When you have a visually handicapped child in your classroom: Suggestions for teachers* (2d ed., pp. 32–33) New York: American Foundation for the Blind.

fied students for further visual evaluation and follow-up to ensure that the recommendations have been carried out.

● *Functional Vision Assessment* In addition to the medical evaluations just discussed, it is critical to test the functional vision of students with visual impairments—in other words, how well they use the vision that they do possess. If, for example, it is noted during a functional vision assessment that a student has difficulty moving and performing tasks in limited lighting, teachers will be more prepared to accommodate him in low-lighting situations.

Functional vision assessments vary according to the type of information needed. Commercially produced functional vision assessments are available, such as the Program to Develop Efficiency in Visual Functioning (American Printing House for the Blind) and Project IVEY: Increasing Visual Efficiency in Young Children (Florida Department of Education), but most functional vision assessments are informal and may be a compilation of other assessments. Functional vision assessments are usually conducted by a vision specialist and an orientation and mobility specialist and may include the following (http://www.afb.org; Erin & Paul, 1996):

In addition to medical evaluations of vision, it is critical to test a student's functional vision.

- Information on the student's visual disability and prognosis
- Current print functioning and classroom modifications for distance and near vision tasks
- Assessment of reading level and reading speed

- Informal assessments of visual field, color vision, eye preference, and light sensitivity
- Equipment adaptations for classes
- Travel skills

Functional vision assessments are individualized. By carefully considering the information provided by the assessment, teachers can make more informed decisions about educational programming.

● *Assessment for Teaching*   Students who are visually impaired must demonstrate knowledge through both informal classroom evaluations and formal standardized tests, just as their sighted peers do. Accommodations can be made in the way the test is presented (for example, in Braille or large print, or using a magnification device); in the way the student responds (marking responses on a large print answer sheet, using a computer or communication board); or in the setting, timing, and scheduling of the test (take the test alone, take more time, take more breaks—it generally takes longer to read material in Braille or in large print) (Allman, 2002). Most commercially produced achievement tests are available in Braille and large-print versions. A vision specialist will be able to obtain copies of these tests. Visit Test Central at the American Printing House for the Blind (**http://www.aph.org**).

> Most commercially produced achievement tests are available in Braille and large print.

Finally, interpretation of test results should take into consideration the modification of test items and the testing situation as well as whether any test items rely heavily on visual experiences for correct answers. The scores of students who are visually impaired should not be compared with standardized scores since standardized scores do not reflect modifications for these students. Vision specialists can assist in the interpretation of test results for individual students.

Students with visual impairments should also be assessed in the areas of the expanded core curriculum (the areas that support learning of the core curriculum), which you will read about below, and they will also require assistive technology assessments, which will determine the need for such equipment as screen readers, screen magnification, scanners, adaptive keyboards, portable note-takers, closed-circuit televisions, augmentative communication devices, Braille translation software, Braille embossers, and Braille writing equipment. Finally, students must be assessed to determine their learning medium: whether he or she should read using Braille, large print, or regular print, and which instructional materials and methods should be used (Koenig & Holbrook, 2002).

Curriculum

Students who are visually impaired require instruction not only in academic areas but also in skills needed to compensate for their loss of vision. These skills are critical to students' success in life after school and so are an important part of the curriculum. Instruction in most of these areas should begin during early childhood, and spiral through elementary and high school. Phillip Hatlen (2000b) has described the necessary school program for students with visual impairments as the **expanded core curriculum**—the existing core curriculum plus the additional areas of learning needed by students who are visually impaired, including those with additional disabilities (see Table 11.2).

> The expanded core curriculum includes the specialized skill areas that students with visual impairments need.

For Hatlen, the **compensatory academic skills** of the expanded core curriculum are the skills that students with visual impairments need to access the

Table 11.2 Curriculum for Students with Visual Impairments

Existing Core Curriculum	Expanded Core Curriculum
English language arts	All of the existing core curriculum, PLUS
Other languages, to the extent possible	Compensatory academic skills, including communication modes
Mathematics	Orientation and mobility
Science	Social interaction skills
Health	Independent living skills
Physical education	Recreation and leisure skills
Social studies	Career education
History	Use of assistive technology
Economics	Visual efficiency skills
Business education	
Fine arts	
Vocational education	

core curriculum. They include concept development, spatial understanding, study and organizational skills, and speaking and listening skills. Communication modes might include Braille, large print, print with the use of optical devices, regular print, tactile symbols, a calendar system, sign language, recorded materials, or combinations of these means. These skills might be taught by the teacher who is a visual impairment specialist, or by other specialists; some, like concept development, could be taught by the general education teacher.

Not every student who is blind or has low vision will need instruction in every component of the expanded core curriculum. Each student's needs must be determined individually through careful, comprehensive assessment. Let's take a closer look at the most common of these components.

● **Braille**   Learning Braille is essential for students who are so severely visually impaired that they cannot read print. It is also recommended for students who are legally blind and those with visual impairments that are progressive (will worsen over time). **Braille** was devised by Louis Braille, a French musician and educator, in 1829. It is a code that uses raised dots instead of printed characters (letters). A unit in Braille is called a *cell*. Each cell consists of six dots, three dots high and two dots wide. The dots are numbered from 1 through 6, and the Braille alphabet is made of combinations of these six dots (Figure 11.4). The Braille alphabet is only a small part of the literary Braille code, which also consists of contractions (or combinations of letters). Braille is produced on a Braillewriter or on a hand-held slate and stylus. A computer can also produce it with a Braille printer.

Students who are blind read by using Braille, a tactile code of raised dots.

Learning to read Braille should begin long before a student enters school, just as learning to read print should (Koenig & Holbrook, 2002; McComiskey, 1996). Sighted children begin the reading process by recognizing symbols in the environment. For example, children at an early age might learn to associate a hamburger and french fries with the golden arches of McDonald's. Children who are sighted have experience watching adults read books, looking at picture

The six dots of the Braille cell are arranged and numbered thus:

$$
\begin{array}{ccc}
1 & \bullet\ \bullet & 4 \\
2 & \bullet\ \bullet & 5 \\
3 & \bullet\ \bullet & 6
\end{array}
$$

The capital sign, dot 6, placed before a letter makes it a capital. The number sign, dots 3, 4, 5, 6, placed before a character, makes it a figure and not a letter.

1	2	3	4	5	6	7	8	9	10
a	b	c	d	e	f	g	h	i	j

11	12	13	14	15	16	17	18	19	20
k	l	m	n	o	p	q	r	s	t

21	22	23	24	25	26	Capital	Number		
u	v	w	x	y	z	sign	sign	Period	Comma

Figure 11.4

Braille Alphabet and Numerals

Source: Division for the Blind and Physically Handicapped, Library of Congress, Washington, DC 20542.

books, and having books read to them long before they know how to read. They also build background experiences through observation and participation.

In contrast, children who are severely visually impaired will not have experiences equating symbols with their meanings unless they are given tactile symbols. Children who are blind cannot watch adults read books, so they gain knowledge about books only if they have the opportunity to explore Braille books prior to school. Parents who give children opportunities to become familiar with Braille and tactile symbols help them achieve readiness for Braille reading. Without these experiences, it becomes necessary for the teacher to begin the process of developing an understanding of symbols. Children with visual impairments also need to be provided with the experiences that are described in their school reading series—usually the games and routines of sighted children (Koenig & Farrenkopf, 1997). All children need experiential background to fully understand what they read, but it is especially important to provide background experiences for children who are blind, for they may not have developed symbolic meanings for themselves (Koenig & Holbrook, 2000). Classroom teachers should request Braille copies of all classroom materials so that the student who reads Braille can be included in all activities.

Classroom teachers should request Braille copies of all classroom materials for students who need them.

● ***Low-Vision Aids and Training***   Many students who are visually impaired do not use Braille as their primary literacy medium; instead, they can learn to use large print or even regular print with magnification or low-vision aids. In other words, their primary source of information is still visual (Hatlen, 2000a).

Students with low vision get most of their information through their vision.

This brother and sister read side-by-side. She is normally sighted and reads print; he is blind and reads the Braille equivalent. (Laura Dwight)

Professionals in visual impairment no longer believe that using vision can damage it. In fact, professionals who work with students who are visually impaired now realize that instruction can actually help children develop better use of their vision.

Instruction in the use of low vision touches on three areas: environmental adaptations, which may involve making changes in distance, size, contrast, illumination, or time; enhancement of visual skills, such as attention, scanning, tracking, and reaching for objects, through integration of these skills into functional activities; and integration of vision into activities, or teaching skills within the actual activities where they are needed (Erin & Paul, 1996). Teaching these skills is usually the responsibility of the teacher specialist in visual impairment.

Some examples of low-vision aids are optical aids, such as a hand-held magnifying glass; closed-circuit television (CCTV) sets that enlarge printed material onto a screen; computer software that varies type size and type; computer hardware such as large monitor screens and screen magnifiers; large-print textbooks; and materials used to provide greater contrast in written and printed matter: yellow acetate, bold-line paper, felt-tip markers (Zimmerman, 1996). Low-vision instruction is designed to help the student make the best possible use of the vision that he or she has.

● **_Developing Listening Skills_**   Since students who are visually impaired receive a large percentage of information through their auditory sense, it is important to give them instruction and experience in using this sense to the fullest. Many people believe that people who are blind automatically have superior auditory skills, but this is not true.

Listening to recorded materials does not replace reading print or Braille as a means for developing literacy; however, it is important for students who are blind since it allows for efficient gathering of large amounts of materials over a short period of time. With instruction, a student can become more efficient in the use of listening for learning.

Students with visual impairments benefit from instruction in listening skills.

● *Orientation and Mobility*   In addition to academic skills, students with visual impairment must develop skills to ensure that they can be independent adults, able to work and to move around in their environment with as little assistance as possible (Fazzi & Petersmeyer, 2001). For this reason, instruction in orientation and mobility is a critical component of the curriculum for students who are blind (see the accompanying Closer Look box entitled, "Who Are the Professionals Interacting with the Student Who Is Visually Impaired?"). Orientation and mobility training is "teaching the concepts and skills necessary for

---

A Closer Look — Who Are the Professionals Interacting with the Student Who Is Visually Impaired?

Anumber of professionals with different educational backgrounds and specialized skills will likely work with the student who is visually impaired, and you as the teacher will have the opportunity to collaborate with some of them to provide services to the student.

The *teacher of students with visual impairments* has advanced training in providing specialized skills—reading skills, including Braille and large print; concept development; daily living skills; and so on. The teacher may provide direct services to students on an itinerant basis or in a special day class, resource room, or residential school; or may consult with the general education teacher. The *orientation and mobility specialist* teaches the skills for safe and independent travel, from toddlerhood through adulthood, as well as the use of specialized travel devices. Orientation and mobility instructors help students learn to detect obstacles and eventually to cross streets alone; they will be required whenever a student needs to become familiar with a new setting, such as a new school. The *vocational rehabilitation counselor*, usually associated with a state or private agency, assists adolescents with visual impairments making the transition from school to work by helping them and their families plan for post-high-school education and training, as well as job placement.

Lisa Pruner, a teacher-consultant with students with visual impairments, developed these tips for working with a consultant:

1. Use the telephone! Your consultant won't know that you have questions or concerns unless you let him or her know. Don't try to "make do" until the next scheduled visit. That can be frustrating for everyone. When in doubt, call your consultant.

2. Set aside a block of time to talk to your consultant during her visit. It's important to be able to share observations and concerns immediately in a relatively distraction-free environment.

3. Let your consultant know what you need. If you need an observation, some suggestions for adaptations, or if you want to observe the consultant interacting directly with a student, tell your consultant. Every classroom has different needs, and every teacher has a different level of comfort with vision issues. Let your consultant know what he or she can do for you.

4. Make a list of questions to ask before each visit.

5. Contact therapists, specialists, administrators, and parents regarding the consultant's visit. Invite them to join you or submit questions through you if they can't attend.

6. Remember, the consultant's job is to provide technical assistance in an area in which classroom teachers aren't usually trained. Make good use of your consultant.

Sources: Adapted from Appendix A, Who are the professionals who work with visually impaired people? In I. Torres & A. L. Corn (1990). *When you have a visually impaired child in your classroom: Suggestions for teachers* (2nd ed.). New York: American Foundation for the Blind; and Lisa W. Pruner (1994). Tips for working with a consultant. *RE:view, 25*(4), 174.

students to travel safely and efficiently in their environmental settings" (Griffin-Shirley, Trusty, & Rickard, 2000, p. 530). Orientation and mobility specialists (again, refer to the Closer Look box for further information) should begin their work as soon as a child is identified with visual impairment—even in infancy! The skills needed to travel within the environment are rooted in the child's early experiences at home (Anthony et al., 2002).

Orientation and mobility consist of two equally important subparts: **orientation**, the ability to use one's senses to establish where one is in space and in relation to other objects and people, and **mobility**, the ability to move about in one's environment. Skill in orientation and mobility is crucial for several reasons:

- Psychological reasons, including the development of a positive self-concept
- Physical reasons, including the development of fitness
- Social reasons, including the increase of opportunities for social interactions through independent travel
- Economic reasons, including the increase of employment opportunities and options

There are four generally accepted orientation and mobility systems: **human guide**, **cane travel**, **dog guide**, and **electronic travel aids**. The first three systems will be discussed in this section, and electronic travel aids in the section on assistive technology. People who are blind often use a combination of these systems, depending on the nature of the task they wish to accomplish.

Orientation is the ability to use one's senses to establish one's relationship to objects and people; mobility is the ability to move about the environment.

Human Guide   In this system, the person who is blind can travel safely through the environment, including maneuvering around stairs and obstacles, by holding lightly onto the elbow of a sighted person and following the movement of that person as he or she walks. Even though these techniques are relatively safe and efficient, and human guides are often able to assist the person who is blind in the development of kinesthetic awareness (awareness of movement), the continuous use of a human guide may also lead to a level of dependence instead of the independence that is the goal of instruction in orientation and mobility (Griffin-Shirley, Trusty, & Rickard, 2000). It is also difficult to use human guide techniques—those used to optimally support and guide a person who is blind—properly, since few members of the general public are aware of them. For information about Human Guide Techniques, visit **http://www.brailleinstitute.org/Education-guide.html**.

A human guide can help a person who is blind travel safely but may also lead to a high level of dependence.

Cane Travel   One of the most common systems of orientation and mobility is the use of the long cane for independent travel. Students who are visually impaired and use a cane must learn a variety of techniques in order to travel efficiently and safely. The canes used today are generally made from aluminum and vary in length according to a person's height, stride, and the time it takes him or her to respond to information gathered by moving the cane (Hill, 1986). Instruction in the use of the cane is very specialized and should be provided individually. This instruction is very important, since in many cases the safety of the student depends on the use of proper techniques. Instruction is most commonly given by an orientation and mobility specialist. Orientation and mobility specialists must undergo hundreds of hours of training while blindfolded themselves in order to learn to teach independent travel skills to people who are visually impaired.

With proper training, students who are visually impaired can use a cane to travel independently.

Dog guides are used only by a small percentage of people with visual impairments.

Dog Guides   The use of dog guides, though well publicized, is very limited. Only a small percentage of people with visual impairments use a dog guide for travel. Not everyone is suited to the strict relationship that a dog guide and its owner must maintain, and they are not typically used by children for that reason. Dog guides are trained to assist people who are blind in safe travel; however, it is the person who is blind who makes decisions regarding travel route and destination. The use of a dog guide does not negate the need for a person who is blind to have good independent orientation and mobility skills.

One of the responsibilities of the vision specialist is to teach independent living skills.

● *Development of Independent Living Skills*   An important element in the expanded core curriculum is the development of **independent living skills** for students with visual impairments, which increases their ability to accomplish daily routines, such as selecting and caring for clothes, managing (including identifying) money, preparing food, shopping, and so on (Hill, 1986).

Children who are sighted learn most daily living skills through observation and imitation or instruction from parents or family members. Children who are blind may not be able to observe daily living activities with enough detail to imitate, and their parents may be unaware of adapted techniques for instruction. It is usually the responsibility of the vision specialist to provide this instruction. Consider, for example, Roberto's predicament:

Case Study

The vision specialist was unaware until Roberto was in the eighth grade that he was unable to tie his shoes. After investigating, the teacher found out that Roberto's parents had attempted several times to teach him, but he had difficulty accomplishing the task as it was described to him and consequently took a very long time to tie his shoes. As in most families, the mornings were hectic, so, two minutes before Roberto's bus arrived each morning, his mother gave in and tied his shoes. The problem came in junior high school, when Roberto had to get dressed and undressed for gym class, and no one was there to tie his shoes. Had instruction in independent living skills been a priority in earlier grades, this difficulty (and embarrassment for Roberto) might have been avoided. The vision specialist immediately began intensive instruction in independent living skills with Roberto. She taught him not only how to tie his shoes but also how to fold the bills in his wallet so that he could tell the difference between a $5 bill and a $10 bill and how to make healthy after-school snacks. As a result, Roberto is more confident and more independent.

See Table 11.3 for examples of daily living skills that can be taught to children who are visually impaired.

Social Interaction Skills   Think about how much of what we have learned about interacting with others came through watching others—through vision. Posture, eye contact, facial expression, when to shake hands, when to touch and not to touch—for all these skills and more we unconsciously imitate what we see. Without vision, these skills must be taught explicitly, so that people with visual impairments can be accepted by others and form friendships (Sacks & Silberman, 2000). Teachers can help by quietly requesting that the student with a visual impairment conform to the social expectations of the situation: "Josh, shake hands

Table 11.3	Typical Independent Living Activities for Children with Visual Impairments
Preschool	Dressing
	Mealtime routines
	Toileting
	Use of eating utensils
Elementary years	Selection of clothes according to preference and weather
	Washing and caring for hair
	Household chores
	Handling small amounts of personal money
High school years	Grooming
	Self-care
	Organization of personal possessions
	Ordering and maintaining special devices and equipment
	Application of appropriate social skills

Source: N. C. Barraga & J. N. Erin (1992). *Visual handicaps and learning.* Austin, TX: Pro-Ed. (pp. 152–153).

with Mr. Hudson"; "Lupe, stand up straight." If this is done without embarrassment, it should lead to greater social acceptance in the long run.

Recreation and Leisure Skills   Many students with visual impairments may not know how many options there are for the use of leisure time (McGregor & Farrenkopf, 2000). Learning about these options and acquiring the skills needed to perform them are part of the responsibility of the specialized teacher. Among the options that can be learned by people with visual impairments are cross-country and downhill skiing, bicycling, sailing and canoeing, running, skating, bowling, swimming, waterskiing, scuba diving, snorkeling, and martial arts—you name the activity, it can be adapted. For information on world-class mountain climber and author Erik Weihenmayer, who is blind, go to **http://www.nfb.org/everest/seven.htm** or **www.touchthetop.com/**.

Use of Assistive Technology   The technological adaptations for people with visual impairments are impressive, although not all students have access to them. We will discuss technology separately later in the chapter.

Career Education   Career education must start early for the child with visual impairment and must focus on developing knowledge of the range of possible careers and interest and skills in particular areas (Hatlen, 2000b). Since underemployment is a serious issue for adults with visual impairment, this is an essential part of the core curriculum (Wolffe, 2000).

Visual Efficiency   The term *visual efficiency* refers to the best possible use of the remaining vision in the person who is blind or has low vision. The specialized teacher must assess functional vision, plan learning activities, and teach students to use their functional vision effectively (Hatlen, 2000b).

Table 11.4	Expanding the Teaching of Concepts Through the Principles of Special Methods		
	Principles of Special Methods		
Unique Skill	**Concrete Experiences**	**Learning by Doing**	**Unifying Experiences**
Making lemonade	Use real ingredients, real utensils, and real dinnerware.	Make the lemonade, completing each step in the process with or without guidance or prompting from the teacher.	Purchase ingredients from a grocery store. Integrate measurement concepts learned in math class. Drink lemonade as part of an after-school party for peers and parents.
Writing with slate and stylus	Use the actual slate and stylus. Use slate instructional tool from the American Printing House for the Blind to introduce cell configurations.	Use the slate and stylus with guidance from the teacher, as needed. Explore other specialty slates, such as one-liner notecard slate, full-page slate, and cassette-labeling slate.	Use the slate and stylus to jot assignments. Use the slate and stylus to take notes in a classroom. Use a slate and stylus at home to label CDs.

Source: A. J. Koenig & M. C. Holbrook (2000). *Foundations of education: Instructional strategies for teaching children and youth with visual impairments*, Vol. II (2nd ed., p. 200). New York: American Foundation for the Blind.

Allen Koenig and Cay Holbrook (2000) describe Lowenfeld's (1973) three principles of special methods for teaching students with visual impairments: the need for concrete experiences, the need for learning by doing, and the need for unifying experiences. Table 11.4 gives examples of how to use those special methods.

School Settings for Students Who Are Blind or Have Low Vision

Students with visual impairments can be found in every kind of educational setting. Each decision about *where* the child learns is made on the basis of the individual student's needs, by the IEP team. Here are some of the options, ranging from the least restrictive to residential schools.

Most children with visual impairments are now educated in public schools.

● **Public School Programs**   Public school programs are today the most frequently used service delivery model for students who are visually impaired. The major educational models used within public schools are consultative services, itinerant services, resource rooms, and self-contained classrooms.

In the **consultant model**, the general education teacher and specialized teacher set up the needed classroom adaptations together, and the specialized teacher is available to the general education teacher for help as needed. This model might be appropriate for the blind student functioning at grade level or for the student with multiple disabilities that include visual impairment (Lewis & Allman, 2000).

Itinerant services, in which a trained teacher travels from school to school within a specific area, providing direct or indirect services to students with visual impairments, are available for students enrolled in public schools who need additional assistance.

In **resource room programs**, the student who is visually impaired is enrolled in the general education classroom, where he or she receives most instruction. Self-contained classrooms are classrooms within a public school in which only children with visual impairments are enrolled. The teacher of the class is certified in special education that focuses on the needs of students with visual impairments. Self-contained classrooms may be very useful in the education of very young children who are blind in order to prepare them for full, successful inclusion in general education classrooms.

Itinerant teachers travel from school to school to provide services to students with visual impairments.

● *Residential School Programs*   Residential schools, in which students go to classes and live on campus, have traditionally offered comprehensive services, providing instruction in academic skills, daily living skills, and vocational skills.

Lewis and Allman (2000) see the following advantages for residential schools:

Residential schools have played a major role in the education of children with visual impairments and today offer support for regular public schools.

- All the adults are trained and knowledgeable about the complex educational needs of students with visual impairments.
- The students spend all day learning, rather than spending time waiting while sighted students are instructed visually.
- Students continue learning beyond the six-hour school day, since instruction occurs in dormitories and in community-based settings on weekends and after school.
- Goals related to the expanded core curriculum are infused into all activities by knowledgeable specialists.
- Students have the opportunity to interact with other students with visual impairments.

In science lab, Jeremy is using his sense of touch to determine the type of animal bones found at a mountain site. This skill will be crucial for him in every aspect of his life. (© Sean Cayton/The Image Works)

These advantages must be weighed against the drawbacks of being separated for long periods from family and community.

One of the most critical decisions to be made for children with visual impairments and their families is placement, or school setting—*where* they will go to school. It is difficult to obtain the "ideal" placement for the student who is blind or has low vision, since each student has such complex needs (Lewis & Allman, 2000). Following the initial placement decision, it is important that the appropriateness of the decision be re-evaluated frequently so that the child will receive not only the best possible instruction, taking into account the need for adaptive skills, but also the social interactions and experiences that will prepare the child for adult life in a competitive world.

Education for Students with Additional Disabilities

Students with visual impairment and other disabilities will also need specialized instruction.

As we discussed earlier in the chapter, many students with visual impairment have additional disabilities such as deafness, emotional disturbance, mental retardation, learning disabilities, and physical impairment. Regardless of additional disabilities, students with visual impairments should be encouraged to make use of their functional vision and also be taught adaptive techniques for independent living and vocational skills. In most cases, special education teachers who have students with multiple disabilities in their classroom will receive consultation services from the vision teacher in order to provide them with adaptive instruction (Erin, 1996).

? Pause and Reflect

Is there a "best" setting for students with visual impairments? Can you think of an advantage and a disadvantage of each of the options we have described? ●

Assistive Technology

Assistive technology allows people who are blind or have low vision to function independently.

Technological changes have had a significant effect on the educational and vocational outlook for students with visual impairments. Many assistive technology devices are now available to increase a student's ability to function independently in educational and employment settings, and, most important, to increase access to print. (See the Technology Focus feature.) Teachers have a role to play, though, in making this technology accessible and understandable to their students (Mack, Koenig, & Ashcroft, 1990; Spungin, 2002). Teachers need to provide effective instruction, to maximize time management, and to advocate for the purchase of equipment. There are four major categories of available technology:

1. *Devices to increase visual access to print* often start with closed-circuit televisions (CCTV) that enlarge print size on a television screen. A student may use such devices to magnify all or some of her classwork. The CCTV should be available in a place where the student has easy access and is still a part of the class. Some students may have access to a portable version with a small hand-held camera that is TV compatible. As soon as the student is introduced to the CCTV, he or she will receive instruction from the vision specialist on its use and should, within a short time, be able to use it independently. The student should then be allowed to use the CCTV whenever he or she believes it will help accomplish the classwork. Software that enlarges the size of

Technology Focus

What Special Devices Will the Student with Visual Impairment Use?

Students who are visually impaired may use a variety of equipment, devices, and tools to assist them with various academic and everyday tasks. Some students may need only a few adaptive devices, while others need to use several in combination.

OPTICAL DEVICES

Eyeglasses with special prescriptions
Magnifiers
Telescopes

The student who is blind can use this Braille note-taker to take notes using Braille. The notes can be read back via voice, through the speaker on top, or via Braille, using the "refreshable Braille" display at the bottom. (Davis Barber/PhotoEdit)

NONOPTICAL DEVICES

. . . to enhance VISUAL FUNCTIONING

Book stands
Wide felt-tipped pens and markers
Acetate
Lamps
Large-print books
Bold-line paper
Line markers and reading windows
Sun visors and other shields
Measurement tools
Additional tools (many other adaptations are readily available, like calculators with large displays and keys with large print, etc.)

. . . to enhance TACTILE FUNCTIONING

Braille
Tactile graphics
Braillewriter
Slate and stylus
Raised-line paper
Templates and writing guides
Raised-line drawing boards and other tactile writing devices
Raised marks
Braille labeler
Measurement tools with Braille and raised markings
Abacus
Teacher-made materials
Additional tactile materials and tools

. . . to enhance AUDITORY FUNCTIONING

Cassette tape recorders
Talking books, recorded books, and e-books
Talking calculators
Voice organizers and recorders
Audible gym equipment
Additional auditory devices (talking watches, alarm clocks, thermometers, money identifiers, etc.)

ASSISTIVE TECHNOLOGY DEVICES

CCTV
Braille translation software
Braille printer
Synthetic speech

Screen-enlargement software
Refreshable Braille displays
Audible and Braille note-takers
Electronic Braillewriter

Optical character recognition (OCR) with speech and scanner
Tactile graphics maker

Source: Adapted from S. Spungin (Ed.) (2002). *When you have a visually impaired student in your classroom: A guide for teachers.* New York: AFB Press.

print and images on the computer screen (for example, Zoom Text) is another essential for many low-vision computer users.

2. *Devices to increase auditory access to print,* including voice output devices for personal computers and devices that convert print to auditory output, are now widely available. For students who are unable to read the print on a computer screen, a voice output device with screenreading software may allow them to use the computer to complete assignments. Headphones are available so that the student can use the device without disturbing other students.

Technology can improve access to print through visual, auditory, or tactile modalities.

3. *Devices to increase tactile access to print,* including Braille printers that can be attached to word processors for immediate access to print work and devices that convert print to a tactile output. In the past, students who were blind would complete assignments in Braille, but the classroom teacher who was unable to read Braille would have to wait for the vision specialist to transcribe the Braille into print before grading the assignment. With the introduction of devices that can convert print into Braille and Braille into print, students can print their assignments in both Braille and English.

For the student, though, the most helpful tool may be the Braille note-taker (for example, Braille Lite). With these devices, students can take notes on a Braille keypad, and receive auditory output or download their notes to their computer.

4. *Devices to increase independent travel,* including **electronic travel aids** that are independent or provide supplementary information about the environment. There are a variety of devices, such as the laser cane, which use sonar and/or laser technology to aid in the detection of obstacles or drop-offs while traveling. The future may hold an increase in the talking sign technology, already in use in some spots, and the global positioning satellite with speech as an orientation aid. Although these devices are not directly relevant to academic work, the classroom teacher should know as much as possible about any device the student is using, including how it works, when the student should use it, and how to reinforce the student's proper use of the device. An orientation and mobility specialist will be able to answer all these questions.

Using some of these adaptive devices, people with visual impairments can also use the Internet. Websites that are "Bobby-approved" (see Chapter 10) are accessible for users who are blind or have low vision. See the accompanying Teaching Strategies box entitled, "When Should Technology Skills Be Taught?" for guidelines for grade-appropriate technology skills.

As you know, changes in technology occur so quickly that it can be difficult to keep up to date. Consult the Useful Resources section at the end of this chapter for some websites that can provide you with the most current information about assistive technology.

❓ *Pause and Reflect*

The needs of students with visual impairments present us with a significant challenge. We know that, given the appropriate instruction and supports, they can become successful, productive adults, but providing the instruction and the supports takes considerable expertise and teamwork on the part of the student, the family, and the professionals working on the student's behalf. Do you think you could be part of that "support team"? ●

Teaching Strategies & Accommodations

When Should Technology Skills Be Taught?

Primary Grades (K–3)

In these grades, the teacher teaches or fosters the following:

- An awareness of technology, by having students explore the layout of equipment and how components are connected
- The basic rules of computer use, such as shutting down the computer properly
- How to navigate the screen using screen readers with synthesized speech or a refreshable Braille display
- Prekeyboarding activities using touch tables and tactile overlays
- Keyboarding skills when a student has the necessary motor and academic skills for the task using "touch-typing" techniques
- Early word-processing skills, such as naming, saving, and printing files; inserting and deleting text; and completing written assignments
- The use of screen-enlargement features, including built-in features of word-processing programs and specialized software
- The use of screen-reading programs to read sentences, then words and characters; spell out individual words; adjust voice and punctuation settings; and so forth
- The use of refreshable Braille displays, either alone or in conjunction with speech synthesis when a student is proficient in uncontracted Braille

Middle School (Grades 4–8)

In these grades, the specialist instructs students in these skills:

- More advanced word-processing skills, such as cutting and pasting text, using a spell checker, using formatting features (including centering and underlining), and using the dictionary feature
- More advanced screen-reading skills, such as using customized screen-reading settings and skimming long documents with search-and-find features
- The use of portable note-takers, beginning with simple applications (such as word-processing file management, and using the calendar and calculator functions)
- Internet applications, such as using email, a Web browser, off-line browsing, and search engines
- The use of Braille-translation software and Braille embossing

High School (Grades 9–12)

In high school, the specialist helps students master advanced skills:

- Advanced functions of applications
- More detailed use of the Internet and World Wide Web, such as using advanced email features and creating webpages
- The use of scanners and optical character recognition (OCR) software to create Braille documents from print materials
- Higher-level functions, including advanced mathematics and computer programming
- The use of an electronic Brailler and other types of specialized equipment

---

Source: F. M. D'Andrea & K. Barnicle (1997). Adapted from *Access to information: Technology and Braille.* In D. P. Wormsley & F. M. D'Andrea (Eds.), *Instructional strategies for Braille literacy* (pp. 269–307). New York: AFB Press.

SUMMARY

- Students with visual impairments make up a relatively small percentage of school-age children. This low-incidence population includes children who are blind, who have low vision, and who are visually impaired and have additional disabilities. Although legal blindness is required for some services, educational services are also offered to students with less severe visual impairments.

- The process of seeing involves the passage of light through the eye and interpretation of the image by the brain. Damage to any of the eye structures, the nerves connecting them to the brain, or the brain itself can result in visual impairment.

- Visual impairments may affect a child's development by limiting one source of sensory feedback from the environment. In language, children may use verbal expressions without understanding what they mean; in physical development, children may be less motivated to move and explore; in cognitive development, children may interact less with the environment, which may result in poorer concept development.

- Early intervention involves allowing the child to explore and touch and helping parents make the most of learning opportunities in daily life.

- Teachers are often the first to recognize milder visual impairments. The most common screening test is the Snellen Chart. Ideally, vision screening is the product of a team approach, with continuous observation in the classroom, referral for evaluation, and follow-up provided by appropriate professionals.

- A functional vision assessment is used to make decisions about the student's educational program. Interpretation of test results should take into account modifications to the test and items that rely heavily on visual experience.

- The expanded core curriculum for students who are blind or have low vision includes instruction in the core academic areas and in specialized skill areas such as instruction in Braille, instruction in low-vision aids, development of listening skills, and orientation and mobility.

- Placement options for students who have visual impairments were initially limited to residential schools; however, public schools now provide self-contained classrooms, as well as resource programs, itinerant services, and consultation services for students included in the general education classroom.

- Advances in assistive technology have resulted in increasing visual, auditory, and tactile access to print; new technology for mobility has also been developed.

KEY TERMS

visual impairment	functionally blind	pupil
legal blindness	low vision	lens
visual acuity	functional vision	vitreous humor
educational definitions	cornea	iris

retina	compensatory academic skills	dog guide
optic nerve		electronic travel aids
cortical visual impairment	Braille	independent living skills
	orientation	consultant model
expanded core curriculum	mobility	itinerant services
	human guide	resource room programs
	cane travel	

USEFUL RESOURCES

- Susan Spungin (Ed.) (2002). *When you have a visually impaired child in your classroom: A guide for teachers.* New York: AFB Press. This small book is available at low cost from the American Foundation for the Blind (AFB). It is just about the most useful resource a teacher whose class includes a student with vision loss could have.

- The American Printing House for the Blind (APH) also publishes a book for teachers *Teaching the student with a visual impairment: A primer for the classroom teacher.* It is available through the APH website at **http://www.aph.org**. APH provides special media, tools, and material needed for education and daily life by people with visual impairments.

- The American Foundation for the Blind annually publishes the *AFB directory of services for blind and visually impaired persons in the United States and Canada* (with an accompanying CD-ROM) available through AFB Press in New York. This directory, updated yearly, is a compilation of schools, agencies, organizations, and programs that serve individuals who are blind or have low vision and their families. The CD-ROM contains the same information, making it accessible to users with vision loss with adaptive equipment. Contact the AFB website at **http://www.afb.org**, or call its InfoLine at (800) 232-5463. The InfoLine provides information about Talking Books, as well as other AFB services.

- The Blind Children's Center in Los Angeles publishes a series of booklets that are useful, inexpensive, and reader-friendly on topics such as communicating and encouraging movement with the young child with visual impairments. They are written with parents in mind but are helpful for early intervention specialists and teachers, too. Contact them at 4120 Marathon Street, Los Angeles, CA 90020, (800) 222-3566, or at **http://www.blindcntr.org**.

- Helen Keller's autobiography *The story of my life* (Garden City, NY: Doubleday, 1954) has inspired many a reader; for even more detail, read *Helen and teacher* by Joseph Lash (republished in 1997 by AFB Press), or rent the movie version of *The Miracle Worker,* which tells the story of Helen's discovery of the meaning of language with the help of her teacher Annie Sullivan.

- Sandra Lewis and Carol B. Allman have written *Seeing eye to eye: An administrator's guide to students with low vision* (New York: AFB Press, 2000), an ideal resource for administrators and educators. The booklet explains the needs of students with low vision and the practical services essential for helping them become literate and successful.

- The Library of Congress National Library Service for the Blind and Physically Handicapped is a free lending library of Braille and recorded materials circulated to eligible borrowers through a network of cooperating libraries. Call (202) 707-9275, or visit their website at **http://www.loc.gov/nls**.

- See Frances Mary D'Andrea and Carol Farrenkopf (2000). *Looking to learn: Promoting literacy for students with low vision.* New York: AFB Press. This handbook provides teachers with practical tips and advice on improving literacy skills for students with low vision.

- The APH currently houses a database called the *Louis Database of Accessible Materials for People Who Are Blind or Visually Impaired.* Louis contains information about more than 152,000 titles of accessible materials, including Braille, large print, sound recordings, and computer files from over 200 agencies throughout the United States. You can access Louis several ways: through the Internet at **http://www.aph.org/louis.htm2**, by phoning (800) 223-1839, by e-mailing them at **resource@aph.org**, or by faxing your inquiries to (502) 899-2363.

- The *Braille Is Beautiful Kit* is a disability awareness package for use with elementary or high-school students. The activities give students opportunities to read and write Braille, and there are two videos included. It's available through the Council for Exceptional Children; contact them at (888) 232-7733.

- *AccessWorld: Technology for Consumers with Visual Impairments* is a bimonthly journal from the AFB that covers assistive technology and visual impairment. It is available online, in large print and Braille, or on tape or disk. Go to **http://www.afb.org/law/main.asp/** for more information.

 PORTFOLIO ACTIVITIES

1. Now that you've read the chapter, have your assumptions about what it is like to have a visual impairment changed? Try a simulation exercise: Wear a blindfold during the first half of class. Concentrate on orientation and mobility, using listening skills, and memorizing spatial relationships. What were your impressions? Write a short paper for your portfolio describing them.

   ✓*Standards* This activity will help the student meet CEC Content Standard 3: Individual Learning Differences.

2. What are the limitations of the simulation exercise you just experienced? Now that you've experienced the simulation, what are you going to do to improve the quality of life for people with visual impairments? Write a one-page plan for your portfolio.

   ✓*Standards* This activity will help the student meet CEC Content Standard 1: Foundations.

3. Contact the Office for Students with Disabilities on your campus and ask if there is a need for readers for blind students. Some textbooks are not

immediately available in Braille or large print, so listening to a book on audiotape is the only way students have access to text material. Your journal describing your experiences as a reader could be included in your portfolio.

✓ *Standards* This activity will help the student meet CEC Content Standard 4: Instructional Strategies.

4. Plan a social studies or science unit and modify it to meet the needs of students who are blind. Include this unit plan in your portfolio.

✓ *Standards* This activity will help the student meet CEC Content Standard 10: Collaboration.

 To access an electronic portfolio template for these activities, visit our text website through http://www.education. college.hmco.com/students/.

12 Children with Physical Disabilities and Health Impairments

Outline

Terms and Definitions
    Physical Disabilities
    Health Impairment
    Prevalence
Types of Physical Disabilities
    Neurological Conditions
    Musculoskeletal Conditions
    Traumatic Injury
Types of Health Impairments
    Asthma
    Juvenile Diabetes
    Cystic Fibrosis
    Acquired Immune Deficiency Syndrome
      (AIDS)
    Childhood Cancer
    Attention Deficit/Hyperactivity Disorder
      (ADHD)
    Multiple Disabilities
Characteristics of Individuals with Physical
     Disabilities and Health Impairments
    Cognitive Development
    Communication and Language Development
    Social and Emotional Development
    Effects on the Family
Teaching Strategies and Accommodations
    Early Intervention
    Educational Planning
    Accessing Instruction
    Integrating Technology
Adult Life
SUMMARY
KEY TERMS
USEFUL RESOURCES
PORTFOLIO ACTIVITIES

Learning Objectives:

After reading this chapter, the reader will:

- Describe the general differences between physical disabilities and health impairments

- Discuss how knowing the cause and treatment of a student's condition can help you work effectively with the student

- Identify how the age of onset and severity of a condition can affect a child's social and emotional development

- Discuss the ways technology can facilitate communication and social interaction among all students in a classroom, including those with significant physical disabilities

- Define the transdisciplinary approach and describe how it is implemented in the classroom

Children with physical disabilities and health impairments are a diverse group. This category includes students with a wide range of individual differences, abilities, and challenges. Because many people with physical disabilities and health impairments acquire their disabilities after infancy or have short life expectancies, they often face emotional stress, in addition to their primary disability.

Many individuals with physical disabilities or health impairments play a pivotal role in the ongoing fight for civil and human rights due all people with disabilities. Their participation in this struggle resulted not only in many legal and physical changes in the environment, but also in a long tradition of self-advocacy. The visibility of physical disabilities creates a common bond among individuals with disabilities and allows advocates to make powerful statements. That visibility, however, can also set up nonphysical barriers and other difficulties in interpersonal situations, particularly for young children with disabilities. For example, imagine having to explain many times a day why you have no hair, why your hands are in splints, or why you have to rest a few seconds between words. In this chapter, we will rely frequently on the voices of persons with physical disabilities and health impairments as they answer these types of questions to help you learn more about them as people—friends, relatives, and students.

Terms and Definitions

Probably more than any other disability, the presence of a physical disability makes us explore the meaning of such words as *disability, handicap,* and *severity*. This is because the degree of physical involvement and the degree to which the disability affects an individual's life are not necessarily correlated. You might consider paralysis from the neck down to be an extremely severe disability. Yet, the many persons with this condition who lead fulfilling lives may not view themselves as "handicapped" at all. Individuals with physical disabilities adjust, adapt, and contribute to the community: Their disabilities become handicaps only when society uses them as a reason to discriminate against and segregate people.

Physical Disabilities

Many people with physical disabilities prefer to use the term **physically challenged**. They view their physical conditions as a challenge to be faced rather than as a situation that disables or handicaps their existence. "Living as a spinal cord-injured individual is really no different than living as an able-bodied individual, except that you're doing it on wheels. Some of the technical aspects of living on wheels are different" (Corbet, 1980, p. 54).

Physical disability refers to a condition that incapacitates the skeletal, muscular, and/or neurological systems of the body to some degree. Many individuals with physical disabilities have no concurrent mental disability. This is an important point for us to keep in mind. Later in the chapter we will discuss conditions of coexisting mental and physical disabilities.

The Individuals with Disabilities Education Act (IDEA) identifies students who experience physical disabilities as "orthopedically impaired":

> "Orthopedically impaired" means having a severe orthopedic impairment. The term includes impairments caused by a congenital anomaly (e.g., clubfoot, absence of some member, etc.), an impairment caused by

Many people with physical disabilities view their physical condition as a challenge rather than a handicapping condition.

disease (e.g., poliomyelitis, bone tuberculosis, etc.), and an impairment from any other cause (e.g., cerebral palsy, amputations, and fractures or burns which cause contractures). (Individuals with Disabilities Education Act, 1990, Sec. 300.6[6])

Health Impairment

The term **health impairment** also focuses on the physical condition of individuals. It includes conditions in which one or more of the body's systems are affected by diseases or conditions that are debilitating or life-threatening or that interfere with the student's ability to perform in a regular classroom setting. The definition of health impairment found in IDEA is as follows:

> "Other health impaired" means having limited strength, vitality, or alertness, due to chronic or acute health problems such as heart condition, tuberculosis, rheumatic fever, nephritis, asthma, sickle cell anemia, hemophilia, epilepsy, lead poisoning, leukemia, or diabetes. (Amendments to the Individuals with Disabilities Education Act, 1990, Sec. 300.5[7])

Prevalence

Children with physical disabilities and other health impairments are among the smallest groups served under the federal laws known as IDEA. The *Twenty-fourth Annual Report to Congress on the Implementation of the Individuals with Disabilities Act* (USDOE, 2002) reported 73,057 children from the ages of 6 to 21 with orthopedic impairments, 291,850 with other health impairments, and 14,844 with traumatic brain injury in the 2000–2001 school year. Although listed as a separate category of special education, we will define and discuss traumatic brain injury later in this chapter, as many individuals with traumatic brain injury also have physical disabilities.

? Pause and Reflect

Individuals with physical disabilities or health impairments may clearly distinguish between the use of the terms challenge, disability, and handicap. Do you believe that these words can affect the way you or others perceive students with physical challenges? ●

Types of Physical Disabilities

Within each disability category, the individual range of ability varies greatly.

In this section, we will look at the most prevalent types, causes, and treatments of physical disabilities in children. There are several reasons why you, as a prospective teacher, should know about particular disabilities. Understanding the cause may help you to know what to expect from a student, since certain causes lead to characteristic behavior. Understanding treatment requirements can also help you plan classroom time (for example, a student may need to miss class for dialysis) and become comfortable with helping the student with in-school treatment such as tube feeding. Once you know what to expect, you will be better able to plan instruction and to prepare the classroom from a physical perspective.

Between friends, the focus is on fun, not on disability. (© Michael Pole/CORBIS)

The abilities of students within each type of physical disability can vary widely. Resist stereotyping and base your expectations on the abilities and efforts of each individual student.

Neurological Conditions

A neurological condition is one that affects the nervous system—the brain, nerves, and spinal cord (Fraser, Hensinger, & Phelps, 1990). The muscles and bones are healthy, but the neurological messages sent to them are faulty or interrupted. Three of the neurological conditions are cerebral palsy, spina bifida, and seizure disorders.

● *Cerebral Palsy*   **Cerebral palsy** is a condition involving disabilities in movement and posture that results from damage to the brain before or during birth, or in infancy (Fraser, Hensinger, & Phelps, 1990). The muscles and the nerves connecting the muscles to the brain are normal; the problem lies in the "communication" process between the brain and the muscles. Events like cerebral hemorrhages (bleeding in the brain), anoxia (lack of oxygen at birth), and fetal strokes can cause neurological damage that results in some type of cerebral palsy. Other possible causes include abnormal brain development, insufficient circulation to the brain before or after birth, infection in/or beside the brain, or the indirect effects of the mother's immune system that may occur while she fights infection (Mayo Clinic, 2002). However, in many instances of cerebral palsy, no specific cause can be identified, and the condition is not considered to be preventable given our current level of knowledge (Hankins, 2003).

The area and severity of brain injury, the cause of the injury, and when it occurs determine the type of cerebral palsy that appears and the extent of its effect on the body. Prevalence figures suggest that about 8000 infants and 1500 preschool children are identified with cerebral palsy each year—a figure that appears constant over the past thirty years (Hankins, 2003; UCPA, 2001).

Cerebral palsy—caused by damage to the brain before birth or infancy—results in disabilities in movement and posture.

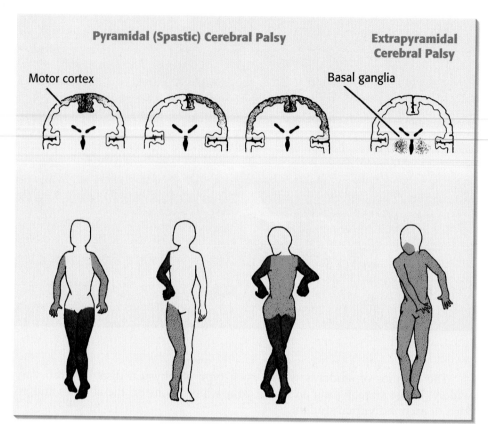

Figure 12.1

Regions of the Brain Affected in Various Forms of Cerebral Palsy

Source: M. L. Batshaw & Y. M. Perret (1992). *Children with handicaps: A medical primer* (3rd ed., p. 444). Baltimore: Paul H. Brookes.

Note: The darker the shading, the more severe the involvement.

Some children are identified as having cerebral palsy at birth, whereas others are not definitively diagnosed until they are a year old or even older. Young children are often identified as having cerebral palsy because of delay in meeting the milestones of motor development, such as walking at twelve months, and the persistence of certain infant reflexes. Cerebral palsy also can be diagnosed in children up to age 6 who have brain damage due to external causes such as suffocation, near drowning, or encephalitis.

Cerebral palsy is often classified by type of motor dysfunction (see Figure 12.1). The most common type of dysfunction is *spasticity,* or hypertonia. Spasticity involves a mild to severe exaggerated contraction of muscles when the muscle is stretched. It is present in about 70 to 80 percent of all cases of cerebral palsy and occurs when the area injured is on the surface of the brain or on the nerves leading from the surface to the interior of the brain (UCPA, 2001). Spasticity can involve the entire body or only some parts of the body.

Dyskenesia is a type of cerebral palsy characterized by involuntary extraneous motor activity, especially under stress. This type of cerebral palsy occurs in 10 to 20 percent of all cases and is caused by injury to the basal ganglia, the brain's motor switchboard (UCPA, 2001). The involuntary movements sometimes accompany the individual's attempts at voluntary movement. One type of movement (*athetosis*) involves a slow, writhing type of movement. The person may appear to be repeatedly and slowly stretching his or her arms or legs when simply trying to reach for a book. *Choreoathetosis* refers to quick, jerky movements that may accompany the athetoid movements. Movements also may be slow and rhythmic and involve the entire limb or trunk (*distonia*).

Ataxia, a third type of cerebral palsy, is much less common. It occurs in about 5 to 10 percent of all cases, when the injury has occurred in the cerebellum. Ataxia refers to a lurching walking gait. People with ataxia also experience difficulty maintaining their balance.

Some individuals with cerebral palsy have a mixture of types. For example, a student might have spastic quadriplegia and ataxia. As we have already mentioned, the range of severity and involvement can be great. Some individuals may only experience slight difficulty in muscle control—difficulty that may be undetectable by an observer. Others have almost no voluntary movement—they are not able to smile, move a hand, or turn a head intentionally.

Some children with cerebral palsy also experience learning disabilities, mental retardation, ADHD, or other disabilities such as visual impairment and hearing loss. The coexistence of other types of disabilities depends on the extent and location of brain injury as well as on early interventions. Recent statistics suggest that approximately 70 percent of individuals with cerebral palsy experience one or more of these additional disabilities (National Center on Birth Defects and Developmental Disabilities, 2002).

Historically, the variability in the estimates of IQ ranges for children with cerebral palsy was largely due to difficulties in administering intelligence tests to individuals with severe physical disabilities. Because many children with severe cerebral palsy may have significant difficulties in both speech and motor abilities, even nonverbal IQ tests may be difficult to administer. The student may have difficulty articulating a response, and difficulty pointing to the correct answer. Parents, teachers, and psychologists must therefore attend closely to academic, task-oriented, and behavioral characteristics of students with cerebral palsy to get a clearer idea of each student's abilities. Characteristics such as maturity, determination and persistence, goal orientation, insight, and the use of one's intellect to cope with disability have been coupled with early academic success in students with severe cerebral palsy (Willard-Holt, 1998). Although typical standardized tests may be difficult to administer, students will find other ways of revealing their potential. Assistive technology has greatly improved our ability to administer tests to children with extensive physical disabilities, and will continue to do so. Clearly, identifying a truly efficient method of communication is the critical factor in both the assessment and instruction of students with cerebral palsy.

Medical interventions such as braces, surgery, and prescribed therapies can help a student with cerebral palsy. For example, physical and occupational therapies exercise, strengthen, and position muscles, bones, and joints. Prevention of serious and painful contractures, dislocations, and rigidity is critical for individuals with cerebral palsy. Physical and occupational therapies facilitate the development of normal reflexes and maximize the control a person can have over the environment.

Positioning is a critical intervention for persons with limited mobility, especially in helping them meet the demands of the classroom. For example, although a physically capable individual can change positions when uncomfortable or fatigued, a student in a wheelchair or one who wears braces may need assistance for minor repositioning. A student with cerebral palsy may need an adult, such as the teacher, to provide physical assistance related to positioning, feeding, and other everyday needs. In the classroom, use of a tape recorder or a "note buddy" for writing notes are simple accommodations that teachers commonly arrange. Assistive technology, another significant intervention for students with cerebral palsy, will be discussed later in the chapter. To learn more about cerebral palsy and to find resources for parents and teachers, go the United Cerebral Palsy Association website at **http://www.ucpa.org**.

In spina bifida, the spine does not close properly during fetal development, resulting in varying degrees of paralysis.

● *Spina Bifida*   **Spina bifida**, or open spine, and *neural tube defects* (NTDs) are general terms used to describe the incomplete development of the brain, the spinal cord, or their protective coverings during prenatal development. An estimated 1 out of every 1000 births is affected (SBAA, 2003). Spina bifida is most common in persons of Irish, Scotch, and English ancestry, and high-incidence regions in the United States, such as southern Appalachia, North and South Carolina, and Tennessee, reflect this heritage. Spina bifida and other NTDs have been correlated with a lack of folic acid, a vitamin found in green vegetables and fresh fruit, in the diet early in the pregnancy. Studies have found that minimal intakes of folic acid before and during pregnancy significantly decrease the incidence of spina bifida and other NTDs even in women who have had children with NTDs. Women of childbearing age should carefully evaluate their diets for proper amounts of folic acid or consult with a doctor about appropriate vitamin supplements.

Children with spina bifida have spines that did not properly close during development, so the spinal cord protrudes from the weak point. As a result,

FIRST PERSON

My Life

Hi! My name is Jessica Smallman. I am 14 years of age; I was born May 3, 1982, in Halifax, Nova Scotia. Before I was born my parents, Faye Smallman and John Smallman, Jr., were told that I had a birth defect called spina bifida. I also had something called hydrocephalus, which means I had water on and near the brain. After I was born the doctors did an operation on me to insert a shunt (a tube from my head to my stomach to drain the water from my head to my stomach). I was hospitalized for a little while after birth.

As I got older I needed special equipment to help me go to the washroom, stand, walk, and just for mobility reasons. Since my dad is in the navy, we move a lot and I went to several elementary schools and a new hospital in Montreal. When I went to new schools it was very hard because of the students at these schools. The kids didn't know what was wrong with me and they didn't know how to react around me. In class they would call me stupid. One day, I just could not take it anymore and I did a presentation in front of my grade five classmates on spina bifida. After the presentation they stopped bugging and teasing me. My parents pushed me to be more active and independent even though they saw how much I was hurting. In the summer I went to the rehabilitation centre for four weeks. They taught me how to live on my own, how to keep fit, and how to protect myself. They also taught me not to be so upset about the way people treat me since the reason they act this way is because they don't understand me. They think they have to do everything for me, and if they move me a certain way I will break. This is not true because I'm very, very strong, and I'm not glass or something fragile or delicate.

nerves that control the lower parts of the body are not properly connected to the brain. When the spinal cord protrudes outside of the body, surgery typically is done within twenty-four hours of birth, in order to protect the spinal cord and to reduce the probability of additional nerve damage. Spina bifida usually results in limited or even no muscle control of the affected area. The extent of the defect depends on the location of the spinal cord damage. If the damage is at the base of the spine, the weakness may be limited to the muscles of the ankles and feet and the child may require only short leg braces for walking. A defect in the middle of the spine may result in paralysis below the waist, necessitating the use of a wheelchair. Bladder control problems and recurring kidney infections are also present (SBAA, 2003).

Hydrocephalus, a condition in which cerebrospinal fluid builds up in the skull and puts pressure on the brain, occurs in about 80 percent of cases of spina bifida. Untreated hydrocephalus may cause brain damage and mental retardation. Since spina bifida and other NTDs can now be detected early in pregnancy, children with this disability are likely candidates for prenatal surgery. Shunts

In hydrocephalus, cerebrospinal fluid builds in the skull, sometimes causing brain damage and mental retardation.

I also have to say that I am not lazy and I don't like people saying that. People used to laugh because I couldn't do some of the things they could, but I try my best to do many things. I think I am almost the same as any kid I know. I think like everyone else and I talk like everyone else. The only things I don't do like everyone else is walk and go to the bathroom by myself. That is why I have to wear diapers and I do self-catheterizations every four hours, and I can't drink much after I do my catheters. If I do I will leak a lot more than I usually do. I also get infections a lot easier than other people. If I could tell people one thing, it is "please don't treat me like I'm fragile."

LIFE

Life is like an elevator, some days are good
some days are bad.

Life is like a book, some parts are boring
and some are lots of fun.

Life is a bunch of songs, some are happy
ones and some are sad ones.

Life is about heartaches and headaches and
other different feelings.

Life is like school, you're always being
educated.

And some things you may not like, but
you've got to continue.

Life is full of surprises that are waiting for
us to discover them.

Some may cause pain and some may cause
happiness.

And life is having friends around you that
care about you no matter what.

They won't do stuff behind your back or
not believe you or the things you say,

And that's what life is all about (at least
that's what my life is all about).

Jessie Smallman

Jessie Smallman is a grade nine student at
Gaetz Brook Junior High, Nova Scotia.

Source: Jessica Smallman (1996/1997). My life. *Ability Network Magazine, 5*(2).

(artificial openings) can be inserted while the fetus is still in the uterus to minimize damage to the brain from excess spinal fluid. Although the paralysis itself cannot be corrected, shunt implants, physical therapy, and surgery can help minimize the effects of the disability (SBAA, 2003).

● *Seizure Disorders*   Seizures occur when the normally ordered pattern of movement of electricity along the nerve pathways of the brain is disrupted by an unorganized burst of electric impulses. These bursts periodically disrupt the normal functioning of the brain. The sudden change in how the cells of the brain communicate with each other results in a seizure. Seizure disorders occur in about 3 percent of the population. A condition of the nervous system that makes us susceptible to seizures is known as **epilepsy**; the occurrence of seizures is the primary characteristic of epilepsy (Epilepsy Foundation, 2003). There are a number of possible causes, including any direct injury to the brain, conditions such as cerebral palsy, or scarring of the brain as a result of infections or illness such as meningitis or rubella. In some instances, there appears to be a genetic component or predisposition. In many instances of epilepsy, however, there is no identifiable cause. Not all seizures are epileptic in nature. For example, sometimes a young child with a high fever has an isolated seizure.

Epilepsy is a neurological condition characterized by recurrent seizures.

About 15,000 school-age children through the age of 14 have epilepsy. Two types of seizures found frequently in children are grand mal seizures and petit mal seizures. **Grand mal seizures**, also called generalized tonic-clonic seizures, are experienced by about 60 percent of all individuals with seizure disorders. The seizures, which involve the whole body, usually last a few minutes and often result in a loss of consciousness. Most people experience a warning (called an *aura*) before the occurrence of a grand mal seizure. The aura may be characterized by unusual feelings or numbness. The seizure itself begins with a *tonic phase*, in which there is a stiffening of the body, often a loss of consciousness, heavy and irregular breathing, and drooling. In a few seconds, the seizure goes into the second or *clonic phase*. At this time, the muscles alternately clench and relax, in a jerking motion. Finally, the seizure is followed by a period of fatigue or disorientation. (See the accompanying Teaching Strategies box entitled, "What to Do If Someone Has a Tonic-Clonic Seizure.")

Petit mal seizures, also called absence seizures, occur most frequently in children between the ages of 4 and 12. Petit mal seizures often disappear as the child grows older; however, one-third to one-half of children with a history of petit mal seizures are likely also to have or eventually develop grand mal seizures. Petit mal seizures are very brief—usually lasting between fifteen and thirty seconds. The episodes are sometimes difficult to recognize. The child will lose consciousness, but this is not accompanied by any observable physical changes. In other words, the child may appear to be just blinking his or her eyes or staring into space for a few seconds.

Medications are used extensively in the treatment of seizure disorders. In most cases, appropriate medication can prevent seizures; some adjustment in prescription may be necessary as the child gets older or if different types of seizures begin to occur. It is important for teachers to know when students are receiving medication for seizures because medication can affect school performance by causing changes in alertness and other school-related behaviors. A few children who experience a number of different kinds of seizures or who have extensive brain damage may have seizures that are difficult to keep under control. A recently approved treatment for epilepsy, especially for people who do not benefit from medications, is electrical stimulation of the vagus nerve. An

Teaching Strategies & Accommodations

What to Do If Someone Has a Tonic-Clonic Seizure

- Keep calm. Reassure the other children that the child will be fine in a minute.

- Ease the child gently to the floor and clear the area of anything that could hurt him.

- Put something flat and soft (like a folded jacket) under his head so it will not bang against the floor as his body jerks.

- Turn him gently onto his side. This keeps his airway clear and allows any fluid in his mouth to drain harmlessly away.
  Don't try to force his mouth open.
  Don't try to hold on to his tongue.
  Don't put anything in his mouth.
  Don't restrain his movements.

- When the jerking movements stop, let the child rest until full consciousness returns.

- Breathing may have been shallow during the seizure and may even have stopped briefly.

This can give the child's lips or skin a bluish tinge, which corrects naturally as the seizure ends. In the unlikely event that breathing does not begin again, check the child's airway for any obstruction. It is rarely necessary to give artificial respiration.

Some children recover quickly after this type of seizure; others need more time. A short period of rest, depending on the child's alertness following the seizure, is usually advised. However, if the child is able to remain in the classroom afterward, he or she should be encouraged to do so.

Source: Epilepsy Foundation of America (1992). From *Children and epilepsy: The teacher's role* (1992, pp. 3–4). Copyright © 1992. Reprinted by permission of the Epilepsy Foundation of America, Landover, MD.

electrode implanted in the chest sends signals to the vagus nerve, which is located in the neck. Research indicates that this procedure significantly reduces the occurrence of seizures (Finesmith, Zampella, & Devinsky, 1999). Other possible treatment options include surgery and a ketogenic diet, which is a diet high in fats and low in carbohydrates (Epilepsy Foundation, 2003).

Musculoskeletal Conditions

In addition to physical disabilities caused by damage to the brain are conditions that directly affect muscles and bones. These musculoskeletal and neuromuscular conditions debilitate the muscles, bones, or joints to such a degree that they cause limitations in their functional use.

● *Muscular Dystrophy*   **Muscular dystrophy** is a neuromuscular condition in which the voluntary muscles of the body are affected by progressive weakness. Although there are several types of muscular dystrophy, the most common in school-age children is Duchenne muscular dystrophy. This genetically transmitted condition, which primarily affects boys, is usually diagnosed between the ages of 2 and 6. Neither the cause of Duchenne muscular dystrophy nor a specific treatment has yet been discovered, although many therapies, including drug and physical therapies, are available to lessen symptoms. The incidence is usually cited as 1 per 3500 live male births (NCBI, 2003).

In muscular dystrophy, the voluntary muscles of the body progressively weaken.

UNDERSTANDING THE THREE PERSPECTIVES: A MAP OF CONCERNS

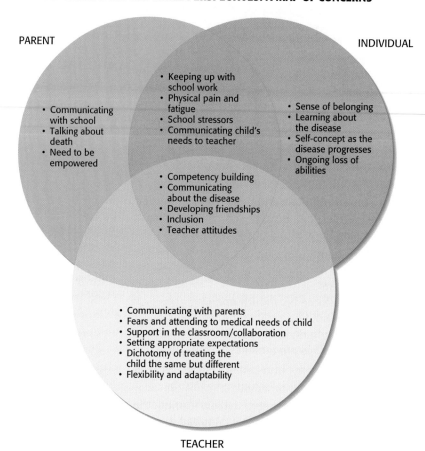

PARENT

INDIVIDUAL

• Keeping up with
  school work
• Physical pain and
  fatigue
• School stressors
• Communicating child's
  needs to teacher

• Communicating
  with school
• Talking about
  death
• Need to be
  empowered

• Sense of belonging
• Learning about
  the disease
• Self-concept as the
  disease progresses
• Ongoing loss of
  abilities

• Competency building
• Communicating
  about the disease
• Developing friendships
• Inclusion
• Teacher attitudes

• Communicating with parents
• Fears and attending to medical needs of child
• Support in the classroom/collaboration
• Setting appropriate expectations
• Dichotomy of treating the
  child the same but different
• Flexibility and adaptability

TEACHER

Figure 12.2

Common and Unique Concerns for Students with Neuromuscular Disabilities

Source: K. Strong & J. Sandoval (1999). Mainstreaming children with a neuromuscular disease: A map of concerns. *Exceptional Children,* 65, 358.

Because muscular dystrophy is a progressive condition, the child becomes increasingly weak and less mobile with age. A young child with muscular dystrophy may have barely noticeable weakness; by the time the child reaches his teens, however, walking may no longer be possible. The muscle weakness usually begins in the shoulders and hips and then spreads to other areas, including the heart muscles and muscles that affect the lungs. Secondary effects of muscular dystrophy include scoliosis (curvature of the spine) and a gradual loss of cardiac and respiratory function. Respiratory disease is often a cause of death of individuals with muscular dystrophy, whose life expectancy is now in the early 20s (MDA, 2003).

Teachers of students with muscular dystrophy must develop individualized modifications in the curriculum, depending on the child's age and the condition's progress. It is important to be aware of the social and emotional effects that muscular dystrophy may have on the child's understanding of his or her own mortality. See Figure 12.2 for an illustration of related concerns.

● *Juvenile Rheumatoid Arthritis*   Juvenile rheumatoid arthritis (JRA) is a condition that affects the tissue lining of the joints, primarily the joints of the knees, ankles, elbows, hips, wrists, and feet, causing them to become painful and stiff. JRA is found in children between the ages of 3 and adolescence, affects

Juvenile rheumatoid arthritis affects the tissue lining of the joints, making them painful and stiff.

twice as many girls as boys, and typically is diagnosed before age 16. It is estimated that approximately 285,000 children have JRA. Although the cause of JRA is unknown, it is suspected that infections may serve as triggers for JRA (American College of Rheumatology, 2003).

One complication of JRA is *iridocyclitis,* an inflammation of the eye that occurs without warning. If a student with JRA complains about bright lights or painful eyes, a teacher should help the student seek immediate medical attention. Some children with JRA may have difficulty holding pencils or typing on a keyboard; others may have difficulty walking, going up stairs, or participating in some physical education activities.

● *Congenital Malformations*   A **congenital malformation** is an incomplete or improperly formed part of the skeletal or muscular system that is present at birth. Congenital malformations occur in 2–3 percent of all live births (Medline, 2003). Often, there is no known cause for these malformations, although many of the risk factors discussed in Chapter 2 have been partially implicated. In some instances, there may be a genetic component. In other cases, birth defects have been associated with medications or drugs taken during pregnancy, with illness, such as rubella, and with infections experienced by the mother during pregnancy. As discussed in Chapter 2, the use of the drug thalidomide by pregnant mothers during the 1950s resulted in a number of infants born with absent or shortened limbs (Batshaw & Perret, 1992).

Congenital malformations can take many forms; a few of them have particular implications for physical movement. One example is a clubfoot, in which the foot is structured so that the forefoot and heel are turned in and down toward the body and the toes are turned down and away from the body. A clubfoot is sometimes hereditary, with an incidence of 2 per every 1000 live births. Surgery, physical therapy, and the use of casts are treatment options for children with this condition. Other malformations that can affect mobility are congenital hip dislocations, discrepancies of leg length, shortened or missing limbs, and scoliosis, or curvature of the spine. In some instances, treatment options include surgery, braces, special shoes, physical therapy, and the use of artificial limbs, or prostheses.

Many students with congenital physical malformations have no other accompanying disabilities. When the condition interferes with the student's regular education—because of surgery-related absences, for example—the student may qualify for special education and related services, such as physical or occupational therapy and transportation.

Traumatic Injury

Traumatic injury refers to damage inflicted to the brain or body after birth. There are many possible causes of traumatic injury, including child abuse and accidents, spinal cord injury, and closed-head injury.

> Traumatic injury is damage to the brain or body that occurs after birth.

● *Spinal Cord Injuries*   Spinal cord injuries, in which the spinal cord is damaged or severed, occur most frequently in adolescents and young adults. Diving, automobile, and motorcycle accidents are frequent causes of this injury in young people. As in spina bifida, the location of the injury determines its effects. A lower-spine injury may result in limited use or paralysis of the legs. An injury higher up the spine or to the neck may result in more extensive involvement, including the arms, trunk, and neck. In some cases, respiration is greatly affected and only facial muscles can be moved voluntarily.

Consider a student who falls from a tree or is involved in a car accident. The student recovers but must now use a wheelchair. The student has missed several months of school, his friends have moved on to the next grade, and he must adjust to a new perception of himself. A severe spinal cord injury may change how the student approaches all aspects of education. One very promising area for assisting students is technology. Technological advances have provided new opportunities for mobility of individuals with spinal cord injury. We will discuss these advances in more detail later on in this chapter.

Traumatic brain injuries are caused by an external physical force and may result in functional disability or psychosocial impairment.

● *Traumatic Brain Injuries*   **Traumatic brain injury (TBI)**, or acquired brain injury, is a a separate diagnostic category in the Individuals with Disabilities Education Act (IDEA, 1990). Traumatic brain injury is defined as:

> an acquired injury to the brain caused by an external physical force, resulting in total or partial functional disability or psychosocial impairment, or both, that adversely affects a child's educational performance. The term applies to open and closed head injuries resulting in impairments in one or more areas, such as cognition; language; memory; attention; reasoning; abstract thinking; judgment; problem-solving; sensory, perceptual, and motor abilities; psychosocial behavior; physical functions; information processing; and speech. The term does not apply to brain injuries that are congenital or degenerative, or brain injuries induced by birth trauma. [Code of Federal Regulations, Title 34, Sec. 300.7(b)(12)]

Since the brain controls and processes how one acts, damage to the brain can cause serious disabilities. The student who survives an automobile accident but who suffers a moderate or severe brain injury may physically recover well, but changes in memory, problem solving, attention span, impulse control, and overall cognition are likely to persist. The student may look the same, but these changes in behavior have a significant impact on school, home, and friends.

Statistics suggest that over 1 million children each year receive head injuries, and over 165,000 of these children will require hospitalization. TBI is the most common cause of death and disability among children living in the United States. The leading causes of TBI for infants are falls and violent shaking by adults; the most common causes of TBI for adolescents and young adults are automobile and motorcycle accidents, and violent crimes (NICHY, 2000). Most cases involve individuals between the ages of 15 and 24, but the number of younger children affected is almost as high (NIDCD, 2002). A small school district can anticipate having several children with traumatic brain injury; a large district can anticipate having over a hundred such students. Although the use of seat belts and bike and motorcycle helmets has reduced the rate of death and of severe brain injury, improvements in emergency medical services and technology have increased the number of students who become TBI survivors (Mira, Tucker, & Tyler, 1992; Witte, 1998).

An individual who survives TBI will usually be in a coma for a period of time. The length of the coma is one of the predictors of how severe the injury is. A mild brain injury usually results in loss of consciousness for less than an hour without skull fracture. A moderate injury results in one to twenty-four hours of unconsciousness and may be complicated by swelling of the brain and skull fractures. These symptoms persist for some time. A severe injury results in loss of consciousness for more than twenty-four hours. Bruising of the brain tissue (*contusion*) or bleeding in the brain (*intracranial hematoma*) is usually present. These serious conditions can result in lifelong cognitive deficits and difficulty with learning new information. Some deficits will be apparent immediately, and some will appear only after a period of time (Mira, Tucker, & Tyler, 1992; Witte, 1998).

On average, children return to school between three and twenty-four months after a brain injury; approximately one-third of these children will need special education services (Keyser-Marcus et al., 2002). Teachers should be aware that the student returning to school with a traumatic brain injury will fatigue quickly for the first few months. Adjustment to schedules, reduction in the amount of reading and writing, memory helpers, and organizers are strategies that will help the student who survives brain injury become adjusted to school. Generally, the establishment of specific routines and highly structured learning environments is recommended for students returning to the classroom. Teachers must be flexible and must remember that each student with a traumatic brain injury will have different symptoms and may respond to different interventions (Witte, 1998).

> Brain injuries affect each individual differently.

? *Pause and Reflect*

When we hear the word disabilities, many of us picture first a person with a physical disability, perhaps someone in a wheelchair. Yet, many kids with physical disabilities don't need special education services at all. What do you think may be the most important services these students do need to succeed in class? ●

Types of Health Impairments

Many conditions and diseases can significantly affect a child's health, and the ability to function successfully in school. Most health impairments are chronic conditions; that is, they are always present or recur. Unfortunately, many of these conditions result in gradual deterioration of health and eventual death.

Students with health impairments typically receive their education in the regular classroom as long as their health allows. Some require home-based instruction for periods of time or support services when they must miss school for an extended time. Teachers will need to be sensitive to the obstacles to learning that can arise from the condition itself, the side effects of prescribed treatments, and the emotional challenges the student faces. Knowledge of the condition and the individual student's treatment regimen will help you plan and prepare appropriate educational programs.

> Students with health impairments typically stay in the regular classroom for as long as possible.

Let's look at some conditions that can fall into the category of health impairment. In some cases, only some forms of the condition are severe enough to warrant special education or support services.

Asthma

Asthma is a chronic obstructive lung condition characterized by an unusual reaction to a variety of stimuli that cause difficulty in breathing and coughing, wheezing, and shortness of breath. Approximately 1 in 12, or as many as 5 million children in the United States have some level of asthma, making it the most common chronic health impairment of young children (Feldman, 1996; Getch & Neuharth-Pritchett, 1999). Many things can trigger an asthma attack. Some of the more common irritants are smoke, a cold or other infection, chalk dust, exercise, cold air, pollen, animal hair, emotional stress, and classroom pets. Asthma most frequently appears for the first time in children during their first five years.

Asthma can be managed. Special attention should be paid to the child's overall fitness. Allergens that cause the reactions can be removed or minimized wherever possible. Children can also receive *bronchodilators,* which are drugs that reverse the narrowing of the airways (Ranshaw et al., 2001). Because there may be side effects to any drug treatment, parents and teachers should learn the possible side effects of the particular medications a child is receiving.

Some forms of exercise are better tolerated than others by children with asthma. Running may result in narrowing of the airways and severe wheezing. Swimming is less likely to cause wheezing, but the child should be carefully watched, for obvious reasons. Overall participation in regular games and activities is encouraged, and many students have little or no difficulty participating in active sports.

Much attention has been given to the psychosocial effects of asthma. Loss of sleep is a frequent problem when attacks flare up at night, and it can be terrifying for a parent to watch a child fighting to breathe. Sometimes parents hesitate to discipline their child or to set limits for fear of triggering an asthmatic reaction. The child may also experience low self-esteem from a deformity in the chest cavity caused by the condition. In general, however, the prognosis for future health is good for these children.

As a teacher, you need to know the recommended physical activity levels for the student with asthma. Also, you should know the early warning signs of asthmatic episodes and what emergency procedures to take if a student has an asthma attack. Visit our website (at **http://www.college.hmco.com/students/**) to view a sample of a detailed asthma care plan for teachers or caregivers of a child with asthma. This care plan can serve as a model for children with other health impairments or physical disabilities that require emergency action and special procedures.

Juvenile Diabetes

Juvenile diabetes is a disorder of the metabolism caused by little or no insulin being produced by the body, which results in difficulties in digesting and obtaining energy from food. It is estimated that **juvenile onset diabetes** affects over 1.5 million children, and the disorder's overall prevalence appears to be increasing at the rate of 6 percent a year.

Juvenile onset diabetes can appear at any point between birth and the age of 30; it cannot be cured, but it can be controlled by daily intake of insulin, by exercise, and by a special diet (Rosenthal-Malek & Greenspan, 1999). Sometimes diabetes can also affect the eyes and the kidneys; unmanaged or severe diabetes may result in early blindness.

Even when children are receiving treatment for diabetes, teachers should be aware of two possible emergency conditions caused by insulin reactions. One condition, which results from low blood sugar and can cause unconsciousness and seizures, is called **hypoglycemia**. Symptoms include confusion, drowsiness, perspiration, a pale complexion, sudden hunger, lack of coordination, trembling, or the appearance of intoxication. Hypoglycemia is most likely to occur if the child has gone without eating for a while or has been exerting him- or herself physically. Although parents should be informed of the reaction, certain foods, such as sugar, can be given to the child immediately to mitigate the condition. A can of cake frosting is a good thing to keep on hand, since it not only contains sugar but is also easy to administer.

Another condition, **hyperglycemia**, results from high blood sugar. Its symptoms include extreme thirst, lethargy, dry hot skin, heavy labored breathing, and eventual unconsciousness. Severe hyperglycemia can result in ketoacidosis, which may result in unconsciousness, coma, and death (Rosenthal-Malek & Greenspan, 1999). Students experiencing hyperglycemia will need to drink water, diet soda, or other sugarless fluids.

If you have a child with juvenile diabetes in your class, it is a good idea to have a complete list of symptoms and emergency actions handy. You will need to be flexible regarding certain aspects of your classroom management. For example, students with juvenile diabetes must have immediate bathroom privileges, immediate access to a nurse, and may need to eat at specific times during the day. Teachers should communicate regularly with parents regarding classroom activities, patterns of high and low blood sugar episodes, and any deviations from those patterns (Rosenthal-Malek & Greenspan, 1999).

Cystic Fibrosis

Cystic fibrosis is a progressive and usually fatal disorder characterized by lung damage, abnormal mucus production within the lungs, and difficulties in the absorption of protein and fat. Damage to the lungs results in inadequate amounts of oxygen being delivered to the body, which stresses the heart. Children with cystic fibrosis are susceptible to lung infections, pneumonia, and collapsed lungs.

The disorder is an inherited recessive gene disorder; that is, both parents must be carriers in order for the child to have the condition. Parents who both are carriers have a 25 percent chance per pregnancy of having a child with cystic fibrosis. Parents can be tested to determine if they are carriers, but the test is not accurate for many populations, and there are many possible genetic mutations involved. The test is most accurate for Caucasian populations of Northern European descent and Ashkenazi Jews, and most often recommended for parents with a known family history of cytic fibrosis (CFF, 2003). The condition occurs in approximately 1 of every 3200 births of Caucasian infants and 1 of every 3900 births in the general population—about 32,000 Americans each year (CFF, 2003). Children with cystic fibrosis often die at a young age; the average lifespan is about 33.4 years. With early and continuous treatment, however, individuals with cystic fibrosis continue to live longer. In 1990, the gene carrying cystic fibrosis was identified; this is the crucial first step in finding a cure or treatment for this condition. This discovery led to the establishment of the first gene therapy centers. Although treatment is still in the earliest stages, it is apparent that a major breakthrough is at hand (Welsh & Smith, 1995).

Treatment for cystic fibrosis is extremely vigorous and often painful, including physical therapy (in some cases daily) to loosen the mucus secretions in the lungs. Because of problems in digestion, children must have dietary supplements of vitamins and enzymes, as well as antibiotics to fight off frequent infections. Hospitalization may be required because of bouts with pneumonia, other serious lung conditions, or lung collapse.

Teachers must be aware of the reduced energy level characteristic of children with cystic fibrosis and must understand that they may miss school because of therapy or hospitalization. Particularly difficult aspects, of course, are the child's awareness of the course of the disease, the fact that it is often a very painful condition, and the prospect of early death.

FIRST PERSON

My Midlife Crisis

JANUARY 2000

I am having a midlife crisis. Tomorrow I will be nineteen. It sounds melodramatic. But technically I should have had this crisis five years ago—my life expectancy according to average statistics is twenty-eight years.

However, most without cystic fibrosis (also known as CF) have a midlife crisis at age forty and some die at sixty-five, so I imagine it's okay for mine to be a little late. Had I been born ten years earlier, in 1971, I would've had my midlife crisis at age five. How does a kindergartner have a midlife crisis? Friends tell me not to worry, that I should be more optimistic. So, I sit in my dorm room each morning with Irish Breakfast tea in my Coffee Exchange mug, the sky blue carpet scattered with papers, books newly bought from the bookstore, and an unmade bed.

. . .

I'm a typical college student, if there is such a thing. Except that I won't be able to look back on my life from an old age. The minute I begin to hypothesize about when and where and who—it upsets me. I often imagine scenarios in my head as I fall asleep—my lung collapses, they rush me to the hospital, I have to take a leave of absence from Brown, or I suddenly spike a high fever and I'm coughing up blood. . . . I could go on and on, but it even makes me queasy. I think about death every day. I wrote a poem about my funeral when I was seventeen.

Part of me wants to grow as old as I can, to live, but the other part is worried about living.

Laura Rothenberg

Laura Rothenberg, a young woman with cystic fibrosis wrote the autobiography *Breathing for a Living*. She died in 2003.

Source: L. Rothenberg (2003). *Breathing for a living.* (New York: Hyperion), pp. 1–3.

Acquired Immune Deficiency Syndrome (AIDS)

Acquired immune deficiency syndrome (AIDS) is a condition that has had a great impact on health concerns in recent years, and its effect on children has been recognized for some time (see the HIV/AIDS fact sheet in Chapter 2). AIDS is a disease caused by the human immunodeficiency virus (HIV) that breaks down the body's immune system, destroying its ability to fight infections (AIDS Organization, 2003). When a child gets even the slightest cold or infection, the symptoms linger as the child weakens. AIDS is progressive, resulting in increasingly greater weakness and illness, particularly lung disease and pneumonia, which are frequently the immediate cause of death. AIDS also can affect many areas of child development, including cognitive development as the infection attacks the central nervous system (Lesar, Gerber, & Semmel, 1995).

AIDS is transmitted by the exchange of body fluids from an infected individual engaged in unprotected, high-risk behavior, such as unprotected sexual contact or sharing needles. AIDS also can be transmitted through blood transfusions, and passed from infected mothers to infants in utero and at birth. Tragically, the number of children born with AIDS is increasing each year. In the United States, 14,000 to 20,000 children are infected with HIV each year (CAAF, 2003). Although much money and effort have been devoted to research on the virus that causes AIDS, no cure or vaccine is available yet.

AIDS is the only condition we have discussed that can be transmitted to others. So, in addition to the health maintenance procedures, hospitalization, and medication required for children with this condition, children often face the unwarranted prospect of social isolation. There have been many instances in which children with AIDS have been avoided or ostracized because of fear.

Although transmission of AIDS in the normal course of school activities has never been documented, many parents—and therefore their children—have an extreme fear of this condition and sometimes fight the presence of the child with AIDS in the regular classroom. When a teacher is aware of a student with AIDS, he or she must work to facilitate appropriate and normal social interaction and to educate other children in the classroom. Children with AIDS and their families have the most difficult task of not only dealing with a painful and probably fatal illness but also of fighting for love and acceptance from the people around them.

Children with AIDS often face social isolation.

Childhood Cancer

Although the prognosis for children with cancer is steadily improving, cancer continues to result in more fatalities among school-age children than any other disease. Current statistics suggest that approximately 35 percent of children affected with childhood cancer will not survive to adulthood (Childhood Cancer Foundation, 2003). The extent to which childhood cancer will affect a child's school performance depends on whether the child is undergoing active treatment such as chemotherapy, the immediate state of the disease, and the general prognosis for the child.

Attention Deficit/Hyperactivity Disorder (ADHD)

Although we have already discussed ADHD in some detail in Chapter 7, educational practice also places it in the category of Other Health Impaired. Because ADHD is a specific diagnosis but is not a separate category of special education, teachers and particularly parents seeking comprehensive services must find a category that will include their children. Many children may not meet the specific identification criteria of categories that commonly co-occur with ADHD, such as learning disabilities or behavioral disorders. The category of health impairments is defined in fairly general terms, and many school districts include some children with ADHD in this category. The use of this category to serve children with ADHD, not surprisingly, has resulted in great increases in the number of children served who are identified as Other Health Impaired. Remember, however, that despite the name of the category, the interventions used with students with ADHD will parallel those presented in Chapters 4 and 5.

Multiple Disabilities

This chapter focuses on individuals whose primary disability is a physical disability or health impairment. Some children born with other disabilities, including mental retardation, hearing or visual impairments, and communication disorders, also experience physical disabilities or health impairments. For example, some children with Down syndrome experience congenital heart problems, and some children born with cerebral palsy have mental retardation. The IDEA Amendments of 1990 (Sec. 300.6[5]) define multiple disabilities as "concomitant impairments (such as mental retardation-blindness, mental retardation-orthopedic impairments, etc.) the combination of which causes such severe educational problems that they cannot be accommodated in special education programs solely for one of the impairments. The term does not include deaf-blindness."

Children whose multiple disabilities include physical or health disabilities may need comprehensive treatment and educational programming. A child with both severe cerebral palsy and mental retardation, for example, requires an effective avenue for communication, mobility instruction, physical and occupational therapy, and a program that facilitates maximum physical, social, and intellectual development.

? Pause and Reflect

Perhaps you are surprised to see that children with chronic diseases like cancer, or even asthma, may receive special education and related services. Remember, it is the extent to which the condition affects school performance that is the determining factor. How might you adjust your instruction for a child who has a severe and chronic illness? Where might you look to find resources or ideas? ●

Characteristics of Individuals with Physical Disabilities and Health Impairments

Many things contribute to the way a disability manifests in a child. The severity of the disability, the level of support a student requires, life expectancy, family support, and the resilience of the child all can affect the impact of a disability on an individual's life. In some instances, mobility or communication may be the areas in which a child feels the greatest effect; in others, the child's overall energy and motivation for making it through a day may be his or her most difficult task. The visibility of the disability may also play a major role, but not always in the way you might think. A mild disability or condition such as infrequent asthma attacks may affect the child a great deal if unwanted attention during an attack makes the child feel embarrassed. A child with a visible orthopedic disability may adjust well to challenges. It's important for you as a teacher to understand that each child is an individual with unique needs and abilities, rather than a collection of characteristics of a particular condition.

Cognitive Development

In most instances, a physical disability or illness has no direct effect on intellectual growth or development. The presence of a physical disability, even a severe physical disability, does not mean that the individual's intellectual ability has been affected. Sometimes, however, both physical and cognitive disabilities occur. Cerebral palsy, for example, may include mental retardation, and some children who experience extensive brain damage are affected in many areas of functioning, including intellectual ability. Some conditions result in the gradual deterioration of both physical and cognitive abilities. For example, Rett syndrome, a condition that affects 8000–10000 girls in the United States, will cause significant and progressively more severe deficits in motor skills, cognitive functioning, and communication abilities (Katsiyannis et al., 2001).

In most cases, a physical disability has no direct effect on intellectual disability.

A health impairment can interfere directly with learning by affecting the speed of mental processing or the ability to focus for long periods of time. Children with asthma, muscular dystrophy, or other chronic or progressive conditions may require extensive therapy or stays in the hospital, which may interrupt their academic progress. A serious illness or condition also might greatly affect the child's stamina. As children tire more and more easily and lose energy, they may require school accommodations so that they can more readily handle academic work and attend to tasks.

Finally, cognitive development is closely dependent on communication abilities. This is particularly obvious in educational settings. Students with severe physical disabilities are most likely to succeed in academic subjects, particularly in regular classroom settings, if they are able to communicate visually, orally, or in writing. Students with physical disabilities who are able to speak and write may experience no exceptional difficulty with their academic tasks. We discuss communication further in the next section.

Communication and Language Development

Many of the physical disabilities we've discussed, such as cerebral palsy and muscular dystrophy, can affect a child's ability to communicate. The effects of a congenital disability, however, may be quite different from the effects of a condition with a gradual or sudden onset. If a child is born with a serious physical disability that affects speech, he or she may learn to communicate using various methods and materials at once—such as a communication board, maybe signs, scanning equipment, perhaps some speech. This will be difficult not only for the student, but also a challenge for others in the environment. On the other hand, most persons with progressive conditions, or those who experienced a sudden onset of a disability, have had a number of years during which they could communicate using more conventional means. Their intellectual abilities were probably tested using standard assessment instruments, and there was time to plan for the future and teach alternative communication systems to the student and to others in his or her home, school, and social environments.

Because many children born with severe physical disabilities are frequently unable to communicate clearly, their cognitive capabilities may remain hidden until they are old enough to use an alternative system, several of which we will describe later in the chapter. Throughout the years, people born with severe physical disabilities have faced extreme bias concerning their intellectual abilities, largely because of their inability to communicate with those around them.

People with severe physical disabilities find their intellectual abilities underestimated because they communicate differently.

The assumption that severe physical disabilities were automatically associated with severe mental retardation resulted in the placement of many individuals in institutional settings with very little, if any, attempt to engage in reciprocal social interaction or communication. As you might imagine, this was not only a deplorable condition in its own right, but extremely frustrating and painful for the people involved. One eloquent spokesperson, Ruth Sienkiewicz-Mercer, who lost bodily control and speech at age 5 due to encephalitis, describes her first communication breakthrough with her caretakers in a residential placement. At this point she had lived in the institution for three years without communicating with any of the adults present.

> As she brought the next spoonful of food to my mouth, she noticed that I was doing something funny with my eyes, obviously in reaction to what she had just said. I kept looking up at the ceiling, but Wessie couldn't figure out why I was doing that. She put the spoon down and thought for a few seconds, then asked, "Ruthie, are you trying to tell me something?"
>
> With a broad grin on my face, I looked at her squarely. Then I raised my eyes up to the ceiling again with such exaggeration that I thought my eyes would pop up through the top of my head.
>
> Wessie knew she was on to something, but she wasn't sure just what. She pondered for a few more seconds . . . then it clicked! A silent conversation flashed between us as loud and clear as any spoken words. Even before she asked me a dozen times over, and before I exuberantly answered a dozen times with my eyes raised skyward, Wessie knew. And I knew that she knew.
>
> I was raising my eyes to say yes.
>
> We both started laughing. Then I started laughing really hard, and before I knew it I was crying so uncontrollably that I couldn't see because of the tears. They were tears of pure joy, the kind of tears a person sheds on being released from prison after serving three years of what she had feared would be a life sentence. (Sienkiewicz-Mercer & Kaplan, 1989, p. 110)

Social and Emotional Development

Children with physical disabilities and health impairments are faced with an incredible array of stressful emotions—both their own and the emotions of others. They must struggle with perceptions of themselves, the reactions of others, and the impact on their families.

Young people with physical disabilities or health impairments may experience difficulty making friends, or just meeting new children. Sometimes, we avoid interacting with persons with physical disabilities not because we are insensitive or uncaring, but because we are confused about how to act. Sometimes, it's difficult to judge whether or not you should provide assistance to someone, and often we become aware that we are noticing the disability—and this makes us uncomfortable with ourselves. Unfortunately, these concerns may result in the appearance of indifference or actual avoidance of persons with physical disabilities. Regardless of our reasons, the result is the same—a lack of communication and interaction with someone simply because of his or her physical appearance.

As you consider your reactions to persons with physical disabilities, past and future, remember our axiom of looking at the *person* first. We've alluded to the fact that sometimes our fear of acting patronizing or too helpful will insult or embarrass the individual with whom we are interacting. People with physical disabilities realize your apprehension (many may have experienced these feelings themselves if their disability is injury-related) and appreciate the fact that any meaningful social interaction must be reciprocal in nature.

Most of us are only too aware of the importance society places on appearance. As children get older, teasing someone who looks different is, unfortunately, fairly common. Unkind and humiliating situations are encountered. This happens, of course, to most children—but children with disabilities often get more than their share. The child with a disability must have the opportunity to cry, vent anger, and talk in order to learn to deal with these situations. A key factor in a child's ability to develop a positive self-image is the extent to which he or she can accept his or her physical differences.

Another significant source of stress is the struggle for independence. For people with certain types of disabilities, such as seizure disorders or diabetes, it is very difficult to accept the fact that a certain level of dependence on others or on medications will be a continuing part of their lives. The protectiveness of parents and other family members, and the possible adjusted expectations of others, may make the process of growing up very difficult.

Some children with progressive illness or deteriorating conditions must face the inevitable fact of an early death. Clearly, family, friends, and other support services and people can help children as they try to face this possibility. Experts advise teachers and other adults to be gentle, yet direct, with children who want to discuss death. Often, because children find it difficult to discuss this emotional topic with their parents, they may need to confide in another trusted adult. Although many children display incredible courage and consideration of others in the face of their disabilities, it is only natural for a part of this process to include the inevitable questions of "why me?" and "what if . . . ?" Sometimes these questions are directed at the condition itself, and sometimes at the pain or discomfort involved.

> A key factor in a child's positive self-image is accepting his or her physical disability.

Effects on the Family

The impact of a child's physical disability or health impairment on a family can vary as greatly as the types of disabilities. The effects on the family of a child with cerebral palsy will be very different from the effects on the family of a child with muscular dystrophy, cancer, an amputated leg, or epilepsy. Yet parents of children with special needs do share many common experiences, such as dealing with medical professionals, educators, community prejudices, and the joys of loving a child.

There is no uniform reaction to disability. Some families appear able to accept the child for who he is and become strong while dealing with challenges and decisions that may overwhelm most of us. Other families seem frayed as the child with the disability siphons all their emotional and physical energies. Some families face a potentially lifelong commitment to the education of their child; others must face daily the agony of watching their child's physical abilities and health deteriorate. Children are often well aware of the impact of their disability on their families and may themselves feel a sense of guilt or responsibility for the ensuing emotional or financial strain. Sometimes, children will respond to this by avoiding discussion of their condition with their parents or by being careful of what they say or do. The child may focus on "taking care" of his or her parents. This unexpected interaction is illustrated in a touching passage from Frank Deford's book *Alex: The Life of a Child*, the story of his young daughter, who died of complications from cystic fibrosis.

> And so then Alex and I laughed. Unfortunately, at that point, late in her life, it was difficult for her to laugh without coughing and starting to choke. So she made sure she laughed gently, and I laughed extra hard, for both of us. Then she came over, sat in my lap, and this is what she said: "Oh, Daddy, wouldn't this have been great?"
>
> That is what she said, exactly. She didn't say, "Hasn't this been great?" She said, "Oh, Daddy, wouldn't this have been great?" Alex meant her whole life, if only she hadn't been sick.
>
> I just said, "Yes," and after we hugged each other, she left the room, because, I knew, she wanted to let me cry alone. Alex knew by then that, if I cried in front of her, I would worry about upsetting her, and she didn't want to burden me that way. She was the only one dying. (Deford, 1983, p. 9)

Because physical disabilities and deteriorating health are usually apparent to others, families also try to cope with the emotional pain faced by their children as they integrate into educational and social settings and deal with the countless questions about "what happened to you?" or "what's wrong with you?" Although it is important for families to encourage independence for their children, it is often difficult for them to let go of their desire to protect the child from more potentially painful situations. One of the greatest emotional challenges faced by families of children with physical or health disabilities is encouraging their children to experience life and take risks, just as they would with children without disabilities. Parents worry about the social and emotional well being of their children, and report that their greatest concerns for their school-age children with physical disabilities are not the physical barriers they face, but rather the attitude barriers that can result in their child becoming isolated and having low self-esteem (Pivik, McComas, & LaFlamme, 2002).

Practical issues faced by the family include decisions about treatment and placement.

Practical issues faced by the family include treatment decisions. Families must make constant decisions about the type or extent of therapy they will select for the child involved. In some instances, these decisions may be relatively simple (selecting a type of medication, choosing a particular kind of prosthesis). When the child has a severe illness or disability, however, these decisions can be very complex and include considerations of time allocated to the child and other family members; finances; emotional stress on the part of the parents, siblings, and involved child; and sometimes the actual physical abilities of the family caretakers. Certainly, one of the biggest decisions related to treatment is whether the child with severe physical involvement, particularly a child with multiple disabilities, should be at home or in a residential placement. These decisions are never easy, and each family's financial resources, personal obligations to siblings and spouse, and the simple physical and emotional strength of caregivers all figure into the decision. Although there may be some similarities in the ways families deal with the impact of a physical disability or health impairment, families are composed of individuals. The child with the disability and the other family members develop the pattern of interaction that works for them. Educators must be aware of the needs of individual families and the type of support services that might help them make informed decisions about the education and placement of their children.

Fortunately, the emphasis on parent services and training available through P.L. 99-457 enables greater education and support for parents of young children with physical disabilities and health impairments. Parents and families of older children who incur physical or health disabilities need immediate and continued information and assistance. Social, spiritual, and physical support are all important predictors of more successful family adaptations (Lin, 2000). Often, local, state, or national groups related to a specific disability area can be a great source of available services, information, and emotional support. The website of the Muscular Dystrophy Association compiled by individuals with disabilities is full of information for parents and others interested in making contributions. Visit **http://www.mdausa.org**.

❓ *Pause and Reflect*

The range of characteristics of individuals with physical disabilities and health impairments is arguably wider than in any other categories of special education. One of the greatest errors we've made, as a society, is assuming that individuals with significant physical disabilities also have severe cognitive disabilities. How can this type of assumption affect expectations of individuals with physical disabilities? ●

Teaching Strategies and Accommodations

In the past, the diverse educational needs of children with physical disabilities and health impairments often kept them away from public education. Today's teachers need to know, however, that in most cases, these children can be part of the regular class with accommodations and support.

Early Intervention

For many children with physical disabilities or health impairments, the first educational issue to arise is the appropriate and early diagnosis of the condition, and assessment of physical, cognitive, and language abilities. The diagnosis tend to be made by physicians rather than school personnel, and many diagnoses of conditions, such as spina bifida or cerebral palsy, are made long before the child reaches school age.

As with other disabilities, early intervention services—both medical and educational—significantly affect the well-being of these children. For some of them, early intervention can mean the difference between life and death. For others, early intervention can mean the difference between a mild disability and a severe and long-term disability. Early and consistent therapy can help children to maximize their physical skills and sometimes prevent the occurrence of muscular atrophy and skeletal deformities.

Early intervention services that focus on family-centered service delivery models may have positive effects on the family as well as the child. Family-centered services can help parents establish a support network, as well as provide them with knowledge about their child's disability and a sense of empowerment (Thompson et al., 1997).

The Connecticut Trails Council of Girl Scouts Brownies of the Dunbar Hill Accelerated School have a traditional ceremonial Girl Scout "Closing Circle" as they sing "Make New Friends." (© Peter Hvizdak/The Image Works)

Educational Planning

Most physical disabilities and health impairments are diagnosed before schooling begins, but some conditions will not be identified until later in the child's life. As a teacher, you should be alert to gradual or sudden changes in children's physical abilities, energy level, and general behavior.

Regardless of the severity of any condition, it is your responsibility continually to assess and address the educational needs of the individual child. If you notice motor difficulties, a physical or occupational therapist may be called in to consult on the case or to provide assistance. See the accompanying Teaching Strategies box entitled, "Some Considerations for Students with Mobility Impairments" for some general recommendations for interacting with students with physical disabilities or health impairments.

In the transdisciplinary model, all interventions are delivered by one or two professionals to ensure continuity for the child.

● **The Transdisciplinary Approach** Integrated, multidisciplinary planning is a requirement for appropriate education (York & Vandercook, 1991). IDEA requires that a multidisciplinary team evaluate each student in special education programs. On a multidisciplinary team, professionals work independently, or directly, with the child. Figure 12.3 illustrates the instructional roles of different team members, including physical therapists, occupational therapists, and special education teachers (Shapiro & Sayers, 2003). According to Orelove and Sobsey (1991), however, the multidisciplinary model lacks methods for coordinating assessment and prioritizing the student's educational needs. Therefore, they recommend the **transdisciplinary model** of service delivery.

The transdisciplinary, or indirect service, model differs from the multidisciplinary approach because all interventions are delivered by one or two professionals. For example, a student who needs physical therapy to learn to walk is helped by his or her regular teacher to complete mobility exercises several times a day. This does not mean that the physical therapist never sees the student. It does mean that the physical therapist works closely with the teacher to carry out therapeutic activities properly and sees the student directly as needed. In a multidisciplinary or interdisciplinary team, the student might be pulled out of the class and given physical therapy once a week for thirty minutes. The teacher and parents would have little idea of how to help the student learn and practice mobility the rest of the week. The accompanying Teaching Strategies box enti-

---

Student Background

Name: George
Age: 14
Present Level of Performance: Walks independently with a slight scissor gait; able to perform reach, grasp, and release skills when accommodations are made for slight upper extremity hypertonicity; eye-hand coordination skills are good but George requires extra time to complete eye-hand coordination tasks; balance is generally good and protective extension is used when balance is challenged.
Annual Goal: Transition to community bowling alley

Role of the Physical Therapist (PT)

The PT will work with George to develop body mechanics of balance and posture needed to transfer weight while walking down the lane from the ball carriage to the foul line and maintaining balance during ball release and follow-through. To accomplish these goals, the PT also will work with George on strength and stability as well as joint mobility.

Role of the Occupational Therapist (OT)

The OT will work with George to develop arm and wrist strength to support the weight of a 9-lb bowling ball as he engages in the pendulum swing action. The OT will also assist George with developing the fine motor skills he needs to release the ball during return arm swing as well as reflex integration.

Role of the Therapeutic Recreation Specialist (TR)

The TR will help George learn about bowling equipment and selection, relevant interpersonal and social skills as it relates to bowling, self-initiated independent behavior in bowling, and appropriate bowling etiquette.

Role of the Adapted Physical Educator (APE)

The APE will provide instruction in the technique of bowling, including arm action, four-step approach, and ball release and follow-through. Skills will be taught in the gymnasium and will be taught in a whole-part-whole method.

Role of the General Physical Educator (PE)/Special Education Teacher

The general PE and/or special education teacher can facilitate the TR specialist's goals by providing opportunities for students to study and research the sport of bowling and practice appropriate interpersonal skills with classmates. Physical therapy goals can be addressed in the classroom by encouraging George to walk throughout the school and outside in the playground as much as possible, giving him opportunities to improve posture and balance. With training the general PE/special education teacher can look for the interaction of reflexes to facilitate and reduce its impact on George's fine motor skills.

Figure 12.3

Combining Expertise in a Sample IEP

Source: D. R. Shapiro & L. K. Sayers (2003). Who does what on the interdisciplinary team regarding physical education for students with disabilities. *Teaching Exceptional Children, 35*(6), 35.

tled, "Continuum of Service Models" illustrates the traditional, multidisciplinary direct service model and the transdisciplinary indirect service model.

A transdisciplinary team of professionals, in conjunction with the family and, when appropriate, the child, works together to assess educational needs in a variety of areas and to determine appropriate program goals. For example, the group would work together to determine what type of computer keyboard is most appropriate for a student with cerebral palsy who cannot use a regular keyboard.

The family's role on the transdisciplinary team is critical because family members are able to give insight into the child's abilities, motivation, emotional adjustment, and goals. Whenever special therapy, communication systems, or adaptive equipment is suggested, the willingness and ability of the family members to accept and use them or to participate must be assessed and evaluated.

Teaching Strategies & Accommodations

Some Considerations for Students with Mobility Impairments

- Many students with mobility impairments lead lives similar to those without impairments. Dependency and helplessness are not characteristics of physical disability.

- A physical disability is often separate from matters of cognition and general health; it does not imply that a student has other health problems or difficulty with intellectual functioning.

- People adjust to disabilities in myriad ways; students should not be assumed to be brave and courageous on the basis of disability.

- When talking with a wheelchair user, attempt to converse at eye level as opposed to standing and looking down. If a student has a communication impairment as well as a mobility impairment, take time to understand the person. Repeat what you understand, and when you don't understand, say so.

- A student with a physical disability may or may not want assistance in a particular situation. Ask before giving assistance, and wait for a response. Listen to any instructions the student may give; by virtue of experience, the student likely knows the safest and most efficient way to accomplish the task at hand.

- Be considerate of the extra time it might take a student with a disability to speak or act.

- Allow the student to set the pace walking or talking.

- A wheelchair should be viewed as a personal assistance device rather than something one is "confined to." It is also part of a student's personal space; do not lean on or touch the chair, and do not push the chair, unless asked.

- Mobility impairments vary over a wide range, from temporary to permanent. Other conditions, such as respiratory conditions, affect coordination and endurance; these can also affect a student's ability to perform in class.

- Physical access to a class is the first barrier a student with a mobility impairment may face, and this is not related only to the accessibility of a specific building or classroom. An unshoveled sidewalk, lack of reliable transportation, or mechanical problems with a wheelchair can easily cause a student to be late.

- Common accommodations for students with mobility impairments include priority registration, note-takers, accessible classroom/location/furniture, alternative ways of completing assignments, lab or library assistants, assistive computer technology, exam modifications, and conveniently located parking.

Source: Used by permission of Disability Services.

One example of a curriculum that incorporates the transdisciplinary approach is the MOVE curriculum (Mobility Opportunities via Education). The MOVE curriculum incorporates six planning and instructional steps to increase functional mobility skills such as walking in the classroom setting. The six steps (testing, setting goals, task analysis, measuring prompts, reducing prompts, and specific skill instructions) are each addressed by the transdisciplinary team (Barnes & Whinnery, 2002). When interventions are integrated into the home and classroom setting, not only does the student learn meaningful and useful skills, but the teacher and parents get a better understanding of how to reinforce those skills on a day-to-day basis. To learn more about the MOVE curriculum and intervention strategies, visit the website of MOVE International at **http://www.move-international.org**.

> When interventions are integrated into the classroom, teachers better understand how to help students learn useful skills.

Accessing Instruction

Today, most children with physical disabilities or hearth impairements are served primarily in the general education classroom. In the past, children whose only disabilities were physical or health-related were placed in a variety of edu-

---

Teaching Strategies & Accommodations

Continuum of Service Models

Direct Service Model

- **One-on-one therapy.*** The therapist treats the student in a separate therapy room or a segregated portion of the classroom.
- **Small group therapy.*** The therapist treats several students with similar needs at one time.
- **One-on-one therapy (inclusive).** The therapist works with the student during a classroom activity to facilitate his or her participation. Therapy can also occur during activities in the gymnasium, on the playground, or at a community site.
- **Small-group therapy (inclusive).** The therapist works with the student with special needs and a group of his or her classmates on an educationally appropriate activity. The activity also promotes the therapeutic goal for the student with special needs. For example, the therapist leads a craft project that facilitates the fine motor manipulation for all students, yet the project is modified to include and instruct the student with special needs.

Transdisciplinary Indirect Service Model

- **Consultation.** The therapist recommends and instructs educators, paraprofessionals, or caregivers to carry out therapeutic programs. This may include instruction modification, activity enhancement, environmental modification, adaptation of materials, routine or schedule alterations, or team member training.
- **Monitoring.** The therapist maintains contact with the student to monitor his or her status. Effective monitoring consists of check-ups scheduled on a regular basis in the student's educational environment.

*Restrictive model of treatment used only as a last resort. Therapy should be provided in a manner that facilitates integration with peers.

Source: J. L. Szabo (2000). Maddie's story. *Teaching Exceptional Children, 33*(2), 49–53.

cational settings, ranging from a state hospital or institution to the regular classroom. Although there are still separate classes for children with "orthopedic handicaps," they are no longer the primary educational placement for children with physical disabilities (McLesky, Henry, & Hodges, 1999). Instead, these classes provide a setting for initial instruction in skills such as mobility and language, which can then be used in regular class settings. Support or special education services are often provided in physical therapy, occupational therapy, speech or language therapy, counseling, and, in some instances, homebound instruction for periods of time.

> Special education services should be structured to support placement in the regular classroom.

● *Academic Access*   Because placement options now focus on the general education classroom, general education teachers are largely responsible for educating students with physical or health impairments in their classrooms. In some instances, it is not necessary to make any specific instructional modifications for the student; in other cases, you will need assistance from special education teachers or other members of the student's education team to learn the best

Teaching Strategies & Accommodations

Specific Strategies for Integrating Students with Physical Disabilities or Health Impairments in the Classroom

- Place students with limited physical movement front and center in a traditional classroom setting, to facilitate access to the teacher's presentation and material on the board. There are exceptions to this guideline; for example, a student with a traumatic brain injury might have a limited field of vision on one side and might follow the visual presentation of material more easily if seated at an angle.

- If students gather around small tables or learning centers, make sure the tables are at an appropriate height for the student who is in a wheelchair. If the students gather in groups on the floor, try to use chairs instead, so the child in a wheelchair is not sitting above and apart from the group. This is important for social integration as well as physical accessibility.

- Use bookshelves, material drawers, pencil sharpeners, and cubbies that are the appropriate height and can be reached by a student in a wheelchair. If a student cannot physically reach and grasp, make sure he or she has a trustworthy assistant for retrieving and putting away materials.

- Avoid the use of carpet squares or other floor materials, such as number lines, with raised sides or edges.

- Classrooms with fixed furnishings, such as science labs, can be particularly problematic for the student in a wheelchair. Creating an accessible work area may require significant changes in the classroom construction, so that the student will be truly integrated into the classroom setting.

- If a student requires assistive technology for communication, establish clear signals for typical classroom activities such as hand raising and asking a question. These signals should be clearly recognized by all students in the classroom, as well as the teacher. Provide training to all the students in the classroom on how to communicate with the student using his or her specific assistive device. Always be careful to allow the student time to respond.

- Become an expert at identifying and creating learning experiences that allow all students in the classroom to participate fully.

ways to encourage and facilitate communication, class participation, class inter-action, and physical movement or activity. See the accompanying Teaching Strategies box entitled, "Specific Strategies for Integrating Students with Physical Disabilities or Health Impairments in the Classroom."

In fact, some of the responsibilities of general education teachers who work with children with physical disabilities and other health impairments can be quite challenging. Even special education teachers often feel unprepared to deal with situations such as working with terminally ill students and their families, or identifying appropriate forms of augmentative communication and assistive technology (Heller et al., 1999). Salisbury, Evans, and Palombaro (1997) found that general education teachers in the primary grades used collaborative problem-solving activities with all students to identify solutions to help students with significant disabilities participate more actively in the classroom. Teachers often use children's literature on topics such as HIV/AIDS to educate both peers and themselves about specific conditions of children in their classrooms and to gain new perspectives on dealing with illness and disability (Prater & Sileo, 2001).

Sometimes, individuals with severe physical disabilities may have a para-professional, an aide, who travels with them to assist in educational and health-care activities. The major role of the paraprofessional should be to promote the student's independence. It is important for the aide to step back whenever pos-sible to allow full integration of the student and to encourage communication and other interactions with peers (Giangreco et al., 1997). The specific responsi-bilities of paraprofessionals should be delineated in each child's IEP. Figure 12.4 illustrates one framework that can be used to clarify the role of the paraprofes-sional in the classroom (Muellor & Murphy, 2001).

When a student is too sick to attend school, he or she may receive a home-bound program, either in the student's home or at a hospital. This homebound program should always include plans for the student to re-enter school as soon as possible. The teacher who visits the student at home or in the hospital coordi-nates with the student's regular teachers so that proper assignments, home-work, tests, and other activities are completed.

Technology is quickly improving the quality of homebound programs. In some school districts, distance learning is now available, which permits the stu-dent to watch educational television programs along with classroom peers. For students with long-term homebound needs, telephones can be set up in the classroom that allow the student to listen to the teacher and respond to ques-tions just like the other students. The homebound teacher makes sure the stu-

Specify Class Activity	Identify need for paraeducator	Identify areas to increase socialization (utilize natural supports, peers)	Identify how independence will be encouraged	Total time needed for paraeducator support	Total anticipat-ed time reduc-tion in para-educator support by annual review

Figure 12.4

Plan for Paraeducator Assistance

Source: P. H. Mueller & F. V. Murphy (2001). Determining when a student requires paraeducator support. *Teaching Exceptional Children, 33* (6), 25.

dent has the necessary materials each week to follow along with the class. Fax machines and Web access are also used to connect the homebound student to the regular classroom.

● *School Accessibility*   With the passage of the Americans with Disabilities Act in 1990, all public facilities and buildings were required to be barrier-free by 1994. Your classroom, therefore, will probably be adapted to the needs of students with physical disabilities.

Sometimes, however, schools may not take into account accessibility to such items as play equipment, furniture, or educational equipment. One potential problem area is the surface of floors and walls. For example, carpeting, rugs, or uneven floor surfaces can cause difficulties for students using wheelchairs or other types of assistance for walking. Pivik, McComas, and LaFlamme (2002) interviewed a number of students with physical disabilities, including those who used wheelchairs and walkers. The students were asked questions about the accessibility of their schools. Many of these students reported that they still experienced difficulty negotiating the physical school environment. Specific barriers identified by the students were as follows: entering school—because the ramps were located in the back of the school, heavy doors, narrow passageways, the height of lockers, types of locks, and inaccessible recreation equipment. Most of the students were also very worried about what would happen to them in case of fire.

Although some of these areas should be addressed by working in conjunction with the student's therapists, you, as a classroom teacher, can take some simple precautions yourself to ensure optimum accessibility. Widening aisles between desks and placing equipment such as computers, tape recorders, and bookshelves appropriately are some tasks that teachers can attend to in their classes. When planning field trips, it is always a good idea to call ahead and check to ensure that the visiting site has been adapted to accommodate students with disabilities. Although adapted school buses are quite common, some public buses still cannot be used by persons in wheelchairs. The student then needs to be lifted onto the bus and the wheelchair folded up and carried along. This may present difficulties, particularly with an older student, so advance planning will be necessary.

> Teachers should be sure that equipment and furniture are arranged for maximum accessibility.

● *Physical Supports*   As a teacher, you may be required to assist students with physical disabilities in the use of equipment for moving, eating, breathing, and other bodily functions. These aspects of care are called physical handling and health maintenance.

Physical handling involves moving the student from one place to another or adjusting his or her placement in a fixed setting. For example, you might need to move a student from a wheelchair to another setting such as a group activity on the floor. There are very specific professional guidelines for picking up and carrying students with physical disabilities. It is important that you not try to lift or move students until you have received the information necessary to do it appropriately. In some instances, more than one person is needed to move a child, and in others, a specially trained aide or nurse will assist or do the lifting.

Other aspects of physical handling include adjusting physical placement, or using physical props to allow greater range of motion. If students have a tendency to lean to one side or have difficulty reaching needed materials, you can make simple adjustments such as by using pillows to prevent leaning, having armrests or trays attached to wheelchairs to allow the closer placement of manipulative materials, or providing wedge-shaped props that children can lie on to allow greater range of arm movement. Again, the physical and occupational therapists on each child's team can provide needed information and equipment.

Health maintenance involves assisting students in eating, drinking, and using the bathroom. A student with severe cerebral palsy, for example, might be unable to feed herself. Some students run the risk of choking when they eat or drink, so it is important that the person feeding the student be skilled in CPR. Often a nurse or trained aide will assist in this process, as they will when medically oriented processes such as catheterization are required. Because the courts consistently rule that the school is responsible for providing any and all medical care to students in school as long as it does not require a physician, children with very severe medical needs may be in your classroom (Katsiyannis & Yell, 2000). Students requiring medical technology for support, such as ventilators for breathing, and students with other conditions requiring constant health maintenance, such as gastrostomies and tracheostomies, may be placed in the general education class for instruction and require monitoring and maintenance procedures by nurses or other health-care professionals (Levine, 1996; Thomas & Hawke, 1999).

Other health maintenance activities may include administration of medication, injections, and monitoring students for signs of distress such as diabetic shock. School nurses typically are responsible for the administration of any medical procedures, but as we mentioned previously, it is important for you to be aware of any particular signs or symptoms that signal a specific health problem. If you assist students with these activities, you must be taught correct procedures and be aware of potential risks. Federal guidelines and school district interpretations regulate who may or may not perform health-care services (Rapport, 1996). These guidelines should be reviewed by the teachers, administrators, and parents on the IEP team when decisions are being made about the delivery of these services in school.

Integrating Technology

Throughout this chapter, we have alluded to the importance of technology for many individuals with physical disabilities and health impairments. For individuals with physical disabilities, most of the technological assistance is either medical technology or assistive technology that is designed to help the individual perform life tasks. For school-age students with disabilities, assistive technology may be considered special education or a related service. Teachers, parents, students, and other members of the evaluation team must evaluate the student's needs and indicate the need for appropriate assistive technology on the student's IEP (Menlove, 1996). When selecting appropriate technology for a student, it is most important to look at the way the individual functions in his or her environment and to determine what specific pieces of equipment or training may help to support the student in various settings (Blackhurst, 1997). It is also important to keep in mind cultural issues related to the use of assistive technology. Parette (1999) suggests that areas of cultural sensitivity include (1) the family's desire for the degree of independence that assistive technology can provide, (2) the balance between providing technological assistance and what may be perceived as the stigma of drawing attention to an individual because of technology use, (3) the information a given family desires about the choices, costs, and goals of assistive technology, (4) the impact of assistive technology on family routines and demands, and (5) the experiences with assistive technology of the child and the family. Teachers must be sensitive to these issues as they work with families and students to identify appropriate assistive technology for students.

Technology Focus

Assistive Technology Assessments: Determining a Student's Needs

CONDUCT AN ASSISTIVE TECHNOLOGY ENVIRONMENTAL USE ASSESSMENT

- List times and subjects in which student needs assistance to satisfactorily complete assignments.
- List times student needs assistance to satisfactorily function in his or her school environment.
- List adaptations currently in use (shortened assignment, note-takers, etc.).
- List an assistive technology device currently used by student, what setting, and time used.

CONDUCT AN ASSISTIVE TECHNOLOGY FUNCTIONAL USE ASSESSMENT

- Describe student's present level of functioning.
- List characteristics of student.

- What are the student's academic skills?
- Does student have keyboarding skills and at what level?
- What are the student's preferences for types of assistive technology?
- What technology courses are available in the current curriculum?
- What technology instructional services are available at the school site?

MATCH ENVIRONMENTAL USE ASSESSMENT WITH FUNCTIONAL USE ASSESSMENT TO IDENTIFY APPROPRIATE ASSISTIVE TECHNOLOGY SERVICES

Source: B. J. Webb (2000). Planning and organizing assistive technology resources in your school. *Teaching Exceptional Children,* *43*(4), 51.

Lau (2000) suggests that technology also can serve an important role as a focal activity for prompting social interaction among young children with physical disabilities and their peers. She suggests that when an appropriate software program is used in a well-structured cooperative learning group, young children can learn social interaction skills. This type of instructional activity can be used to teach young children with or without physical disabilities skills such as turn taking, group decision-making, and helping. Table 12.1 provides a checklist for teachers to use to determine proper positioning at the computer for children with physical disabilities.

Although social interaction is a new and exciting application of technology, technology use by students with physical disabilities and health impairments typically focuses on instructional accommodations, mobility, and communication skills.

● *Instructional Accommodations*   An increasingly important area of technological interventions is the development of materials for use in the classroom. Technology allows children with physical disabilities to have access to materials they would not otherwise be able to enjoy or use. Beck (2002) describes the successful use of assistive technology in preschool classes to promote early literacy skills in young children. As you can imagine, a three- or four-year-old child with fine or gross motor disabilities might not be able to hold books, turn pages, or follow along with group literacy activities. Beck found that by creating

Table 12.1 Classroom Checklist for Proper Positioning at the Computer for Social Interaction

Criterion	Met	Not Met
1. Is the child's head at midline? (e.g., ears are directly over shoulders and face is facing forward)		
2. Is the child's pelvis at midline? (e.g., hips are in the back of the seat and are not tilted to one side)		
3. Is the child's trunk at midline? (e.g., trunk is not tilted to one side)		
4. Are the child's shoulders at midline? (e.g., shoulders are not hunched forward)		
5. Are the child's forearms supported? (e.g., elbows are flexed at 90 degrees and supported by the table, arm rest, or tray)		
6. Are the child's legs in a neutral position? (e.g., thighs are slightly apart; knees and ankles are bent at 90 degrees)		
7. Are the child's feet in a neutral position and supported? (e.g., feet are directly under the knees and facing forward; feet are supported by the floor or foot rest)		
8. Is the child seated at the same height as other children at the computer? (e.g., eye contact and verbal exchange can easily be achieved among children in the group)		
9. Is the computer monitor at the child's eye level? (e.g., the child can easily see the monitor without tilting his or her head)		
10. Is the computer table accessible to the child? (e.g., the child can easily reach the computer peripherals)		

Source: C. Lau (2000). I learned how to take turns. *Teaching Exceptional Children, 32*(4), 8.

electronic books, or e-books, preschool children were able to participate fully in classroom activities. The e-books she used were created using Intellipics (Intelli-tools, 2000). By activating a single switch, the pages of the text turned on the computer screen, story illustrations moved, and the text on the screen was read. Such e-books have three basic components: (1) hardware to serve as the reader of the program (e.g., computer, PDA); (2) software, the reader software program that displays the book; and (3) book files, the electronic data files that contain the content of the actual book (Cavanaugh, 2003). Teachers can use existing technology available online to create electronic books for their own classes. To learn more about creating e-books for your own classroom, visit **http://www. ebookexpress.com**.

● *Mobility*   New designs in wheelchairs and controls for wheelchair move-ment have resulted in opportunities for independence for people who previ-ously were dependent on others for even limited transportation. For example, individuals with very severe disabilities were unable to use conventionally de-signed wheelchairs to move because they had limited or no arm movement. A now-common mouth apparatus allows them to control wheelchair movement by blowing puffs of air through a tube.

Muscles that are not used because of injury (typically a spinal cord injury) can be given electronically stimulated "exercise" to prevent atrophy, contrac-tions, and skeletal deformities. Researchers currently are examining the use of electronic stimulation to reactivate paralyzed muscles. This process is referred to as Functional Electrical Stimulation or FES (Loeb, 2001, 2002). Some experiments using electrical stimulation and feedback have taken place. They have allowed paralyzed individuals to walk a few steps, even though they could not feel the movement of their legs (Dickey & Shealy, 1987).

Technology has also made it possible for people with physical disabilities to control some aspects of their home environment. Through the use of switches from a wheelchair panel or a voice-activated control device, it is possible to open doors, turn on lights from across the room, use keys to enter their homes, and opearate alarm systems (Access Ingenuity, 2003; Bigge, 1991a). These devices provide an option for independent living that might not otherwise be available. Home accounting and banking software are examples of how technology has facilitated personal life-skills management for individuals with severe physical disabilities. When software is not available for printed materials, alternative format services can translate documents from print and diskettes into alternative, accessible formats (Access Ingenuity, 2003; Bigge, 1991b).

● *Communication* The most critical factor in using technology to meet communication needs is to identify processes that meet the individual's needs, allow and encourage intellectual and physical growth and development, and can be used by others in the environment. This last point is of the greatest importance. The latest high-tech system is useless if no one else takes the time to understand how it is used and to participate in the communication process. In this section we discuss some of the major developments in communication technology for people with physical disabilities.

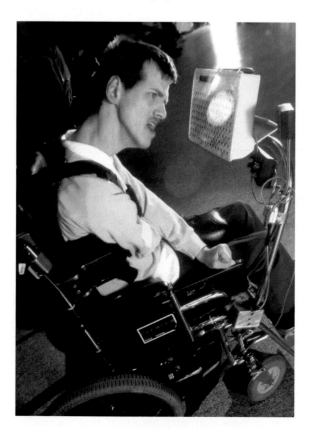

Technology provides many opportunities for communication and mobility to individuals with extensive physical challenges. (© Bill Aron)

Most advances in communication technology provide access to the symbols of written or oral language. The majority of these advances are associated with computer use. **Eye-gazing scanning systems** are a good example. As the individual scans a keyboard and focuses, a small and very sensitive camera detects the direction of the person's eyes and registers the letters, words, or phrases. A typed message or voice message can then be produced.

Augmentative communication aids are used in addition to the individual's existing speech or vocalizations (Bigge, 1991). A person using an augmentative communication aid can directly select the desired message elements (such as words or pictures) from the display or can scan and then identify one of a series of potential message elements. In direct selection, the individual points to the desired message or message component using a finger, an adapted handpiece with a pointer attached, or a light beam attached to the head. In school settings, direct selection aids often take the form of alternative computer keyboards and overlays. These keyboards can look like an enlarged version of the typical keyboard, may contain numbers, pictures, or other symbols, and are designed to accommodate specific difficulties a person with limited motor control might encounter (such as difficulty pressing two keys at one time) (Intellitools, 1996).

In scanning, message elements are presented one at a time on flashcards, transparent charts, or a computer screen. As the potential messages are presented, the individual indicates which message(s) he or she wants to choose by making a sound, flexing a muscle, or fixing a visual gaze for a few seconds. This process eliminates the need for great mobility. An adapted form of scanning is a multisignal process, in which the individual:

1. Scans groups (for example, fifteen groups of four messages)
2. Selects a group (for example, group 9: I want to go see a movie. I want to see a television show. I want to turn the television off. Let's go to the video store.)
3. Scans the message elements in that group to select the appropriate message (I want to see a television show). This type of encoding allows the individual with limited movement and a large message vocabulary to cover a wide range of potential messages. Computers facilitate scanning because they can store and present many groups of messages quickly.

Another communication option available through advanced technology is synthesized and digitized speech. **Digitized speech** is the storage of words or phrases that can be recalled as needed; **synthesized speech** is the storage of speech sounds—a phonetic alphabet that can be put together to form any word using a sound-by-sound process similar to the spelling process (Bigge, 1991). Synthesized speech allows greater variety of words and phrases but can be a much slower process. These devices can be designed in various sizes and can be portable or connected to a large computer screen. Digitized speech devices can be designed with customized keyboard overlays and can present language at various speeds (Breakthroughs, 1997). Recent research suggests that synthetic speech can do more than serve as augmentative communication. Blischak (1999) found that young children with severe speech difficulties who used synthetic speech during language training sessions significantly increased their production of natural speech, when compared to students who used graphic or pictoral representations of speech. This research suggests that children can actually improve their speech while using synthesized speech technology.

Technological advances clearly have opened many new avenues for individuals with severe difficulties in communication. Not all procedures need to have a high-tech component; many augmentative communication processes can be integrated in very simple ways. The role of technology is to expand these options, particularly for individuals with limited movement or advanced cognitive capabilities.

? Pause and Reflect

Look around your college classroom or the classroom in which you teach. Can you identify ways you could adapt the physical or instructional environment to address the instruction, mobility, or communication needs of a student with severe physical disabilities? ●

Adult Life

Legislation has refined the legal requirements of accessibility for schools, public services and places of employment. The **Americans with Disabilities Act (ADA) of 1990 (P.L. 101-336)** extends civil rights protection to individuals with disabilities in private-sector employment. In addition, the law requires that public services such as transportation make accommodations for individuals with disabilities. For example, transportation systems such as buses and railroads must include access for individuals with physical disabilities. Other public accommodations and facilities (stores, hotels, schools) must be accessible and must provide any supporting material necessary to allow individuals to use their services (Council for Exceptional Children, 1990).

For young adults with physical disabilities, accessibility to colleges and universities is an important and logical extension of school programs. Although individuals with other health impairments or physical disabilities attend postsecondary institutions at about twice the rate of many other students with disabilities (Blackorby and Wagner, 1996), the process often is difficult and frustrating. Colleges and universities do provide a range of technological support for students with disabilities; however, a recent survey found that many schools provide limited resources, primarily because of the cost (Michaels, Prezant, & Jackson, 2002). For example, resources such as scanners and screen magnification devices were found at only three-fourths of campuses, and items such as recorded textbooks and adapted keyboards were only found at one-half of the campuses surveyed. Lehmann, Davies, and Laurin (2000) organized a summit of a number of college students with disabilities, including a number with physical disabilities and other health impairments. These students identified barriers to their successful transition to postsecondary programs. The students then listed specific suggestions for students and teachers at both the secondary and postsecondary levels. These suggestions are found in the accompanying Teaching Strategies box entitled, "Tips for Eliminating Barriers to Postsecondary Education."

Young adults with disabilities typically will establish and maintain contact with the **adult service agencies** that can provide guidance and assistance once the students have graduated from high school or college. Adult service agencies can provide medical and psychological examinations and counseling, training and job placement, and financial assistance for adaptive equipment, prostheses, and basic living costs during training. Once a person is determined to be eligible for vocational rehabilitation services, a vocational rehabilitation counselor will

Teaching Strategies & Accommodations

Tips for Eliminating Barriers to Postsecondary Education

- Ask students to conduct workshops that describe the nature of various disabilities to faculty and staff.

- Provide staff development to postsecondary faculty regarding adaptations and accommodations they can implement.

- Reward faculty who are willing to adapt instruction to address the learning needs of students.

- Evaluate transportation availability to campus and on campus.

- Inform students about the documentation requirements of the local postsecondary institution before their senior year in high school.

- Identify potential financial resources for students entering into postsecondary settings.

- Teach high-school students time and money management skills.

- Tour the college campus with interested students during transition planning.

- Provide summer classes addressing compensatory strategies on college campuses for high-school students interested in obtaining a postsecondary education.

- Role-play with students ways of communicating to college faculty about students' disability and learning needs.

- Encourage networking between college students via focus groups, student meetings, and informational workshops.

Source: J. P. Lehmann, T. G. Davies, & K. M. Laurin (2000). Listening to student voices about postsecondary education. *Teaching Exceptional Children, 32*(5), 63.

serve as case manager and outline specific employment goals and needed services in an Individual Plan of Employment (IPE) (Neubert & Moon, 2000). Although such services may be provided automatically for persons under the care of state-run facilities, individuals with disabilities who are living on their own will need to seek out and secure available services. Each state has a vocational rehabilitation department. To find a list of contacts for the vocational rehabilitation department in your state and a description of the services it provides, visit **http://www.jan.wvu.edu/SBSES/VOCREHAB.htm**.

In addition to postsecondary education and employment opportunities, residential options are important considerations for individuals with physical disabilities and health impairments. Historically, many individuals with extensive physical disabilities, such as severe cerebral palsy, lived in institutional settings. Today, most of the individuals who in times past lived in segregated settings have moved directly and successfully into the community in group homes, or apartments. Some, however, continue to live in smaller segregated settings such as nursing homes. Many individuals with physical disabilities or health impairments live independently in homes within the community. Sometimes adaptive equipment is necessary or a personal attendant is required, so financial resources may be the factor that determines independent living for some people.

Important aspects of adult life include forming relationships, marrying, and perhaps having children. Of course, many individuals with physical disabilities and health impairments become parents. Often, they face challenges related to their personal mobility, in addition to accommodating the constant needs of a young child. The website of Parents with Disabilities On-Line offers a great site for parents, who also have physical disabilities, to find resources, share their stories, and learn about recent research and technology. Visit this website at **http://www/disabledparents.net**.

Individuals with physical disabilities and health impairments are increasingly participating fully and successfully in all aspects of adult life. Because many of us view a disability as an adverse condition, we may ascribe certain characteristics to the person with a disability who has been able to get a successful job and conduct a relatively normal existence. We speak frequently of the bravery of people who must deal with sensory impairments, debilitating illnesses, or physical conditions. Sometimes we wonder if we would be able to exhibit the same strength if we were in similar situations. There is no doubt that many people with disabilities are engaged in mighty struggles and exhibit courage and tenacity.

People with disabilities may struggle more with physical and social barriers imposed by others than with their own disabilities.

It is important for us to realize, however, that these struggles are often due to the physical and social barriers imposed by others—they are not a necessary consequence of disability. As in all historical battles for human and civil rights, ordinary people must become heroes in order to gain their rightful place in society. Although we admire the risks heroes take and the strength they show, it is unfortunate that we live in a society in which heroic acts are still necessary before basic rights and acceptance can be obtained.

Educating people about the challenges faced by individuals with physical disabilities has an important purpose—to facilitate change. Although it's been a long time coming, public awareness and technology are combining to create a much more accessible environment for persons facing physical challenges. Change in interpersonal areas—efforts at communication, comfortable social exchanges, and acceptance—cannot be legislated and must be instigated at an individual level.

We hope that by listening to our words as well as to the words of children and adults who have experienced disabilities, you have gained some insight into their strength, optimism, struggles, and educational needs. The past decade has resulted in great strides in medical management and technology, which have dramatically increased the options for individuals with physical disabilities and health impairments. We look forward to the doors that will be opened in the future through continued advances in science, social awareness, and knowledge. Visit our website at **http://www.college.hmco.com/students/** to read articles written by Harriet McBryde Johnson, a lawyer and advocate in Charleston, SC, who also happens to face significant physical challenges.

❓ *Pause and Reflect*

Adults with physical disabilities are among the most vocal advocates for personal and civil rights. In what ways can you participate as an advocate, whether or not you have a physical disability, in your community or at the national level? ●

Summary

- Physical disabilities and health impairments as currently defined by IDEA include a wide range of conditions. Physical disabilities can be grouped into neurological conditions, musculoskeletal conditions, and traumatic injuries. Health impairments include debilitating or life-threatening diseases or conditions such as cystic fibrosis and AIDS. Being familiar with what is known about the causes, prevalence, and treatment of these various conditions may help you to understand what to expect from the student, plan time for the student's treatment, and become comfortable with helping the student with in-school treatment.

- One of the most difficult aspects of physical disabilities and health impairments is the issue of mortality, since many conditions involve shortened life expectancy. Another issue is the continual need to educate others.

- Educational issues to be aware of include transdisciplinary planning, the importance of early intervention, and the use of technology to increase access for students in the regular class as well as to provide opportunities to students at home.

- New technologies for environmental control and communication have allowed people with physical disabilities and health impairments to participate more fully in many aspects of life. Legislation provides safeguards and regulations that facilitate the integration of individuals with physical disabilities and health impairments into the work force and the community.

Key Terms

physically challenged

physical disability

health impairment

cerebral palsy

spina bifida

hydrocephalus

epilepsy

grand mal seizure

petit mal seizure

muscular dystrophy

juvenile rheumatoid
   arthritis (JRA)

congenital malformation

traumatic brain injury
   (TBI)

asthma

juvenile onset diabetes

hypoglycemia

hyperglycemia

cystic fibrosis

acquired immune
   deficiency syndrome
   (AIDS)

transdisciplinary model

physical handling

health maintenance

eye-gazing scanning
   systems

augmentative communi-
   cation aid

digitized speech

synthesized speech

Americans with Disabil-
   ities Act (ADA) of 1990
   (P.L. 101-336)

adult service agency

USEFUL RESOURCES

- Visit *The Ragged Edge* at **http://www.ragged-edge-mag.com**. Formerly the *Disability Rag*, this is a magazine created by and for people with disabilities. It includes scathing editorials and calls to political action, and reviews relevant legislation.

- Access the Disability Rights Civilian Defense Fund (DREDF) at **http://www.dredf.org**. This website provides information to individuals with disabilities and their parents and advocates about legal rights and courses of political action.

- Contact World Communications, ACS Software, for software designed for students who use scanning techniques for communication: Freedom Writer Software, Academics with Scanning: Language Arts and Math. **http://www. m-media.com/products/remotes/interlink/freedomwriter**.

- Visit the National Organization for Rare Disorders (NORD) at **http://www.pcnet.com/~orphan**. NORD is a unique federation of voluntary health organizations dedicated to helping people with rare "orphan" diseases and assisting the organizations that serve them. NORD is committed to the identification, treatment, and cure of rare disorders through programs of education, advocacy, research, and service. Since its inception in 1983, NORD has served as the primary nongovernmental clearinghouse for information on over 5000 rare disorders. NORD also provides referrals to additional sources of assistance and ongoing support.

- Contact the National Sports Center for the Disabled, P.O. Box 36, Winter Park, CO 80482, (303) 726-5514. It provides information and contacts for individuals with disabilities who wish to engage in a variety of sports.

- Access the Office of Disability Employment Policy at **http://www.dol.gov/odep**. Provides information in many areas related to the employment of individuals with disabilities, including laws, benefits, publications, federal programs, and special projects.

- Laura Rothenberg (2003). *Breathing for a living*. This is the thoughtful autobiography of a young woman with cystic fibrosis who was a college student at the time of the book's writing. Rothenberg died in March 2003. In addition to her book, she created a video diary and radio diary "My So-Called Lungs" that aired on National Public Radio (NPR) and may be obtained through their archives **http://discover.npr.org**.

PORTFOLIO ACTIVITIES

1. Make an appointment with a physical therapist or occupational therapist who serves your school district. Discuss with him or her the types of activities typically provided to the students he or she serves. Accompany the therapist on a visit to a local school to observe individual service delivery and describe your observations.

   ✔*Standards* This activity will help students meet CEC Content Standard 2: Development and Characteristics of Learners.

2. Visit the center for disability services at your college or university. Review the services and materials that are available for college students with physical disabilities. Talk to some of the students who provide services, or, if possible, with some of the college students who receive services. Based on your interviews, identify the services the college students find most helpful.

   ✔*Standards* This activity will help students meet CEC Content Standard 3: Individual Learning Differences.

3. Create an annotated bibliography of children's literature on a variety of physical disabilities and health impairments. Create a series of learning objectives and lesson plans designed to integrate the literature into a curriculum.

   ✔*Standards* This activity will help students meet CEC Content Standard 2: Development and Characteristics of Learners.

4. Identify a job in your community often held by high-school students (working in a fast-food restaurant or music store). Observe and identify the specific skills that are required. Describe the adaptations that would be needed for a student who is in a wheelchair to hold that job.

   ✔*Standards* This activity will help students meet CEC Content Standard 5: Learning Environments and Social Interactions.

5. Invite an adult with a physical disability to visit your class and talk about work, living, social opportunities, challenges to acceptance, and achievement. Perhaps an adult with a disability is in your class and would also be interested in sharing his or her experiences. Describe your personal and professional reactions to the presentation.

   ✔*Standards* This activity will help students meet CEC Content Standard 5: Learning Environments and Social Interactions.

 To access an electronic portfolio template for these activities, visit our text website through http://www.education. college.hmco.com/students/.

13 Children Who Are Gifted and Talented

Outline

Terms and Definitions
    Early Scholars and Their Ideas on Giftedness
    Current Definitions of Giftedness
    Criteria for Identification
Factors Contributing to Giftedness
    Hereditary and Biological Factors
    Environmental Factors
    Prevalence
Characteristics of Students Who Are Gifted and Talented
    Cognitive Characteristics
    Social and Emotional Characteristics
    Physical Characteristics
    Personal Characteristics
    Special Populations of Gifted Students
Teaching Strategies and Accommodations
    Early Intervention
    Identification and Assessment: The Teacher's Role
    Placement Alternatives
    Program Models
    Curriculum Modifications in the General Education Classroom
    Is Special Education for Gifted Students Necessary?
SUMMARY
KEY TERMS
USEFUL RESOURCES
PORTFOLIO ACTIVITIES

Learning Objectives

After reading this chapter, the reader will:

- Construct a definition of giftedness using his or her own words and reflecting his or her own values, as well as understand the federal definition of giftedness

- Describe the traditional means of identifying gifted and talented students

- Describe contemporary theories of intelligence

- Identify the major program models and curriculum adaptations recommended for exceptionally able and/or talented students

Giftedness is not just a gift—much practice is required. (Plomin & Price, 2003, p. 114)

Each of us has something that we are very good at, and each of our students has an ability or potential that deserves nurturing. But who is *gifted*? Who is *talented*? And once we've decided, what should be done about it? What kinds of school programs, curriculum, and teaching strategies are the ones that will nurture and develop our students' gifts and talents and keep them from becoming underachievers or dropouts? How can we provide students with meaningful incentives?

In order to develop gifts and talents, children need *opportunities*. Would you have developed your own talents without the opportunity to practice? Would Yo-Yo Ma have become a cellist if his parents hadn't been musicians? Would Colin Powell have become a leader without the opportunities to advance available in the military? Would J. K. Rowling have become a writer without the encouragement of family and teachers? Some families can provide many opportunities to their children—lessons, summer camp, traveling, meeting accomplished people. And some cannot. In either case, the school is the place where opportunities for all students should be found—opportunities to find their strengths and develop their talents. For many of today's accomplished adults, a teacher was the first person to identify their strengths. Perhaps you can be that teacher for the next generation of gifted and talented adults.

Terms and Definitions

Generally, it would be appropriate to begin a chapter on giftedness with a definition of that term. However, defining giftedness is not a straightforward task. Giftedness exists in a cultural and historical context—it is defined according to the values of the time and place. So instead of jumping directly to the federal definition, in this section you will read about the various concepts of giftedness that have evolved over the past hundred years or so. You will also read about some individuals who have devoted their lives to studying students with gifts and talents, as well as current ideas about intelligence and giftedness.

As you read, think about someone you know (or know of) whom *you* consider gifted or talented. What are the characteristics of that individual that distinguish him or her? In short, how would *you* define giftedness?

It's hard to find two "experts" who agree on a single definition of giftedness. For that matter, it is difficult to find two experts who agree on whether **giftedness** and **talent** are synonyms or merely related terms. Giftedness often refers to exceptional intelligence or academic ability, whereas talent is often used to indicate exceptional artistic or athletic ability. Jane Piirto (1999) says that "to be talented is to possess the skills to do something well" (p. 16). You will see as you read this chapter, however, that these distinctions are too simplistic in a time when new theories and research are challenging our traditional ideas about intelligence, giftedness, and talents.

Although the problem of defining giftedness has perplexed educators and psychologists for generations, everyone seems to agree on at least one thing: There is a universal fascination with people—especially children—who are intellectually very capable, or exhibit precocious talents.

Giftedness is a complex and controversial subject.

Early Scholars and Their Ideas on Giftedness

According to early views of giftedness, it is a step away from insanity, and environment plays no role in developing talent.

From the time of the earliest scholars to today's most influential theorists, debate has centered on whether abilities and talents are born or made. This question continues to be of interest to teachers, who have a considerable stake in the belief that experiences can make a difference. In the 1800s, giftedness was often considered a personality flaw. Cesare Lombroso, a nineteenth-century physician, proffered a popularly held view that genius was just a short step from insanity. Other nineteenth-century theorists believed that each individual had only so much brain power to expend and that if a person used up this intellect early in life, she or he could expect an adulthood filled with madness or imbecility. This "early ripe, early rot" theory, though scientifically groundless, was believed by many nineteenth-century scholars.

● *Galton*   When Sir Francis Galton began his study of eminent scientists (*English Men of Science*, 1890), he concluded that "genius" (the nineteenth-century term for *giftedness*) was a natural talent composed of three traits: intellectual capacity, zeal, and the power of working. However, Galton believed fully in the idea that geniuses were born, not made. He dismissed the role of environment in the development of talent, even going so far as to suggest that "inferior specimens—for example, the mentally handicapped" (Kitano & Kirby, 1986, p. 36) be sterilized to safeguard society from the further production of mental defectives.

● *Terman*   Using Galton's work as the cornerstone of his own, Lewis M. Terman is credited with being the "father" of gifted education in the United States. Beginning with the publication of his article "Genius and Stupidity" (1906) and continuing until his death in the 1960s, Terman left his mark on all psychological research with his longitudinal study of over 1500 children determined to be gifted after scoring an IQ of 140+ on the Stanford–Binet Intelligence Test. Today, this original group of 1500 "Termites" is still being studied (Friedman et al., 1995). The Terman legacy can be found in his five-volume series *Genetic Studies of Genius* (Terman et al., 1925, 1926, 1930, 1947, 1959). See **http://www.radcliffe.edu/murray/data/ds/ds0882.htm** for information on the Terman Life Cycle Study.

Terman's longitudinal study of 1500 gifted children dispelled many misconceptions about giftedness.

Terman's work did much to dispel the above-mentioned myths of the eventual mental breakdown of individuals with gifts or talents, for his picture of highly able children was one of absolute mental health—of children who were immune from social and emotional crises. As his career progressed and his knowledge of gifted persons deepened, Terman realized how complex the phenomenon of giftedness was. Near the end of his career, Terman acknowledged the powerful influence of family, marriage, self-confidence, work habits, and mental health on the development of talent, for even among his 1500 high-IQ subjects, vast discrepancies existed in their contributions to society (Delisle, 2000).

● *Hollingworth*   Leta S. Hollingworth, a contemporary of Terman at Columbia University, added another dimension to the understanding of people with gifts and talents. A psychologist by training, she had tested thousands of children with mental disabilities before becoming interested in extreme intelligence. Hollingworth, who began a public school program for gifted elementary students in New York City, is best remembered for her recognition of the vulnerability that she knew to be a characteristic of these very bright children.

Hollingworth's research and writing concentrated on the humanity of children with gifts and talents and on the idea that individual students had unique personalities in addition to their IQs. In effect, Hollingworth presented a middle ground: She identified specific social and emotional concerns that might affect the behavior of students with gifts and talents (Delisle, 2000).

> Hollingworth identified social and emotional concerns that might affect students who are gifted and talented.

Current Definitions of Giftedness

A complete history of ideas about giftedness, talent, or intelligence cannot be written in these few pages. More thorough analysis of these topics is available elsewhere (Thurstone, 1924; Gould, 1981), and you may wish to consult such work once you have completed this book and this course. Now let us turn to the theorists who are influential today in the education of gifted children.

Contemporary views on the nature and scope of giftedness are still tied to concepts of that nebulous construct, **intelligence**. As you recall from Chapter 4, intelligence is thought of as the capacity to acquire, process, and use information. Terman's early work suggested that giftedness was limited to a select few who scored 140+ on an IQ test. One important contributor to contemporary understanding, Paul Witty, moved the thinking in a different direction. Witty suggested that anyone "whose performance is consistently remarkable in any potentially valuable area" (1940, p. 516) should be considered gifted. He based this assertion less on statistical evidence and more on observation of the world around him. Thus, the poet whose words make you weep, the teacher who inspires you to learn, and the architect who causes you to look skyward in awe would be considered gifted, regardless of their IQ scores. Today, psychologist Nancy Ewald Jackson echoes Witty; she defines giftedness "simply as exceptional performance or exceptionally rapid learning" (2000, p. 38).

Taking this thought a few steps further, Joseph Renzulli (1978) elaborated on the idea that giftedness lies not so much in the traits you have as in the deeds

For these gifted young musicians, the payoff for hours of practicing is the pleasure of making music with others. (© Gabe Palmer/CORBIS)

According to Renzulli, giftedness includes creativity and task commitment as well as above-average intellectual ability.

you do. His conception of giftedness highlights the importance of combinations of **creativity** (the ability to generate original or imaginative ideas) and **task commitment** (the ability to stay focused on a task to its completion), in addition to above-average intellectual abilities, in the development of gifted behaviors (see Figure 13.1). Like Witty, Renzulli believed that IQ alone provides insufficient

FIRST PERSON

Unexpected Light

I remember years ago sitting in a movie theatre watching Stanley Kubrick's film *2001* when it was still the future. I was crazy for anything having to do with space, and the thought of starscapes and zero-G space stations had a special fascination for me. But I'll never forget the disorienting feeling I had the first time I saw that sequence of the astronaut jogging around the circumference of the space station. You couldn't tell what was up and what was down. It was all just one continuous circular motion. I had never seen anything like it. This was space. Well, I think that was it for me because that was the moment I began to wonder what music would be like in zero-gravity. I didn't know it at the time but looking back I can see that that night at the movies was a transformational moment for me. It changed the way I thought about sound.

In my experience as an improviser I've found that knowledge comes from the most unexpected places. Some of the most profound things I've learned—the core concepts and ideas that at the heart of my work, are thoughts that have evolved from exposure to subjects beyond my music training. I've realized that what you carry with you from your education isn't so much "what you think" as it is "how you think." That it's the quality of your think-

ing—your mind's openness and ability to process your experience artistically, intellectually, and emotionally in a fresh and spontaneous way. That's what makes a difference.

As a jazz improviser and now a teacher of improvisation at the New School I'm constantly reminding my students that there's a great responsibility that comes with performing "in the moment." Jazz musicians meticulously rehearse spontaneity. In the jazz tradition music practice, theory, and history all combine to inform the choices that improvisers make when they perform. But creativity and imagination can't grow in a vacuum and for students, having an open mind to ideas outside their own discipline holds the potential to completely reshape their work.

I've improvised a living in jazz by allowing many of my interests to intersect with music. Whether it's writing music for NASA or setting Jackson Pollock's painting to music—I've allowed my mind to draw inspiration from thought and experience outside the world of jazz. I realize now that one of the ways this kind of lateral thinking was made possible was by introducing myself to different subjects when I was in school. I could never in a million years have anticipated how taking courses like Art in the Machine Age, Modern Drama or Develop-

evidence of giftedness, and only after a student, an architect, or a poet creates a visible product can an analysis be made of that person's intellect. This product-based formula for giftedness fits right in with our own culture's current emphasis on performance and educational accountability. For these reasons, Renzulli's concept of giftedness has enjoyed wide popularity among educators.

Jane Ira Bloom posing with her saxophone.
(Time Life Pictures/Getty Images)

mental Psych 101 would resonate in my work today. Studying abstract painting helped me imagine a jazz quartet that could swing around sound the way Jackson Pollock threw paint. Exploring Freud and unconscious processes helped inform a whole new spontaneous approach to composition. My interest in zero-gravity found expression in imagining orchestras that use circular movement to create changes in sound.

In a university you also have a unique opportunity to get close to great minds from diverse fields. Learning from them may not only be about the information that they have to offer, but about learning how they think. What they question, how they organize ideas, how they consider information—not only what is said but what is unsaid, how they put ideas in context,

how they focus or allow their thoughts to flow freely. These are insights that you can take with you wherever you go. These are insights that can transform your mind.

I'll never forget the first time I spoke with the great jazz innovator Ornette Coleman on the phone. I was about 20, full of fire and ready to move to New York and begin my career as an improviser. I thought surely he'd have some extraordinary advice for me. Well, the phone call wasn't quite what I expected. I'd introduce a question and Ornette would seem to respond to it but then would arc off in an abstract way onto subjects that seemed to connect but I wasn't sure. There was a passion and mystery in his voice that I could feel but not quite understand. Well, many years later as I'm teaching his music to students at the New School, I realize that the quality of his language is exactly what characterizes the genius of his music—melodies that seem to randomly crystallize in different directions but retain a beautiful continuity at the same time. That's the genius of his thought. It just took some time to understand.

Jane Ira Bloom

Jane Ira Bloom teaches in the Jazz Studies Program at the New School University in New York City. Her instrument is the soprano saxophone. This essay is adapted from her address to the university opening convocation on August 29, 2002. Used with permission. Jane's latest CD is "Chasing Paint," on the Arabesque Jazz Label.

Source: "Aims of Education" address, the New School University opening convocation, August 29, 2002.

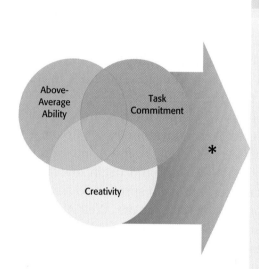

General Performance Areas		
Mathematics	Visual Arts	Physical Sciences
Philosophy	Social Sciences	Law
Religion	Language Arts	Music
Life Sciences		Movement Arts

Specific Performance Areas		
Cartooning	Demography	Electronic Music
Astronomy	Microphotography	Child Care
Public Opinion Polling	City Planning	Consumer Protection
Jewelry Design	Pollution Control	Cooking
Map Making	Poetry	Ornithology
Choreography	Fashion Design	Furniture Design
Biography	Weaving	Navigation
Film Making	Play Writing	Genealogy
Statistics	Advertising	Sculpture
Local History	Costume Design	Wildlife Management
Electronics	Meteorology	Set Design
Musical Composition	Puppetry	Agriculture
Landscape	Marketing	Research
Architecture	Game Design	Animal Learning
Chemistry	Journalism	Film Criticism
etc.	etc.	etc.

*This arrow should be read as "brought to bear upon. . ."

Figure 13.1

Graphic Representation of Renzulli's Definition of Giftedness

Source: Joseph S. Renzulli, Conception of giftedness and its relation to social capital. From Nicholas Colangelo and Gary Davis (Eds.), *Handbook of gifted education* (3rd ed., p. 76). Published by Allyn and Bacon, Boston, MA. Copyright 2003 by Pearson Education. Reprinted by permission of the publisher.

> Gardner postulates at least eight kinds of intelligence.

Robert Sternberg and Howard Gardner, two psychologists whose work has revitalized the debate on intelligence, propose broader views of human capabilities. Gardner defines intelligence as "a biophysical potential" and giftedness as "a sign of early or precocious biophysical potential in the domains of a culture" (2000, pp. 78–79). Gardner is best known in education for his **theory of multiple intelligences** (1983; Von Károlyi, Ramos-Ford, & Gardner, 2003), which postulates that there are at least eight distinct intelligences (see Table 13.1). An abundance of talent in any of these areas constitutes giftedness, according to Gardner, and although people may be capable in several different intelligences, one does not have to excel in every area to be considered gifted. Gardner points out that the manifestation of intelligence depends on what is valued in a culture; if a person is good at something that is not valued in a culture, then that capacity would not be considered an intelligence (Gardner, 2000).

> Sternberg proposes knowledge-based skills, social/practical intelligence, and fluid abilities.

Robert J. Sternberg adds yet another tile to this mosaic with his **triarchic theory**, which includes three kinds of intellectual giftedness: analytic, creative, and practical (Sternberg, 1997; Sternberg & Clinkenbeard, 1995). Students who are analytically gifted are effective at analyzing, evaluating, and critiquing; those who are creatively gifted are skillful at discovering, creating, and invent-

Table 13.1 Gardner's Multiple Intelligences

Category	Core Operations	Example
Linguistic Mastery, sensitivity, desire to explore, and love of words and spoken and written language(s).	Comprehension and expression of written and oral language, syntax, semantics, pragmatics.	William Shakespeare, Toni Morrison.
Logical-mathematical Confront, logically analyze, assess and empirically investigate objects, abstractions, and problems, discern relations and underlying principles, carry out mathematical operations, handle long chains of reasoning.	Computation, deductive reasoning, inductive reasoning.	Paul Erdos, Isaac Newton.
Musical Skill in producing, composing, performing, listening, discerning, and sensitivity to the components of music and sound.	Pitch, melody, rhythm, texture, timbre, musical, themes, harmony.	Charlie Parker, Wolfgang Amadeus Mozart.
Spatial Accurately perceive, recognize, manipulate, modify and transform shape, form, and pattern.	Design, color, form, perspective, balance, contrast, match.	Leonardo da Vinci, Frank Lloyd Wright.
Bodily-kinesthetic Orchestrate and control body motions and handle objects, skillfully, to perform tasks or fashion products.	Control and coordination, stamina, balance, locating self or objects in space.	Martha Graham, Tiger Woods.
Interpersonal Be sensitive to, accurately assess, and understand other's actions, motivations, moods, feelings, and other mental states and act productively on the basis of that knowledge.	Ability to inspire, instruct, or lead others and respond to their actions, emotions, motivations, opinions, and situations.	Virginia Woolf, Dalai Lama.
Intrapersonal Be sensitive to, accurately assess, understand and regulate oneself and act productively on the basis of one's actions, motivations, moods, feelings, and other mental states.	Knowledge and understanding of one's strengths and weaknesses, styles, emotions, motivations, self-orientation.	Mahatma Gandhi, Oprah Winfrey.
Naturalist Expertise in recognition and classification of natural objects, i.e., flora & fauna, or artifacts, i.e., cars, coins, or stamps.	Noting the differences that are key to discriminating among several categories or species of objects in the natural world.	Charles Darwin, Jane Goodall.
Existential* Capturing and pondering the fundamental questions of existence; an interest and concern with "ultimate" issues.	Capacity to raise big questions about one's place in the cosmos.	Soren Kierkegaard, Martin Luther King, Jr.

*Unconfirmed ninth intelligence.

Source: C. Von Károlyi, V. Ramos-Ford, & H. Gardner (2003). Multiple intelligences: A perspective on giftedness. From Nicholas Colangelo & Gary Davis (Eds.), *Handbook of gifted education* (3rd ed. p. 102). Published by Allyn and Bacon, Boston, MA. Copyright 2003 by Pearson Education. Reprinted by permission of the publisher.

ing; and those who are practically gifted are good at implementing, utilizing, and applying (see Figure 13.2). In Sternberg's view, "the big question is not how many things a person is good at, but how well a person can exploit whatever he or she is good at and find ways around the things that he or she is not good at" (1991, p. 51). Sternberg now describes this combination as "successful intelligence" (Sternberg, 2003; Sternberg & Grigorenko, 2000). (For a look into the development of Sternberg's own intelligence, see the Closer Look box entitled, "Robert J. Sternberg.")

A Closer Look   Robert J. Sternberg

The Child is father of the Man. . . .

—William Wordsworth

Psychologist Robert Sternberg of Yale University, the creator of the triarchic theory of intelligence and past president of the American Psychological Association, is the author of over fifty books on a wide variety of topics—from intelligence and gifted children to wisdom, love, and hate, as well as countless professional journal articles. He must have been the epitome of the gifted child, correct? You'll be surprised . . . let Sternberg tell his own story (2000, pp. 21–22):

As an elementary school student, Sternberg failed miserably on the IQ tests he had to take. He was incredibly test-anxious. Just the sight of the school psychologist coming into the classroom to give a group IQ test sent him into a wild panic attack. And by the time the psychologist said "Go!" to get the class started, he was in such a funk that he could hardly answer any of the test items. He still remembers being on the first couple of problems when he heard other students already turning the page as they sailed through the test. For him, the game of taking the test was all but over before it even started. And the outcome was always the same: He lost.

Sternberg was an ordinary student, convinced of his mediocrity,—"one more loser in the game of

life"—until he reached Mrs. Alexa's fourth grade class:

. . . Mrs. Alexa did not know or did not care much about IQ test scores. She believed Sternberg could do much better than he was doing, and she expected more of him. In fact, she demanded more of him. And she got it. Why? Because he wanted to please her. . . .

Mrs. Alexa did not seem particularly surprised, but her student was astonished when he actually exceeded her expectations. He became a straight-A student very quickly. For the first time, he saw himself as someone who could be an A student, and he was one thereafter. But at the time, it never occurred to him that he had become an A student *because* he was smart; on the contrary, he felt that he had become an A student *in spite* of his low intelligence, as witnessed by his low test scores.

In this painful memory of the little boy who was father to a brilliant man, it is not difficult to see the genesis of a psychologist who would widen our definition of intelligence. Read more of Sternberg's story, and explore his work, in *Teaching for Successful Intelligence*, cowritten with his colleague Elena Grigorenko. For more about Sternberg's work, visit our textbook website.

―――――――――
Source: R. J. Sternberg & E. Grigorenko. (2000). *Teaching for successful intelligence* (pp. 21–22). Arlington Heights, IL: Skylight Training and Publishing, Inc.

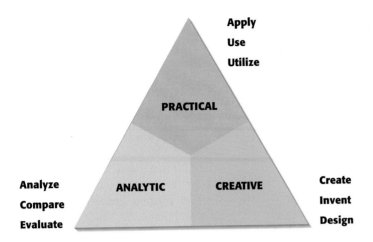

Figure 13.2

Sternberg's Triarchic Theory of Intelligence

According to Robert Sternberg, intelligence comprises analytic, creative, and practical abilities. In *analytical thinking,* we try to solve familiar problems by using strategies that manipulate the elements of a problem or the relationships among the elements (for example, comparing, analyzing). In *creative thinking,* we try to solve new kinds of problems that require us to think about the problem and its elements in a new way (for example, inventing, designing). In *practical thinking,* we try to solve problems that apply what we know to everyday contexts (for example, applying, using).

Source: From *In Search of the Human Mind* by Robert J. Sternberg, copyright © 1995 by Harcourt Brace & Company, reproduced by permission of the publisher.

One of Sternberg's current interests lies in the nature of *wisdom* as a form of giftedness (2000). He asks that we think, for example, of four extremely gifted individuals of the twentieth century—Mahatma Gandhi, Mother Theresa, Dr. Martin Luther King, Jr., and Nelson Mandela. Would their gifts have been identified through any kind of test, or with the definitions we identify in this chapter? Perhaps not. But they instigated change that led to great good in the world, the scope of which few others can claim. Sternberg argues that we need to start developing wisdom in children:

> For example, students need to learn how to think dialogically, understanding points of view other than their own, and to think not only in terms of their own interests, but in terms of the interests of others and of the society, as well. . . . Unless students are specifically taught to focus upon the common good, rather than only upon the good of themselves and those close to them, they may simply never learn to think in such a fashion. (2000, p. 252)

The accompanying Teaching Strategies box entitled, "Developing Wisdom in Children" provides Sternberg's suggestions for this endeavor. These strategies would be particularly successful with teenagers.

The National Association for Gifted Children notes that most definitions of giftedness have one element in common: A gifted person is

Someone who shows, or has the potential for showing, an exceptional level of performance in one or more areas of expression. Some of these abilities are very general and can affect a broad spectrum of the person's life, such as

Sternberg identifies wisdom as a form of intelligence, and believes that schools should try to teach wisdom.

Teaching Strategies & Accommodations

Developing Wisdom in Children: The Work of Robert Sternberg

What we consider wisdom, argues Sternberg, is inextricably tied to our values, and we must begin by valuing wisdom itself and what it can contribute to society. Do we? Think of how older people are perceived in our culture to answer that question.

Here are Sternberg's own words (2000, pp. 257–258):

Wisdom is a form of giftedness that can be developed in a number of ways. Seven of these are particularly important:

- *First*, provide students with problems that require wise thinking.

- *Second*, help students think in terms of a common good in the solution of these problems.

- *Third*, help students learn how to balance their own interests, the interests of others, and the interests of institutions in the solution of these problems.

- *Fourth*, provide examples of wise thinking from the past and analyze them.

- *Fifth*, model wisdom for the students. Show them examples of wise thinking you have done and perhaps not-so-wise thinking that has taught you lessons.

- *Sixth*, help students to think dialectically. . . . Most problems in the world do not have right or wrong answers, but better or worse ones, and what is seen as a good answer can vary with time and place.

- *Seventh*, show your students that you value wise information processing and solutions.

Finally, carry what you learn and encourage students to carry what they learn outside the classroom. The goal is not to teach another "subject" that will serve as the basis for an additional grade to appear on a report card. The goal is to change the way people think about and act in their own lives.

For more information on teaching wisdom, read Sternberg's "Wisdom as a Form of Giftedness."

Source: Copyright material from the National Association for Gifted Children (NAGC), 1707 L Street, NW, Suite 550, Washington, DC 20036 (202) 785-4268. http://www.nagc.org. This material may not be reproduced without permission from NAGC.

---

leadership skills or the ability to think creatively. Some are very specific talents and are only evident in particular circumstances, such as a special aptitude in mathematics, science, or music. (National Association for Gifted Children, 2003)

Finally, the "official" definition of giftedness is the one in federal law, which states that gifted children are those

> . . . who give evidence of high performance capability in areas such as intellectual, creative, artistic, leadership capacity, or specific academic fields, and who require services or activities not ordinarily provided by the school in order to fully develop such capabilities. (P.L. 103–382, Title XIV, p. 388)

Federal law defines giftedness as high performance in intellectual, creative, artistic, leadership, and academic areas.

The federal definition specifies areas of giftedness; it allows for gifted traits and gifted behaviors; and it connects the definition with the need to provide special educational programs for children identified as gifted. Overall, it is a comprehensive definition that is now widely used in the United States.

Federal law does not *require* educational services for students identified as gifted, nor does it provide any funds for the implementation of gifted programs. Since its enactment, however, many individual states have incorporated the federal definition into state legislation; and, since more than half the states now require special educational provisions for students identified as gifted or talented, this federal definition has encouraged a substantial increase in state-based initiatives for serving students with gifts or talents.

It is doubtful that one definition of giftedness will ever be written that satisfies every theorist, educator, and parent. Nor is it likely that all gifted children will ever be identified for the special education they require. Still, it is important for you to realize that if you are unsure about "exactly" who is gifted, you share your lack of certainty with some of the world's experts on the theory and measurement of intelligence.

> Federal law does not require educational services for gifted students but encourages state initiatives for serving these students.

Criteria for Identification

If a child begins to read independently at the age of 3 or a 15-year-old graduates as high-school valedictorian, it is quite apparent that you are observing atypical behavior—not "abnormal" behavior, but behavior that appears in advance of its usual developmental onset.

Advanced development is one of the most commonly applied criteria in the identification of students with gifts and talents. Measurement of this advanced development historically has been through standardized tests commonly given by school psychologists or teachers.

Individual IQ tests, like the WISC-IV or the Stanford–Binet (see Chapter 4), can be used to assess intellectual capacity. However, the extensive costs in terms of time and money needed to administer and score the tests have caused most school districts to forgo their use. Instead, standardized group intelligence tests are often used. When given as part of the annual battery of achievement tests administered to all students, these group tests provide a general assessment of how students compare intellectually with their classmates. Those students who score two or more standard deviations above the mean of the test (which generally results in an IQ of 130–135) are often classified as gifted. (See Figure 13.3.) Similarly, students who score at the 95th percentile or above on standardized achievement tests of reading, math, and other content areas are often identified as academically gifted.

> Students scoring two or more standard deviations above the mean on IQ tests are usually classified as gifted.

The criteria for qualifying for special programs for gifted students varies; check with your local school district to determine the criteria in your area. In the Los Angeles Unified School District (LAUSD), for example, students can qualify for gifted programs in one of three ways:

1. Demonstrate ability in *all four* critical-thinking and problem-solving skills in their primary language
   - Explain meanings or relationships among facts, information, or concepts that demonstrate depth and complexity
   - Formulate new ideas or solutions and elaborate on the information
   - Use alternative methods in approaching new or unfamiliar mathematical problems
   - Use extensive vocabulary easily and accurately to express creative ideas or demonstrate creative ideas nonverbally

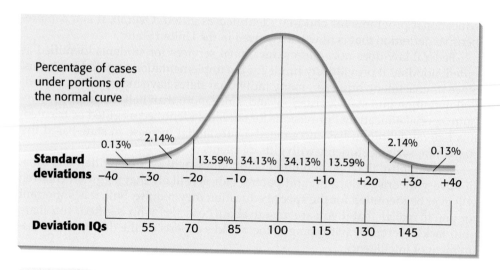

Figure 13.3

The Normal Curve and Average IQ Score Distribution

Source: S. A. Kirk & J. J. Gallagher (1988). *Educating exceptional children* (6th ed., p. 11), Boston: Houghton Mifflin. Copyright © 1988. Used with permission.

2. National stanine scores of 7 or above in total reading *and* total mathematics on standardized tests

3. Identification as gifted in any of the categories by an LAUSD school psychologist (LAUSD, 2004)

But qualification for the **highly gifted** programs comes through an IQ score alone—in this case, a score on an individually administered IQ test equivalent to 99.9 percent.

> Standardized tests that determine giftedness are criticized because they may lead to underrepresentation of children from minority groups.

Achievement and IQ tests, though, have been criticized as being too narrow in focus; they concentrate on analytic abilities (Sternberg, 2003), and the traditional areas of linguistic and logico-mathematical reasoning (Von Károlyi, Ramos-Ford, & Gardner, 2003). Many scholars have noted that using IQ tests as the primary means of identifying candidates for gifted programs inevitably leads to underrepresentation of children from culturally and linguistically diverse backgrounds as well as those with disabilities (Salvia & Ysseldyke, 2004). Any standardized test-based identification of giftedness leads to the underidentification of students who are American Indian/Alaskan Native, African American, and Hispanic (Donovan & Cross, 2002). Ensuring that gifted programs are inclusive of *all* children, regardless of race, home language, or disability, will involve developing more sensitive assessment procedures and changes in our reliance on tests and test scores.

Informal assessment by parents, teachers, peers, and community members who know the student can provide school personnel with non-test-based information about the range of a student's specific skills or talents. The yardsticks for measuring giftedness should be many and varied. The teacher's role in identifying and assessing giftedness and talent is discussed later in the chapter. For more information, visit the Center for Gifted Education and Talent Development at **http://www.gifted. uconn.edu**.

? Pause and Reflect

Conceptualizing giftedness is more complicated than you might have thought. What qualities do you think make someone gifted? Can you put your own definition of giftedness into writing? How is your definition influenced by your culture and values? ●

Factors Contributing to Giftedness

For as long as gifts and talents have been recognized and studied, the question of nature versus nurture has been pondered. Are individuals with gifts and talents endowed with a pool of superior genes, or is their environment responsible for the emergence of superior performance?

Hereditary and Biological Factors

Scientists and educators agree that genes are but one element in the complex development of human intelligence. Even geneticists disagree about the relative contributions of our genes to our abilities—estimates range from about 40–80 percent. Gage and Berliner (1998) see the influences of heredity and environment on intelligence as about equal; Plomin and Price (2003) explain that "genes merely contribute to the odds that development will proceed in a certain direction . . . *genetic* does not mean innate" (p. 113). Vernon (1989), in arguing against overemphasizing any one element—genes, environment, or opportunity—in the development of intelligence, reminds us that since none of these factors occurs in total isolation from the others, it is impossible to tell where the effects of heredity end and the impact of environment takes over.

Both genetics and environment play crucial roles in determining giftedness.

While innate ability appears essential, it may not emerge without an added dimension: hard work. Ericsson, Krampe, and Tesch-Romer (1993; Winner, 2000a) found that the highest achievers in ballet, violin, piano, chess, bridge, and athletics were those who engaged in the most "deliberate practice"—consistent effort designed to improve performance.

Environmental Factors

Abraham J. Tannenbaum writes: "Giftedness requires a social context that enables it to mature. These contexts are as broad as society itself and as restricted as the sociology of the classroom. Human potential needs nurturance, urgings, encouragement, and even pressures from a world that cares" (2003, p. 54). In other words, many aspects of the child's environment contribute to the development of abilities.

The role played by the family in the development of gifts and talents has been studied extensively, and virtually every study has shown the importance of nurturance. Benjamin Bloom (1985), in his study of Olympic athletes, musical prodigies, and others of exceptional achievement, points to the vital role played by the family (not just the parents) in channeling these remarkable talents and downplays the role of the school in the realization of noteworthy accomplishments. Sternberg (2003) reminds us that an individual's intelligence must be viewed within the context of the *opportunities* he or she has had—and people of

Family encouragement of the child's talents is of critical importance.

higher socioeconomic status tend to have more opportunities than those of lower socioeconomic status.

The role played by peers, especially among economically disadvantaged children, has also been shown to have a significant impact on the desire to achieve academically (Reis & McCoach, 2000). In short, the debate over the development of gifts and talents has grown far beyond the nature–nurture arguments of past generations. Today, the emphasis is on the practical: designing structure and strategies at home and at school that encourage these talents to blossom.

Prevalence

In most states, the prevalence of giftedness among the population is placed at 5 percent.

Considering the variety of definitions of giftedness, it is not surprising that the prevalence of gifts and talents in the population is also open to debate. For example, if you were to use the criterion of an IQ of 140 as the baseline for intellectual giftedness, you would exclude 99 percent of the population. (See Figure 13.3 again for a visual representation of this concept.) If, however, you were to use the federal definition of giftedness, 3–5 percent of the school-age population would qualify as having gifts or talents. Renzulli's concept of giftedness (1978) identifies a set of behaviors that can emerge in students who are above-average (although not necessarily superior) in ability. Thus, he suggests a figure of 15–20 percent of the population as capable of performing gifted behaviors. And Henry Levin (1996) believes that if we take time to look, we will find that almost every student in a class is above-average in some skill, ability, or knowledge area—everyone is gifted in some way.

Many theorists and researchers, although arguing about the exact prevalence of gifts and talents, do agree that for funding purposes the figure of 5 percent is useful. Thus, despite the fact that experts may disagree philosophically on where giftedness begins and ends, the prevalence figure of 5 percent is common in most states (National Association for Gifted Children, 2003).

? Pause and Reflect

Gifted performance seems to depend on a combination of innate ability and environmental factors such as opportunity and support. What are the opportunities you have had—or wish you had had—to develop your own areas of talent or interest? How do you plan to provide these opportunities to the students you teach? ●

Characteristics of Students Who Are Gifted and Talented

Students who are gifted and talented represent a cross-section of humanity: All races, cultures, sizes, and shapes are represented. Yet as different as these individual students seem at first glance, their intelligence has affected their cognitive and social-emotional development in similar ways. The following sections highlight some of these effects.

Cognitive Characteristics

Cognitive development is frequently accelerated in children with exceptional abilities, and although we may see this as a positive factor, it can cause problems in the classroom. For example, a child who learned to read independently at the age of 3 may have difficulty in a kindergarten class where he or she is expected to learn the alphabet. A junior-high student well versed in algebra may question the point of completing pages of long-division problems. A 10-year-old who perceives subtle distinctions in moral reasoning may be frustrated by agemates who see only cut-and-dried, right-and-wrong solutions.

Exceptionally gifted students may ponder questions deeply and consider many possible answers; they often pose complex philosophical questions themselves (Lovecky, 1994). If there is no special program available for students like these, problems and frustrations may occur for both the student and the teacher. In fact, these sophisticated cognitive characteristics may pose unique challenges even for the teacher who is committed to providing an enriched curriculum to gifted and talented students. See Table 13.2 for more on this topic.

Social and Emotional Characteristics

Very closely tied to the cognitive effects of giftedness and talents is the social and emotional impact of these talents on students' performance. While many students have the same social and emotional characteristics as other children their age, some students may feel "different," misunderstood, and socially isolated. They may benefit from the support of other gifted peers, as well as understanding families and teachers.

Some gifted students experience social isolation.

Some people assume that gifted students must have plenty of friends of their own age in order to be socially "healthy." Schultz and Delisle (2003) believe that for gifted students, peers are not necessarily of the same age, but share the same abilities and interests—their commonalities may have nothing to do with age. Most would agree that relationships with peers of all ages can be appropriate for students who are gifted and talented.

The interplay between intellect and emotion is clear to people who work with students with talents and gifts. An intellectually able 6-year-old may cry uncontrollably when confronted with inequity or injustice, either on the schoolyard or while watching the evening news. A fastidious high-school junior may consider herself a failure if she receives a grade of B+ in advanced physics. Perfectionism is a scourge for many high-performing students, and a source of underachievement for others—impossibly high goals may provide an excuse for lack of effort (Rimm, 2003). It is your job, as a teacher, to understand that intellectually capable students, whatever their ages, must be appreciated for their strengths and their vulnerabilities; even though these young people are smart, they are not small adults—they still need support and guidance from the grown-ups in their lives.

Physical Characteristics

Early research by Terman (1925) showed students with high IQ test scores to be stronger, bigger, and healthier than their agemates. In fact, Terman's findings did much to dissolve the stereotype of the gifted student as a bespectacled weakling who carries a briefcase to school instead of a backpack. However,

The gifted student cannot be identified by appearance.

Table 13.2 Cognitive Characteristics of Gifted Students and Their Implications for Teaching

Differentiating Characteristics	Possible Problems	Teaching Strategies
Extraordinary quantity of information; unusual retentiveness	Boredom with regular curriculum; impatience with "waiting for the group."	Expose the student to new and challenging aesthetic, economic, political, social, and educational information about the culture and the environment.
Advanced comprehension	Poor interpersonal relationships with same-age peers; adults consider the child a "smart aleck."	Provide access to challenging curriculum and intellectual peers.
Unusually varied interests and curiosity	Difficulty in conforming to group tasks; overextending energy levels, taking on too many projects at one time.	Expose student to varied subjects and concerns; allow student to pursue individual ideas as far as interest itakes him or her.
High level of language development and verbal ability	Perception as a "show off" by same-age peers; domination of discussion; use of verbalism to avoid difficult thinking tasks.	Provide uses for increasingly difficult vocabulary and concepts; expect student to share ideas verbally in depth.
Unusual capacity for processing information	Resentment at being interrupted; perceived as too serious; dislike of routine and drill.	Expose student to ideas at many levels and in large variety.
Accelerated pace of thought processes	Frustration with inactivity and absence of progress.	Expose student to ideas at rates appropriate to individual pace of learning—often accelerated.
Comprehensive synthesis	Frustration with demand for deadlines and for completion of each level prior to starting new one.	Allow a longer incubation time for ideas.
Ability to generate original ideas and solutions	Difficulty with rigid conformity; may be penalized for not following directions; may deal with rejection by becoming rebellious.	Build skills in problem-solving and creative thinking; provide the opportunity to contribute to solutions of meaningful problems.

Source: Barbara Clark, *Growing up gifted: Developing the potential of children at home and at school*, 6th edition, © 2002. Reprinted by permission of Pearson Education Inc., Upper Saddle River, NJ.

Terman's research included primarily children from advantaged backgrounds whose physical prowess was bolstered by nurturing and well-off home environments. Today, as gifted programs expand to embrace students from all cultures and socioeconomic backgrounds, we see an array of physical characteristics that defies any simple categorization. In effect, a gifted student has no certain look or appearance. Indeed, students with physical disabilities must not be overlooked in the identification of giftedness; they may have an impressive store of knowledge despite limited experiences, and they use exceptional creativity in finding ways of communicating and accomplishing tasks (Willard-Holt, 1999).

School-age students who are gifted may face a physical challenge if they are accelerated. **Acceleration** involves skipping grades to provide a more appropriate curriculum. As a result, accelerated students can be significantly younger than classmates. Especially in junior high and high school, this becomes an important consideration, since few adolescents want to be left behind when growth spurts occur for everyone but them. This possibility, which can also have social side effects, should be reviewed before acceleration is undertaken.

Acceleration may have social implications for students, particularly in adolescence.

Personal Characteristics

Ellen Winner (2000a) adds another perspective to our picture of gifted students. She describes the anecdotal evidence that highly gifted students may be qualitatively different in motivation than other students; they display an intense drive, or "rage to master": "They work for hours with no parental prodding or external reinforcement. As they work, they pose challenges for themselves. . . . They make discoveries on their own, and much of the time they appear to teach themselves" (p. 154). Winner suggests that these students may develop and think differently from others, but cautions that research is needed to determine whether high ability and these cognitive and motivational differences always appear together.

Ethical and spiritual issues may become important to gifted students at an earlier age than is typically expected. Clark and Hankins (1985) posed twenty-five philosophical questions to children ages 6 to 10 who were matched on all variables except intellectual ability. They found that in response to such questions as "What is the worst thing that could happen in the world?" and "Who is the best person in the world, living or dead?" the gifted children were found to be more knowledgeable about the world and more pessimistic about the future.

Ethical and spiritual issues may be especially important to gifted students during adolescence.

❓ Pause and Reflect

Throughout this book we have provided you with descriptions of the characteristics of students in each category. Remember that these lists of characteristics are general statements that are true of *many*—but not *all*—students in that group. Are there general statements made about a group that *you* identify with, perhaps based on your age or gender, that you have found untrue in your own experience? ●

Special Populations of Gifted Students

The following sections address some special populations of gifted students and the special needs these young people may have.

● *Gifted Adolescents*   Struggling for social acceptance, experiencing physical changes, and conducting inner searches for meaning in one's life are some of the benchmarks of adolescence. Gifted adolescents are as concerned about these issues as are their agemates, but there may be unique implications for them.

Schultz and Delisle (2003) point out that adolescence for gifted students involves special concerns in the social and emotional, educational, ethical and spiritual, and career and lifestyle domains. In the area of social and emotional issues, gifted females may struggle with decisions related to the often conflicting needs for social acceptance and the full expression of their talents (Kerr &

Gifted adolescent girls often feel they must suppress or disguise their abilities to be accepted.

Nicpon, 2003). In effect, gifted girls may feel they must suppress or disguise their abilities to be accepted by boys. Conversely, Alvino (1989) contended that most gifted males feel obligated to use their academic talents, often at the cost of the emotional aspects of their lives; the result may be increased stoicism and the tendency to overwork. Teachers should be aware of these potential issues and be prepared to provide appropriate support.

Educationally, adolescents with gifts and talents tend to question how best to further their intellectual development. For example, if they are admitted to college after their junior year in high school, do they stay in high school and not miss the senior prom and varsity football, or do they go on to college and seek social outlets there? Or, given the opportunity to pursue intellectual challenges independently, do they choose this route and forgo other options? Chad Gervich, a 15-year-old gifted student, summarizes these issues when describing his difficult decision whether to attend a summer residential program for gifted students:

> The biggest problem I encountered was my friends. They never let me forget I was applying to "Nerd Camp," "Geek City," and "Dweebville." "It's summer; school's out," they'd say. "Why do you want to go back?" That was a question I couldn't easily answer. Even I didn't know. (Delisle, 1992)

Career and lifestyle issues include a problem that many people see as a benefit: the ability to be successful in so many fields that selecting a career becomes problematic (Schultz & Delisle, 2003). The societal expectation that gifted students should become highly valued professionals (doctors, lawyers, professors) may intrude on an adolescent's personal choice if he or she wishes to enter a career such as artisan, laborer, or homemaker.

Secondary school teachers can help ward off some of these dilemmas by facilitating discussions among adolescents with similar talents, or through academic and curricular programs that address intellectual and emotional growth (Schultz & Delisle, 2003).

Students who are gifted can become depressed and suicidal if their emerging sexual identity does not conform with societal expectations.

● *Gay, Lesbian, and Bisexual Adolescents*   Gifted adolescents who may need special understanding and support are those who are gay, lesbian, or bisexual. Peterson and Rischar (2000) note that exceptional ability may contribute to a sense of "differentness" and may affect social relationships. When a gifted child is also gay, lesbian, or bisexual (GLB), that sense of differentness may intensify. A quest for perfection and a sexual identity that may not be approved of by the student's family and community can combine to form serious feelings of inadequacy in the GLB adolescent who is gifted. Students who fall into these categories may be subject to overt acts of homophobia (Kerr & Nicpon, 2003), and at particular risk of depression and thoughts of suicide. Peterson and Rischar write:

> All educators, particularly those involved in education for the gifted, need to be courageous in their support for GLB students, ensuring that their classrooms are physically and psychologically safe and intervening on behalf of students who are "out" or are bullied or teased when their behaviors fit popular GLB stereotypes. Even quiet acknowledgement that gayness is worthy of discussion, that some respected individuals in textbooks are/were GLB, that concerns about sexual orientation are common during childhood and adolescence, and that GLB individuals are probably present

in all schools and classrooms may help to lessen the distress of those who believe that no one has ever felt as they do. (2000, p. 231)

The Gay Lesbian and Straight Education Network consists of parents, students, educators, and others working to end discrimination against GLB students in schools. Visit **http://www.glsen.org**.

● *Gifted Girls*   Until the impact of the women's movement began to be felt in American education in the 1970s and 1980s, little was done to identify and develop giftedness and talents in girls. Although it is now generally understood that it is illegal to discriminate on the basis of gender in any arena, unconscious biases may still prevent girls who are gifted and talented from being identified and from persevering through rigorous educational programs, particularly in middle and secondary school (Kerr & Nicpon, 2003). Girls may receive differential treatment in the classroom because of teacher attitudes that (as an example) stereotype girls as weaker than boys in math and science (Secada, Fennema, & Adajian, 1995). Teachers may give less attention to girls, and respond to their questions and answers differently than to those of boys (Sadker & Sadker, 1994). Gifted girls should be encouraged to take the most challenging coursework available, to engage in play activities that are physically challenging and occasionally competitive, and to speak out and defend their opinions in groups (Kerr, 1997). Both girls and boys may need support from their families, counselors, and mentors if they deviate from the stereotyped gender roles of their communities (Kerr & Nicpon, 2003). For more information on gender equity, go to **http://www.sadker.org/index.htm**.

> Gifted girls must be identified, supported, and challenged, particularly in the middle-school years.

● *Gifted Students with Disabilities*   As early as 1942, Hollingworth saw the possibility that disabilities could coexist with giftedness. But only recently have the needs of these "twice exceptional" students been addressed.

June Maker (1977) was among the first to suggest that options should be provided in schools for highly able students who also had learning disabilities,

> Some gifted students have learning disabilities, sensory impairments, or motor limitations.

The development of future scientists depends on opportunities to experience the fun of scientific inquiry. (© LWA-Dann Tardif/CORBIS)

sensory impairments, or physical disabilities. But she warned that her work was merely a beginning, serving to "identify issues and raise questions to a greater degree than it solves or answers them" (p. xi).

Students with learning disabilities are a unique group. Sally Reis and her colleagues (Reis, Neu, & McGuire, 1997; Reis, McGuire, & Neu, 2000) conducted in-depth interviews with twelve young adults who were successful in college while receiving support services for their identified learning disabilities. All had been tested earlier in their schooling and were found to have high IQs. The researchers found that these students uniformly reported negative experiences in elementary and secondary school. Their learning disabilities tended to be identified relatively late in their schooling, despite problems that had appeared early; they reported negative interactions with teachers, some of whom told the students they were lazy and could achieve if they worked harder; and they felt isolated from peers and unaccepted by them. But because these students developed compensation strategies, had parental support, and participated in a university learning disability program, they succeeded despite their early negative experiences (see the accompanying Teaching Strategies box entitled, "Compensation Strategies Used by Gifted Students with Learning Disabilities"). Reis and her colleagues suggest that it was the combination of their high abilities and disabilities that set them up for problems in school, such as the late referrals to special education and poor relationships with teachers.

> **High-ability students with learning disabilities can succeed in college with the right supports.**

These students had other advantages and a secret weapon:

> Each person in this study had a mother who devoted herself to using different strategies to help her child succeed. This assistance was given regardless of whether the mother worked outside of the home and regardless of how many other children were in the family. One may ask, therefore, what happens to children who do not have a similar source of support? (Reis, Neu, & McGuire, 1997, p. 477)

Table 13.3 describes some of the factors that may make it difficult to identify students with learning disabilities as gifted.

There is some concern that students who are gifted might inadvertently be identified as attention deficit-disordered because of the behaviors they display when bored (Willard-Holt, 1999). Children with attention deficit disorder demonstrate the same inattentive behaviors consistently across situations; the behavior of students who are gifted and bored would vary, depending on how engaged in the material the student found him- or herself. Both sets of characteristics *can* exist in the same person, however (Baum & Olenchak, 2002), making the provision of appropriate services all the more complex.

Students with disabilities who are gifted may show their abilities in unusual ways and may need unconventional assessment techniques because traditional assessments are not appropriate. In the end, underlying all approaches to locating and serving gifted children with disabilities is a need to change society's attitudes and perceptions. There remains a need for each of us to see that *capability* is more important than *disability*.

> **Some gifted students do not achieve at the level of their potential.**

● *Underachieving Gifted Students*   Think of someone you knew in school who was always told by teachers, "You're a smart kid; I know you could do better if you wanted to." Usually, this type of student frustrates teachers and parents, for they see a lot of talent going to waste. The technical term applied to students whose aptitude is high but whose performance is low (or mediocre) is

Teaching Strategies & Accommodations

Compensation Strategies Used by Gifted Students with Learning Disabilities

Students who had high-ability levels and also had learning disabilities found that the following strategies and supports helped them succeed in college work:

Strategy	Components
Study and performance strategies	Notetaking
	Test-taking preparation
	Time management
	Monitoring daily, weekly, and monthly assignments and activities
	Using weekly and monthly organizers to maximize use of time; chunking assignments into workable parts
	Library skills
	Written expression
	Reading
	Mathematical processing
Cognitive/ learning strategies	Memory strategies such as mnemonics and rehearsal using flash cards
	Chunking information into smaller units for mastery
Compensation supports	Word processing
	Use of computers
	Books on tape

These students also had other supports and strengths:

Parental Support

- Parents, particularly mothers, were energetic advocates for their children.
- The students in the university learning disabilities program cited help with study skills, a network of support, and a consistent program director as important components of the program.

Self-Perceived Strength and Future Aspirations

- Students had a strong work ethic and the conviction that they could succeed.

Sources: S. M. Reis, T. W. Neu, & J. M. McGuire (1997). Case studies of high-ability students with learning disabilities who have achieved. *Exceptional Children 63*(4), 463–479, and S. M. Reis, J. M. McGuire, & T. W. Neu (2000). Compensation strategies used by high-ability students with learning disabilities who succeed in college. *Gifted Child Quarterly 44*(2), 123–134.

gifted underachiever, but the less technical terms are the ones that sting—terms like *lazy*, *unmotivated*, or *disorganized*. Whatever you call these students, one thing is certain: When *you* get one in *your* classroom, you'll wish there was some magic elixir available that would cause this "underachievement" to disappear.

What causes this disheartening underachievement? Hollingworth (1942) believed that students with an IQ of 140 spend half of each school day in activities that are unchallenging and monotonous, and the result is often a poor attitude toward school ("school is boring") or even misbehavior, as shown by the comment of this 12-year-old girl: "I learned I was gifted in third grade. I would finish my work early and disturb others because I had nothing to do" (Delisle,

Intellectually gifted students who dislike school may not develop their talents.

Table 13.3 Giftedness and Learning Disabilities

Common Attributes of Giftedness

- Motivation
- Problem-solving ability
- Well-developed memory
- Insight
- Imagination–creativity
- Advanced ability to deal with symbol systems

- Advanced interests
- Communication skills
- Inquiry
- Reasoning
- Sense of humor

Characteristics of Gifted Students with Learning Disabilities

Characteristics that hamper identification as gifted:

- Frustration with inability to master certain academic skills
- Learned helplessness
- General lack of motivation
- Disruptive classroom behavior
- Demonstration of poor listening and concentration skills
- Absence of social skills with some peers
- Deficiency in tasks emphasizing memory and perceptual abilities

- Lack of organizational skills
- Failure to complete assignments
- Supersensitivity
- Perfectionism
- Low self-esteem
- Unrealistic self-expectations

Characteristic strengths:

- Advanced vocabulary use
- High levels of creativity
- Specific aptitude (artistic, musical, or mechanical)
- Ability to think of divergent ideas and solutions
- Task commitment

- Exceptional analytic abilities
- Advanced problem-solving skills
- Wide variety of interests
- Good memory
- Spatial abilities

Sources: Adapted from M. M. Frasier & A. H. Passow (1994). *Towards a new paradigm for identifying talent potential.* Storrs, CT: University of Connecticut, the National Research Center on the Gifted and Talented. Also adapted from S. M. Reis, T. W. Neu, & J. M. McGuire (1995). *Talent in two places: Case studies of high ability students with learning disabilities who have achieved.* Storrs, CT: University of Connecticut, the National Research Center on the Gifted and Talented.

1984, p. 11). Family, cultural, and peer issues may contribute to underachievement as well when education is not highly valued (Reis & McCoach, 2000). Boys may be somewhat more likely than girls to "disengage" from both leadership and academic activities in school (Kerr & Nicpon, 2003).

Methods of modifying school curriculum and structure for students with gifts and talents are discussed later in this chapter. What is important to note here is the intimate link between school achievement and school attitude; for if intellectually able students perceive school as drudgery, not stimulating, or irrelevant, it is unlikely that they will develop their talents fully (Whitmore, 1980).

Joanne Whitmore (1980) has produced the definitive work on gifted underachievers, and her approach combines curricular changes (focusing on a child's strengths and interests), family involvement (parent conferences and "partnership" in rewarding even small improvements in performance), and self-concept education (based on the premise that students who feel good about themselves will choose to achieve).

Others have suggested more mechanistic solutions—like behavioral contracts—and more coercive measures—like punishment (Rimm, 1986). These efforts, though possibly successful in the short term, tend to be less effective than the approaches described by Whitmore. Reis and McCoach (2000) point out that none of the suggested interventions has been well-researched, but it is likely that a combination of curricular modifications, counseling, and self-regulation training will be most effective.

However, there is one point on which all researchers agree: The earlier the problem of underachievement is detected and addressed, the more hopeful is the prognosis for positive change. The problem of underachieving behaviors will not be easy to solve, but if you look toward making the gifted child's school time relevant, interesting, and intellectually stimulating, chances are good that the student's response will be positive.

> When underachievement is detected early, the prognosis for positive change is good.

● **Culturally Diverse Gifted Students**   Gifts and talents exist in children of every race, culture, and socioeconomic group. However, school districts have often been criticized for not looking hard enough to find talents in children who may not represent the majority culture or its values. Indeed, African American students are overrepresented in all categories of special education except for one, gifted education, where they are significantly underrepresented (Daniels, 2002; Baldwin & Vialle, 1999). Disproportionate representation occurs for children from other ethnic minority groups as well (Coleman, 2003). Figure 13.4 depicts the over and underrepresentation of gifted students from traditional minority groups in programs for gifted students. So, although every thinking person agrees that one's skin color and primary language are not intrinsic limitations to the expression of one's talents, many gifted programs are filled with students from the white, middle-class culture of our population.

> Using non-test-based indicators, children with gifts and talents can be found in every race, culture, and socioeconomic group.

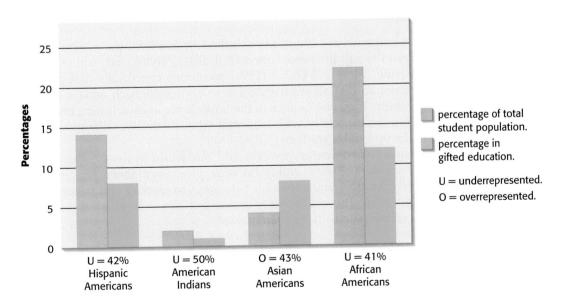

Figure 13.4

Representation of Students from Diverse Groups in Gifted Education Programs

Source: Adapted from Donna Y. Ford (2003). Equity and excellence: Culturally diverse students in gifted education. In N. Colangelo & G. A. Davis (Eds.). *Handbook of gifted education* (3rd ed., p. 507, Table 39.1), Boston: Allyn and Bacon.

Cohen (1990) saw this as a problem related to *misuse* and *nonuse*: misuse of assessment instruments (like IQ tests) that were normed on middle-class students with middle-class experiences and nonuse of alternative methods of non-test-based indicators of giftedness—like nominations from parents or community leaders or a portfolio of a student's work samples that indicate superior performance. Paul Torrance (1969), ever conscious of the fact that different cultures have different standards of appropriate behavior, reminded us to look for qualities such as *expressive speech, enjoyment and leadership in group-based activities,* and *the ability to improvise with commonplace materials and objects* as indicators of giftedness in culturally diverse groups.

Identifying gifted children from diverse cultural backgrounds has become a major goal of professionals involved in gifted child education (Clark, 2002). The National Research Council recently recommended that research be conducted on early identification and intervention of advanced performance in children from minority backgrounds (Donovan & Cross, 2002). Baldwin notes that this change will involve "accepting new paradigms." Among the new assumptions we must embrace, according to Baldwin (2002), are:

- Giftedness can be expressed through a variety of behaviors and the expression of giftedness in one dimension is just as important as giftedness expressed in another.

- Intelligence is a broad concept that goes beyond language and logic to encompass a wide range of human abilities.

- Carefully planned subjective assessment techniques can be used effectively along with objective measures.

- Giftedness in any area can be a clue to the presence of potential giftedness in another.

- All cultures have individuals who exhibit behaviors that are indicative of giftedness.

Once the students are identified as gifted or talented, the program itself must be tailored to suit the needs, interests, learning styles, and cultural values of its participants. Ford and Harris (1999) encourage approaches that promote multiculturalism so that all students come to appreciate each other's cultures and backgrounds. They also believe in the importance of establishing links with the child's family, especially with someone who is familiar with the cultural heritage of the program's students.

As the twenty-first century evolves and our world becomes even smaller through the wonders of travel and technology, program planners for gifted students, and *all* educators, must look for new ways to identify and foster the talents of each child. The challenge is great, but the individual and societal benefits, should we succeed, are even greater.

Most highly gifted children are placed in general education classrooms, which often don't meet their needs.

● *Highly Gifted Students*   Just as educators who work with students with developmental disabilities classify disabilities by level of severity—mild, severe, or profound, for example—gifted child educators sometimes do the same thing regarding the label of gifted. Often, an IQ score is used to define a population that has come to be called the **highly gifted**. Terman and Merrill (1973) and Whitmore (1980) use an IQ score of 140 to classify a child as highly gifted, while McGuffog, Feiring, and Lewis (1987) call an IQ of 164 "extremely gifted." And Hollingworth (1942), in an early and classic study, used an IQ of 180 as the point at which giftedness is manifest in an extreme form.

A regular classroom placement for a child whose intellect surpasses that of 99.99 percent of his or her classmates can pose problems. Yet Gaunt (1989) found that most highly gifted children are placed in regular school classes, and even though many of these students are involved in part-time enrichment programs, the majority of their time is spent in classes that take their exceptional intelligence into account only minimally (Kearney, 1988).

Gallagher (2000) believes that highly gifted students (who may constitute less than 1 percent of the total student population) need something different from other very capable students and suggests the following:

- These students should be the instructional responsibility of the specialist in gifted education rather than the general education teacher.
- Highly gifted students need more individual attention, perhaps through tutoring, acceleration, or individualized studies and projects.

> Highly gifted students make up less than 1 percent of the school-aged population.

The problems and solutions involving highly gifted students are complex and varied, but the highly gifted child has been receiving increasing attention over the past years. Advocates for this population of students point out that even the best school program that includes opportunities for **academic enrichment** (broadening the experience base of the students without changing the instructional objectives) and acceleration may fall far short of meeting the needs of highly gifted children. **Radical acceleration** (for example, skipping several grades), early entrance to college (some preteen students have attended university full time), and home schooling are some options that have been used effectively to meet the needs of this population. (See the Closer Look box entitled "The EEPsters" on page 501.)

Teaching Strategies and Accommodations

Early Intervention

Children are often not formally identified as gifted or talented until sometime during their school career, usually in third or fourth grade. Because of particular advanced behaviors, though, many gifted young children show signs of high potential before they enter the classroom, and the people who identify these talents are often the child's parents.

Disagreement exists regarding the appropriateness of early identification of gifts and talents. On the one hand, some educators believe that it is imperative to identify and challenge talents at the youngest age possible. Eby and Smutny (1990) argue that such identification helps not only the child but also the child's caregivers, for if teachers, child-care workers, and parents are informed of a young child's strengths, they will be better able to provide academic and creative options that match those strengths. Joanne Whitmore (1980), in her classic study of underachieving gifted students, found that patterns of underachievement were developed during the primary school years, yet intervention seldom occurred until the intermediate grades. This unwillingness to address problems as they emerge means that much remediation will have to be done later, whereas preventive measures could have been less extreme yet equally effective.

On the other hand, critics of early identification of gifts and talents point to the "superbaby syndrome" as a problem that cannot be ignored. Parents who replace their gifted children's toys and free play with flash cards and classical concerts are, according to the critics, misguided in their attempts to challenge their children. Eby and Smutny (1990), in critiquing these efforts, state that such

> Some professionals are concerned that early identification of gifts and talents creates the "superbaby syndrome."

"programs impose adult agendas on their young participants and forget that children learn best through experience" (p. 158).

The label of "gifted" tells us little about a child's specific unique talents. As parents and teachers work together to match a child's needs with appropriate services, they must keep in mind that the child's individual physical, emotional, and intellectual needs must be considered in order to provide a healthy balance of rigor and fun.

Identification and Assessment: The Teacher's Role

It was once considered easy to identify gifted students. An individual intelligence test on which a student scored 130 or higher qualified him or her as intellectually gifted. A student who scored 126 was summarily excluded.

Today, as the validity of standardized intelligence test scores has become more suspect, especially for students from minority cultures, and as educators and parents have become more involved in the assessment of exceptional children, best practices call for multiple measures to be used to identify giftedness in students (Delisle, 2000). Most often, classroom teachers will be asked to supplement information about a child through the use of behavioral checklists. These checklists come in many varieties, but they generally require the teacher to rate a child on a scale of 1 to 4 (1 = seldom; 4 = always) on how often he or she observes behaviors such as these:

> Today there is a greater likelihood that multiple measures will be used to identify giftedness.

- Learns rapidly, easily, efficiently
- Prefers to work alone
- Has a vocabulary above that of classmates
- Displays curiosity and imagination
- Goes beyond the minimum required with assignments
- Follows through on tasks
- Is original in oral and written expression

Essentially, teachers are being asked to select children who "go to school well" and whom teachers love to have in their classes. Yet if teachers are asked to consider only positive student traits and behaviors, they may not identify some gifted children who could surely benefit from advanced instruction. Some researchers have cautioned against teacher referral as the method of identifying gifted students, for two reasons:

1. Teacher judgments may be influenced if they hold low expectations for children from culturally and linguistically diverse learners.
2. Teachers may not recognize characteristics of giftedness when exhibited in the nontraditional behaviors of minority children.

While some scholars cite these as reasons for underrepresentation of students from culturally and linguistically diverse backgrounds in programs for gifted students, Donovan and Cross (2002) remind us that research evidence on teacher bias is inconclusive. As we have emphasized, teachers must take care to look for manifestations of gifted behavior in all children.

Consider your own education. Were you ever in a class where you felt that your time was being wasted or your talents ignored? Perhaps it was a class that was repetitive to you, or one that provided few challenges or little outlet for creative expression. Whatever the reason for your dissatisfaction, do you recall how you acted in that class? It's unlikely that you led an animated discussion or that you were overly eager to answer the teacher's easy questions. In fact, if someone were to observe you in that class, he or she might find that you appeared bored, off-task, or looking for excitement in all the wrong places (like talking to your friends or passing notes). These would hardly seem to be behavioral indicators of giftedness but, in fact, they might be exactly that.

The point is this: When you, as a teacher, are asked to select children for gifted program services, remember that some indicators of giftedness in children are those very behaviors that teachers usually find distasteful—boredom, misbehavior, even incomplete assignments on easy tasks or worksheets. This is not to say that all gifted children display negative behaviors in class, but it is a reminder to you that some gifts are wrapped in packages (that is, "behaviors") that are not so pretty. Be aware of this possibility when you question why a seemingly bright child is responding negatively to a class assignment or lecture.

> Some indicators of giftedness are behaviors that teachers find irritating.

Renzulli and Reis (2003) described two kinds of giftedness: *Schoolhouse giftedness*, which can be identified through standardized tests as well as some of the techniques we have described, and *creative-productive giftedness*, which may result in "the development of original material and products that are purposefully designed to have an impact on one or more target audiences" (p. 185). Ellen Winner (2000b) uses the term "big-C creativity"—the type of work that changes the way people think, or alters whole domains of thought (think of Darwin or Freud, for example). Creativity and potential for innovation are much harder to recognize, but teachers should be open to ways in which those gifts might show themselves in children.

The identification of gifted children is a complex, ongoing process, and it sometimes appears that the main goal is not to locate talents in children but to find ways to exclude them from gifted program services. (In most states, very little funding is available for gifted programs. Often districts simply cannot afford to provide services to all the students who might be identified under a broad definition of giftedness.) However, with the insights that can be provided by using a variety of methods of identification of giftedness, and students' prior projects or portfolios as evidence of talent, we will do a better job of locating the variety of abilities that students display both inside and outside of school.

Placement Alternatives

The majority of students who are gifted and talented are served in the general education classroom—both those who have been identified and those who have not. Even though elementary and secondary classroom teachers can provide rich intellectual stimulation for gifted students, many school districts offer other options that take place outside of a regular classroom setting. Probably the most common service delivery model is **enrichment**. According to Barbara Clark (2002), "Enrichment can refer to adding disciplines or areas of learning not normally found in the regular curriculum, using more difficult or in-depth material to enhance the core curriculum, or enhancing the teaching strategies used to present instruction" (p. 264). Typically, students identified as gifted participate in pullout or afterschool enrichment activities. Clark believes that enrichment is the least desirable option for the gifted student, since it involves the least change in learning opportunities.

> Enrichment activities supplement the core curriculum for students identified as gifted.

Some school districts have special schools or self-contained classes for students who are gifted and talented. In other locales, a resource room model is preferred. Just as there are a variety of ways to serve students with gifts and talents within a classroom setting, there are multiple options for meeting the needs of these students in other settings. See Figure 13.5 for an overview of the models. Some of the more popular out-of-class methods are reviewed here.

Placement Options

The general education classroom	The general education classroom with resource room	Self-contained classes on general education campuses	Special schools
Possible teaching arrangements: • No special attention • Clustering gifted students together • Differentiated instruction by the general education teacher	Differentiated content for gifted students in the resource room	All content designed for gifted students	All content designed for gifted/talented students. Examples: • Magnet schools • State-sponsored residential schools • Visual and performing arts academies

Figure 13.5

Placement Options for Gifted and Talented Students

A Closer Look   Where Budding Geniuses Can Blossom

A private school for children with exceptionally high IQs nurtures an unfettered, unapologetic appetite for knowledge. Experiments in terminal velocity, anyone?

At 10 a.m. on a Wednesday morning, the 5-year-olds were writing. Not, mind you, their ABCs, as most kindergartners would be doing. No, these tots were composing sentences, an entire paragraph—and with few errant periods or funny spellings. Their topic: "What I Would Do if I Were President."

In another room, the 11-year-olds were doing math. Not long division, not multiplication of fractions, but algebraic equations. X intercept, Y axis, eyes gleaming at the very mention. Manipulating fancy graphing calculators, these kids were not merely paying attention to the lesson, they were absorbed in it.

In the science lab, the 13-year-olds were furiously swaddling eggs in typing paper, masking tape and paper clips, which they soon would launch from the roof of a nearby building. They were conducting a physics experiment in terminal velocity—splat rate, for you dimwits out there. By the time these teens enter high school, they'll be years ahead of the crowd in physics and chemistry.

Extracurricular reading? Of course, plenty of it. But forget Harry Potter. Try "The Nothing That Is: A Natural History of Zero."

"It was brilliant," said Nicholas Sofroniew, the 13-year-old who gobbled up math teacher Robert Kaplan's weighty work of nonfiction in his free time.

If you've guessed that we're inside a school for geniuses, you are partially correct. To be labeled gifted, an IQ of 132 will do, but that still isn't enough to win passage through the black iron gate of the Mirman School in Bel-Air.

Mirman, a private school founded in 1962, is one of a handful in the country to cater to the tip-top of the intelligence scale: Only the highly gifted—children with an IQ of 145 and above—may apply.

Such exclusivity comes at a price. First of all, there's tuition—more than $12,000 a year for most of the 355 students (about 10 percent are on scholarship). The school, which serves youngsters ages 5 to 14, admits only about 40 new students a year, most of them at the earliest level.

Then there is the social fallout. Some parents feel that Mirman admission gives them bragging rights, a colossal turnoff for other parents who may already feel that schools for geniuses are undemocratic.

Mirman may be Egghead Central, but not in any stereotypical way. The students don't wear ink-smeared pocket protectors and they "don't all have big round glasses or oversized heads," says Norman Mirman, the octogenarian former Los An-

● *Resource Rooms*   The most popular option at the elementary school level may be the resource room approach. Similar in design and structure to such programs for children with disabilities, the gifted education resource room allows gifted students to work together. Often, cross-age grouping is used, and it is not unusual to see third-grade students working alongside fifth-grade students. However, some consequences of resource rooms are undesirable, as this 10-year-old girl expresses:

> Last year I wasn't at school one day a week (my gifted program was in another school), so I didn't finish all my classwork. I would have finished, but my teacher wouldn't let me bring anything home as homework. When my mother asked her about my grade, the teacher said that "if I was smart enough to go to another school I should be smart enough to keep up with my own classwork." (Delisle, 1984, p. 75)

geles city schoolteacher who founded the school with his wife, Beverly.

Socially and emotionally, the students, most of them Anglo, generally act their ages. Eight-year-olds still get in trouble for throwing sand—even the one who left at age 9 to attend Loyola University in Chicago. Eleven-year-olds study high school Spanish, but sometimes they forget their homework and cry.

In other ways, though, Mirman clearly is beyond the norm. It has no grades per se, just flexible age groups that allow students to learn at their own accelerated pace, studying material typically tackled by youngsters three to five years older. Here, if a 6-year-old, for instance, is especially talented in math, she's not stuck with others of her age; she can move up to an older class for part of the school day. By the time students finish Mirman, they have covered at least a ninth-grade curriculum and some far more. Over the years, about half a dozen prodigies have gone straight to college—a leap frowned on by Mirman but often pushed by parents.

Eight decades after influential psychologist Lewis Terman warned against indifference to the special needs of budding geniuses, the general attitude hasn't changed: Why invest in the high-IQ child who'll learn fine wherever he is? It's the struggling masses who need the help. "The argument is, if we just have limited resources, why do we help the kids who don't need help? But that assumes they don't need help," said Ellen Winner, a Boston College psychology professor and author of the 1996 book *Gifted Children: Myths and Realities.* "They need education that is challenging but don't often get it," Winner noted. "These children are miserable in school when they are forced to work way below their level."

Take 10-year-old Sydney Ember. At the private San Fernando Valley school she attended until this year, she was the know-it-all who stuck her hand in the air every time the teacher asked a question. It got to the point that teachers told her, "Stop raising your hand, we know you know the answer." One teacher didn't understand why she begged for more homework, suggesting she should be happy that she had more time for TV.

Now, Sydney "comes home every day happy," said her mother, Laurie Ember. Sydney, whose 5-year-old sister, Jamie, also attends Mirman, has only one complaint: "Why didn't I come here sooner?"

Source: Excerpted from Elaine Woo (2000). Where budding geniuses can blossom. *Los Angeles Times*, November 22, 2000, Living Section, pp. 1 and 3.

The resource room is a part-time solution to the full-time challenge of educating gifted students.

"Makeup work"—needing to complete worksheets and text assignments in addition to the work in the gifted program—can cause students stress and prompt them to question the benefits of their resource room participation. The conscientious classroom teacher, by testing to determine what the student already knows and using curriculum telescoping (see page 504), can relieve many of these problems.

Another problem occurs when the classroom teacher relinquishes responsibility for educating gifted students by assuming that "they're getting all they need in the resource room." Teachers must remember that the resource room presents only a part-time solution to the full-time challenge of educating gifted students (Cox, Daniel, & Boston, 1985). The resource room works best when its teachers communicate frequently with regular classroom teachers, and both work together to benefit gifted students.

A Closer Look Norah Jones

Early in 2003, Los Angeles Times *music critic Robert Hilburn spoke with Grammy-award-winning singer Norah Jones. He was interested in the question of whether Jones' musical talents were something she was born with (her father is Indian sitar master Ravi Shankar; her mother Sue Jones, a concert producer and music enthusiast), or whether they were formed by nurturing and experiences. Hilburn's question: Is talent born or made? This question is important for teachers as well. Here are some excerpts from Hilburn's article:*

Norah Jones enjoys the recognition of her talent as she holds her five 2003 Grammy awards. (© PA/Topham/The Image Works)

Numerous people, from her mom to teachers in Texas, talked about watching [Norah's] talent blossom and helping steer her to various arts programs in high school and college. By the time Jones got to Blue Note Records, she had been well schooled, with more than 1,000 hours of piano lessons. But—and this is where the mystery comes in—the pop vocal sensation never had a single singing lesson.

"Some people have the touch of God on their head," [says Bruce Lundvall, the head of Blue Note Records]. "They're born with a certain gift, but what gives them taste? That's the mystery."

Jones' path to a pop career was far from straight. She started piano lessons around 6 or 7, but she was no child prodigy. She was, she says, a lazy student who gave up piano for several years. If others didn't recognize her talent and help mentor her, she might have easily given up music.

The 5-foot-1 Jones does come with great musical genes. Jones' mom encouraged the youngster, but she wasn't a controlling "stage mother." Looking back at Norah's early years, she says, "Norah did so many other things, painting, drawing. Everything pretty much came easy for her, especially the singing. I just let her do her own thing. She always had a sense of the songs that were good for her voice."

● *Self-Contained and Homogeneously Grouped Classes*   Often the option of choice a generation ago, the self-contained gifted classroom is still used today, but less frequently. In this type of class, gifted students are identified and placed together for instruction. This placement limits participation to a select group of gifted children—enough to fill one classroom—while denying gifted program services to those students who may have talents only in particular areas.

> The self-contained gifted education classroom denies program services to students who may have talents only in one area.

● *Special Schools*   Some schools are exclusively designed for gifted/talented students. Magnet schools, for example, may be designed to place special emphasis on science, the arts, or some other content area and to attract students with interests or talents in that specific area. (See the Closer Look box entitled, "Where Budding Geniuses Can Blossom" for a description of a private school for gifted children.)

When Jones expressed an interest in the piano, her mom bought one and arranged for classical lessons from Renetta Frisque, who remembers the quiet young girl with the same words you hear over and over from people who knew her: "She had a feeling for the notes that you can't teach."

But Norah got bored with the lessons after a few years and didn't resume studying until around the seventh grade, when she studied jazz piano with Julie Bonk, who noticed that the teenager sometimes liked to sing along as she played. Bonk was so impressed she helped Jones get into the same magnet arts school in the Dallas area that Erykah Badu had attended, and later into Interlochen, the prestigious summer arts camp in Michigan.

"She had a sense of phrasing and style and quality that just seemed to be well beyond her years," recalls Kent Ellingson, her piano teacher at the Booker T. Washington School for the Performing Arts and Visual Arts in Dallas. "She was ready for a professional career from the moment I met her."

Two years into studying piano and theory in the jazz program at the University of North Texas outside Dallas, Jones saw her future when some New York musicians visited the campus and told her about the exciting underground jazz scene there. One of them was Jesse Harris, who wrote "Don't Know Why." Much to her mother's chagrin, Jones quit college and headed to Manhattan, where she began focusing more on singing than piano because it was easier to get singing gigs.

Hilburn's conversation with Jones draws to a close:

Near the end of the two-hour dinner, Jones pauses when asked whether she thinks talent is born or made. She stares out the window at the traces of snow on the ground as she thinks about the question.

"I was lucky to tap into it early and be exposed to a lot of great music around the house. If I didn't have the upbringing I had with my mom and a lot of wonderful teachers, it might not have amounted to anything, genes or no genes."

Source: Excerpted from Robert Hilburn (2003). A sweet mystery; Norah Jones' artistry stands out in a world of prefab pop. Where'd it come from? *Los Angeles Times*, January 26, 2003.

State-sponsored residential schools for gifted and talented students have increased in popularity.

State-sponsored residential schools, often called "governor's schools" because they are established by an individual state's legislature and governor, have continued to increase in popularity in recent years. Highly competitive, these schools seek nominations from across the state's high schools for unusually talented juniors and seniors who will spend up to two years in the residential setting. The first governor's schools focused almost exclusively on math and science, but now many states have incorporated the arts and humanities into their stringent curricula.

Some urban school districts have developed special high schools for talented students in the visual and performing arts. Students often go through competitive auditions in order to enter these schools. These special "academies" focus on *making* art—painting, dancing, instrumental and vocal music. Many well-known performers (see the Closer Look box entitled, "Norah Jones" for one such example) have come out of such settings to flourish in the entertainment business; other students go on to study their discipline in college.

In mentorships, secondary students learn specific skills, trades, or crafts from community members.

● ***Other Options***   Not all educational options for gifted students take place within the school building or, for that matter, within the school year. **Mentorships**, during which time secondary students work with a community member to learn, firsthand, a specific skill, trade, or craft, are becoming increasingly common. Mentors can assume the interlocking roles of teacher, expert, guide, advisor, friend, and role model for the gifted/talented student (Clasen & Clasen, 2003). Research on the effectiveness of mentorships shows the very positive results of these community-school interactions, since participating students learn from the mentor's skill and expertise, receive valued and substantive praise and encouragement, and have as a role model a person who loves his or her field of study as much as the student does (Torrance, 1984).

Summer and weekend programs are also offered for gifted students at many colleges and universities. Purdue University's Super Saturday Program,

You don't have to be gifted to succeed in a course in advanced placement calculus ... but it helps! (© Elizabeth Crews/The Image Works)

for example, serves children from preschool through high school with a variety of accelerated and enrichment classes each semester (Feldhusen, 1991). The Purdue model has been replicated across the country.

Summer programs can be either day programs or residential in nature, depending on the student's age. In Ohio, each of the thirteen state universities and several private colleges offer one- to three-week "summer institutes" that are financially supported by the state. Michigan and Iowa also offer extensive summer programs for gifted students.

In addition, early entrance to college or dual enrollment programs allow gifted secondary-school students to progress through high school and college at a more rapid pace. (See the Closer Look box entitled, "The EEPsters" for further discussion of this.) In high schools, students enrolled in advanced placement

> With summer and weekend programs gifted children remain with their peers; in other programs they progress rapidly through high school and college.

A Closer Look — The EEPsters

The Early Entrance Program (EEP) at California State University, Los Angeles, provides highly gifted young people the opportunity to enter college as young as 11 years old. (The average entering age is currently 13.5 years.) These "EEPsters" as they are affectionately known on campus, enroll in the General Education Honors Program, which provides select faculty and specially designed small classes with other University Honors students. They typically earn their degrees in 4–5 years.

The Early Entrance Program admissions procedures favor students with the following qualifications:

- One who is not yet in the tenth grade unless accelerated by one or more grades, and is not yet over 16 years of age.
- One who consistently scores in the very top ranges on standardized ability and achievement tests.
- One who has a demonstrated ability to perform at an outstanding level in school.
- One whose educational needs will not be met in the school he/she is presently attending or would be attending.

The student likely to be admitted to the EEP is one who:

- Demonstrates a strong desire to attempt a challenging educational program.

- Possesses adequate maturity for self-motivation and appropriate behavior on a college campus, including appropriate verbal skills and critical thinking abilities.
- Has the support of the parents to undertake a program of radical educational acceleration.
- Has a history of advanced intellectual and academic achievement.
- Performs at a level indicating a readiness for college level work on the Washington Pre-College Test and University entrance exams for specific disciplines.

This kind of acceleration is unusual, and it is not for every bright student, but the program has had a good measure of success since its inception in 1982. Many EEP graduates have gone on to receive M.D., Ph.D., and law degrees at the country's most selective universities. Ryan Montgomery, an EEP graduate at 17, now works at the Jet Propulsion Lab on the Mars Rover team. Two physician graduates of the program recently married; Richard Maddox, Program Director, hailed it as "the first EEP wedding." He emphasized the importance of the support system available to the 100 students enrolled. "We create a high school within the university for them—they just take college classes, and experience little of the boring repetition of material they would have in a regular high school." So if you are sitting next to a young teenager in class—be respectful!

courses may earn up to a year's worth of transferable college credit by taking rigorous courses and advanced placement tests, generally in their junior and senior years. Also, many colleges have an "honors college" component, which offers rigorous and often accelerated courses to highly able students. Some colleges encourage full-time enrollment by students as young as 15. Simon's Rock in Great Barrington, Massachusetts (affiliated with Bard College), has been doing this for over twenty-five years, and Mary Baldwin College in Staunton, Virginia, has a similar program, called PEG (Program for the Exceptionally Gifted), which is open only to young women; these students generally attain both a high-school diploma and a college degree within five years.

Program Models

Acceleration and enrichment options for gifted students, as we have seen, have existed for generations. But only within the past fifteen years have organizational models been developed. These models structure the activities in which gifted children participate to provide a "skeleton" format for teachers and gifted program planners.

- ● **The Enrichment Triad Model (Grades 4–6)**   The **Enrichment Triad Model** (ETM) (Renzulli, 1977) is based on the following premises:

  - Some types of academic and creative enrichment are good for all children.
  - Students must master certain "process skills" (such as research skills and creative problem solving) if they are to master curriculum content.
  - Students should investigate problems of their own interest, rather than topics chosen by teachers, and they should share the results of their work with audiences outside of their school.

  The ETM builds in the teaching strategies from gifted education for a wider group of students, and allows children to express their talents to others in visible ways.

- ● **Schoolwide Models**   With so many interesting and innovative teaching strategies and models designed for students identified as gifted and talented, why not use them to benefit all children? Two school reform efforts attempt to do just that. The **Accelerated Schools Project** (Levin, 1996) operates on the principle that every child is a gifted child (Hopfenberg, Levin et al., 1993). According to Levin,

  > All students are treated as gifted and talented students, because the gifts and talents of each child are sought out and recognized. Such strengths are used as a basis for providing enrichment and acceleration. As soon as one recognizes that all students have strengths and weaknesses, a simple stratification of students no longer makes sense. Strengths include not only the various areas of intelligence identified by Gardner (1983), but also areas of interest, curiosity, motivation, and knowledge that grow out of the culture, experiences, and personalities of all children. (1996, p. 17)

Accelerated schools operate with the philosophy that building on the strengths of each student is more successful than identifying and remediating weaknesses. For more information, visit the Accelerated Schools website at **http://www.acceleratedschools.net**.

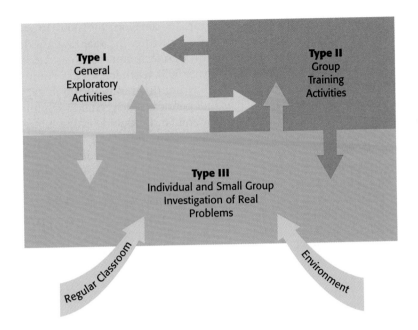

Figure 13.6

The Schoolwide Enrichment Model

Source: From J. S. Renzulli, & S. M. Reis (2003). The Schoolwide Enrichment Model: Developing creative and productive giftedness. In Nicholas Colangelo and Gary Davis (Eds.), *Handbook of gifted education* (3rd ed., pp. 184–203). Published by Allyn and Bacon, Boston, MA. Copyright © 2003 by Pearson Education. Reprinted by permission of the publisher.

Renzulli's **Schoolwide Enrichment Model** was originally developed for gifted education programs just as the ETM was (1977; see above). It is now being used on a schoolwide basis to improve the creative productivity and academic achievement of *all* students (Renzulli & Reis, 2003). The model serves as a framework for organizational and curricular changes and rests on specific curriculum modification techniques, enrichment learning and teaching, and the recognition and development of student talents. See Figure 13.6 for a graphic description of this model. For more information, visit the website for National Research Center for the Gifted and Talented at **http://www.ucc.uconn.edu/~wwwgt/nrcgt.html**.

Schoolwide enrichment models help teachers differentiate the curriculum for all students.

Curriculum Modifications in the General Education Classroom

Much of what is written about curriculum and instruction for highly able students is based on the belief that programming should be *differentiated* for gifted learners. **Differentiation** is the adaptation of educational programs and teaching methods to meet the unique needs of gifted learners. Differentiation can involve modifications in *content*, by putting more depth in the curriculum; *process*, by using a variety of methods and materials; *products, classroom environment*, and *teacher behavior* (Renzulli, 1997, in Dinnocenti, 1998). For teachers to individualize their teaching for gifted students, they must have models of differentiation, such as those prepared by van Tassel-Baska in science (1997) and language arts (1999) or Stepien and Gallagher (1997) in social studies. A commitment to differentiating learning for students who are gifted and talented takes time, energy, and some inspiration, especially for those middle- and high-school teachers who see large numbers of students at all ability levels throughout the day. Read Joyce van Tassel-Baska on differentiating the language arts at **http://www.ericec.org/digests/e640.html**.

Differentiated instruction can involve modifications in content, process, products, classroom environment, and teacher behavior.

Every classroom teacher has (or can develop) the skills to work with gifted students within a regular classroom structure. By adapting, modifying, and differentiating the basic curriculum through techniques such as curriculum telescoping and content acceleration (see page 505), teachers can determine when students have mastered particular skills, allowing them to move on to explore new ideas. Effective use of options such as independent study, cluster grouping, and cooperative learning can help satisfy students' individual learning interests. Finally, the appropriate use of higher-level thinking strategies and creative thinking skills can benefit *all* students, including those who are highly able. We'll discuss each of these methods in further detail.

Curriculum telescoping allows students to explore new concepts or subjects.

● ***Curriculum Telescoping***   **Curriculum telescoping**, or compacting, involves an analysis of the specific subject matter (for example, spelling, math, language arts) to determine which parts of those subjects are inappropriate for gifted students because they have already mastered them. Return for a minute

---

IEP COMPACTOR

Name Wendy, Mike, Carol, Paul, Chris, Kurt   **Age** _____   **Teacher(s)** _____

School Smith   **Grade** _____   **Parent(s)** _____

Individual conference dates and persons participating in planning of IEP _____

CURRICULUM AREAS TO BE CONSIDERED FOR COMPACTING: Describe basic material to be covered during this marking period and the assessment information or evidence that suggests the need for compacting.	PROCEDURES FOR COMPACTING BASIC MATERIAL: Describe activities that will be used to guarantee proficiency in basic curricular areas.	ACCELERATION AND/OR ENRICHMENT ACTIVITIES: Describe activities that will be used to provide advanced levels of learning experiences in each area of the regular curriculum.
Math: Houghton Mifflin Mathematics Level 6	Pre- and posttests will be used to check skill proficiency.	Selected enrichment masters
This group scored above 90% ile on CTBS math.	No assignment of math text examples or basic masters for skills already mastered.	Pre-algebra with Pizzaz and After-Math materials
		Logic puzzles: mind benders, logic box
	Students will be individually assigned student text pages and skill sheets as indicated by pretests.	Individual or small-group advanced-level independent study.

Figure 13.7

Individual Educational Programming Guide: The Compactor

Source: Alane J. Starko (1986). Meeting the needs of the gifted throughout the school day: Techniques for curriculum compacting. *Roeper Review, 9*(1), 27–33.

to your fourth-grade class. It's math time, and let's assume you are a strong math student. As the teacher hands out worksheets, you have a sinking sense of dèja vu, for you are confronted with fifty problems like these: 26×247; 69×189; 24×790; $126 \div 4$; $4216 \div 57$. You think to yourself, "Didn't I see these yesterday? And the day before, too?" A conscientious math teacher would know that not all students in the class need extensive instruction in the basic math operations involved in these problems. In fact, a teacher who knew something about curriculum telescoping would probably not even require good math students like you to complete basic skill worksheets once you had mastered the concepts involved. What would be the point? If you already know how to multiply and divide large numbers, what possible benefit could there be to your completing more of these problems? There are dozens of more difficult concepts in math that you could probably work on instead of these basic skills.

That is the core of curriculum telescoping: determining what individual students already know and giving them the chance to explore concepts, subjects, or topics that better tap into their talents (Renzulli & Reis, 1985, 1991). Several authors have addressed the logistical problems of curriculum telescoping. Starko (1986) recommends several management techniques, including **group telescoping**, in which the teacher uses preexisting "top groups" in reading or math as the core group to telescope a particular concept or content area. The Teaching Strategies box entitled, "Steps in Curriculum Telescoping" will provide you with more information, and Figure 13.7 presents documentation for curriculum telescoping or "compacting."

● *Content Area Acceleration*   Content area acceleration is another modification available to regular classroom teachers. Most often, educators equate *acceleration* with grade skipping, a practice that is not endorsed as enthusiastically today as in past generations (Schiever & Maker, 2003). However, **content area acceleration** can occur within regular classes at virtually every grade level and within virtually every subject area. It happens every time a teacher allows students to "jump ahead" at a faster pace than most of their classmates. Thus, the first-grade teacher who provides literature to a child who has outgrown a basal reader is accelerating curriculum content for that child; so is the high school science teacher who works with a tenth-grader on physics experiments, even though physics is generally taken by twelfth-graders.

> With content acceleration, students proceed at a faster pace than most of their classmates.

Teaching Strategies & Accommodations

Steps in Curriculum Telescoping

1. Provide evidence of students' mastery (left column of Figure 13.7).

2. Describe how students may have their basic curriculum modified (center column of Figure 13.7).

3. List options for enrichment activities that take advantage of students' talents (right column of Figure 13.7).

Source: A. J. Starko (1986). Meeting the needs of the gifted throughout the school day: Techniques for curriculum compacting. *Roeper Review, 9*(11), 27–33.

When you accelerate a student's curriculum in a basic skill area, there is always the possibility that other teachers (especially those in subsequent grades) will disapprove of this strategy. Some may prefer that students pursue areas of study that do not infringe on the content they will teach. Others may believe that content acceleration complicates their role as teachers since not all students are taught the same thing at the same time.

The most important consideration, however, remains the student's learning needs, even if fulfilling those needs complicates scheduling or planning. If teachers lose sight of this basic principle, students may be deprived of instruction or content that matches their level of ability. In extreme cases, students may adopt a negative attitude toward school.

Content area acceleration can be a nonobtrusive way to modify the curriculum for gifted students, but like any other activity, it will take practice for you to perfect. See the accompanying Teaching Strategies box entitled, "Guidelines for Modifying Curriculum" for some tips.

● *Independent Study and Self-Directed Learning*   Independent study is one of the more popular forms of classroom modification for gifted students. **Independent study** provides "a chance for students to inquire about topics of interest to them in a manner that allows extensive exploration" (Parke, 1989, pp. 99–100). Teachers have come to realize, however, that even highly able students need differentiated levels of support for directing their own learning.

Like any strategy, independent study can be done improperly. Perhaps the most common mistake teachers make is to assume that since they're so smart, gifted students can succeed without any help. Teachers should introduce research skills such as library and computer information searching, hypothesis generation, and basic statistical analysis, which will give students tools for higher-level independent study. Unless a student selects a topic that is specific enough to be manageable, even a gifted student may wallow in a sea of confusion. As a teacher, you will need to provide appropriate direction as well as support for the independent work.

> In independent study, students pursue topics on their own, under teacher supervision.

Teaching Strategies & Accommodations

Guidelines for Modifying Curriculum

1. Assess the student's skill level accurately, making sure he or she understands each of the concepts involved in any material that might be replaced or skipped over.

2. Talk with the student's teachers from the previous year and the teacher(s) who may be receiving this student the following year. Team planning can avoid many problems of miscommunication.

3. Remember that an option other than accelerating content is enriching it. So, if a student skilled in reading and language arts wants something more complex to do, consider activities such as playwriting, cartooning, interviewing, or designing posters for a schoolwide project. These projects increase the student's breadth and depth of understanding of a subject.

4. Speak with your school district's director of curriculum or assistant superintendent about materials, resources, and options about which you might be unaware.

● *Cluster Grouping*   In **cluster grouping**, students who are identified as gifted at a given grade level are grouped together in the same classroom with a teacher who (ideally) has training in educating students who are gifted. The rest of the class is a diverse group of learners. The cluster arrangement allows the gifted learners to be grouped together for some activities and to be mixed with their age peers for others. Cluster grouping appears to be an increasingly popular option (Schuler, 1997).

Cluster grouping allows gifted learners to be grouped for some activities and not others.

● *Cooperative Learning*   **Cooperative learning** operates under the assumption that "all students are learners and teachers; all have an equal responsibility to explain to others and discuss with others. The pace of instruction is similar to what it would be in a traditional class, so high achievers are exposed to the same material they would have otherwise been taught" (Slavin, 1990, pp. 6–7). Under cooperative learning strategies, students are placed in mixed ability clusters of five or six, and they learn material by capitalizing on the strengths each member brings to the "team." Often, the same grades are awarded to all group members, which is meant to engender a team spirit in which everyone pulls his or her own weight.

Critics of cooperative learning contend that gifted students can be passive and disengaged in cooperative learning groups (Robinson, 2003). One opponent enumerates the objections:

> The disadvantages of cooperative learning for academically talented students are primarily those of limiting instruction to grade level materials, presented at the pace of a grade level group and evaluated primarily on basic skill measures. The corollary is that opportunities which can meet intellectual needs may be made unavailable to talented students because cooperative learning is assumed to be a substitute. (Robinson, 1990, p. 22)

Since there is no clear-cut agreement as to whether cooperative learning will benefit gifted students, the new teacher should approach this technique cautiously.

Teachers should be cautious in using cooperative learning with highly able students.

● *Creative and Higher-Level Thinking*   Creative and higher-level thinking processes are another area in which the curriculum can be modified. Consider the following two questions, either of which could appear on an elementary-level geography test:

1. What is the capital of Massachusetts?
2. Considering the geography of the state of Massachusetts, why might Boston have been chosen to be the state's capital?

The first question requires little thought, merely a good memory. Students need to know nothing about Boston other than that it is the state capital. The second question, though, requires analytical thought and some comprehension of the role that geography, location, and politics may have played in choosing the site for a state's capital.

Gifted students often think naturally—with little direction from parents or teachers—about these "bigger questions," the ones that require the use of more complex levels of thinking. When they are in a classroom setting where the majority of time is spent on activities or questions that have one right answer requiring only rote memorization to deliver, they often feel stifled intellectually. To compound this problem, classroom materials and texts usually emphasize

Higher-level thinking skills should be incorporated into the curriculum for gifted students.

the acquisition of low-level thinking skills (such as memorization) rather than the more sophisticated thinking patterns required to answer questions like the second one (Raths et al., 1986).

There are, however, methods and systems for incorporating higher-level thinking skills into your curriculum. Benjamin Bloom (1956) developed a taxonomy of educational objectives to distinguish among the various ways that questions and teaching strategies can be designed to promote varied levels of thinking. Figure 13.8 shows how to use this taxonomy in designing curriculum for gifted students. Another scholar proposed that teachers should train their students to use three distinct types of critical thinking strategies; see the Teaching Strategies box entitled, "Promoting Critical Thinking" (Ennis, 1985).

Some problems, however, do not require analytical thinking as much as they

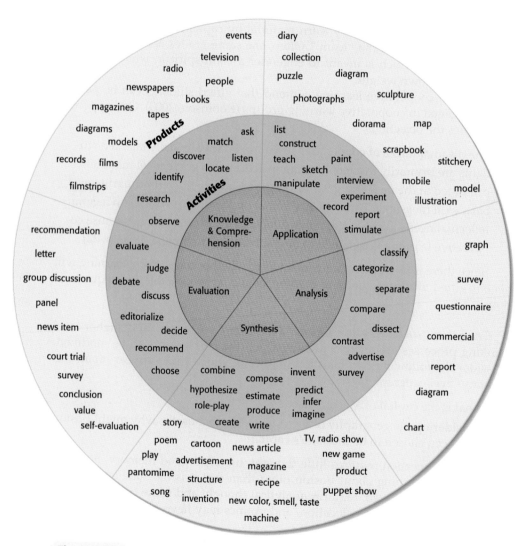

Figure 13.8

Cognitive Taxonomy Circle
The wheel was developed by Barry Ziff and a class of teachers of gifted students. They found it very useful in curriculum building.

Source: Barbara Clark, *Growing up gifted: Developing the potential of children at home and at school,* 6th edition, © 2002. Reprinted by permission of Pearson Education, Inc., Upper Saddle River, NJ.

Teaching Strategies & Accommodations

Promoting Critical Thinking

Ask your students to:

- Define and clarify problems, which includes the ability to identify a problem's central issue, identify assumptions underlying a problem, and identify appropriate questions to ask to better understand a situation.
- Judge information, which includes the ability to determine the relevance of information and the credibility of sources and observations.
- Infer solutions, which includes the ability to make deductive and inductive conclusions and to predict probable consequences of particular actions.

These classroom strategies should prompt independent and logical thinking in your students, especially in problem-solving situations encountered in math, science, social studies, and interpersonal relationships.

Source: R. H. Ennis (1985). A logical basis for measuring thinking skills. *Educational Leadership, 43*(2), 44–48.

---

require creative thinking. That is, rather than trying to find a *solution* to a problem, it is more important to first determine what the problem itself really is. **Brainstorming** (Osborn, 1963) is a basic, creative problem-solving technique. In brainstorming, there are no right or wrong answers, students cannot criticize each others' responses, and "piggybacking" an idea on someone else's is encouraged. Group brainstorming can be the first step in positive problem solving.

> In brainstorming, participants come up with many ideas on a specific subject.

- *Problem-Based Learning*   **Problem-based learning** is a method used in medical schools to focus on an "ill-structured problem" as a way for students to ask questions and hypothesize about how to clarify and solve the problem (Delisle, 2000). See the box on page 510 entitled, "Problem-Based Learning."

Is Special Education for Gifted Students Necessary?

Ellen Winner (2000b) argues eloquently and persuasively that special programs (and the increased resources they require) are necessary for our most highly gifted students—not simply because they are our future leaders and innovators, but because they need an appropriate level of challenge for their own well-being and happiness. The National Association for Gifted Children (2003) offers additional reasons for providing differentiated instruction to gifted learners:

- Gifted learners must be given stimulating educational experiences appropriate to their level of ability if they are to realize their potential.
- Each person has the right to learn and to be provided challenges for learning at the most appropriate level where growth proceeds most effectively.
- Only slightly over one-half of the possible gifted learners in the United States are reported to be receiving education appropriate to their needs.
- Traditional education currently does not sufficiently value bright minds.
- When given the opportunity, gifted students can use their vast amount of knowledge to serve as a background for unlimited learning.

- Providing for our finest minds allows both individual and societal needs to be met.

For more information, visit **http://www.nacg.org/About NAGC.htm**.

Teaching Strategies & Accommodations

Problem-Based Learning (PBL)

What Is Problem-Based Learning?

Problem-based learning instruction is built on "ill-structured and complex problems" just like those encountered in real life. The problems require that students "search beyond the readily available information to solve the problem" which is offered to them (Torp & Sage, 1998). Students become inquirers and active learners, collaborating, creating, and using knowledge to construct solutions. Teachers facilitate, model, and coach students as they work together in small groups.

Why Is This Model Used?

Students learn best when they must "do" and when they are asked to think in authentic ways rather than abstractly. Use this model when you want students to apply, analyze, synthesize, and extend knowledge, and when you wish students to apply research skills.

What Are "Ill-Structured and Complex Problems" for PBL and What Are Some Examples?

Delisle (2000) explains:

> Unlike a thinking exercise that includes all necessary information or a traditional project that requires students to use information they already know, PBL problems should be designed so that students must perform research to gather the information needed for possible solutions. It should require students to think through information they already know and find additional information, interpreting preexisting knowledge in light of new data they discover. In addition, the problem should

lead students to discover that there may be a number of solutions.

Here are two examples of problems used from elementary through middle school:

- Some students and our cafeteria staff have been complaining that the cafeteria is becoming so loud that it is hard to hear. We have been asked by our School Council to investigate this challenge and make a recommendation to them by next week. You will need to prepare a presentation for the council that includes the facts and conclusions we have reached.

- You are part of the Natural Science Museum Display team. You design all the display areas in the museum so that the people who come to the museum can easily see and learn from such displays. This week, the museum was given $50,000 to create an area of the museum for four wolves who cannot be released into the wild because they have lived all their lives in a zoo. The museum staff wants to construct an area that is as similar as possible to the natural habitat of the wolf and with a safe (for both wolves and the public) viewing area. The museum curator wants your team plans within two weeks so that preparations for construction can then be made. The curator would like you to present the background information your team used to develop its plans, as well as sketches or a model of what your team suggests.

Source: National Center for the Accelerated Schools Project, University of Connecticut Neag School of Education, 2131 Hillside Road, Unit 3224, Storrs, CT 06269-3224.

Technology Focus

Uses and Abuses of Technology with Gifted Children

Technology is an essential tool for research and creative efforts for students who are gifted and talented. Access to various kinds of software and to the Internet is vital for students who can learn independently, and the computer skills of these students grow quickly—often they teach *us* in this arena.

Michael Pyryt (2003) provides some examples of the advantages of technology use by gifted students:

- Technology use can provide *enrichment* through such programs as Odyssey of the Mind, a competition in which students respond to creative challenges, and the Center for Critical Thinking website. Technology-savvy teachers will find more such sites on the Internet for their students. Visit **http://www.odysseyofthemind.org** and **http://www.criticalthinking.org**.

- Technology can also provide *content-area acceleration* for advanced students through distance-learning courses provided by universities.

- Technology can provide experiences that lead to *personal and social growth*. For example, email correspondence with other students all over the world—fostered and monitored by teachers—can broaden one's social milieu, reduce feelings of isolation, and create a worldwide community of students interested in a range of topics.

But Pyryt (2003) also describes the potential "dark side" of technology use by very capable students, and the steps teachers must take to avoid the misuse of technology:

- Teachers must teach ethics and integrity in the use of technology and absolutely insist on their practice. It's the most capable technology users who can also wreak the most havoc, both on the Internet and within computer networks.

- Teachers must manage "controlled curiosity" in Internet use so that students stay focused on their academic topic and do not use their Internet time on inappropriate or irrelevant exploration (and this is easier said than done, as many of you know).

- Teachers must demonstrate to students that the Internet has some limitations in terms of the breadth of information, and libraries and other compendiums of knowledge still play an important role.

- Finally, "educators need to remember that there is an affective dimension to giftedness that can be enhanced through positive human interaction" (Pyryt, 2003, p. 586). There's no substitute for the human face or a pat on the back!

Keep in mind that technology is an area in which disadvantaged gifted students are potentially left out because of lack of access—the so-called digital divide (Solomon, Allen, & Resta, 2003). Students who do not have access to the Internet at home must obtain exposure at school so that they will not fall behind others in experience.

In this age of technology, with the proliferation of information and widening access to our "global village," the sky's the limit for our very capable students. They may need our guidance, though, to use their knowledge wisely and well.

 Some other teaching websites for gifted students, as suggested by Pyryt, are National Geographic expeditions at **http://www.nationalgeographic.com/xpiditions** and biographical information at **http://www.biography.com**. Pyryt also recommends **http://www.hoagiesgifted.com** for additional insight on educational resources for gifted and talented students.

Nevertheless, in turn, Winner (2000b) believes, gifted children should be required to give back—a commitment to service should be built into their school experiences. The fulfillment of giftedness in adulthood is not just the optimal development of the self, according to Winner, but the use of ability and talents in service to others. Let's close this chapter with Winner's words:

> The moral value of service, of giving back to a society that has devoted extra resources to the gifted, ought to be considered as important as the value of self-actualization of the gifted. All children should be taught the value of service, and gifted children are no exception. (p. 167)

SUMMARY

- The concept of giftedness has changed greatly over time, as has our view of students who are gifted. Giftedness has been described in terms of creativity and task commitment, multiple intelligences, successful manipulation of the environment, and heightened sensitivity and understanding.

- Standardized test scores are one criterion for identifying giftedness, but they should be supplemented by other measures, as well as by informal observations by teachers and parents.

- Although biological factors may play a role in giftedness, educators focus on environmental factors, especially family support, guidance, and encouragement, that can contribute to the full expression of a student's gifts.

- The prevalence of giftedness varies because of differing definitions and criteria; for funding purposes many states use a figure of 5 percent. Gifted females, students who are gifted and disabled, gifted underachievers, culturally diverse students, and the highly gifted are often underserved.

- Teachers usually play a central role in identifying gifted students through multiple measures, including observations of behavior (which might include negative as well as positive behaviors) as well as test scores and grades.

- The curriculum can be differentiated through telescoping, content area acceleration, independent study, cluster grouping, and cooperative learning. Modifications should be based on the student's needs and interests. Gifted students are usually served in the regular classroom and pulled out for resource room time. If self-contained classes are used, the students may be grouped according to their level or type of ability. Magnet schools are another setting in which students can receive a special emphasis on a specific type of ability.

- Many models for organizing gifted education have been proposed. These models help teachers plan curriculum modifications and activities to fulfill the needs of gifted students.

KEY TERMS

giftedness

talent

intelligence

creativity

task commitment

theory of multiple
  intelligences

triarchic theory

acceleration

gifted underachiever

highly gifted

academic enrichment

radical acceleration

enrichment

mentorships

Enrichment Triad Model

Accelerated Schools
  Project

Schoolwide Enrichment
  Model

differentiation

curriculum telescoping

group telescoping

content area acceleration

independent study

cluster grouping

cooperative learning

brainstorming

problem-based learning

USEFUL RESOURCES

- Susan Winebrenner (2001). *Teaching gifted kids in the regular classroom* (2nd ed.). Minneapolis: Free Spirit Publishing. This book is an excellent source for teaching ideas.

- James R. Delisle (2000). *Once upon a mind: The stories and scholars of gifted child education*. Fort Worth: Harcourt Brace. Delisle has written a textbook for readers interested in gifted child education that is unconventional, creative, informative, and entertaining.

- The ERIC Clearinghouse on Disabilities and Gifted Education has assembled the Gifted Education Searchable Online Database of selected gifted and talented programs in the United States. Using the database, educators may gather information on a wide variety of service options that match the needs of their student populations. The database enables professionals working in both general education and gifted education to find current programs and take advantage of research findings and work that was accomplished by using those programs. The database is available on the ERIC EC website GIFTED menu at **http://ericec.org/gifted/gt-menu.htm**.

- National Association for Gifted Children (NAGC), 1701 L Street, NW, Suite 550, Washington, DC 20036, telephone: (202) 785-4268, fax: (202) 785-4248.

- *Parenting for High Potential* is a publication of NAGC available at **http://www.nagc.org**. This quarterly magazine is designed for parents who want to develop their children's gifts and talents, and help them develop their potential to the fullest. Each issue includes special features, expert advice columns, software and book reviews, ideas from parents, and a pullout children's section.

- Carol Ann Tomlinson has written a series of books on differentiated instruction. The newest is *Fulfilling the promise of the differentiated classroom: Strategies and tools for responsive teaching* (2003). All are published by the Association for Supervision and Curriculum Development (ASCD); visit **http://shop.ascd.org**.

- Prufrock Press has useful publications for teachers of gifted students. Among them are Jim Delisle and Barbara Lewis's *Survival guide for teachers of gifted kids* (2003).

- Another Prufrock Press publication shines light on some of the "special populations" of gifted students we wrote about in this chapter. It is Maureen Neihart, Sally Reis, Nancy Robinson, and Sidney Moon (2001) *The social and emotional development of gifted children: What do we know?*

 PORTFOLIO ACTIVITIES

1. Select one or two books or articles about gifted students from the list in the Useful Resources section or the references that appear in this chapter. Compare the authors' perspectives with your own knowledge of and experiences with giftedness and talents. Make a chart contrasting the authors' views and your own, and place the chart in your portfolio.

   ✓ *Standards* This activity will help the student meet CEC Content Standard 2: Development and Characteristics of Learners.

2. Investigate popular culture and media images.

   - How do films and television shows portray gifted children? How have those images changed? Are stereotypes evident?

   - Interview a gifted student, classmate, or other person and note how that person differs from media stereotypes. Why might these stereotypes exist?

   - Rent a film about a gifted person (some suggestions: *A Beautiful Mind, Little Man Tate, My Left Foot, Good Will Hunting*). Do you consider the portrait in the film realistic? Write a review of the movie based on your analysis. Place the review in your portfolio.

   ✓ *Standards* This activity will help the student meet CEC Content Standard 3: Individual Learning Differences.

3. Identify an individual whom you consider gifted or talented. This person could be a public figure, a friend or family member, or a student you have known. Using the characteristics described in this chapter, write an analysis of how this person fits or does not fit the criteria for giftedness. Place the analysis in your portfolio.

   ✓ *Standards* This activity will help the student meet CEC Content Standard 2: Development and Characteristics of Learners.

4. Survey attitudes in your class.

   - Find out what stereotypes or preconceptions students hold about gifted students.

   - Have the other students write about one area in which they feel they are gifted. Does this ability shape their view of themselves, or is it just one characteristic?

   - Compile the responses about individual areas of giftedness in a poster showing the range of gifts in the class.

✓**Standards**   This activity will help the student meet CEC Content Standard 3: Individual Learning Differences, and CEC Content Standard 9: Professional and Ethical Practice.

5. Using the information on curriculum modifications provided in this chapter and the recommended readings, develop some activities that would allow gifted students to enrich their learning in the general education classroom. Write up the activities as lesson plans and add them to your portfolio.

✓**Standards**   This activity will help the student meet CEC Content Standard 7: Instructional Planning.

6. Where are gifted students in your school district served? Arrange to visit a local public school and see what combination of the general education classroom, resource room, and self-contained class instruction gifted students receive. If possible, observe students in each of these environments. How do the settings vary? Write up your observations and add them to your portfolio.

✓**Standards**   This activity will help the student meet CEC Content Standard 5: Learning Environments and Social Interactions.

 To access an electronic portfolio template for these activities, visit our text website through http://www.education. college.hmco.com/students/.

PART 3

Current Issues in Special Education

Having assimlated the foundational knowledge in the field of special education, conclude your reading with a comprehensive look at the special education issues that are making the pages of today's newspapers.

Part Outline

Chapter 14
The Special and General
Education Relationship: New
Trends and Challenges

14

The Special and General Education Relationship: New Trends and Challenges

Outline

Educational Reform: General
    Implications
Issues in Assessment
    Purposes of Assessment
    High-Stakes Testing
    School Accountability:
        Perceptions of Disability
Access to the General Education
    Curriculum
    Curriculum Standards
    Universal Design for
        Learning
Providing Instruction
    Teacher Preparation
    Instructional Options
SUMMARY
KEY TERMS
USEFUL RESOURCES
PORTFOLIO ACTIVITIES

Learning Objectives

After reading this chapter, the reader will:

- Identify the purposes and practices involved in high-stakes assessment, and the implications for students with disabilities

- Describe some of the issues involving accountability measures and special education practices

- Explain how the principles of universal curriculum can be applied in general education settings

- Identify and describe a number of teaching options, such as co-teaching, which are designed to facilitate the success of students with disabilities in the general education classroom

As we've learned in earlier chapters, special education gradually has become accepted as an important part of public education. We've discussed the history of special education and its legal foundations. In the text, we've also examined the principles and practices of philosophical movements such as inclusion, and the effects of these factors on our perceptions of kids with disabilities and on the value we put on their place within school communities. We've also looked at the growing relationships among teachers, parents, and other professionals as they learn to work together to create beneficial educational experiences for all children.

In this chapter, we look to the future relationship of special education and general education. Today, education is undergoing significant changes. Now, almost thirty years after the first laws mandating that all children receive a free and appropriate education, new laws are altering the ways we go about making educational decisions for children with disabilities. So, in the face of new challenges in all aspects of education, we must once again re-examine how general education and special education fit together. New laws and new regulations will require adjustments in the areas of assessment, curriculum, and teaching practices. First, however, we will look at some of the national changes that are driving a new age of educational reform.

Educational Reform: General Implications

As more children with disabilities are spending some or all of their school time in general education classrooms, we recognize that virtually all teachers may be teaching students with disabilities. In fact, 82 percent of all children with disabilities between 2000 and 2001 were in general education services for all or part of the school day (*Twenty-fourth Annual Report to Congress,* 2002). Therefore, each educational team—including special educators and general educators—works and plans to deliver appropriate instruction to children with disabilities across various classroom settings.

> Almost all teachers will teach students with disabilities.

Historically, the conversation among parents, special educators, administrators, and other professionals focused on instructional decisions, such as the type and amount of specialized services each child needs, who would deliver instruction, specialized curriculum, or instructional support, and what accommodations might be necessary in the general education classroom. The instructional decisions that were reached were documented in the child's IEP—all services, methods, materials, curricula, and assessment approaches were recorded. The IEP, as we describe in Chapter 1, served as the vehicle by which education was described and provided, student progress was documented, and accountability was established. While the IEP continues to be a critical component of special education programming, its role is changing—some question whether it will continue to be an integral part of how we plan for children in the future. Why? The separate, though often parallel systems of general education and special education practice, are being challenged more vigorously than ever before, due to new national educational requirements that apply to both general and special education. Most of these requirements have come about through educational reform, including the education act (P.L. 107-110) entitled No Child Left Behind (NCLB).

NCLB calls for major changes in assessment and accountability practices.

No Child Left Behind, the reauthorization of the Elementary and Secondary Education Act, was signed by President George W. Bush in January 2002. This act calls for major changes in assessment, instruction, accountability, and programming in general education and special education. All components of public education received the same directives. The major tenets of NCLB include an increased emphasis on public school accountability. Some of these requirements are as follows:

- Each state must develop curriculum standards in reading and math.
- All states must develop tests that address the curriculum standards, and all students in grades 3–8 must be tested annually.
- Test data will be clustered into groups for analysis, according to ethnicity, poverty, race, disability, and proficiency in English.
- Each school will be evaluated annually to determine if all groups of students in the school are making basic academic progress. This measure is referred to as Annual Yearly Progress (AYP). Evaluations will determine eligibility for incentives, as well as the need for state-supported remediation.
- School districts will provide parents with school choice if their child is in a failing school.
- Schools will identify and use research-based reading programs; every child will read by the end of the third grade.
- All teachers will be highly qualified.

Children with disabilities are specifically included in NCLB.

When we examine some of the components of NCLB, we see that both curriculum and assessment procedures are identified and proscribed for public schools. We also see that the law doesn't exclude children with disabilities; in fact, it specifies that children with disabilities participate in the same curriculum content, and be evaluated the same way as all children. Clearly, these mandates affect special education. From one perspective, we can celebrate the fact that children with disabilities are included so thoroughly in national educational mandates. We can assume that this inclusion reflects a high level of academic expectations for children with disabilities, and that the effectiveness of special education is considered an important part of every school's evaluation. On the other hand, we might be concerned that some children will spend years trying to learn a curriculum they don't need, that state-level testing may be inappropriate for some children, and that a year's progress in a year's time is an unrealistic expectation for many children with disabilities.

The fact that schools are directed to use research-based reading programs is good for all children and probably will reduce the number of children identified as needing special education in reading. On the other hand, will all children with disabilities—even mild to moderate disabilities—read by the end of the third grade? Because many of the changes are so new, we don't have resolutions to many of these issues, or answers to many of our questions. It is likely that practice will work to refine and adapt policy, over time.

In the rest of this chapter, we will look at the ways educational reform interacts with other efforts, such as teaching techniques, educational philosophies, and technology, to integrate special education and general education services. We also will examine possible benefits, issues, and concerns related to the emerging face of education. Read the executive summary or the full text of No Child Left Behind (signed January 8, 2002) by going to **http://www.ed.gov/nclb/landing.jhtm**.

❓ *Pause and Reflect*

As you can see, the emphasis on educational programs in public schools may be greatly and immediately affected by public policy and national legislation. What educational rights for children, both with and without disabilities, do you believe should be protected by or identified through law? ●

Issues in Assessment

Assessment, or evaluating student performance, is an integral part of education in general, and special education in particular. You've seen the word assessment often throughout this text—mainly within the context of assessment used for identification and placement. Assessment is at the heart of special education practice; teachers must determine what a student knows and needs to know in order to individualize instruction. There are other reasons for assessing children and many types of assessment instruments or tests.

Purposes of Assessment

In Chapter 4 we presented two major purposes for assessing students that are related directly to special education: (1) to evaluate or identify the student's need for special education or other support services if a student is referred, and (2) to assess for purposes of instruction: learning where to begin instruction, monitoring a student's performance, and evaluating the effectiveness of instruction. This assessment allows for teachers to provide appropriate and individualized instruction to students with disabilities. In contrast to these types of assessment, some testing is done on a large scale. State and national tests—largely achievement tests—have been used to provide parents and teachers with a sense of how their children are performing relative to other students in the state or across the country. Often, these scores are provided in percentiles to allow consumers a better means of comparison. For example, you might learn that, on a state-wide achievement test, Jason, a fourth-grade student, scored in the 91st percentile in math calculation, or at the 45th percentile in reading comprehension. There may be many uses for this type of assessment, but historically, they've been utilized for general information purposes.

In the wake of the educational reform movement, we see testing taking on increasing importance. Testing may be used as educators seek to set and maintain high-performance standards in the classroom, and to demonstrate that each school or school district is performing as expected. Instead of a test simply providing information that can be used to target instruction, tests are now employed to determine what child is eligible for certain classes, who passes to the next grade, and which students graduate from school (Heubert & Hauser, 1999). Students' test scores are also used now to grade schools, evaluate school districts, and determine the effectiveness of teachers and school administrators. When the consequences of testing are great—when students can fail, principals can lose their jobs, and schools can be considered as failing—we say that tests are used to make high-stakes decisions (Heubert & Hauser, 1999). Today, tests completed for

High-stakes testing refers to the ways test scores are used in education decision-making.

the purpose of making these important and critical decisions have come to be known as *high-stakes tests.*

High-Stakes Testing

High-stakes testing is quickly becoming the driving force in school reform and is drawing both praise and criticism. Some people praise the current use of **high-stakes testing** because they feel it promotes a standardized curriculum, provides a uniform level of expectations for students across schools, and helps parents to evaluate effective schools (Heubert & Hauser, 1999). On the other hand, many criticize the use of high-stakes testing because of the traditionally poor performance of students with disabilities, English-language learners, and students who are members of minority groups. Disparities in the test performance of students in these groups may result in inappropriate tracking and lower expectations. In addition, the performance differences appear to result in more grade retention and higher drop-out rates, not necessarily increases in student learning (Horn, 2003).

There appear to be few instructional benefits of high-stakes testing.

The instructional benefits of high-stakes testing for students with cognitive and academic disabilities appear to be limited. Additionally, because of the importance of the IEP as an assessment tool as well as an instructional plan, many students with disabilities have not participated in state-wide assessment, in the form of achievement tests, over the years. In 1997 IDEA reflected concern about schools' lack of accountability regarding the education of students with disabilities, by requiring schools to include children with disabilities in their assessment system and to report results. Although schools could attend to the scores of students with disabilities, they were not actually held accountable for the degree of progress students with disabilities were making each year. This complacence has changed drastically with the requirements of NCLB. As we've indicated earlier, this law asserts that *all* children must make a year's worth of progress each year at their grade level. By law, every child in grades 3–8 will take a state-wide, content-area test in reading and math. Each student will receive a score, and although the terms used to grade scores may vary from state to state, the bottom line is that each student must demonstrate proficiency, or a passing grade in each area. States are responsible for developing their own tests and competency scores. Each school is responsible for demonstrating that all children regardless of poverty, ethnicity, or level of disability can make adequate yearly progress.

Although the law recognizes that there are some children with disabilities so severe they cannot possibly take the standard test, accepted alternative assessments are strictly limited to approximately 1 percent of all students, or 9 percent of all students with disabilities (NCLB, 2002). The scores of most students with disabilities must be counted by each school and school district, and a few additional rules were set forth, including:

- Accommodations for testing must be provided when necessary. Accommodations may include increased time allowed to complete tests or taking the test in a room separate from the rest of the class.
- At least 95 percent of all students must participate in state tests.
- Test scores taken below grade level (to match the student's instructional level) cannot be counted, if the student scores proficient.

State-wide assessments are based on the educational standards established by each state, and because schools must demonstrate the progress each child makes, participation in the general education curriculum for all children is critical. Consequently, several questions and concerns have been raised by advocates for children with disabilities. Because the NCLB requirements seem to dictate participation in testing and the curriculum, some professionals and parents are concerned about the continued importance of the IEP in preserving individualized educational programs. For many, the big picture emphasis of NCLB is contradicted by the individualized focus of the IEP (Olson, 2004). For others, it seems incongruous to expect children with academic or cognitive disabilities to make a year's work of progress each year—particularly when failure to progress in the general education curriculum is necessary for identification in many categories of special education. A number of organizations developed guidelines and position papers hoping to preserve the rights of individuals in the testing system, to assure test validity and accurate reporting, and to emphasize the importance of using test scores in a responsible manner (National Center for Learning Disabilities, 2003).

Some educators voice concern that legislation such as NCLB is contradictory to the individual focus of the IEP.

The International Dyslexia Association, the National Center for Learning Disabilities, and the Learning Disabilities Association of America have endorsed a set of thirteen principles designed to provide guidelines for students with learning disabilities as they participate in high-stakes assessment. Visit the International Dyslexia Association's website at **http://www.interdys.org** and click on first, About IDA, and second, Public Policy, to view these thirteen principles as well as related advocacy statements.

In addition to the effects of testing on individuals with disabilities, great concerns have emerged about the effects of high-stakes assessment on the interactions among administrators, teachers, and students in general education and special education. NCLB is requiring general education to attend to the performance of students with disabilities for the first time (Olson, 2004). On the one hand, we can perceive this attention as a good thing—the performance of students with disabilities is no longer irrelevant and can no longer be ignored. On the other hand, a school needs to demonstrate that all groups of kids make adequate yearly progress. If the students with disabilities don't make that progress, neither will the school as a whole—regardless of how the other students do.

All educators are now paying attention to the academic success of children receiving special education services.

School Accountability: Perceptions of Disability

During 2002–2003, the first full school year after the NCLB was signed, high-stakes tests were administered, schools received report cards, and data were collected from all states that participated. Although the states were just beginning to implement the new procedures, the results at the local and state level were clear: Students with disabilities were not doing well, and many schools failed because of their performance. Quality Counts (2004), a report on special education and testing requirements, collected data from the thirty-nine states that participated in testing during 2002–2003. The data included proficiency (or passing) rates for both general education and special education students in fourth-grade reading and math, and eighth-grade math. A summary of that data reveals:

- Thirty of thirty-nine states had proficiency gaps between general education and special education students of more than thirty percentage points on fourth-grade reading.

- Six states had gaps in fourth-grade reading of fifty percentage points or more.
- Thirty-four of thirty-nine states had gaps of thirty percentage points or more in eighth-grade reading (Ansell, 2004).

How will testing results like those above affect the successful inclusion of children with disabilities in schools? The first year of assessment resulted in an outcry by individual schools, teachers, and parents, because of the poor performance by students with disabilities. It became clear that some changes in the law would be necessary or children with disabilities would not be welcome in schools—the implications were frightening. Fortunately, the government responded fairly quickly to the many concerns expressed by the public and by special education organization. In December 2003 a new provision to NCLB (Council for Exceptional Children, 2003) gave schools more flexibility in meeting the assessment requirements. For example, states can now create their own definition of severe disabilities—children with severe disabilities participate in alternative assessments. Alternative assessments may vary across states, but often portfolios documenting student learning are used to replace tests. A student's successful performance in alternative assessments, can now count as proficient—a score that wasn't allowed before. Although the new provision doesn't alter the requirement that no more than one percent of students participate in alternative assessments, they do allow states and schools to appeal this percentage.

It is not clear if the changes established by the new federal provision for NCLB will give schools needed relief and take the pressure off of students with disabilities. It is clear that it is a difficult task to develop high-stakes testing so that it serves its purpose in a fair and instructive way. Perhaps changes will continue to shape NCLB and other educational reform measures over time, so that they serve all children well.

New provisions of NCLB allow states more flexibility to meet its legal mandates.

? Pause and Reflect

The extent to which students with disabilities participate in standardized state testing will probably continue to change over the next five years. As you reflect on the advantages and disadvantages of including the vast majority of students with disabilities in these assessment programs, what direction should these changes take? Can you think of regulations or criteria that you would use to determine if students should or should not participate in high-stakes assessment? ●

Access to the General Education Curriculum

Throughout this text, we've mentioned curriculum options for students with disabilities. Curriculum options range from the general education curriculum, to specialized curricula such as social skills or study skills, the expanded core curriculum for students with visual impairments, to a functional or life-skills curriculum. Traditionally, the IEP team determines what skills a student needs to be taught and the IEP serves as the curriculum blueprint for instruction. Today, however, special education can be defined as the services required by a student

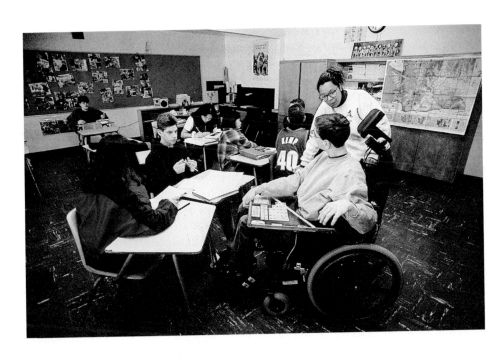

Many students with disabilities require only a few accommodations to work successfully in general education classes. (© Paul Conklin/PhotoEdit)

to facilitate access to the general education curriculum. All students must participate in the general education curriculum—teachers must even tie alternative curriculum content to the curriculum standards.

Curriculum Standards

In 1994 Goals 2000: Educate America Act encouraged states to develop two sets of academic standards. The first set of academic standards was called **content standards**: broad descriptions of the knowledge and skills students should acquire in a particular subject area (P.L. 103-227, Sec. 3[4]). The second set of standards was termed **performance standards**: concrete examples and explicit definitions of what students have to know and be able to do to demonstrate that they are proficient in the skills and knowledge framed by the content standards (P.L. 103-227, Sec. 3[9]) (McDonnel, McLaughlin, & Morison, 1997). Content standards identify what should be taught and performance standards describe the ways students can demonstrate their skills. Both assessment instruments and the curriculum taught in schools today reflect content and performance standards.

In the ten years since Goals 2000, states have been required to establish grade-level content standards in reading and math and to coordinate these standards with high-stakes assessment. The content standards that each state develops determine which curriculum school districts choose for their schools, as well as determine the pace and breadth of instruction taking place in the classroom. How do these standards fit in with the IEP? IEP teams develop instructional goals and objectives that can be tied directly to the state standards. While this may not be too difficult for children with mild disabilities, it can be quite a challenge when trying to relate community-based instruction in vocational skills to standards in reading, math, or social studies. To some educators, it is unnecessary and time-consuming to have to relate, for example, life-skills curriculum objectives, determined by the student's need to function successfully in

Content standards provide specific guidelines for what material should be taught in each subject area.

The information we teach all students with disabilities must be related to the content standards of our state.

his or her environment, to state standards that are based on academic learning. Others find it important to demonstrate the full inclusion of all students in the general education curriculum—even if it is only in a tangential way. From either perspective, it is clear that what we teach to students with disabilities must be related to what we teach to all students. How can we increase accessibility to the general education curriculum? In some instances, we will modify the way we teach or the order in which we present certain skills. In other situations, we will provide students with additional classroom tools—tapes, readers, note-takers, calculators, keyboards, or software. A comprehensive approach to presenting curriculum, universal design, was created to promote curriculum and classroom accessibility for all students. To view the curriculum content standards for your state, visit the website of your state's Department of Education. At the following website, you can find links to the curriculum standard section for all fifty states: **http://education.umn.edu/nceo/TopicAreas/Standards/StatesStandards.htm**.

Universal Design for Learning

Universal Design for Learning (UDL) is a general approach to curriculum development.

When we think about accessibility, typically we think of entering a building and the need to adapt existing structures to accommodate individuals with disabilities. The term accessibility, however, also is used to refer to gaining information from curriculum. **Universal Design for Learning (UDL)** is a concept that grew out of the idea of architectural accessibility, but was adapted to encompass the diversity of all learners and to accommodate the needs of all learners from the beginning of curriculum design (Dolan & Hall, 2001). In other words, instead of developing a curriculum and then looking at ways to accommodate diverse learners, according to the principles of UDL, the curriculum would be created with all learners in mind, so there would not be a need to alter the program's structure to accommodate the needs of various learners. UDL focuses on accessing the curriculum without lowering academic standards or restricting content coverage. The accessibility focus of UDL can easily be interpreted in light of physical design. The following Teaching Strategies box entitled, "Three Essential Qualities of Universal Design for Learning" illustrates the basis for general curriculum applications.

UDL focuses on allowing all students to have access to curriculum content and related activities.

Although UDL represents a general approach to curriculum development, it is a philosophy that is emerging in special education. Many of the principles of UDL are based in or revolve around the use of technology. There are seven basic principles of UDL:

- **Equitable use.** Materials are created that are accessible to everyone.
- **Flexibility in use.** Choice is incorporated to appeal to individual likes and abilities.
- **Simple and intuitive use.** Designs are uncomplicated and easy to understand.
- **Perceptible information.** Necessary information is clearly and effectively communicated.
- **Tolerance for error.** The consequences of making a mistake are minimal.
- **Low physical effort.** Minimal physical effort is required.
- **Size and space and approach and use.** Designs allow for easy use regardless of physical abilities or mobility (CAST, 2003).

Teaching Strategies & Accommodations

Three Essential Qualities of Universal Design for Learning

(1) Curriculum Provides Multiple Means of **Representation**	(2) Curriculum Provides Multiple Means of **Expression**	(3) Curriculum Provides Multiple Means of **Engagement**
Alternative modes of presentation reduce perceptual and learning barriers. Multiple presentations can adjust to the different ways that students recognize objects and information.	With **different means of expression**, students can respond to information using their preferred means of control. Multiple means of expression can accommodate different strategic and motor systems of students.	With **different ways to become engaged** with the curriculum, students can match their interests in learning with the mode of presentation and response. Such a curriculum can better motivate more students to learn.

Digital formats provide the greatest flexibilty in presenting and using curricular materials.

Digital materials are transformable (they can be changed easily from one mode of presentation to another; the means of expression can be changed).	**Digital materials are transportable** (amount and complexity of content can be customized for individual needs).	**Digital materials are recordable** (they "learn and remember" user patterns; can track progress over time and identify areas of difficulty and strength).

The source materials for these principles of Universal Design for Learning were developed by CAST. For a more in-depth explanation of the principles and further discussion of Universal Design for Learning, jump to the CAST website through these links: The Three Principles of Universal Design for Learning, Overview of Concepts, and Issues in Universal Design for Learning.

Source: Council for Exceptional Children. Retrieved from http://www.cec.sped.org/osep/ud-fig2.html, Dec. 2003.

Educators today are beginning to apply the principles and qualities of UDL in their everyday instruction. In the Teaching Strategies box entitled, "Example of Teaching U.S. History Using UDL," you can see how these principles look when integrated into classroom instruction. To learn more about UDL and its applications for teachers, visit the website for Universal Design Education Online at **http://www.udeducation.org**.

Teaching Strategies & Accommodations

Example of Teaching U.S. History Using UDL

A U.S. history teacher using the UDL approach might ask her students to construct an essay that compares and contrasts the industrial North and the agricultural South in the 1800s. Her focus is the thinking behind the essay, the methods of comparing and contrasting as a means to help her students gain a deeper understanding of the historical period and geographic locations.

The teacher emphasizes that there are many different approaches to constructing the essay and offers examples: outlines, diagrams, concept maps, digitally recorded think-alouds, and drawings. She uses tools supporting each of these approaches, so that students who need extra structure can choose the supports that work for them, and she creates templates with partially completed sections and links to more information.

Because this is a long-term assignment, the teacher breaks the research and the writing into sections and incorporates group sharing and feedback in the process to help students revise their essays as they work. The teacher also provides models by sharing the work of previous students who approached the same problem in varied ways.

Source: C. Hitchcock, A. Meyer, D. Rose, & R. Jackson (2002). Providing new access to the general curriculum: Universal design for learning. *Teaching Exceptional Children, 35*(2), 13. Copyright © Council for Exceptional Children.

? Pause and Reflect

The controversy about the extent to which a standards-based curriculum is appropriate for over 95 percent of the school population is one that will remain with us for a while. Discuss this issue with general education and special education teachers you know. What are your opinions on current curriculum requirements? How would you defend your position to teachers or parents? ●

Providing Instruction

There is a wide range of abilities and disabilities within the group of students with learning disabilities. Consequently, the range of program options discussed in Chapter 1, from itinerant service to pullout resource to self-contained programs, should be available within most school districts so that the unique needs of each student can be met. The national education reforms of the early 1990s calling for a restructuring and reorganization of educational programs resulted in an increased emphasis on the access of all students to the general education curriculum, and ongoing controversy about the effectiveness of resource or pullout programs have contributed to this movement. This emphasis was reflected in the IDEA amendments (1997), which called for goals and objectives for students with disabilities that were as similar as possible to those in general education (Ansell, 2004). As schools attempted to devise effective service delivery systems for general education curriculum to students with disabilities, a focus on innovative teaching techniques emerged—particularly approaches that focused on educational collaboration (Hourcade, Parette, & Anderson, 2003). Although many teachers in both general and special education were willing to collaborate, other teachers were not prepared for the type of instruction they would be asked to deliver.

Diverse approaches to instruction reflect innovative attempts to address the needs of all of the students included in general education classrooms.

Teacher Preparation

The traditional undergraduate route for teacher preparation is a fairly straightforward one. When a high-school graduate decides to enter college to become a teacher, she decides what age level she wants to teach (early childhood, elementary, middle school, or high school), and the subject area she wants to teach, such as biology or history, if she's chosen high school. The student then follows a course of study to prepare her; she may become certified after completing her degree and passing state teaching exams. If an individual is interested in teaching children with disabilities, he follows a course of study that either focuses on a specific age group (preschool special education), a specific disability (mental retardation), or a general degree that includes several areas of disability (mild disabilities or severe disabilities). The specific names and types of special education certifications differ from state to state, but they require certifications separate from those in general education. Some colleges provide the option for students to become certified in both one area of general education and one area of special education (elementary education and learning disabilities).

When general education teachers are prepared only in general education and special education teachers are prepared only in special education, difficulties arise when both types of teachers are faced with providing general education curriculum to students with disabilities in general education classrooms—both sets of teachers have sometimes felt incompetent and unprepared. Over the past decade, teacher preparation standards have become more inclusive for both groups of teachers. Although they continue to be evaluated separately, standards for general education teachers are beginning to include knowledge of some special education content, and special education standards are beginning to include knowledge of general education content.

Teacher preparation programs sometimes fail to prepare teachers to teach all of the students who might be in their classrooms.

Surprisingly, however, most of the current teachers in general education receive little, if any, coursework or fieldwork in special education. Although 82 percent of general education teachers in public schools are providing instruction for students with disabilities at any given time, only fourteen states and the District of Columbia require teachers to take at least one course in special education before becoming certified (Ansell, 2004). In special education, many teachers at the secondary level, particularly those who teach children with mild disabilities, may provide the students primary instruction in biology, algebra, geography, or English. However, because these teachers are certified only in special education, they may have little or no preparation in these subjects. In fact, not one state requires secondary special education teachers to complete a degree, pass a test, or complete a minimum amount of hours in any of the subject areas he or she might teach (Quality Counts, 2004).

As more and more students with disabilities participate in the general education curriculum, it seems clear that some changes in preparation should occur for both general and special education teachers. The nature of these changes is now defined, in part, both by federal law (NCLB) and each state's interpretation of it. One of the tenets of NCLB, as we mentioned earlier, is the mandate for **highly qualified teachers**. According to the law, a highly qualified teacher holds a license

Each state determines the criteria a teacher must meet before he or she can be considered a highly qualified teacher.

or teaching certificate, and can demonstrate knowledge in all the subjects he or she teaches. At the early childhood or elementary level, teachers must pass a test on basic subjects. A special education teacher for children at the elementary level might need to pass tests or hold certificates in both special education and elementary education. A secondary teacher would need to pass an exam or hold teaching certificates in all subjects he or she teaches (Keller, 2004). As each state struggles to interpret these requirements, it is likely that the preparation program of teachers, especially special education teachers, will expand to accommodate new requirements. In the meantime, teachers continue to work together and learn from each other as they share teaching experiences. To view the new standards for preparing teachers in special education, visit the performance-based standards section of the Council for Exceptional Children's website at **http://www.cec.sped.org**. These standards are also outlined at the beginning of this book.

Instructional Options

● *Teacher-Directed*   Students with disabilities who are served in regular classroom settings receive the same basic curriculum as other students in the classroom. As we've discussed, the general education curriculum may present obstacles for students with disabilities. Some of these obstacles can be addressed through curriculum modifications, and others can be addressed through educational collaboration—between teachers or among peers. Chief among the teacher-directed instructional alternatives are consultation, collaboration, co-teaching, and classroom tutoring. In all these options, the teacher who has expertise in special education or a specific area of instructional support, such as educational technology or mobility, comes into the regular classroom and works with the classroom teacher or student. Some schools employ all these models, whereas others select one or two, depending on the needs of the students and regular classroom teacher.

> The presence of more than one teacher allows for more careful attention to student performance.

Let's review some of the terms introduced in Chapter 1. In **consultation**, the special education teacher observes the student in the regular classroom and provides suggestions concerning how the regular classroom teacher might adapt

Co-teaching can provide rich opportunities for student-teacher interaction and improved learning. (© Will Hart/PhotoEdit)

instruction or materials to meet the specific needs of the student with learning disabilities in his or her class. **Collaboration** describes the process whereby both regular and special education teachers identify the problems or difficulties a child is experiencing and work together to find intervention strategies (Dettmer, Thurston, & Dyck, 1993). Sometimes, the special education teacher works with the general education teacher in the classroom. This method, called **co-teaching**, has many different forms. Co-teaching could involve the special educator teaching a specific subject area to the entire class (math or social skills) or teaching a specific group of students that includes a student with a disability (often a subject such as reading or a content area requiring reading skills). See the accompanying Teaching Strategies box entitled, "Co-Teaching Models" for a description of the various co-teaching formats. A final alternative is individual tutoring of the student with a learning disability by a teacher, peer, or older student within the classroom setting.

> Co-teaching provides opportunities for general education and special education teachers to work together in the classroom.

Teaching Strategies & Accommodations

Co-Teaching Models

One Person Teaching in Classroom

1. One teacher prepares materials and offers strategies but does not actually teach in the classroom. This model frequently coexists with all the other models.

2. One teach–one observe: One teacher observes a student in the classroom and perhaps takes data, evaluates student responses to instruction, etc. One teacher provides classroom instruction. Could be occasional or structured.

Two Teachers in Classroom: One Supplementing General Instruction

1. One teach–one drift: One teacher circulates around the room helping students with particular needs, and the co-teacher instructs the entire group. Can be most beneficial when roles are reversed regularly.

2. Alternative teaching: One teacher provides remediation, enrichment, or specialized instruction for students who need it, while the other provides instruction for the rest of the group. This may be done occasionally, on an as-needed basis, or as regular alternative reading instruction, for example.

Two Teachers in Classroom: Both Delivering General Instruction

1. Station teaching: Curriculum content is broken into components; each teacher teaches one part of content to a group of children, then students switch to the other teacher. Could also include cooperative learning or an independent group station.

2. Parallel teaching: Class is broken into two groups of students; each teacher teaches the same content material to one group of students. (Don't separate all special education students into one group.)

3. Team teaching: Both teachers deliver the instruction together at the same time, sharing leadership in the classroom. This may be done for one class a day or more, but it should be consistent across time so that students perceive both teachers as the teachers in charge.

Source: Adapted from M. Friend (1996). *The power of 2: Making a difference through co-teaching.* Bloomington: Indiana University Press.

• *Peer-Directed*   Although several models of peer-tutoring and cooperative learning strategies have been suggested as means of integrating students with disabilities into general education classes, few have strong research supporting their effectiveness. Teachers believe there is much potential in these types of interventions, however, and report that cooperative learning and peer tutoring are the most useful approaches for working with multicultural students with disabilities (Utley et al., 2000). One peer-tutoring program that has been well researched and found to be effective for many students with mild disabilities is Peer-Assisted Learning Strategies (PALS) (Fuchs et al., 1997). PALS, outlined in the accompanying Teaching Strategies box, is based on the Classwide Peer Tutoring Program (Greenwood, Delquadri, & Hall, 1989) and designed to focus on reading instruction in general education classrooms. What

Some peer-based interventions, such as the Peer-Assisted Learning Strategies, are effective strategies in general education classes.

Teaching Strategies & Accommodations

Peer-Assisted Learning Strategies (PALS)

Preparation

PALS involves preparation of students: Teachers prepare students with a series of scripted lessons. Students are grouped into dyads; typically, one student is a stronger reader than the other. Reading material is selected that is at the lower reader's level.

Implementation

PALS sessions are implemented three times a week, for thirty-five minutes each session. Students receive points for correct performance and appropriate tutoring when necessary. Both students participate in tutoring activities, but the stronger reader begins the session. No answer keys are provided.

Activities

• **Partner reading.** The peer tutor, and then the other student, each read the text for five minutes. The peer tutor stops the reader when an error occurs and asks the student to try to figure out the mistake. If the reader cannot do this in four seconds, the tutor supplies the word. Then the sentence is re-read by the student who made the error.

• **Paragraph shrinking.** The students read the text aloud, stopping at the end of each paragraph to state the main idea and eventually presenting it in no more than ten words. The tutor prompts the identification of the main idea by asking questions. He or she asks the other student to try again if the response is incorrect and to shorten the response if it is too long.

• **Prediction relay.** The reader makes predictions about the content of a half page of text and then reads the text. While this student is reading, the tutor corrects errors, evaluates predictions, and presents the main idea of the text. The correction procedures used in the first two activities are included in this activity, and the tutor solicits new predictions if he or she deems the initial ones unreasonable.

For more program information, see D. Fuchs, L. S. Fuchs, P. G. Mathes, and D. C. Simmons (1996), *Peer-Assisted Learning Strategies in Reading: A Manual* (available from Box 328 Peabody, Vanderbilt University, Nashville, TN 37203 on go to PALS website at http://kc.vanderbilt.edu/kennedy/pals/.

Source: D. Fuchs, L. S. Fuchs, & P. Burish (2000). Peer-assisted learning strategies: An evidence-based practice to promote reading achievement. *Learning Disabilities Research and Practice, 15,* 85–91.

distinguishes PALS from other classroom tutorial programs is the use of structured peer interactions, including specific task strategies, and the incorporation of effective instructional practices. The PALS program was created for students in grades 2 through 6, but it has since been adapted for use with kindergarten children, first-graders, and high-school students (Fuchs, Fuchs, & Burish, 2000; Mathes et al., 1999).

? *Pause and Reflect*

As you prepare to become a teacher, you often imagine having your own classroom—what you would do to organize the class, how you would create learning opportunities, and the ways you and your students interact. Co-teaching involves sharing your classroom and your students, and may involve compromise to determine learning strategies and activities. Can you imagine participating in a co-teaching setting? What do you think would help make co-teaching an attractive option for you? ●

In spite of the emphasis on serving students with disabilities in the general education classroom, other service delivery options, such as the resource room and self-contained classrooms, continue in most schools. The new emphases on teacher preparation, curriculum standards, and high-stakes testing will make it exceedingly difficult, however, for students to receive general education curriculum content in special education settings, and for the curriculum for most children with disabilities to be anything but academic and standards-based. Children with severe disabilities are exempt from high-stakes testing and, therefore, may continue to participate in curriculum that is functional in nature, emphasizing life skills, such as preparation for work activities, social interaction skills, and exposure to domestic and recreational activities. What will happen to the middle-school or high-school child who is reading on the second-grade level and still has difficulty writing a legible paragraph? Where can he or she receive the instruction in life skills needed? What will school teach such a student if he or she is exposed only to an academic curriculum and fails state achievement tests year after year? These are the types of questions posed by special educators, parents, and students in the face of educational reform. We've discussed many of the proactive strategies—approaches to curriculum and instruction—that attempt to facilitate learning and allow for many students to be more successful in school. The fact remains, of course, that there are many unanswered questions to the dilemmas facing schools and families as they continue to negotiate appropriate and individualized instructional programs for children with disabilities. We wish you luck as you become part of the solutions to these problems.

SUMMARY

- The move toward accountability in general education and special education is reflected in the educational reform movement, which includes legislation such as the federal No Child Left Behind act.

- High-stakes testing is used in schools not only to evaluate individual student progress, but also to evaluate the performance of subgroups of students and to rate the success of schools.

- Most children with disabilities participate in the general education curriculum, which is now a standards-based curriculum. High-stakes testing is tied to the curriculum standards.

- Universal Design for Learning is a philosophical approach to creating a curriculum that is more accessible to all students.

- Teachers use a variety of approaches, including co-teaching, to provide special education services to children with disabilities in general education classes.

KEY TERMS

No Child Left Behind   Universal Design for   collaboration
high-stakes testing   Learning (UDL)   co-teaching
content standards   highly qualified teachers
performances standards   consultation

USEFUL RESOURCES

- Visit the Center for Applied Special Technology (CAST) at **http://www.cast.org**. This center is a not-for-profit organization that focuses on creating opportunities for accessibility for all people via technology. The contributors to CAST engaged in much of the pioneer research in the Universal Design for Learning.

- Marquita Grenot-Scheyer, Mary Fisher, and Debbie Staub (Eds.) (2001). *At the end of the day: Lessons learned in inclusive education.* Baltimore: Paul H. Brookes. This book examines the inclusive programs available to eight students with disabilities. It describes successes and the barriers to inclusive education.

- Mary Susan E. Fishbaugh (2000). *The collaboration guide for early career educators.* Baltimore: Paul H. Brookes. This text focuses on specific teacher collaboration strategies for new teachers.

- For data and reports from its national research project, visit State Accountability for All Students Project (SAAS) at **http:// www.ssco.org/saas**. SAAS is a federally funded project that is designed to study the effects of high-stakes testing on students with disabilities.

- Wolfgang Preiser and Elaine Ostroff (2001). *Universal design handbook.* New York: McGraw-Hill. This book contains the American and international standards, American with Disabilities Act code requirements, and ideas for increasing accessibility in areas such as communication, transportation, Internet use, and buildings.

● *Exceptional Parent Magazine* (September 2000 issue). This special issue includes short descriptions of inclusion programs that received Models of Excellence in Education awards. Available online at **http://www. eparent.com**.

 ## PORTFOLIO ACTIVITIES

1. Visit your state's Department of Education website and review the schools' testing reports. Compare the passing scores of two school districts or of schools within one district. Summarize the performances of the schools as a whole and the performances of various subgroups reported.

   ✓**Standards** This activity will help students meet CEC Content Standard 8: Assessment.

2. Examine the curriculum used for science at the middle-school level. Consider the principles of Universal Design for Learning and describe at least five ways you could create a curriculum more accessible for students with disabilities.

   ✓**Standards** This activity will help students meet CEC Content Standard 10: Collaboration.

3. Review the early elementary level reading standards for your state (Grades 1–3). Use the descriptions of academic challenges in reading that you may find in Chapters 4, 5, 7, and 8 of this text, to identify the additional skills you will need to teach these standards to children with mild to moderate academic disabilities.

   ✓**Standards** This activity will help students meet CEC Content Standard 7: Instructional Planning.

4. Create a notebook of articles and firsthand descriptions of special education programs delivered in a general education setting. Record and compare the models of instruction used by the teachers and the strategies or materials that you find particularly interesting and potentially useful in your own classroom.

   ✓**Standards** This activity will help students meet CEC Content Standard 5: Learning Environments and Social Interactions.

 To access an electronic portfolio template for these activities, visit our text website through http://www.education. college.hmco.com/students/.

Glossary

AAMR Adaptive Behavior Scale one of the most widely used instruments for measuring adaptive behavior.

academic enrichment broadening the experience base of the students in an academic content area without changing the instructional objectives.

Accelerated Schools Project school reform model that extends the expectations and strategies used in gifted education to all students in the school.

acceleration providing a more appropriate program for a gifted student by moving the student ahead in the curriculum; the most common example is grade-skipping.

acquired hearing loss a hearing loss acquired at any time after birth.

acquired immune deficiency syndrome (AIDS) a viral disease that breaks down the body's immune system, destroying its ability to fight infections; AIDS is transmitted by the exchange of body fluids that can occur through sexual contact or sharing contaminated needles to inject intravenous drugs.

adaptive behaviors the age- and situation-specific social, maturational, self-help, and communicative acts that assist each individual in adapting to the demands of his or her environment.

adult service agencies agencies that provide medical and psychological examinations and counseling, training and job placement, and financial assistance for adaptive equipment, prostheses, and basic living costs during training to adults with disabilities.

age-appropriate behavior behavior considered normal for a particular age.

albinism a congenital lack of pigmentation which can cause vision loss.

alcohol-related neurodevelopmental disorder (ARND) a spectrum of learning and behavioral characteristics in a child caused by maternal alcohol ingestion during pregnancy.

American Sign Language (ASL) the sign language considered by many deaf adults to be their "native language"; it has the same vocabulary as English but a different grammatical structure.

Americans with Disabilities Act of 1990 (P.L. 101-336) a law that extends civil rights protection to individuals with disabilities in private-sector employment and requires that public services like telecommunications and transportation make accommodations for individuals with disabilities.

amniocentesis a prenatal testing technique that analyzes amniotic fluid to identify certain chromosomal and neural tube abnormalities.

anxiety-withdrawal behaviors, such as extreme sensitivity or depression, reflecting fear of performance and avoidance.

Asperger's syndrome A syndrome in which individuals have social and behavioral deficits similar to those experienced by children with autism, but do not experience delays in language and cognition.

asthma a chronic obstructive lung condition characterized by an unusual reaction to a variety of stimuli that causes difficulty in breathing; coughing, wheezing, and shortness of breath.

at-risk infants and young children who have a higher likelihood of developing a disability because of factors like extreme prematurity, chronic poverty, or medical problems.

attention the ability to focus on information.

attentional deficits the inability to come to attention, to maintain attention, or to pay attention selectively.

attention deficit disorder (ADD) a condition determined by difficulty in focusing on information and in sustaining attention.

attention deficit/hyperactivity disorder (ADHD) a condition determined by difficulty in focusing on information, sustaining attention, and hyperactive behavior.

audiogram the chart on which the audiologist records an individual's responses to a hearing test.

audiologist the professional who tests and measures hearing.

auditory training enhancing the residual hearing of a student with hearing loss by teaching listening skills.

augmentative communication aid a system designed to give individuals assistance in communication, such as a scanning system or communication board.

autism a severely incapacitating lifelong developmental disability characterized by certain types of behaviors and patterns of interaction and communication. Symptoms include disturbance in the rate of appearance of physical, social, and language skills; abnormal response to sensation; delayed or absent speech and language; and abnormal ways of relating to people, objects, and events. It usually appears during the first three years of life.

Autism Spectrum Disorders a term used to refer to the range of syndromes and conditions that fall under the category of pervasive developmental disorder. Children with Autism Spectrum Disorders may exhibit a few or many of the characteristics historically associated with autism to varying degrees of severity.

behavior disordered a term used by some states instead of "serious emotional disturbance" to classify children with behavior and emotional disorders.

behavior intervention plan (BIP) an empirically based individual program to address problem behavior that contains positive behavior support strategies designed to teach appropriate behavior.

behavior-rating scale an observation form that allows teachers, parents, and psychologists to rate patterns of behavior.

Bell, Alexander Graham 19th-century teacher of speech to deaf children; inventor of the telephone.

bilateral hearing loss hearing loss in both ears.

biological aging the physiological changes that occur over the lifespan.

biological risk the risk associated with damage to a child's developing systems before, during, or after birth.

Board of Education of Hendrick Hudson School District* v. *Rowley a 1982 Supreme Court decision that an "appropriate" education does not mean that a student must reach his or her maximum potential, only that the student have access to educational opportunity.

Bobby-approved symbol indicating that website content is accessible to people with disabilities.

Braille a system of reading that uses raised dots to signify numbers and letters.

brainstorming a basic creative thinking technique used in problem solving; participants are asked to come up with as many ideas as possible relative to a certain topic—there are no right or wrong answers; responses cannot be criticized; piggybacking an idea onto someone else's is encouraged.

Brown v. Board of Education of Topeka, Kansas a 1954 Supreme Court ruling prohibiting the use of "separate but equal" schools for African American and white students.

cane travel using a long white cane to scan the environment while walking.

caregiver any person who takes care of or raises a child.

cataract a clouding of the lens of the eye.

cerebral palsy a neurological condition resulting from damage to the brain before or during birth or in infancy; it is characterized by disabilities in movement and posture.

chorionic villous sampling (CVS) a prenatal testing technique that analyzes cells from the chorion to determine if certain genetic abnormalities are present.

civil rights movement the 1960s movement for social and political equality for African Americans; it provided a model for activists seeking similar rights for people with disabilities.

classroom discourse the verbal interactions of the classroom.

classroom discourse strategies ways in which teachers communicate their expectations for learning to students.

Clerc, Laurent 19th-century Frenchman who became the first teacher at the school for deaf children founded by T.H. Gallaudet. Clerc was deaf himself.

closed captioning captions that parallel the verbal content of a television show; they are made visible through decoders built into all television sets manufactured after July 1, 1993, which allow viewers to select captioning of all available programs.

cluster grouping students who are identified as gifted at a given grade level are grouped together in the same classroom with a teacher who has training in educating students who are gifted. The rest of the class is a diverse group of learners.

cochlear implants tiny processors that are surgically implanted in the cochlea and serve to electrically stimulate the auditory nerve fibers and improve perception of sound.

code-emphasis approach an approach to reading instruction that focuses on teaching regular sound-symbol relationship in a structured and sequential way.

cognitive style the cognitive activity that takes place between the time a student recognizes the need to respond to something and actually does respond; cognitive styles are categorized along a continuum ranging from impulsive to reflective.

collaboration professionals working together with a shared purpose in a supportive, mutually beneficial relationship.

collaborative consultation teachers and other school professionals working together on an equal footing to solve students' problems.

communication the exchange of ideas, information, thoughts, and feelings.

communication disorders a language or speech disorder that adversely affects a child's educational performance.

communicative intent the intention or purpose of a behavior in communication with another.

community-based instruction working on a student's instructional goals in the community setting in which they would naturally be used.

compensatory academic skills skills needed to access the core curriculum.

conduct disorder individual disruptive, aggressive, noncompliant behaviors.

conductive hearing loss hearing loss resulting from damage or blockage to the outer or middle ear that disrupts the efficient passage or conduction of sound; most conductive losses can be treated medically.

congenital a condition present at birth.

congenital hearing loss a hearing loss present at birth.

congenital malformation an incomplete or improperly formed part of the skeletal or muscular system that is present at birth.

consultation a means of providing specialized services in the general education classroom whereby the special education teacher observes students with disabilities and provides suggestions to the teacher about adapting instruction or materials to meet students' needs.

consultation model special education resource teacher meets with classroom teachers to plan instructional adaptations for students and provide direct services in the classroom.

content area acceleration a curriculum modification for gifted students that allows students to proceed at a faster pace than their classmates.

content standards descriptions of the knowledge and skills children should acquire in specific content areas, such as reading, arithmetic, and science. Each state develops content standards that reflect the curriculum goals for students at each grade level.

contingency intervention curriculum the immediate and distinct presentation of consequences in order to facilitate an understanding of the relationship between actions and their results; this curriculum is used to give infants with severe disabilities the opportunity to develop purposeful behavior and interact with the environment in a meaningful way.

cooperative learning a learning strategy that involves providing small groups of students of various skill levels with a task to complete so that each student makes a significant contribution.

coping strategies things people do to enhance a sense of well-being and avoid being upset by stressful events.

cornea the transparent outer membrane of the eye.

cortical visual impairment vision loss resulting from damage to the brain rather than the eye.

creativity the ability to generate original or imaginative ideas.

cultural competence a respect for and knowledge of cultural differences and a willingness to accept that there are many ways of viewing the world.

cultural reciprocity a two-way process of information sharing and understanding between school professionals and families that can be truly reciprocal and lead to genuine mutual understanding and cooperation.

culture a way of perceiving, believing, evaluating, and behaving shared by a group of people.

curriculum-based assessment (CBA) a method of assessment based on materials in the child's curriculum rather than on a general achievement test.

curriculum telescoping a curriculum modification for gifted students that involves determining what the students already know and allowing them the chance to explore concepts, subjects, or topics that they have yet to learn.

cystic fibrosis a progressive and usually fatal disorder characterized by lung damage, abnormal mucus production, and difficulties in the absorption of protein and fat.

cytomegalovirus (CMV) a relatively common infection that if contracted by a pregnant woman can cause microcephaly, mental retardation, neurological impairments, and hearing loss in the surviving infant.

Deaf community those adults bound together by their deafness, the use of American Sign Language, and their culture, values, and attitudes.

Deaf culture the view of life manifested by the mores, beliefs, artistic expression, and language particular to deaf people.

deafness a hearing loss that precludes the learning of language through hearing.

deinstitutionalization the movement away from housing people with mental retardation in residential institutions and toward integrating them more fully into the community.

diabetic retinopathy a condition of the eye that can cause blindness; it occurs when the circulation problems associated with diabetes result in damage to the blood vessels of the retina.

diagnostic assessment the gathering of information about a child's developmental levels, usually through observation, interview, and formal testing, to determine whether the child has a disability.

dialect a variation of a spoken language used by a group of individuals that reflects and is determined by shared regional, social, or cultural/ethnic factors.

Diana v. Board of Education a 1970 California decision that children must be tested in their primary language when special education placement is being considered.

differentiation modifying the curriculum to meet the needs of learners with different levels of ability.

differentiated teaching teaching designed to meet the individual needs of students.

direct instruction the identification and instruction of specific academic skills and the use of teaching techniques that have been empirically demonstrated to be effective with students with learning difficulties.

disability a limitation, such as difficulty learning to read or inability to see.

discourse shared communication or conversation.

discrepancy the gap between a student's performance in school and his or her intellectual potential.

dog guide a trained dog used to identify obstacles to safe travel.

double deficit hypothesis the hypothesis that phonemic awareness and rapid naming difficulties are at the root of significant reading disabilities.

Down syndrome a condition caused by an extra twenty-first chromosome that results in mental retardation and physical anomalies.

DSM-IV *The Diagnostic and Statistical Manual of Mental Disorders of the American Psychiatric Association,* fourth edition. A classification system for behavior and emotional disorders.

dual diagnosis the coexisting conditions of mental retardation and behavioral disorders.

due process hearing a procedure to resolve a conflict between school and family over the evaluation, program, or placement of a student with a disability.

duration the length of time a behavior lasts.

early intervention a comprehensive set of services provided to children from birth to 3 years and their families designed to minimize the effects of risk status or disability.

echolalia the immediate or delayed repetition of someone else's utterance.

ecocultural theory seeks to explain family adaptations and activities through an understanding of the family's goals, dreams, and beliefs and the reality of the physical, material, and socio-cultural environment in which they live.

educational definitions those definitions of degrees of vision loss focusing on academic functioning and reading medium.

electronic travel aids devices that use sonic waves to detect obstacles in the environment.

emotional disturbance a condition including one or more of the following characteristics over a long period of time and to a marked degree, which adversely affects educational performance: an inability to learn, an inability to build satisfactory interpersonal relationships, inappropriate types of behavior, a general mood of unhappiness or depression, and a tendency to develop fears associated with personal or school problems.

enclave a small group of individuals with disabilities who are placed in a work setting, usually within a large business or corporation, and receive on-the-job training from job coaches or social service agencies and from the business itself.

encoding processes processes used to organize information so it can be learned.

enrichment adding disciplines or areas of learning not normally found in the regular curriculum, using more difficult or in-depth material to enhance the core curriculum, or enhancing the teaching strategies used to present instruction.

enrichment triad model (ETM) a program option for upper-elementary gifted children that exposes students to new curricular areas they might wish to explore in greater depth.

environmental analysis *see* environmental inventory.

environmental inventory (environmental analysis) a technique used to identify skills for instruction; it involves a visit to the settings in which the student lives or works so a list can be made of the specific skills needed to be successful in that environment.

environmental risk risk factors related to the environment in which a child develops.

epilepsy a condition of the nervous system that results in seizures that disrupt the normal functioning of the brain.

ethnicity the common history, values, attitudes, and behaviors that bind a group of people.

exceptional the label used to describe the range of students who receive special education services in the school.

exclusion clause the sentence in the federal definition of learning disabilities that excludes from the definition learning problems that are primarily the result of visual, hearing, or motor handicaps, mental retardation, emotional disturbance, or environmental, cultural, or economic disadvantage.

expanded core curriculum the existing core curriculum plus the additional areas of learning needed by students who are visually impaired.

expert consultation the special educator advises the regular educator about the management and instruction of students with special needs.

expressive language the language abilities involved in generating and presenting information.

extended family grandparents, aunts, uncles, cousins, and other relations who may or may not live with a child and parent(s).

externalizing behavior overtly expressed behavior directed toward others or the environment.

eye-gazing scanning system a system that allows an individual to select letters, words, and phrases from a display by simply focusing his or her eyes on the display; a small, sensitive camera detects the direction of the person's eyes and registers the selected elements so a typed message can be produced.

families with multiple risks those families that experience a number of social stressors that place the development of their children in jeopardy.

family two or more people who live together and are related by birth, marriage, or adoption.

family characteristics the traits, such as size, socioeconomic status, cultural background, and geographic location, that give each family its unique identity.

family configuration the adults present in a family.

family functions all the life tasks of the family necessary for meeting family needs, including economic, daily care, recreation, socialization, self-identity, affection, and educational/vocational functions.

family interaction the relationships among family members.

family life cycle the lifespan of a family, starting with the marriage of a man and a woman and evolving through the birth and growth of their children.

family quality of life family members' sense of overall satisfaction with family life.

family size the number of children in a family.

family systems approach a framework for understanding the family as an interrelated social system with unique characteristics and needs.

fetal alcohol syndrome (FAS) a syndrome resulting from maternal alcohol intake during pregnancy; it is characterized by altered facial features, developmental delays in language and cognition, and behavior problems.

field independent student a student who does well on independent projects and on analytical tests.

field independent teacher a teacher who prefers to use the lecture approach, with limited interactions with students, and who encourages student achievement and competition among students.

field sensitive student a student who performs well in group work and cooperative learning situations.

field sensitive teacher a teacher who prefers to use interpersonal teaching methods, such as personal conversations.

fingerspelling spelling the manual alphabet with the fingers.

first trimester the first three months of pregnancy.

fluency disorder an interruption in the flow of speaking that significantly interferes with communication.

formal assessment using standardized tests to compare a student's performance with that of his or her peers.

fragile X syndrome an inherited disorder, caused by chromosomal abnormalities, that may result in mental retardation, social, and communication deficits.

Framework of Support an outline of the supports necessary for a student with disabilities to meet the goals of education in the general education classroom.

functional academics basic academic skills taught in the context of real-life activities; a curricular emphasis on academic skills that are meaningful and useful for daily living.

functional behavior analysis the planned observation and analysis of the antecedents and consequences of a behavior.

functional communication verbal or nonverbal communication that is efficient, useful, understandable, and easy to use.

functional curriculum a curriculum that emphasizes preparation for life and includes only skills that will be useful to the student in home, community, school, or work environments.

functionally blind describes a person who uses his/her senses of touch or hearing as the primary means of learning.

functional vision how well a student uses whatever vision he or she may possess.

Gallaudet, Thomas Hopkins 19th-century minister and educator who was instrumental in starting the first school for deaf children in the United States.

generalization see skill transfer.

genetic counseling the process of discussing with a trained counselor the likelihood that a child will inherit a genetic condition.

giftedness high performance capability in intellectual, creative, artistic, leadership, or academic areas.

gifted underachiever the term applied to students whose aptitude is high but whose performance is low.

glaucoma a disease of the eye that can lead to blindness if untreated; it occurs when fluid within the eye cannot drain properly, resulting in a gradual increase of pressure within the eye.

grand mal seizure an epileptic seizure that involves the whole body, usually lasts a few minutes, and often results in a loss of consciousness.

group telescoping an analysis of subject matter to determine which parts are inappropriate for a small group of gifted students because they have already mastered them.

handicap the limitations imposed by the environment of a person with a disability or by people's attitudes toward disability.

hard of hearing a term that describes a hearing loss less severe than deafness that usually permits the understanding of oral speech through the use of hearing aids.

health impairment a term used to describe a condition in which one or more of the body's systems are affected by debilitating or life-threatening conditions or diseases.

health maintenance the assisting of or instruction of a student with a physical disability or health impairment in eating, drinking, or using the bathroom.

hearing impairment a term that refers to all degrees of hearing loss from slight to profound.

hearing loss a term used to describe hearing problems.

highly gifted a term used to designate someone whose IQ score is in the 140+ range.

Highly Qualified teachers a term used in the *No Child Left Behind* legislation that refers to a status bestowed on teachers who meet criteria of content and skill knowledge in their field. The certification, testing, and skill requirements that determine if a teacher can be called highly qualified are defined by individual states.

high-stakes testing or high-stakes assessment refers to testing that is used to make educational decisions. The term high stakes refers to the importance of the test result to the students taking the tests and to the teachers, schools, and educational agencies administering them.

home- or hospital-based instruction instruction provided by a special education teacher to students with chronic illness or other medical needs; it is usually temporary.

household one or more people, members of a family and others, who live under the same roof.

Howe, Samuel Gridley 19th-century educator and advocate for people with disabilities.

human guide a person, usually sighted, accompanying someone with vision loss while walking.

human immunodeficiency virus (HIV) the virus that causes AIDS.

hydrocephalus a condition in which cerebrospinal fluid builds up in the skull and puts pressure on the brain; if untreated, it can cause brain damage and mental retardation.

hyperglycemia a condition in which individuals with juvenile onset diabetes have high blood sugar, with potentially serious side effects, including unconsciousness and coma.

hypoglycemia a condition in which individuals with juvenile onset diabetes have low blood sugar, with potentially serious side effects including unconsciousness and seizures.

hypoxia decreased availability of oxygen during pregnancy, labor, delivery, or newborn life; it can result in death or brain damage.

immature behavior behavior that exhibits a low level of frustration tolerance and the inability to say and do socially appropriate things.

inclusion the provision of services to students with disabilities in the general education classroom.

independent living skills the skills and practices necessary for living everyday life on one's own.

independent study a curriculum modification for gifted students that allows them to explore topics of interest to them; the student does require teacher guidance to be sure a manageable topic is selected.

individual supported job model a form of supported employment in which a job coach provides on-site training and problem solving for a single individual; the goal is to gradually decrease the level of support until the individual is ready for independent competitive employment.

individualized education the concept that each student should have a program tailored to his or her unique learning needs.

individualized education program (IEP) the written plan for each student's individual education.

individualized family service plan (IFSP) a written account of the personal and social services needed to promote and support the child and family for the first three years of an exceptional child's life.

individualized transition plan the written plan designed to help prepare a student with a disability for life after schooling.

Individuals with Disabilities Education Act (IDEA) the name given in 1990 to what was formerly known as the Education for All Handicapped Children Act, Public Law 94-142 and its amendments.

informal assessment measures of student performance and progress in academic or behavioral tasks; focuses on individual growth and skill acquisition rather than on a comparison of one child's performance with that of others.

informal inventories a series of sequential passages or tasks, on different grade levels, used to assess the specific difficulties a student is having with reading, writing, or math skills.

inoculation vaccination against such infectious diseases as rubella, pertussis, measles, mumps, and polio.

institution a large, segregated, residential building used to house individuals with mental retardation, mental illness, or physical disabilities.

instructional discourse strategies classroom interactions between teacher and students which are designed to teach.

intelligence the capacity to acquire, process, and use information.

intensity the strength or magnitude of a behavior.

interdisciplinary team a group of professionals from a variety of disciplines who work with a family to plan, coordinate, and deliver services.

intermediate-care facility (ICF) a community-based residential placement comprised of a number of individuals with disabilities living together in a supervised setting.

internalizing behavior self-directed behavior, such as withdrawal, avoidance, or compulsiveness.

iris the colored part of the eye.

Irving Independent School District v. Tatro a 1984 U.S. Supreme Court decision that schools must provide medical services that a nonphysician can perform if a child needs them to remain in school.

Itard, Jean-Marc-Gaspard early 19th-century French physician who attempted to teach the "wild boy of Aveyron" to talk.

itinerant services services provided by a specialized teacher who travels from school to school to work with students or to consult with teachers.

job coach a person trained in special education who trains people on the job and works with on-site supervisors to help integrate the person with disabilities into the employment setting.

joint attention two or more individuals attending to the same experiences, activities, or objects.

juvenile onset diabetes a metabolic disorder caused by an insufficient amount of insulin produced by the body, which results in difficulties in digesting and obtaining energy from food; it can appear at any point between birth and age 30.

juvenile rheumatoid arthritis a condition that affects the tissue lining of the joints.

Kennedy, John F. U.S. president with a strong personal interest in improving the quality of life for people with mental retardation.

language the verbal means by which humans communicate.

language delay a delay in the acquisition of normal language milestones.

language disorders the impaired comprehension and/or use of spoken, written, and/or other symbol systems that may involve the form, content, or function of language.

language sample a written excerpt of a student's verbal communication over a specified period of time.

Larry P. v. Riles a 1979 California state court decision that IQ tests not be used in placing African American students in classes for students with mental retardation.

learning disability a disorder in one or more of the basic psychological processes involved in understanding or using language. A student who has a learning disability does not achieve at the expected age and ability level in one or more academic areas and shows a severe discrepancy between achievement and intellectual ability.

learning style the way a student approaches learning.

Learning Strategies Curriculum a well-known curriculum developed at the University of Kansas Institute for Research in Learning Disabilities that focuses on strategy instruction.

least restrictive environment the setting that allows each child to be educated with his or her nondisabled peers to the maximum extent appropriate.

legal blindness a visual acuity of 20/200 or worse in the better eye after correction or a visual field of no greater than 20 degrees; this level of visual impairment qualifies a person for a variety of legal and social services.

lens the clear structure between the iris and the tissue inside the eyeball, which focuses light on the retina.

level system an educational program that involves a stepwise progression through a predetermined set of behavioral requirements, restrictions, and responsibilities that allow students to achieve higher levels of freedom and responsibility once they demonstrate appropriate behavior.

life-skills curriculum a course of study intended to provide the skills necessary to enable a student to live and work independently.

low birthweight a weight less than five and a half pounds at birth.

low vision a visual impairment in which there is enough remaining vision to use as the primary source of information.

macroculture the core, or universal, culture of a country; in the United States it is characterized by traits such as individualism, industriousness, ambition, competitiveness, self-reliance, and independence.

Macy, Anne Sullivan teacher and companion of Helen Keller.

manual communication approach an approach to teaching students who are deaf or hard-of-hearing that emphasizes the use of signs and sign language; its basic components are fingerspelling and signs.

mediation discussion between families and school districts over a point of disagreement, for the purpose of resolving the disagreement before a due process hearing can be held.

meningitis a serious illness that can cause brain damage and result in a range of disabling conditions such as hearing and vision loss and mental retardation.

mental retardation a mild, moderate, or severe condition that is manifested in childhood and characterized by subaverage intellectual functioning and impairments in adaptive behavior.

mentorship an arrangement whereby a student works with a community member to learn a specific skill, trade, or craft.

metacognition "thinking about thinking"; the ability to identify how one learns and to evaluate, monitor, and adapt the learning process.

metalinguistic awareness the ability to think about one's own communication and language.

microculture a subculture that has its own distinctive cultural patterns while at the same time sharing core values with the macroculture.

Mills v. Washington, D.C. Board of Education a 1972 decision that required the District of Columbia to provide a free, appropriate public education for students with disabilities.

minority a numerical minority; it also suggests a subordinate position in society.

minority group a group that can be categorized by ethnicity, gender, language, religion, handicap, or socioeconomic status.

mixed hearing loss a hearing loss with both conductive and sensorineural components.

mobile work crew a group of individuals with disabilities who have learned a specific trade or set of skills that can be applied in the community.

mobility the ability to move about in one's environment.

Montessori, Maria early 20th-century Italian physician, teacher, and advocate of children with developmental disabilities; developed method of teaching used with typically developing children today.

morphemes the smallest units of meaning in a language.

morphology the rules that govern how word meanings may be changed by adding prefixes, suffixes, and other forms that specifically indicate tense and number.

multiple intelligences Howard Gardner's theory that there are at least eight distinct intelligences. An abundance of talent in any of these areas constitutes giftedness, according to Gardner.

muscular dystrophy a condition in which the voluntary muscles of the body are affected by progressive weakness.

natural environment one in which a child would spend time if he or she did not have special needs.

neonatal intensive care unit a specialized unit of the hospital for the care of high-risk newborns.

neonatology the study of high-risk newborns.

neurotoxins substances that adversely effect the developing central nervous system.

No Child Left Behind or NCLB, is a phrase used to refer to a law, previously known as the Elementary and Secondary Education Act, which was reauthorized in 2002 and amended to call for greater accountability by local schools and state education agencies.

nondiscriminatory evaluation evaluation procedures conducted with fairness in the child's native language.

normalization an emphasis on conventional or normal behavior and attitudes in all aspects of education, socialization, and other life experiences for people with disabilities.

nystagmus a repetitive, involuntary, rhythmic movement of the eyes common among children with visual impairments.

occupational hazards risks to health and life in the workplace.

optic nerve the nerve that connects the eye to the brain.

optic nerve hypoplasia faulty development or deterioration of the optic nerve, resulting in vision loss.

oral communication approach an approach to teaching students who are deaf and hard-of-hearing that emphasizes the development of speech and auditory skills through a combination of speech reading and use of residual hearing.

organization a cognitive skill that involves the ability to see and use similarities and differences and to categorize, arrange, and plan.

orientation the ability to use one's senses to establish where one is in space and in relation to other objects and people.

orientation and mobility the skills involved in being able to move around in the environment for a person with visual impairment.

otitis media middle ear infection; the most common cause of conductive hearing loss in children.

otologist a physician who specializes in diseases of the ear.

overrepresentation a representation in a specific group or class that is greater than would be expected based on actual population numbers.

parent-to-parent model a model for parent support that links experienced parents of children with disabilities to parents who are new to the programs and processes.

partial participation performing parts of a skill or activity that are in an individual's ability range.

pegwords a word that rhymes with a piece of information to be learned, that is then associated with a picture to assist in remembering.

Pennsylvania Association for Retarded Citizens (PARC) v. Commonwealth of Pennsylvania a 1972 state decision that required Pennsylvania to provide a free, appropriate public education for students with mental retardation.

people-first language language that describes the person first, then the disability.

perception the ability to organize and interpret what one experiences through the senses.

perinatal period the period from the twelfth week of pregnancy to the twenty-eighth day of life.

perinatal stress traumatic events such as difficult or prolonged labor and delivery, hypoxia, low birthweight, or illness that occur during birth or the first twenty-eight days after birth.

pervasive developmental disorders a term given to a collection of developmental disabilities including autism, Asperger's syndrome, and other disorders including autistic-like behavior.

petit mal seizure an epileptic seizure that occurs most frequently in children between the ages of 4 and 12; these seizures are very brief—usually only a few seconds—and although the child may lose consciousness, there may be no observable physical changes.

phoneme the smallest unit of speech.

phonological awareness the ability to recognize the sounds contained in words.

phonological disorders problems with the consistent articulation of phonemes, the individual sounds of speech.

phonology the rules for combining sounds in permissible ways to form words.

physical disability a condition that incapacitates to some degree the skeletal, muscular, and/or neurological systems of the body.

physical handling the moving of a student with a physical disability from place to place.

physically challenged the descriptive term preferred by many people with a physical disability; it describes their physical condition as a challenge to be faced rather than as a handicap.

polysubstance abuser someone who uses a combination of illegal drugs and alcohol.

positive behavior support preventive and positive interventions designed to create and maintain a supportive and successful environment.

postlingual deafness deafness that occurs after language is acquired.

postnatal period the period from the twenty-eighth day of life through the end of the first year.

pragmatic language the ability to use language effectively in different settings and for different purposes.

pragmatics the rules governing language use in differing situations.

predictive validity how accurately a test can predict academic performance.

performance standards descriptions of the ways students must be able to demonstrate that they have acquired specific skills and content. They focus on how students can illustrate their content knowledge. Performance standards are developed by all state departments of education.

prelingual deafness deafness that occurs before language is acquired.

premature a baby born before thirty-seven weeks' gestation.

prenatal care the care provided to an expectant mother during pregnancy by her physician, usually an obstetrician.

prenatal period the period from conception to birth.

prereferral intervention team a team of teachers and other professionals that works to keep children in the general education classroom instead of referring them to special education.

preterm *see* premature.

prevalence the number of students within a given special education category.

problem-based learning classroom learning based upon a real-life problem.

profound mental retardation a level of retardation characterized by an IQ of less than 20 and deficits in adaptive behavior.

projective test an open-ended test that provides an opportunity for a child to express himself or herself and perhaps reveal evidence of behavioral or emotional trauma.

prompt a cue or guide that helps a student attend to or learn the appropriate material.

Public Law 94-142 a 1975 federal law (known now as the Individuals with Disabilities Education Act, or IDEA) that requires that every child between

the ages of 3 and 21 with a disability be provided a free, appropriate public education in the least restrictive environment.

pullout program a service that involves the student leaving the classroom to receive specialized instruction.

pupil the opening in the center of the eye.

quality of life an index of adult performance, adjustment, and happiness.

radical acceleration skipping several grades or early entry to college.

rate how often a behavior occurs in a given time period.

reading comprehension the ability to understand the meaning of sentences and passages.

receptive language the language abilities involved in understanding and interpreting information.

reciprocal speech using language to give and receive information appropriately.

related services those services, such as speech, adaptive physical education, and others, which the student with disabilities requires in order to benefit from schooling. Related services must be specified on the IEP.

refractive errors myopia, hyperopia, and astigmatism resulting from differences in the shape of the eye.

relational meaning the meaning that goes beyond the individual meanings of words and links word meanings together into topics.

remedial instruction teaching the basic skill or content subject in which a student is having difficulty.

residential school a special school where students live during the school year.

residual hearing the remaining hearing most people with hearing loss possess.

resiliency the ability to resist stress, overcome risk factors, and develop well.

resource room a service that involves students leaving the regular classroom for specialized instruction in academic areas of need.

respite care care given to a family member with a disability by a trained substitute caregiver.

retina a layer of specialized cells at the back of the eye that are highly sensitive to light.

retinitis pigmentosa a hereditary condition of the eye characterized by degeneration of the retina caused by a deposit of pigment in the back of the eye; it is a progressive disease that results in tunnel vision.

retinopathy of prematurity damage to the eye that can cause vision loss in premature infants.

right to due process a procedure to resolve a conflict between a school and family over the evaluation, placement, or program of a child with a disability.

risk factors biological and environmental conditions associated with the increased probability of developmental problems.

rubella also known as German measles; a highly contagious virus that can cause severe damage to the fetus if contracted by a mother in the first sixteen weeks of pregnancy.

scaffolding the guidance an adult or peer provides through verbal communication as a way of doing for the student what the student cannot yet do alone.

screening quick evaluation of large numbers of children for developmental and health problems.

Schoolwide Enrichment Model Joseph Renzulli's model for school change that is based on curriculum modifications and enrichment strategies used with gifted students.

Section 504 of the Rehabilitation Act of 1973 a law requiring that all facilities that receive federal funds be accessible to people with disabilities and prohibiting discrimination against people who are disabled.

Seguin, Edouard 19th-century teacher and advocate for children with mental retardation.

semantics the rules used to create and understand meaning in words and word combinations.

sensorineural hearing loss permanent hearing loss that usually results from damage to the cochlea or auditory nerve.

severe disabilities disabilities that require ongoing support in one or more major life activity, such as mobility, communication, self-care, and learning, in order to participate in integrated community settings and enjoy a quality of life available to people with fewer or no disabilities.

severe mental retardation a level of retardation characterized by an IQ of less than 40 and deficits in adaptive behavior.

sexually transmitted diseases (STDs) diseases spread through sexual intercourse.

sheltered employment contract work conducted in settings designed for individuals with disabilities—usually assembly-line workshops.

sheltered workshops large facilities for people with disabilities that provide simple contract work.

signs manual symbols for a word or concept.

skill transfer (generalization) the ability to apply a specific skill learned in one context to a different context.

Snellen Chart the most common visual screening test; it consists of eight rows of letters, each row smaller in size than the previous one; the person being tested is asked to read the letters with each eye while the other eye is covered. Each row represents the distance at which a person with normal vision can see the letters.

social integration inclusion, acceptance, and the development of friendships for students with disabilities.

socialized aggression aggressive and disruptive behaviors on the part of a group.

socioeconomic status a measure of a family's social and economic standing based on family income, education, and employment of the parents.

special class a class within an elementary or high school that groups children by exceptionality; a specialist teacher instructs these students together.

special education the educational program designed to meet the unique learning and developmental needs of exceptional students.

special school a school designed exclusively for students with exceptionalities.

specific language impairment primary difficulty in learning and using language that cannot be attributed to another disability.

speech the spoken component of the language system produced by complex, well-coordinated activity from respiration to phonation to articulation.

speech disorders impairments of articulation, fluency, or voice.

speech-language pathologist the specialist concerned with the identification, assessment, and treatment of students with communication disorders.

spina bifida a midline defect of the skin, spinal column, and spinal cord that occurs during fetal development; it is characterized by varying degrees of paralysis.

stage theory an assumption that changes occur in a predictable order

and that movement to the next stage depends on successful resolution of the prior stage.

Stanford-Binet a widely used standardized test of intelligence that places great emphasis on verbal judgments and reasoning.

stereotypic behaviors repetitive, nonharmful behaviors sometimes exhibited by people with severe mental retardation and autism; examples include rocking, twirling of objects, clapping of hands.

strabismus a structural defect associated with the muscles of the eye resulting in the appearance of crossed eyes or wall eyes; the result of this deviation is that the eyes focus on two different things at the same time, leading the brain to suppress one of the images.

strategy instruction an approach to teaching students with learning disabilities that involves first breaking down the skills involved in a task or problem into a set of sequential steps and then preparing the steps so that students may read and later memorize them in order to perform the task correctly.

stuttering the habit of repeating a sound, syllable, or word while speaking, which significantly interferes with communication.

supported employment an employment setting in which a job coach trains a student at the job site, and a support system is established to help the student maintain the job and adjust to new job requirements over time.

syntax rules governing how words may be combined to form sentences.

synthesized speech the storage of words or phrases that can be recalled as needed, or the storage of speech sounds that can be put together to form words using a sound-by-sound process.

talent a mental or physical aptitude or ability.

task analysis the process of breaking down a task or skill into its component parts.

task commitment the ability to stay focused on a task to its completion.

teacher assistance team a group of teachers and other professionals who work together to assist the general education teacher.

team teaching shared instruction of a lesson, a subject area, or an entire instructional program.

telecommunication devices for the deaf (TDDs) telephones with screens and keyboards that allow people who are deaf to communicate with others.

teratogen a substance that can cause birth defects.

Thalidomide a drug prescribed to pregnant women in the 1950s that caused severe birth defects.

total communication the philosophy that advocates the use of whatever communication system is appropriate for a given child with a hearing loss at a given time.

transdisciplinary model an approach to assessment and planning in which professionals with differing specializations work together on an equal footing.

transition movement from one life period or event to another. In special education, the transition most frequently prepared for is that from school to work and adult life.

transition coordinator a person designated by the state, school district, or school to plan, coordinate, and supervise transition services.

transition programs programs designed to facilitate movement from school to work, from segregated to integrated settings, and from isolated living to community living and employment.

traumatic brain injury an acquired injury to the brain caused by an external physical force resulting in total or partial functional disability or psychosocial impairment.

triarchic theory Robert Sternberg's theory that describes three kinds of intelligence: analytic, creative, and practical.

tutorial instruction helping the student in the specific subject in which he or she is having difficulty.

underrepresentation representation in a specific group or class that is less than would be expected based on actual numbers in the population.

unilateral hearing loss normal hearing in one ear and hearing loss in the other.

Universal Design for Learning (UDL) a philosophy and an approach to curriculum construction that emphasizes maximizing access of all individuals to both content and performance requirements.

verbalism the use of words without concrete knowledge of their meanings.

very low birthweight weight at birth of $3\frac{1}{2}$ pounds or less.

Vineland Adaptive Behavior Scale one of the most widely used instruments for measuring adaptive behavior.

visual acuity sharpness of vision.

visual impairment a term that describes all levels of vision loss, from total blindness to uncorrectable visual limitations.

vitreous humor liquid-filled "eyeball."

vocational rehabilitation counselor person who assists adolescents and adults with disabilities in making the transition from school to work by helping them plan for post high school education and training, and job placement.

voice disorder any disorder resulting from difficulties in breathing, abnormalities of the larynx, or dysfunctions in the oral and nasal cavities that can affect the pitch, loudness, and/or quality of a voice.

Wechsler Intelligence Scale for Children, Third Edition (WISC-III) a test frequently used to predict academic achievement in school-age children.

word analysis the process of identifying written words; it involves the use of phonics, sight words, and context clues.

zero reject the principle that no child with a disability shall be refused an appropriate education by the schools.

References

A. G. Bell Association for the Deaf and Hard of Hearing (2000). *So your child has a hearing loss: Next steps for parents.* Washington, DC: A. G. Bell Association for the Deaf and Hard of Hearing. http://www.agbell.org/information/brochures_parent_so.cfm.

Abelson, A.G. (1999). Respite care needs of parents of children with developmental disabilities. *Focus on autism and other developmental disabilities, 14* (2), 96–100.

Abuzaitoun, O.R., & Hanson, I.C. (2000). Organ-specific manifestations of HIV disease in children. In M. F. Rogers (Ed.), *The pediatric clinics of North America, 47*(1), 109–126.

Access Ingenuity (2003). http://www.accessingenuity.com/Disabilities/PhysicalDisability.htm/.

Adams, G. L. and Englemann, S. (1996). *Research on direct instruction: 25 years beyond Distar.* Seattle: Educational Achievement Systems.

Adams J. W. (2002). *You and your deaf child: A self-help guide for parents of deaf and hard of hearing children.* Washington, DC: Gallaudet University, Pre-College National Mission Programs.

Adelman, H.S. (1996). Appreciating the classification dilemma. In W. Stainback & S. Stainback (Eds.), *Controversial issues confronting special education: Divergent perspectives* (2nd ed.) (pp. 96–111). Boston: Allyn and Bacon.

Adger, C.T., Snow, C.E., & Christian, D. (Eds.) (2002). *What teachers need to know about language.* Washington, DC: ERIC Clearinghouse on Languages and Linguistics/Center for Applied Linguistics.

AIDS.ORG. (2003) /http://www.aids.org/factsheets/.

Alberto, P.A., & Troutman, A.C. (2003). *Applied behavior analysis for teachers* (6th Ed.). Upper Saddle River, NJ: Merrill/Prentice Hall.

Alessi, S.M., & Trollip, S.R. (2001). *Multimedia for learning: Methods and development* (3rd ed.). Boston: Allyn and Bacon.

Allinder, R.M., Dunse, L., Brunken, C.D., & Obermiller-Krolikowski, H.J. (2001). Improving fluency in at-risk readers and students with learning disabilities. *Remedial and Special Education, 22,* 48–54.

Allman, C. (2002). *Guidelines for providing state assessments in alternate formats for students with visual impairments.* Austin, TX: Texas School for the Blind and Visually Impaired (Last revision: July 30, 2002). http://www.tsbvi.edu/Education/state-assess.htm.

Allor, J.H. (2002). The relationships of phonemic awareness and rapid naming to reading development. *Learning Disability Quarterly, 25,* 47–56.

Alvino, J. (1989). From the editor. *Gifted Children Monthly, 10*(2), 23.

American Association for Mental Retardation (2002). Definition of mental retardation. Retrieved in September, 2003: www.aamr.org/Policies/faq_mental_retardation.shtml.

American College of Medical Genetics (1996). Statement on guidance for genetic counseling in advanced paternal age. http://www.acmg.net/resources/policies/pol-016.asp.

American College of Obstetricians and Gynecologists. (1997). Smoking and women's health. *ACOG Educational Bulletin,* number 240.

———. (2002). Illegal drugs and pregnancy. Retrieved May 14, 2004 from http://www.medem.com/medlb/article_detaillb.cfm?article_ID=ZZZN0X8997C&sub_cat=3/.

American College of Rheumatology (2003). /http://www.rheumatology.org/patients/factsheet/.

American Foundation for the Blind. (2001). *AFB directory of services for blind and visually impaired persons in the US and Canada* (print and online). New York: AFB Press.

American Printing House for the Blind (N.D.): *Program to develop efficiency in visual functioning.* http://www.aph.org/products/progdev.html/ (retrieved May 14, 2004).

———. (2002). Distribution of eligible students based on the Federal Quota Census of January 2, 2001 (Fiscal Year 2002). Retrieved from http://sun1.aph.org/fedquotpgm/dist01.html/ May 24, 2004.

Amish, P.L., Gesten, E.L., Smith, J.K., Clark, H.B., & Stark, C. (1988). Social problem-solving training for severely emotionally and behaviorally disturbed children. *Behavioral Disorders, 13,* 175–186.

Anderson, J.A., Kutash, K., & Duchnowski, A.J. (2001). A comparison of academic progress of students with EBD and LD. *Journal of Emotional and Behavioral Disorders, 9,* 106–121.

Anderson, P.P., & Fenichel, E.S. (1989). *Serving culturally diverse families of infants and toddlers with disabilities.* Arlington, VA: National Center for Clinical Infant Programs.

Ansell, S. E. (2004). Quality counts 2003: Put to the test. *Education Week, 23*(17), 75–76, 78–79.

Anthony, T.L., Bleier, H., Fazzi, D.L., Kish, D., & Pogrund, R.L. (2002). Mobility focus: Developing early skills in orientation and mobility. In R.L Pogrund & D.L. Fazzi, (Eds.). *Early focus: Working with young children who are blind or visually impaired and their families* (2nd ed.). New York: AFB Press.

Arick, J.R, Young, H.E., Falco, R.A., Loos, L.M., Krug, D.A., Gense, M.H., & Johnson, S.B. (2003). Designing an outcome study to monitor the progress of students with Autism Spectrum Disorders. *Focus on Autism and Other Developmental Disabilities, 18,* 75–87.

Arnold, L., Christopher, J., & Huestis, R. (1978). Megavitamins for minimal brain dysfunction: A placebo-controlled study. *Journal of the American Medical Association, 240,* 2642.

Arnos, K.S. (1999). Genetic counseling for hearing loss. In S. Epstein (Ed.), *Medical aspects of hearing loss for the consumer and the professional. The Volta Review, 99*(5): 85–96.

Artiles, A.J., & Ortiz, A.A. (2002). *English language learners with special education needs: Identification, assessment, and instruction.* McHenry, IL: Center for Applied Linguistics/Delta Systems Co.

Artiles, A.J., Harry, B., Reschly, D.J., & Chinn, P.C. (2002). Over-identification of students of color in special education: A critical overview. *Multicultural Perspectives, 4,* 3–10.

ASHA (American Speech-Language-Hearing Association) (1980). Committee on Language Speech and Hearing Services in the Schools. Definitions for communicative disorders and differences. *ASHA, 22,* 317–318.

———. (1991). The prevention of communication disorders tutorial. *ASHA, 33* (Suppl. 6), 15–41.

———. (1993a). Definitions of communication disorders and variations. *ASHA, 35* (Suppl. 10), 40–41.

———. (1993b). Implementation procedures for the standards for the certificates of clinical competence. *ASHA, 35*(3), 76–83.

———. (1997). *Assistive listening devices.* Rockville, MD: American Speech-Language-Hearing Association.

———. (1997). *Preventing speech and language disorders.* Rockville, MD: American Speech, Language, and Hearing Association.

———. (2002). *Guidelines for the roles and responsibilities of the school-based speech-language pathologist.* Rockville, MD: American Speech-Language-Hearing Association.

———. (2003). Late blooming or language problem? Retrieved from http://www.asha.org/public/speech/disorders/ Late-Blooming-or-Language-Problem.htm/ May 24, 2004.

Augusto, C. (1996). Foreword. In A.L. Corn & A.J. Koenig (Eds.), *Foundations of low vision: Clinical and functional perspectives* (p. v). New York: AFB Press.

Aveno, A., & Renzaglia, A. (1988). A survey of attitudes of potential community training site staff toward persons with severe handicaps. *Education and Training in Mental Retardation, 23,* 213–223.

Babyak, A.E., Koorland, M., & Mathes, P.G. (2000). The effects of story mapping instruction on the reading comprehension of students with behavioral disorders. *Behavioral Disorders, 25,* 239–258.

Bailey, D.B., Bruer, J.T., Symons, F.J., Lichtman, J.W. (Eds.) (2001). *Critical thinking about critical periods.* Baltimore: Paul H. Brookes.

Bailey, D.B., Hatton, D.D., Mesibov, G., Ament, N., & Skinner, M. (2000). Early development, temperament, and functional impairment in Autism and Fragile X Syndrome. *Journal of Autism and Developmental Disorders, 30,* 49–59.

Bailey, D.B., Skinner, D., Rodriguez, P., Gut, D., & Correa, V. (1999). Awareness, use, and satisfaction with services for Latino parents of young children with disabilities. *Exceptional Children, 65* (3), 367–381.

Bain, B.A., & Olswang, L.B. (1995). Examining readiness for learning two-word utterances by children with specific expressive language impairment: Dynamic assessment validation. *American Journal of Speech-Language Pathology, 4,* 81–91.

Baker, C., & Cokely, D. (1980). *American Sign Language: A teacher's resource on grammar and culture.* Silver Spring, MD: T.J. Publishers.

Baker, R.L., Mednick, B.R., & Hunt, N.A. (1987). Academic and social characteristics of low-birth-weight adolescents. *Social Biology, 34*(1–2), 94–109.

Baldwin, A.Y. (2002). Culturally diverse students who are gifted. *Exceptionality, 10*(2), 139–147.

Baldwin, A. & Vialle, W. (1999). *The many faces of giftedness: Lifting the masks.* Belmont, CA: Wadsworth.

Barkley, R.A. (1998). *Attention deficit hyperactivity disorders: A handbook for diagnosis and treatment.* New York: Guilford Press.

Barnard, K.E., & Kelly, J.F. (1990). Assessment of parent-child interaction. In S.J. Meisels & J.P. Shonkoff (Eds.), *Handbook of early childhood intervention* (pp. 278–302). New York: Cambridge University Press.

Barnes, S.B., & Whinnery, K.W. (2002). Effects of functional mobility skills training for young students with physical disabilities, *Exceptional Children, 68,* 313–324.

Barraga, N. C., & Erin, J. N. (1992). *Visual handicaps and learning.* Austin, TX: Pro-Ed.

Barton, D.D. (1984). Uncharted course: Mothering the blind child. *Journal of Visual Impairment and Blindness, 78*(2), 66–69.

Bashir, A.S., & Scavuzzo, A. (1992). Children with language disorders: Natural history and academic success. *Journal of Learning Disabilities, 25,* 53–64.

Batshaw, M.L. (Ed.) (1997). *Children with disabilities* (4th ed.). Baltimore: Paul H. Brookes.

Batshaw, M.L., & Conlin, C.J. (1997). Substance abuse: A preventable threat to development. In M.L. Batshaw (Ed.), *Children with disabilities* (4th edition) (pp. 143–162). Baltimore: Paul H. Brookes.

Batshaw, M.L., & Perret, Y.M. (1992). *Children with handicaps: A medical primer* (3rd ed., p. 444). Baltimore: Paul H. Brookes.

Batshaw, M.L., & Rose, N.C. (1997). Birth defects, prenatal diagnosis, and prenatal therapy. In M.L. Batshaw (Ed.), *Children with disabilities* (4th edition) (pp. 35–52). Baltimore: Paul H. Brookes.

Bauer, A.M., & Shea, T.M. (2002). *Parents and schools: Creating a special partnership for students with special needs.* Englewood Cliffs, NJ: Prentice-Hall.

Baum, S.M., & Olenchak, F.R. (2002). The alphabet children: GT, ADHD, and more. *Exceptionality, 10*(2), 77–91.

Beck, J. (2002). Emerging literacy through assistive technology. *Teaching Exceptional Children, 35*(2), 44–48.

Beirne-Smith, M., Ittenbach, R.E., & Patton, J.R. (2002). *Mental retardation* (6th ed.). Upper Saddle River, NJ: Merrill/Prentice-Hall.

Belsky, J., Lang, M.E., & Rovine, M. (1985). Stability and change in marriage across the transition to parenthood: A second study. *Journal of Marriage and the Family, 47,* 855–865.

Bennett, D.S., Bendersky, M., & Lewis, M. (2002). Children's intellectual and emotional/behavioral adjustment at 4 years as a function of cocaine exposure, maternal characteristics, and environmental risk. *Developmental Psychology, 38* (5), 648–658.

Berko, J. (1958). The child's learning of English morphology. *Word, 14,* 150–177.

Bernheimer, L.P., Gallimore, R., & Weisner, T.S. (1990). Ecocultural theory as a context for the Individualized Family Service Plan. *Journal of Early Intervention, 14* (3), 219–233.

Bernheimer, L.P., & Keogh, B.K. (1995). Weaving assessment into the fabric of everyday life: An approach to family assessment. *Topics in early childhood special education, 15*(4), 415–433.

Berry, J.O., & Hardman, M.L. (1998). *Lifespan perspectives on the family and disability.* Boston: Allyn and Bacon.

Berry, M.R., Lindstrom, L., & Vovanoff, P. (2000). Improving graduation outcomes of students with disabilities: Predictive factors and student perspectives. *Exceptional Children, 66,* 509–529.

Bettleheim, B. (1967). *The empty fortress: Infantile autism and the birth of the self.* New York: Free Press.

Biederman, G.B., Fairhall, J.L., Raven, K.A., & Davey, V.A. (1998). Verbal prompting, hand-over-hand instruction, and passive observation with developmental disabilities. *Exceptional Children, 64,* 503–511.

Bigge, J. (1991a). Self care. In J. Bigge, *Teaching individuals with physical and multiple disabilities* (3rd ed.) (pp. 379–398). New York: Merrill.

———. (1991b). Life management. In J. Bigge, *Teaching individuals with physical and multiple disabilities* (3rd ed.) (pp. 399–427). New York: Merrill.

———. (1991c). Augmentative communication. In J. Bigge, *Teaching individuals with physical and multiple disabilities* (3d ed.) (pp. 199–246). New York: Merrill.

Bigler, E.D. (1992). The neurobiology and neuropsychology of adult learning disorders. *Journal of Learning Disabilities, 25,* 488–506.

Blachman, B.A. (1991a). Getting ready to read: Learning how to print maps of speech. In J.F. Kavanagh (Ed.), *The language continuum: From infancy to literacy* (pp. 41–62). Parkton, MD: York Press.

———. (1991b). Early intervention for children's reading problems: Clinical applications of the research in phonological awareness. *Topics in Language Disorders, 12*(1), 51–65.

Blackhurst, A.E. (1997). Perspectives on technology in special education. *Teaching Exceptional Children, 29*(5), 41–48.

Blackorby, J., & Wagner, M. (1996). Longitudinal postschool outcomes of youth with disabilites: Findings from the National Longitudinal Transition Study. *Exceptional Children, 62,* 399–413.

Blatt, B. (1966). *Christmas in purgatory.* Boston: Allyn and Bacon.

Blischak, D.M. (1999). Increases in natural speech production following experience with synthetic speech. *Journal of Special Education Technology, 7*(2), 44–53.

Bloom, B. (Ed.). (1956). *Taxonomy of educational objectives, Handbook I: Cognitive domain.* New York: David McKay.

———. (1985). *Developing talent in young people.* New York: Ballantine.

Blumenthal-Kelly, A. (1995). Fingerspelling interaction: A set of deaf parents and their deaf daughter. In C. Lucas (Ed.). *Sociolinguistics in deaf communities* (pp, 62–73). Washington, DC: Gallaudet University.

Bock, S.J., & Myles, B.S. (1999). An overview of characteristics of Asperger Syndrome. *Education and Training in Mental Retardation and Developmental Disabilties, 34,* 511–520.

Boland, M.G. (2000). Caring for the child and family with HIV disease. In M. F. Rogers (Ed.), *The pediatric clinics of North America, 47*(1), 189–202.

Bondy, A., & Frost, L., (2001). *A picture's worth: PECS and other visual communication strategies in autism.* Bethesda, MD: Woodbine House.

Bowe, F.G (1991). *Approaching equality: Education of the deaf.* Silver Spring, MD: TJ Publications.

———. (2002). Deaf and hard of hearing Americans' instant messaging and email use: A national survey. *American Annals of the Deaf, 147*(4), 6–10.

Boyle, J.R., & Weishaar, M. (2001). The effects of strategic notetaking on the recall and comprehension of lecture information for high school students

with learning disabilities. *Learning Disabilities Research and Practice, 16,* 133–141.

Bradbury, J. (2002). Could treatment of neonatal RDS improve further? *Lancet, 360* (9330), 394.

Brady, M.P., & Rosenberg, H. (2002). Job observation and behavior scale: A supported employment assessment instrument. *Education and Training in Mental Retardation and Developmental Disabilities, 37,* 427–433.

Brady, N.C., & Halle, J.W. (1997). Functional analysis of communicative behaviors. *Focus on Autism and Other Developmental Disabilities, 12,* 95–104.

Branham, R.S., Collins, B.C., Schuster, J.W., & Kleinert, H. (1999). Teaching community skills to students with moderate disabilties: Comparing combined techniques of classroom simulation, videotape modeling, and community-based instruction. *Education and Training in Mental Retardation and Developmental Disabilities, 34,* 170–181.

Breakthroughs. (1997). Augmentative communication product catalog. Pittsburgh, PA: Sentient Systems Technology, Inc.

Breslau, N., Staruch, K.S., & Mortimer, E.A. (1982). Psychological distress in mothers of disabled children. *American Journal of the Disabled Child, 136,* 682–686.

Bronfenbrenner, U. (1993). Forward. In T. Luster and L. Okagaki (Eds.): *Parenting: An Ecological Perspective.* Hillsdale, NJ: Lawrence Erlbaum.

Brooke, V., Wehman, P., Inge, K., & Parent, W. (1995). Toward a customer-driven approach of supported employment. *Education and Training in Mental Retardation and Developmental Disabilities, 30,* 308–320.

Browder, D.M., & Minarovic, T.J. (2000). Utilizing sight words in self-instruction training for employees with moderate mental retardation in competitive jobs. *Education and Training in Mental Retardation and Developmental Disabilities, 35,* 78–89.

Bruns, D.A. (2000). Leaving home at an early age: Parents' decisions about out-of-home placement for young children with complex medical needs. *Mental Retardation, 38,* 50–60.

Bruns, D.A., & Fowler, S.A. (1999). Culturally sensitive transition plans for young children and their families. *Teaching Exceptional Children, 31*(5), 26–30.

Bryan, T. (1991). Social problems and learning disabilities. In B. Wong (Ed.),

Learning about learning disabilities (pp. 196–231). San Diego: Academic Press.

Buck, G.H., Polloway, E.A., Smith-Thomas, A., & Cook, K.W. (2003). Prereferral intervention processes: A survey of state practices. *Exceptional Children, 69*(3), 349–360.

Bufkin, J.A., & Altman, R. (1995). A developmental study of nonverbal pragmatic communication in students with and without mild mental retardation. *Education and Training in Mental Retardation and Developmental Disabilities, 30,* 199-207.

Bullis, M., Yovanoff, P., Mueller, G., & Havel, E. (2002). Life on the "outs"—examination of the facility-to-community transition of incarcerated youth. *Exceptional Children, 69,* 7–22.

Burton, B.K., Schultz, C.J., & Burd, L.I. (1992). Limb abnormalities associated with chorionic villous sampling. *Obstetrics and Gynecology, 79,* 726–730.

Butterfield, N., & Arthur, M. (1995). Shifting the focus: Emerging priorities in communication programming for students with a severe intellectual disability. *Education and Training in Mental Retardation and Developmental Disabilities, 31,* 41–50.

Buysse, V., Goldman, B.D., & Skinner, M.L. (2002). Setting effects on friendship formation among young children with and without disabilities. *Exceptional Children, 68,* 503–517.

Campbell, P.H., Bellamy, G.T., & Bishop, K.K. (1988). Statewide intervention systems: An overview of the new federal program for infants and toddlers with handicaps. *Journal of Special Education, 22,* 25–40.

Carlson, C.I. (1987). Social interaction goals and strategies of children with learning disabilities. *Journal of Learning Disabilities, 20,* 306–311.

Carnine, D. (1991). Curricular interventions for teaching higher order thinking to all students: Introduction to the special series. *Journal of Learning Disabilities, 24,* 261–269.

Carnine, D., Silbert, J., & Kameenui, E.J. (1990). *Direct instruction reading* (2nd. ed.), New York: Merrill/Macmillan.

Caro P., & Snell, M.E. (1989). Characteristics of teaching communication to people with moderate and severe disabilities. *Education and Training in Mental Retardation, 24,* 63–77.

Carter, S. (2002). *The impact of parent/family involvement on student outcomes: An annotated bibliography of research from the past decade.* Eugene, OR: Consortium for Appropriate Dispute Resolution in Special Education

(CADRE). Available at http://www. directionservice.org/cadre/ parent_family_involv.cfm.

Cartledge, G., Kea, C.D., & Ida, D.J. (2000). Anticipating differences—celebrating strengths: Providing culturally competent services for students with serious emotional disturbance. *Teaching Exceptional Children, 32*(3), 30–37.

CAST (2003). CAST: Center for Applied Special Technology: Summary of universal design for learning concepts. Retrieved from (http://www.cast.org/udl/) January 4, 2004.

Catts, H.W. (1991). Facilitating phonological awareness: Role of speech-language pathologists. *Language, Speech, and Hearing Services in Schools, 22,* 196–203.

Cavanaugh, T. (2003). Ebooks and accommodations: Is this the future of print accommodations? *Teaching Exceptional Children, 35*(2), 56–61.

Cawley, J.F., Parmar, R.S., Yan, W.F., & Miller, J.H. (1996). Arithmetic computation abilities of students with learning disabilities: Implications for instruction. *Learning Disabilities Research and Practice, 1,* 230–237.

Center for Children's Health and the Environment (2002). Neurotoxins and the health of children. http://www.childrenvironment.org/factsheets/neurotoxins.htm.

Centers for Disease Control, Division of Sexually Transmitted Diseases (1997). Sexually transmitted diseases: Facts & information. Retrieved from http://www.cdc.gov/nchstp/dstd/disease_info.htm/ May 24, 2004.

——— (2003). STDs and pregnancy. http://www.cdc.gov/std/STDFact-STDs&Pregnancy.htm.

Chan, S. (1986). Parents of exceptional Asian children. In M.K. Kitano & P.C. Chinn (Eds.), *Exceptional Asian children and youth* (pp. 36–53). Reston, VA: Council for Exceptional Children.

Chan, S. (1998). Families with Asian roots. In E.W. Lynch & M.J. Hanson (Eds.), *Developing cross-cultural competence: A guide for working with children and their families* (2nd ed.). Baltimore: Paul H. Brookes.

Chandler, L.K., Dahlquist, C.M., Repp, A.C., & Feltz, C. (1999). The effects of team-based functional assessment on the behavior of students in classroom settings. *Exceptional Children, 66,* 101–122.

Chapman, R.S., Streim, N.W., Crais, E.R., Salmon, D., Strand, C.A., & Negri, N.A. (1992). Child talk: Assumptions of a developmental process model for early language learning. In R.S. Chapman (Ed.), *Processes in language acquisition and disorders* (pp. 3–19). St. Louis: Mosby Year-Book.

Chedd, N.A. (1995). Genetic counseling. *Exceptional Parent, 25*(8), 26–27.

Chen, D. (Ed.) (1999). *Essential elements in early intervention: Visual impairment and multiple disabilities.* New York: American Foundation for the Blind.

Chen, D., & Dote-Kwan, J. (1995). *Starting points: Instructional practices for young children whose multiple disabilities include visual impairment.* Los Angeles: Blind Children's Center.

Cheng, A.K., & Niparko, J.K. (2000). Analyzing the effects of early implantation and results with different causes of deafness: Meta-analysis of the pediatric cochlear implant literature. In J.K. Niparko, K.I. Kirk, N.K. Mellon, A.M. Robbins, D.L. Tucci, & B.S. Wilson (Eds.), *Cochlear implants: Principles and practices* (pp. 259–265). Philadelphia: Lippincott Williams & Wilkins.

Cheng, I. (1987). Cross-cultural and linguistic considerations in working with Asian populations. *ASHA 29*(6), 33–38.

Cheng, L.L. (1987). *Assessing Asian language performance: Guidelines for evaluating limited English proficient students.* Rockville, MD: Aspen.

Chez, M.G., Buchanan, C.P., Bagan, B.T., Hammer, M.S., McCarthy, K.S., Ovrutskaya, I., Nowinski, C.V., & Cohen, Z.S. (2000). Secretin and autism: A two-part clinical investigation. *Journal of Autism and Developmental Disorders, 30,* 87–94.

Childhood Cancer Foundation (2003). http://www.candlelighters.org/.

Children Affected by Aids Foundation (CAAF) (2003). http://www.caaf4kids.org/hivaid.html.

Children's Defense Fund. (2000). *The state of America's children yearbook.* Washington, DC: Children's Defense Fund.

——— (2002). Frequently asked questions. http://www.childrensdefense.org/fs_cpfaq_facts.php.

Cho, S.J., Singer, G.H.S., & Brenner, M. (2000). Adaptation and accommodation to young children with disabilities: A comparison of Korean and Korean American parents. *Topics in Early Childhood Special Education, 20*(4), 236–249.

Christensen, K.M. (1993). A multicultural approach to education of children who are deaf. In K.M. Christensen & G.L. Delgado (Eds.), *Multicultural issues in deafness.* White Plains, NY: Longman.

Christiansen, J., & Leigh, I. (2002). *Cochlear implants in children: Ethics and choices.* Washington, DC: Gallaudet University Press.

Civil Rights Project (2002). Racial inequity in special education: Executive summary for federal policy makers. Retrieved in September, 2003; www.civilrightsproject.harvard.edu.

Clark, B. (2002). *Growing up gifted* (6th edition). Upper Saddle River, NJ: Merrill/Prentice-Hall.

Clark, G.M., & Patton, J.R. (1997). *Transition planning inventory: Administration and resource guide.* Austin, TX: Pro-Ed.

Clark, W., & Hankins, N. (1985). Giftedness and conflict. *Roeper Review, 8,* 50–53.

Clasen, D.R., & Clasen, R.E. (2003). Mentoring the gifted and talented. In N. Colangelo and G.A. Davis (Eds.), *Handbook of gifted education* (3rd ed.) (pp. 254–267). Boston: Allyn and Bacon.

Clement-Heist, K., Siegel, S., & Gaylord-Ross, R. (1992). Simulated and *in-situ* vocational social skills training for youths with learning disabilities. *Exceptional Children, 58,* 336–345.

Cohen, L.M. (1990). Meeting the needs of gifted and talented minority language students ERIC EC Digest E480. Reston, VA: ERIC Clearinghouse on Disabilities and Gifted Education, Council for Exceptional Children.

Cohen, S.E., & Parmalee, A.H. (1983). Prediction of five-year Stanford-Binet scores in preterm infants. *Child Development, 54,* 1242–1253.

Coleman, M., & Vaughn, S. (2000). Reading interventions for students with emotional/behavioral disorders. *Behavioral Disorders, 25,* 93–105.

Coleman, M.R. (2003). The identification of students who are gifted. ERIC EC Digest E644. Reston, VA: ERIC Clearinghouse on Disabilities and Gifted Education, Council for Exceptional Children.

Coles, R. (1977). *Children of crisis: Vol. IV. Eskimos, Chicanos, Indians.* Boston: Little, Brown.

Committee on Disability Issues in Psychology (2003). *Guidelines for non-handicapping language in APA journals.* http://www.apastyle.org/ disabilities.html, retrieved 7/2/03.

Connor, L.E. (1986). Oralism in perspective. In D.M. Luterman (Ed.), *Deafness in perspective* (pp. 117–129). San Diego: College-Hill.

Conture, E.G. (1990). *Stuttering* (2nd ed.). Englewood Cliffs, NJ: Prentice-Hall.

Cook, B.G. (2001). A comparison of teachers' attitudes toward their included students with mild and severe disabilities. *The Journal of Special Education, 34,* 203–213.

Cook, B.G., & Semmel, M.I. (1999). Peer acceptance of included students with disabilities as a function of severity of disability and classroom composition. *Journal of Special Education, 33,* 50–61.

Cook, R., Klein, M.D., & Tessier, A. (2004). *Adapting early childhood curricula for children in inclusive settings* (6th ed.). Englewood Cliffs, NJ: Merrill/Prentice-Hall.

Cook, R.E., Tessier, A., & Klein, M.D. (2000). *Adapting early childhood curricula for children in inclusive settings* (5th ed.). Englewood Cliffs, NJ: Merrill.

Copeland, S.R., McCall, J., Williams, C.R., Guth, C., Carter, E.W., Fowler, S.E., Presley, J.A., & Hughes, C. (2002). High school peer buddies: A win-win situation. *Teaching Exceptional Children, 35,* 16–21.

Corbet, E.B. (1980). Elmer Bartels. *Options: Spinal cord injury and the future* (pp. 145–147). Denver: Hirschfield Press.

Corn, A.L, DePriest, L.B., & Erin, J.N. (2000). Visual efficiency. In A.J. Koenig and M.C. Holbrook (Eds.), *Foundations of Education: Vol. II* (2nd ed., pp.464–499). New York: American Foundation for the Blind.

Cott, A. (1972). Megavitamins: The orthomolecular approach to behavioral disorders and learning disabilities. *Academic Therapy, 7,* 245–257.

Council for Exceptional Children (1990). Americans with Disabilities Act of 1990: What should you know? *Exceptional Children, 57,* Supplement.

———. (1997). *CEC policy manual: Basic commitments and responsibilities to exceptional children.* http://www.cec. specl.org/pp/policies/ch3.htm#35.

——— (2001). Improving family involvement in special education. *Research Connections in Special Education, 9.* Reston, VA: Council for Exceptional Children.

———. (2003). Press release: New regulations on No Child Left Behind's annual yearly progress requirements give states and districts more flexibility. Arlington, VA: www.cec.sped.org.

Cox, J., Daniel, N., & Boston, B. (1985). *Educating able learners: Programs and promising practices.* Austin: University of Texas Press.

Craig, S., Hull, K., Haggart, A.G., & Perez-Selles, M. (2000). Promoting cultural competence through teacher assistance teams. *Teaching Exceptional Children, 32*(7), 6–12.

Crittenden, J.B. (1993). The culture and identity of deafness. In P.V. Paul & D.W. Jackson, *Toward a psychology of deafness.* Boston: Allyn and Bacon.

Cullinan, D. (2002). *Students with emotional and behavior disorders: An introduction for teachers and other helping professionals.* Upper Saddle River, NJ: Merrill/Prentice Hall.

Culpepper, B. (2003). Identification of permanent childhood hearing loss through universal newborn hearing programs. In Bodner-Johnson, B., & Sass-Lehrer, M., *The young deaf or hard-of-hearing child* (pp. 99–122). Baltimore: Paul H. Brookes.

Cutsforth, T.D. (1932). The unreality of words to the blind. *Teachers Forum, 4,* 86–89.

———. (1951). *The blind in school and society.* New York: American Foundation for the Blind.

Cystic Fibrosis Foundation (CFF) (May, 2003)/http://www.cff.org/about-cf/.

D'Andrea, F.M., & Barnicle, K. (1997). Access to information: Technology and Braille. In D.P. Wormsky & F.M. D'Andrea, (Eds.). *Instruction strategies for Braille literacy* (pp. 269–307). New York: AFB Press.

D'Andrea, F.M., & Farrenkopf, C. (2000). *Looking to learn: Promoting literacy for students with low vision.* New York: AFB Press.

Daniels, V.I. (2002). Maximizing the learning potential of African-American learners with gifts and talents. In F.E. Obiakor & B.A. Ford (Eds.), *Creating successful learning environments for African-American learners with exceptionalities.* Thousand Oaks, CA: Corwin Press.

Davidovitch, M., Glick, L., Holtzman, G., Tirosh, E., & Safir, M.P. (2000). Developmental regression in autism: Maternal perception. *Journal of autism and Developmental Disorders, 30,* 113–119.

Davies, D.K., Stock, S.E., & Wehmeyer, M.L. (2002). Enhancing independent task performance for individuals with mental retardation through use of a handheld self-directed visual and audio prompting system. *Education and Training in Mental Retardation and Developmental Disabilities, 37,* 209–218.

Dawson, G., & Osterling, J. (1997). Early intervention in autism. In M.J. Guralnick (Ed.), *The effectiveness of early intervention.* Baltimore: Paul H. Brookes.

Dawson, L., Venn, M.L., & Gunter, P.L. (2000). The effects of teacher versus computer reading models. *Behavioral Disorders, 25,* 105–113.

Deford, F. (1983). *Alex: The life of a child.* New York: Viking Press.

DeFries, J.C., Gillis, J.J., & Wadsworth, S.J. (1993). Genes and genders: A twin study of reading disability. In A.M.

Galaburda (Ed.), *Dyslexia and development: Neurological aspects of extra-ordinary brains* (pp.187–204). Cambridge, MA: Harvard University Press.

De La Paz, S., & Graham, S. (1997). Strategy instruction in planning: Effects on the writing performance and behavior of students with learning difficulties. *Exceptional Children, 63,* 167–181.

De La Paz, S., Owen, B., Harris, K.R., & Graham, S. (2000). Riding Elvis' motorcycle: Using self-regulated strategy development to PLAN and WRITE for a state writing exam. *Learning Disabilities Research and Practice, 15,* 101–109.

Delisle, J.R. (1984). *Gifted children speak out.* New York: Walker.

———. (1992). *Kidstories: Biographies of twenty young people you'd like to know.* Minneapolis: Free Spirit.

———. (2000). *Once upon a mind: The stories and scholars of gifted child education.* Fort Worth: Harcourt Brace College Publishers.

Delisle, J.R., & Lewis, B.A. (2003). *The survival guide for teachers of gifted kids: How to plan, manage, and evaluate programs for gifted youth K–12.* Minneapolis, MN: Free Spirit.

Denning, C.B., Chamberlain, J.A., & Polloway, E.A. (2000). Guidelines for mental retardation: Focus on definition and classification practices. *Education and Training in Mental Retardation and Developmental Disabilities, 35,* 226–232.

Dennis, R.E., Williams, W., Giangreco, M.F., & Cloninger, C.J. (1993). Quality of life as context for planning and evaluation of services for people with disabilities. *Exceptional Children, 59,* 499–512.

Desai, M., Pratt, L.A., Lentzner, H., & Robinson, K.N. (2001). Trends in vision and hearing among older Americans. *Aging trends, No. 2.* Hyattsville, MD: National Center for Health Statistics.

Deshler, D.D., Warner, M.M., Schumaker, J.B., & Alley, G.R. (1983). Learning strategies intervention model: Key components and current status. In J.D. McKinney & L. Feagans (Eds.), *Current topics in learning disabilities.* Norwood, NJ: Ablex.

Dettmer, P., Thurston, L.P., & Dyck, N. (1993). *Consultation, collaboration, and teamwork for students with special needs* (pp. 1–35). Boston: Allyn and Bacon.

Devlieger, P.J., & Trach, J.S. (1999). Mediation as a transition process: The impact on postschool employment outcomes. *Exceptional Children, 65,* 507–523.

Devlin, S.D., & Elliott, R.N. (1992). Drug use patterns of adolescents with behavioral disorders. *Behavioral Disorders, 17*, 264–272.

Diagnostic and Statistical Manual of Mental Disorders (4th ed., TR) (2000). Washington, DC: American Psychiatric Association.

Dickey, R., & Shealy, S.H. (1987). Using technology to control the environment. *American Journal of Occupational Therapy, 41*(11), 717–721.

Dingle, M., & Hunt, N. (2001). *Home literacy practices of Latino parents of first graders.* Paper presented at the American Educational Research Association Annual Meeting, Seattle.

Dinnocenti, S.T. (1998). Differentiation: Definition and description for gifted and talented. *National Research Council for the Gifted and Talented.* Retrieved from http://www.sp.uconn.edu/~nrcgt/news/spring98/sprng985.html.

DiSalvo, C.A., & Oswald, D.P. (2002). Peer-mediated interventions to increase the social interaction of children with autism: Consideration of peer expectancies. *Focus on Autism and Other Developmental Disabilities, 17*, 198–207.

Division for Early Childhood, Council for Exceptional Children (1998). Position statement on inclusion. Retrieved from http://www.cdc.gov/nchstp/dstd/disease_info.htm/ May 24, 2004.

Dolan, R.P., & Hall, T.E. (2001). Universal design for learning: Implications for large-scale assessment. *IDA Perspectives, 27*(4), 22–25.

Donahue, M., Cole, D., & Hartas, D. (1994). Links between langage disorders and emotional/behavioral disorders. *Education and Treatment of Children, 17*, 244–255.

Donovan, M.S., & Cross, C.T. (2002). *Minority students in special and gifted education.* Washington, DC: National Academy Press.

Dorris, M. (1989). *The broken cord.* New York: Harper Perennial.

Dote-Kwan, J. (1995). Impact of mothers' interactions on the development of their young visually impaired children. *Journal of Visual Impairment and Blindness, 89*, 47–58.

Downey, D., Mraz, R., Knott, J., Knutson, C., Holte, L., & Van Dyke, D. (2002). Diagnosis and evaluation of children who are not talking. *Infants and young children, 15*(2), 38–48.

Drasgow, E. (1998). American sign language as a pathway to linguistic competence. *Exceptional Children, 64*(3).

Drew , C.J., Logan, D.R., & Hardman, M. (1992). *Mental retardation: A life cycle approach* (5th ed.), (pp. 233–341). New York: MacMillan.

Dunlap, G., & Childs, K.E. (1996). Intervention research in emotional and behavioral disorders: An analysis of studies from 1980–1993. *Behavioral Disorders, 21*, 125–136.

Dunn, L.M. (1968). Special education for the mildly retarded: Is much of it justifiable? *Exceptional Children, 35*, 5–22.

Dunst, C.J. (2002). Family-centered practices: Birth through high school. *The Journal of Special Education, 36*, 139–147.

Durand, V.M., & Carr, E.G. (1985). Self-injurious behavior: Motivating conditions and guidelines for treatment. *School Psychology Review, 14*, 171–176.

Dykens, E., & Volkmar, F.R. (1997). Medical conditions associated with autism. In D.J. Cohen & F.R. Volkmar (Eds.), *Handbook of autism and pervasive developmental disorders* (2nd. ed., pp. 388–410). New York: Wiley.

Eby, J.W., & Smutny, J.F. (1990). *A thoughtful overview of gifted education.* New York: Longman.

Eccarium, M. (1997). Educating children who are deaf or hard of hearing: Assessment. ERIC EC Digest E550. Reston, VA: ERIC Clearinghouse on Disabilities and Gifted Education, Council for Exceptional Children.

Eddy, J.M., Reid, J.B., & Fetrow, R.A. (2000). An elementary school-based prevention program targeting modifiable antecedents of youth delinquency and violence: Linking the Interests of Families and Teachers (LIFT). *Journal of Emotional and Behavioral Disorders, 8*, 165–176.

Edgar, E. (1988). Employment as an outcome for mildly handicapped students: Current status and future directions. *Focus on Exceptional Children, 2*(1), 1–8.

Educating Children with Autism. (2001). Committee on Educational Interventions for Children with Autism, Washington, DC: National Research Council.

Ehlers, S., & Gillberg, C. (1993). The epidemiology of Asperger Syndrome: A total population study. *Journal of Child Psychology and Psychiatry, 34*, 1327–1350.

Ehren, B.J. (2000). Maintaining a therapeutic focus and sharing responsibility for student success: Keys to in-classroom speech-language services. *Language, Speech, and Hearing Services in Schools, 31* (3), 219–229.

Ehri, L.C. (1989). Movement into word reading and spelling. In J.M. Mason (Ed.), *Reading and writing connections* (pp. 65–81). Boston: Allyn and Bacon.

Elbaum, B. (2002). The self-concept of students with learning disabilities: A meta-analysis of comparisons across different placements. *Learning Disabilities Research and Practice, 17*, 216–226.

Ellerd, D.A., Morgan, R.L., & Salzberg, C.L. (2002). Comparison of two approaches for identifying job preferences among persons with disabilities using video CD-ROM. *Education and Training in Mental Retardation and Developmental Disabilities, 37*, 300–309.

Eng, T.R., & Butler, W.T. (Eds.).(1997). *The hidden epidemic: Confronting sexually transmitted diseases.* Committee on Prevention and Control of Sexually Transmitted Diseases, Institute of Medicine, Division of Health Promotion and Disease Prevention. Washington, DC: National Academy Press.

Englemann, S., & Bruner, E. (1995). *Reading mastery II, fast cycle,* (Rainbow Edition). Columbus, OH: SRA./MacMillan-McGraw-Hill.

Engelmann, S., & Carnine, D. (1982). *Corrective mathematics program.* Chicago: Science Research Associates.

Engelmann, S., Carnine, D., & Steely, D.G. (1991). Making connections in mathematics. *Journal of Learning Disabilities, 24*, 292–303.

Engelmann, S., & Hanner, S. (1982). *Reading mastery, level III: A direct instruction program.* Chicago: Science Research Associates.

Englemann, S. et al. (1999). *Corrective reading revised.* Columbus, OH: SRA./MacMillan-McGraw-Hill.

Englemann, S. et al. (2002). *Reading mastery plus* Columbus, OH: SRA./MacMillan-McGraw-Hill

Ennis, R.H. (1985). A logical basis for measuring critical thinking skills. *Educational Leadership, 43*(2), 44–48.

Epilepsy Foundation (1992). *Children and epilepsy: The teacher's role.* Landover, MD.

Epilepsy Foundation (2003). http://www.epilepsyfoundation.org/

Epstein, M., & Cullinan, D. (1998). *Scales for assessing emotional disturbance.* Austin, TX: Pro-Ed.

Epstein, M.H., Polloway, E.A., Patton, J.R., & Foley, R. (1989). Mild retardation: Student characteristics and services. *Education and Training in Mental Retardation, 24*, 7–16.

Ericsson, K.A., Krampe, R., & Tesch-Romer, C. (1993). The role of deliberate practice in the acquisition of expert performance. *Psychological Review, 199*, 363–406.

Erin, J.N. (1996). Functional vision assessment and instruction of children and youths with multiple disabilities.

In A.L. Corn & A.J. Koenig (Eds.), *Foundations of low vision: Clinical and functional perspectives* (pp. 221–245). New York: AFB Press.

Erin, J.N., & Paul, B. (1996). Functional vision assessment and instruction of children and youths in academic programs. In A.L. Corn & A.J. Koenig (Eds.), *Foundations of low vision: Clinical and functional perspectives* (pp. 185–220). New York: AFB Press.

Executive Committee of the Council for Children with Behavioral Disorders (1989). White paper on best assessment practices for students with behavioral disorders: Accommodation to cultural diversity and individual differences. *Behavioral Disorders, 14,* 263–278.

Fahey, K.R. (2000a). Language problems exhibited in classrooms. In K.R. Fahey & D.K. Reid (Eds.). *Language development, differences, and disorders* (pp. 247–296). Austin, TX: Pro-Ed.

———. (2000b). Speech problems in classrooms. In K.R. Fahey & D.K. Reid (Eds.). *Language development, differences, and disorders* (pp. 297–325). Austin, TX: Pro-Ed.

Falk, G.D., Dunlap, G., & Kern, L. (1996). An analysis of self-evaluation and videotape feedback for improving the peer interactions of students with externalizing and internalizing behavior problems. *Behavioral Disorders, 21,* 261–276.

Falk-Ross (2002). *Classroom-based language and literacy intervention: A programs and case studies approach.* Boston: Allyn and Bacon.

Falvey, M. (1995). *Inclusive and heterogeneous schooling.* Baltimore: Paul H. Brookes.

Fazzi, D.L., & Klein, M.D. (2002). Cognitive focus: Developing cognition, concepts, and language. In R.L Pogrund & D.L. Fazzi, (Eds.). *Early focus: Working with young children who are blind or visually impaired and their families* (2nd ed.). New York: AFB Press.

Fazzi, D.L., & Petersmeyer, B.A. (2001). *Imagining the possibilities: A creative approach to orientation and mobility instruction for people who are visually impaired.* New York: AFB Press.

Federal Register. (1992). Washington, DC: U.S. Government Printing Office, September 29.

Feelings Game (2002). Do2learn (http://www.dotolearn.com/games/learningames.htm).

Feil, E.G., Walker, H., Severson, H., & Ball, A. (2000). Proactive screening for emotional/behavioral concerns in Head Start preschools: Promising practices and challenges in applied research. *Behavioral Disorders, 26,* 13–25.

Feingold, B.F. (1975). Hyperkinesis and learning disabilities linked to artificial food flavors and colors. *American Journal of Nursing, 75,* 797–803.

Feldhusen, J.F. (1991). Saturday and summer programs. In N. Colangelo & G.A. Davis (Eds.), *Handbook of gifted education* (pp. 197–208). Boston: Allyn and Bacon.

Feldman, W. (1996). Chronic illness in children. In R.H.A. Haslam & P.J. Valletutti (Eds.), *Medical problems in the classroom: The teacher's role in diagnosis and management* (3rd ed., pp. 115–123). Austin, TX: Pro-Ed.

Felko, K.S., Schuster, J.W., Harley, D.A., & Collins, B.C. (1999). Using simultaneous prompting to teach a chained vocational task to young adults with severe intellectual disabilities. *Education and Training in Mental Retardation and Developmental Disabilities, 34,* 318–329.

Ferguson, D.L. (1987). *Curriculum decision making for students with severe handicaps: Policy and practice.* New York: Teachers College Press.

Ferrell, K.A. (1986). Infancy and early childhood. In G.T. Scholl (Ed.), *Foundations of education for blind and visually handicapped children and youth: Theory and practice.* New York: American Foundation for the Blind.

———. (2000). Growth and development of young children. In M.C. Holbrook and A.J. Koenig (Eds.), *Foundations of Education: Vol.1* (2nd ed., pp. 111–134). New York: American Foundation for the Blind.

Fidler, D.J., Hodapp, R.M., & Dykens, E.M. (2002). Behavioral phenotypes and special education: Parent report of educational issues for children with Down Syndrome, Prader-Willi Syndrome, and Williams Syndrome. *The Journal of Special Education, 36,* 80–88.

Finesmith, R.B., Zampella, E., & Devinsky, O. (1999). Vagal nerve stimulator: A new approach to medically refractory epilepsy. *National Journal of Medicine, 96*(6), 37–40.

Firman, K.B., Beare, P., & Lloyd, R. (2002). Enhancing self-management in students with mental retardation: Extrinsic versus intrinsic procedures. *Education and Training in Mental Retardation and Developmental Disabilities, 37,* 163–171.

First Step Kid Tools (2003). The Kid Tools Support System (http://kidtools.missouri.edu).

Fishbaugh, M.S.E. (2000). *The collaboration guide for early career educators.* Baltimore: Paul C. Brookes.

Fitzsimmons M.K. (1998). Beginning reading and phonological awareness for students with learning disabilities. ERIC EC Digest E565. Reston, VA: ERIC Clearinghouse for Special and Gifted Education, Council for Exceptional Children.

Flexer, C. (1994). *Facilitating hearing and listening in young children.* San Diego: Singular.

Florida Department of Education (1992). *Project IVEY: Increasing visual efficiency.* Tallahassee: State of Florida Department of Education.

Foorman, B.R., Francis, D.J., Fletcher, J.M., Schatschneider, C., & Mehta, P. (1998). The role of instruction in learning to read: Preventing reading failure in at-risk children. *Journal of Educational Psychology, 90,* 37–55.

Ford, A., Schnorr, R., Meyer, L., Davern, L., Black, J., & Dempsey, P. (1989). General community functioning. In A. Ford, R. Schnorr, L. Meyer, L. Davern, J. Black, & P. Dempsey (Eds.), *The Syracuse community-referenced curriculum guide for students with moderate and severe disabilities* (pp. 77–88). Baltimore: Paul H. Brookes.

Ford, D.Y. (2003). Equity and excellence: Culturally diverse students in gifted education. In N. Colangelo & G. A. Davis (Eds.), *Handbook of gifted education* (3rd ed.). Boston: Allyn and Bacon.

Ford, D.Y., & Harris, J.J. (1999). *Multicultural gifted education.* New York: Teachers College Press.

Forness, S.R., Sweeney, D.P., & Toy, K. (1996). Psychopharmacologic medication: What teachers need to know. *Beyond Behavior, 7*(2), 4–11.

Fowler, M. (1995). *Maybe you know my kid.* New York: Carol Publishing Group.

Frank, A.R., & Sitlington, P.L. (2000). Young adults with mental disabilities: Does transition planning make a difference? *Education and Training in Mental Retardation and Developmental Disabilities, 35,* 119–134.

Fraser, B., Hensinger, R.N., & Phelps, J. (1990). *Physical management of multiple handicaps.* Baltimore: Paul H. Brookes.

Frasier, M.M., & Passow, A.H. (1994). *Towards a new paradigm for identifying talent potential.* Storrs, CT: University of Connecticut, the National Research Center on the Gifted and Talented.

Freeman, B.J., Cronin, P., & Candela, P. (2002). Asperger Syndrome or Autistic Disorder? The Diagnostic dilemma. *Focus on Autism and Other Developmental Disabilities, 17,* 145–151.

Frey, K.S., Hirschstein, M.K., & Guzzo, B.A. (2000). Second step: Preventing aggression by promoting social competence. *Journal of Emotional and Behavioral Disorders, 8,* 102–112.

Friedman, H.S., Tucker, J.S., Schwartz, J.E., Tomlinson-Keasey, C., Martin, L.R., Wingard, D.L., & Criqui, M.H. (1995). Psychosocial and behavioral predictors of longevity: The aging and death of the "Termites." *American Psychologist, 50*(2), 69–78.

Friedrich, O. (1983, August). What do babies know? *Time,* pp. 70–76.

Friend, M. (1996). *The Power of 2: Making a difference through co-teaching.* Bloomington, IN: Indiana University Press.

Friend, M., & Cooke, L. (2000). *Interactions: Collaboration skills for school professionals.* White Plains, NY: Longman.

Fuchs, D., Fuchs, L., & Burish, P. (2000). Peer-Assisted Learning Strategies: An evidence-based practice to promote reading achievement. *Learning Disabilities Research and Practice, 15,* 85–91.

Fuchs, D., Fuchs, L.S., Mathes, P.G., & Simmons, D.C. (1997). Peer-assisted learning strategies: Making classrooms more responsive to diversity. *American Educational Research Journal, 34,* 174–206.

Fuchs, L.S., Fuchs, D., & Speece, D.L. (2002). Treatment validity as a unifying construct for identifying learning disabilities. *Learning Disability Quarterly, 25,* 33–45.

Fueyo, V. (1997). Below the tip of the iceberg: Teaching language-minority students. *Teaching Exceptional Children, 30*(1), 61–65.

Fujiura, G.T., & Yamaki, K. (2000). Trends in demography of childhood poverty and disability. *Exceptional Children, 66*(2), 187–199.

Furlong, M., & Morrison, G. (2000). The school in school violence: Definitions and facts. *Journal of Emotional and Behavioral Disorders, 8,* 71–82.

Gage, N.L., & Berliner, D. (1998). *Educational psychology* (6th ed.). Boston: Houghton Mifflin Co.

Gajar, A. (1992). Adults with learning disabilities: Current and future research priorities. *Journal of Learning Disabilities, 25,* 507–519.

Gajira, M., & Salvia, J. (1992). The effects of summarization instruction on text comprehension of students with learning disabilities. *Exceptional Children, 58,* 508–516.

Gallagher, J.J. (2000). Unthinkable thoughts: Education of gifted students. *Gifted Child Quarterly, 45,* 5–12.

Gallaudet Research Institute (2002). *Regional and national summary report of data from the 2000-01 Annual Survey of Deaf and Hard of Hearing Children and Youth.* Washington, DC: Gallaudet University.

———. (2003). *Regional and national summary report of data from the 2001–02 Annual Survey of Deaf and Hard of Hearing Children and Youth.* Washington, DC: Gallaudet University.

Gallimore, R., Bernheimer, L.P., & Weisner, T.S. (1999). Family life is more than managing crisis: Broadening the agenda of research on families adjusting to childhood disability. In R. Gallimore, L.P. Bernheimer, D.L. MacMillan, D.L. Speece, & S. Vaughn (Eds.) *Developmental perspectives on children with high-incidence disabilities.* Mahwah, NJ: Lawrence Erlbaum Associates.

Garbarino, J. (1990). The human ecology of early risk. In S.J. Meisels & J.P. Shonkoff (Eds.), *Handbook of early childhood intervention.* Cambridge: Cambridge University Press.

———. (1997). Educating children in a socially toxic environment. *Educational Leadership, 54*(7), 12–16.

Gardill, M.C., & Jitendra, A.K. (1999). Advanced story map instruction: Effects on the reading comprehension of students with learning disabilities. *Journal of Special Education, 33,* 2–17, 28.

Gardner, H. (1983). *Frames of mind.* New York: Basic Books.

———. (2000). The giftedness matrix: A developmental perspective. In R.C. Friedman & B.M. Shore (Eds.), *Talents unfolding: Cognition and development,* pp. 77–88. Washington DC: American Psychological Association.

Gardner, J.E., & Edyburn, D.L. (2000). Integrating technology to support effective instruction. In J.D. Linsey (Ed.). *Technology and exceptional individuals* (3rd ed.). Austin, TX: Pro-Ed.

Garretson, M.D. (1976). Total communication. *Volta Review, 78*(4), 107–112.

Gaunt, R.I. (1989). A comparison of the perceptions of parents of highly and moderately gifted children. Doctoral dissertation, Kent State University. *Dissertation Abstracts International, 50,* A.

Gee, J.P.(1990). *Social linguistics and literacies: Ideology in discourse.* Bristol, PA: Falmer Press.

Gerber, P.J., Ginsberg, R., & Reiff, H.B. (1992). Identifying alterable patterns in employment success for highly successful adults with learning disabilities. *Journal of Learning Disabilities, 25,* 475–487.

Gersten, R., & Baker, S. (2000).What we know about effective instructional practices for English-language learners. *Exceptional Children, 66*(4), 454–470.

Gersten, R., & Woodward, J. (1994). The language-minority student and special education: Issues, trends, and paradoxes. *Exceptional Children, 60,* 310–322.

Getch, Y.Q., & Neuharth-Pritchett, S. (1999). Children with asthma: Strategies for educators. *Teaching Exceptional Children, 31*(3), 30–36.

Ghaziuddin, M. (2002). Asperger Syndrome: Associated psychiatric and medical conditions. *Focus on Autism and Other Developmental Disabilities, 17,* 138–144.

Giangreco, M.F., Edelman, S.W., Luiselli, T.E., & MacFarland, S.Z.C. (1997). Helping or hovering? Effects of instructional assistant proximity on students with disabilities. *Exceptional Children, 64,* 7–18.

Gibbs, D.P., & Cooper, E.B. (1989). Prevalence of communication disorders in students with learning disabilities. *Journal of Learning Disabilities, 22,* 60–63.

Glassberg, L.A., Hooper, S.R., & Mattison, R.E. (1999). Prevalence of learning disabilities at enrollment in special education students with behavioral disorders. *Behavioral Disorders, 25,* 9–21.

Goldstein, L. (2003). IDEA reauthorization languishes as election year looms. *Education Week, 23*(10), 30.

Gollnick, D.M., & Chinn, P.C. (2002). *Multicultural education in a pluralistic society* (6th ed.). Columbus, OH: Macmillan.

Gomaa, A, Tsaih, S., Hu, H., Schwartz, J., Bellinger, D., Gonzalez-Cossio, T., Hernandez-Avila, M., Schnaas, L., Peterson, K., Aro, A. (2002). Maternal bone lead as an independent risk factor for fetal neurotoxicity: A prospective study. *Pediatrics, Vol. 110* (1), 110–118.

Goodenough, N. (1987). Multi-culturalism as the normal human experience. In E.M. Eddy & W.L. Partridge (Eds.), *Applied anthropology in America* (2nd ed.). New York: Columbia University Press.

Gorski, P.A., & VandenBerg, K.A. (1996). Infants born at risk. In M.J. Hanson (Ed.), *Atypical infant development* (2nd ed.) (pp. 85–114). Austin, TX: Pro-Ed.

Gould, S.J. (1981). *The mismeasure of man.* New York: Norton.

Graham, E.M., & Morgan, M.A. (1997). Growth before birth. In M.L. Batshaw (Ed.), *Children with disabilities* (4th ed.) (pp. 53–69). Baltimore: Paul H. Brookes.

Graham, S., Harris, K.R., & Larsen, L. (2001). Prevention and intervention of writing difficulties for students with learning disabilities. *Learning Disabilities Research and Practice, 16,* 74–84.

Gray, C. (2003). The Gray Center Retrieved 7/14/03 from (http://www.thegraycenter.org./sample_social_stories.htm).

Green, G. (1996). Evaluating claims about treatments for autism. In C. Maurice, G. Green, & S.C. Luce, (Eds.), *Behavioral intervention for young children with autism: A manual for parents and professionals* (pp. 15–28). Austin, TX: Pro-Ed.

Green, L. (2002). P.A. Parents try to save ill daughter. *San Jose Mercury News.* Retrieved from Sophia's Garden Foundation (www.sophiasgarden.org/in_the_news.html), 2003.

Greene, G. (1999). Mnemonic multiplication fact instruction for students with learning disabilities. *Learning Disabilities Research and Practice, 14,* 141–148.

Greenwood, C.R., Delquadri, J.C., & Hall, R.V. (1989). Longitudinal effects of classwide peer tutoring. *Journal of Educational Psychology, 81,* 371–383.

Gresham, F. (2001). Responsiveness to intervention: An alternative approach to the identification of learning disabilities. Paper presented at the Learning Disabilities Summit. Retrieved online at http://www.air.org/ldsummit//.

Gresham, F.M., & MacMillan, D.L. (1997). Social competence and affective characteristics of students with mild disabilities. *Review of Educational Research, 67,* 377–415.

———. (1997). Autistic recovery? An analysis and critique of the empirical evidence on the Early Intervention Project. *Behavioral Disorders, 22,* 185–201.

Griffin, D.K., Rosenberg, H., Cheyney, W., & Greenburg, B. (1996). A comparison of self-esteem and job satisfaction of adults with mild mental retardation in sheltered workshops and supported employment. *Education and Training in Mental Retardation and Developmental Disabilities, 31,* 142–150.

Griffin-Shirley, N., Trusty, S., & Rickard, R. (2000). Orientation and mobility. In A.J. Koenig and M.C. Holbrook (Eds.), *Foundations of Education: Vol. II* (2nd ed., pp. 529–568). New York: American Foundation for the Blind.

Griffith, P.L., & Olson, M.W. (1992). Phonemic awareness helps beginning readers to break the code. *The Reading Teacher, 45,* 516–523.

Grigal, M., Neubert, M., & Moon, M.S. (2002). Postsecondary options for students with significant disabilities, *Teaching Exceptional Children, 35*(2), 68–73.

Griswold, D.E., Barnhill, G.P., Myles, B.S., Hagiwara, T., & Simpson, R.L. (2002). Asperger Syndrome and academic achievement. *Focus on Autism and Other Developmental Disabilities, 17,* 94–102.

Gunn, B., Biglan, A., Smolkowski, K., & Ary, D. (2000). The efficacy of supplemental instruction in decoding skills for Hispanic and non-Hispanic students in early elementary school. *Journal of Special Education, 34,* 90–103.

Gunter, P.L., Hummel, J.H., & Venn, M.L. (2000). Are effective academic instructional practices used to teach students with behavior disorders? *Beyond Behavior, 9*(3), 5–13.

Guralnick, M.J. (1997). *The effectiveness of early intervention.* Baltimore: Paul H. Brookes.

Hack, M., & Fanaroff, A.A. (2000). Outcomes of children of extremely low birthweight and gestational age in the 1990s. *Seminars in Neonatology, 5* (2), 89–106.

Hafer J.C., & Wilson, R.M. (2002). *Come sign with us: Sign language activities for children.* Washington, DC: Gallaudet University Press.

Hallahan, D.P., Kauffman, J.M., & Lloyd, J.W. (1999). *Introduction to learning disabilities* (2nd ed.). Boston: Allyn and Bacon.

Halpern, A.S. (1993). Quality of life as a conceptual framework for evaluating transition outcomes. *Exceptional Children, 59,* 486–498.

Halvorsen, A.T., Doering, K., Farron-Davis, P., Usilton, R., & Sailor, W. (1989). The role of parents and family members in planning severely disabled students' transitions from school. In G.H.S. Singer and L.K. Irwin (Eds.), *Support for caregiving families* (pp. 253–268). Baltimore: Paul H. Brookes.

Hankins, C.S. (2003). Temporal and demographic trends in cerebral palsy fact and fiction. *American Journal of Obstetrics and Gynecology, 188,* 628–633.

Hanline, M.F., & Halvorsen, A. (1989). Parent perceptions of the integration transition process: Overcoming artificial barriers. *Exceptional Children, 55,* 487–492.

Hans, S.L. (1999). Demographic and psychosocial characteristics of substance-abusing pregnant women. *Clinics in Perinatology* (1), 55–74.

Hanson, M.J. (1998). Ethnic, cultural, and language diversity in intervention settings. In E.W. Lynch & M.J. Hanson (Eds.), *Developing cross-cultural competence* (2nd ed.) (pp. 3–22). Baltimore: Paul H. Brookes.

Hanson, M.J, & Carta, J.J. (1996). Addressing the challenges of families with multiple risks. *Exceptional Children, 62*(3), 201–212.

Hanson, M.J., Ellis, L., & Deppe, J. (1989). Support for families during infancy. In G.H.S. Singer & L.K. Irvin (Eds.), *Support for caregiving families* (pp. 207–219). Baltimore: Paul H. Brookes.

Harley, R.K., & Lawrence, G.A. (1984). *Visual impairment in the schools.* Springfield, IL: Thomas.

Harris, C.A., Miller, S.P., & Mercer, C.D. (1995). Teaching initial multiplication skills to students with disabilities in general education classrooms. *Learning Disabilities Research and Practice, 10,* 180–195.

Harris, S.L., & Handleman, J.S. (2000). Age and IQ at intake as predictors of placement for young children with autism: A four- to six-year follow-up. *Journal of Autism and Developmental Disorders, 30,* 137–142.

Harry, B. (1992a). Making sense of disability: Low-income, Puerto Rican parents' theories of the problem. *Exceptional Children, 59*(1), 27–40.

———. (1992b). Restructuring the participation of African-American parents in special education. *Exceptional Children, 59*(2), 123–131.

———. (2002). Trends and issues in serving culturally diverse families of children with disabilities. *Journal of Special Education, 36*(3), 131–138, 147.

Harry, B., Allen, A., & McLaughlin, M. (1995). Communication versus compliance: African-American parents' involvement in special education. *Exceptional Children, 64*(4), 364–377.

Harry, B., Kalyanpur, M., and Day, M. (1999). *Building cultural reciprocity with families: Case studies in special education.* Baltimore: Paul H. Brookes.

Harry, B., Rueda, R., & Kalyanpour, M. (1999). Cultural reciprocity in sociocultural perspective: Adapting the normalization principle for family collaboration. *Exceptional Children, 66* (1), 123–136.

Hartman, R., & Stage, S.A. (2000). The relationship between social information processing and in-school suspension for students with behavioral disorders. *Behavioral Disorders, 25,* 183–195.

Harvey, H.M., & Sall, N. (1999). Profiles of the expressive communication skills of children and adolescents with severe cognitive disabilities. *Education and Training in Mental Retardation and Developmental Disabilities, 34,* 77–89.

Hasazi, S., Furney, K., & DeStefano, L. (1999). School and agency implementation of the IDEA transition mandates: Perspectives from nine sites. *Exceptional Children, 65*(4), 555–567.

Hatlen, P. (2000a). Historical perspectives. In M.C. Holbrook and A.J. Koenig (Eds.), *Foundations of Education: Vol.1* (2nd ed., pp.1–54). New York: American Foundation for the Blind.

———. (2000b). The core curriculum for blind and visually impaired students, including those with additional disabilities. In A.J. Koenig and M.C. Holbrook (Eds.), *Foundations of Education: Volume II* (2nd ed., pp. 779–784). New York: American Foundation for the Blind.

Hatton, D.D., McWilliam, R.A., & Winton, P.J. (2002). Infants and toddlers with visual impairments: Suggestions for early interventionists. ERIC EC Digest E636. Reston, VA: The ERIC Clearinghouse on Disabilities and Gifted Education, Council for Exceptional Children.

Hauser-Cram, P., Warfied, M.E., Shonkoff, J.P., & Krauss, M.W. (2001). The development of children with disabilities and the adaptations of their parents: Theoretical implications and empirical evidence. *Monographs of the Society for Research in Child Development, 66,* 3.

Hayden, M., Gersten, R., & Carnine, D. (1992). Using computer networking to increase active teaching in general education math classes containing students with mild disabilities. *Journal of Special Education Technology, 11,* 167–177.

Hayes et al. (1997). Ten-year survival of Down syndrome births, *International Journal of Epidemiology, 26,* 822–829.

Haynes, W.O., Moran, M.J., & Pindzola, R.H. (1990). *Communication disorders in the classroom.* Dubuque, IA: Kendall/Hunt Publishing.

Health Indicators (2000). National Health Interview Survey, National Center for Health Statistics. Atlanta: Centers for Disease Control and Prevention.

Heflin, L.J., & Simpson, R.L. (1998). Interventions for children and youth with autism: Prudent choices in a world of exaggerated claims and empty promises. Part I: Intervention and treatment option review. *Focus on Autism and Other Developmental Disabilities, 13,* 194–211.

Heller, K.W., Fredrick, L.D., Dykes, M.K., Best, S., & Cohen, E.T. (1999). A national perspective of competencies for teachers of individuals with physical and health disabilities. *Exceptional Children, 65,* 219–234.

Henley, M., Ramsey, R.S., & Algozzine, R. (1984). *Education of exceptional learners.* (3rd ed.). Boston: Allyn and Bacon.

Henley, M., Ramsey, R.S., & Algozzine, R. (1993). *Characteristics of and strategies for teaching students with mild disabilities* (pp. 69–110). Boston: Allyn and Bacon.

Hentoff, N. (1985). The awful privacy of Baby Doe. *The Atlantic Monthly,* January, 54–62.

Hernandez, B. (2000). Employer attitudes towards workers with disabilities and their ADA employment rights: A literature review. *Journal of Rehabilitation, 66*(4), 4–16.

Heubert, J.P. & Hauser, R.M. (Eds.) (1999). *High-stakes testing for tracking, promotion, and graduation.* Committee on Appropriate Test Use, National Research Council, Washington, DC: National Academy Press.

Hewett, F.M., & Forness, S.R. (1984). *Education of exceptional learners* (3rd ed.). Boston: Allyn and Bacon.

Hilburn, R. (2003). A sweet mystery; Norah Jones' artistry stands out in a world of prefab pop. Where'd it come from? *The Los Angeles Times,* January 26, p. E.1.

Hill, E.W. (1986). Orientation and mobility. In G.T. Scholl (Ed.), *Foundations of education for blind and visually handicapped children and youth: Theory and practice.* New York: American Foundation for the Blind.

Hitchcock, C., Meyer, A., Rose, D., & Jackson, R. (2002). Providing new access to the general curriculum: Universal design for learning. *Teaching Exceptional Children, 35*(2) 8–17.

Hitchings, W.E., Luzzo, D.A., Ristow, R., Horvath, M., Retish, P., & Tanners, A. (2001). The career development needs of college students with learning disabilities: In their own words. *Learning Disabilities Research and Practice, 16,* 8–17.

Hobbs, N. (1975). *The futures of children: Categories, labels, and their consequences.* Nashville: Vanderbilt Institute for Policy Studies.

Hodapp, R.M., & Fidler, D.J. (1999). Special education and genetics: Connections for the 21st century. *Journal of Special Education, 33,* 130–137.

Holbrook, M.C., & Koenig, A.J. (2000). Basic techniques for modifying instruction. In A.J. Koenig & M.C. Holbrook (Eds.), *Foundations of education* (2nd ed.) *Volume II: Instructional strategies for teaching children and youths with visual impairment* (pp. 173–193). New York: AFB Press.

Holcomb, T.K. (1997). Social assimilation of deaf high school students: The role of school environment. In I. Parasnis (Ed.), *Cultural and language diversity and the Deaf experience.* Cambridge, UK: Cambridge University Press.

Hollingsworth, M., & Woodward, J. (1993). Integrated learning: Explicit strategies and their role in problem-solving instruction for students with learning disabilities. *Exceptional Children, 59,* 444–455.

Hollingworth, L.A. (1942). *Children above 180 I.Q. Stanford-Binet: Origin and development.* Yonkers-on-Hudson, NY: World Book Company.

Hom, J.L., O'Donnell, J.P., & Leicht, D.J. (1988). Phonetically inaccurate spelling among learning-disabled, head-injured, and nondisabled young adults. *Brain and Language, 33,* 55–64.

Hopfenberg, W.S., Levin, H.M., Chase, C., Christensen, S.G., Moore, M., Soler, P., Brunner, I., Keller, B., & Rodriguez, G. (1993). *The Accelerated Schools resource guide.* San Francisco: Jossey-Bass.

Horn, C. (Winter, 2003). High-stakes testing and students: Stopping or perpetuating a cycle of failure? *Theory into Practice,* 1–15.

Hourcade, J., Parette, P., & Anderson, H. (2003). Accountability in collaboration: A framework for evaluation. *Education and Training in Developmental Disabilities, 38,* 398–404.

Hourcade, J.J., Parette, H.P., & Huer, M.B. (1997). Family and cultural alert! Considerations in assistive technology assessment. *Teaching Exceptional Children, 30*(1), 40–44.

Huebner, K.M. (2000). Visual impairment. In M.C. Holbrook and A.J. Koenig (Eds.), *Foundations of Education: Vol. 1* (2nd ed., pp. 55–76). New York: American Foundation for the Blind.

Hughes, C., Copeland, S.R., Agran, M., Wehmeyer, M.L., Rodi, M.S., & Presley, J.A. (2002). Using self-monitoring to improve performance in general education high school classes. *Education and Training in Mental Retardation and Developmental Disabilities, 37,* 262–272.

Hughes, C.A., Ruhl, K.L., Schumaker, J.B., & Deshler, D.D. (2002). Effects of instruction in an assignment completion strategy on the homework performance of students with learning disabilities in general education classes. *Learning Disabilities Research and Practice, 17,* 1–18.

Humphries, T., & MacDougall, F. (1997). *Adding links to the chain: Discourse strategies in American Sign Language teaching.* Unpublished manuscript. Teacher Education Program, University of California, San Diego.

Humphries, T., Padden, C., & O'Rourke, T.J. (1980). *A basic course in American Sign Language.* Silver Spring, MD: T.J. Publishers.

Hunt, N.A. (1982). *The relationship of medical, social, and familial variables with school-related performance of adolescents born at low weight.* Doctoral dissertation, University of Southern California.

Hunt, P., Soto, G., Maier, J., & Doering, K. (2003). Collaborative teaming to support students at risk and students with severe disabilities in general education classrooms. *Exceptional Children, 69*(3), 315–332.

Hurlbutt, K., & Chalmers, L. (2002). Adults with Autism speak out: Perceptions of their life experiences. *Focus on Autism and Other Developmental Disabilities, 17*(2), 103–111.

Hutchinson, M.K., & Sandall, S.R. (1995). Congenital TORCH infections in infants and young children: Neurodevelopmental sequelae and implications for intervention. *Topics in Early Childhood Special Education, 15*(1), 65–82.

Hwang, B., & Hughes, C. (2000). The effects of social interactive training on early social communicative skills of children with autism. *Journal of Autism and Developmental Disorders, 30,* 331–343.

Iacono, T.A., & Miller, J.F. (1989). Can microcomputers be used to teach communication skills to students with mental retardation? *Education and Training in Mental Retardation, 24,* 32–44.

Individuals with Disabilities Education Act Amendments of 1997. (1997). P.L. 105–17, 105th Cong., 1st sess.

Individuals with Disabilities Education Act of 1990, 20 U.S.C. § 1400 et seq.

Inge, K.J., Banks, P.D., Wehman, P., Hill, J.W., & Shafer, M.S. (1988). Quality of life for individuals who are labeled mentally retarded: Evaluating competitive employment versus sheltered workshop employment. *Education and Training in Mental Retardation, 23,* 97–104.

Inspiration Software (1988–1993). Portland, OR: Inspiration.

Iovannone, R., Dunlap, G., Huber, H., & Kinkaid, D. (2003). Effective educational practices for students with autism spectrum disorders. *Focus on Autism and Other Developmental Disabilities, 18,* 150–165.

Ishii-Jordan, S.R. (2000). Behavioral interventions used with diverse students. *Behavioral Disorders, 25,* 299–309.

Jackson, N.E. (2000). Strategies for modeling the development of giftedness in children. In R.C. Friedman & B.M. Shore (Eds.), *Talents unfolding: Cognition and development,* pp. 27–54. Washington, DC: American Psychological Association.

Jansson, L.M., & Velez, M. (1999). Understanding and treating substance abusers and their infants. *Infants and Young Children, 11*(4), 79–89.

Jimenez Gonzalez, J.E., & Garcia Espinel, A.I. (2002). Strategy choice in solving arithmetic word problems: Are there differences between students with learning disabilities, poor performance, and typical achievement students? *Learning Disability Quarterly, 25,* 113–122.

Jiménez, R.T., & Gersten, R. (1999). Lessons and dilemmas derived from the literacy instruction of two Latina/o teachers. *American Educational Research Journal, 36,* 265–301.

Joe, J.R., & Malach, R.S. (1998). Families with Native-American roots. In E.W. Lynch & M.J. Hanson (Eds.), *Developing cross-cultural competence* (2nd ed.). Baltimore: Paul H. Brookes.

Johnson, H.M. Unspeakable conversations. *New York Times,* February 16, 2003, section 6, p. 5.

Joint Committee on Infant Hearing (2000). Year 2000 Position Statement: Principles and Guidelines for Early Hearing Detection and Intervention Programs. http://www.asha.org/infant_hearing/y2kpstn_stmnt.htm

Jolivette, K., Wehby, J.H., Canale, J., & Massy, N.G. (2001). Effects of choice-making opportunities on the behavior of students with emotional and behavioral disorders. *Behavioral Disorders, 26,* 131–145.

Kalyanpur, M., and Harry, B. (1999). *Culture in special education: Building reciprocal family-professional relationships.* Baltimore: Paul H. Brookes.

Kalyanpur, M., Harry, B., & Skrtic, T. (2000). Equity and advocacy expectations of culturally diverse families' participation in special education. *International Journal of Disability, Development, and Education, 47*(2), 119–136.

Kamhi, A.G. (1992). Three perspectives on language processing: Interactionism, modularity, and holism. In R.S. Chapman (Ed.), *Processes in language acquisition and disorders* (pp. 45–64). St. Louis: Mosby Yearbook.

———. (1993). Some problems with the marriage between theory and clinical practice. *Language, Speech, and Hearing Services in the Schools, 24,* 57–60.

———. (1998). Trying to make sense of developmental language disorders. *Language, Speech, and Hearing in the Schools,* January, 35–44.

Kamps, D., Kravits, T., Rauch, J., Kamps, J.L., & Chung, N. (2000). A prevention program for students with or at risk for ED: Moderating effects of variation in treatment and classroom structure. *Journal of Emotional and Behavioral Disorders, 8,* 141–154.

Kamps, D.M., & Tankersley, M. (1996). Prevention of behavioral and conduct disorders: Trends and research issues. *Behavioral Disorders, 22,* 41–48.

Kamps, D., Royer, J., Dugan, E., Kravits, T., Gonzalez-Lopez, A., Garcia, J., Carnazzo, K., Morrison, L., & Kane, L.G. (2002). Peer training to facilitate social interaction for elementary students with autism and their peers. *Exceptional Children, 68,* 173–187.

Kanner, L. (1943). Inborn disturbances of affective contact. *Nervous Child, 2,* 217–250.

Katsiyannis, A., & Yell, M.L. (2000). The Supreme Court and school health services: Cedar Rapids v. Garret F. *Exceptional Children, 66,* 317–326.

Katsiyannis, A., Ellenberg, J.S., Acton, O.M., & Torrey, G. (2001). Addressing the needs of students with Rett Syndrome. *Teaching Exceptional Children, 33*(5), 74–78.

Katsiyannis, A., Yell, M.L., & Bradley, R. (2001). Reflections on the 25th anniversary of the Individuals with Disabilities Education Act. *Remedial & Special Education, 22* (6), 324–335.

Kauffman, J.M. (2001). *Characteristics of emotional and behavioral disorders of children and youth* (7th ed.). Upper Saddle River, NJ: Merrill/Prentice Hall.

Kavale, K.A., & Forness, S.R. (1983). Hyperactivity and diet treatment: A meta-analysis of the Feingold hypothesis. *Journal of Learning Disabilities, 16,* 324–330.

———. (1996). Social skill deficits and learning disabilities: A meta-analysis. *Journal of Learning Disabilities, 29,* 226–237.

Kearney, K. (1988). The highly gifted. *Understanding Our Gifted, 1*(1), 13.

Keller, B. (2004). Rigor disputed in standards for teachers. *Education Week, 23*(18), 1,14.

Keller, H. (1954). *The story of my life.* Garden City, NY: Doubleday.

Kelly, J.F., & Barnard, K.E. (2000). Assessment of parent-child interaction: Implications for early intervention. In J.P. Shonkoff & S.J. Meisels (Eds.), *Handbook of early childhood intervention* (2nd ed.). Cambridge, UK: Cambridge University Press.

Kendrick, D. (1997). Can girls with impaired vision be mommies? *Envision,* 5–7.

Keogh, B.K., Gallimore, R., & Weisner, T. (1997). A sociocultural perspective on learning and learning disabilities. *Learning Disabilities Research and Practice, 12,* 107–113.

Kerr, B.A. (1997). *Smart girls two: A new psychology of girls, women, and giftedness.* Dayton, OH: Ohio Psychology Press.

Kerr, B.A., & Nicpon, M.F. (2003). Gender and giftedness. In N. Colangelo and G.A. Davis (Eds.), *Handbook of gifted education* (3rd ed.) (pp. 493–505). Boston: Allyn and Bacon.

Keyser-Marcus, L., Briel, L., Sherron-Targett, P., Yasuda, S., Johnson, S., & Wehman, P. (2002). Enhancing the schooling of students with traumatic brain injury. *Teaching Exceptional Children, 34*(4), 62–67.

KidsSource (2000). http://www.kidsource.com/NICHCY/brain.html.

Kiernan, W.E., & Stark, J.A. (1986). *Pathways to employment for adults with developmental disabilities.* Baltimore: Paul H. Brookes.

Kinder, D., & Bursuch, W. (1991). The search for a unified social studies curriculum: Does history really repeat itself? *Journal of Learning Disabilities, 24,* 270–275.

King, C., & Quigley, S. (1985). *Reading and deafness.* San Diego: College-Hill.

Kirk, K.I. (2000). Challenges in clinical investigations of cochlear implant outcomes. In J.K. Niparko, K.I. Kirk, N.K. Mellon, A.M. Robbins, D.L. Tucci, & B.S. Wilson, (Eds.), *Cochlear implants: Principles and practices* (pp. 225–255). Philadelphia: Lippincott Williams & Wilkins.

Kitano, M.K., & Kirby, D.F. (1986). *Gifted education: A comprehensive view.* Boston: Little, Brown.

Kitchel, E., Murphy, R., & Gevers, M., (2002). *Teaching the student with a visual impairment: A primer for the classroom teacher.* Louisville, KY: American Printing House for the Blind.

Kittrell, A., & Arjmand, E. (1997). The age of diagnosis of sensorineural hearing impairment in children. *International Journal of Pediatric Otorhinolaryngology, 40,* 97–106.

Klein, M.D., & Chen, D. (2001). *Working with children from culturally diverse backgrounds.* Albany, NY: Delmar.

Klein, M.D., Chen, D., & Haney, M. (2000). *Project PLAI.* Baltimore: Paul H. Brookes.

Klin, A., Lang, J., Cicchetti, D.V., & Volkmar, F.R. (2000). Brief report: Interrater reliability of clinical diagnosis and DSM-IV Criteria for Autistic Disorder: Results of the DSM-IV Autism field trial. *Journal of Autism and Developmental Disorders, 30,* 163–167.

Knapczyk, D.R. (1988). Reducing aggressive behaviors in special and regular class settings by training alternative social responses. *Behavioral Disorders, 14,* 27–39.

Knoblauch, B., & McLane, K. (1999). An overview of the Individuals with Disabilities Education Act Amendments of 1997 (P.L. 105–17): Update 1999. ERIC EC Digest E576. Reston, VA: ERIC Clearinghouse on Disabilities and Gifted Education, Council for Exceptional Children.

Knoblauch, B., & Sorenson, B. (1998). IDEA's definition of disabilities. ERIC EC Digest E560. Reston, VA: ERIC Clearinghouse on Disabilities and Gifted Education, Council for Exceptional Children.

Koegel, R.L., Koegel, L.K., Frea, W.D., & Smith, A.E. (1995). Emerging interventions for children with autism: Longitudinal and lifestyle implications. In R.L. Koegel & L.K. Koegel (Eds.), *Teaching children with autism: Strategies for initiating positive interactions and improving learning opportunities* (pp. 1–16). Baltimore: Paul H. Brookes.

Koenig, A.J., & Farrenkopf, C. (1997). Essential experiences to undergird the early development of literacy. *Journal of Visual Impairment and Blindness, 91*(1), 14–24.

Koenig, A.J., & Holbrook, M.C.(2000). Planning instruction in unique skills. In A.J. Koenig and M.C. Holbrook (Eds.), *Foundations of Education: Vol. II* (2nd ed., pp. 196–224). New York: American Foundation for the Blind.

———. (2002). Literacy focus: Developing skills and motivation for reading and writing. In R.L Pogrund & D.L. Fazzi, (Eds.). *Early focus: Working with young children who are blind or visually impaired and their families* (2nd ed.). New York: AFB Press.

Kolb, S.M., & Hanley-Maxwell, C. (2003). Critical social skills for adolescents with high incidence disabilities: Parental perspectives. *Exceptional Children, 69,* 163–179.

Kolominsky, Y., Igumnov, S., & Drozdovitch, V. (1999). The psychological development of children from Belarus exposed in the prenatal period to radiation from the Chernobyl atomic power plant. *Journal of Child Psychology and Psychiatry and Allied Disciplines, 40*(2), 299.

Konstantareas, M.M., & Homatidis, S. (1999). Chromosomal abnormalities in a series of children with autistic disorder. *Journal of Autism and Developmental Disorders, 29,* 275–285.

Kopp, C.B. (1983). Risk factors in development. In M. Haith & J. Campos (Eds.), *Infancy and the biology of development* (Vol. II). In P. Mussen (Ed.), *Manual of child psychology.* New York: Wiley.

Kraijer, D. (2000). Review of adaptive behavior studies in mentally retarded persons with autism/pervasive developmental disorder. *Journal of Autism and Developmental Disorders, 30,* 39–47.

Krauss, M.W. (1990). New precedent in family policy: Individualized family service plan. *Exceptional Children, 56*(5), 388–395.

Kuhse, H., & Singer, P. (1985). *Should the baby live? The problem of handicapped infants.* New York: Oxford University Press.

Kupfer, F. (1997). Home is not for everyone (http:www.psych-health.com/fern.htm). Retrieved November 2, 2003.

Kutscher, M.L. (2003). Autism spectrum disorders: Sorting it out. Retrieved from http://www.pediatricneurology.com/autism.htm on November 23, 2003.

Lagomarcino, T.R., & Rusch, F.R. (1989). Utilizing self-management procedures to teach independent performance. *Education and Training in Mental Retardation, 24,* 297–323.

Landrigan, P.J., Schechter, C.B., Lipton, J.M., Fahs M.C., & Schwartz, J. (2002). Environmental pollutants and disease in American children: Estimates of morbidity, mortality, and costs for lead poisoning, asthma, cancer, and developmental disabilities. *Environ-*

mental Health Perspectives, 110(7), pp. 721–728

Langenbacher, D., Nield, T., & Poulsen, M.K. (2001). Neurodevelopmental outcome of ECMO survivors at five years of age: The potential for academic and motor difficulties. *The Journal of Special Education, 35,* 156–160.

Langone, J., & Mechling, L. (2000). The effects of a computer-based instructional program with video anchors on the use of photographs for prompting augmentative communication. *Education and Training in Mental Retardation and Developmental Disabilities, 35,* 90–105.

Lardieri, L.A., Blacher, J., & Swanson, H.L. (2000). Sibling relationships and parent stress in families of children with and without learning disabilities. *Learning Disability Quarterly, 23*(2), 105–116.

Laureate Learning (2003). Retrieved 7/11/03 from http://www.laureate learning.com/images/tvlg.gif.

Le Grice, B., & Blampied, N.M. (1994). Training pupils with intellectual disability to operate educational technology using video prompting. *Education and Training in Mental Retardation and Developmental Disabilities, 29,* 321–330.

Leffert, J.S., Siperstein, G.N., & Millikan, E. (2000). Understanding social adaption in children with mental retardation: A social-cognitive perspective. *Exceptional Children, 66,* 530–545.

Lehmann, J.P., & Baker, C. (1995). Mothers' expectations for their adolescent children: A comparison between families with disabled adolescents and those with non-labeled adolescents. *Education and Training in Mental Retardation and Developmental Disabilities, 31,* 27–40.

Lehmann, J.P., Davies, T.G., & Laurin, K.M. (2000). Listening to student voices about postsecondary education. *Teaching Exceptional Children, 32*(5), 60–65.

Leiberman, L.M. (1996). Preserving special education . . . for those who need it. In W. Stainback & S. Stainback (Eds.), *Controversial issues confronting special education: Divergent perspectives* (2nd ed.) (pp. 16–27). Boston: Allyn and Bacon.

Lerner, J. (1993). Young children with disabilities. *Learning disabilities: Theories, diagnosis, and teaching strategies* (6th ed.) (pp. 245–271). Boston: Houghton Mifflin.

Lerner, J.W., Lowenthal, B., & Lerner, S. (1995). *Attention deficit disorders: Assessment and teaching.* Pacific Grove, CA: Brooks/Cole.

Lesar, S., Gerber, M.M., & Semmel, M.I. (1995). HIV infection in children: Family stress, social support, and adaptation. *Exceptional Children, 62,* 224–236.

Levendoski, L.S., & Cartledge, G. (2000). Self-monitoring for elementary school children with serious emotional disturbances: Classroom applications for increased academic responding. *Behavioral Disorders, 25,* 211–224.

Levin, H.M. (1996). Accelerated Schools: The background. In C. Finnan, E.P. St. John, J. McCarthy & S.P. Slovacek (Eds.), *Accelerated Schools in action: Lessons from the field* (pp. 3–23). Thousand Oaks, CA: Corwin Press.

Levine, J.M. (1996). Including children dependent on ventilators in school. *Teaching Exceptional Children, 28*(3), 24–29.

Levy, S., & Chard, D.J. (2001). Research on reading instruction for students with emotional and behavioral disorders. *International Journal of Disability, Development, and Education, 48,* 429–444.

Lewis, B.A. (1992). Pedigree analysis of children with phonology disorders. *Journal of Learning Disabilities, 25,* 586–597.

Lewis, R.B. (1993). *Special education technology: Classroom applications* (pp. 176–219). Pacific Grove, CA: Brooks/Cole.

Lewis, S., & Allman, C.B. (2000). Educational programming. In M.C. Holbrook and A.J. Koenig (Eds.), *Foundations of Education: Vol.1* (2nd ed., pp. 218–259). New York: American Foundation for the Blind.

———. (2000). *Seeing eye-to-eye: An administrator's guide to students with low vision.* New York: AFB Press.

Lim, L., Browder, D.M., & Bambara, L. (2001). Effect of sampling opportunities on preference development for adults with severe disabilities. *Education and Training in Mental Retardation and Developmental Disabilities, 36,* 188–195.

Lin, S.L. (2000). Coping and adaptation in families of children with cerebral palsy. *Exceptional Children, 66,* 201–218.

Linan-Thompson, S., & Jean, R.E. (1997). Completing the parent participation puzzle: Accepting diversity. *Teaching Exceptional Children, 30*(2), 46–50.

Lindegren, M.L., Steinberg, S., & Byers, R.H. (2000). Epidemiology of HIV/AIDS in children. In Martha F. Rogers (Ed.), *The pediatric clinics of North America, 47*(1), 1–20.

Lindsey, J.D., & Stewart, D.A. (1989). The guardian minority: Siblings of children with mental retardation. *Edu-*

cation and Training in Mental retardation, 24, 291–296.

Loeb, G.E. (2001). Learning from the spinal cord. *Journal of Physiology, 533,* 111–117.

Loeb, G.E. (2002). Reanimating paralyzed limbs—Coping with spatially distributed multimodal systems. Texas: Proceedings of the IEEE-EMBS. Retrieved from: http://ami.usc.edu/publications.asp.

Lopez-Reyna, N.A. (1996). The importance of meaningful contexts in bilingual special education: Moving to whole language. *Learning Disabilities Research and Practice, 11,* 120–131.

Los Angeles Unified School District (2004). Gifted/Talented Programs. Retrieved from http://www.lausd.k12.ca.us/lausd/offices/GATE/prog-opt-4.html/.

Losardo, A., & Notari-Syverson, A. (2001). *Alternative approaches to assessing young children.* Baltimore: Paul H. Brookes.

Lovecky, D.V. (1994). Exceptionally gifted children: Different minds. *Roeper Review, 17,* 116–120.

Lowenfeld, B. (1981). *On blindness and blind people.* New York: American Foundation for the Blind.

Lue, M.S. (2001). *Survey of communication disorders for the classroom teacher.* Boston: Allyn and Bacon.

Lueck, A.H., Chen, D., & Kekelis, L.S. (1997). *Developmental guidelines for visually impaired infants: A manual for infants birth to two.* Louisville, KY: American Printing House for the Blind.

Luetke-Stahlman, B. (1999). *Language across the curriculum: When students are deaf or hard of hearing.* Hillsboro, OR: Butte Publications.

Luetke-Stahlman, B., & Luckner, J. (1991). *Effectively educating students with hearing impairments.* New York: Longman.

Luterman, D.M. (2001). *Counseling persons with communication disorders and their families.* Austin, TX: Pro-Ed.

Lyon, J.S. (1985). *Playing God in the nursery.* New York: Norton.

Maag, J.W., & Katsiyannis, A. (2000). Recent legal and policy developments in special education. *NASSP Bulletin,* February, 1–8.

Maccini, P., & Hughes, C.A. (2000). Effects of a problem-solving strategy on the introductory algebra performance of secondary students with learning disabilities. *Learning Disabilities Research and Practice, 15,* 10–21.

Mack, C.G., Koenig, A.J., & Ashcroft, S.C. (1990). Microcomputers and access technology in programs for teachers of visually impaired students. *Journal of Visual Impairment and Blindness, 84*(10), 526–530.

MacMillan, D.L., Gresham, F.M., Lopez, M.F., & Bocian, K.M. (1996). Comparison of students nominated for pre-referral interventions by ethnicity and gender. *The Journal of Special Education, 30,* 133–151.

MacMillan, D.L., Semmel, M.I., & Gerber, M.M. (1994). The social context of Dunn: Then and now. *Journal of Special Education, 27,* 466–480.

Maker, C.J. (1977). *Providing programs for the gifted handicapped.* Reston, VA: Council for Exceptional Children.

Male, M. (1997). *Technology for inclusion: Meeting the special needs of all students* (3rd ed). Boston: Allyn and Bacon.

Malone, L.D., & Mastropieri, M.A. (1992). Reading comprehension instruction: Summarization and self-monitoring training for students with learning disabilities. *Exceptional Children, 58,* 270–279.

Mank, D., Cioffi, A., & Yovanoff, P. (1998). Employment outcomes for people with severe disabilities: Opportunities for improvement. *Mental Retardation, 36,* 205–216.

Maratens, B.K., Muir, K.A., & Meller, P.J. (1988). Rewards common to the classroom setting: A comparison of regular and self-contained room student ratings. *Behavioral Disorders, 13,* 169–174.

March of Dimes (2000). Smoking during pregnancy. Retrieved from http://www.marchofdimes.com/professionals/681_1171.asp May 18, 2004.

———. (2002a). Facts you should know about teenage pregnancy. Retrieved from http://www.marchofdimes.com/professionals/681_1159.asp May 18, 2004.

———. (2002b). Pregnancy after 35. Retrieved from http://www.marchofdimes.com/professionals/681_1155.asp May 18, 2004.

Masten, A.S., & Coatsworth, J.D. (1998). The development of competence in favorable and unfavorable environments: Lessons from research on successful children. *American Psychologist, 53,* p.212.

Mastropieri, M.A., Jenne, T., & Scruggs, T.E. (1988). A level system for managing problem behaviors in a high school resource program. *Behavioral Disorders, 13,* 202–208.

Mastropieri, M.A., & Scruggs, T.E. (1991). *Teaching students ways to remember: Strategies for learning mnemonically.* Cambridge, MA: Brookline Books.

———. (2000). *The inclusive classroom: Strategies for effective instruction.* Columbus, OH: Merrill.

Mathes, P.G., Grek, M.L., Howard, J.K., Babyak, A.E., & Allen, S.H. (1999). Peer-Assisted Learning Strategies for first-grade readers: A tool for preventing early reading failure. *Learning Disabilities Research and Practice, 14,* 50–60.

Matson, J.K. & Mulick, J.A. (1991). *Handbook of mental retardation* (2nd ed.) Boston: Allyn and Bacon.

Maurice, C. (1993). *Let me hear your voice: A family's triumph over autism.* New York: Fawcett Columbine.

Mayo Clinic (2002). http://www.mayoclinic.com/.

McComiskey, A.V. (1996). The Braille readiness skills grid: A guide to building a foundation for literacy. *Journal of Visual Impairment and Blindness, 90*(3), 190–193.

McCormick, L. (2003a). Introduction to language acquisition. In L. McCormick, D.F. Loeb, & R.L Schiefelbusch, *Supporting children with communication difficulties in inclusive settings* (2nd ed.). Boston: Allyn and Bacon.

———. (2003b). Language intervention in the inclusive preschool. In McCormick, L., Loeb, D.F., & Schiefelbusch, R.L. *Supporting children with communication difficulties in inclusive settings* (2nd ed.). Boston: Allyn and Bacon

McCormick, L., & Loeb, D.F. (2003). Characteristics of students with language and communication difficulties. In L. McCormick, D.F. Loeb, & R.L Schiefelbusch. (2003). *Supporting children with communication difficulties in inclusive settings* (2nd ed.) (pp. 71–112). Boston: Allyn and Bacon.

McCormick, L., Loeb, D.F., & Schiefelbusch, R.L. (2003). *Supporting children with communication difficulties in inclusive settings* (2nd ed.). Boston: Allyn and Bacon.

McDonald, H. (2002). Perinatal care at the threshold of viability. *Pediatrics, 110*(5) 1024–1027.

McDonnel, L.M., McLaughlin, M.J., & Morison, P. (Eds.). (1997). *Educating one and all: Students with disabilities and standards-based reform.* Committee on Goals 2000 and the Inclusion of Students with Disabilities, National Research Council. Washington, DC: The National Academy Press.

McDonnell, J.J., Hardman, M.L., & McDonnell, A.P. (2003). *An introduction to persons with moderate and severe disabilities: Educational and social issues* (2nd ed.). Boston: Allyn and Bacon.

McEvoy, A., & Welker, R. (2000). Antisocial behavior, academic behavior, and school climate: A critical review. *Journal of Emotional and Behavioral Disorders, 8,* 130–140.

McGregor, D., & Farrenkopf, C. (2000). Recreation and leisure skills. In A.J. Koenig and M.C. Holbrook (Eds.), *Foundations of Education: Vol. II* (2nd ed., pp. 653–678). New York: American Foundation for the Blind.

McGuffog, C., Feiring, C., & Lewis, M. (1987). The diverse profile of the extremely gifted child. *Roeper Review, 10*(2), 82–89.

McIntosh, R., Vaughn, S., & Zaragoza, N. (1991). A review of social interventions for students with learning disabilities. *Journal of Learning Disabilities, 24,* 451–458.

McKinney, J.D., Hocutt, A.M., Giambo, D.A., & Schumm, J.S. (2000). *Research on a teacher-implemented phonological awareness intervention for Hispanic kindergarten children.* Paper presented at the Council for Exceptional Children Convention, Vancouver, BC.

McLesky, J., Henry, D., & Hodges, D. (1999). Inclusion: What progress is being made across disability categories? *Teaching Exceptional Children, 31*(3), 60–64.

McLloyd, V.C. (1998). Socioeconomic disadvantage and child development. *American Psychologist, 53* (2), 185–204.

McLoughlin, J.A., & Lewis, R.B. (1986). *Assessing special students* (2nd ed.). Columbus, OH: Merrill.

McWilliam, R.A. & Scott, S. (2001). A support approach to early intervention: A three-part framework. *Infants and Young Children, 13*(4), 55–66.

Meadow, K. (1968). Parental responses to the medical ambiguities of deafness. *Journal of Health and Social Behavior, 9,* 299–309.

Meadow-Orlans, K.P. (1980). *Deafness and child development.* Berkeley: University of California Press.

Meadow-Orlans, K.P., & Orlans, H. (1990). Responses to loss of hearing in later life. In D.F. Moores & K.P. Meadow-Orlans (Eds.), *Educational and developmental aspects of deafness* (pp. 417–429). Washington, DC: Gallaudet University Press.

Mechaty, I.R., & Thompson, J.E. (Eds.). (1990). *New perspectives on prenatal care.* New York: Elsevier.

Mechling, L.C., & Gast, D.L. (1997). Combination audio/visual self-prompting system for teaching chained tasks to students with intellectual disabilities. *Education and Training in Mental Retardation and Developmental Disabilities, 32,* 138–153.

Medline Plus (2003). *Down syndrome.* Retrieved from http://search.nlm. nih.gov/medlineplus/, September, 2003.

Meisels, S.J., & Provence, S. (1989). *Screening and assessment: Guidelines for identifying young disabled and developmentally vulnerable children and their families.* Washington, DC: National Center for Clinical Infant Programs.

Menlove, M. (1996). A checklist for identifying funding sources for assistive technology. *Teaching Exceptional Children, 28*(3), 20–24.

Mercer, C.D., & Mercer, A.R. (1993a). Assessing and teaching handwriting and written expression skills. *Teaching students with learning problems* (4th ed.) (pp. 533–581). New York: Merrill.

———. (1993b). Teaching math skills. In *Teaching students with learning problems* (4th ed.) (pp. 273–342). New York: Merrill.

Mercer, C.D., & Miller, S.P. (1992). *Multiplication facts 0 to 81.* Lawrence, KS: Edge Enterprises.

Mercer, J. (1973). *Labeling the mentally retarded.* Berkeley: University of California Press.

Merrill, E.C. (1990). Attentional resource allocation and mental retardation. In N.W. Bray (Ed.), *International review of research in mental retardation, Vol. 16,* 51–88. San Diego, CA: Academic Press.

Mesibov, G.B. (1994). A comprehensive program for serving people with autism and the families: The TEACCH model. In J.L. Matson (Ed.), *Autism in children and adults: Etiology, assessment, and intervention* (pp. 85–97). Belmont, CA: Brooks/Cole.

———. (1997). Formal and informal measures on the effectiveness of the TEACCH programmme. *Autism: The International Journal of Research and Practice, 1,* 25–35.

Michaels, C.A., Prezant, F.P., & Jackson, K. (2002). Assistive and instructional technology for college students with disabilities: A national snapshot of postsecondary service providers. *Journal of Special Education Technology, 17*(1), 5–14.

Millward, C., Powell, S., Messer, D., & Jordan, R. (2000). Recall for self and other in autism: Children's memory for events experienced by themselves and their peers. *Journal of Autism and Developmental Disorders, 30,* 15–28.

Milstead, S. (1988). Siblings are people, too! *Academic Therapy, 23,* 537–540.

Mira, M., Tucker, B.F., & Tyler, J.S. (1992). *Traumatic brain injury in children and adolescents: A source book for teachers and other school personnel.* Austin, TX: Pro-Ed.

Mithaug, D.K. (2002). "Yes" means success: Teaching children with multiple disabilities to self-regulate during independent work. *Teaching Exceptional Children, 35,* 22–27.

Moats, L.C., & Lyon, G.R. (1996). Wanted: Teachers with knowledge of language. *Topics in Language Disorders, 16*(2), 23–86.

Modell, S.J., & Cox, T.A. (1999). Let's get fit! Fitness activities for children with severe/profound disabilities. *Teaching Exceptional Children, 31*(3), 24–29.

Moores, D.F. (2001). *Educating the deaf: Psychology, principles, and practices* (5th ed.). Boston: Houghton Mifflin.

Modell, S.J., & Valdez, L.A. (2002). Beyond bowling: Transition planning for students with disabilities. *Teaching Exceptional Children, 34,* 46–53.

Moores, D.F. (2001). *Educating the deaf: Psychology, principles, and practices.* Boston: Houghton Mifflin.

Morgan, J. (2000). Good things come in small packages. *The Exceptional Parent. 30*(7), 100.

Morgan, R.L., Gerity, B.P., & Ellerd, D.A. (2000). Using video and CD-ROM technology in a job preference inventory for youth with severe disabilities. *Journal of Special Education Technology, 15*(3), 25–33.

Morrice, P. (2002). Few options for treating autism. *New York Times,* November 12, 2002, p. 27.

Morse, T.E., & Schuster, J.W. (2000). Teaching elementary students with moderate intellectual disabilities how to shop for groceries. *Exceptional Children, 66,* 273–288.

Morton, K. (1985). Identifying the enemy: A parent's complaint. In H.R. Turnbull & A.P. Turnbull. *Parents speak out: Then and now* (pp. 143–147). Columbus, OH: Merrill.

Mortweet, S.L. (1999). Classwide peer tutoring: Teaching students with mild mental retardation in inclusive classrooms. *Exceptional Children, 65,* 524–536.

Mueller, P.H., & Murphy, F.V. (2001). Determining when a student requires paraeducator support. *Teaching Exceptional Children, 33,* 22–27.

Mull, C., Sitlington, P.L., & Alper, S. (2001). Postsecondary education for students with learning disabilities: A synthesis of the literature. *Exceptional Children, 68,* 97–118.

Muñoz, M.L. (1998). *Language assessment and intervention with children who have visual impairments: A guide for speech-language pathologists.* Austin, TX: Texas School for the Blind and Visually Impaired.

Murray, C., Goldstein, D.E., Nourse, S., & Edgar, E. (2000). The postsecondary school attendance and completion rates of high school graduates with learning disabilities. *Learning Disabilities Research and Practice, 15,* 119–127.

Myer, J.A., & Minshew, N.J. (2002). An update on neurocognitive profiles in Asperger Syndrome and higher functioning autism. *Focus on Autism and Other Developmental Disabilities, 17,* 152–160.

Myklebust, H. (1964). *The psychology of deafness* (2nd ed.). New York: Grune & Stratton.

National Association for Gifted Children (retrieved November 24, 2003). *Parent information.* http://www.nagc. org/ParentInfo/index.html/.

National Center for Biotechnology Information (NCBI) (2003). http://www. ncbi.nim.nih.gov/.

National Center for Education Statistics (1999). Inclusion of students with disabilities in the least restrictive environment. Section 2: *The Condition of Education.* Retrieved from http:// nces.ed.gov/pubs99/condition99/ pdf/section2.pdf/ May 18, 2004.

———. (2003). Racial/ethical distribution of public school students. http://nces.ed.gov/programs/coe/ 2002/section1/indicator03.asp. Retrieved 9/17/03.

National Center for Infectious Diseases (2002). *Cytomegalovirus (CMV) infection.* http://www.cdc.gov/ncidod/ diseases/cmv.htm.

National Center for Learning Disabilities (2003). *High stakes assessments and students with learning disabilities.* Retrieved from http:www.ld.org/ advocacy/high_stakes.cfm, January 4, 2004.

National Center on Birth Defects and Developmental Disabilities (2002). http://www.cdc.gov/ncbddd/.

National Down Syndrome Society website (2003). Information retrieved from http://www.ndss.org/, September, 2003.

National Education Association (2003). High-stakes testing can limit access for special needs students. Retrieved from http://www.nea.org/specialed/ saasresults.html, January 4, 2004.

National Information Center for Children and Youth with Disabilities

(NICHCY) (2003). http://www. nichcy.org/pubs/.

National Institute on Alcohol Abuse and Alcoholism (2003). *Frequently asked questions.* Updated March 2003. http://www.niaaa.nih. gov/faq/q-a.htm#question 14/.

National Institute on Deafness and Other Communication Disorders (NICCD) (2002). http://www.nidcd. nih.gov/.

National Research Council (2002). *Minority students in special and gifted education.* Washington, DC: National Academy Press.

Needleman, H.L. (1992). Childhood exposure to lead: A common cause of school failure. *Phi Delta Kappan, 74*(1), 35–37.

Needleman, H.L., Gunnoe, C., Leviton, A., Peresie, H., Maher, C., Barret, P. (1979). Deficits in psychological and classroom performance of children with elevated dentine lead levels. *New England Journal of Medicine, 300,* 689–695.

Needleman, H.L., & Reiss, J.A. (1996). Bone lead levels and delinquent behavior. *JAMA: Journal of the American Medical Association, 275* (5), 363–368.

Needleman, H.L., Schell, A., Bellinger, D., Leviton, A., & Allred, E.N. (1991). The long-term effects of exposure to low doses of lead in childhood. An 11-year follow-up report. *New England Journal of Medicine, 322* (2), pp. 83–88.

Neel, R.S., Meadows, N., Levine, P., & Edgar, E.B. (1988). What happens after special education: A statewide follow-up study of secondary students who have behavioral disorders. *Behavioral Disorders, 1,* 209–216.

Neihart, M., Reis, S.M., Robinson, N.M., Moon, S.M. (Eds.) (2001). *The social and emotional development of gifted children: What do we know?* Waco, TX: Prufrock Press.

Nelson, N.W. (1998). *Childhood language disorders in context: Infancy through adolescence* (2nd ed.). Boston: Allyn and Bacon.

Neubert, D.A., & Moon, M.S. (2000). How a transition profile helps students prepare for life in the community. *Teaching Exceptional Children, 33*(2), 20–25.

Neubert, D.A., Tilson, G.P., & Ianacone, R.N. (1989). Postsecondary transition needs and employment patterns of individuals with mild disabilities. *Exceptional Children, 55,* 494–500.

Newborn Screening Task Force (2000). Newborn screening: A blue print for the future. *Exceptional Parent, 30* (10), 69–73.

Newcomer, P.L., & Barenbaum, E.M. (1991). The written composing ability of children with learning disabilities. A review of the literature from 1980–1990. *Journal of Learning Disabilities, 24,* 578–593.

Newell, W. (1991). ASL is not a four-letter word: Deaf education can dance with the boogieman. In S. Polowe-Aldersley, P. Schragle, V. Armour, & J. Polowe (Eds.), *Profession on parade: Proceedings of the Fifty-fifth Biennial Meeting, Convention of American Instructors of the Deaf and the Sixty-third Annual Meeting of the Conference of Educational Administrators Serving the Deaf, New Orleans, Louisiana, June 1991* (pp. 74–75). Silver Spring, MD: Convention of American Instructors of the Deaf.

Nietupski, J.A., & Hamre-Nietupski, S.M. (1987). An ecological approach to curriculum development. In L. Goetz, D. Guess, & K. Stremel-Campbell (Eds.), *Innovative program design for individuals with dual sensory impairments.* Baltimore: Paul H. Brookes.

Nihira, K., Leland, H., & Lambert, N. (1993). AAMR Adaptive Behavior Scale - Residential and Community (2nd. ed.). Austin, TX: Pro-Ed.

NIMH (National Institute of Mental Health). (1999). *Attention deficit hyperactivity disorder.* http://www. nimh.nih.gov. Retrieved October, 2003.

———. (2003). Retrieved November, 2003 from http://www.nimh:nih. gov/publicat/autism.cfm#aut 6.

Niparko, J.K. (2000). Introduction. In J.K. Niparko, K.I. Kirk, N.K. Mellon, A.M. Robbins, D.L. Tucci, & B.S. Wilson, (Eds.), *Cochlear implants: Principles and practices* (pp. 1–6). Philadelphia: Lippincott Williams & Wilkins.

Nissenbaum, M.S., Tollefson, N., & Reese, R.M. (2002). The interpretative conference: Sharing a diagnosis of autism with families. *Focus on Autism and Other Developmental Disabilities, 17,* 30–43.

No Child Left Behind (2002). Reauthorization of the Elementary and Secondary Education Act. Washington, DC: U.S. Department of Education.

Noonan, M.J., & Kilgo, J.L. (1987). Transition services for early age individuals with severe mental retardation. In R.N. Ianacone & R.A. Stodden (Eds.), *Transition issues and directions* (pp. 25–37). Reston, VA: Council for Exceptional Children.

Northern, J.L., & Downs, M.P. (1991). *Hearing in children* (4th ed.). Baltimore: Williams & Wilkins.

Northern, J.L., & Downs, M.P. (2002). *Hearing in children* (5th ed.). Philadelphia: Lippincott Williams & Wilkins.

Office of Communications (2003). *Fingertip facts 2003–2004.* Los Angeles: Los Angeles Unified School District.

Oller, D.K., & Eilers, R.E. (1982). Similarity of babbling in Spanish- and English-learning babies. *Journal of Child Language, 9,* 565–577.

Oller, D.K., Weiman, L.A., Doyle, W.J., & Ross, C. (1976). Infant babbling and speech. *Journal of Child Language, 3,* 1–11.

Orel-Bixler, D. (1999). Clinical vision assessment for infants. In D. Chen (Ed.), *Essential elements in early intervention: Visual impairment and multiple disabilities.* New York: American Foundation for the Blind.

Orelove, F.P., & Sobsey, D. (1987). *Educating children with multiple disabilities: A transdisciplinary approach* (pp. 285–314). Baltimore: Paul H. Brookes.

Orelove, F.P., & Sobsey, R. (1991). *Multiple disabilities: A transdisciplinary approach.* Baltimore: Paul H. Brookes.

Ortiz, A.A. & Yates, J.R. (2002). Considerations in the assessment of English language learners referred to special education. In A.J. Artiles & A.A. Ortiz, *English language learners with special education needs: Identification, assessment, and instruction* (pp. 65–86). McHenry, IL: Center for Applied Linguistics/Delta Systems Co.

Osborn, A. (1963). *Applied imagination.* New York: Scribners.

Osberger, M.J., & Lane, H. (1993). The debate: Cochlear implants in children. *Hearing Health, 9* (2), 19–22.

O'Shea, D.J., O'Shea, L.J., Algozzine, R., & Hammitte, D.J. (2001). *Families and teachers of individuals with disabilities.* Boston: Allyn and Bacon.

Ostrosky, M.M., Drasgow, E., & Halle, J.W. (1999). How can I help you get what you want? *Teaching Exceptional Children, 31*(4), 5–61.

Owen, L., & Dreker, L.A. (2003). How to spell success for secondary students labeled EBD: How students define effective teachers. *Beyond Behavior, 12*(2), 21.

Owen, R.L., & Fuchs, L.S. (2002). Mathematical problem-solving strategy instruction for third-grade students with learning disabilities. *Remedial and Special Education, 23,* 268–278.

Owens, R.E. (1991). *Language disorders: A functional approach to assessment and intervention.* New York: Merrill

———. (2001). *Language development: An introduction* (5th ed.). Boston: Allyn and Bacon.

———. (2004). *Language disorders: A functional approach to assessment and intervention* (4th ed.). Boston: Allyn and Bacon.

Owens, R.E., Metz, D.E., & Haas, A. (2003). *Introduction to communication disorders: A life span perspective* (2nd ed.). Boston: Allyn and Bacon.

Padden, C. (1980). The deaf community and the culture of deaf people. In C. Baker & D. Cokely (Eds.), *Sign language and the deaf community: Essays in honor of William C. Stokoe* (pp. 89–103). Silver Spring, MD: National Association for the Deaf.

Padden, C. & Humphries, T. (1988). *Deaf in America: Voices from a culture*. Cambridge, MA: Harvard University Press.

Pahl, J., & Quine, L. (1987). Families with mentally handicapped children. In J. Oxford (Ed.), *Treating the disorder, treating the family*. Baltimore: Johns Hopkins University Press.

Paneth, N. (1995). The problem of low birth weight. *Future of Children, 5*(3), 19–34.

Parakeshwar, N., & Pargament, K.I. (2001). Religious coping in families of children with autism. *Focus on Autism and Other Developmental Disabilities, 16*(4), 14, 247.

Parasnis, I. (1996). Interpreting the Deaf experience within the context of cultural and language diversity. In I. Parasnis (Ed.), *Cultural and language diversity and the Deaf experience* (pp. 3–19). New York: Cambridge University Press.

Parette, P. (1999). Transition and assistive technology planning with families across cultures. *Career Development for Exceptional Individuals, 22*, 213–231.

Parette, P., & McMahan, G.A.(2002). What should we expect of assistive technology? Being sensitive to family goals. *Teaching Exceptional Children, 35*(1), 56–61.

Park, C.C. (1998). Exiting nirvana. *The American Scholar, 67*(2), 28–43.

Park, J., Turnbull, A.P., & Turnbull, H.R. (2002). Impacts of poverty on quality of life in families of children with disabilities. *Exceptional Children, 68*(2), 151–170.

Parke, B.N. (1989). *Gifted students in regular classrooms*. Boston: Allyn and Bacon.

Patterson, D. (1987). The causes of Down syndrome. *Scientific American, 257*(2), 52–57.

Paul, P. (1998). *Literacy and deafness: The development of reading, writing, and literate thought*. Boston: Allyn and Bacon.

Paul, P.V., & Jackson, D.W. (1993). *Toward a psychology of deafness*. Boston: Allyn and Bacon.

Paul, P.V., & Quigley, S.P. (1990). *Education and deafness*. New York: Longman.

PECS (Picture Exchange Communication System). http://pyramidproducts.com.

Pembrey, M. (1992). Genetics and language disorder. In P. Fletcher & D. Hall (Eds.), *Specific speech and language disorders in children* (pp. 51–62). San Diego: Singular Publishing.

Pena, E., Iglesias, A. & Lidz, C.S. (2001). Reducing test bias by dynamic assessment of children's word-learning ability. *American Journal of Speech-Language Pathology, 10*, 138–154.

Perla, F., & O'Donnell, B. (2002). Reaching out: Encouraging family involvement in orientation and mobility. *RE:view, 34*(3), 103–109.

Persson, B. (2000). Brief report: A longitudinal study of quality of life and independence among adult men with autism. *Journal of Autism and Developmental Disorders, 30*, 61–66.

Peterson, J., & Rischar, H. (2000). Gifted and gay: A study of the adolescent experience. *Gifted Child Quarterly, 44*, 231–246.

Peushel, S.M. (1991). Ethical considerations relating to prenatal diagnosis of fetuses with Down syndrome. *Mental Retardation, 29*, 185–190.

Picture Reading Literacy Project. http://busboy.sped.ukans.edu.

Piirto, J. (1999). *Talented children and adults: Their development and education* (2nd ed.). Columbus, OH: Prentice Hall/Merrill.

Pintner, R., & Patterson, D. (1917). A comparison of deaf and hearing children in visual memory span for digits. *Journal of Experimental Psychology, 2*(2), 76–88.

Pivik, J., McComas, J., & LaFlamme, M. (2002). Barriers and facilitators to inclusive education. *Exceptional Children, 69*, 97–107.

P.L 103-382, Title XIV. (1994). Reauthorization of the Jacob K. Javits Gifted and Talented Students Education Act of 1988, p. 388.

Plomin, R., & Price, T.S. (2003). The relationship between genetics and intelligence. In N. Colangelo and G.A. Davis (Eds.), *Handbook of gifted education* (3rd ed.) (pp. 113–123). Boston: Allyn and Bacon.

Pogrund, R.L., & Fazzi, D.L. (Eds.) (2002). *Early focus: Working with young children who are blind or visually impaired and their families* (2nd ed.). New York: AFB Press.

Polloway, E.A., & Patton, J.R. (1997). *Strategies for teaching learners with special needs* (5th. ed.). Upper Saddle River, NJ: Merrill/Prentice Hall.

Polloway, E.A., Smith, J.D., Patton, J.R., & Smith, T.E.C. (1996). Historic changes in mental retardation and developmental disabilities. *Education and Training in Mental Retardation and Developmental Disabilities, 31*, 3–12.

Polloway, E.A. & Smith, T.E.C. (2000). *Language instruction for students with disabilities* (2nd ed.). Denver: Love Publishing Company.

Potvin, F.R. (2000). Newborn screening: Testing for disorders at birth. *Exceptional Parent*, 90–93.

Powell, T.H., & Gallagher, P.A. (1993). *Brothers and sisters: A special part of exceptional families* (2nd ed.). Baltimore: Paul H. Brookes.

Prater, L.P. (2002). African-American families: Equal partners in general and special education. In F.E. Obiakur & B.A. Ford (Eds.), *Creating successful learning environments for African-American learners with exceptionalities*. Thousand Oaks, CA: Corwin Press.

Prater, M.A., & Sileo, N.M. (2001). Using juvenile literature about HIV/AIDS: Ideas and precautions for the classroom. *Teaching Exceptional Children, 33*(6), 34–45.

Preiser, W., & Ostroff, E. (2001). *Universal design handbook*. New York: McGraw-Hill.

Prelock, P.A.(2000). Epilogue: An intervention focus for inclusionary practice. *Language, Speech, and Hearing Services in Schools, 31*(3), 296–298.

Prendergast, S.G., Lartz, M.N., & Fiedler, B.C. (2002). Ages of diagnosis, amplification, and early intervention of infants and young children with hearing loss: Findings from parent interviews. *American Annals of the Deaf, 147*(1), 24–29.

Presley, J.A., & Hughes, C. (2000). Peers as teachers of anger management to high school students with behavioral disorders. *Behavioral Disorders, 25*, 114–130.

Prevent Blindness America (2003). *Children's eye problems*. http://www.preventblindness.org/children/ch_eye_problems.html/.

Price-Hughes, D. (2002). *Aquamarine blue 5: Personal stories of college students with autism*. Athens, OH: Ohio University Press & Swallow Press.

Pruher, L.W. (1994). Tips for working with a consultant. *RE:view, 25*(4), 174.

Pyle, A. (1996). Teaching the silent student. *Los Angeles Times,* June 11, p. 1.

Pyryt, M.C. (2003). Technology and the gifted. In N. Colangelo and G.A. Davis (Eds.), *Handbook of gifted education* (3rd ed.) (pp. 584–589). Boston: Allyn and Bacon.

Quality Counts (2002). Building blocks for success [Special Report]. Bethesda, MD: *Education Week.*

———. (2004). Count me in: Special education in an era of standards. Executive Summary: Special Needs, Common Goals. *Education Week, 23*(17), 7.

Quay, H.C., & Peterson, D.R. (1983). *Behavior problem checklist: Revised.* Coral Gables, FL: University of Miami.

Quigley, S.P., & Paul, P.V. (1984). *Language and deafness.* San Diego: College-Hill.

Rais-Bahrami, K., Short, B.L., & Batshaw, M.L. (2002). Premature and small-for-dates infants. In Mark L. Batshaw (Ed.), *Children with disabilities* (5th ed.), pp. 85–103. Baltimore: Paul H. Brookes.

Ranshaw, H.S., Woodcock, J.M., Bagley, C.J., McClure, B.J., Heraus, T.R., & Lopez, A.F. (2001). New approaches in the treatment of asthma. *Immunology and Cell Biology, 79,* 154–162.

Rapport, M.K. (1996). Legal guidelines for the delivery of special health care services in schools. *Exceptional Children, 62,* 537–549.

Raskind, M.H., Goldberg, R.J., Higgins, E.L., & Herman, K.L. (1999). Patterns of change and predictors of success in individuals with learning disabilities: Results from a twenty-year longitudinal study. *Learning Disabilities Research and Practice, 14,* 35–49.

Raths, L.E., Wassermann, S., Jonas, A., & Rothstein, A. (1986). *Teaching for thinking.* New York: Teachers College Press.

Ratner, V., & Harris, L. (1994). *Understanding language disorders: The impact on learning.* Eau Claire, WI: Thinking Publications.

Ravitch, D. (2003). *The language police: How pressure groups restrict what students learn.* New York: Alfred A. Knopf.

Reese, L. Goldenberg, C., Loucky, J., & Gallimore, R. (1995). Ecocultural context, cultural activity, and emergent literacy of Spanish-speaking children. In S.W. Rothstein (ed.) *Class, culture and race in American schools: A handbook,* pp. 199–224. Westport, CT: Greenwood Press.

Reichard, A. (1995). The value of prenatal testing. *Exceptional Parent, 25*(8), 29–31.

Reid, D.K. (2000). Discourse in classrooms. In K.R. Fahey & D.K. Reid (Eds.). *Language development, differences, and disorders.* (pp. 31–38). Austin, TX: Pro-Ed.

———. (2000). Ebonics and Hispanic, Asian, and Native American dialects of English. In K.R. Fahey & D.K. Reid (Eds.), *Language development, differences, and disorders,* pp. 219–244. Austin, TX: Pro-Ed.

Reid, D.H., Everson, J.M., & Green, C.W. (1999). A systematic evaluation of preferences identified through person-centered planning for people with profound multiple disabilities. *Journal of Applied Behavior Analysis, 32,* 467–477.

Reid, R., Riccio, C.A., Kessler, R.H., DuPaul, G.J., Anastopoulos, A.D., Rogers-Adkinson, D., & Noll, M.B. (2000). Gender and ethnic differences in ADHD as assessed by behavior ratings. *Journal of Emotional and Behavioral Disorders, 8,* 38–48.

Reis, S.M., & McCoach, D.B. (2000). The underachievement of gifted students: What do we know and where do we go? *Gifted Child Quarterly, 44*(3), 152–170.

Reis, S.M., McGuire, J.M., & Neu, T.W. (2000). Compensation strategies used by high-ability students with learning disabilities who succeed in college. *Gifted Child Quarterly, 44*(2), 123–134.

Reis, S.M., Neu, T.W., & McGuire, J.M. (1995). *Talent in two places: Case studies of high ability students with learning disabilities who have achieved.* Storrs, CT: University of Connecticut, the National Research Center on the Gifted and Talented.

———. (1997). Case studies of high-ability students with learning disabilities who have achieved. *Exceptional Children, 63*(4), 463–479.

Renner, P., Klinger, L.G., & Klinger, M.R. (2000). Implicit and explicit memory in autism: Is autism an amnesic disorder? *Journal of Autism and Developmental Disorders, 30,* 3–14.

Renzulli, J.S. (1977). *The Enrichment Triad Model.* Mansfield Center, CT: Creative Learning Press.

———. (1978). What makes giftedness? *Phi Delta Kappan, 60,* 180–184.

———. (Ed.). (1986). *Systems and models for developing programs for the gifted and talented.* Mansfield Center, CT: Creative Learning Press.

———. (2003) Conception of giftedness and its relation to social capital. In N. Colangelo and G.A. Davis (Eds.), *Handbook of gifted education* (3rd ed., p. 76). Boston: Allyn and Bacon.

Renzulli, J.S., & Reis, S.M. (1985). *The schoolwide enrichment model: A comprehensive plan for educational excellence.* Mansfield Center, CT: Creative Learning Press.

———. (1991). The schoolwide enrichment model: A comprehensive plan for the development of creative productivity. In N. Colangelo & G.A. Davis (Eds.), *Handbook of gifted education.* Boston: Allyn and Bacon.

———. (2003). The Schoolwide Enrichment Model: Developing creative and productive giftedness. In N. Colangelo and G.A. Davis (Eds.), *Handbook of gifted education* (3rd ed.) (pp. 184–203). Boston: Allyn and Bacon.

Rescorla, L. (2002). Language and reading outcomes to age 9 in late-talking toddlers. *Journal of Speech, Language, and Hearing Research, 45*(2), 360–371.

Rimland, B. (1964). *Infantile autism: The syndrome and its implication for a neural theory of behavior.* Englewood Cliffs, NJ: Prentice-Hall.

Rimm, S.B. (1986). *Underachievement syndrome: Causes and cures.* Watertown, WI: Apple Publishing Company.

———. (2003). Underachievement: A national epidemic. In N. Colangelo and G.A. Davis (Eds.), *Handbook of gifted education* (3rd ed.) (pp. 424–443). Boston: Allyn and Bacon.

Rivers, J.W., & Stoneman, Z. (2003). Sibling relationships when a child has autism: Marital stress and support coping. *Journal of Autism and Developmental Disorders, 33*(4), 383–394.

Roberts, C.D., Stough, L.M., & Parrish, L.H. (2002). The role of genetic counseling in the elective termination of pregnancies involving fetuses with disabilities. *The Journal of Special Education, 36,* 48–55.

Roberts, J.E., Wallace, I.F., & Henderson, F.W. (1997). *Otitis media in young children.* Baltimore: Paul H. Brookes.

Robertson, C.M., & Finer, N.N. (1993). Long-term follow-up of term neonates with perinatal asphyxia. *Clinics in Perinatology, 20*(2), 483–500.

Robinson, A. (1990). Cooperation or exploitation? The argument against cooperative learning for talented students. *Journal for the Education of the Gifted, 14*(1), 9–27.

———. (2003). Cooperative learning and high ability students. In N. Colangelo and G.A. Davis (Eds.), *Handbook of gifted education* (3rd ed.) (pp. 282–292). Boston: Allyn and Bacon.

Rodier, P. (2000). The early origins of autism. *Scientific American, 282*(2), 56–63.

Rogan, J. (2001). Learning strategies: Recipes for success. *Beyond Behavior, 10*(1), 18–22.

Rogers-Dulan, J. (1998). Religious connectedness among urban African-American families. *Mental Retardation, 36*(2), 91–103.

Rosen, L.A., Gabardi, L., Miller, C.D., & Miller, L. (1990). Home-based treatment of disruptive junior high school students: An analysis of the differential effects of positive and negative consequences. *Behavioral Disorders, 15,* 227–232.

Rosenshine, B., & Stevens, R. (1986). Teaching functions. In M.C. Wittrock (Ed.), *Handbook of research on teaching* (3rd ed.) (pp. 376–391). New York: Macmillan.

Rosenthal-Malek, A., & Greenspan, J. (1999). A student with diabetes is in my class. *Teaching Exceptional Children, 31*(3), 38–43.

Rothenberg, L. (2003). *Breathing for a living.* New York: Hyperion.

Rylance, B.J. (1998). Predictors of post–high school employment for youth identified as severely emotionally disturbed. *The Journal of Special Education, 32,* 184–192.

Sacks, O. (1989). *Seeing voices: A journey into the world of the deaf.* New York: HarperCollins.

Sacks, S.Z. (1996). Psychological and social implications of low vision. In A.L. Corn & A.J. Koenig (Eds.), *Foundations of low vision: Clinical and functional perspectives.* New York: American Foundation for the Blind.

Sacks, S.Z., & Silberman, R.K. (2000). Social skills. In A.J. Koenig and M.C. Holbrook (Eds.), *Foundations of Education: Vol. II* (2nd ed.), (pp. 616–652). New York: American Foundation for the Blind.

Sadker, M., & Sadker, D. (1994). *Failing at fairness: How America's schools cheat girls.* New York: Charles Scribner's Sons.

Safran, J.S. (2002). Supporting students with Asperger's Syndrome in general education. *Teaching Exceptional Children, 34*(5), 60–66.

Saigal, S. (2000). Follow-up of very low birthweight babies to adolescence. *Seminars in Neonatology, 5*(2), 107–118.

Salisbury, C.L., Evans, I.M., & Palombaro, M.M. (1997). Collaborative problem-solving to promote the inclusion of young children with significant dis-

abilities in primary grades. *Exceptional Children, 63,* 195–209.

Salvia, J., & Ysseldyke, J. (2004). *Assessment in special and inclusive education* (9th ed.). Boston: Houghton Mifflin.

Sameroff, A.J. (1998). Environmental risk factors in infancy. *Pediatrics, 102*(5) (Supplement), 1287–1292.

Sampson, P.D., Streissguth, A.P., Bookstein, F.L., Little, R.E., Clarren, S.K., Dehaene, P., Hanson, J.W., & Graham, J.M. (1997). Incidence of fetal alcohol syndrome and prevalence of alcohol-related neurodevelopmental disorder. *Teratology, 56*(5), 317–26.

Sandall, S., McLean, M., & Smith, B.J. (Eds.) (2000). *DEC recommended practices in early intervention/early childhood special education.* Longmont, CO: Sopris West.

Sandall, S.R. (1997a). The family service team. In A.H. Widerstrom, B.A. Mowder & S.R. Sandall (Eds.), *Infant development and risk* (2nd ed.). Baltimore: Paul H. Brookes.

———. (1997b). The individualized family service plan. In A.H. Widerstrom, B.A. Mowder & S.R. Sandall (Eds.), *Infant development and risk* (2nd ed.). Baltimore: Paul H. Brookes.

Santamaria, L.J., Fletcher, T.V., & Bos, C.S. (2002). Effective pedagogy for English language learners in inclusive classrooms. In A.J. Artiles & A.A. Ortiz, *English language learners with special education needs: Identification, assessment, and instruction* (pp. 133–157). McHenry, IL: Center for Applied Linguistics/Delta Systems Co.

Savelle, S., & Fox, J.J. (1988). Differential effects of training in two classes of social initiations on the positive responses and extended interactions of preschool-aged autistic children and their nonhandicapped peers. In R.B. Rutherford, Jr. & J.W. Maag (Eds.), *Monograph in behavioral disorders: Severe behavior disorders of children and Youth, 11,* 75–86.

Scanlon, D., & Mellard, D.F. (2002). Academic participation profiles of school-age dropouts with and without disabilities. *Exceptional Children, 68,* 239–257.

Scarborough, H. (2001). Connecting early language and literacy to later reading (dis)abilities: Evidence, theory, and practice. In S.B. Neumann & D.K. Dickinson (Eds.), *Handbook of early literacy research.* New York: Guilford Press.

Scarborough, H.S., & Dobrich, W. (1990). Development of children with early language delay. *Journal of Speech and Hearing Disorders, 33,* 70–83.

Scheuermann, B., & Webber, J. (1996). Level systems: Problems and solutions. *Beyond Behavior, 7*(2), 12–17.

Schildroth, A.N. (1994). Congenital cytomegalovirus and deafness. *American Journal of Audiology* (July).

Schiever, S.W., & Maker, C.J. (2003). New directions in enrichment and acceleration. In N. Colangelo and G.A. Davis (Eds.), *Handbook of gifted education* (3rd ed.) (pp. 163–173). Boston: Allyn and Bacon.

Schirmer, B.R. (1994). *Language and literacy development in children who are deaf.* New York: Merrill.

Schleper, David R. (1997). *Reading to deaf children: Learning from deaf adults.* Washington, DC: Gallaudet University, Pre-College National Mission Programs.

———. (2000). Fingerspelling: Critical for literacy development. *Odyssey,* Summer, p. 10.

Schoem, S.R. (1999). Update on otitis media in children. *Volta Review, 99*(5), 97–111.

Scholl, T.O., Hediger, M.L., & Belsky, D.H. (1994). Prenatal care and maternal health during adolescent pregnancy: A review and meta-analysis. *Journal of Adolescent Health, 15*(6), 444–456.

Schuler, P.A. (1997). Cluster grouping coast to coast. *Newsletter of the National Research Center on the Gifted and Talented* (Winter).

Schultz, R.A., & Delisle, J.R. (2003). Gifted adolescents. In N. Colangelo and G.A. Davis (Eds.), *Handbook of gifted education* (3rd ed.) (pp. 483-492). Boston: Allyn and Bacon.

Schumaker, J.B., & Hazel, J.S. (1984). Social skills assessment and training for the learning disabled: What's on second? Part I. *Journal of Learning Disabilities, 17,* 422–431.

Scorgie, K., Wilgosh, L., & McDonald, L. (1999). Transforming partnerships: Parents' life management issues when a child has mental retardation. *Education and Training in Mental Retardation and Developmental Disabilities, 34,* 395–405.

Scott, J., Clark, C., & Brady, M. (2000). *Student with autism: Characteristics and instructional programming.* San Diego, CA: Singular.

Scott, T.M., & Shearer-Lingo, A. (2002). The effects of reading fluency instruction on the academic and behavioral success of middle school students in a self-contained EBD classroom. *Preventing School Failure, 46,* 167–173.

Scott, T.M., Liaupsin, C.J., Nelson, C.M., & Jolivette, K. (2003). Ensuring student success through team-based functional behavioral assessment. *Teaching Exceptional Children, 35*(5), 16–21.

Scruggs, T.E., & Mastropieri, M.A. (2001). Mnemonic interventions for students with behavior disorders. *Beyond Behavior, 10*(1), 13–17.

Scruggs, T.E., & Mastropieri, M.A. (1996). Teacher perceptions of mainstreaming/inclusion, 1958–1995: A research synthesis. *Exceptional Children, 63*(1), 59–74.

Secada, W., Fennema, E., & Adajian, L.B. (1995). *New directions for equity in mathematics education.* New York: Cambridge University Press.

Seidel, J.F., & Vaughn, S. (1991). Social alienation and the learning disabled school dropout. *Learning Disabilities Research and Practice, 3,* 152–157.

Seligman, M., & Darling, R.B. (1997). *Ordinary families, special children* (2nd ed.). New York: The Guilford Press.

Serna, L., Nielsen, E., Lambros, K., & Forness, S. (2000). Primary prevention with children at risk for emotional or behavioral disorders: Data on a universal intervention for Head Start Classrooms. *Behavioral Disorders, 26,* 70–84.

Shapiro, D.R., & Sayers, L.K. (2003). Who does what on the interdisciplinary team? *Teaching Exceptional Children, 35*(6), 32–38.

Shaywitz, S.E., & Shaywitz, B.A. (2001). The neurobiology of reading and dyslexia. *Focus on Basics, 5,* Issue A. Retrieved online at: http://ncsall.gse.harvard.edu/fob/2001/Shaywitz.html.

Shiono, P.H., & Behrman, R.E. (1995). Low birth weight: Analysis and recommendations. *Future of Children, 5*(3), 4–18.

Shonkoff, J.P., & Meisels, S.J. (2000). Preface. In J.P. Shonkoff & S.J. Meisels, (Eds.), *Handbook of early childhood intervention* (2nd ed.), pp. xvii–xviii. Cambridge, UK: Cambridge University Press.

Siegel-Causey, E., McMorris, C., McGowen, S., & Sands-Buss, S. (1998). In Junior High you take Earth Science: Including a student with severe disabilities into an academic class. *Teaching Exceptional Children, 31*(1), 66–72.

Sienkiewicz-Mercer, R., & Kaplan, S.B. (1989). *I raise my eyes to say yes.* Boston: Houghton Mifflin.

Sigafoos, J. (2000). Communication development and aberrant behavior in children with developmental disabilities. *Education and Training in Mental Retardation and Developmental Disabilities, 35,* 168–176.

Sigman, M. & Whaley, S.E. (1998) The role of nutrition in the development of intelligence. In Ulric Neisser (Ed.). *The rising curve: Long-term gains in IQ and related measures.* Washington, DC: American Psychological Association.

Silberman, R.K. (2000). Children and youths with visual impairments and other disabilities. In M.C. Holbrook and A.J. Koenig (Eds.), *Foundations of Education: Vol.1* (2nd ed., pp. 173–196). New York: American Foundation for the Blind.

Simeonsson, R.J. (Ed.). (1994). *Risk, resilience, and prevention: Promoting the well-being of all children.* Baltimore: Paul H. Brookes.

Simpson, R.L., & Souris, L.A. (1988). Reciprocity in the pupil-teacher interactions of autistic and mildly handicapped preschool children. *Behavioral Disorders, 13,* 159–168.

Singer, L.T., Arendt, R., Minnes, S., Farkas, K., Salvator, A., Kirchner, H.L., & Kliegman, R. (2002). Cognitive and motor outcomes of cocaine-exposed infants. *JAMA, 287*(15), 1952–1960.

Singer, P. (1996). *Rethinking life and death: The collapse of our traditional ethics* (2nd ed.). New York: St. Martin's Press.

Singleton, D.K., Schuster, J.W., Morse, T.E., & Collins, B.C. (1999). A comparison of antecedent prompt and test and simultaneous prompting procedures in teaching grocery words to adolescents with mental retardation. *Education and Training in Mental Retardation and Developmental Disabilities, 34,* 182–199.

Siperstein, G.N., Leffert, J.S., & Widaman, K. (1996). Social behavior and the social acceptance and rejection of children with mental retardation. *Education and Training in Mental Retardation and Developmental Disabilities, 31,* 271–281.

Skinner, D., Bailey, D.B., Correa, V., & Rodriguez, P. (1999). Narrating self and disability: Latino mothers' construction of identities vis-à-vis their child with special needs. *Exceptional Children, 65,* 481–495.

Skinner, R. (1990). Genetic counseling. In A.E.H. Emery & D.L. Rimoin (Eds.), *Principles and practice of human genetics* (2nd ed.) (Vol. 2). New York: Churchill Livingstone.

Slavin, R.E. (1988). Synthesis of research on grouping in elementary and secondary schools. *Educational Leadership* (Sept.), 67–77.

———. (1990). Ability grouping, cooperative learning and the gifted. *Journal for the Education of the Gifted, 14*(1), 3–8.

Smith, J.D. (1989). On the right of children with mental retardation to life-sustaining medical care and treatment: A position statement. *Education and Training in Mental Retardation, 24,* 3–6.

Smith, T. (1996). Are other treatments effective? In C. Maurice, G. Green, & S.C. Luce (Eds.), *Behavioral intervention for young children with autism: A manual for parents and professionals.* Austin, TX: Pro-Ed.

Smith, T., & Lovaas, O.L. (1997). The UCLA young autism project: A reply to Gresham and MacMillan. *Behavioral Disorders, 22,* 202–218.

Smith, T.E.C., Finn, D.M., & Dowdy, C.A. (1993). *Teaching students with mild disabilities.* Orlando, FL: Harcourt Brace Jovanovich.

Smith, T.M. (1994). Adolescent pregnancy. In R.J. Simeonsson (Ed.), *Risk, resilience, and prevention: Promoting the well-being of all children.* Baltimore: Paul H. Brookes.

Snell, M.E. (1988). Curriculum and methodology for individuals with severe disabilities. *Education and Training in Mental Retardation, 23,* 302–314.

Snell, M.E., & Brown, F. (2000). *Instruction of students with severe disabilities* (5th ed.). Columbus, OH: Merrill.

Snell, M.E., & Drake, G.P. (1994). Replacing cascades with supported education. *Journal of Special Education, 27,* 393–409.

Snell, M.E., & Janney, R.E. (2000). Teachers' problem-solving about children with moderate and severe disabilities in elementary classrooms. *Exceptional Children, 66,* 472–490.

Snider, V.E. (1997). Transfer of decoding skills to a literature basal. *Learning Disabilities Research and Practice, 12,* 54–62.

Snow, C.E., Burns, M.S., & Griffin, P. (Eds.). (1998). *Preventing reading difficulties in young children.* Washington, DC: National Academy Press.

Solomon, G., Allen, N.J., & Resta, P. (Eds.) (2003). *Toward digital equity: Bridging the divide in education.* Boston: Allyn and Bacon

Sonnier-York, C., & Stanford, P. (2002). Learning to cooperate: A teacher's perspective. *Teaching Exceptional Children, 34,* 40–45.

Sontag, J.C., & Schacht, R. (1994). An ethnic comparison of parent participation and information needs in early intervention. *Exceptional Children, 60,* 422–433.

Sparrow, S.S., Balla, D.A., & Cicchetti, D.V. (1984). *Vineland adaptive behavior scales: Interview edition, survey form manual.* Circle Pines, MN: American Guidance Service.

Spencer, K.C., & Sands, D.J. (1999). Prediction of student participation in transition-related actions. *Education and Training in Mental Retardation and Developmental Disabilities, 34,* 473–484.

Spina Bifida Association of America (SBAA) (2003). http://www.sbaa.org/.

Sprague, J., & Walker, H. (2000). Early identification and intervention for youth with antisocial and violent behavior. *Exceptional Children, 66,* 367–379.

Spungin, S. (Ed.) (2002). *When you have a blind or visually impaired child in your classroom: A guide for teachers.* New York: AFB Press.

Stafford, A., Alberto, P.A., Fredrick, L.D., Heflin, L.J., & Heller, K.W. (2002). Preference variability and the instruction of choice making with students with severe intellectual disabilities. *Education and Training in Mental Retardation and Mental Disabilities, 37,* 70–88.

Stagni, K. (2000). Newborn screening and parent support groups. *Exceptional Parent, 30*(10), 66–68.

Stainback, G.H., Stainback, W.C., & Stainback, S.B. (1988). Superintendents' attitudes toward integration. *Education and Training in Mental Retardation, 23,* 92–96.

Stainback, S., Stainback, W., & Ayres, B. (1996). Schools as inclusive communities. In W. Stainback & S. Stainback (Eds.), *Controversial issues confronting special education: Divergent perspectives* (2nd ed.) (pp. 31–43). Boston: Allyn and Bacon.

Starko, A.J. (1986). Meeting the needs of the gifted throughout the school day: Techniques for curriculum compacting. *Roeper Review, 9*(1), 27–33.

Stecker, P.M., & Fuchs, L.S. (2000). Effecting superior achievement using curriculum-based measurement: The importance of individual progress monitoring. *Learning Disabilities Research and Practice, 15,* 128–134.

Steere, D.E., & Cavaiuolo, D. (2002). Connecting outcomes, goals, and objectives in transition planning. *Teaching Exceptional Children, 34*(6), 54–59.

Stein, M., & Davis, C.A. (2001). Direct instruction as a positive behavioral support. *Beyond Behavior, 10*(1), 7–12.

Stein, M., & Davis, C.A. (2000). Direct instruction as a positive behavioral support. *Beyond Behavior, 10,* 7–12.

Stella, J., Mundy, P., & Tuchman, R. (1999). Social and nonsocial factors in the Childhood Autism Rating Scale. *Journal of Autism and Developmental Disorders, 29,* 307–317.

Stephenson, J.R., & Dowrick, M. (2000). Parent priorities in communication intervention for young students with severe disabilities. *Education and Training in Mental Retardation and Developmental Disabilities, 35,* 25–35.

Stepien, W.J., & Gallagher, S. (1997). *Problem-based learning across the curriculum professional inquiry kit.* Alexandria, VA: ASCD.

Sternberg, R.J. (1991). Giftedness according to the triarchic theory of human intelligence. In N. Colangelo & G.A. Davis (Eds.), *Handbook of gifted education* (pp. 45–54). Boston: Allyn and Bacon.

———. (1995). *In search of the human mind.* Belmont, CA: International Thomson Publishing.

———. (1997). What does it mean to be smart? *Educational Leadership, 54*(6), 16–20.

———. (2000). Wisdom as a form of giftedness. *Gifted Child Quarterly, 44*(4), 252–260.

———. (2003). Giftedness according to the theory of successful intelligence. In N. Colangelo and G.A. Davis (Eds.), *Handbook of gifted education* (3rd ed.) (pp. 88–99). Boston: Allyn and Bacon.

Sternberg, R.J., & Clinkenbeard, P. (1995). A triarchic view of identifying, teaching, and assessing gifted children. *Roeper Review, 17,* 225–260.

Sternberg, R.J. & Grigorenko, E.L. (2000). *Teaching for successful intelligence.* Arlington Heights, IL: Skylight Training and Publishing Inc.

Stewart, D.A., & Clarke, B.R. (2003). *Literacy and your deaf child: What every parent should know.* Washington, DC: Gallaudet University, Pre-College National Mission Programs.

Stewart, D.A., & Kluwin, T.N. (2001). *Teaching deaf and hard of hearing students: Content, strategies, and curriculum.* Boston: Allyn and Bacon.

Stewart, D.A., & Luetke-Stahlman, B. (2002). *The signing family: What every parent should know about sign communication.* Washington, DC: Gallaudet University, Pre-College National Mission Programs.

Stokoe, W. (1960). Sign language structure: An outline of the visual communication system of the American deaf. *Studies in Linguistics Occasional Papers No. 8.* Washington, DC: Gallaudet College Press.

Stoneman, Z., Brody, G.H., Davis, C.H., & Crapps, J.M. (1988). Childcare responsibilities, peer relations, and sibling conflict: Older siblings of mentally retarded children. *American Journal of Mental Retardation, 93,* 174–183.

Storey, K. (1997). Quality of life issues in social skills assessment of persons with disabilities. *Education and Training in Mental Retardation and Developmental Disabilities, 32,* 197–200.

Storey, K., & Provost, O. (1996). The effect of communication skills instruction on the integration of workers with severe disabilities in supported employment settings. *Education and Training in Mental Retardation and Developmental Disabilities, 31,* 123–141.

Stotland, J. (1984). Relationships of parents to professionals: A challenge to professionals. *Journal of Visual Impairment and Blindness, 78*(2), pp. 69–74.

Strauss, et al. (1999). Causes of excessive mortality in cerebral palsy. *Developmental Medicine and Child Neurology, 9,* 580–585.

Strauss, M. (1999). Hearing loss and cytomegalovirus. *Volta Review, 99*(5), 71–74.

Strong, K., & Sandoval, J. (1999). Mainstreaming children with a neuromuscular disease: A map of concerns. *Exceptional Children, 65,* 353–366.

Sturm, J.M., & Rankin-Erikson, J.L. (2002). Effects of hand-drawn and computer-generated concept mapping on the expository writing of middle school students with learning disabilities. *Learning Disabilities Research and Practice, 17,* 124–139.

Sullivan, C.A.C., Vitello, S.J., & Foster, W. (1988). Adaptive behavior of adults with mental retardation in a group home: An intensive case study. *Education and Training in Mental Retardation, 23,* 76–81.

Summers, J.A., Behr, S.K., & Turnbull, A.P. (1989). Positive adaptation and coping strengths of families who have children with disabilities. In G.H.S. Singer & L.K. Irvin (Eds.), *Support for caregiving families* (pp. 27–40). Baltimore: Paul H. Brookes.

Sutherland, K.S., Wehby, J.H., & Yoder, P.J. (2002). Examination of the relationship between teacher praise and opportunities for students with EBD to respond to academic requests. *Journal of Emotional and Behavior Disorders, 10,* 1–19.

Swanson, H.L. (1993). Principles and procedures in strategy use. In L.J. Meltzer (Ed.), *Strategy assessment and instruction for students with learning disabilities* (pp. 61–92). Austin, TX: Pro-Ed.

———. (1999). Instructional components that predict treatment outcomes for students with learning disabilities: Support for a combined strategy and direct instruction model. *Learning*

Disabilities Research and Practice, 14, 129–140.

Swanson, H.L., Cochran, K.F., & Ewers, C.A. (1990). Can learning disabilities be determined from working memory performance? *Journal of Learning Disabilities, 23,* 59–67.

Sweetow, R.W., & Luckett, E. (2001). Selecting the "best" hearing aids for yourself or your child. *Volta Voices,* March/April, 18–21.

Szabo, J.L. (2000). Maddie's story: Inclusion through physical and occupational therapy. *Teaching Exceptional Children, 33*(2), 12–18.

Talking Verbs, The Talking Series, Laureate Learning Systems. http://www. laureatelearning.com/professionals 602/.

Tannenbaum, A.J. (2003). Nature and nurture of giftedness. In N. Colangelo and G.A. Davis (Eds.), *Handbook of gifted education* (3rd ed.) (pp. 45–59). Boston: Allyn and Bacon.

TASH (The Association for Individuals with Severe Handicaps). (2000). TASH Resolutions and Policy Statement. http:www.TASH.org. Retrieved June, 2003.

Taylor, B.A., & McDonough, K.A. (1996). Selecting teaching programs. In C. Maurice, G. Green, & S.C. Luce (Eds.), *Behavioral intervention for young children with autism: A manual for parents and professionals* (pp. 63–177). Austin, TX: Pro-Ed.

Taylor, S.E. (1983). Adjustment to threatening events: A theory of cognitive adaptation. *American Psychologist, 38,* 1161–1173.

Taylor, S.J., Lakin, K.C., & Hill, B.K. (1989). Permanency planning for children and youth: Out-of-home placement decisions. *Exceptional Children, 55,* 541–549.

Taylor, S.J., Racino, J.A., & Walker, P.M. (1992). Inclusive community living. In W. Stainback & S. Stainback (Eds.) *Controversial issues confronting special education: Divergent perspectives* (pp. 299–312). Boston: Allyn and Bacon.

Tellus 2. (2002) Voice Output Communication Aids, Techcess Ltd.

Temple, E., Deutsch, G.K., Poldrack, R.A., Miller, S.L., Tallal, P., Merzenich, M.M., & Gabrieli, J.D.E. (2003). Neural deficits in children with dyslexia ameliorated by behavioral remediation: Evidence from functional MRI. PNAS Online, February 25, 2003 (http://www.pnas.org/cgi/content/abstract/.

Terman, L.M., & Merrill, M.A. (1973). *Stanford-Binet Intelligence Scale-Third Revision Form L-M.* Boston: Houghton Mifflin.

Terman, L.M., et al. *Genetic studies of genius.* I. *The mental and physical traits of a thousand gifted children,* 1925; II: *The early mental traits of three hundred geniuses,* 1926; III: *The promise of youth,* 1930; IV: *The gifted child grows up,* 1947; V: *The gifted group at mid-life,* 1959. Stanford, CA: Stanford University Press.

Terpstra, J.E., Higgins, K., & Pierce, T. (2002). Can I play? Classroom-based interventions for teaching play skills to children with autism. *Focus on Autism and Other Developmental Disabilities, 17,* 119–126.

Terrell, S.L., & Jackson, R.S. (2002). African Americans in the Americas. In D.E. Battle (Ed.), *Communication disorders in multicultural populations* (3rd ed.). Boston: Butterworth Heinemann.

Tharp, R.G., Estrada, P., Dalton, S.S., & Yamauchi, L.A. (2000). *Teaching transformed: Achieving excellence, fairness, inclusion, and harmony.* Boulder, CO: Westview.

Thomas, C.C., Correa, V.I., and Morsink, C.N. (2001). *Interactive teaming: Enhancing programs for children with special needs* (3rd ed.). Upper Saddle River, NJ: Merrill/Prentice-Hall.

Thomas, S.B., & Hawke, C. (1999). Health-care services for children with disabilities: Emerging standards and implications. *Journal of Special Education, 32,* 226–237.

Thompson, L., Lobb, C., Elling, R., Herman, S., Jurkiewicz, T., & Hulleza, C. (1997). Pathways to family empowerment: Effects of family-centered delivery of early intervention services. *Exceptional Children, 64,* 7–18.

Thurstone, L.L. (1924). *The nature of intelligence.* London: Kegan Paul, Trench, Trubner.

Torgeson, J.K. (2000). Individual differences in response to early interventions in reading: The lingering problem of treatment resisters. *Learning Disabilities Research and Practice, 15,* 55–64.

Tomlinson, C.A. (2003). *Fulfilling the promise of the differentiated classroom: Strategies and tools for responsive teaching.* Alexandria, VA: Association for Supervision & Curriculum Development.

Tomlinson, C.A., Kaplan, S.N., Renzulli, J.S., Purcell, J., Leppien, J., & Burns, D. (2002). *The Parallel Curriculum.* Thousand Oaks, CA: Corwin Press.

Torp, L. & Sage, S. (1998). *Problems as possibilities: Problem-based learning for K-12 education.* Alexandria, VA: Association for Supervision and Curriculum Development.

Torrance, E.P. (1969). Creative positives of disadvantaged children and youth. *Gifted Child Quarterly, 13,* 71–81.

———. (1984). *Mentor relationships: How they aid creative achievement, endure, change and die.* Buffalo: Bearly Limited.

Torres, I., & Corn, A.L. (1990). *When you have a visually handicapped child in your classroom: Suggestions for teachers.* (2nd ed.). New York: American Foundation for the Blind.

Toscano, R.M., McKee, B., & Lepoutre, D. (2002). Success with academic English: Reflections of deaf college students. *American Annals of the Deaf, 147*(1), 5–23.

Townsend, B.L. (2000). The disproportionate discipline of African American learners: Reducing school suspensions and expulsions. *Exceptional Children, 66,* 381–391.

Treiman, R. (1993). *Beginning to spell.* New York: Oxford University Press.

Turnbull, H.R., Buchele-Ash, A., & Mitchell, L. (1994). *Abuse and neglect of children with disabilities: A policy analysis.* Lawrence, KS: Beach Center on Families and Disability, University of Kansas.

Turnbull, A.P., Patterson, J.M., Behr, S.K., Murphy, D.L., Marquis, J.G., & Blue-Banning, M.J. (1993). *Cognitive coping, families, and disability.* Baltimore: Paul H. Brookes.

Turnbull, A.P., & Ruef, M. (1997). Family perspectives on inclusive lifestyle issues for people with problem behavior. *Exceptional Children, 63,* 211–227.

Turnbull, A.P., Sumness, J.A., & Brotherson, M.J. (1984). *Working with families with disabled members: A family systems approach.* Lawrence: University of Kansas, Beach Center on Families and Disabilities.

Turnbull, A.P. and Turnbull, H.R. (1993b). Participatory research on cognitive coping: From concepts to research planning. In A.P. Turnbull, J.M. Patterson, S.K. Behr, D.L. Murphy, J.G. Marquis, & M.J. Blue-Banning (Eds.), *Cognitive coping, families, and disability.* Baltimore: Paul H. Brookes.

———. (1997). *Families, professionals, and exceptionality: A special partnership* (3rd ed.) Upper Saddle River, NJ: Merrill/Prentice Hall.

———. (2001). *Families, professionals, and exceptionality: Collaborating for empowerment* (4th ed.). Upper Saddle River, NJ: Merrill/ Prentice-Hall.

Tuttle, D.W., & Tuttle, N.R. (2000). Psychosocial needs of children and youths. In M.C. Holbrook and A.J. Koenig (Eds.), *Foundations of Education: Vol.1* (2nd ed., pp. 161–172). New York: American Foundation for the Blind.

United Cerebral Palsy Association (UCPA) (2001). http://www.ucpa.org/.

U.S. Advisory Board on Child Abuse and Neglect. (1995). *A nation's shame: Fatal child abuse and neglect in the United States.* Washington, DC: U.S. Department of Health and Human Services.

U.S. Census Bureau (2002). *Current population survey (CPS)—definitions and explanations.* Population Division, Fertility & Family Statistics Branch. Retrieved 12/24/02 from www. census.gov/population/www/cps/cpsdef.html.

U.S. courts affirm the need for a full continuum of services (1996). *CEC Today, 3*(6), 4–5.

U.S. Department of Education. (1977, December 29). Education of handicapped children. Assistance of the states: Procedures for evaluating specific learning disabilities. *Federal Register, Part III.* Washington, DC: U.S. Department of Health, Education and Welfare.

U.S. Department of Education (1977). *Federal Register 42* [163], August 23, 1977, p. 42, 478.

U.S. Department of Education. (1995). www.ed.gov. IDEA/amend95. backgrnd.html.

U.S. Department of Education. (2000). Twenty-second Annual Report to Congress on the Implementation of the Individuals with Disabilities Education Act. Washington, DC.

U. S. Department of Education (2001). Twenty-third Annual Report to Congress on the Implementation of the Individuals with Disabilities Education Act. Washington, DC: U.S. Department of Education.

U.S. Department of Education, National Center for Education Statistics (2002). *The condition of education 2002,* NCES 2002–025. Washington, DC: U.S. Government Printing Office.

U. S. Department of Education (2002). Twenty-fourth Annual Report to Congress on the Implementation of the Individuals with Disabilities Education Act. Washington, DC: U.S. Department of Education.

Utley, C.A., Delquadri, J.C., Obiakor, F.E., & Mims, V.A. (2000). General and special educators' perceptions of teaching strategies for multicultural students. *Teacher Education and Special Education, 23,* 34–50.

VanTassel-Baska, J. (1997). *Guide to teaching a problem-based science curriculum.* Dubuque, IA: Kendall/Hunt.

VanTassel-Baska, J., Johnson, D.T., Boyce, L.N. & Little, C.A. (1999). *Guide to teaching a language arts curriculum for high-ability learners.* Dubuque, IA: Kendall/Hunt.

Vaughn, S. (1991). Social skills enhancement in students with learning disabilities. In B. Wong (Ed.), *Learning about learning disabilities* (pp. 409–440). San Diego: Academic Press.

Vaughn, S., Chard, D.J., Bryant, D.P., Coleman, M., Tyler, B.J., Linan-Thompson, S., & Kouzekanani, K. (2000). Fluency and comprehension interventions for third-grade students. *Remedial and Special Education, 21,* 325–340.

Vaughn, S., Levy, S., Coleman, M., & Bos, C.S. (2002). Reading instruction for students with LD and EBD: A synthesis of observation studies. *Journal of Special Education, 36,* 2–11.

Vaughn, S., Schumm, J., & Arguelles, M.E. (1997). The ABCDEs of co-teaching. *Teaching Exceptional Children, 30* (2), 4–10.

Vernon, P.E. (1989). *Intelligence: Heredity and environment.* San Francisco: Freeman.

Villa, R.A., Thousand, J.A., Meyers, H., & Nevin, A. (1996). Teacher and administrator perceptions of heterogeneous education. *Exceptional Children, 63*(1), 29–45.

Von Károlyi, C., Ramos-Ford, V., & Gardner, H. (2003). Multiple intelligences: A perspective on giftedness. In N. Colangelo and G.A. Davis (Eds.), *Handbook of gifted education* (3rd ed.) (pp. 100–112). Boston: Allyn and Bacon.

Vygotsky, L. (1978). *Mind in society: The development of higher psychological processes.* Cambridge, MA: Harvard University Press.

Wakschlag, L.S., & Hans, S.L. (2000). Early parenthood in context: Implications for development and intervention. In C.H. Zeanah (Ed.), *Handbook of Infant Mental Health* (2nd ed.), 129–144. New York: Guilford Press.

Walker, H.M., Colvin, G., & Ramsey, E. (1995). *Antisocial behavior in school: Strategies and best practices.* New York: Brooks/Cole.

Walker, H.M., Severson, H., Stiller, B., Williams, G., Haring, N., Shinn, M., & Todis, B. (1988). Systematic screening of pupils in the elementary age range at risk for behavior disorders: Development and trial testing of a multiple

gating model. *Remedial and Special Education, 9*(3), 8–14.

Walker, H.M., Todis, B., Holmes, D., & Horton, G. (1988). *The Walker social skills curriculum: The ACCESS Program.* Austin, TX: Pro-Ed.

Walker, N. (1985). Impulsivity in learning disabled children: Past research findings and methodological inconsistencies. *Learning Disabilities Quarterly, 8,* 85–94.

Wallace, G., Larsen, S.C., & Elksnin, L.K. (1992). The nature of assessment. *Educational assessment of learning problems: Testing for teaching* (2nd ed.) (pp. 1–29). Boston: Allyn and Bacon.

Wallace, G., & McLoughlin, J.A. (1988). *Learning disabilities: Concepts and characteristics* (3rd ed.). Columbus, OH: Merrill.

Ward, M.E. (2000). The visual system. In M.C. Holbrook and A.J. Koenig (Eds.), *Foundations of Education: Vol.1* (2nd ed.) (pp. 77–110). New York: American Foundation for the Blind.

Warren, D.H. (1984). *Blindness and early childhood development* (2nd ed.). New York: American Foundation for the Blind.

Watlawick, J., Beavin, J., & Jackson, D. (1967). *The pragmatics of communication.* New York: Norton.

Webb, B.J. (2000). Planning and organizing assistive technology resources in your school. *Teaching Exceptional Children, 32*(4), 50–55.

Webb-Johnson, G. (2003). Behaving while black: A hazardous reality for African American learners? *Beyond Behavior, 12*(3), 3–7.

Wedemeyer, N.V. & Grotevant, H.D. (1982). Mapping the family system: A technique for teaching family systems theory concepts. *Family Relations, 82,* 185–193.

Wehman, P., & Kregel, J. (Eds.). (2004). *Functional curriculum for elementary, middle, and secondary students with special needs* (2nd ed.). Austin, TX: Pro-Ed.

Wehman, P., & Targett, P. (2002). Supported employment: The challenges of new staff recruitment, selection, and retention. *Education and Training in Mental Retardation and Developmental Disabilities, 37,* 434–446.

Wehman, P., West, M., & Krege, J. (1999). Supported employment program development and research needs: Looking ahead to year 2000. *Education and Training in Mental Retardation and Developmental Disabilities, 17,* 3–19.

Wehman, P., Wood, W., Everson, J., Marchant, J. & Walker, R. (1987). Transition services for adolescent age individuals with severe mental retardation. In R.N. Ianacone & R.A. Stodden (Eds.), *Transition issues and directions* (pp. 49–76). Reston, VA: Council for Exceptional Children.

Wehmeyer, M.L., & Kelchner, K. (1994). Interpersonal cognitive problem-solving skills of individuals with mental retardation. *Education and Training in Mental Retardation and Developmental Disabilities, 29,* 265–278.

Welsh, M.J., Smith, A.E. (1995). Cystic fibrosis. *Scientific American,* December, 52–59.

Werner, E.E. (1986). The concept of risk from a developmental perspective. In *Advances in special education* (Vol. 5) (pp. 1–23). Greenwich, CT: JAI Press.

————. (1999). Risk and protective factors in the lives of children with high-incidence disabilities. In R. Gallimore, L.P. Bernheimer, D.L. MacMillan, D.L. Speece, S. Vaughn (Eds.), *Developmental perspectives on children with high-incidence disabilities.* Mahwah, NJ: Lawrence Erlbaum.

Werner, E.E., Smith, R.S. (1982). *Vulnerable, but invincible: A longitudinal study of resilient children and youth.* New York: McGraw-Hill.

Westling, D.L., & Fox, L. (2000). *Teaching students with severe disabilities.* Upper Saddle River, NJ: Merrill/Prentice Hall.

What Color? (2002). Do2learn. http://www.dotolearn.com/games/learninggames.htm.

Whitmore, J.R. (1980). *Giftedness, conflict and underachievement.* Boston: Allyn and Bacon.

Whitney-Thomas, J., & Hanley-Maxwell, C. (1996). Packing the parachute: Parents' experiences as their children prepare to leave high school. *Exceptional Children, 63*(1), 75–87.

Widerstrom, A.H., & Nickel, R.E. (1997). Determinants of risk in infancy. In A.H. Widerstrom, B.A. Mowder, & S.R. Sandall (Eds.), *Infant development and risk: An introduction.* Baltimore: Paul H. Brookes.

Will, M.C. (1984). *OSERS programming for the transition of youth with disabilities: Bridges from school to working life.* Washington, DC: Office of Special Education and Rehabilitative Services, U.S. Department of Education.

Willard-Holt, C. (1998). Academic and personality characteristics of gifted students with cerebral palsy: A multiple case study. *Exceptional Children, 65,* 37–50.

————. (1999). Dual exceptionalities. *ERIC Digest E574.* Available at http://www.ed.gov/databases/ERIC_Digests/ed430344.html/.

Winebrenner, S. (2001). Teaching gifted kids in the regular classroom (2nd ed.). Minneapolis: Free Spirit Publishing.

Winner, E. (2000a). Giftedness: Current theory and research. *Current Directions in Psychological Science, 9*(5), 153–156.

————. (2000b). The origins and ends of giftedness. *American Psychologist, 55*(1), 159–169.

Winterman, K.G., & Sapona, R.H. (2002). Everyone's included: Supporting young children with autism spectrum disorders in a responsive classroom learning environment. *Teaching Exceptional Children, 35*(1), 30–35.

Withrow, F.B. (1976). Applications of technology to communication. *Volta Review, 78*(4), 107–112.

Witte, R. (1998). Meet Bob, a student with traumatic brain injury. *Teaching Exceptional Children, 30*(1), 56–60.

Witty, P.A. (1940). Some considerations in the education of gifted children. *Educational Administration and Supervision, 26,* 512–521.

Wolfensberger, W. (1977). The principle of normalization. In B. Blatt, D. Biklen & R. Bogden (Eds.), *An alternative textbook in special education* (pp. 305–327). Denver: Love.

————. (1983). Social role valorization: A proposed new term for the principle of normalization. *Mental Retardation, 21,* 234–239.

Wolffe, K., & Sacks, S.Z. (1997). The lifestyles of blind, low vision, and sighted youths: A quantitative comparison. *Journal of Visual Impairment & Blindness, 91*(3), part 1 of 2, pp. 245–257.

Wolffe, K.E. (2000). Growth and development in middle childhood and adolescence. In M.C. Holbrook and A.J. Koenig (Eds.), *Foundations of Education: Vol.1* (2nd ed., pp. 135–160). New York: American Foundation for the Blind.

Wong, B.Y.L. (1991). The relevance of metacognition to learning disabilities. In B.Y.L. Wong (Ed.), *Learning about learning disabilities* (pp. 232–261). San Diego: Academic Press.

Woo, E. (2000). Where budding geniuses can blossom. The *Los Angeles Times,* November 22, Living Section, pp. 1 and 3.

Wood, D.K., & Frank, A.R. (2000). Using memory-enhancing strategies to learn multiplication facts. *Teaching Exceptional Children, 32*(5), 78–82.

Wood, D.K., Frank, A.R., & Wacker, D.P. (1998). Teaching multiplication facts to students with learning disabilities.

Journal of Applied Behavior Analysis, 31, 323–338.

Woodward, J., Baxter, J., & Robinson, R. (1999). Rules and reasons: Decimal instruction for academically low achieving students. *Learning Disabilities Research and Practice, 14,* 15–24.

Wunsch, M.J., Conlon, C.J., & Scheidt, P.C. (2002). Substance abuse: A preventable threat to development. In M.L. Batshaw (Ed.), *Children with disabilities* (5th ed.), 107–122. Baltimore: Paul H. Brookes.

www.afb.org. (2002). *Specific assessments for students with low vision.* Retrieved 3/10/03.

www.aph.org. (2003). Distribution of eligible students based on the federal quota census of January 2, 2001 (Fiscal Year 2002). American Printing House for the Blind, retrieved March 1, 2003.

Wynant, J. (2003). A few facts on captioning. *Volta Voices,* (March/April) 4–6.

Yairi, E. (1998). Is the basis for stuttering genetic? *American Speech Language and Hearing Association, 70*(1), 29–32.

Yell, M.L., & Drasgow, E. (2000). Litigating a free appropriate public education: The Lovaas hearings and cases. *The Journal of Special Education, 33,* 205–214.

Yell, M.L., & Shriner, J.G. (1997). The IDEA amendments of 1997: Implications for special and general education teachers, administrators, and teacher trainers. *Focus on Exceptional Children, 30*(1), 1–19.

Yetman, N.R. (1985). *Majority and minority: The dynamics of race and ethnicity in American life* (4th ed.). Boston: Allyn and Bacon.

York, J., & Vandercook, T. (1991). Designing integrated programs for learners with severe disabilities. *Teaching Exceptional Children, 23*(2), 22–29.

Yoshinaga-Itano, C., Sedley, A., Coulter, D.K., & Mehl, A.L. (1998). Language of early and late identified children with hearing loss. *Pediatrics,102*(5), 1161–1171.

Yu, D.C.T., Spevack, S., Hiebert, R., Martin, T.L., Goodman, R., Martin, T.G., Harapiak, S., & Martin, G.L. (2002). Happiness indices among persons with profound and severe disabilities during leisure and work activities: A comparison. *Education and Training in Mental Retardation and Developmental Disabilities, 37,* 421–426.

Zamora-Duran, G., & Reyes, E. (1997). From tests to talking in the classroom: Assessing communicative competence. In A. Artiles & G. Zamora-Dunn (Eds.), *Reducing disproportionate representation of culturally diverse students in special and gifted education.* Reston, VA: Council for Exceptional Children.

Zeaman, D., & House, B.J. (1963). The role of attention in retardate discrimination of learning. In N.R. Ellis (Ed.), *Handbook of mental deficiency.* New York: McGraw-Hill.

———. (1979). A review of attention theory. In N.R. Ellis (Ed.), *Handbook of mental deficiency: Psychological theory and research.* (2nd ed.). Hillsdale, NJ: Erlbaum.

Zimmerman, G.J. (1996). Optics and low vision devices. In A.L. Corn & A.J. Koenig, (Eds.), *Foundations of low vision: Clinical and functional perspectives* (pp. 115–142). New York: AFB Press.

Zirpoli, T.J. (1986). Child abuse and children with handicaps. *Remedial and Special Education, 7*(2), 39–48.

Zuckoff, M. (2003). *Choosing Naia: A family's journey.* Boston: Beacon Press.

Zuniga, M. (1998). Families with Latino roots. In E.W. Lynch & M.J. Hansen (Eds.), *Developing cross-cultural competence* (2nd ed.) (pp. 209–245). Baltimore: Paul H. Brookes.

Credits

Chapter 1

p. 5 (box): "It's the 'Person First'—Then the Disability," *Pacesetter* (September 1989), p. 13. Reprinted by permission from PACESETTER. PACESETTER is published by the PACER Center, Minneapolis, Minnesota.

p. 10, Fig. 3.1: From "Special Education as Developmental Capital," by G. Deno, *Exceptional Children, 37,* 1970, pp. 229–237. Copyright 1970 by the Council for Exceptional Children. Reprinted with permission.

p. 11 (box): "Teacher Perceptions of Mainstreaming/Inclusion, 1958–1995: A Research Synthesis," T. E. Scruggs and M. A. Mastropieri, *Exceptional Children, 63*(1) (1996), 72. Copyright © 1996 by the Council for Exceptional Children. Reprinted by permission.

pp. 14–15 (box): "Lessons from a Boy Named David" by Sandy Banks, *Los Angeles Times,* February 21, 1999. Copyright, 1999, Los Angeles Times. Reprinted with permission.

pp. 15–16: Excerpt from Harriet McBryde Johnson, "Unspeakable Conversations," *New York Times Magazine,* February 16, 2003. Copyright © 2003, Harriet McBryde Johnson. Reprinted by permission of The New York Times.

p. 19: From "Student Access: A Resource Guide for Educators," by Council of Administrators of Special Education, 1992, Council for Exceptional Children. Copyright 1992 by The Council for Exceptional Children. Reprinted with permission.

p. 25, Tab. 1.3: Adapted from "Legal Foundations: The Individuals with Disabilities Education Act (IDEA)," from *Teaching Exceptional Children* (Winter 1993), pp. 85–87. Copyright 1993 by The Council for Exceptional Children. Reprinted with permission.

p. 32. Tab. 1.4: From "The Ins and Outs of Special Education Terminology," by G. Vergason and M. L. Anderegg, *Teaching Exceptional Children, 29* (5), May/June 1997, p. 36. Copyright 1997 by The Council for Exceptional Children. Reprinted with permission.

p. 38 (box): Excerpt from "What Should We Expect from Assistive Technology?" by Phil Parette amd Gale A. McMahan, from *Teaching Exceptional Children 2002, 35* (1), pp. 56–61. Copyright 2002 by The Council for Exceptional Children. Reprinted with permission.

Chapter 2

p. 48, Fig. 2.3: Adapted from *Before We Are Born,* Fifth Edition by K. L. Moore. Copyright © 1998, with permission from Elsevier.

p. 59 (box): Children's Defense Fund Website. Reprinted by permission.

p. 65 (box): PACER Center, Inc. Families and Advocates Partnership for Education (FAPE) Project web site: www.pacer.org. PACER Center, Inc., FAPE Coordinating Office, 8161 Normandale Blvd., Minneapolis, MN 55437. 952-838-9000 voice; 952-838-0190 TTY; 952-838-0199 fax; 1-888-248-0822 toll-free; email: pacer@pacer.org. Reprinted by permission.

p. 73, Tab. 2.3: From "The Development of Competence in Favorable and Unfavorable Environments: Lessons from Research on Successful Children," by A. S. Masten and J. D. Coatsworth (1998). From *American Psychologist, 53,* p. 212. Copyright © 1998 by the American Psychological Association. Reprinted with permission.

Chapter 3

pp. 81–82 (box): Janice Fialka, excerpted and adapted from "You Can Make a Difference in Our Lives," by Janice Fialka, *DEC Communicator,* November 1996 23(1), p. 8. Reprinted by permission of the author.

p. 86 (box): Harry B., Kalyanpur, M., & Day, M. (1999). *Building Cultural Reciprocity with Families: Case Studies in Special Education* (pp. 7–11). Baltimore: Paul H. Brookes. Reprinted with permission.

p. 87, Fig. 3.1: A. P. Turnbull, J. A. Summers, and M. J. Brotherson. *Working with Families with Disabled Members: A Family Systems Approach* (Lawrence, KS: University of Kansas, Beach Center on Families and Disabilities, 1984), p. 60. Adapted by permission.

p. 88, Fig. 3.2: Nancy V. Wedemeyer & Harold D. Grotevant (1982). "Mapping the Family System: A Technique for Teaching Family Systems Theory Concepts." *Family Relations,* Issue 8204, *31*:2, 185–193. Copyrighted 1982 by the National Council on Family Relations, 3989 Central Ave. NE, Suite 550, Minneapolis, MN 55421

p. 95, Fig. 3.3: From "Impacts of Poverty on Family Quality of Life in Families of Children with Disabilities" by Jiyeon Park, Ann P. Turnbull, & H. R. Turnbull (2002). *Exceptional Children, 68*(2), p. 154. Copyright 2002 by The Council for Exceptional Children. Reprinted with permission.

p. 100 (box): From "Principles of Support and Intervention for Children and Their Families," adapted from M. J. Hanson & J. J. Carta, "Addressing the Challenges of Families with Multiple Risks," *Exceptional Children 62*(3), 1996, pp. 201–212. Copyright 1996 by The Council for Exceptional Children. Reprinted with permission.

pp. 106–107 (box): *Interactive Teaming: Enhancing Programs for Students,* Third Edition by Thomas/Correa/Morsink, © 2001. Adapted by permission of Pearson Education, Inc., Upper Saddle River, NJ.

p. 108 (box): Adapted from the ERIC/OSEP Special Project, *IDEAS That Work: News Brief,* February 10, 2003, www.ericec.org (ERIC Clearinghouse on Disabilities and Gifted Education.

Chapter 4

pp. 120–121 (box): Caitlin Norah Callahan, "Advice About Being an LD Student. Reprinted by permission of *LD OnLine.* http://www.ldonline.org/article.php?id=535&loc=11

p. 141, Fig. 4.4: "Using Memory-Enhancing Strategies to Learn Multiplication Facts" by D. K. Wood and A. R. Frank, *Teaching Exceptional Children, 32,* 2000, pp. 78–82. Copyright 2000 by The Council for Exceptional Children. Reprinted with permission.

p. 142, Fig. 4.6: Maccini, P., & Hughes, C. A., "Effects of a Problem-Solving Strategy on the Introductory Algebra Performance of Secondary Students with Learning Disabilities," *Learning Disabilities and Practice, 15,* 10–21. Reprinted with permission of Lawrence Erlbaum Associates, Inc.

p. 158, Fig. 4.8: Archive Vernon Huff, Jr., "The History of South Carolina," in *The Building of the Nation* (Greenville, SC: Furman, 1991). Copyright © 1991. Reprinted by permission.

p. 159, Fig. 4.9: Archive Vernon Huff, Jr., "The History of South Carolina," in *The Building of the Nation* (Greenville, SC: Furman, 1991). Copyright © 1991. Reprinted by permission.

p. 160, Fig. 4.10: Archive Vernon Huff, Jr., "The History of South Carolina," in *The Building of the Nation* (Greenville, SC: Furman, 1991). Copyright © 1991. Reprinted by permission.

Chapter 5

p. 168, Fig. 5.1: S. A. Kirk and J. J. Gallagher, *Educating Exceptional Children,* Sixth Edition. (Boston: Houghton Mifflin, 1998), p. 11. Copyright © 1998. Used with permission.

p. 170, Fig. 5.2: K. Nihira, H. Leland, and N. Lambert, *AAMR Adaptive Behavior Scale: Residential and Community,* Second Edition. (Austin, TX: PRO-ED, 1993). Copyright © 1993 by The American Association on Mental Retardation. Reprinted by permission.

p. 172, Fig. 5.3: From "Promoting Cultural Competence Through Teacher Assistance

Teams" by S. Craig et al, *Teaching Exceptional Children, 32,* 2000, pp. 6–12. Copyright 2000 by The Council for Exceptional Children. Reprinted with permission.

p. 177 (box): "My Name is John Kellerman," FAS Community Resource Center, Tucson, AZ. www.fasstar.com. Reprinted by permission.

p. 191, Fig. 5.4: M. E. Cronin and J. R. Patton, *Life Skills Instruction for All Students with Special Needs: A Practical Guide for Integrating Real-Life Content into Curriculum* (Austin, TX: PRO-ED, 1993), p. 57. Copyright © 1993. Used by permission of PRO-ED.

p. 193, Fig. 5.5: A, B and C from "Connecting Outcomes, Goals, and Objectives in Transition Planning, " *Teaching Exceptional Children,* Vol. 34, (6), July/August 2002, pp. 56–57. Copyright 2002 by The Council for Exceptional Children. Reprinted with permission.

Chapter 6

p. 209 (box): From "How Can I Help You Get What You Want?" by M. M. Ostrosky et al., *Teaching Exceptional Children, 31,* 1999, pp. 56–61. Copyright 1999 by The Council for Exceptional Children. Reprinted with permission.

pp. 212–213 (box): "Keeping Sophia Healthy & Alive" is from "P.A. Parents Try to Save Ill Daughter," by Loretta Green, *San Jose Mercury News,* July 1, 2002. Copyright © 2002 San Jose Mercury News. All rights reserved. Reproduced with permission.

p. 219 (box): "Home Is Not for Everyone" by Fern Kupfer from *Newsweek,* December 8, 1997. Reprinted by permission of the author.

p. 221 (box): From "In Junior High You Take Earth Science: Including a Student with Severe Disabilities into an Academic Class" by E. Siegel-Causey et al, *Teaching Exceptional Children, 31,* 1998, pp. 66–72. Copyright 1998 by The Council for Exceptional Children. Reprinted with permission.

p. 223, Fig. 6.1: M. E. Cronin and J. R. Patton, *Life Skills Instruction for all Students with Special Needs: A Practical Guide for Integrating Real-Life Content into Curriculum* (Austin, TX: PRO-ED, 1993) p. 57. Copyright © 1993. Used by permission of PRO-ED.

pp. 224–225, (box): From Ford, A., Schnorr, R., Meyer, L., Davern, L., Black, J., & Dempsey, P. (1989). *The Syracuse Community-Referenced Curriculum Guide for Students with Moderate and Severe Disabilities* (p. 78). Baltimore: Paul H. Brookes Publishing Co.; reprinted by permission.

p. 227 (box): From "Postsecondary Options for Students with Significant Disabilities" by Meg Grigal, Debra A. Neubert and M. Sherrill Moon, *Teaching Exceptional Children Magazine,* Vol. 35, #2, November/December 2002. Copyright 2002 by The

Council for Exceptional Children. Reprinted with permission.

p. 228 (box): From "Culturally Sensitive Transition Plans for Young Children and Their Families" by D. A. Bruns and S. A. Fowler, *Teaching Exceptional Children, 31,* 1999, pp. 26–30. Copyright 1999 by The Council for Exceptional Children. Reprinted with permission.

Chapter 7

p. 248, Fig. 7.1: Figure "The Path to Negative Outcomes" pg. 391, from Sprague/Walker. From *Exceptional Children,* Summer 2000, (v66 n3), p. 391. Copyright 2000 by The Council for Exceptional Children. Reprinted with permission.

p. 257 (box): Diagnostic Criteria for Attention-Deficit/Hyperactivity Disorder, from *Diagnostic and Statistical Manual of Mental Disorders,* Fourth Edition, 1994. Reprinted with permission from *The Diagnostic and Statistical Manual of Mental Disorders,* Fourth Edition, Text Revision. Copyright 2000 American Psychiatric Association.

p. 263 (box): From "Anticipating Differences—Celebrating Strengths" by Cartledge et al. *Teaching Exceptional Children,* February 2000 (v32 n2). Copyright 2000 by The Council for Exceptional Children. Reprinted with permission.

p. 265, Fig. 7.3: From "Ensuring Student Success Through Team-Based Functional Behavioral Assessment" by Terrance M. Scott, Carl J. Liaupsin, C. Michael Nelson, and Kristine Jolivette from *Teaching Exceptional Children,* May/June 2003. Copyright 2003 by The Council for Exceptional Children. Reprinted with permission.

p. 268 (box): From "How to Spell Success for Secondary Students Labeled EBD: How Students Define Effective Teachers" by Laura Owens and Lisa A. Dieker, *Beyond Behavior,* Winter 2003, 12 (2), p. 21. Copyright 2003 by The Council for Children with Behavioral Disorders. Reprinted with permission.

p. 269, Fig. 7.4: From "Preventing School Violence: The Use of Office Discipline Referrals to Assess and Monitor School-Wide Discipline Interventions" by G. Sugai, J. R. Sprague, R. H. Horner, and H. M. Walker, *Journal of Emotional and Behavioral Disorders,* 8, Issue 2, pp. 94–101. Copyright 2000 by PRO-ED, Inc. Reprinted with permission.

p. 274 (box): Vern Jones, "Responding to Student Behavior Problems," *Beyond Behavior* (Winter 1990), p. 20. Copyright 1990 by The Council for Children with Behavioral Disorders. Reprinted with permission.

Chapter 8

p. 280 (box): Excerpts from "Exiting Nirvana" by Claira Claiborne Park. Reprinted from *The American Scholar,* 67, (2), Spring 1998. Copyright © 1998 by the author.

p. 283 (box): "How Doctors Diagnose Autism" from *Newsweek,* Donna Foote and Heather Won Tesoriero. © 2000 Newsweek, Inc. All rights reserved. Reprinted by permission.

p. 286, Fig. 8.1: "Autism's Effects" from "The Early Origins of Autism" by Patricia M. Rodier. From *Scientific American, 282* (2), pp. 56–63. © 2000 Terese Winslow. Reprinted with permission.

p. 289 (box): Reprinted by permission of the author.

p. 293, Fig. 8.2: From *Behavioral Intervention for Young Children with Autism: A Manual for Parents and Professionals* edited by Catherine Maurice, Gina Green, and Stephen Luce. Copyright © 1996 by PRO-ED. Reprinted with permission.

p. 294, Tab. 8.2: Adapted from "Selecting Teaching Programs" by B. A. Taylor and K. A. McDonough, in *Behavioral Intervention for Young Children with Autism: A Manual for Parents and Professionals,* edited by Catherine Maurice, Gina Green, and Stephen C. Luce. Copyright © 1996. Reprinted by permission from PRO-ED.

p. 304, Fig. 8.4: The Gray Center Website. Reprinted by permission.

p. 307 (box): From "Adults with Autism Speak Out: Perceptions of Their Life Experiences" by Karen Hurlbutt and Lynne Chalmers, Summer 2002, *Focus on Autism and Other Developmental Disabilities,* 17, (2), pp. 103–111. Copyright 2002 by PRO-ED, Inc. Adapted with permission.

p. 309 (box): Reprinted by kind permission of Claira Claiborne Park.

Chapter 9

p. 314, Fig. 9.1: M. Diane Klein, Division of Special Education, California State University, Los Angeles. Used with permission.

p. 333, Tab. 9.3: From *Language Instruction for Students with Disabilities,* Second Edition, by E. A. Polloway and Tom E. C. Smith, p. 38. Copyright © 2000. Reproduced by permission of Love Publishing Company.

p. 333 (box): American Speech–Language–Hearing Association (1993). "Implementation Procedures for the Standards for the Certificates of Clinical Competence," *ASHA,* 35, (3), 76–83. Reprinted by permission of the American Speech–Language–Hearing Association.

p. 334 (box): Adapted from "Teaching the silent student," by Amy Pyle, *Los Angeles Times,* June 11, 1996. Copyright, 1996, Los Angeles Times. Reprinted with permission.

p. 335, Fig. 9.7: From "Tests to Talking in the Classroom: Assessing Communicative Competency" by G. Zamora-Duran and E. I. Reyes, *Reducing Disproportional Representation of Culturally Diverse Students in Special and Gifted Education,* edited by A. J. Artiles and F. Zamora-Duran. Copyright 1997 by The Council for Exceptional Children. Reprinted with permission.

p. 342, Tabs. 9.7 and 9.8: From Santamaria L. J., Fletcher, T. V., and Bos, C. S. (2002). "Effective Pedagogy for English Language Learners in Inclusive Classrooms." In A. J. Artiles and A. A. Ortiz (Eds.) *English Language Learners with Special Education Needs* (pp. 140–141). Washington, D.C. and McHenry, IL: Center for Applied Linguistics & Delta Systems, Inc.

p. 345 (box): "Introduction to Augmentative and Alternate Communication, "American Speech–Language–Hearing Association at http://www.asha.org/public/speech/disorders/Augmentative+and+Alternative/htm. Copyright by the American Speech–Language–Hearing Association. Reprinted by permission.

p. 346–347 (box): "I Can Even Stutter Now," American Speech–Language–Hearing Association at http://www.asha.org/public/speech/disorders/I-Can-Even-Stutter-Now.htm.

Chapter 10

p. 355, Tab. 10.3: From *Hearing in Children*, Fourth Edition, by Jerry L. Northern and Marion P. Downs. Copyright © 1991. Used by permission of Lippincott Williams & Wilkins, and the author.

p. 360, Fig. 10.2: "Understanding Your Audiogram" by Dr. Allan S. Mehr, *Consumer Guides, FAAA.* Downloaded from www.audiology.org/consumer/guides/uya.php November 2003. Reprinted by permission of Allan S. Mehr.

pp. 364–365 (box): "Making the Grade" by Debra Cappella as found at <www.handsandvoices.org>. Reprinted by permission of the author.

p. 373, Fig. 10.3: T. Humphries, C. Padden, and T. J. O'Rouke. *A Basic Course in American Sign Language.* (Silver Spring, MD: T. J. Publishers, 1980.) Reprinted by permission.

Chapter 11

p. 394, Fig. 11.2: Used by permission of American Printing House for the Blind.

p. 398 (box): *Early Focus: Working with Young Children Who Are Blind or Visually Impaired and Their Families*, (2nd ed.) by Pogrund, R. L., & Fazzi, D. L. (Eds.). Copyright © 2002 by American Foundation for the Blind. Reproduced with permission of American Foundation for the Blind in the format Textbook via Copyright Clearance Center.

p. 401 (box): "Can Girls With Impaired Vision Be Mommies?" by Deborah Kendrick, *Envision*, August 1997, pp. 5–7. Copyright © 1997. Reprinted by permission of The Lighthouse Inc.

p. 404 (box): Reproduced from "Strategies to Promote Social Inclusion at Home and at School" by Sharon Zell Sacks and Rosanne K. Silberman in *Foundations of Education: Instructional Strategies for Teaching Children and Youths with Visual Impairments*, Vol. II, 2nd Edition, pp. 633–634. New York: AFB Press. Copyright © by AFB Press. Reproduced with permission from the American Foundation for the Blind. All rights reserved.

p. 415, Tab. 11.3: From N. C. Barraga and J. N. Erin, *Visual Handicaps and Learning*, 1992, pp. 152–153. Copyright © 1992. Used by permission of PRO-ED Inc.

p. 416, Tab. 11.4: Reproduced from "Applications of the Principles of Special Methods" in *Foundations of Education: Instructional Strategies for Teaching Children and Youth with Visual Impairments* by Alan J. Koenig and M. Cay Holbrook, Vol. II, 2nd Edition, pp. 196–221. Copyright © by AFB Press. Reproduced with permission from the American Foundation for the Blind. All rights reserved.

p. 419 (box): Reproduced from "Scope and Sequence of Technology Skills and Applications" by Gaylen Kapperman and Jodi Sticken in *Foundations of Education: Instructional Strategies for Teaching Children and Youths with Visual Impairments*, Vol. II, 2nd Edition, p. 508. New York: AFB Press. Copyright © by AFB Press. Reproduced with permission from the American Foundation for the Blind. All rights reserved.

Chapter 12

p. 430, Fig. 12.1: M. L. Batshaw and Y. M. Perret, *Children with Handicaps: A Medical Primer*, Third Edition (Baltimore: Paul H. Brookes, 1992), p. 444. Copyright © 1992. Used by permission of the author.

p. 433 (box): "My Life," by Jessica Smallman, *Ability Network Magazine*, 5, (2), Winter 1996/97. Reprinted by permission of Ability Network Publishing Inc.

p. 436, Fig. 12.2: From "Mainstreaming Children with Neuromuscular Disease: A Map of Concerns" by Kristine Strong and Jonathan Sandoval, *Exceptional Children*, Spring 1999, pp. 353–366. Copyright 1999 by The Council for Exceptional Children. Reprinted with permission.

p. 451, Fig. 12.3: From "Who Does What on the Interdisciplinary Team Regarding Physical Education for Students with Disabilities," *Teaching Exceptional Children*, 35, (6), July/August 2003, p. 35, Figure 2. Copyright 2003 by The Council for Exceptional Children. Reprinted with permission.

p. 452 (box): Used by permission of Disability Services.

p. 453 (box): From "Maddie's Story: Inclusion Through Physical and Occupational Therapy" by Joanne Lockard Szabo, *Teaching Exceptional Children*, Nov/Dec 2000, v33 (n2), pp. 49–53. Copyright 1999 by The Council for Exceptional Children. Reprinted with permission.

p. 455, Fig. 12.4: From "Determining When a Student Requires Paraeducator Support," *Teaching Exceptional Children*, 33, (6), July/August 2001, p. 25, Figure 3. Copyright 2001 by The Council for Exceptional Children. Reprinted with permission.

p. 458 (box): From "Planning and Organizing Assistive Resources in Your Schools" by B. J. Webb, *Teaching Exceptional Children*, v43 (n4), March/April 2000, pp. 50–55. Copyright 2000 by The Council

for Exceptional Children. Reprinted with permission.

p. 463 (box): From J. P. Lehmann, T. G. Davies, K. M. Laurin (2000), "Listening to Student Voices About PostSecondary Education," *Teaching Exceptional Children, v32* (n5), May/June 2000, p. 63. Copyright 2000 by The Council for Exceptional Children. Reprinted with permission.

Chapter 13

p. 473 (box): Jane Ira Bloom's essay, "Unexpected Light," is reprinted by permission of the author.

p. 478 (box): Copyright material from the National Association for Gifted Children (NAGC), 1707 L Street, NW, Suite 550, Washington, DC 20036 (202) 785-4268. http://www.nagc.org. This material may not be reproduced without permission from NAGC.

p. 480, Fig. 13.3: S. A. Kirk and J. J. Gallagher, *Educating Exceptional Children*, Sixth Edition (Boston: Houghton Mifflin, 1998), p. 11. Copyright 1988. Used with permission.

p. 490 Tab. 13.3: Adapted from *Talent in Two Places: Case Studies of High Ability Students with Learning Disabilities Who Have Achieved*, by S. M. Reis, T. W. Neu, and J. M. McGuire, 1995, Storrs, CT, University of Connecticut, The National Research Center of the Gifted and Talented. Reprinted by permission.

p. 497 (box): From "Where Budding Geniuses Can Blossom," by Elaine Woo, *Los Angeles Times*, November 22, 2000. Copyright, 2000, Los Angeles Times. Reprinted with permission.

p. 499 (box): Excerpted from "A Sweet Mystery: Norah Jones' artistry stands out in a world of prefab pop. Where'd it come from?" *Los Angeles Times*, January 26, 2003, p. E1 Copyright, 2003, Los Angeles Times. Reprinted with permission.

p. 504, Fig. 13.7: Alane J. Starko (1986). "Meeting the Needs of the Gifted Throughout the School Day: Techniques for Curriculum Compacting." *Roeper Review*, 9 (1), 27–33. Copyright © 1986. Reprinted by permission of Roeper Review, P. O. Box 329, Bloomfield, MI 48303, and the author.

p. 509 (box): Reprinted by permission from National Association for the Accelerated School Project.

Chapter 14

p. 527 (box): Council for Exceptional Children website (http://www.cec.sped.org/osep/ud-fig2.html). Copyright 2003 by The Council for Exceptional Children. Reprinted with permission.

p. 532 (box): Fuchs, D., Fuchs, L. S., & Burish, P. (2000) Peer-assisted learning strategies: An evidence-based practice to promote reading achievement. *Learning Disabilities Research and Practice*, 15, 85–91. Reprinted by permission of Lawrence Erlbaum Associates, Inc.

Name Index

Abelson, A. G., 102
Abuzaitoun, O. R., 50
Access Ingenuity, 460
Adams, G. L., 149
Adelman, 31
Adger, C. T., 336, 338
AIDS Organization, 442
Alberto, P. A., 192
Alessi, S. M., 152, 153
Algozzine, R., 124, 136
Allen, N. J., 511
Allinder, R. M., 133
Allman, C. B., 408, 416, 417
Allor, J. H., 131
Alper, S., 162
Altman, R., 181
Alvino, J., 486
American Association for Mental Retardation, 173
American College of Medical Genetics, 56
American College of Obstetricians and Gynecologists, 51, 53
American College of Rheumatology, 437
American Printing House for the Blind, 392
American Psychiatric Association, 243, 244, 279
American Psychological Association, 3
American Speech, Language, and Hearing Association (ASHA), 320, 325, 326, 328, 333, 336, 345, 347, 386
Amish, P. L., 271
Anderson, H., 529
Anderson, J. A., 250
Anderson, P. P., 80
Ansell, S. E., 524, 528, 529
Anthony, T. L., 399, 413
Arguelles, M. E., 33
Arick, J. R., 297, 298
Arjmand, E., 356
Arnold, L., 122
Arnos, K. S., 356
Arthur, M., 208
Artiles, A. J., 23, 332, 336
Ashcroft, S. C., 418
Association for Persons with Severe Handicaps (TASH), 202
Augusto, C., 393
Aveno, A., 230, 232
Ayres, B., 218

Babyak, A. E., 267
Bailey, D. B., 104, 399
Bain, B. A., 336
Baker, C., 211, 372
Baker, R. L., 94

Baker, S., 344, 346
Baldwin, A. Y., 491, 492
Balla, D. A., 169
Bambara, L., 215
Banks, S., 13
Barenbaum, E. M., 137
Barkely, R. A., 256, 259
Barnard, K. E., 98
Barnes, S. B., 453
Barnicle, K., 421
Barton, D. D., 403
Bashir, A. S., 322
Batshaw, M. L., 63, 174, 437
Bauer, A. M., 104
Baum, S. M., 488
Baxter, J., 141
Beare, P., 183
Beavin, J., 314
Beck, J., 458
Behr, S. K., 100, 101, 356
Behrman, R. E., 53
Beirne-Smith, M., 168, 174, 188
Bellamy, G. T., 211
Belsky, D. H., 54
Belsky, J., 97
Bendersky, M., 52
Bennett, D. S., 52
Berko, J., 315
Berliner, D., 481
Bernheimer, L. P., 89, 96
Berry, J. O., 94
Berry, M. R., 162
Bettleheim, B., 285
Biederman, G. B., 192
Bigge, J., 460, 461
Bigler, E. D., 121
Bishop, K. K., 211
Blacher, J., 92, 99
Blachman, B. A., 330
Black, J., 224
Blackhurst, A. E., 457
Blackorby, J., 462
Blampied, N. M., 192
Blischak, D. M., 461
Bloom, B., 481, 508
Bock, S. J., 281
Boland, M. G., 50
Bondy, A., 302
Bos, C. S., 341
Boston, B., 498
Bowe, F., 387
Boyle, J. R., 154
Bradbury, J., 55
Brady, M., 197, 285, 286, 290, 301
Branham, R. S., 196
Breakthroughs, 461
Brenner, M., 96, 104
Breslau, N., 97
Bronfenbrenner, U., 60
Brooke, V., 230, 232
Browder, D. M., 192, 215

Brown, F., 188
Bruner, E., 149
Bruns, D. A., 211, 228, 229
Bryan, T., 142
Buchele-Ash, A., 60
Buck, G. H., 35
Bufkin, A., 181
Bullis, M., 143
Burd, L. I., 63
Burish, P., 533
Burns, M. S., 330
Bursuck, W., 161
Burton, B. K., 63
Butler, W. T., 50
Butterfield, N., 208
Buysse, V., 182
Byers, R. H., 50

Callahan, C. N., 121
Campbell, P. H., 211
Candela, P., 281
Carlson, C. I., 142
Carnine, D., 131, 137, 139, 147, 148, 149, 161
Caro, P., 222
Carta, J. J., 99, 100
Carter, S., 107
Cartledge, G., 255, 262, 270
Catts, H. W., 330, 331
Cavaiuolo, D., 192
Cavanaugh, T., 459
Cawley, J. F., 139
Center for Applied Special Technology (CAST), 526, 527
Center for Children's Health and the Environment, 57
Centers for Disease Control, 48
Chalmers, L., 307
Chamberlain, J. A., 171
Chan, S., 23, 82, 83
Chandler, L. K., 294, 295
Chapman, R. S., 318
Chard, D. J., 266
Chedd, N. A., 62, 63
Chen, D., 69, 82, 90, 358, 398, 406
Cheng, A. K., 376
Chez, M. G., 303
Childhood Cancer Foundation, 443
Children Affected by AIDS Foundation (CAAF), 443
Children's Defense Fund, 58, 59, 94
Chinn, P. C., 23, 82, 83
Cho, S. J., 96, 104
Christensen, K. M., 367
Christian, D., 336, 338
Christiansen, J., 375
Christopher, J., 122

Cicchetti, D. V., 169
Cioffi, A., 232
Civil Rights Project, 171
Clark, B., 31, 290, 301, 485, 492, 495
Clark, C., 285, 286
Clark, G. M., 110
Clasen, D. R., 500
Clasen, R. E., 500
Clement-Heist, K., 154
Clinkenbeard, P., 474
Coatsworth, J. D., 73
Cochran, K. F., 127
Cohen, S. E., 72
Cohen, L. M., 492
Cokely, D., 372
Cole, D., 252
Coles, R., 96
Colvin, G., 252, 275
Conlon, C. J., 52
Connor, L. E., 372
Conture, E. G., 324
Cook, B. G., 219
Cook, L., 33, 34
Cook, R. E., 4, 324
Cooper, E. B., 136
Copeland, S. R., 194
Corbet, E. B., 427
Corn, A. L., 393, 407, 412
Correa, V. I., 107
Cott, A., 122
Council for Exceptional Children, 33, 462, 524
Cox, J., 498
Cox, T. A., 208
Craig, S., 171
Crittenden, J. B., 366
Cronin, P., 281
Cross, C. T., 21, 22, 55, 61, 75, 480, 494
Cullinan, D., 244, 252, 254
Culpepper, B., 356
Cutsforth, T. D., 397
Cystic Fibrosis Foundation (CFF), 441

D'Andrea, F. M., 421
Daniel, N., 498
Daniels, V. I., 491
Darling, R. B., 99
Davern, L., 224
Davidovitch, M., 287, 291
Davies, T. G., 462
Davis, C. A., 267
Dawson, G., 301
Dawson, L., 267
Day, M., 82, 85, 86
Decker, L. A., 268
Deford, F., 448
De Fries, J. C., 123
De La Paz, S., 150
Delaquadri, J. C., 532

Delisle, J. R., 470, 471, 483, 485, 486, 489, 494, 497, 509
Dempsey, P., 224
Denning, C. B., 171
Dennis, R. E., 235
Deppe, J., 64
DePriest, L. B., 393
Desai, M., 358
Deshler, D. D., 150
DeStefano, L., 190
Dettmer, P., 531
Devinsky, O., 435
Devlieger, P. J., 190
Devlin, S. D., 252
Diagnostic and Statistical Manual of Mental Disorders (DSM-IV), 243, 244, 256
Dickey, R., 460
Dingle, M., 89
Dinnocenti, S. T., 503
DiSalvo, C. A., 302
Dobrich, W., 322
Dolan, R. P., 526
Donahue, M., 252
Donovan, M. S., 21, 22, 55, 61, 75, 480, 494
Dorris, M., 96
Dote-Kwan, J., 358, 398
Dowdy, C. A., 151
Downey, D., 326
Downs, M. P., 352, 354, 355, 356
Dowrick, M., 211, 291, 296
Drake, G. P., Jr., 222
Drasgow, E., 208, 209, 300, 375
Drew, C. J., 181, 188
Drozdovich, V., 56
Duchnowski, A. J., 250
Dunlap, G., 270
Dunn, L., 20, 23
Dunst, C. J., 74, 211
Dyck, N., 531
Dykens, E. M., 185, 283

Eby, J. W., 493
Eccarius, M., 362, 380
Eddy, J. M., 255
Edgar, E., 197
Edyburn, D. L., 153
Ehlers, S., 281
Ehren, B. J., 340, 343
Ehri, L. C., 331
Eilers, R. E., 320
Elbaum, B., 143
Elksnin, L. K., 147
Ellerd, D. A., 216
Elliott, R. N., 252
Ellis, L., 64
Eng, T. R., 50
Engelmann, S., 139, 148, 149, 161
Ennis, R. H., 508, 509
Epilepsy Foundation, 434, 435
Epstein, M., 182, 244
Ericsson, K. A., 481
Erin, J. N., 393, 407, 411, 418
Evans, I. M., 455
Everson, J. M., 215

Ewers, C. A., 127
Executive Committee of the Council for Children with Behavioral Disorders, 262

Fahey, K. R., 324, 326
Falk, G. D., 270
Falk-Ross, F., 341
Falvey, M., 109
Fanaroff, A. A., 55
Farrenkopf, C., 410, 415
Fazzi, D. L., 397, 398, 412
Federal Register, 320
Feil, E. G., 260
Feingold, B. F., 122
Feiring, C., 492
Feldhusen, J. F., 501
Feldman, W., 439
Felko, K. S., 226
Fenichel, E. S., 80
Ferguson, D. L., 236
Ferrell, K., 397, 398, 402, 405
Fetrow, R. A., 255
Fialka, J., 81
Fidler, D. J., 185, 204
Fiedler, B. C., 356
Finer, N. N., 54
Finesmith, R.B., 435
Finn, D. M., 151
Firman, K. B., 183
Fitzsimmons, M. K., 330
Fletcher, T. V., 341
Flexer, C., 372
Foorman, B. R., 131
Foote, D., 280, 283
Ford, A., 224
Ford, D. Y., 492
Forness, S. R., 6, 122, 142, 249
Foster, W., 209
Fowler, M., 258
Fowler, S. A., 228, 229
Fox, J. J., 292
Fox, L., 179
Frank, A. R., 141, 197
Fraser, B., 429
Freeman, B. J., 281
Freidrich, O., 399
Frey, K. S., 269
Friedman, H. S., 470
Friend, M., 33, 34, 531
Frost, L., 302
Fuchs, D., 119, 533
Fuchs, L., 119, 147, 150, 532, 533
Fueyo, V., 155
Fujiura, G. T., 60, 94
Furlong, M., 251
Furney, K., 190

Gage, N. L., 481
Gajar, A., 162
Gajira, M., 134
Gallagher, J. J., 493
Gallagher, P. A., 99
Gallagher, S., 503
Gallaudet Research Institute, 357, 375, 376, 380
Gallimore, R., 83, 89, 96
Garbarino, J., 58, 60, 63, 99

Garcia Espinel, A. I., 139
Gardill, M. C., 134
Gardner, H., 474, 480, 502
Gardner, J. E., 153
Garretson, M. D., 375
Gaunt, R. I., 493
Gaylord-Ross, R., 154
Gee, J. P., 326
Gerber, M. M., 99, 176, 443
Gerber, P. J., 162
Gerity, B. P., 216
Gersten, R., 149, 156, 344, 346
Getch, Y. Q., 439
Ghazuddin, M., 283
Giangreco, M. F., 455
Gibbs, D. P., 136
Gillberg, C., 281
Gillis, J. J., 123
Ginsberg, R., 162
Glassberg, L. A., 250
Goldman, B. D., 182
Goldstein, L., 17
Gollnick, D. M., 82, 83
Goodenough, N., 79
Gorski, P. A., 45
Gould, S. J., 471
Graham, E. M., 51, 56
Graham, S., 137, 140, 150
Gray, C., 302
Green, C. W., 208, 215
Greene, G., 141
Greenspan, J., 440, 441
Greenwood, C. R., 532
Gresham, F. M., 119, 251, 300
Griffin, D. K., 190
Griffin, P., 330
Griffin-Shirley, N., 413
Griffith, P. L., 330
Grigal, M., 226
Grigorenko, E. L., 476
Griswold, D. E., 282
Gunn, B., 155
Gunter, P. L., 266, 267
Guralnick, M. J., 67
Guzzo, B. A., 269

Haas, A., 322
Hack, M., 55
Hall, R. V., 532
Hall, T. E., 526
Hallahan, D. P., 120
Halle, J. W., 208, 209
Halpern, A. S., 235
Halvorsen, A. T., 109, 229
Hamre-Nietupski, S. M., 222
Handleman, J. S., 297
Haney, M., 358, 406
Hankins, C. S., 429, 485
Hanley-Maxwell, C., 109, 183
Hanline, M. F., 229
Hanner, S., 148
Hans, S. L., 52, 53
Hanson, I. C., 50
Hanson, M. J., 64, 79, 80, 85, 99, 100
Hardman, M. L., 94, 181, 188, 207, 210, 211, 215
Harley, R. K., 406
Harris, C. A., 139, 141

Harris, J. J., 492
Harris, K. R., 137, 140
Harris, S. L., 297
Harry, B., 8, 23, 82, 83, 85, 86, 96, 104, 105, 107
Hartas, D., 252
Hartman, R., 270
Harvey, H. M., 208
Hasazi, S., 190
Hatlen, P., 393, 408, 410, 415
Hatton, D. D., 405
Hauser, R. M., 521, 522
Hauser-Cram, P., 94
Hawke, C., 457
Hayden, M., 149
Hayes, C., 205
Haynes, W. O., 316, 324
Hazel, J. S., 142
Health Indicators, 58
Hediger, M. L., 54
Heflin, L. J., 304, 305
Heller, K. W., 455
Henderson, F. W., 354
Henley, M., 124, 136
Henry, D., 454
Hensinger, R. N., 429
Hentoff, N., 235
Hernandez, B., 232
Heubert, J. P., 521, 522
Hewett, F. M., 6
Higgins, K., 302
Hilburn, R., 499
Hill, B. K., 230
Hill, E. W., 413, 414
Hirschstein, M. K., 269
Hitchcock, C., 528
Hitchings, W. E., 162
Hobbs, N., 31
Hodapp, R. M., 185, 204
Hodges, D., 454
Holbrook, M. C., 401, 408, 409, 410, 416
Holcomb, T., 367
Hollingsworth, M., 150
Hollingworth, L. A., 489, 492
Hom, J. L., 135
Homatidis, S., 290
Hooper, S. R., 250
Hopfenberg, W. S., 502
Horn, C., 522
Hourcade, J., 85, 529
House, B. J., 179
Hu, H., 57
Huebner, K. M., 395
Huer, M. B., 85
Huestis, R., 122
Hughes, C., 141, 151, 183, 271, 292
Hummell, J. H., 266
Humphries, T., 366
Hunt, N. A., 60, 89, 94
Hunt, P., 38
Hurlbutt, K., 307
Hutchinson, M. K., 50
Hwang, B., 292

Iacono, T. A., 206
Ianacone, R. N., 192
Ida, D. J., 255

Iglesias, A., 336
Igumnov, S., 56
Individuals with Disabilities Education Act (IDEA), 279, 438
Individuals with Disabilities Education Act (IDEA) Amendments, 262, 273, 528
Inge, K. J., 209
Intellitools, 459, 461
Iovannone, R., 298
Ishii-Jordan, S. R., 272
Ittenbach, R. E., 168, 174, 188

Jackson, D., 314
Jackson, K., 462
Jackson, N. E., 471
Jackson, R., 528
Jackson, R. S., 326, 362
Janney, R. E., 195
Jansson, L. M., 52
Jean, R. E., 85
Jenne, T., 272
Jiminez Gonzalez, J. E., 139
Jitendra, A. K., 134
Joe, J. R., 96
Johnson, H. M., 13
Joint Committee on Infant Hearing, 368
Jolivette, K., 249
Jones, V., 273

Kalyanpur, M., 8, 82, 83, 85, 86, 104
Kameenui, E. J., 131, 147, 148
Kamhi, A. G., 317, 321, 339
Kamps, D., 260, 269, 302
Kanner, L., 284, 285
Kaplan, S. B., 445
Katsiyannis, A., 445, 457
Kauffman, J. M., 120, 244, 262
Kavale, K. A., 122, 142
Kea, C., 255, 262
Kearney, K., 493
Kegel, J., 197
Kekelis, L. S., 398
Kelchner, K., 178, 182
Keller, B., 530
Kelly, J. F., 98
Kendrick, D., 401
Keogh, B. K., 83, 89
Kern, L., 270
Kerr, B. A., 485, 486, 487, 490
Keyser-Marcus, L., 439
KidTools, 130
Kiernan, W. E., 197
Kilgo, J. L., 230
Kinder, D., 161
King, C., 362
Kirby, D. F., 470
Kirk, K. I., 376
Kitano, M. K., 470
Kittrell, A., 356
Klein, M. D., 4, 82, 90, 324, 358, 397, 406
Klin, A., 281
Klinger, L. G., 288
Klinger, M. R., 288

Kluwin, T., 367, 378, 379
Knapczyk, D. R., 271
Knoblauch, B., 13, 14, 29, 392
Koegel, R. L., 289
Koenig, A. J., 401, 408, 409, 410, 416, 418
Kolb, S. M., 183
Kolominsky, Y., 56
Konstantareas, M. M., 290
Koorland, M., 267
Kopp, C. B., 43, 45
Kraijer, D., 291
Krampe, R., 481
Krauss, M. W., 214
Krege, J., 197
Kuhse, H., 17
Kutash, K., 250
Kutscher, M. L., 281

LaFlamme, M., 448, 456
Lagomarcino, T. R., 232
Lakin, K. C., 230
Lambert, N., 169
Landrigan, P. J., 57
Lane, H., 377
Lang, M. E., 97
Langone, J., 216
Lardieri, L. A., 99
Larsen, L., 138, 140
Larsen, S. C., 147
Lartz, M. N., 356
Lau, C., 459
Laureate Learning, 305
Laurin, K. M., 462
Lawrence, G. A., 406
Leffert, J. S., 182
Le Grice, B., 192
Lehmann, J. P., 211, 462
Leiberman, L. M., 33
Leicht, D. J., 135
Leigh, I., 375
Leland, H., 169
Lepoutre, D., 363, 376, 377
Lerner, J., 117, 139, 147, 256
Lerner, S., 256
Lesar, S., 99, 443
Levendoski, L. S., 270
Levin, H., 482, 502
Levy, S., 266
Lewis, M., 52, 492
Lewis, R. B., 123
Lewis, S., 415, 418
Lidz, C. S., 336
Lim, L., 215
Lin, S. L., 449
Linan-Thompson, S., 85
Lindegren, M. L., 50
Lindsey, J. D., 211
Lindstrom, L., 162
Lloyd, J. W., 120
Lloyd, R., 183
Loeb, G. E., 313, 321, 324, 460
Logan, 181, 188
Lopez-Reyna, N. A., 155
Los Angeles Unifed School District, 479, 480
Lovaas, O. J., 300
Lovecky, D. V., 483
Lowenfeld, B., 399, 416, 417

Lowenthal, B., 256
Luckett, E., 385, 386
Luckner, J., 379
Lue, M. S., 324
Lueck, A. H., 398
Luetke-Stahlman, B., 379
Luterman, D. M., 331
Lyerla, 150
Lyon, G. R., 340
Lyon, J. S., 235

Maccini, P., 141
Mack, C. G., 418
MacMillan, D. L., 22, 176, 251, 300
Maier, J., 38
Maker, C. J., 487, 505
Malach, R. S., 96
Male, M., 152
Malone, L. D., 134
Mank, D., 232
Maratens, B. K., 272
March of Dimes, 53
Masten, A. S., 73
Mastropieri, M. A., 10, 18, 134, 141, 267, 272
Mathes, P. G., 267, 533
Mattison, R. E., 250
Maurice, C., 280, 290, 294, 295
Mayo Clinic, 429
McCoach, D. B., 482, 491
McComas, J., 448, 456
McComiskey, A. V., 409
McCormick, L., 313, 315, 321, 324, 339, 344, 347
McDonald, H., 54
McDonald, L., 185
McDonnel, L. M., 525
McDonnell, A. P., 207, 210, 211, 215
McDonnell, J. J., 207, 210, 211, 215
McEvoy, A., 249
McGee, B., 363, 376, 377
McGregor, D., 415
McGuffog, C., 492
McGuire, J. M., 488, 489
McIntosh, R., 154, 155
McKinney, J. D., 155
McLane, K., 29
McLaughlin, M. J., 525
McLean, M., 66
McLesky, J., 454
McLloyd, V. C., 58
McLoughlin, J. A., 123
McMahan, G. A., 38, 85, 108, 209
McMorris, S. J., 219, 221
McWilliam, R. A., 85, 405
Meadow, K., 356
Meadow-Orlans, K. P., 358, 361, 363
Mechaty, I. R., 63
Mechling, L., 216
Medline, 437
Medline Plus, 175
Mednick, B. R., 94
Meisels, S. J., 64, 71
Mellard, D. F., 162

Meller, P. J., 272
Menlove, M., 457
Mercer, A. R., 141
Mercer, C. D., 137, 139, 141
Mercer, J., 20, 23
Mercer, S. P., 137
Merrill, E. C., 179
Merrill, M. A., 492
Mesibov, G. B., 301
Metz, D. E., 322
Meyer, A., 528
Meyer, L., 224
Meyers, H., 10
Michaels, C. A., 462
Miller, J. F., 206
Miller, S. P., 139, 141
Millikan, E., 182
Millward, C., 288
Milstead, S., 99
Minarovic, T. J., 192
Minshew, N. J., 281
Mira, M., 438, 439
Mitchell, L., 60
Mithuag, D. K., 183
Moats, L. C., 340
Modell, S. J., 182, 208
Montague, M., 141
Moon, M. S., 226, 463
Moores, D., 7, 46, 357, 362, 378, 384
Moran, M. J., 316
Morgan, R. L., 141
Morgan, J., 205
Morgan, M. A., 51, 56
Morgan, R. L., 216
Morison, P., 525
Morrice, P., 295
Morrison, G., 251
Morse, T. E., 196
Morsink, C. V., 107
Mortimer, E. A., 98
Morton, K., 94
Mortweet, S. L., 194
Mueller, P. H., 455
Muir, K. A., 272
Mull, C., 162
Mullis, L., 67
Mundy, P., 281
Munoz, M. L., 398
Murphy, F. V., 455
Murray, C., 162
Muscular Dystrophy Association (MDA), 436
Myer, J. A., 281
Myles, B. S., 281

National Association for Gifted Children, 478, 482, 509
National Center for Biotechnology Information (NCBI), 435
National Center for Education Statistics, 9, 20
National Center for Infectious Diseases, 48
National Center for Learning Disabilities, 523

National Center on Birth Defects and Developmental Disabilities, 431
National Down Syndrome Society, 175
National Information Center for Children and Youth with Disabilities (NICHCY), 204, 438
National Institute of Mental Health, 283
National Institute on Alcohol Abuse and Alcoholism, 52
National Institute on Deafness and Other Communication Disorders (NIDCD), 438
National Research Council, 297
Needleman, H. L., 57
Neel, R. S., 197
Nelson, N. W., 322, 329, 338, 339
Neu, T. W., 488, 489
Neubert, D. A., 226, 463
Neubert, M., 192
Neuharth-Pritchett, S., 439
Newborn Screening Task Force, 47
Newcomer, P. L., 137
Newell, W., 375
Nickel, R. E., 51
Nicpon, M. F., 486, 487, 490
Nietupski, J. A., 222
Nihira, K., 169
Niparko, J. K., 376
Nissenbaum, M. S., 295, 296
No Child Left Behind, 522
Noonan, M. J., 230
Northern, J. L., 352, 354, 355, 356

O'Donnell, B., 404
O'Donnell, J. P., 135
Olenchak, F. R., 488
Oller, D. K., 320
Olson, L., 523
Olson, M. W., 330
Olswang, L. B., 336
Orel-Bixler, D., 399
Orelove, F. P., 235, 450
Ortiz, A. A., 332, 333, 336
Osberger, M. J., 377
Osborn, A., 509
O'Shea, D. J., 79
Osterling, J., 301
Ostrosky, M. M., 208, 209
Oswald, D. P., 302
Owen, R. L., 150
Owens, R. E., 268, 317, 322, 328

Padden, C., 366
Pahl, J., 97
Palombaro, M. M., 455
Paneth, N., 54
Parakeshwar, N., 96
Parasnis, I, 367
Parette, P., 38, 85, 108, 209, 457, 529

Park, C. C., 290, 308
Park, J., 95
Parke, B. N., 506
Parmalee, A. H., 72
Parrish, L. H., 235
Patton, J. R., 110, 168, 174, 180, 188
Paul, P., 362, 373, 375, 379, 380, 407, 411
Pembrey, M., 326
Pena, E., 336
Perla, F., 404
Perrett, Y. M., 437
Persson, B., 301
Petersmeyer, B. A., 412
Peterson, D. R., 245
Peterson, J., 486
Peushel, S. M., 234
Phelps, J., 429
Picture Reading Literacy Project, 302
Pierce, T., 302
Piirto, J., 469
Pindzola, R. H., 316
Pivik, J., 448, 456
Plomin, R., 469, 481
Pogrund, R. L., 398
Polloway, E. A., 35, 171, 180, 321
Potvin, F. R., 47
Powell, T. H., 99
Prater, L. P., 104
Prater, M. A., 455
Prelock, P. A., 340
Prendergast, S. G., 356
Presley, J. A., 271
Prevent Blindness America, 406
Prezant, F. P., 462
Price, T. S., 469, 481
Provence, S., 71
Provost, O., 210
Pruner, L. W., 412
Pryt, M., 511
Pyle, A., 334

Quality Counts, 523, 529
Quay, H. C., 245
Quigley, S. P., 362, 373, 375, 380
Quine, L., 97

Racino, J. A., 217
Ramos-Ford, V., 474, 480
Ramsey, E., 252, 275
Ramsey, R. S., 124, 136
Rankin-Erikson, J. L., 137
Ranshaw, H. S., 440
Rapport, M. K., 457
Raskind, M. H., 162
Raths, L. E., 508
Ravitch, D., 5
Reese, L., 295
Reese, R. M., 89
Reichard, A., 64
Reid, D. H., 208, 215
Reid, D. K., 262, 326, 344
Reid, J. B., 255
Reiff, H. B., 162

Reis, S. M., 482, 488, 489, 491, 495, 503, 505
Renner, P., 288
Renzaglia, A., 230, 232
Renzulli, J. S., 471, 482, 495, 502, 503, 505
Reschly, D. J., 23
Rescorla, L., 328
Resta, P., 511
Reyes, E., 333
Rickard, R., 413
Rimland, B., 285
Rimm, S. B., 483, 491
Rischar, H., 486
Rivers, J. W., 99
Roberts, C. D., 235
Roberts, J. E., 354
Robertson, C. M., 54
Robinson, A., 507
Robinson, R., 141
Rodier, P., 284, 285, 290
Rogan, J., 266
Rogers-Dulan, J., 96
Rose, D., 528
Rose, N. C., 63, 174
Rosen, L. A., 255
Rosenberg, H., 197
Rosenshine, B., 149
Rosenthal-Malek, A., 440, 441
Rothenberg, L., 441
Rovine, M., 97
Rueda, R., 8
Ruef, M., 211
Rusch, F. R., 232
Rylance, B. J., 275

Sacks, O., 367
Sacks, S. Z., 400, 401, 404, 414
Sadker, D., 487
Sadker, M., 487
Safran, J. S., 35, 281
Saigal, S., 55
Salisbury, C. L., 455
Sall, N., 208
Salvia, J., 134, 380, 480
Salzberg, C. L., 500
Sameroff, A., 72
Sandall, S., 50, 68, 69, 105
Sands, D. J., 190
Sands-Buss, S., 221
Santamaria, L. J., 341
Sapona, R. H., 303
Savelle, S., 292
Sayers, L. K., 450
Scanlon, D., 162
Scarborough, H., 322, 330
Scavuzzo, A., 322
Schacht, R., 85
Scheidt, P. C., 52
Scheuermann, B., 272
Schiefelbusch, R. L., 313, 321
Schiever, S. W., 505
Schirmer, B. R., 367, 379
Schleper, D. R., 379, 380
Schnorr, R., 224
Schoem, S. R., 356
Scholl, T. O., 54
Schuler, P. A., 507
Schultz, C. J., 63

Schultz, R. A., 483, 486
Schumaker, J. B., 142, 150
Schumm, J., 33
Schuster, J. W., 196
Scorgie, K, 185
Scott, J., 285, 286, 290, 301
Scott, S., 85
Scott, T. M., 266
Scruggs, T. E., 10, 18, 141, 267, 272
Secada, W., 487
Seidel, J. F., 144
Seligman, M., 99
Semmel, M. I., 99, 176, 219, 443
Serna, L., 269
Severson, H., 260
Shapiro, D. R., 450
Shaywitz, B. A., 122, 130
Shaywitz, S. E., 122, 130
Shea, T. M., 104
Shealy, S. H., 460
Shearer-Lingo, A., 266
Shiono, P. H., 53
Shonkoff, J. P., 64
Shriner, J. G., 273
Shultz, R. A., 485
Siegel, S., 154
Siegel-Causey, E., 219, 221
Sienkiewicz-Mercer, R., 445
Sigafoos, J., 210, 292
Sigman, M., 55
Silberman, R. K., 395, 414
Silbert, J., 131, 147, 148
Sileo, N. M., 455
Simeonsson, R. J., 61
Simon, C., 136
Simpson, R. L., 292, 304, 305
Singer, G. H. S., 96, 104
Singer, L. T., 51
Singer, P., 17
Singleton, D. K., 192
Siperstein, G. N., 182
Sitlington, P. L., 162, 197
Skinner, M. L., 182
Skinner, R., 56, 184
Skrtic, T., 104
Slavin, R. E., 507
Smallman, J., 433
Smith, A. E., 441
Smith, B. J., 66
Smith, J. D., 235, 321
Smith, R. S., 73, 94
Smith, T., 300, 301
Smith, T. E. C., 151
Smith, T. M., 53
Smith-Thomas, A., 35
Smutny, J. F., 493
Snell, M. E., 188, 195, 217, 220, 222
Snider, V. E., 135
Snow, C. E., 330, 336, 338
Sobsey, D., 235
Sobsey, R., 450
Solomon, G., 511
Sonnier-York, C., 194
Sontag, J. C., 85
Sorenson, B., 13, 14, 392
Soto, G., 38

Souris, L. A., 292
Sparrow, S. S., 169
Speece, D. L., 119
Spencer, K. C., 190
Spina Bifida Association of America, 432, 433, 434
Sprague, J., 269
Spungin, S., 418, 419
Stafford, A., 215
Stage, S. A., 270
Stagni, K., 47
Stainback, G. H., 218, 227
Stainback, S. G., 227
Stainback, W. C., 218, 227
Stanford, P., 194
Stark, J. A., 197
Starko, A. J., 505
Staruch, K. S., 97
Stecker, P. M., 147
Steeley, D. G., 139, 161
Steere, D. E., 192
Stein, M., 267
Steinberg, S., 50
Stella, J., 281
Stephenson, J. R., 211, 291, 296
Stepien, W. J., 503
Sternberg, R. J., 474, 476, 477, 478, 482
Stevens, R., 149
Stewart, D. A., 211, 367, 378, 379, 380
Stokoe, W., 373
Stoneman, Z., 99, 185
Storey, K., 210, 235
Stotland, J., 402
Stough, L. M., 235
Strauss, M., 205
Sturm, J. M., 137
Sullivan, C. A. C., 209
Summers, J. A., 100, 101, 356
Sutherland, K. S., 249
Swanson, H. L., 99, 127, 145, 150
Sweeney, D. P., 249
Sweetow, R. W., 385, 386
Szabo, J. L., 453

Tankersley, M., 260
Targament, K. I., 96
Targett, P., 197

TASH (Association for Persons with Severe Handicaps), 202
Taylor, S. E., 101
Taylor, S. J., 217, 230
Temple, E., 122
Terman, L. M., 470, 471, 483, 492
Terpstra, J. E., 302
Terrell, S. L., 326
Tesch-Romer, C., 481
Tesoriero, H. W., 280, 283
Tessier, A., 4, 324
Tharp, R., 341
Thomas, C. C., 107
Thomas, S. B., 457
Thompson, J. E., 63
Thompson, L., 449
Thousand, J. A., 10
Thurston, L. P., 531
Thurstone, L. L., 471
Tilson, G. P., 192
Tollefson, N., 295
Torgesen, J., 131
Torrance, E.P., 492, 500
Torres, I., 407, 412
Toscano, R. M., 363, 376, 377
Townsend, B. L., 272
Toy, K., 249
Trach, J. S., 190
Treiman, R., 330
Trollop, S. R., 152, 153
Troutman, A. C., 192
Trusty, S., 413
Tuchman, R., 281
Tucker, B. F., 438, 439
Turnbull, A. P., 86, 95, 100, 101, 106, 110, 211, 356, 405
Turnbull, H. R., 60
Turnbull, R., 86, 95, 101, 106, 110, 405
Tuttle, D. W., 400
Tuttle, N. R., 400
Tyler, J. S., 438, 439

United Cerebral Palsy Association, 430
U.S. Advisory Board on Child Abuse and Neglect, 60
U.S. Census Bureau, 79, 80

U.S. Department of Education, 6, 10, 12, 119, 204, 242, 245, 260, 284, 428
U.S. Office of Special Education, 109
Utley, C. A., 532

Valdez, L. A., 182
VandenBerg, K. A., 45
Vandercook, T., 450
Van Tassel-Baska, J., 503
Vaughn, S., 33, 133, 143, 144, 154, 155, 266
Velez, M., 52
Venn, M. L., 266, 267
Vernon, P. E., 481
Vialle, W., 491
Villa, R. A., 10
Vitello, S. J., 209
Volkmar, F. R., 283
Von Karolyi, C., 474, 480
Vovanoff, P., 162
Vygotsky, L., 341

Wacker, D. P., 141
Wadsworth, S. J., 123
Wagner, M., 462
Wakschlag, L. S., 53
Walker, H., 269
Walker, H. M., 155, 252, 260, 269, 275
Walker, N., 129
Walker, P. M., 217
Wallace, G., 147
Wallace, I. F., 123, 354
Ward, M. E., 394, 396
Warger, C., 141
Warren, D. H., 397, 402
Watlawick, J., 314
Webb, B. J., 458
Webber, J., 272
Webb-Johnson, G., 247, 262
Wehby, J. H., 249
Wehman, P., 197, 230
Wehmeyer, M. L., 178, 182
Weishaar, M., 154
Weisner, T. S., 83, 89, 96
Welker, R., 249
Welsh, M. J., 441
Werner, E. E., 73, 74, 94

West, M., 197
Westling, D. L., 179
Whaley, S. E., 55
Whinnery, K. W., 453
Whitmore, J., 490, 491, 492
Whitney-Thomas, J., 109
Widerstrom, A. H., 51
Wilgosh, L., 185
Will, M. C., 109
Willard-Holt, C., 431, 484, 488
Williams, D. F., 324
Winner, E., 481, 485, 495, 497, 509, 512
Winterman, K. G., 303
Winton, P. J., 405
Withrow, F. B., 387
Witte, R., 439
Wolfensberger, W., 216
Wolffe, K. E., 401, 402, 415
Wong, B. Y. L., 127
Woo, E., 497
Wood, D. K., 141
Woodward, J., 141, 150, 156
Wormsley, D. P., 421
Wunsch, M. J., 52
Wynant, J., 387

Yairi, E., 324
Yamaki, K., 60, 94
Yates, J. R., 333
Yell, M. L., 13, 273, 300, 457
Yetman, N. R., 83
Yoder, P. J., 249
York, J., 450
Yoshinaga-Itano, C., 368
Yovanoff, P., 232
Ysseldyke, J., 380, 480
Yu, D. C. T., 210

Zamora-Duran, G., 333
Zampella, E., 435
Zaragoza, N., 154, 155
Zeaman, D., 179
Zimmerman, G. J., 411
Zirpoli, T. J., 254
Zuckoff, M., 185
Zuniga, M., 82, 96

Subject Index

Note: Page numbers followed by f indicate figures; t indicates tables; and d indicates display material.

AAMR Adaptive Behavior
  Scale, 169, 170f
Abbreviated Conner's Behavior-
  Rating Scales, 260, 261f
ABC's of behavior observation,
  263–264, 265f
Ability-achievement
  discrepancy, 118
Absence seizures, 434, 435d
Abuse, child, 60
Academic enrichment, 493, 495,
  496f, 502–503
Accelerated Schools Project, 502
Acceleration, 485, 493, 501–502,
  501d, 505–506
  content area, 505–506
  radical, 493
Acceptance, parental, 92. See also
  Family response
Accessibility, for physically
  disabled, 456–457
ACCESS Program, 155
Accidents, 57–58
Accommodation, 37f
Accountability, No Child Left
  Behind and, 523–524
Achievement-ability
  discrepancy, 118
Achievement tests. See also
  Assessment
  high-stakes, 522–523
  No Child Left Behind and,
  520, 521–522
Acquired hearing loss, 353t
Acquired immunodeficiency
  syndrome (AIDS). See
  Human immunodeficiency
  virus infection
Adaptation, coping strategies
  and, 100–101
Adaptive behavior, 168–169
  assessment of, 169
  in mental retardation, 164
Adaptive equipment. See also
  Assistive technology
  for physically disabled, 456
Adjustment, parental, 92
Adolescents, gifted and
  talented, 485–487
Adulthood, domains of, 223f
Adult service agencies, 462–463
Advanced placement courses,
  501–502
Advance organizers, 157, 158,
  160f
African American English
  (AAE), 325–326, 327t
African Americans. See also
  Minority groups
  disproportionate
    representation of among
    mentally retarded, 171
  overrepresentation of in
    special education, 20–24
  underrepresentation of in
    gifted education, 20–24
Age
  maternal, as fetal risk factor,
    53–54, 53t

paternal, as fetal risk factor,
  56
Age-appropriate behavior,
  242–243
Aggression, in behavior
  disorders, 251–252
Aides, for physically disabled,
  455, 455f
AIDS. See Human
  immunodeficiency virus
  infection
Albinism, 396d
Alcohol-related
  neurodevelopmental
  disorder, 52
Alcohol use/abuse, during
  pregnancy, 50, 51, 51f,
  176d–177d, 177
American Association on
  Mental Retardation
  (AAMR), 170–172
  Adaptive Behavior Scale of,
    169, 170f
American Psychiatric
  Association (APA). See
  Diagnostic and Statistical
  Manual of Mental Disorders
  (DSM-IV)
American Sign Language, 361,
  366, 374
  as first language, 375
  interpreters for, 381d, 382
  vs. oral approach, 374–377
American Speech-Language-
  Hearing Association
  (ASHA), 333d
Americans with Disabilities Act,
  13t, 18, 109, 456, 462
Amniocentesis, 63
Anger, parental, 92. See also
  Family response
Anger management, 271–272
Antisocial behavior. See
  Behavior disorders
Apple/House/Umbrella
  Screening, 406
Applied behavior analysis
  in autism, 298–300
  in Lovaas method, 300
Arithmetic. See Mathematics
Arthritis, juvenile rheumatoid,
  436–437
Articulation, definition of, 324
Articulation disorders, 324
Asian Americans. See also
  Minority groups
  acceptance of disability by,
    95–96
  communication patterns of,
    325–326, 327t
  underrepresentation of in
    special education, 22
Asperger's syndrome, 280,
  281–282. See also Autism
Assessment
  alternative, 524
  best practices in, 71
  computers in, 153d
  diagnostic, 71

ecological, 337–338, 338t
  flexibility in, 524
  formal, 145, 146f
  high-stakes testing and,
    522–523
  individual vs. group focus in,
    523
  informal, 145–147
  intelligence testing in. See
    Intelligence testing
  purposes of, 521–522
  referral for, cultural factors in,
    21, 23–24
  school accountability and,
    523–524
  screening in. See Screening
  for severely disabled, 524
Assistive listening devices, 386
Assistive technology, 65d,
  418–420, 419d
  for communication, 65d,
    302–303, 303f, 304f, 305d,
    345d–347d, 460–462
  cultural aspects of, 457
  family acceptance of, 108d
  instructional uses of, 458–459
  for mobility, 459–460
  needs assessment for, 457,
    458d
  for physically disabled,
    457–462
  self-determination and, 216d
  for visually impaired, 418–421
Assistive technology device, 38d
Assistive technology service, 38d
Association for Persons with
  Severe Handicaps (TASH),
  202
Asthma, 438–439
Ataxia, in cerebral palsy, 431
Athetosis, in cerebral palsy, 430
Athletics, for mentally retarded,
  182
At risk children, definition of, 4,
  43
At risk infants, identification
  and assessment of, 70–75
Attachment, parental, 91–92
Attention
  in autism, 290–291
  joint, 290
  learning disabilities and,
    125–126
  in mental retardation, 179–180
  selective, 126, 179
  teaching strategies for, 181d
Attention deficit disorder
  (ADD), 125–126, 256–259
  giftedness and, 488
  teaching strategies for, 127d
Attention deficit/hyperactivity
  disorder (ADHD), 125–126,
  243, 256–259, 443
  assessment of, 256–257
  autism and, 283
  diagnosis of, 256–257, 257d
  drug therapy for, 248–249, 259
  educational programs for,
    258–259

features of, 258
Audiogram, 359, 360f
Audiologist, 359
Auditory training, 372
Augmentative communication
  aids, 65d, 302–303, 303f,
    304f, 305d, 345d–347d,
    460–462
Aura, 434
Autism, 278–311
  applied behavior analysis in,
    298–300
  attention in, 290–291
  behavior in, 293–295, 294f
  brain abnormalities in, 286,
    286f
  causes of, 284–287
  cognitive function in, 287–290
  communication aids in,
    302–303, 303f, 304f, 305d
  diagnosis of, 279–280,
    282d–283d, 295
  drug therapy for, 303–305
  dual diagnosis in, 282–283,
    291
  early intervention in, 297–298,
    299t
  educational settings for, 297,
    298
  employment in, 305–307, 307d
  environmental factors in, 285,
    287
  environmental interventions
    in, 300–302
  family's response to, 280d,
    285, 288d–289d, 295–296,
    296d, 308d
  features of, 287–296
  federal definition of, 279–280
  first-person accounts of,
    288d–289d, 308d
  fragile-X syndrome and,
    282–283
  genetic factors in, 286, 290
  information resources for, 284
  intelligence in, 281–282, 287
  language and communication
    in, 291–292, 292t, 293f,
    295
  living situations in, 307
  Lovaas method for, 300
  mental retardation in,
    282–283, 283, 287–288,
    291
  pervasive developmental
    disorders and, 280–282
  physical characteristics in, 290
  prevalence of, 284
  Project TEACCH for, 300–302
  rigidity in, 289–290, 294
  school-based programs for,
    298
  screening for, 280
  social interaction in, 290–291,
    302–303
  social skills instruction in,
    301–302
  special abilities in, 287–288
  support groups for, 295–296

teaching strategies and accommodations in, 296–307
transition to adulthood in, 305–307, 307d
treatment of, 303–307, 306t
Autism Society of America, 296
Autism spectrum disorders, 280–282

Babbling, 320
Behavior
age appropriateness of, 242–243
in autism, 293–295, 294f
communication and, 252, 314, 314f, 322–323
duration of, 242
externalizing, 245, 251
intensity of, 242
internalizing, 245, 251
measures of, 242–243
rate of, 242
self-destructive, 253–254
stereotypic, 294, 294f
suicidal, 253–254
unusual, 243
Behavior disorders, 240–277
academic programming in, 266–268
addressing inappropriate behavior in, 268–270
anger management for, 271–272
assessment of, 242–243, 259–264
attention deficit/hyperactivity disorder and, 256–259
behavior-change interventions for, 268–272
case studies of, 246d, 250d
causes of, 246–249
classification of, 243–245
classroom management in, 272–275, 273d
cognitive strategies for, 270
criminal behavior in, 251–252
cultural factors in, 262, 263d
curriculum focus in, 264–266
depression and, 254
diagnosis of, 243–244, 259–262
dropping out of school and, 252
drug abuse and, 252
drug therapy for, 248–249, 250d
environmental factors in, 247–248, 248f
externalizing behaviors in, 245, 251
family's response to, 254–256
federal definition of, 241–242
first-person account of, 250d
internalizing behaviors in, 245, 251
language and communication in, 252
learning disabilities and, 249–250
level system in, 272, 274d
parent-school cooperation for, 255–256
physiological factors in, 248–249
positive behavior support in, 267
prevalence of, 245–246

prevention of, 268–270, 269f
residential care for, 253–254
school achievement and, 249–250
school-based programs for, 272–275
screening for, 260
self-destructive behavior in, 253–254
self-management instruction in, 270, 271d
severe, 253–254
social adjustment in, 251–252
suicidal behavior in, 253–254
teaching new behaviors in, 270–272
teaching strategies and accommodations for, 259–275
universal interventions for, 269, 269f
unusual behavior in, 243
violent behavior in, 251–252
vs. disability-related behavior problems, 273
vs. isolated episodes, 243
Behavior intervention plan (BIP), 262–263, 264d
Behavior management, in behavior disorders, 255–256, 270–272
Behavior problems, 29, 29d
disability-related, 273
in mental retardation, 182–183
Behavior rating scales, 260–262, 261f
Bell, Alexander Graham, 8f
Best practice, 10–11
Bilateral hearing loss, 353t
Bilingual students. See Non native English speakers
Biological risk factors, 45–55
definition of, 45
environmental risk factors and, 57, 60
in perinatal period, 54–55
in postnatal period, 55
in prenatal period, 46–54, 56
Birth defects. See Congenital malformations
Birthweight, low, 54–55, 55t
Black English, 325–326, 327t
Blindness. See also Visual impairment
functional, 393
legal, 392
Blissymbols, 346d–347d
Board of Education of Hendrick Hudson Central School District v. Rowley, 20, 21t
Bodily-kinesthetic intelligence, 475t
Body language, 252
in mental retardation, 181
Bonding, parental, 91–92
Books
Braille, 409–410, 410f
electronic, 458–459
large-print, 410–411
Braille, 409–410, 410f
Brain damage
from head trauma, 438–439
learning disabilities and, 121–122
perinatal, 54
Brain imaging studies, 121–122, 122f
Brain stem, in autism, 286, 286f

Brainstorming, 509
Bridgeman, Laura, 9f
Brother. See Siblings
Brown v. Board of Education, 21t, 23

Canavan's disease, 218d
Cancer, 443
Cane travel, 413, 420
Captioning, for hearing impaired, 387
Caregiver, definition of, 79
Cataracts, 396d
Categorization, 128d
Cause-and-effect relationships, 206–207
CD-ROMs. *See also* Technology
instructional, 152d–153d, 216d
Cedar Rapids Community School District v. Garret F.., 20, 21t
Cells, Braille, 409, 410f
Cerebral palsy, 429–431, 430f
communication disorders in, 346d–347d
Certificate of Clinical Competence, 333d
Certification, of speech-language pathologists, 333d
Checklist for Autism in Toddlers (CHAT), 280
Child abuse/maltreatment, 60
in behavior disorders, 254
Childhood disintegrative disorder, 281. *See also* Autism
Children. *See also* Adolescents; Infant(s)
resilient, 73–75, 73t
Chlamydia, in pregnancy, 48–50
Choral response, 148d
Chorioathetosis, in cerebral palsy, 430
Chorionic villus sampling (CVS), 63
Chronic illness, 55
Chronic otitis media, 55
hearing loss and, 55, 354–356
Chunking, 128d
Classroom discourse, 341
Classroom management, 29, 29d
behavior disorders and, 272–275, 273d
Classroom materials, modifications for, 156–162
Classroom modifications, for physical disabilities, 454d, 456–457
Clerc, Laurent, 8f
Closed captioning, for hearing impaired, 387
Closed-circuit television, 418–420
Clubfoot, 437
Cluster grouping, 507
Cocaine, fetal effects of, 51–52
Cochlear implants, 376d–377d, 386
Code-emphasis approaches, 131
Cognitive coping, 101
Cognitive development
in gifted and talented, 483
hearing loss and, 362
learning disabilities and, 124–130
means-end relationship and, 206–207

in mental retardation, 178–180, 206–207
visual impairment and, 397–399, 399
Cognitive skills, teaching strategies for, 181d
Cognitive style, 129, 258
Cognitive taxonomy, 508, 508f
Collaboration, 33–36, 34d, 531
College
for gifted, 501–502, 501d
integration into, 226, 227d
transition to, 109, 462–463, 463d. *See also* Transition programming
Combined risk, 45f
Communication. *See also* Language; Speech
augmentative and alternative, 345d–347d
in autism, 291–292, 292, 292t, 293f, 295, 302–303
behavior and, 252, 314, 314f, 322–323
in behavior disorders, 252
cultural aspects of, 325–326, 327t, 332–336, 332–337, 337d
in cultural competency, 85
definition of, 313–314
dialects and, 325–326, 327t
functional, 208–209, 209d, 222
in health impairments, 445–446
hearing loss and, 361, 366–367, 368–377
interpreters and, 104
language and, 85, 252. *See also* Language
with non-English speakers, 85, 104
nonverbal, 181, 252, 294–295, 314, 314f, 322–323
in physical disabilities, 445–446
Picture Exchange Communication System and, 302, 303f
self-awareness in, 84, 85
in severe/profound mental retardation, 208–209, 209d, 222
social stories and, 302–303, 304f
types of, 314f
Communication aids, 65d, 302–303, 303f, 304f, 305d, 345d–347d, 460–462
in autism, 302–303, 303f, 304f, 305d
Communication disorders, 312–350, 320–348
assessment for, 331–338
augmentative and alternative communication and, 345d–347d
in bilingual children, 332–336, 334d
case example of, 334d, 337d
causes of, 326–327
collaborative team for, 341–344, 343d
communication aids in, 65d, 302–303, 303f, 304f, 305d, 345d–347d, 460–462
cultural aspects of, 325–326, 327t, 332–337, 337d
definition of, 320

Communication disorders (continued)
first-person accounts of, 338d–339d, 346d–347d
genetic factors in, 326–327
hearing impairment and, 355, 355t. See also Hearing impairment
identification of, 328–331, 370d–371d
integrative language and literacy learning for, 340–341
interventions for, 344–348
in kindergarten and early school years, 329–330
of language, 320–323, 321f, 334d
language delay in, 334d
language/literacy instruction and, 340–341, 342t
learning disabilities and, 329–330
in mental retardation, 180–181
metalinguistic awareness and, 330
phonological awareness and, 330, 330d
placement and service options for, 338–340
in preschool years, 328–329
prevalence of, 327–328, 328f
pull-out vs. classroom-based interventions for, 338–340, 339d
risk indicators for, 328–331, 332f
of speech, 321f, 323–325, 325d
speech-language pathologist in, 332, 333d
teaching strategies and accommodations for, 331–348
vs. dialects, 325–326, 327t
Communicative competence, 333, 335f, 340–341
Communicative intent, 323
Community-based instruction, 188–189, 195–196, 222–223, 224d–225d
Community-based residential facilities, 231d
Compacting, 504–505, 504f
Compensatory academic skills, in visual impairment, 408–409, 409t
Composition. See Writing
Computers. See also Assistive technology
instructional uses of, 152d–153d, 216d
positioning for, 459t
in self-management instruction, 271d
Concept map, 137, 139d
Concrete experiences method, 416, 416t
Conductive hearing loss, 354–356, 354t
Congenital hearing loss, 353t
Congenital infections, 46–48
Congenital malformations
biological factors in, 46–54, 46f
environmental factors in, 56, 56f
physical disability due to, 437
sensitive periods for, 46, 48f
Conner's Behavior-Rating Scales, 260, 261f

Consent, informed, 102
Construct, intelligence as, 167
Consultation, 530–531
Consultation model, 35, 416
Content area acceleration, 505–506
Content standards, 525
Context cues, 132
Contusion, 438–439
Cooperative learning, 194–195, 507
Coping strategies, 100–101
Cornea, 395, 395f
Corrective Reading–Revised, 149
Cortical visual impairment, 396d
Co-teaching, 33, 531, 532d
Creativity, 472, 474–476, 477f, 507–509
Criminal behavior, in behavior disorders, 251–252
Cultural awareness, 84, 85
Cultural competence, 84–86, 172f
teacher assistance teams and, 171, 172f
Cultural factors
in assistive technology, 457
in behavior disorders, 262, 263d
in communication disorders, 325–326, 327t, 332–337, 337d, 340–341, 342t
in concept of disability, 83, 95–96
in Deaf culture, 365–367, 367d
in IQ testing, 22, 23–24, 24, 171
in learning disabilities, 155–156
in referral, 22
in representation in gifted education, 21, 23–24, 491
in representation in special education, 20–24
in social constructs, 89
in speech and language, 325–326, 327d
Cultural inversion, 263d
Cultural reciprocity, 85–86, 86d
Culture
Deaf, 352, 365–366, 367d, 375, 379–380, 379d
definition of, 79–80
language and, 325–326, 327t
macroculture and, 82, 82d
microculture and, 82, 82d
minority groups and, 83. See also Minority groups
vs. ethnicity, 83
Curriculum
environmental inventory for, 222
expanded core, 408–416, 409t
functional, 220–222, 222d
general education, access to, 524–528
inclusion, 220–222, 222d
life-skills, 188–189, 194d
Curriculum-based measurement (CBM), 147
Curriculum development, Universal Design for Living and, 526–527, 527d, 528d
Curriculum modification, 161–162. See also Teaching strategies and accommodations

for gifted and talented, 488–489, 503–509
for mentally retarded, 186–192, 220–223
in reading instruction, 156–159
Curriculum standards, 525–526
Curriculum telescoping, 504–505, 504f
Cystic fibrosis, 441, 442d
Cytomegalovirus infection, in pregnancy, 47–48
hearing loss and, 357d

Deaf community, 352
Deaf culture, 352, 365–367, 367d, 375
cochlear implants and, 376d–377d
in school curriculum, 379–380, 379d
Deafness
definition of, 352. See also Hearing impairment
postlingual, 353t
prelingual, 353t
Deaf studies, 379–380, 379d
Deinstitutionalization, 8
Depression, behavior disorders and, 254
Diabetes, 439–441
Diabetic retinopathy, 396d
Diagnostic and Statistical Manual of Mental Disorders (DSM-IV), 243–244
autism in, 279–280
behavior disorders in, 243–244
Diagnostic assessment, 71
Dialects, 325–326, 327t
Diana v. Board of Education, 21t, 23, 171
Differentiated instruction, 38, 503–504
Digitized speech, 461
Digivox, 194d
Direct instruction, 147d, 148–149
assessment of, 267d
in behavior disorders, 267
checklist for, 267d
Directions, modifications of, 160
Direct service model, 452, 453d
Disability(ies)
behavior problems due to, 273
concept of, cultural factors in, 83, 95–96
culture and, 83
definition of, 3
degree of, 94
demands of, 94
due to child abuse, 60
family response to, 89–97. See also Family response
giftedness and, 487–488, 489d
medical model of, 83
multiple, 444
physical. See Physical disabilities
positive adaptation to, 100–101
positive aspects of for family, 110
predictors of, 71–72, 72f
severe, 201–239. See also Mental retardation, severe/profound
as social construct, 89
vs. handicap, 3–4

Disciplinary problems, 29, 29d
behavior disorders and, 272–275, 273d
Discipline
Individuals with Disabilities Education Act guidelines for, 12–17, 29
manifestation determination for, 273
Discourse, 315
Discrepancy, achievement-ability, 118
Dog guides, 414
Double deficit hypothesis, 131
Down syndrome, 174t. See also Mental retardation
causes of, 173f, 175d
chromosomal defect in, 173f, 175d
educational potential in, 175d
Individualized Family Service Plan for, 69, 70f
maternal age and, 53, 53t
paternal age and, 56
personal account of, 66–67
physical problems in, 182
range of abilities in, 175d
Drills, computer, 152d
Dropping out, in behavior disorders, 252
Drug abuse
behavior disorders and, 252
during pregnancy, 50–52, 176d–177d, 177
Drug therapy
for attention deficit/hyperactivity disorder, 248–249, 259
for autism, 303–305
for behavior disorders, 248–249, 250d
during pregnancy, 50–52
DSM-IV. See Diagnostic and Statistical Manual of Mental Disorders (DSM-IV)
Dual diagnosis, in autism, 282–283, 291
Dual programs, for gifted, 501–502
Duchenne muscular dystrophy, 435–436
Due process, 103
Dyskinesia, in cerebral palsy, 430
Dystonia, in cerebral palsy, 430

Ear, structure of, 353, 353f
Ear infections, hearing loss and, 354–356
Early entrance programs, 501–502, 501d
Early intervention, 44, 64–69
for autism, 297–298, 299t
definition of, 4, 64
effectiveness of, 67, 68d
eligibility for, 66, 70–71
family-centered services in, 211–214, 449
family involvement in, 66d–67d, 68–69, 105
for gifted and talented, 493–494
goals of, 64
for health impairments, 449
for hearing loss, 368, 370d
identification and assessment for, 70–75
Individualized Family Service Plan for, 69, 70f
interdisciplinary team in, 69, 70f

key components of, 66, 68d
for mental retardation, 186, 211–214
models for, 67–68
in natural environments, 67d, 68
for physical disabilities, 449
settings for, 67–68
specialists in, 64
for visual impairment, 405–406
E-books, 458–459
Echolalia
in autism, 291
in visual impairment, 397
Ecocultural theory, 89
Ecological assessment, in communication disorders, 337–338, 338t
Economic factors. *See* Socioeconomic status
Ecosystem assessment, 263d
Education
right to, 236
teacher, 529–530
Educational achievement. *See* School achievement
Educational definitions, 393
Educational reform, 519–524
assessment and, 520–524
No Child Left Behind and, 520, 522–523
school accountability and, 523–524
Educational settings, 31–38
examples of, 34f, 36f
least restrictive environment and, 9, 31–33
for visually impaired, 416–418
Education for All Handicapped Act. *See* Individuals with Disabilities Education Act (IDEA)
EEPsters, 501d
Elaboration, 128d
Electronic books, 458–459
Email, for hearing impaired, 387
Emergency care, for seizures, 435d
Emotional development. *See* Social and emotional development
Emotional disturbance. *See also* Behavior disorders
federal definition of, 241–242
Employment
in autism, 305–307, 307d
in community-based instruction, 188–189, 195–196
health impairments and, 463–464
independent competitive, 197d
in mental retardation, 188–189, 194d, 197d, 198d, 230–232
mentors for, 307d
physical disabilities and, 463–464
self-management procedures for, 232, 233f
sheltered, 197d, 232
social skills training for, 154–155
supported, 197d
transition to, 109, 191–193, 230–232. *See also* Transition programming
for visually impaired, 415

Empowerment, 215
Enclave, 197d
Encoding processes, 127
English as a second language learners. *See* Non native English speakers
Enrichment programs, 493, 495, 496f, 502–503
Enrichment Triad Model (EMT), 502
Environmental analysis, 222
Environmental inventory, 222
Environmental modifications, for physical disabilities, 454d, 456–457
Environmental risk factors, 45f, 55–61, 72, 72f, 99
biological risk factors and, 57, 60
occupational, 56
postnatal, 56
prenatal, 56
social toxins and, 99
Epilepsy, 434–435, 435d
Ethical issues
regarding severe disabilities, 233–236
right to life, 234–235
Ethnicity. *See also* Culture; Minority groups
definition of, 83
Ethnocentrism, 83
Euthanasia, 234–235
Exceptionality. *See also* Disability(ies)
definition of, 3
labeling and, 31, 32t
prevalence of, 6
Exclusion clause, 118–119
Existential intelligence, 475t
Expanded core curriculum, in visual impairment, 408–416, 409t
Expressive language, 292
problems with, 322
Extended family, 79
response of to disability, 99
Externalizing behaviors, 245, 251
Eye, structure and function of, 394–395, 395f
Eye-gazing scanning systems, 461

Family. *See also* Parent(s); Siblings
assistive technology and, 108d
characteristics of, 87, 87f
coping strategies of, 100–101
definition of, 79
in early intervention, 66d–67d, 68–69, 211–214
extended, 79
future options and, 110
language of, 80–81. *See also* Home language; Non native English speakers
with multiple risks, 99
noninvolvement of, 104–105
single-parent, 60–61
size of, 94
study of
ecocultural theory approach in, 89
family systems approach in, 86–87, 87f, 88f
support for, 90–91, 99, 100d, 101–102. *See also* Support/support groups

in transitional programming, 228–230, 228d
unstable, 60
Family configuration, response of to disability and, 94
Family functions, 87, 87f
impact of disability on, 97
Family interactions, 87, 87f
impact of disability on, 97–99
Family life cycle, 87, 87f
Family map, 87, 88f
Family quality of life
definition of, 95
poverty and, 95, 95f
Family response
to autism, 280d, 285, 288d–289d, 295–296, 296d, 308d
to behavior disorders, 254–256
cultural factors in, 83, 95–96
to disability, 89–97. *See also* Disability, family response to
disability characteristics and, 93–94
family characteristics and, 94–97
to health impairments, 447–449
to mild/moderate mental retardation, 184–185
parent-child relationship and, 98
to physical disabilities, 447–449
religious beliefs and, 96
to severe/profound mental retardation, 209–214, 218d–219d
to visual impairment, 402–404
Family systems approach, 86–87, 87f, 88f
Family theories, 89
Family Village website, 229, 229f
Father. *See also* Family; Parent(s)
age of, as fetal risk factor, 56
Feedback, corrective, 148d
Females, gifted and talented, 487
Fetal alcohol syndrome, 50, 51, 51f, 174t, 176d–177d, 177. *See also* Mental retardation
first person account of, 176d–177d
Fingerspelling, 372–373, 373f, 374d
First aid, for seizures, 435d
First trimester, 46
Fluency disorders, 324–325
Foreign language speakers, 80–81. *See also* Home language; Non native English speakers
communication with, 85, 104
interpreters for, 85, 104
Formal assessment, 145, 146f
Formal supports, 215
Fragile-X syndrome, 174t, 282–283
Framework of Support, 37–38, 37f, 39f
Functional academics, 187–188, 195
Functional behavior assessment (FBA), 262–263, 264d, 265f
in communication disorders, 323
Functional blindness, 393

Functional communication, 208–209, 209d, 222
Functional curriculum, 220–222, 222d
language instruction in, 222
Functional electrical stimulation (FES), 459–460
Functional flexibility, 136
Functional vision, 393
Functional vision assessment, 407–408

Galactosemia, 174t
Gallaudet, Thomas Hopkins, 8f
Gallaudet University, 367d, 377d
Galton, Francis, 470
Games, computer, 153d
Gardner, Howard, 474, 475t
Gay adolescents, gifted and talented, 485–487
Gender, giftedness and, 487, 490
General education curriculum. *See also* Curriculum
access to, 524–528
General education teachers
collaboration with, 33, 531, 532d
support for, 11d
Generalization
in mental retardation, 180
teaching strategies for, 181d
Genetic counseling, 61–63, 62d
Genetic disorders
genetic counseling for, 61–63, 62d
mental retardation in, 174t, 204, 208, 212d–213d, 214, 218d–219d
neonatal screening for, 47d
prenatal testing for, 63–64
German measles
immunization for, 61
in pregnancy, 46–47, 356
Gifted and talented, 468–515
accelerated instruction for, 485, 493, 505–506
adolescent, 485–486
advanced placement courses for, 501–502
assessment of, 494–495
attention deficit disorder in, 488
cluster grouping for, 506, 507
cognitive characteristics of, 483
college for, 501–502, 501d
cooperative learning for, 507
creativity in, 507–509
creativity of, 472, 474–476, 477f, 495
cultural diversity and, 21, 23–24, 474, 480, 491–492, 491f, 494
current concepts of, 471–479
curriculum modification for, 488–489, 503–509
curriculum telescoping for, 504–505, 504f
definitions of, 471–479
disabilities of, 487–488, 489d
early intervention for, 493–494
early theories of, 470–471
educational settings for, 493, 495–502, 496f
enrichment programs for, 493, 495, 502–503
environmental influences and, 481–482

Gifted and talented (continued)
   extracurricular programs for,
      500–502
   federal definition of, 478–479
   female, 487, 490
   first-person account of,
      472d–473d
   gay/lesbian/bisexual,
      486–487
   heredity and biological
      factors and, 481
   higher-level thinking by,
      507–509
   highly gifted, 492–493
   identification of, 479–481,
      494–495
   independent study/self-
      directed learning for, 506
   intelligence in, 471–477,
      479–481, 483, 484t
      multiple, 474–477, 475t,
         477f, 478d
   IQ in, 479, 480f
   learning disabilities in, 488,
      489d, 490t
   mentors for, 500
   minority, 21, 23–24, 480,
      491–492, 492f, 494
   motivation of, 485, 488–491
   performance areas for, 473,
      474d
   personal characteristics of,
      485
   physical characteristics of,
      483–484
   physical disabilities of, 484
   physically disabled, 484, 487
   prevalence of, 480f, 482
   problem-based learning for,
      509, 510d
   productivity of, 471–472, 495
   resource room for, 495, 496f,
      497–498
   schoolhouse, 495
   self-contained classrooms for,
      499
   social and emotional
      characteristics of, 483
   special education for, pros
      and cons of, 509–510
   special schools for, 496f, 499
   task commitment in, 472
   technology and, 511d
   underachieving, 488–489
   wisdom of, 477, 478d
Gifted underachiever, 488–491
Girls, gifted and talented, 487
Glaucoma, 396d
Governor's schools, 500
Grade skipping, 485, 493
Grammar, 315
Grand mal seizures, 434, 435d
Grandparents. See also Family
   impact of disability on, 98
Grief, parental, 91–92
Group homes, 231
Group telescoping, 505
Guide dogs, 414
Guides, for visually impaired,
   413

Handicap
   definition of, 3
   vs. disability, 3–4
Hard of hearing, 352. See also
      Hearing loss
Head injuries, 438–439
Health impairments
   acceptance of, 447

   access to instruction and,
      453–457
   cognitive development in, 445
   communication and language
      development in,
      445–446
   early intervention for, 449
   educational planning and,
      450–453
   family response to, 447–449
   federal definition of, 428
   first-person account of, 442d
   health maintenance and, 457
   inclusion and, 455–456, 455f
   physical supports and,
      456–457
   postsecondary education and,
      462–463, 463d
   social and emotional
      development in, 446–447
   teaching strategies and
      accommodations for,
      452d
   transdisciplinary approach
      for, 450–453
   transition to adulthood in,
      462–464
   treatment of, 448
   types of, 438–444
   vs. physical disabilities, 428
Health maintenance, 457
Hearing
   organs of, 353, 353f
   physiology of, 353, 353f
   residual, 353t, 354
Hearing aids, 384–386
Hearing impairment, 352. See
      also Hearing loss
Hearing loss, 352–390
   acquired, 353t
   additional disabilities in,
      356–358, 358t
   assistive listening devices for,
      386
   auditory training for, 372
   bilateral, 353t
   causes of, 354–356, 357d
   cognitive development and,
      362
   communication in
      controversy over, 374–377
      manual approaches in,
         372–377
      oral approach in, 368, 369t,
         371–372, 374–377
      tips for, 382d–383d
      total communication
         approach in, 371t,
         375–376
   conductive, 354–356, 354t
   congenital, 353t
   curriculum modifications for,
      378–380, 378d, 379d
   Deaf culture and, 352,
      365–367, 367d, 375,
      376d–377d, 379–380,
      379d. See also Deaf
      culture
   degrees of, 355t, 360f
   diagnosis of, 359, 360, 368,
      370d
   early identification and
      intervention for, 368,
      370d
   educational assessment in,
      364d–365d, 380
   educational settings and,
      380–384, 381f
   features of, 359–367

   fingerspelling in, 372–373,
      373f, 374d
   first-person account of,
      364d–365d
   genetic factors in, 356
   hearing aids for, 384–386
   instant messaging/email and,
      387
   interpreters and, 381d, 382
   language development and,
      355, 361–362
   literacy instruction and, 379
   manual approach in, 361, 366,
      372–374, 373f
   measurement of, 358–359
   mixed, 354
   otitis media and, 55, 354–356
   prevalence of, 358
   reading and, 379
   residential schools and, 384
   residual hearing in, 372
   school achievement and,
      362–363, 364d–365d,
      380–384
   sensorineural, 354–356, 354t
   sign language and, 361,
      366–367, 372–377,
      374–377, 381d, 382
   special classes and, 383–384
   speech instruction in, 372,
      374–377
   support groups for, 377d
   teaching strategies and
      accommodation for,
      368–384
   technologic aids for, 384–387,
      385d
   telecommunication devices
      for, 386–387
   terminology of, 352, 353t,
      365–367, 367d
   unilateral, 353t
   visual impairment and, 358,
      358t
Hearing tests, 358–359, 360f
Hematoma, intracranial,
   438–439
Herpes infection, in pregnancy,
   48–50
Higher education
   for gifted, 501–502, 501d
   integration into, 226, 227d
   transition to, 109, 226, 227d,
      462–463, 463d. See also
      Transition programming
Higher-level thinking, 507–509
Highly gifted, 492–493
Highly qualified teachers,
   529–530
High-stakes testing, 522–523. See
      also Assessment
Hispanic Americans. See
      Latinos; Minority groups
HIV infection. See Human
      immunodeficiency virus
      infection
Hollingworth, Leta S., 470–471,
   487
Homebound instruction,
   455–456
Home care, vs.
   institutionalization,
   218d–219d
Home language, 80–81. See also
      Non native English
      speakers
   communication and, 85
   interpreters and, 104
Homework contract, 130, 130f

   Homosexual adolescents, gifted
      and talented, 485–487
   Honig v. Doe, 20, 21f
   Horner, Rob, 270
   Household, 79
   Howe, Samuel Gridley, 7, 8f
   Human guides, for visually
      impaired, 413
   Human immunodeficiency
      virus infection
      in children, 442–443
      educational services and,
         51d
      incidence of, 49d, 50
      statistics on, 49d
      in pregnancy, 50
   Hydrocephalus, 174t, 432,
      433–434
   Hyperglycemia, in diabetes, 441
   Hypermedia, 152d
   Hypertonia, in cerebral palsy,
      430, 430f
   Hypoglycemia, in diabetes,
      440–441
   Hypoxia, perinatal, 54

   IDEA. See Individuals with
      Disabilities Education Act
      (IDEA)
   IEP. See Individualized
      Education Program (IEP)
   IFSP (Individualized Family
      Service Plan), 24–26, 25t,
      105
   Ilan, Leah, 381d
   Illness
      chronic, 55
      in pregnancy, 46–50, 174
      hearing loss and, 356, 357d
   Immature behaviors. See also
      Behavior disorders;
      Behavior problems
      in mental retardation, 182–183
   Immunizations, 61
   Impulsive cognitive style, 129,
      258
   Inclusion, 9–11, 217–220. See also
      Integration
      advantages and
         disadvantages of, 9–10
      continuum of, 9–10, 10f
      definition of, 9
      of severely disabled, 217–220,
         221d
      support for general education
         teachers for, 11d
      trends in, 10
      vs. segregation, 9–10
   Independent competitive
      employment, 197d
   Independent living skills, in
      visual impairment,
      414–416, 415t
   Independent study, 506
   Indirect service model, 450–453,
      453d
   Individualized education,
      24–30
      components of, 25t
   Individualized Education
      Program (IEP), 17, 18f,
      26–29, 103, 519
      components of, 25t, 28–30
      curriculum standards for,
         525–526
      family involvement in,
         103–105
      guide to, 26–30
      sample, 451f

transition plan in. *See*
    Individualized Transition
    Plan (ITP)
Individualized Family Service
    Plan (IFSP), 24–26, 25t, 69,
    70f, 85, 105
Individualized Transition Plan
    (ITP), 17, 25t, 26–30,
    190–192, 191f, 223. *See also*
    Transition programming
    components of, 25t
    sample, 191f
Individual supported job
    model, 197d
Individuals with Disabilities
    Education Act (IDEA),
    236
    amendments to, 17
    disciplinary guidelines of,
        12–17, 29
    eligibility criteria of, 19f
    emotional disturbance
        definition in, 241–242
    exclusion clause in, 118–119
    learning disability definition
        in, 117–119
    provisions of, 12–17, 24
    reauthorization of, 12–17
Infant(s)
    chronic illness in, 55
    premature. *See* Prematurity
Infant-parent bonding, 91–92
Infection, in pregnancy, 46–50,
    174
    hearing loss and, 356, 357t
Informal assessment, 145–147
Informal inventories, 147
Informed consent, 102
Injuries
    accidental, 57–58
    brain, 438–439
    from child abuse, 60, 254
    physical disabilities due to,
        437–439
Inoculations, 61
Instant messaging, for hearing
    impaired, 387
Institutionalization, 218d–219d,
    446. *See also* Residential care
Instruction. *See* Teacher(s);
    Teaching
Instructional discourse
    strategies, 341
Instructional technology,
    152d–153d, 216d
    for gifted, 511d
    for mentally retarded, 194d
    in self-management
        instruction, 271d
Integration, 222–223. *See also*
    Inclusion
    into college, 226, 227d
    transition to, 226–230. *See also*
        Transition programming
Intelligence, 167–168
    in Asperger's syndrome,
        281–282
    in autism, 281–282, 287
    bodily-kinesthetic, 475t
    in cerebral palsy, 431
    as construct, 167
    existential, 475t
    genetic vs. environmental
        factors in, 176–177
    in gifted and talented,
        471–477, 483, 484t, 495
    hearing loss and, 362
    interpersonal, 475t
    intrapersonal, 475t

learning disabilities and,
    124–130
linguistic, 475t
logical-mathematical, 475t
multiple, 474–477, 475t, 477f,
    478d
musical, 475t, 498d–499d
naturalist, 475t
physical disabilities and,
    445–446
productivity and, 471–472,
    495
spatial, 475t
successful, 476
triarchic theory of, 474–477,
    477f, 478d
visual impairment and, 399
Intelligence quotient (IQ),
    167–168
    of gifted and talented, 479,
        480f, 492
    in mental retardation, 168,
        168f, 203
Intelligence testing, 167–168
    cultural factors in, 22, 23–24,
        171
    in gifted and talented
        identification, 479, 480f,
        492
    hearing loss and, 362
    score distribution in, 168, 168f
Intensive care unit, neonatal, 55
Interdisciplinary team, 69
Intermediate-care facilities, 231d
Internalizing behaviors, 245, 251
International Dyslexia
    Association, 523
Internet
    for hearing impaired, 387
    learning via, 153d
Interpersonal intelligence, 475t
Interpreters, sign language,
    381d, 382
Interview, teacher, in formal
    assessment, 145–146, 146f
Intracranial hematoma,
    438–439
Intrapersonal intelligence, 475t
IQ. *See* Intelligence quotient (IQ)
Iridocyclitis, 437
Iris, 395, 395f
*Irving Independent School District
    v. Tatro*, 20, 21t
Isolation.
    social, 99. *See also* Peer
        relationships; Social and
        emotional development
Itard, Jean-Marc-Gaspard, 7, 8f
Itinerant services, for visually
    impaired, 417
ITP. *See* Individualized
    Transition Plan (ITP)

Jobs. *See* Employment
Johnson, Harriet McBryde,
    15–17, 16f
Joint attention, 290
Jones, Norah, 498d–499d
Jordan, King, 367d
Juvenile diabetes, 439–441
    retinopathy in, 396d
Juvenile rheumatoid arthritis,
    436–437

Kanner, Leo, 284–285
Keller, Helen, 9f
Kennedy, John F., 7
Kennedy, Rosemary, 7
Kinesthetic intelligence, 475t

Labeling
    pros and cons of, 30–31
    social change and, 32t
Language, 315
    in behavior disorders, 252
    body, 252
    communication and, 85, 252.
        See also Communication
    components of, 315f
    cultural aspects of, 325–326,
        327t
    definition of, 315
    expressive, 292
    of family, 80–81, 104. *See also*
        Home language; Non
        native English speakers
    functional flexibility and, 136
    interpreters and, 104
    oral. *See* Speech
    people-first, 4–5, 5d
    pragmatic, 136
    receptive, 292, 322
    structure of, 315
    written. *See* Writing
Language arts, learning
    disabilities and, 135–138
Language delay, 328, 334d
Language development,
    316–320
    in autism, 291–292, 292t, 293f,
        302–303
    in health impairments,
        445–446
    hearing loss and, 355, 361–362
    identification of, 370d–371d
    language acquisition in,
        317–318, 319t, 370d
    in mental retardation,
        180–181, 208–209
    milestones in, 318, 319t,
        370d–371d
    models of, 317, 317t
    in physical disabilities,
        445–446
    rate of, 318, 319t, 370d–371d
    speech production in, 319t,
        320, 370d–371d
    visual impairment and,
        397–399, 398d
Language disorders, 320–323,
    321f, 322t. *See also*
    Communication disorders
Language instruction
    in functional curriculum, 222
    in hearing loss, 364d–365d,
        368–377
    for non native English
        speakers, 340–341, 342t
Language sample, 337
Large-print books, 410–411
Larry P. v. Riles, 21t, 24, 171
Late talkers, 328
Latinos. *See also* Minority
    groups
    acceptance of disability by,
        95–96
    communication patterns of,
        325–326, 327t
    overrepresentation of in
        special education, 20–24
    underrepresentation of in
        gifted education, 20–24
Law. *See* Legal issues;
    Legislation
Lawsuits, 18–20
Lead poisoning, 57
Learning. *See also* Cognitive
    development; School
    achievement

brain changes in, 122, 122f
cooperative, 194–195, 507
problem-based, 509, 510d
self-directed, 506
self-monitoring in, 128, 129d,
    183
Learning by doing method, 416,
    416t
Learning disabilities, 116–165
    academic performance and,
        130–142
    achievement-ability
        discrepancy in, 118
    in Asperger's syndrome, 281
    attention and, 125–126
    behavior disorders and,
        249–250
    of bilingual students, 155–156
    brain damage and, 121–122,
        122f
    causes of, 120–123
    cognitive processes and,
        124–130
    cognitive style and, 129
    coping with, 162d
    cultural diversity and,
        155–156
    definitions of, 117–119
    emotional development and,
        142–144
    employment and, 162d
    federal criteria for, 117–119
    genetic factors in, 123
    giftedness and, 488, 489d, 490t
    information processing in, 122
    language arts and, 135–138
    language disorders and, 321,
        329–330
    learning style and, 123
    memory and, 126–127
    metacognition and, 127–128
    organization and, 128–130
    perception and, 124–125, 125d
    perinatal stress and, 122–123
    prevalence of, 119
    reading skills and, 130–135
    self-esteem and, 143–144
    social aspects of, 142–144,
        154–155
    spelling and, 135–136
    teaching strategies and
        accommodations for,
        144–162
Learning Disabilities
    Association of America, 523
Learning Strategies Curriculum,
    150–151
Learning style, 123
Least restrictive environment, 9,
    31–33
Lectures, modifications for,
    156–157
Legal blindness, 392. *See also*
    Visual impairment
    reading media for, 394f
Legal issues. *See also* Legislation;
    Litigation
    criminal behavior, 252
    informed consent, 103
    mediation, 103
    rights of mentally retarded,
        196
    right to due process, 103
Legislation, 12–18. *See also*
    Public Law *and specific*
    statues
    chronology of, 13t
    foundations of, 13t
Lens, of eye, 395, 395f

Lesbian adolescents, gifted and talented, 485–487
Lesson planning, modifications for, 156, 157d. *See also* Curriculum modifications; Teaching strategies and accommodations
Letter reversals, 125
Level system, 272, 274d
Licensure, for speech-language pathologists, 333d
Life-skills curriculum, 188–189
technology in, 194d
Linguistic intelligence, 475t
Listening skills, 372
Literacy instruction, in hearing loss, 379
Litigation, 18–20
due process hearing and, 103
important cases in, 21t
regarding availability of services, 18–20, 21t
regarding minority representation, 21t, 23–24
Logical-mathematical intelligence, 475t
Loneliness, 99. *See also* Peer relationships; Social and emotional development
Lovaas method, 300
Low birthweight, 54–55, 55t
Low vision, 393. *See also* Visual impairment
aids for, 410–411
Lysosomal storage disorders, 212d–213d, 214

Macroculture, 82, 82d. *See also* Culture
Macy, Anne Sullivan, 9f
Magnet schools, 496f, 499, 500
Mainstreaming, 9. *See also* Inclusion
Malnutrition, in infants, 55
Manifestation determination, 273
Manual communication approach, 372–374
American Sign Language in, 361, 366, 374
fingerspelling in, 372–373, 373f, 374d
Maternal age, as fetal risk factor, 53–54, 53t
Maternal-infant bonding, 91–92
Mathematics
learning disabilities and, 139–141
teaching strategies for, 140–141, 141f, 142f
Means-end relationship, 206–207
Mediation, 103
Medical model, of disability, 83
Memory
aids to, 128d
in autism, 288
encoding processes in, 127
learning disabilities and, 126–127
in mathematics, 139, 141, 141f
in mental retardation, 178–179, 181d
in spelling, 135–136
teaching strategies for, 128d, 181d
working, 127

Meningitis, 55
in pregnancy, hearing loss and, 357d
Mental retardation, 166–200
advocacy for, 198
in autism, 282–283, 287–288, 291
in cerebral palsy, 429–431
classification of, 170–172
definition of, 167
in Down syndrome. *See* Down syndrome
in dual diagnosis, 282–283
mild/moderate
adaptive behavior and, 168–169
attention in, 179–180
behavior problems in, 182–183
biomedical factors in, 174–175
causes of, 173–178, 174t
cognitive development in, 178–180, 181d
community-based instruction in, 188–189
curriculum modifications for, 186–192
definition of, 171
early intervention in, 186
educational settings for, 186–187
employment in, 188–189, 194d, 197d, 198d
environmental factors in, 176–177
family's response to, 184–185
first-person account of, 176d–177d
generalization in, 180
genetic factors in, 176–177
instructional materials in, 195–196
instructional methods in, 192–195
IQ in, 168, 168f
language development in, 180–181
life-skills curriculum for, 188–189
manifestations of, 169–170
personal/civil rights in, 196–198
physical development in, 181–182
prevalence of, 172–173
skill transfer in, 180
social and emotional development in, 182–183
support groups for, 185
teaching strategies in, 186–198, 189d, 195d
transition programming in, 190–192, 191f
physical disabilities and, 445–446
severe/profound, 171, 201–239
causes of, 204–205
cognitive development in, 206–207
communication in, 208–209, 209d, 222
community-based instruction in, 222–223, 224d–225d

curriculum modifications in, 220–223
definition of, 201–239
educability in, 236
environmental supports in, 215
ethical issues in, 233–236
family's response to, 209–214, 218d–219d
first person account of, 205d, 212d–213d
inclusion in, 217–220, 221d
institutionalization in, 218d–219d, 231d
integration in, 222–223
IQ in, 203
living situations in, 230, 231d
normalization in, 216–217
physical problems in, 204–205, 207–208
prevalence of, 203–204
quality of life in, 234–235
right to education in, 236
social and emotional development in, 209–210
support groups for, 211, 229, 229f
teaching strategies in, 214–233
technological aids in, 216d
transition between school levels in, 226
transition from school to work in, 226–233
transition from segregated to integrated settings in, 226–230
transition programming in, 223–232
severity of, 170–172
Mentors
for gifted, 500
job, 307d
Metacognition
learning disabilities and, 127–128
in mental retardation, 178–179, 181d
Metalinguistic awareness, 330
Mexican Americans. *See* Latinos
Microcephaly, 174t
Microculture, 82, 82d. *See also* Culture
Mills v. the Washington D.C. Board of Education, 18, 21t
Minority groups. *See also* Culture
definition of, 83
disproportionate representation of among mentally retarded, 171
disproportionate representation of in special education, 20–24, 171
family involvement in educational plan and, 103–105
underrepresentation of in gifted education, 21, 23–24, 491–492, 492f, 494
Mirman School, 496d–497d
Mixed hearing loss, 388
Mobile work crew, 197d
Mobility
definition of, 413

in visual impairment, 399, 412–413. *See also* Orientation
Mobility aids, for physically disabled, 459
Mobility impairments. *See* Physical disabilities
Modeling, in direct instruction, 148
Modification, 37f
Montessori, Maria, 7, 8f, 9f
Morere, Donna, 376d–377d
Morphemes, 315
Morphology, 315
problems with, 323t
Mother. *See also* Family; Parent(s)
age of, as fetal risk factor, 53–54, 53t
refrigerator, 285
Mother-infant bonding, 91–92
Motivation, in gifted and talented, 485, 488–491
Motor development, visual impairment and, 399
MOVE curriculum, 453
Movies, captioned, 387
Moyamoya disease, 205d
Multidisciplinary service model, 452, 453d
Multiple disabilities, 444
Multiple intelligences, 474–477, 475t, 477f, 478d
Muscular dystrophy, 435–436, 449
Muscular Dystrophy Association, 449
Musculoskeletal disorders, physical disabilities in, 435–437
Musical intelligence, 475t, 498d–499d

National Advisory Committee on Handicapped Children, 117
National Association for Gifted Children, 477–478, 509
National Center for Learning Disabilities, 523
National Organization of the Deaf (NAD), 377d
Native Americans. *See also* Minority groups
acceptance of disability by, 95–96
underrepresentation in gifted education and, 22
Natural environments, in early intervention, 67d, 68
Naturalist intelligence, 475t
Natural supports, 215
Neglect, 60
Neonatal intensive care unit (NICU), 55
Neurological disorders, physical disabilities in, 429–435
Neurotoxins, 57
Newborns
low-birthweight, 54–55, 55t
premature, 54–55, 55t
screening of, 47d
Niemann-Pick disease, 212d–213d
No Child Left Behind, 520–524. *See also* Assessment
highly qualified teachers and, 529–530

Non native English speakers
  communication disorders in,
    332–336, 334d, 361–362
  communicative competence
    of, 333, 335d, 340–341
  with hearing loss, 361–362
  IEP for, 23–24
  IQ testing for, 23–24
  language development in,
    332–336, 334d, 361–362
  language instruction for,
    340–341, 342t
  representation of in special
    education, 22, 23–24
Nonverbal communication, 252,
  314, 314f, 322–323
  in autism, 294–295
  in mental retardation, 181
Normalization, 8, 216–217
Note buddy, 431
Note-taking, 154
Nutritional deficiencies, in
  infants, 55

Observation, in informal
  assessment, 145–147
Occupational concerns. See
  Employment
Occupational risk factors, 56
Opportunity factors, 74–75
Optical devices, 419d
Optic nerve, 395, 395f
  atrophy/hypoplasia of, 396d
Oral communication approach,
  368, 369t, 371–372
Oral language. See Speech
Organization, learning
  disabilities and, 128–130
Orientation, definition of, 413
Orientation and mobility aids,
  413, 420
Orientation and mobility
  specialist, 412d, 413
Orientation and mobility
  training, 399, 412–413
Orthopedic impairment,
  427–428. See also Physical
  disabilities
Osberger, Mary Jo, 376d
Otitis media, 55
  hearing loss and, 55, 354–356
Otologist, 359
Overrepresentation, in special
  education, 20–24
Oxygen deprivation, perinatal,
  54

Pacing, of lessons, 148d
Paraeducators, 455, 455f
Paragraph shrinkage, 532d
Paralysis, 437–438
Paraprofessional aides, for
  physically disabled, 455
Parent(s). See also Family
  age of, as fetal risk factor,
    53–54, 53t
  noninvolvement of, 104–105
  reaction of to disability,
    87–98. See also Family
    response
  support for, 99, 101–102
Parent-child relationship, 98
Parent-infant bonding, 91–92
Parent-teacher relationship,
  107–109
Parent-to-parent model, 101
Partial participation, 217
Partner reading, 532d

Paternal age, as fetal risk factor,
  56
Peer-assisted leaning strategies
  (PALS), 532–533, 532d
Peer relationships
  in autism, 290–291, 302–303
  of gifted and talented, 483
  health impairments and,
    446–447
  hearing loss and, 363–364
  learning disabilities and,
    154–155
  in mental retardation,
    182–183, 195, 217–220
  physical disabilities and,
    446–447
  social skills instruction and,
    154–155
  visual impairment and,
    400–401, 403–404, 404d,
    414–415
Pegwords, 141, 141f
Pennsylvania Association for
  Retarded Citizens (PARC) v.
  Commonwealth of
  Pennsylvania, 18, 21t
People-first language, 4, 5d
Perception, learning disabilities
  and, 124–125, 125d
Perfectionism, 483
Performance standards, 525
Perinatal period
  definition of, 45
  risk of injury in, 54–55, 55t
  sensitive periods in, 48f
Perinatal stress, learning
  disabilities and, 122–123
Person-centered planning, 215
Pervasive developmental
  disorders, 280–282. See also
  Autism
Peterson-Quay Behavior-Rating
  Scales, 260
Petit mal seizures, 434, 435d
Phenomes, 316
Phenylketonuria (PKU), 174t,
  175
Phonemes, 315
Phonological awareness, 330,
  330d
Phonological disorders, 323–324
Phonology, 315
  problems with, 323t
Physical development, in
  mental retardation,
  181–182, 207–208
Physical disabilities, 427–439
  acceptance of, 447
  access to instruction and,
    453–457
  cognitive development in, 445
  communication aids in, 65d,
    302–303, 303f, 304f, 305d,
    345d–347d, 460–462
  communication and language
    development in, 445–446
  definitions of, 427–428
  due to congenital
    malformations, 437
  due to traumatic injuries,
    437–439
  early intervention for, 449
  educational planning and,
    450–453
  family response to, 447–449
  first-person account of,
    432–434
  giftedness and, 484, 487

health maintenance and, 457
  inclusion and, 455–456, 455f
  intelligence and, 445–446
  in neurological disorders,
    429–435
  physical supports for, 456–457
  postsecondary education and,
    462–463, 463d
  prevalence of, 428
  school accessibility for, 456
  social and emotional
    development in, 446–447
  teaching strategies and
    accommodations for, 452d
  technology aids for, 457–462
  transdisciplinary approach
    for, 450–453, 451f
  transition to adulthood in,
    462–464
  treatment of, 448
  types of, 428–439
  vs. health impairment, 428
Physical education, in mental
  retardation, 182
Physical handling, 456
Physically challenged persons,
  427
Physical therapy, 208
Picture Exchange
  Communication System,
  302–303, 303f
Picture story board, 196
PKU (phenylketonuria), 174t,
  175
Placement, 36. See also
  Educational settings
Pollution, toxins in, 57
Polysubstance abuse, during
  pregnancy, 51d
Positioning, for computer use,
  459t
Positive behavior interventions
  and support, 267, 270
Postlingual deafness, 353t
Postnatal period
  biological risk in, 55
  definition of, 45
Postsecondary education,
  transition to, 109, 226, 227d,
  462–463, 463d. See also
  Transition programming
Poverty, 58–59
  demographics of, 59d
  economic vs. social, 58–59
  family quality of life and, 95
  family response to disability
    and, 94–96, 95f
  malnutrition and, 55
  over/underrepresentation in
    special education and,
    22–24
  as risk factor, 58–60
  in single-parent families,
    60–61
Pragmatic language skills, 136
Pragmatics, 315
  problems with, 323t
Prediction relay, 532d
Pregnancy. See also Perinatal;
  Prenatal
  biological risk in, 46–54
  early prenatal care in, 63
  genetic testing in, 63–64
  healthy, guidelines for, 45d
  maternal age in, 53–54, 53t
  maternal illness/infection in,
    46–50, 174
  hearing loss and, 356, 357d

premature delivery in, 54–55,
  55t
  hearing loss and, 357d
  mental retardation and,
    174t
  sensitive periods in, 48f
  substance abuse during,
    50–53, 176d–177d, 177
Prelingual deafness, 353t
Prematurity, 54–55, 55t
  hearing loss and, 357d
  mental retardation and, 174t
Prenatal care, 63
Prenatal period, 45. See also
  Pregnancy
Prenatal testing, 63–64
Prereferral intervention team, 35
Preschool Grants Program, 17
President's Commission on
  Mental Retardation, 7
Preterm delivery. See
  Prematurity
Private schools. See also
  Residential schools
  for gifted and talented, 496f,
    499
Problem-based learning, 509,
  510d
Problem-solution-effect model,
  161–162
Productivity, intelligence and,
  471–472, 495
Profound mental retardation.
  See Mental retardation,
  severe/profound
PROJECT strategy, 151
Project TEACCH, 300–302
Prompts, 192
  in vocational training, 194d
Psycholinguistic theories, 317,
  317t
Public Law 94–142. See
  Individuals with
  Disabilities Education Act
  (IDEA)
Public Law 97–35, 478–479
Public Law 99–457, 13t, 17, 186,
  298, 449
Public Law 101–336. See
  Americans with Disabilities
  Act
Public Law 101–476, 13t, 17,
  117
Public Law 105–17, 13t, 17
Pullout programs, 35–36
Pupil, 395, 395f

Quality of life, 234–235

Race. See Culture; Minority
  groups
Radical acceleration, 493
Reading
  Braille for, 409–410, 410f
  learning disabilities and,
    130–135
  partner, 532d
Reading comprehension
  learning disabilities and,
    133–135
  teaching strategies for, 134d
Reading fluency, 132–133
Reading instruction
  curriculum modifications in,
    157–159
  direct instruction in, 147d,
    148–149, 149f
  in hearing loss, 379

Reading instruction (*continued*)
modifications in, 156–159
strategy instruction in,
150–151
Reading Mastery direct
instruction programs, 149,
149f
Receptive language, 292
problems with, 322
Reciprocal speech, 292
Referral
cultural factors in, 22
to speech-language
pathologist, 332, 336
Reflective cognitive style, 129
Refrigerator mother, 285
Rehabilitation Act of 1973,
Section 504 of, 13t, 17–18,
19f, 109
Rehearsal, 128d
Relationships, importance of,
74–75
Religion, response to disability
and, 96
Repetitive behaviors, in autism,
294, 294f
Residential care. *See also*
Institutionalization
for behavior disorders,
253–254
community-based, 231d
Residential schools
for gifted and talented, 500
for hearing impaired, 384
for visually impaired, 417–418
Residual hearing, 353t, 354
auditory training for, 372
Resiliency, 44, 73–75, 73t
Resource room programs
for gifted, 495, 496f, 497–498
for visually impaired, 417
Respite care, 102
Response signals, 148d
Retina, 395, 395f
Retinopathy
diabetic, 396d
of prematurity, 396d
Rett's disorder, 281, 445. *See also*
Autism
Rezulli, Joseph, 471–473, 495
Rheumatoid arthritis, 436–437
Right to due process, 103
Right to education, 236
Right to life, 234–235
Risk factors
biological, 45–55. *See also*
Biological risk factors
combined, 45f
definition of, 43
environmental, 45f, 55–61, 72,
72f. *See also*
Environmental risk
factors
examples of, 46f
interaction of, 57, 60
multiple, 57, 60, 71–72, 72f
prediction of disabilities from,
71–72, 72f
prevention strategies for,
61–64
types of, 44–45, 45f
Rubella
immunization for, 61
in pregnancy, 46–47, 356

Scaffolding, 341, 342t
School(s)
for gifted and talented, 496f,
499

magnet, 496f, 499
residential. *See* Residential
schools
School accountability, 523–524
School achievement
in Asperger's syndrome,
281–282
in autism, 281–282
behavior disorders and,
249–250
hearing loss and, 362–363,
364d–365d, 380–384
visual impairment and,
401–402
School dropouts, behavior
disorders and, 252
Schoolwide Enrichment
Program, 503
Screening
of at-risk children, 71
for autism, 280
for behavior disorders, 260
definition of, 71
for hearing loss, 368
of newborns, 47d
vision, 406–407
Second language learners. *See*
Non native English
speakers
Secretin, for autism, 303
Section 504 of Rehabilitation Act
of 1973, 13t, 17–18, 109
eligibility criteria of, 19f
Seeing eye dogs, 414
Segregation, educational, 8–9
vs. inclusion, 9–10
Seguin, Edouard, 7, 8f
Seizure disorders, 434–435, 435d
Selective attention, 126
in mental retardation, 179
Self-awareness, in mental
retardation, 183
Self-control, in mental
retardation, 183
Self-destructive behavior,
253–254
Self-determination, transition
programming and, 190–191
Self-directed learning, 506
Self-esteem, learning disabilities
and, 143–144
Self-help groups, 90–91
Self-management, 232, 233f
instruction in, 270, 271d
in mental retardation, 183
Self-monitoring, in learning,
128, 129d, 183
Self-stimulating behaviors, in
autism, 294, 294f
Semantics, 315
problems with, 323t
Sensorineural hearing loss,
354–356, 354t
Service models
multidisciplinary (direct), 452,
453d
transdisciplinary (indirect),
450–453, 453d
Service options, 528–533
Severe disabilities, 201–239. *See*
also Health impairments;
Mental retardation,
severe/profound; Physical
disabilities
definition of, 202
integration into college in,
226, 227d
right to education and, 236
right to life and, 234–235

Sexually transmitted diseases,
in pregnancy, 48–50
Sheltered employment, 197d,
232
Shock, parental, 91. *See also*
Family response
Siblings. *See also* Family
impact of disability on, 98,
185, 211
of mentally retarded, 185, 211
Sienkiewicz-Mercer, Ruth, 446
Sign language, 361, 366–367,
372–377
interpreters for, 381d, 382
vs. oral approach, 374–377
Simulations, computer, 153d
Simulation training, 196
Singer, Peter, 17
Single-parent families, 60–61
Sister. *See* Siblings
Skills transfer
in mental retardation, 180
teaching strategies for, 181d
Small-group instruction, 148d
Smoking, in pregnancy, 53
Snellen Charts, 406
Social and emotional
development
in autism, 290–291
in behavior disorders,
251–252
in gifted and talented, 483
hearing loss and, 363–364
learning disabilities and,
142–144
in mental retardation,
182–183, 195
physical disabilities and,
446–447
visual impairment and,
400–401, 414–415
Social construct, disability as,
89
Social integration, 37
Social interactional theories, of
language development,
317, 317t
Social isolation, 99
Socially toxic environments,
99
Social poverty, 58–59
Social risk factors, 72, 72f. *See*
also Environmental risk
factors
Social skills instruction,
154–155
in autism, 301–302
Social stories, 302–303, 304f
Socioeconomic status, 94–95. *See*
also Poverty
determinants of, 94
Sociolinguistic theories, 317,
317t
Spasticity, in cerebral palsy, 430,
430f
Spatial intelligence, 475t
Special education. *See also*
Teacher(s); Teaching
collaboration in, 33–36, 34d,
531, 532d
definition of, 4–5, 524–525
eligibility criteria for, 19f
family's role in, 102–110
foundations of, 6–24
history of, 6–11
learning environments in, 10,
10f
legislation affecting, 8, 9. *See*
also Legislation

minority representation in,
20–24. *See also* Minority
groups
No Child Left Behind and,
520, 522–523
pioneers of, 7
reforms in, 519–523
segregation vs. inclusion in,
8–9. *See also* Inclusion
settings for, 9, 31–38
student population in, 6, 6f
teacher training in, 529–530
terminology of, 3–5
transition from, 109. *See also*
Transition programming
trends and challenges in,
518–535
Special skills instruction,
151–154
Specific language impairment,
321
Speech. *See also*
Communication; Language
in autism, 291–292
cultural aspects of, 325–326,
327t
definition of, 316
development of, 320
dialects and, 325–326, 327t
digitized, 461
in learning disabilities, 136
in mental retardation, 180–181
organs of, 316, 316f
production of, 316, 316f, 320
reciprocal, 292
synthesized, 461
Speech disorders, 321f, 323–325,
325d. *See also*
Communication disorders
Speech instruction, in hearing
loss, 372, 374–377
Speech-language pathologist,
333d
assessment by, 331–338
collaboration with, 341–344,
343d
referral to, 332, 332t, 336
role of, 331–332, 333d
training and certification of,
333d
Spelling, learning disabilities
and, 135–136
Spina bifida, 432–434
Spinal cord injuries, 437–438
Spoken language. *See* Speech
Sports participation, in mental
retardation, 182
Standards
content, 525
curriculum, 525–526
performance, 525
Stanford-Binet Intelligence
Scale, 167–168
STAR strategy, 141, 142f
Stereotypic behaviors, in
autism, 294, 294f
Sternberg, Robert, 474–477, 477f,
478d
Story board, 196
Strategy instruction, 150–151
in mathematics, 141, 142f
in reading, 150–151
Stress
family, 97–99
perinatal, learning disabilities
and, 122–123
Stress-resistant children, 73–75,
73t
Student support team, 35

Study skills instruction, 151–154
Stuttering, 324–325, 325d
Substance abuse
  behavior disorders and, 252
  during pregnancy, 50–53, 176d–177d, 177
Successful intelligence, 476
Sugai, George, 270
Suicide, 253–254
Sullivan, Anne, 7, 9f
Summer programs, for gifted, 500–501
Superbaby syndrome, 493–494
Supported employment, 197d
Support/support groups, 90–91, 101–102
  for autism, 295–296
  for families, 90–91, 100d, 101–102
  for general education teachers, 36
  for hearing loss, 377d
  for mental retardation, 185, 211, 229, 229f
  for students, 36–38, 37f, 39f
  for stuttering, 325
Switches, in assistive technology, 65d
Syntax, 315
  problems with, 323t
Synthesized speech, 461
Syphilis, in pregnancy, 48–50

Tactile symbols, 410
Talent. See also Gifted and talented
  definition of, 467
TASH (The Association for Persons with Severe Handicaps), 202
Task analysis, 192
Task commitment, 472
Tay-Sachs disease, 174t, 208
TDD devices, 386–387
Teacher(s)
  collaboration among, 33–36, 34d, 531, 532d
  general education collaboration with, 33, 531, 532d
  support for, 11d
  highly qualified, 529–530
Teacher assistance teams, 35
  culturally competent, 171, 172f
Teacher education, 529–530
Teacher interview, in formal assessment, 145–146, 146f
Teacher-parent relationship, 107–109
Teaching, 528–533
  differentiated, 38, 503–504
  direct instruction in, 147d, 148–149, 149f, 267, 267d
  for homebound students, 455–456
  peer-directed instruction and, 532–533, 532d
  preparation for, 529–530
  social skills instruction in, 154–155
  special skills instruction in, 151–154
  strategy instruction in, 150–151
  teacher-directed instruction and, 529–530
  team, 33

Teaching strategies and accommodations
  for attention, 181d
  for attention deficit disorder, 127d
  for autism, 296–307
  for behavior disorders, 259–272, 259–275
  for cognitive skills, 181d
  for communication disorders, 331–348
  for generalization, 181d
  for hearing loss, 368–384
  for learning disabilities, 181d
  for memorization, 128d, 181d
  for mental retardation, 186–192, 189d, 195d, 214–236
  for physical disabilities, 452d
  for reading comprehension, 134d
  for skills transfer, 181d
  student recommendations for, 268d
  for visual impairment, 405–421
  for writing, 140d
Team-teaching, 33, 194–195, 519–520
Technology
  assistive. See Assistive technology
  instructional, 152d–153d, 216d
    for gifted, 511d
    for mentally retarded, 194d
    in self-management instruction, 271d
Telecommunication devices for the deaf (TDD), 386–387
Television
  closed captioning for, 387
  closed-circuit, 418–420
Teratogens, 46
Terman, Lewis M., 470
Testing. See Assessment
Textbooks
  Braille, 409–410, 410f
  large-print, 410–411
  modifications of, 157–159, 159f, 160f
Thalidomide, 51
Tonic-clonic seizures, 434, 435d
Total communication approach, 371t, 375–376
Toxins, environmental, 56–57
Transdisciplinary model, 450–453, 451f
Transition, definition of, 223
Transition programming, 190–192, 191f, 193f
  domains in, 223–233
  family's role in, 228–230, 228d
  for health impairments, 462–464, 463d
  Individualized Transition Plan for, 17, 25t, 26–30, 190–192, 191f
  for mental retardation, 190–192, 223–232
  for physical disabilities, 462–464, 463d
  for transition between school levels, 226, 462–463, 463d
  for transition from school to work, 230–232
  for transition from segregated to integrated settings, 226–230

Translators, 104
Traumatic brain injury (TBI), 438–439
Traumatic injuries, physical disabilities due to, 437–439
Treatment, withholding/withdrawal of, 234–235
Triarchic theory of intelligence, 474–477, 477f, 478d
Trisomy 21. See Down syndrome
Tutorials, computerized, 152d

Underachiever, gifted, 488–491
Underrepresentation, in special education, 21, 23–24
Unified Plan of Support (UPS), 38, 39f
Unifying experiences method, 416, 416t
Unilateral hearing loss, 353t
Unison response, 148d
Universal Design for Living (UDL), 526–527, 527d, 528d

Vaccinations, 61
Vagus nerve stimulation, 434–435
Verbalisms, 397
Very low birthweight, 54–55, 55t
Victor (wild boy of Aveyron), 9f
Videotapes. See also Technology, instructional
  instructional, 152d–153d, 216d
Vineland Adaptive Behavior Scales, 169
Violence, in behavior disorders, 251–252
Vision
  functional, 393
  low, 393
  physiology of, 394–395
Visual acuity
  assessment of, 406–407
  definitions of
    educational, 393
    legal, 392
Visual efficiency, 415–416
Visual impairment, 391–425
  achievement testing and, 408
  assistive technology for, 418–421, 419d
  associated disabilities in, 395, 418
  Braille in, 409–410, 410f
  cane travel in, 413
  career education in, 415
  case examples of, 397d, 414d
  causes of, 395, 396d
  cognitive development in, 397–399, 399
  compensatory academic skills in, 408–409
  concrete experience method in, 416, 416t
  congenital, 395
  consultants for, 412d
  cortical, 396d
  definition of, 392
  dog guides in, 414
  early intervention in, 405–406
  educational definitions for, 393
  expanded core curriculum for, 408–416

family's response to, 402–404
first-person account of, 400d
functional vision and, 393
functional vision assessment in, 407–408
hearing loss and, 358, 358t
human guides in, 413
identification of, 406–407
independent living skills in, 414–416, 415t
language development in, 397–399, 398d
learning by doing method in, 416, 416t
legal blindness in, 392
listening skills in, 411–412
low vision and, 393, 410–411
misconceptions about, 392, 396
nonoptical devices for, 419d
optical devices for, 419d
orientation and mobility training for, 399, 412–414
parenting and, 400–401d
peer relationships and, 400–401, 403–404, 404d, 414–415
prevalence of, 395
reading media in, 394f
residual vision in, 392
school achievement and, 396–397, 397d, 401–402
school settings for, 416–418
social development and, 414–415
social development in, 400–401
student characteristics in, 395–404
tactile symbols in, 410
teaching strategies and accommodations in, 405–421
unifying experiences method in, 416, 416t
visual efficiency and, 415–416
vocational rehabilitation counselor for, 412d
Vitreous humor, 395
Vocal output communication aids (VOCAs), 305v
Vocational rehabilitation counselor, 412d
Vocational training. See also Employment
  for visually impaired, 415
Voice disorders, 324–325

Walker Social Skills Curriculum, 155
Web-based learning, 153d
Webbing, 137, 139d
Wechsler Intelligence Scale for Children (WISC-III), 167–168
Wheelchairs, 459–460
  accessibility for, 456
Wild boy of Aveyron, 9f
Wisdom, 477, 478d
Word-analysis skills, 131, 132d
Work. See Employment
Working memory, 127
Worksheets, modifications of, 159–161
Writing
  learning disabilities and, 136
  spelling and, 135–136
  teaching strategies for, 140d

Content Within This Text Correlates with the Council for Exceptional Children (CEC) Content Standards for Teachers of Special Education

Standard 1: Foundations	Related Portfolio Activities (chapter and activity number)	Emphasized in Chapters
Teachers working with exceptional children are expected to demonstrate knowledge of the following:	3-1, 3-3, 11-2	
Models, theories, and philosophies that form the basis for special education practice.		1, 2, 3, 14 and throughout
Laws, policies, and ethical principles regarding behavior management planning and implementation.		1, 7
Relationship of special education to the organization and function of educational agencies.		1, 14
Rights and responsibilities of students, parents, teachers, other professionals, and schools related to exceptional learning needs.		1, 2, 3
Issues in definition and identification of individuals with exceptional learning needs, including those from culturally and linguistically diverse backgrounds.		1, 2, 3, 4–13
Standard 2: Development and Characteristics of Learners		
Teachers working with exceptional children are expected to demonstrate knowledge of the following:	3-3, 4-1, 7-1, 7-3, 7-4, 8-1, 12-1, 13-1, 13-3	
Typical and atypical human growth and development.		4–13
Educational implications of characteristics of various exceptionalities.		4–13
Characteristics and effects of the cultural and environmental milieu of the individual with exceptional learning needs and the family. Family systems and the role of families in supporting development.		3
Standard 3: Individual Learning Differences		
Teachers working with exceptional children are expected to demonstrate knowledge of the following:	3-2, 4-2, 4-3, 6-3, 6-4, 7-5, 8-3, 10-1, 10-2, 10-3, 11-1, 12-2, 13-2, 13-3	
Effects an exceptional condition(s) can have on an individual's life.		4–13
Impact of learners' academic and social abilities, attitudes, interests, and values on instruction and career development.		4–13
Variations in beliefs, traditions, and values across and within cultures and their effects on relationships among individuals with exceptional learning needs, family, and schooling.		3
Cultural perspectives influencing the relationships among families, schools, and communities as related to instruction.		3
Standard 4: Instructional Strategies		
(This standard consists of skills only)	5-4, 6-2, 7-2, 8-4, 10-2, 10-3, 11-3	4–13
Standard 5: Learning Environments and Social Interactions		
Teachers working with exceptional children are expected to demonstrate knowledge of the following:	4-4, 5-2, 6-1, 8-2, 8-5, 12-4, 12-5, 13-6, 14-4	
Demands of learning environments.		4–13
Basic classroom management theories and strategies for individuals with exceptional learning needs.		7
Effective management of teaching and learning.		4–13
Teacher attitudes and behaviors that influence behavior of individuals with exceptional learning needs.		4–13